The Economics of Innovation and Intellectual Property

The Economics
of Innovation and
Intellectual Property

BRONWYN H. HALL AND CHRISTIAN HELMERS

OXFORD
UNIVERSITY PRESS

OXFORD
UNIVERSITY PRESS

Oxford University Press is a department of the University of Oxford. It furthers
the University's objective of excellence in research, scholarship, and education
by publishing worldwide. Oxford is a registered trade mark of Oxford University
Press in the UK and certain other countries.

Published in the United States of America by Oxford University Press
198 Madison Avenue, New York, NY 10016, United States of America.

Library of Congress Control Number: 2024917075

ISBN 978-0-19-763092-1 (pbk.)
ISBN 978-0-19-763091-4 (hbk.)

DOI: 10.1093/oso/9780197630914.001.0001

Paperback printed by Marquis Book Printing, Canada
Hardback printed by Bridgeport National Bindery, Inc., United States of America

Patent illustrations shown on the cover:
Top right: US174465A, issued to Alexander Graham Bell on 7 March 1876.
Improvements in Telegraphy.
https://patents.google.com/patent/US174465A/en?oq=US174%2c465

Top left: US4136359A, issued to Stephen G. Wozniak on 23 January 1979, assigned to Apple Inc.
Microcomputer for use with video display
https://patents.google.com/patent/US4136359A/en?oq=US4136359

Lower left: US8541575B2, issued to Mauricio Pulizi et al. on 24 September 2013,
assigned to Nerviano Medical Sciences SRL
3,4-diarylpyrazoles as protein kinase inhibitors
https://patentimages.storage.googleapis.com/a7/42/23/3b5c57b9fc5513/US8541575.pdf

Upper left: US9645502B2, issued to Pieter Willem Herman De Jager et al. on 9 May 2017,
assigned to ASML Netherlands BV.
Lithographic apparatus, programmable patterning device and lithographic method
https://patentimages.storage.googleapis.com/aa/bb/cc/7da3378b4c810c/US9645502.pdf

Lower right: US7762994B2, issued to Henrik Sonderskov Klint et al. on 27 July 2010,
assigned to Novo Nordisk AS.
Needle mounting system and a method for mounting a needle assembly
https://patentimages.storage.googleapis.com/e4/1b/18/a2e97dfe5e7ad5/US7762994.pdf

Contents

IV. APPENDICES

Illustrations

Boxes

Figures

Tables

Preface

This book is the joint product of two scholars of different generations and backgrounds (one educated in the United States and one in Europe and the United Kingdom), who are united in their interest in the economics and management of innovation and intellectual property, as well as policies that encourage the former, especially those policies that involve the latter. We undertook the writing of this book because when teaching these topics, we found no comprehensive and up-to-date text that was suitable for our courses. We hope that we have been successful in filling this gap.

A great deal of the material in this book is focused on the United States and Europe. This is mostly a result of the authors' background and research, which has centered on issues in these locations. The substantive focus of the book also reflects the research of its authors, meaning that there may be some omissions or some topics that perhaps deserved more attention, such as international aspects of intellectual property or innovation, competition/antitrust policy, and the emerging field of science of science. This being a book about innovation, we are also aware that the academic field and, more importantly, the real world continue to evolve rapidly. This is particularly evident in the area of artificial intelligence, where significant changes have occurred from the start of our work on this book to its completion. It is impossible for a static book like this to keep pace with such exciting dynamic developments. We hope that we can be excused any omissions, given the already many pages of this book, and hope that we get the opportunity to update and expand its content in a future edition.

Acknowledgments

We are particularly grateful to several anonymous reviewers, as well as Laurie Ciaramella, Andrea Fosfuri, Fabian Gaessler, Bernhard Ganglmair, Stephen Guth, Joachim Henkel, Brian J. Love, Imke Reimers, Bhaven Sampat, Lucy Xiaolu Wang, Beth Webster, and Brian Wright for providing detailed feedback on one or several draft chapters at different stages of this project. We are also indebted to Christine Greenhalgh and David C. Mowery for providing detailed comments on an entire interim draft. William Nachtrieb helped us with our case law references, and Sarah Lane provided valuable editorial assistance. We also received constructive comments on early drafts of chapters from students at the University of Mannheim.

We are additionally indebted to many generations of undergraduate and graduate students at Santa Clara University, where Christian has been teaching courses on innovation and intellectual property since 2014. Their feedback and enthusiasm for the subject have been an important motivation for writing this book. Bronwyn taught courses and a seminar on innovation for undergraduates and graduate students at the University of California at Berkeley and advised many doctoral theses in the area of innovation and intellectual property. She learned a tremendous amount from these students, and this is reflected especially in some of the concrete examples in the book.

Both of us are also very grateful to the many researchers with whom we have worked and published, a list too long to give here, but they have nonetheless contributed a great deal to our understanding of the topics addressed in this work.

In particular, Bronwyn is especially fortunate in having worked with and learned from some of the pioneers in the field: Zvi Griliches at Harvard introduced her to the topic of R&D, patents, and productivity and the use of data in these areas. At Stanford, Paul David and Nathan Rosenberg expanded her understanding of innovation, especially of the history of technological innovation, partly via what was probably the first economics of innovation seminar, begun at Stanford in the very late 1970s. All three of these scholars are greatly missed. In addition, she is grateful to David C. Mowery who jointly managed the innovation seminar with her at Berkeley and shared many of his excellent graduate students with her, greatly enhancing her understanding of the management side of innovation.

How to Use This Book

This text is organized into three parts. Part I is more broadly about innovation and the innovation process. In Part II, we introduce readers to different mechanisms employed by innovators to appropriate returns to their innovations. Part III delves more deeply into the use of intellectual property, in particular patents, in different industries and discusses related topics of interest to stakeholders, including companies and policymakers.

The book is too extensive to cover in a single course. Courses focusing on innovation might want to concentrate on the content in the first part of the book. Courses with a stronger emphasis on intellectual property could use a combination of Parts II and III. Throughout the book, all chapters are intentionally designed to provide instructors with the flexibility to choose and cover specific chapters without having to follow a fixed sequence. As chapters are largely self-contained, there is some overlap in content between them.

Some readers will find that there are sections that use a level of mathematics and econometrics with which they are unfamiliar. We have provided a simple mathematical appendix (Appendix A) to clarify some concepts and included more than a few references to the relevant textbooks in econometrics. But it is perfectly possible to simply skim the book's more difficult sections for the main ideas, which we have tried to explain verbally as well as mathematically.

The primary audience we had in mind for this book are undergraduates who have completed at least an introductory economics course and graduate students in economics, public policy, and management. We nevertheless hope that some scholars and policymakers will also find it useful as an introduction to the fields of innovation and intellectual property or specific topics within those fields.

I.

INNOVATION

1

Innovation and Intellectual Property

1.1 Introduction

Innovation is widely viewed as the engine behind economic growth and improvements in the standard of living. Maximizing the benefits from innovative activity and mitigating its costs require understanding of the innovative process and how to manage it, both at the business- and the economywide level.

This book introduces its readers to the use of economic analysis for the understanding of technical change and the innovative process, its determinants and consequences. The second half of the book hones in on the major system currently used in market economies to provide incentives for the production of innovation, the intellectual property (IP) system. This system provides temporary "ownership" of innovative ideas and their expression to their creators.

What is innovation? At the simplest level, innovation is the introduction of a new idea or new way of doing things. As individuals, we innovate every day: taking a new route to school or work, making a new recipe, or even choosing a new hairstyle. Such innovations are minor and not really new, except to the person that makes them. Other innovations are major but not properly the study of economics—for example, the introduction of universal suffrage (the idea that any person is allowed to vote in a jurisdiction where they are a resident) was a major and overdue innovation during the 19th and early 20th centuries in many countries.

Our focus in this book is a subset of the broader set of innovations: those that have a direct impact on the economy, either via increasing the productivity of its members or by improving and expanding the goods and services available to them. Thus, our focus is the part of innovative activity that is the province of economists, leaving the broader topic to others.[1] In general, this means that we focus largely on technological innovation in the broad sense, that is, including innovation related to all fields of science and technology. On occasion, we will also make reference to organizational or managerial innovation, which additionally contributes to productivity improvements in the economy.

We study innovation and technical change for a number of reasons. Macroeconomists wish to understand the sources of economic growth and how innovation contributes to that growth. Microeconomists want to learn how the process works and what motivates the innovators. Business economists and lawyers want an understanding of innovation to help them choose strategies that increase their profits or defend against competitors. Policymakers seek information to help them choose and design institutions and government policy in this area. Our textbook is intended as an introduction to the topic

---

[1] For an introduction to the broader topic, see Fagerberg et al. (2004) and Rogers (1995).

The Economics of Innovation and Intellectual Property. Bronwyn H. Hall and Christian Helmers, Oxford University Press.
© Oxford University Press 2024. DOI: 10.1093/oso/9780197630914.003.0001

that may aid these various investigations. We expand on such ideas in the remainder of this introduction.

1.2 Innovation and Economic Growth

The United States and many other countries have seen substantial productivity growth and improvements in the standard of living during the past 100 or more years. Economists since Abramovitz and Solow have attributed this growth to four main causes: investment in physical capital leading to more capital per worker, education and other investments in worker skills, scale or size effects from commercial expansion and specialization, and increases in the stock of knowledge via innovation leading to technical and institutional change.

Figure 1.1 illustrates the accelerating growth in Gross domestic product (GDP) per person since 1850 in the United States and the United Kingdom. For comparison, we also include China, whose growth did not take off until after the Cultural Revolution (1966–1976).

Tracking the sources of this growth has shown that only one-half to two-thirds is accounted for by increases in the physical capital stock and the education levels of workers. The remainder has been labeled as due to technical change, that is, new and improved methods of production that mean greater output is obtained from the same inputs. There is evidence that this source of growth has been very important in the United States and other countries during the last 50 years, and a great deal of research time has been devoted to modeling and measuring the magnitude of the contribution of

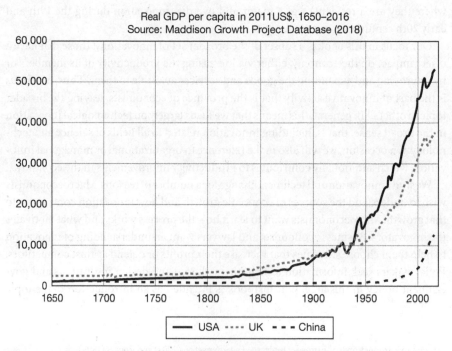

Figure 1.1 GDP per capita for the United States, United Kingdom, and China.

innovation and technical change. Chapter 9 discusses the contributions to growth and how to measure them in more detail.

Most technical change today is an outgrowth of the conscious activities of firms, and this phenomenon has been increasing over time. Empirical innovation scholars frequently focus their attention on the R&D spending by firms and countries as a proxy for innovative activity because these data are the only innovation data that have been collected for a number of countries over a number of years. They are the result of the investment decisions by firms and countries, and therefore represent a measure that reflects a willingness to pay for innovation. In addition, they cover both successful and unsuccessful projects, unlike patents, which may not exist for projects that have failed. So we use them here to examine the broad trends in innovation input across countries and over time, while bearing in mind that some types of economically relevant innovation activity may not be measured by looking only at R&D.

Figure 1.2 shows the trends in R&D spending between 1981 and 2018 for several large economies, in constant dollars and adjusted for purchasing power parity. R&D has grown in all these countries, most dramatically in China (whose data only begin in 1990). Korea also shows substantial growth over this period, as does the United States, while growth in the major European countries and Japan is much more modest. The main message of the figure is that innovative activity has become increasingly important, at least in developed economies as well as China.

Of course, some of this trend growth in R&D reflects growth in the size of the economy, which helps to account for the differences between the rising Asian countries and Europe. In Figure 1.3 we show the ratio of R&D to GDP, in order to examine

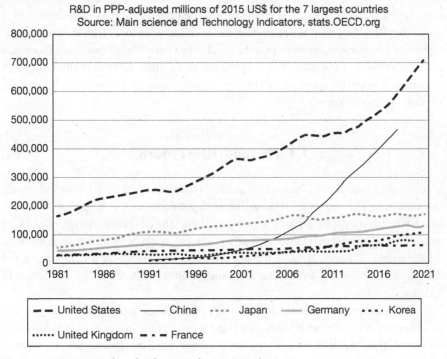

Figure 1.2   R&D spending for the seven largest spenders.

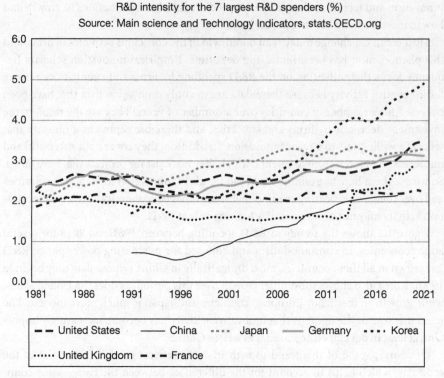

R&D intensity for the 7 largest R&D spenders (%)
Source: Main science and Technology Indicators, stats.OECD.org

Figure 1.3 R&D intensity for the seven largest R&D spenders.

how the R&D intensity in these countries changed over time. This is revealing, as it shows that R&D intensity has been stagnant or falling in Europe, with the possible exception of Germany, in the most recent period. The United States and Japan show only slight increases. On the other hand, for Korea and China, R&D intensity has grown from fairly low levels to parity with the large Western economies (and even beyond the West, in the case of Korea).

1.3 The Innovative Process

Much of the economic analysis of innovation relies on established notions of supply and demand. The supply of innovations is dependent on the supply of inventors, which is affected by the culture in which they reside, the education system, risk-taking attitudes, and tolerance for novelty as well as the conventional financial motives. Additionally, it depends on available and accessible knowledge on which to build, the various costs of turning an idea into an innovation, and therefore the availability of finance.

The demand for innovation is driven first by the willingness of firms, consumers, and governments to pay for innovation. The potential size of the future market for an innovation will also matter because innovation is a quasi-fixed cost that is cheaper if spread over more units.

Other factors include the nature of competition--innovators are more likely to inno-vate if they fear another innovator will get there first and displace them. This means that market structure matters, sometimes in subtle ways. For example, there is considerable debate over the role of large incumbent firms in generating innovation, exemplified by the two views of Joseph Schumpeter. In his 1911 book, he described the creative de-struction in an entrepreneurial industry where each new entrant innovates and destroys the profits of the incumbents. But in his 1934 book, he describes an industry with high entry barriers where innovation is performed by large firms with the deep pockets to support it.[2] We will look at these phenomena in more detail in Chapter 5.

However, as Arrow pointed out long ago, innovation and the associated produc-tion of knowledge are a special kind of good, one whose characteristics mean that a simple supply–demand model is not always the appropriate method for analysis. Briefly stated, the knowledge and ideas associated with creating something new are both non-rival and non-excludible. That is, once an idea has been created, several individuals can use it without diminishing the others' benefit from use (non-rivalry). Nor are these individuals able to prevent others from using it, absent an intellectual property system that guarantees ownership of the idea or invention (non-excludability).

Because of its variety and complexity, the analysis of the innovative process relies on a range of methodologies: historical examples, economic theory, and empirical study. We review what has been learned about the innovative process in the first few chapters of the textbook.

1.4 Innovation Strategy

Increasingly, competition among firms in market economies depends on their innova-tive activity. Competitive strategy is directed toward creating areas or niches in which the firm can capture supra-normal profits or economic rents in a potentially sustain-able way. This is sometimes termed *exploiting core competencies*, that is, things the firm does better than other firms. In the past, such rents often relied on access to natural resources, but in the modern economy they are often due to innovations. In addition to the strategy of creating a new or improved good, the networked economy has enabled another successful strategy: the creation of a standard or of a dominant platform for services. This particular strategy has a tendency to lead to quasi-monopolization. Thus, the innovation process is of major concern to antitrust regulators as well as those re-sponsible for a firm's strategy.

Creating a new or better product or service requires an understanding of the in-teraction between economic forces and technology. Extracting profits from such an innovation also requires an IP strategy in order to ensure these profits are not dissi-pated by imitation. At the same time, exclusion of others via IP also has a downside in terms of facilitating monopolization. In the latter part of this book, we delve more deeply into the management and regulation of intellectual property, especially patents, in Chapters 15–22.

---

[2] These two views are sometimes described as Schumpeter Mark 1 and Schumpeter Mark 2.

1.5   Innovation Policy

The non-rivalry and non-excludability of invention and knowledge and its importance in competitive strategy have led to increased attention by policymakers in the past 70 or so years, dating back to Vannevar Bush's famous manifesto at the end of World War II, *Science: The Endless Frontier.* We discuss this topic in Chapter 10 of the book.

The argument that invention and knowledge will be undersupplied by the market because they create positive externalities implies a need for some kind of policy to encourage its production. These policies take many forms, from direct subsidy to the grant of IP rights. In designing provisions to encourage innovative activity broadly, the first question is which kind of activity do we wish to encourage. That is, we may think that scientific research has very positive externalities and should be shared by all, whereas research that merely generates refinements to an existing product may have few if any benefits for entities than the firm making the product. Because of this variability in the importance of the public good nature of innovative activity, there are a range of policy solutions in use in most economies.

Another consideration that has received somewhat less attention in developed country circles until recently is that knowledge externalities do not respect borders, but policy is generally national. This fact leads to possible variations in optimal policy that depend on the relative size or importance of the economy in the world economy. In particular, it may imply differences in the desirable policies that depend on the development level of an economy and its institutions.

The components of innovation policy consist ordinarily of subsidies to higher education and research, the establishment of technical standards, the IP system, and R&D subsidies and taxes. In addition, various kinds of regulation such as antitrust and technical mandates (e g., fuel economy standards) will play a role. Some government policies will also affect the diffusion of innovations, via mandates, targeted subsidies, and the like. Taken together, these government policies and institutions and their interaction are sometimes referred to as a *national innovation system* (Nelson 1993).

We delve into the design of these policies and the trade-offs in their implementation in Chapter 10.

1.6   Uses of This Book

This book is intended for undergraduate and master's students in economics, management, legal studies, and policy studies. Different courses will emphasize different portions. For example, Chapters 1–10 might be used in a basic course on the economics of innovation, whereas Chapters 11–22 are appropriate for a course in IP strategy and policy. A course in the law of intellectual property and its rationale might only use Chapters 15–22. Any of these courses might find Chapters 1–3, 6, and 7 useful as background reading on innovation.

2

What Is Innovation?

Learning Objectives

After reading this chapter, you will be able to understand and explain the following concepts:

- The basic structure of the innovation process
- The role of learning in the innovative process in the form of feedbacks to scientific understanding, learning by doing, and learning by using
- The importance of technical risk and market risk in the innovation process
- The factors that determine the direction of innovation
- The different types of innovation: incremental and radical, product and process, and user innovation
- The public good characteristics of innovation

2.1 Introduction

In order to study innovation, it is useful to have a fuller understanding of what it is and how it is performed. The word itself comes from the Latin verb *innovare* (*in* = "into" + *novare* = "make new"). Thus, the essence of the word is "new," the creation of something new. In the context of economics and business that we are studying here, innovation is the conversion of an idea for a new product or process into reality, putting the idea or invention into practice. Box 2.1 defines the three stages of the innovative process as usually viewed by those who study innovation.

Economists, technology historians, and others who have studied the innovation process have reached at least four broad conclusions listed below. We will give some examples of all these features later in the chapter.

1. Although economic factors are important for an understanding of the rate and direction of technical change, chance and unpredictability are often seen in the process.
2. Although innovation it is often modeled as a linear process from science to the end product, throughout the process of innovation, there can be feedback from one stage to an earlier stage. Such feedback can be important to the eventual success of the innovation.

The Economics of Innovation and Intellectual Property. Bronwyn H. Hall and Christian Helmers, Oxford University Press.
© Oxford University Press 2024. DOI: 10.1093/oso/9780197630914.003.0002

Box 2.1 Elements of Innovation

---

1. **Invention:** creation of the idea of how to do or make something (usually done by an individual, sometimes a small team of individuals).

"an increment in the set of total technical knowledge of a given society" (Mokyr 1992)

"prescription for a producible product or operable process so new as not to have been obvious to one skilled in the art at the time the idea was put forward" (Schmookler 1966)

2. **Innovation:** making an idea for a new product or process real, putting it into practice; includes development and commercialization; usually done by a team or company.

3. **Diffusion:** the spread of a new invention/innovation throughout society or at least throughout the relevant part of society. Diffusion can also refer to the *diffusion of knowledge* embodied in the new invention/innovation.

---

3. Innovations frequently require a number of factors to come together before they are made; that is, the environment in which the innovation will come to life needs to have the necessary ingredients to make it effective, such as consumer demand for the innovation and the capabilities of necessary complementary products.
4. Although the relevant science is often a precondition for an innovation, some innovations are made *before* the science that lies behind them is completely understood.

The linear model is a useful starting point for thinking about innovation, although it does have its critics. In the next section of this chapter, we outline the model and describe the path by which some example innovations have been achieved, which will help us in generalizing about the process. We emphasize throughout the chapter that this model is very stylized and that, in practice, an innovation process will overlap the different stages or even do things out of order. The next section of the chapter discusses a particularly important example of this reordering: cases where scientific understanding has come after technological innovation.

We go on to discuss the role of learning during the innovative process and its feedback to innovation. We also present different ways to classify innovations: process versus product and radical versus incremental. Invention and innovation have some unique features as quasi-public goods, which we explore briefly. We will discuss the special characteristics of innovation from the point of view of economic analysis later in Chapters 4 and 10.

2.2 The Linear Model of Innovation

When thinking about strategies to produce innovative outcomes, it is quite natural for firms and governments to view innovation as a linear process from basic research through to commercialization. That is, it makes no sense to think about commercialization or diffusion in the abstract without having prior development of a particular innovation in mind, and such an innovation will inevitably be one developed from

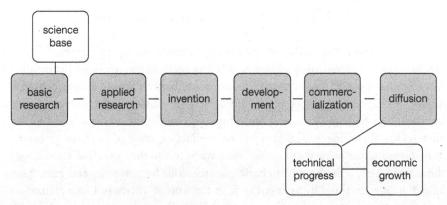

Figure 2.1 The linear model of innovation.

an invention of some kind. This sequence can be characterized by the diagram in Figure 2.1.

The items in grey are those generally viewed as composing the innovative process, although sometimes we might include the development of the science base. With the exception of diffusion and (to some extent) basic research, they are also those activities performed by specialized firms and individuals in the economy. More detailed definitions of these activities that are based on the definitions used by various government data collection agencies are given in Box 2.2 below.

Again, it is important to recognize that although the linear model is a useful stylized view of the structure of the innovation process, many stages in this process will overlap, some stages may be missing, and there will be feedback between stages. Much of the remainder of the chapter discusses these features of the process more thoroughly. However, here we illustrate the basic sequence of the linear model with some examples of present-day innovation in order to make the concepts in Figure 2.1 more concrete.

Box 2.2 Definitions of R&D from the Frascati Manual

Basic research: experimental or theoretical work undertaken primarily to acquire new knowledge of the underlying foundation of phenomena and observable facts, without any particular application or use in view. (OECD 2015a, p. 50)

Applied research: original investigation undertaken in order to acquire new knowledge. It is, however, directed primarily toward a specific, practical aim or objective. (OECD 2015a, p. 51)

Development (experimental): systematic work, drawing on knowledge gained from research and practical experience and producing additional knowledge, which is directed to producing new products or processes or to improving existing products or processes. (OECD 2015a, p. 51)

2.2.1 Example: Pharmaceutical Innovation

The first example is the production of a new pharmaceutical.[1] With the recombinant DNA and gene sequencing revolutions, this process has evolved somewhat over time from one that involved searching hundreds of potential molecules to a more focused endeavor, but the basic elements remain the same. The scientific base is the accumulated knowledge in biology (including biotechnology), organic chemistry, and biomedicine. A typical pharmaceutical firm will be conducting some of this basic research, if only to ensure that researchers in the firm have access to the frontier of knowledge in these areas. They will also rely on basic research done by university and government laboratories, sometimes in partnership with the firm in question. Large pharmaceutical firms may also finance and use applied research conducted by specialized biotechnology firms. Applied research directed at a particular disease involves screening likely compounds in test tubes and testing candidate compounds on animals (typically mice). When a particular compound in the laboratory is successful, it can be patented, although it may not become a successful innovation in the future. This is one example of the difference between an invention and an innovation.

In pharmaceuticals, the development phase consists of a series of clinical trials, denoted Phase I, II, and III. In Phase I, the drug is tested among a few healthy volunteers to check for safety. In Phase II, a few hundred patients with the targeted disease or condition receive the drug, in order to assess its effectiveness and determine the optimal doses. Phase III involves a few thousand patients, divided into treatment and control groups. The first group is given the drug and the second group a placebo, but no individual knows which one they have been given. Comparing the two groups allows the researchers to demonstrate whether or not a drug candidate offers a treatment benefit, in addition to providing more detailed safety data and serving as the basis for product labeling.[2]

After completion of Phase III and its evaluation, the company can submit a New Drug Application (NDA) to the US Food and Drug Administration (FDA; or to other regulatory agencies outside the United States) for consideration for marketing approval. According to a careful study of over 400,000 trials of 20,000 candidate drug compounds by Wong et al. (2019), approximately 20% of the compounds made it through Phase III trials, fewer than 5% in the case of oncology drugs (for cancers). Thus in this sector, a successful invention by no means leads with certainty to a successful innovation. Even after success in Phase III trials, bringing the drug to market will be affected by regulatory decisions. In the Wong et al. data, only 59% of drugs that showed success in Phase III trials made it to approval.

The final phases in Figure 2.1 above are commercialization and diffusion. In this case, commercialization consists of determining the packaging and dosage information, scaling up manufacturing, and marketing the drug to doctors and sometimes to consumers. Diffusion is the process by which use of the drug is spread throughout the relevant doctor and patient population. It may also include the process of satisfying regulators in other countries and adapting the drug delivery to different health care systems (e.g., administration via pill vs. suppository).

---

[1] Chapter 16 reviews the pharmaceutical industry in more detail, focusing on the use of IP in this sector.
[2] This might include such things as the recommended dose and frequency, as well as potential side effects.

> **Box 2.3 Software Testing**
>
> ---
>
> **Alpha testing:** testing performed by a developer or its employees to identify possible issues and bugs before releasing the final product to end users
>
> **Beta testing:** testing performed by users in their environment to identify further issues and bugs that were unanticipated by the developer in their environment

2.2.2 Example: Software Innovation

Now consider the process of developing a new software program or app. The basics of computing rest on mathematics and logic, but the connection to current research in these areas is rather remote and their importance depends on the particular application. Applied research in the areas of cryptography, sorting algorithms, data storage systems, and numerical methods are often far more important for software development. For software, invention would be coming up with the concept of what a useful program would do and specifying its basic features. Development consists of creating detailed specifications, coding, and alpha testing, defined in Box 2.3.

Commercialization is beta testing, marketing, and successful sale. During the diffusion process, there will be adoption by customers, and feedback leading to modifications to the product as a larger customer base finds problems that were not foreseen during development. Like almost all innovators, the goal of software innovators is profit, but they are also concerned with the development of a large market share, guaranteeing future profits. The essential characteristic of software innovation is that it is a prolonged incremental process even after the first sales.

2.2.3 Comparing the Examples

Using these two examples, one can see both commonalities and differences.[3] They both rest on science, albeit of quite different kinds, and both are created in response to perceived consumer demand. They follow the linear process for creating an innovation, but with differences. The costs associated with the pharmaceutical innovation are probably highest for the development phase, while for a software app, success is achieved via investment at the diffusion phase, because generally the development phase is relatively lower-cost. Diffusion is important because success in the software area is to some extent determined by market share. Market share in pharmaceuticals is also important, but given the protected nature of the market for a proprietary drug, it is more or less given by the nature of the disease that is targeted by the drug.

Prior to development of the product, there is a great deal more uncertainty about feasibility in pharmaceuticals than in software, as evidenced by the numbers given above for survival through Phase III trials. Some of this uncertainty is due to the presence of

---

[3] These are somewhat broad generalities, to which there will always be exceptions in the case of a particular product.

another outside actor, the government regulatory agency, that will have an impact on the success of the drug. The uncertainty in software is not whether it can be developed and function as desired, but whether it will get to market before a competing product and whether it will appeal to the potential customers at a cost-covering price. That said, some software projects may fail in development, and we rarely hear about these failures unless they are very large-scale. It is more common for released software to work imperfectly in some situations, hence the many updates issued.

An important characteristic that distinguishes software innovation from pharmaceutical innovation is its modular nature. Although the innovation of a new drug builds on knowledge developed in the past, it does not usually involve combining a large number of separate inventions to produce the drug. A software innovation, in contrast, almost always involves the combination of many pieces (some of which are patented inventions) to create a new product. This fact has important implications for intellectual property management and technical standards, a subject that we discuss later in Chapters 17 and 21.

A final difference between the two types of innovation is in the learning by using possibilities discussed later in the chapter. Software is characterized by continuous development in response to the experience of users, whereas this activity is limited in the case of pharmaceuticals for safety reasons. That is, much of learning by using in pharmaceuticals is done during the original development phase before releasing the product to the public.[4]

2.3 Science from Technology

The description of the innovation process given in the two examples above is reasonably accurate in the modern industrial context. However, the innovation process does not always follow such a simple path, and there are many feedbacks and accidental scientific discoveries in the system. These can be classified as two broad types: cases where the drive to understand why something works leads to new science, and cases where there is a deliberate attempt to improve a technology that requires further understanding of the science behind it. It can also be the case that improved technology makes the science behind it more economically valuable and hence easier to pay for.

For example, during the latter half of the 19th century, Louis Pasteur worked for a vintner trying to improve the fermentation process of beetroot wine, and traced the source of contamination to microorganisms that could be eliminated by heating liquids to temperatures between 60 and 100 degrees Celsius. His work not only invented pasteurization (a commercial innovation) but also led to the germ theory of disease, which is now widely accepted. This is a case where applied research led back to basic research and science, as well as producing a useful invention. There are many such cases. See Table 2.1 below for more examples and Rosenberg (1982c) for further discussion of this topic.

---

[4] An exception to this general rule is informal experience with "off-label" use, driven by doctors' prescription behavior. Off-label use is use of the drug to treat a condition that was not the condition or population for which the development trials were conducted. Wittich et al. (2012) report that about 21% of prescriptions for common drugs were off-label in the United States.

Table 2.1 Science from Technology

Years	Technological Source	Scientific Field Developed
1600s	Torricelli, designing an improved pump	Atmospheric/pressure science
1830s	Carnot, understanding the efficiency of steam engines	Thermodynamics
1850s	Pasteur, studies in the wine industry	Bacteriology/germ theories
1850–1900s	Bessemer process for steel; age-hardening of Duralumin	Metallurgy/materials science
1920s	Davisson, looking for improvements in vacuum tubes	Wave nature of matter
1932	Jansky/Bell labs, identifying sources of radio noise and static	Radio astronomy
1940s	Early semiconductors used as rectifiers (AC/DC converters)	Solid-state physics of free electrons
1950s	Laser technology for cables, increasing capacity while reducing size	Optics

Source: Authors' compilation from Rosenberg (1982c).

A particularly striking example is laser technology, which was invented during the late 1950s and is now used in barcode scanning, navigation, precision measurement, chemical research, surgery, CDs, and printing. A major use is fiber-optic cable for telecommunications. However, Theodore Maiman, who built the first working laser in 1960, reportedly described his invention as "a solution seeking a problem." The scientific origins of the laser are in physics and go back to Einstein, with work by Arthur Schawlow and Charles Townes at Bell Laboratories (the research arm of AT&T) providing the direct theoretical foundation. But the development of the wide range of applications since 1960, especially of fiber-optic cables, has contributed to advances in the science of optics. Thus, laser technology was grounded in basic scientific research in physics and then contributed to further scientific advance in a new (related) area, as the technology was developed.

The examples in Table 2.1 show that there can be feedback from applied research, innovation, and development to the science base. The key idea is that technological knowledge often precedes scientific knowledge and this leads to scientific developments that, in turn, improve technology. In the most striking cases, scientific progress can be an accidental byproduct of searching for an answer to a technological puzzle. This is exemplified by the research of Karl Jansky at Bell Laboratories. While he was studying the problem of static and noise in radio broadcasting during the early 1930s, he found a source of background noise that he was unable to identify. The search for its source led to the discovery that the noise came from stars, and hence led to the science of radio astronomy, which studies stars and galaxies via their radio frequency emissions.

In an influential book, Stokes (1997) defines the phenomenon of scientific discovery coming from applied research as *Pasteur's quadrant*. The idea is illustrated in Table 2.2.

Table 2.2 Applied and Basic Research

		Considerations of use	
		No	Yes
Quest for fundamental understanding	Yes	Pure basic research such as done by the physicist Niels Bohr	Use-inspired basic research such as done by Louis Pasteur
	No		Pure applied research such as done by Thomas Edison

Source: Stokes (1997), p. 196.

Pasteur's quadrant is the upper right quadrant, where the research is inspired by applied needs but leads to fundamental scientific understanding.

2.3.1 Instrumentation for Science

Another channel for improvement in science via technology is the production of better instrumentation, which enables scientific progress. For example, the success of Pasteur in using the microscope to observe fermentation and develop germ theory led to increased demand for improvements in microscopy, which, in turn, aided scientific investigation. The development of huge superconducting magnets for the various particle accelerators such as the supercollider at European Council for Nuclear Research (CERN) has led to improvements in materials science.[5]

In addition to its influence on the science of optics, the development of laser technology led to its use in greatly speeding up DNA sequencing beginning in the 1980s, facilitating scientific research in the biogenetic area (Heather and Chain 2016). As David et al. (1992) suggest, high-energy particle physics research, in general, has led to developments in molecular biology and chemistry. These examples also illustrate the potential for one scientific or technological area to influence the development of a completely different area via the provision of improved instrumentation.

2.4 Learning

Learning by doing and learning by using are twin concepts that describe the ways in which innovation uses results in learning that feeds back into the innovative process. One way to think about the two is that learning by doing pertains to process innovation, while learning by using refers to product innovation, although that clear distinction is not necessarily the way the concepts were introduced into the economic analysis of innovation.

---

[5] CERN is derived from the acronym for the French Conseil Européen pour la Recherche Nucléaire, or European Council for Nuclear Research. This council founded the center for high-energy physics research, which it named CERN (reinterpreted as Centre Européen pour la Recherche Nucléaire), in Switzerland in the 1950s. Today, CERN is the home of the largest particle accelerator in the world, the Large Hadron Collider.

2.4.1 Learning by Doing

Learning by doing was first coined by John Dewey in the education setting, and then used by Arrow (1962a) to describe the process by which technical change leads to knowledge and productivity growth. His idea was that the accumulation of knowledge generated by production would then feed into future productivity growth via enhanced capital goods. That is, the economy is learning all the time as it produces goods and services—better production techniques and improvements to existing products. This adds to the knowledge base and increases productivity. Arrow was influenced by several empirical findings already in use in industry, which suggested that a production process became more efficient as it was repeated, at a diminishing rate. This phenomenon, referred to as the learning curve or the progress curve, had been considered an empirical regularity in the airframe and shipbuilding industries, among others, since the 1930s.[6]

Why does the cost of production fall as experience is gained in producing a particular good, or in the production activities of a particular plant? Past researchers have highlighted several reasons. The first and probably most important is the accumulation of experience on the part of the workers. This channel will be familiar to any of us who have performed a complex task repeatedly. A second reason is learning by management that leads to better organization of productive tasks, better timing in the ordering of parts, and the like. Third, there could be minor improvements in design or materials as time passes. The latter reason suggests that the learning curve could also be due to the passage of time rather than the cumulation of output.[7]

Models of the learning curve typically relate to the cost of producing the next unit of a complex product to the number of such products already produced. In some cases, the cost is instead related to the time since the first unit was produced, and in other cases, the price is used instead of the cost. The idea captured by such a model is that learning takes place when producing something, which increases the efficiency with which it is produced in the future. The simplest model of the learning curve is the following:

$$c = c_0 y^{-b} \quad \text{or} \quad \log(c) = \log(c_0) - b \log(y) \tag{1}$$

where c is unit cost of production, y is past cumulative output, and b is the elasticity of unit cost with respect to past output. c_0 is the cost of producing the first unit, and therefore also converts the units of output to the units of cost. For example, cost might be measured as person-hours and output as counts of widgets. c_0 then measures the number of person-hours used to produce the first widget: $c = c_0(1)^{-b} = c_0$.[8] The presence of c_0 also ensures that whatever units we choose to use for cost and output, the equation will hold with an appropriate adjustment to c_0.

---

[6] The learning curve is also another illustration of the tendency of practice (technology) to precede theory (science) in many cases.

[7] For statistical and econometric reasons, sorting out these two explanations (cumulative output or passage of time) is difficult, but the prevailing evidence seems to prefer cumulative output as an explanatory variable.

[8] Technically, $y = 0$ for the first widget, but the learning curve is undefined at that point, so we assume at least one unit has been produced.

We take the derivative of log(c) with respect to log(y) using equation (1) to obtain b, which is the elasticity of unit cost with respect to cumulative output. That is, b measures the percent reduction in unit cost from a percent increase in output:[9]

$$b = -\frac{\partial \log c}{\partial \log y} = -\frac{y \partial c}{c \partial y} \tag{2}$$

Because output increases while cost falls, an implication of this constant elasticity framework is that the magnitude of the cost benefit from increased output declines as output grows. Another implication is that if unit cost is plotted against cumulative output on a log-log plot, a straight line with a negative slope should be observed. Before the widespread use of computers, this was, in fact, how the learning curve was measured for a wide variety of products, including machine tools, airframes, and ships. For these types of products, the measured values of b usually ranged between 0.25 and 0.4 (25–40%).

We show a typical learning curve plot in Figure 2.2, this time for a more recent product, a laser diode made by Sony. Laser diodes are a semiconductor device that converts electrical energy into light and are widely used in fiber-optic communications, barcode reading, CDs, and DVDs, and so on. The estimated learning curve for this product is given below:

$$\log(price) = \log(5038) - 0.373 \log(shipments)$$

The coefficient 0.373 implies that every time the past number of shipments doubles, unit cost falls 37%, which is consistent with the earlier measures of learning curves.

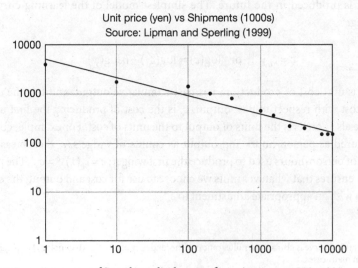

Figure 2.2 Learning curve of Sony laser diode manufacturing costs, 1982–1994.

[9] See Appendix A: Mathematics and Statistics for more on the definition of elasticity.

As the figure illustrates, the fit of a measured learning curve to a straight line is not always perfect, which has led numerous researchers to enhance the model. In particular, as even this figure shows, the learning effect tends to disappear at higher levels of output, suggesting that at some point the gains from learning by doing are exhausted.[10]

2.4.2 Learning by Using

Another feedback in the innovation process is that between commercialization and diffusion on the one hand and development on the other, referred to as *learning by using*, The term learning by using was first used by Rosenberg (1982b), by analogy to *learning by doing*. Learning by using describes the ways in which products are improved and developed and enhanced, based on experience of the product in use.

Of course, learning takes place throughout the innovation process. Basic research uncovers new laws of nature, applied research informs about useful application of knowledge, and so forth. But here we are concerned specifically with the kind of learning that takes place as a result of experience with using a new innovative product. The key idea is that technological change and innovation do not end when the technology is diffused to users. Technologies continue to improve due to feedback from use and users. We are all familiar with the many issues that arise in using a new software application—support websites are full of them. Have you ever had the experience that an app that has stopped working in some way suddenly no longer has the problem you identified? This is doubtless a consequence of learning by using: The developers have observed the user problem reports, made a fix, and updated the program. At least that is how we hope the process works.

Learning by using is especially a feature of complex capital goods, whose performance is not fully understood until they are used. Rosenberg (1982b) studied a key example, the evolution of Boeing aircraft. As time passes, there are many improvements made to planes after their first use. Some are embodied (physical change to the good) and some disembodied (changes to its maintenance or use). In the case of Boeing aircraft, the principal improvement has been to produce longer and longer versions of the same model of aircraft as experience is gained in their use. When the aircraft is first released, there is residual uncertainty about its design, and the developers are cautious about exploiting its full capabilities. As time goes by, experience with the aircraft allows them to stretch it and increase the size of the payloads. There are numerous other changes made also, in the form of engines, configurations, design for freight or particular customers. The history of increasing the capacity of the Boeing 747 is illustrated in Table 2.3.

The development of Boeing aircraft also involved disembodied learning. As the airlines developed experience with maintenance and the jet engines, the requirements for checking performance and scheduling maintenance and overhaul of the plane and its engine changed. Over time, the service intervals lengthened as confidence developed.

---

[10] See Thompson (2010) for a fuller discussion of the learning curve and related issues.

Table 2.3 Example: Stretching the Boeing 747

Model	Year Introduced	Number of Passengers
747-100	1969	366
747-200	1971	NA
747-300	1983	400; stretched upper deck
747-400	1989	416-524
747-8	2005	467

Learning by using also can contribute to product differentiation. Users have specialized needs, and as these are revealed, ways in which the product can be improved to serve a particular group of users will be revealed. Using the previous example, the development of freight and business jets based on commercial Boeing models exhibits this kind of learning by using.

2.5 Uncertainty and Timing

One feature of innovation in the past that is very striking is the inability even by the inventors themselves to forecast the ultimate implications and uses of their inventions. History is replete with examples of this. One of the most famous is the forecast by Thomas Watson, CEO of IBM in 1943 that the worldwide demand for their computers was likely to be only 5. Computers at the time were massive (ENIAC contained 18,000 vacuum tubes and was 100 feet long), and he failed to anticipate the semiconductor revolution, which greatly reduced the size and power needed for computers.[11] Even as late as 1977, Ken Olson, the president, chairman, and founder of Digital Equipment Corporation was quoted as saying "There is no reason anyone would want a computer in their home." That same year, the first West Coast Computer Faire was held in San Francisco and saw the introduction of the Apple II computer created by Jobs and Wozniak, arguably the opening salvo in the PC revolution.

An earlier example of the failure to understand the most important use of an invention is the invention of the radio. Guglielmo Marconi is widely recognized as an important contributor to the invention. However, his goal was a technology useful when wire communication was impossible, such as ship-to-ship communication, something that had been done previously using flags visible from a distance. That is, he envisioned narrowcasting, not the broadcasting that is in major use today.

A more recent example is the development of the internet. During the Cold War between the United States and the Soviet Union, a network entitled ARPANET was created for the US Defense Department using distributed communication protocols as a defense against losing communication ability if a single node goes down. Multiple

---

[11] To give an idea of the change in this technology, one of the authors of this textbook wrote her first computer programs in 1963 on an IBM 7090 that had a memory size of 144 kilobytes (less than a megabyte), and which was big enough with its attendant large tape drives to fill a room. This book is being written on a laptop with a memory size of 16 gigabytes (over 100,000 times as big as that 7090) and that weighs less than 3 pounds.

such networks were linked during the 1970s to create a primitive internet. But (commercial) use did not really take off until Tim Berners-Lee at CERN put together the internet node system and its technologies with hypertext to create the World Wide Web in 1989.

The internet example also illustrates the importance of the availability of complementary inventions and the environment to make an innovation possible and useful. *Hypertext* (see Box 2.4) existed as a concept earlier but was only really implemented in the late 1970s. Widespread commercial use of the internet was not profitable until individuals had PC computers, whose appeal expanded beyond hobbyists with the release of the first IBM PC in 1981 and Apple Mac in 1984. Following these releases, diffusion increased during the 1980s. Even then, specialized communication equipment was necessary for personal computers to access the internet over the phone lines using a slow analog-digital interface, which impeded the diffusion of internet use. The widespread availability of broadband technology, which grew during the 1990s and later encouraged the use of the internet by consumers, at least in developed countries.

The examples above also demonstrate two features of innovation:

1. The length of time between invention and when its larger economic impact becomes apparent, especially for major inventions
2. The need for complementary inventions to enable the first invention to have wider use: semiconductors in the case of computing and hypertext and personal computers in the case of the internet

The examples also illustrate the level of uncertainty and risk involved: Not only is there ordinary risk associated with the process of research and invention, but in addition the true benefit of the invention is very difficult to assess when it is undertaken. That is, there are both "known unknowns" and "unknown unknowns" involved.

From the perspective of the individual or firm that hopes to profit from an invention, it is useful to view the sources of uncertainty as two-fold when evaluating the risk of a project: (1) those related to technical feasibility and (2) those that are due to the state of the market. Briefly, we refer to these as technical risk and market risk. Uncertainty over whether something will work and how it will work is considered technical risk. For example, there was considerable technical uncertainty over Leonardo da Vinci's use of mechanical birdlike wings to achieve human flight, and his project ultimately failed in spite of considerable investment of his time and energy. We have already illustrated the considerable technical risk of developing a new pharmaceutical in Section 2.2.1.

Box 2.4 Hypertext

This is a term coined by T. H. Nelson (1965) to describe the practice of linking items in text on a computer to text in other documents on the same computer, allowing the reader to access them directly. Berners-Lee applied this concept across linked computers to create the World Wide Web.

Market risk is the possibility that the demand for a new product is simply not there, either because it does not fill the needs of enough potential customers, or because there needs to be additional investment in complementary goods by others to make the product useful. For example, the makers of electric cars have faced the risk that they will not sell because of the lack of availability of convenient charging stations. To mitigate this risk, Tesla and others have invested in establishing a large number of charging stations.

An example of an innovation that failed because of market risk is Google Glass for consumers, which was a brand of smart glasses with an optical, head-mounted display, intended to allow interaction with the internet via voice commands. These were launched in 2013, but two years later Google announced they would no longer be producing a consumer version of the glasses. Although the concept will probably succeed eventually, they were somewhat ahead of their time. The technology was not good enough to provide consumers with enough benefit to justify the cost ($1,500), and there were consumer concerns about privacy and safety. Other less expensive and less revolutionary devices such as smart watches, speakers, video games, and televisions appealed more to consumers.

2.5.1 General-Purpose Technologies

One type of innovation where uncertainty and slow evolution are very apparent is the class of innovations referred to by Bresnahan and Trajtenberg (1995) as general-purpose technologies (GPTs). A GPT is technology with many different applications and therefore many spillovers across the economy. When first introduced, its possibilities seem limited, but as it improves, its use spreads to many different areas. It is typical of such technologies that they require the reorganization of production and possibly the broader economy to make them useful, which slows their adoption greatly.

We are familiar with many examples of GPTs that seem to have become more omnipresent in the modern digital economy. Older examples include steam engines, which were used for many applications and required the reorganization of factories to make use of them. Electricity is the quintessential GPT, pervading all parts of the economy. David (1990) investigated the slow contribution of computing to productivity growth in its early years by comparing the diffusion of the computer to the diffusion of the electric dynamo, which enabled newer and cheaper factory layouts that took time to develop and required several interdependent inputs, both tangible capital investment and also human capital in the form of knowledgeable engineers.[12]

At present, the most visible tangible GPT is the semiconductor or microprocessor, which was first used in computers, but is now everywhere: mobile phones, appliances, automobiles, timepieces, audio and television equipment, and so forth. One feature that this GPT exhibits and that was perhaps not as evident in the earlier GPTs is the necessity for standards of interoperability if the technology is to spread across firms and

---

[12] An electric dynamo is an electric generator that creates direct current (DC). Today, this type of generator has been replaced by alternating current (AC) electric generators.

sectors. All modern technologies based on digital technology including the internet use technical standards and, as a result, ownership and regulation of these standards have increased in importance. We discuss this topic at length in Chapter 21.

The newest GPT is arguably technology involving artificial intelligence (AI). AI is defined as the use of computers to perform tasks that are normally performed by human intelligence. Although the idea goes back at least to the analytic machines of the 19th century, and the field of study officially began during the 1950s, it was not until the advent of modern supercomputers that the technology became useful. Probably the most visible early success of AI was the well-publicized 1997 defeat of Gary Kasparov, then World Chess Champion, by Deep Blue, a computer developed by IBM. Furman and Seamans (2018) report a number of statistics on the growth of AI investment, students enrolled in AI courses, research papers on the topic, and jobs requiring AI skills during the past two decades. For example, they report that VC investment in AI startups has increased from a level of less than US $0.5billion during the 2000s to $4billion in 2016.

In addition to the development of large-scale computing, the other ingredients that have made AI a successful innovation are the development of machine learning techniques and the availability of "big data." Machine learning uses various methods to "train" the machine to deliver particular outputs given a set of input variables, basing the algorithm on patterns observed in large datasets. As a technique, it includes a number of related or subsidiary techniques, such as predictive analysis, data mining, neural nets, and various statistical methods. The importance of access to big data for the success of such techniques has led to the development of a new research field called data science in recent years, incorporating much of the work in AI and machine learning.

Applications of AI are already found everywhere. The most familiar might be those used to choose the next video or book to offer you online. One currently attracting a great deal of attention is the use of AI models to automate driving. Essentially, the problem there is to collect a great deal of sensory input continuously and use it to decide how to direct an auto toward its goal, without any untoward events intervening. Other areas that have advanced greatly since the adoption of deep learning (neural nets with many layers) are speech recognition, facial recognition, and machine translation. There are also numerous applications in the medical area. Thus, the idea that AI is a GPT is easy to support.

One difference between AI and previous GPTs is that its use does not necessarily require the complete physical transformation of production to make it useful, because it essentially is being used to replace human intelligence that was already in place. However, its diffusion is affected by a number of potential and actual issues. First, there was delay from the initial excitement generated by the research in the 1950s before it actually became useful, largely because of inadequate computing power and data but also because the algorithms that turn out to be useful were not yet developed. Second, although the public is apparently willing to accept accidents due to human error, they are much less willing to do so when these are due to an errant algorithm. This accounts for the application of more stringent safety standards to driverless than for driver-controlled cars, in the sense that a much lower accident rate might be required to make general use acceptable.

In contexts where AI algorithms are used to inform about individuals (credit rating, likelihood of criminal activity, tax evasion, job applications, even college admission), they are critiqued on two grounds: implicit bias and error rates. The first is probably the most important problem: Algorithms are trained on previous data, and such data are contaminated by human bias, so the algorithm will reproduce this bias.[13] Mitigating such bias is an active area of research in economics, management, and law.

Even without bias, individuals are very concerned when an algorithm that they do not understand makes a prediction error that concerns them. As in the case of auto safety, this concern may be greater than in the case where a human agent makes such an error, due to the lack of transparency in the process. Issues of this kind may inhibit the diffusion of AI techniques and have already led to calls for regulation, similarly to what developed in the pharmaceutical sector during the late 19th and 20th centuries.[14] Regulation of this kind faces the challenge of trading off a risky but beneficial innovation against the certainty that it will certainly do no harm if not approved. Government drug regulatory agencies in many countries have devoted considerable effort in spelling out acceptable risks, and a similar approach may be necessary for the use of AI in predicting the behavior of individuals.

2.6 Direction of Innovation

What kinds of innovation are produced? That is, what determines the direction of innovative activity? Essentially, we can say that innovations produced depend on ease of supply, which innovation economists call technological opportunity, and perceived demand, which is what the consumers in the market appear to want. In Chapter 3, we study the supply and demand for innovation in more detail, but we review a few highlights here.

By technological opportunity, we refer to the availability of science and technology to support a particular innovation. That is, as indicated above, inventions such as machine learning leading to many AI applications were not possible until computers became powerful enough. The DNA revolution introduced by Watson, Crick, and Franklin in 1953 has completely remade the search for new pharmaceuticals, and will doubtless ultimately lead to personalized medicine.

Perceived consumer and customer need will often lead to a focus on a particular line of research, such as improvements in battery technology today. Research in this direction has been driven for the past decades by demand for small batteries with long life for laptops, tablets, and smartphones. More recently, the demand for electric autos has increased the need for reliable longer life and more powerful batteries.

A recent illustration of the role of demand in encouraging innovation is the production of vaccines for COVID-19. In the United States, the clearly defined need for such a vaccine led to the formation of Operation Warp Speed (OWS), a form of large public–private partnership between various government agencies and at least six major pharmaceutical companies designed to accelerate the clinical trials and eventual production of vaccines against SARS-CoV-2 (Slaoui and Hepburn 2020).

---

[13] For a critique of the use of big data in this way, see O'Neil (2016).

[14] For the history of drug regulation in the United States, see https://www.fda.gov/about-fda/fda-history/history-drug-regulation.

Innovations that serve larger markets will tend to be produced. For example, orphan drugs that serve only a few people and are expensive to develop will not be produced in the market without subsidy. In 1983, this fact led the US Congress to pass the Orphan Drug Act, which extends market exclusivity for such drugs as well as providing tax incentives and research subsidies for their development. The act and its subsequent amendments appear to have been a success, as the number of drugs for rare diseases increased dramatically after 1983.[15]

The direction of innovation can also be influenced by the IP system and the ways in which it allows firms to capture profits from innovation. Moser (2005) shows that during the 19th century, the absence of a patent system in several developed economies encouraged firms to specialize in innovations that could be kept secret in order to prevent easy imitation by others (see also Chapter 14).

In addition to the IP system, other features of particular technologies and markets such as increasing returns in production and the ability to sustain markups above marginal cost will influence the profits that can be extracted from innovation. In support of this idea, Acemoglu (2023) uses a model calibrated on the characteristics of the US economy to evaluate whether the direction of innovation is optimal from a social point of view. His computations suggest that health research expenditure is directed more toward curative technologies than preventative technologies that would be socially optimal, mainly because markups tend to be higher in the former than the latter. In the energy research area, his computations suggest an excess of research into dirty technologies relative to clean ones once one takes the social benefit of reduced carbon emission into account.

Finally, there is the role of public procurement: That is, if the government signals that there will be demand for a particular innovation, the guarantee of such a market may induce investment to innovate in that direction. This guidance is especially important in the defense sector, but affects other areas also. For example, government subsidies related to climate change and carbon reduction goals in many countries have led to considerable investment in wind and solar technologies.

2.7 Types of Innovation

2.7.1 Incremental and Radical Innovation

A useful distinction often made with respect to innovation is to classify innovations into two types: incremental and radical. *Incremental innovation* is just what it says—improvements in an existing product or process that enhance its performance or make it more attractive to customers. For example, successive releases of the iPhone or other mobile phones with better cameras, more memory, fancier screens, and the like can be viewed as incremental innovations.

In contrast, *radical innovations* are often viewed as those that create entire new markets. Classic examples are airplanes and automobiles. In the mobile phone example, the first smartphone could be seen as a radical innovation. Radical innovations differ considerably

---

[15] See also Lichtenberg and Waldfogel (2003) for the impact of the 1983 Orphan Drug Act on longevity.

from incremental innovations in a number of ways. First, they are more often serendipitous rather than due to conscious search. Often the true radical nature of the innovation is not even obvious at first (recall the story of Watson and IBM or the invention of the internet). Incremental innovations are more obviously dictated by prior use of the product or process in question. Second, they are more frequently made by new entrants to an industry, whereas incremental innovations are cheaper for incumbents to make since they already have considerably more experience with the existing product. Finally, as we will see later when we look at innovation incentives, the fact that radical innovations have the tendency to threaten existing firms has an impact on the nature of competition with innovation.

2.7.2 Process and Product Innovation

Innovations may also be classified into the two categories of product and process, although, of course, the distinction will not always be entirely clear. Nevertheless, the distinction is useful when modeling innovation. Process innovation is a new way of doing or producing something, usually cost reducing for the firm, even if there is no change to the products being produced. Product innovation is the creation of a new good or service for sale, which may or may not lower costs of production (and may even increase them), but is likely to increase the firm's demand. Firms frequently perform both types of innovation at the same time, of course, because new products often require new processes. In general, process innovation becomes even more important later in a product's life cycle (Klepper 1996).

We illustrate the two types of innovation with some very simple stylized figures below (Figure 2.3). The left-hand panel shows the impact of a cost-reducing innovation in a perfectly competitive market, where price is equal to marginal cost C. Holding the demand curve constant, the process innovation reduces cost to C' and therefore increases quantity produced and sold.[16]

The right-hand panel shows the impact of a product innovation or improvement that shifts demand for the product without increasing the cost of its production. In this

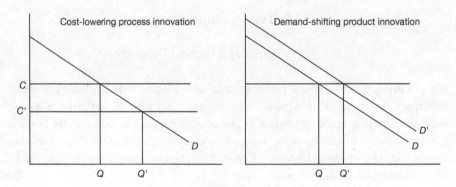

Figure 2.3 Comparing the impact of process versus product innovation.

---

[16] This is a simple stylized picture that assumes the product still sells at the marginal cost of production after the innovation. In practice, we might expect that the reduction in cost would confer some transitory market power on the innovator, raising the price.

Table 2.4 Distribution of Innovation Types for Italian Manufacturing Firms

Type of Innovation	Share of Firms
No innovation	37.1%
Process innovation only	24.0%
Product innovation only	12.0%
Both process and product innovation	26.9%

Source: Hall, Lotti, and Mairesse (2012).

case, cost and price remain unchanged, but the quantity sold is higher because the demand curve has shifted outward. Of course, many innovations produce entirely new products and this simple analysis will be unsatisfactory. We defer a fuller discussion of how to measure the impact of such innovation until Chapter 6.

Table 2.4 shows an example of the frequency of product and process innovation, for Italian manufacturing firms 1996–2005; the results are typical for manufacturing sectors in other countries. The most common type of innovation at the firm level involves both types of innovation, and the least common type is product innovation without process innovation.

Several scholars have tried to categorize product and process innovation using information available in patent claims.[17] For example, Ganglmair and Reimers (2019) look at US patents issued from 1976 to 2006, and find that about half have at least one process patent claim, and a fifth are mostly process claims. This result is consistent with the idea that firms regard patents as more important for product inventions than for pure process inventions, as has been frequently found in surveys. The reason is simple: It is far easier to use secrecy instead of patents to protect process inventions from imitation.

The technology breakdown that Ganglmair and Reimers find is illustrated in Table 2.5. This table shows that newer high-technology areas tend to have more process patents. The largest share of process patents is in computers and communication technologies. Because the number of patents in this area has also grown over time, the net effect is that process patenting is increasing overall relative to product patenting.

2.7.3 User Innovation

Alternatively, users themselves may innovate and modify the product to suit their needs. One prominent example of this phenomenon is in sporting equipment innovation. Shah (2006) reports on her study of innovation in windsurfing, skateboarding, and snowboarding equipment. In all three cases, she found that users developed the original model by modifying a piece of equipment used in related sports. Amateur users developed 57% of all major improvement innovations in her sample, while manufacturers

---

[17] Patent claims are the section of the patent that defines precisely what the invention is for which the patentee seeks protection. We describe them further in Chapter 11. Ganglmair et al. (2022) describes the use of keywords and syntax construction analysis to distinguish the type of patent claim.

Table 2.5 Process Patents by Technology

Broad Technology Class	Share of Patents with Any Process Claim
Computers and communication	73%
Chemicals	56%
Drugs	55%
Electrical	48%
Mechanical	33%
Other	27%

Source: Ganglmair and Reimers (2019), Appendix B.

developed 27% of the major improvement innovations. The remaining 16% were developed by joint user–manufacturer teams or professional athletes.

Von Hippel (2006) has studied user innovation extensively and highlighted the importance of *lead users*, those who are on the frontier in the use of the product and therefore experiencing needs that later users will also experience. Such users, in addition, anticipate large benefits from their innovative activity. In earlier work, von Hippel (1988) found that about 80% of innovations in the domain of four types of scientific instruments were user innovations. In other work, he has found user innovation widespread in industry. Typically, this involves the customers of a firm suggesting modifications to the capital goods they purchase from it. Particularly important examples include semiconductors and users of industrial gases and thermoplastics. His hypothesis that users would innovate when they expected to capture the profits from the innovation was confirmed in his study.

A recent version of the user innovation phenomenon is open-source software (OSS), that is, publicly available software source code that can be inspected, modified, and enhanced by anyone and then redistributed (see also Chapter 17). Such software is to be distinguished from proprietary software such as Microsoft's Office Suite, which requires purchase or rental to use. OSS is usually distributed under some kind of license that allows modification and redistribution, but also restricts subsequent users from making their version proprietary. Much of the internet itself is based on open-source technologies such as the Linux operating system and the Apache Web server application. Netscape was released as open source in 1998, and Mozilla Firefox created using Netscape source code as the base. More recently, companies like Google (with TensorFlow) and Meta (with PyTorch) have released their machine learning software as open source. A popular book by Raymond (2001) described the phenomenon, using the development of Linux as an example.

Lerner and Tirole (2002) provide a brief history of the opensource movement and then suggest an interpretation viewed through the lens of economics. They observe, as have others, that the greatest use of OSS has been in areas where the primary users are other programmers, such as Apache, or Sendmail to handle email.[18] Their analysis of the

---

[18] This point is reinforced by the fact that the earlier open-source browsers based on Netscape have been eclipsed by proprietary (free) browsers as browser use expanded to include the public at large.

contributors to major open-source projects shows that a small minority of contributors make more than one substantial contribution to the code, and they suggest that career concerns may motivate many of these major contributors. This point is reinforced by the fact that signing contributions via comments in the code is highly encouraged, so contributors can be easily identified.

The general phenomenon of open-source, user, and open innovation interacts with the IP system in complex ways. We will take up this broad topic in Chapter 14.

2.8 Innovation as a Quasi-Public Good

In this section of the chapter, we describe some very important features of innovation as an economic activity. These features imply that innovation will probably be undersupplied in the market, both because it is relatively difficult to finance and because it creates knowledge, which is a kind of public good. See Box 2.5 for the definition of a public good and the externalities such a good implies. These attributes mean that innovative activity is often a target of policy in many economies, as we discuss in Chapter 10.

In 1962, Kenneth Arrow published an important paper (Arrow 1962b), the first to use theoretical tools to clearly articulate the problems with the "allocation of resources to invention." Although he used the term invention, the arguments he made also apply more broadly to innovation. He started with the premise that under a set of assumptions, the general equilibrium (GE) theory that he helped to develop and for which he won the Nobel Prize in Economics in 1972 implies that the allocation of resources will be "optimal," in the sense that no other allocation would leave everyone at least no worse off. He then explained how each of these assumptions fails for the production of inventions/information.

The assumptions of GE theory are the following:

1. Utility and production functions are well-defined functions of commodities.
2. No *uncertainty* (now, or in the future, in production or consumer taste).
3. Inputs and outputs are *private property*.
4. No *indivisibility* in production or consumption (convexity).

Assumption 1 simply means that we can write consumers' preferences or tastes as a function of the various goods and services in the market given their prices. Similarly, the production of those goods and services can be written as a function of the inputs needed to produce them, such as labor and capital. In the case of a good called

---

Box 2.5 Public Goods and Externalities

Public good: a good that is both non-excludable (one person cannot prevent others from using it) and non-rivalrous (more than one person can use it at the same time without diminishing its value to the other)

Externality: when the actions of one person influence the production or consumption opportunities of another person, without going through a market

innovation or invention, this assumption could still hold, although perhaps difficult to implement. Moreover, the other three assumptions fail in the case of innovation, rendering Assumption 1 inoperative.

Assumption 2 fails because innovation is highly risky in general and therefore will be undersupplied. In principle, the full GE model allows insurance and futures markets to mitigate these risks, but these are difficult to design and do not function well in the case of innovation. In general, it is not possible to ensure against the risk that an innovation fails, and if it were, the cost would be very high, likely involving an escrow payment to the financier that the innovator is unable to make. Futures markets for all possible innovations and their success or failure are obviously impossible. Therefore, innovation will be underfinanced. See Chapter 3 for a more complete discussion of this point.

Assumption 3 fails because an innovative idea does not act like private property—once in the market, anyone can use it if there are no IP rights. Moreover, IP rights themselves create a welfare cost in the form of temporary monopolies. In the absence of a perfect ability to exclude others, inventors are unable to capture the full returns to their inventions due to imitation and will therefore underprovide them. Arrow called the ability to capture returns to an invention *appropriability*. The fact that the social benefit to an innovation may be greater than the private benefit to an innovator means there is a positive *externality* from research.

Finally, Assumption 4 fails because part of an invention is worth approximately the same as no invention. That is, invention and innovation are discrete rather than continuous, and once made, can be used an arbitrarily large number of times. The implication is increasing returns in the use of information in production caused by fixed costs. This, in turn, implies that the producer of an innovation has a natural monopoly in their product if they can exclude others from producing it, limited only by the existence of substitutes. Even though the first best price for a new product is still the marginal cost of its production, this optimum is not achievable as it does not cover the fixed costs of innovation.

The conclusion from these arguments is that perfectly competitive markets are unlikely to allocate enough resources to invention and innovation because of uncertainty, inappropriability, and indivisibility. This will be especially true for science and basic research, whose returns are even harder to predict and which benefit a broad spectrum of society.[19] Again, given the underprovision of innovation implied by these arguments, there is a role for government policy, which we will cover in Chapter 10.

2.9 Summary

In this chapter, we introduced the concept of innovation, focusing on technological innovation that improves the welfare of society. Our basic model of the innovative process was linear, from the scientific base to the commercialization of new products and processes. However, we emphasized that along this linear path there are many feedback loops that enhance and improve the end result, as well as enabling the knowledge necessary for future innovation.

---

[19] See also Nelson (1959) on policy for basic research.

An important topic in the chapter was the inherent uncertainty and risk in most innovative undertakings. We classified the risk as two broad types: technological (Will it work?) and market (Do enough people want it at the cost-covering price?). The latter can be especially important in the case of general-purpose technologies that require complementary networks to make them useful, which leads to delay in consumer take-up and diffusion.

Innovation comes in many forms, and we presented some classification systems that are sometimes useful for further analysis: incremental versus radical, process versus product, and user as opposed to producer. The radical/incremental or drastic/non-drastic distinction is useful in Chapter 5 when we model the relationship of innovation with competition, whereas the process/product distinction has proved useful in the analysis of the implications of innovation on productivity and employment (Chapter 6).

The final section of the chapter discussed how the knowledge-generating characteristic of innovation makes it a quasi-public good, in the sense that more than one individual can use the ideas produced at the same time, if there are no legal barriers to doing so. This feature of innovative activity lies behind much of the firm strategy and public policy initiatives we will discuss in subsequent chapters here.

3

Supply and Demand for Innovation

Learning Objectives

After reading this chapter, you will be able to understand and explain the following concepts:

- The role of supply factors, including technological opportunity, appropriability, absorptive capacity, and financing, in the innovation process
- The role of demand factors in the innovation process
- The effect of supply and demand factors on the direction of innovation
- Simultaneous innovation

3.1 Introduction

In May 2020, the US federal government introduced OWS, designed to accelerate the development, manufacturing, and distribution of COVID-19 vaccines, therapeutics, and diagnostic tests. OWS was a public–private partnership between various government departments and private firms. The idea was that multiple companies would simultaneously pursue the development of safe and effective vaccines with some government support, and that speedy rollout of effective vaccines would be facilitated in a number of ways: simultaneous FDA review of clinical trials for multiple vaccines; manufacturing candidate vaccines while preapproved so they would be ready for distribution; and use of the Department of Defense to coordinate supply, production, and deployment around the United States.

Eight companies were (partially) funded in August 2020 to pursue several vaccine candidates, and three of the companies produced successful vaccines by the end of 2020 (Johnson and Johnson, Astra-Zeneca, and Moderna). A fourth project, Pfizer-BioNTech, was not funded by OWS, although it did benefit from an advance purchase agreement with the US government. The latter project received €375 million (US$445 million) from the German government in September, so all of the successful projects were partly government-funded.

OWS and the Pfizer initiative are widely viewed as successful, in that less than a year between initiation and vaccine deployment eclipsed the usual vaccine development/diffusion timeline of 10–15 years.[1] This speed was undoubtedly achieved partly

---

[1] https://www.historyofvaccines.org/content/articles/vaccine-development-testing-and-regulation.

The Economics of Innovation and Intellectual Property. Bronwyn H. Hall and Christian Helmers, Oxford University Press.

because of previous recent experience and knowledge acquired with SARS-CoV and MERS-CoV vaccine development as well as the prior research into mRNA vaccines by Pfizer, BioNTech, and Moderna. Nevertheless, this example also illustrates the importance of a clearly identified need sending a strong demand signal that a particular innovation would have a market.

In contrast to the rapid development of the COVID-19 vaccine, consider the long quest for human flight, which goes back to ancient Greece and kite flying in China, and includes extensive design and drawings by Leonardo da Vinci during the 15th century.[2] Most of this early work involved attaching some kind of wing to human arms, with a failure to understand that the arms of humans lacked the strength to move wings enough to support the weight of a human body. The first really successful flight was that by the Montgolfier brothers in 1783, using a hot air balloon.

Modern human flight begins with the Wright brothers and Alberto Santos-Dumont in 1903–1908. Awarding the title "first to fly a heavier than air machine" is controversial because the Wright brothers worked in secrecy until 1908, and Santos-Dumont flew publicly with the media attending in Paris in 1906.[3] Why was human flight achieved in the early 1900s and not earlier? One could argue that an important factor was advances in other mechanical forms of propulsion, such as bicycles and gas-powered internal combustion engines. The Wright brothers themselves started out with bicycles and Santos-Dumont with precursors of the dirigible (lighter than airships). The driving forces for these inventions appear to have been the desire to be first, the supply of the basic components, understanding of the mechanics from previous failures, and in the case of the Wright brothers, the money to be made.[4]

From these examples and many others, it is possible to learn something about the determinants of invention and innovation. Economic analysis views the innovative outcomes as determined by the availability of supply of the inputs and the demand for innovative output. Reviewing these factors is the subject of this chapter. For example, the driving force behind COVID vaccines was immediate and pressing demand, although their development rested heavily on the supply of knowledge from biomedical science. In the case of heavier-than-air flight, one could contemplate future demand, but the driving force appears to be the long felt human desire for flight together with the availability of the relevant technologies (gas-powered engines, steering mechanisms, lightweight construction, wind tunnels for testing) essential for its development, that is, the supply of relevant inputs to the innovation, including the inventors.

In this chapter, we will review the factors that determine both the level and direction of innovation from an economic perspective. As in the case of other goods and services, innovation output can be viewed as the result of the interaction of supply possibilities with marketplace demand. It is therefore useful to examine the role of the different supply and demand factors in order to further our understanding of the innovative process, keeping in mind that the level of uncertainty in this supply–demand interaction is perhaps greater than that for the ordinary production of goods and services.

---

[2] https://airandspace.si.edu/stories/editorial/leonardo-da-vinci-and-flight.

[3] There was also a debate over whether flights that were initiated by towing the plane rather than self-propelled qualified as the first flight.

[4] This can be inferred from the fact that they maintained secrecy until successful and patented their invention; they then litigated the basic design of an aircraft (see also Chapter 20).

3.2 Supply of Innovation

The most important supply factor for innovation is the availability of innovators. This availability will, in turn, depend on two things: the capabilities of individuals and the incentives they face for innovation. Mokyr (1990) catalogs a broad list of mostly noneconomic factors that may have determined this availability across history and various levels of economic development. Some affect individuals directly and some are features of the environment in which they operate. We can classify these according to the ability/incentive dichotomy, although there will obviously be overlap.

Innovators' ability and capability are determined by the following:

1. Nutrition, which increases creative energy.
2. Income level, at least above a minimal level allowing only bare survival.
3. Education and the level of science and technology to which they have access.

Incentives are determined by:

4. The ability to finance and secure returns to innovation.
5. Life expectancy: shorter lives might be expected to mitigate against long horizon investments.
6. Willingness to bear risks, which may depend on the level of economic development. More developed economies can mitigate the worst-case scenarios in the case of failure via their welfare systems. Such systems permit those who fail to at least maintain a minimum standard of living.
7. Religion: using the World Values Survey (Inglehart et al. 2014), Bénabou et al. (2015) have shown a strong negative correlation between religiosity and patenting rates across countries, US states, and individuals. In a much debated thesis, the famous sociologist Max Weber (1905) argued long ago that Protestantism was an important driver of market-driven capitalism, which arguably includes innovation.
8. Values: historically, many societies have valued such characteristics as military success, sports, the arts, administration, and nontechnical learning above economic success, which tended to reduce the status of the inventor in the social hierarchy. This, in turn, means that talented individuals were more likely to pursue other ways to success.

Some of these factors (e.g., life expectancy and nutrition) have become less important over time in developed economies, while others have increased in importance. Today, a key requirement for modern innovation is an educated population, particularly a population educated in scientific and technical subjects, sometimes referred to as science, technology, engineering, and mathematics (STEM) education. Griliches (2000) briefly reviews the literature on the contribution of education and human capital to economic growth and productivity, concluding that the cross-country evidence for a strong relationship is robust. Furman et al. (2002) show that both the number of scientists and engineers in a country and the share of GDP spent on higher education are associated with the country's level of patenting in the United States (a proxy for patenting by inventors and hence for invention in that country). The countries they consider are

---

Box 3.1 CRISPR Technology

CRISPR is short for Clustered Regularly Interspaced Short Palindromic Repeats. Developed by Jenifer Doudna and coworkers in her laboratory at the University of California at Berkeley, CRISPR is a technology that allows research scientists to selectively modify the DNA of living organisms. CRISPR was adapted for use in the laboratory from naturally occurring genome editing systems found in bacteria.

The most widely used editing process is called CRISPR/Cas9, because Cas9 is a CRISPR-associated endonuclease, or enzyme, that acts as "molecular scissors" to cut DNA at a location specified by a guide RNA (ribonucleic acid).

---

developed economies in Europe, as well as Australia, Canada, Japan, New Zealand, and the United States.[5]

A second important supply factor is the state of scientific and technological knowledge. Although as we have seen, some innovations are made in advance of the relevant science, most today rely heavily on scientific discoveries or technological development during the past. For example, the development of the CRISPR technology for editing genes was preceded both by the scientific discovery of the DNA code by Crick, Watson, and Franklin and by the Cohen-Boyer work on splicing DNA (Box 3.1). The development of the integrated circuit rested to some extent on developments in materials science as well as earlier attempts at miniaturization of computer components. The potential for new inventions created by earlier science and technological development is often termed *technological opportunity* by innovation economists.

For many innovators, expected profits and the ability to capture these profits from innovation are important motivators. Expected profits are to some extent a function of projected demand for a product, which we discuss in the next section. They also depend on the costs of producing a new product or the expected reduction in cost from introducing a new process. Kilby (2000) discusses his concern with production costs when trying to come up with an integrated circuit rather than the previously used analog circuits composed of transistors, resistors, capacitors, and the like. He reports that costs of production at Texas Instruments, where he was working in 1958, caused him to settle on semiconductors as a material:[6]

> Probably the only thing they [Texas Instruments] could make cost effectively were semiconductor products. This triggered the thought that maybe you could make everything from semiconductors. (Kilby 2000, p. 110)

We discussed the ability of the inventor to capture the profits of innovation in the previous chapter and termed this characteristic *appropriability*. Appropriability is affected

---

[5] They include a dummy variable in the regression for the United States, as the patenting measure is domestic for that country, and therefore expected to be higher, other things equal.

[6] Kilby filed for a patent on his invention in February 1959, and it was granted in June 1964 (US 3,138,743). Enforcement of this and subsequent patents by Texas Instruments contributed to the explosion of patenting in the semiconductor industry in the 1980s, as we discuss later in the textbook (Chapter 18). Kilby himself received the Nobel Prize in Physics for this invention in 2000.

by the presence and effectiveness of a patent system (including enforcement), which allows the inventor to exclude imitators. *A priori*, we therefore expect innovation to increase when inventors can patent their ideas. As we will discuss later in Chapters 11 and 18, this argument is too simplistic and in some situations the patent system may discourage follow-on innovation that builds on earlier patented inventions. Nevertheless, there is no doubt that some innovators at some times have been encouraged by the availability of patents. Other practices may also increase appropriability (see also Chapter 14):

1. Keeping the invention secret, if that is possible. This tends to be easier for process inventions and improvements.
2. Being (among the) first to market with a new invention, especially if there are network effects that arise due to consumers preferring to purchase a good that other consumers also purchase. These effects are especially strong for communication goods, such as messenger apps.
3. Lowering cost by moving down the learning curve rapidly.
4. Producing complementary output such as sales, marketing, and service activities.

Survey evidence displayed in Chapters 4 and 14 shows that firms use all these techniques in order to profit from innovation, in addition to patenting (Cohen et al. 2000; Levin et al. 1987).

3.2.1 Missing Einsteins and Marie Curies?

Recently, economic research has emphasized that invention, innovation, and entrepreneurship, like much else, are unequally distributed across the population with respect to gender, race, and family background.[7] This suggests that there are "missing" inventors who might contribute to innovation and society if they had the same opportunities as others. Bell et al. (2019) studied millions of individuals in the United States using a range of data sources including tax data, patent data, and a limited sample with test score data. They first confirm that there are huge variations in invention rates across family income, race, and gender, with white males having parents in the top 1% of the income distribution far more likely to be inventors than non-white males, females, and those in the lower parts of the income distribution.

Bell et al. then find that exposure to innovative activity during childhood is a critical factor in determining whether an adult becomes an inventor (files at least one patent). Because minorities are much less likely to come from neighborhoods and families containing inventors, they are less likely to invent, even controlling for schooling and math test scores. Another interesting finding is that exposure is gender-linked, in the sense that female invention is linked to childhood exposure to female invention, and

---

[7] We apply the names used by the authors of the paper in this section, although Einstein and Curie were basic science researchers rather than inventors per se. Better names of potentially missing inventors/innovators might be Steve Jobs and Hedy Lamarr, under her married name Hedy Kiesler Markey (https://patents.google.com/patent/US2292387A/en), the inventor of spread spectrum technology.

not to male invention. The authors conclude that innovation and economic growth would benefit from more attention paid to mentoring and other programs targeted to individuals from low-income and minority backgrounds.

Hoisl et al. (2021) use Danish registry data and European Patent Office (EPO) data to explore the choice by about 1 million individuals born between 1966 and 1985 to become an inventor. They confirm that parental background in the form of STEM education and inventorship predicts entry into inventing, with effects much larger for males than for females. In their sample, 0.12% of women and 0.64% of men become inventors, whereas for those who complete tertiary education with a STEM degree, 1.8% of women and 5.8% of men become inventors. Thus, having a STEM degree improves the odds of women becoming inventors rather than men, but women are less likely to complete a STEM degree in the first place (4.1% vs. 7.6%).

Hoisl et al. also find that maternal STEM education has a greater impact on their daughter's choice to follow a STEM track in high school and university. By comparing first-born women with a second-born female sibling to those with a second-born male sibling, they show that the parental inventorship influence on the female probability to become an inventor disappears if they have a younger brother, but not if they have a younger sister. The comparison also shows no difference in the impact of parental education on the choice to become an inventor. This within-family comparison controls for all the environmental effects that might have affected the probability of becoming an inventor, so it provides fairly convincing evidence that the parental influence on girls' choices does depend on whether that influence is diluted by the presence of a boy in the household. The effect is fairly large—women with female siblings rather than male have 15 more inventors per 1,000.

On the reasonable assumption that innate invention capability does not differ across various groups, all this suggests that we could achieve more innovation as a society if policies could be developed to attract individuals to STEM fields, to familiarize them with the inventive process, and to assist potential inventors with financing when they do not have access to resources.

3.2.2 Absorptive Capacity

In an influential paper, Cohen and Levinthal (1989) pointed out that an important driver of R&D is the desire of firms to build their knowledge capability in order to be able to monitor technological knowledge in their domain and to reduce the cost of future innovation. The term they gave to this capability was *absorptive capacity* (Box 3.2). Thus, one of the determinants of innovation supply is the specific knowledge embodied within a firm as well as that within an economy.

Box 3.2 Absorptive Capacity

This term refers to the ability to recognize the value of new information, assimilate it, and apply it to commercial ends (Cohen and Levinthal 1989).

Cohen and Levinthal built a simple model of R&D competition in an industry with an arbitrary number of symmetric firms n and derived the equilibrium R&D investment as a function of the level of spillovers from competitors' R&D and the absorptive capacity of the firm. They used the model to show that decreases in the ease of learning (e.g., due to increased complexity of knowledge) would lead to net increases in R&D investment by the firm in equilibrium. They also show that if firms can affect their absorptive capacity via investment in R&D, increases in spillovers can lead to increased incentives for R&D. This conclusion is contrary to the earlier work of Nelson (1959) and Arrow (1962b), who assume implicitly that spillovers reduce R&D incentives by making imitation lower-cost than invention.

We sketch the model here, using only two firms rather than n firms for simplicity. The firms are labeled i and j. The model is static and is solved for a Nash equilibrium in R&D investment. Each firm's profits Π depend positively on its own stock of knowledge K and negatively on its rival's stock of knowledge:

$$\Pi_i = g(K_i, K_j) \quad \frac{\partial g}{\partial K_i} > 0, \frac{\partial g}{\partial K_j} < 0 \tag{1}$$

A firm's stock of knowledge is a function of its own R&D R, spillovers from its rival's R&D, and the general knowledge level of the economy T:

$$K_i = R_i + \gamma_i(\theta R_j + T) \quad 0 \leq \theta \leq 1 \tag{2}$$

θ measures the spillovers of rival's R&D. $\theta = 0$ means there are no spillovers, and $\theta = 1$ means that the firm would, in principle, be able to use the rival's R&D as though it was its own R&D. The external knowledge potentially available to the firm is $\theta R_i + T$. However, the firm is only able to actually use a fraction γ of this external knowledge ($0 \leq \gamma \leq 1$). γ is an increasing function of the firm's R&D and a parameter $\beta > 0$ that indexes the ease of learning for a given level of R&D. That is, γ measures the absorptive capacity of the firm, which depends on its own R&D investment, but also varies with β depending on the type of sector and technology. β is assumed to increase the marginal effect of R&D on absorptive capacity but to reduce the level of absorptive capacity.[8] Learning is cheaper when β is higher, but higher β reduces the level of learning. Factors that determine β are technological complexity of the knowledge level in the industry and the extent to which external R&D is related or useful for the firm's own knowledge stock. For example, the introduction of jet travel in the 1960s and the internet in the 1990s have made learning from others at a distance easier, increasing β (Pauly and Stipanicic 2022; Van Alstyne and Brynjolfsson 2005; Forman and van Zeebroeck 2019). However, for a given level of R&D, these may have reduced the fraction of the available knowledge that a firm can make use of (lower γ).

Another example might be a comparison between the level of knowledge required to produce a simple transistor circuit board in 1960 with that necessary to produce a semiconductor chip in 1980. The latter has a higher β than the former, implying that

---

[8] That is, $\partial \gamma / \partial R > 0$, $\partial \gamma / \partial \beta < 0$, and $\partial^2 \gamma / \partial R \partial \beta > 0$.

absorptive capacity is lower for a given stock of knowledge but that a firm's own R&D is more effective in increasing the absorptive capacity of the firm.

Under these assumptions, Cohen and Levinthal are able to derive some propositions about the impact of absorptive capacity and spillovers on a firm's R&D incentives. Because the model cannot be solved easily for a Nash equilibrium, they use numerical methods to find solutions. The return to a firm's R&D is given by the derivative of profit with respect to R&D:

$$\frac{\partial \Pi_i}{\partial R_i} \equiv \rho = \frac{\partial g}{\partial K_i}\left(1 + \frac{\partial \gamma_i}{\partial R_i}(\theta R_i + T)\right) + \frac{\partial g}{\partial K_j}\theta \gamma_i (R_i, \beta) \tag{3}$$

The first term is the positive impact of the firm's knowledge stock on its profits, which includes a spillover term mediated by the impact of the firm's own R&D on its absorptive capacity. The second term is negative because rivalry effects imply a negative impact of the other firm's knowledge stock on profits, one that is larger in absolute value if either spillovers or absorptive capacity are larger. The equilibrium is obtained by setting the return ρ equal to the cost of R&D, which is assumed to be 1.[9]

Cohen and Levinthal are able to show the following results using this model after determining the signs of the various derivatives:[10]

1. If complexity β increases, the return to R&D and the level of R&D will increase because own R&D matters more for absorptive capacity and competitors are less able to exploit spillovers.
2. Given the presence of absorptive capacity, the impact of spillovers on R&D and its return is ambiguous. They increase the profitability of own R&D, but there is a negative effect from their impact on rival's R&D.
3. As in the case of spillovers, another incentive to invest to increase absorptive capacity comes from the presence of technological opportunity T (external knowledge for universities, etc.).

Testing this model using empirical data is challenging due to the lack of specific data on ease of learning that would allow one to characterize β. The authors instead relate R&D investment at the business unit level to various measures of technological opportunity T, appropriability (which is assumed to affect the spillover rate θ), and industry-level demand. They then proxy the ease of learning with a variable that measures the closeness of the industry technology to basic science. The assumption is that industries where basic science is relatively more important have a higher β, that is, learning is more difficult. They test whether the impacts of the technological opportunity and spillover variables are affected by the proximity of the industry technology to basic science and find that they are, and in the ways expected by the model. They find that as the proximity to basic science increases (higher β), R&D responds more positively as predicted.

---

[9] This is a harmless assumption here, which simply means that R&D enters the profit function as an additive expense. The model abstracts from any dynamic effects of an R&D program, depreciation of the knowledge produced by R&D, and so forth.

[10] Ensuring that the solution is an equilibrium requires various assumption on the second derivatives that are plausible, but that we omit here.

That is, the positive impact of spillovers on profitability outweighs the negative incentive impact from spillover to the rival firm.

Numerous subsequent researchers have confirmed empirically that having some kind of research program assists firms in taking advantage of spillovers from others, demonstrating the importance of absorptive capacity. Among other implications of the results in Cohen and Leventhal's paper is the idea that firms will invest in basic research in order to increase their absorptive capacity, in spite of the fact that such research also has broader spillovers, as we discussed earlier (Nelson 1959). Rosenberg (1990) addresses the many additional and related reasons that firms might find it advantageous to do basic research.

3.2.3 Financing Innovation

A key element of innovation cost is the cost of financing the resources needed to develop an invention and bring it to market. As we learned in the previous chapter, the economic theory of innovation says that financing innovation can be problematic for a number of reasons. The basic idea is that unless an entrepreneur is able to finance the development of an innovative idea out of their pocket, they will face a cost of external finance that is higher than their required return, which will lead to some projects not being undertaken. This can happen for at least three reasons: asymmetric information, moral hazard, and a lack of securable assets.

The general definition of asymmetric information is given in Box 3.3. In the innovation setting, the asymmetric information problem is that an inventor frequently has more information about the likelihood of success and the nature of the contemplated innovation project than a potential investor. The implication is that an investor will need a higher return to compensate them for the fact that they may fund a "lemon," that is, a project with little chance of success. Obviously, the inventor will not consciously choose such a project, but inventors are often overly optimistic about the success and potential market for their invention (Astebro et al. 2007). In the most extreme version of the Akerlof (1970) lemons model, the information gap is so large that the market

---

Box 3.3 Asymmetric Information and Moral Hazard

Asymmetric information: when one party in a transaction possesses more information relevant to the transaction than the other. For example, in the sale of used cars, the fact that the seller usually knows more than the buyer about its condition means that buyers' willingness to pay is lower and therefore sellers will supply only cars in bad condition (termed "lemons") in equilibrium. See Akerlof (1970) for this model.

Moral hazard: lack of incentive to guard against risk or perform as contracted when one is protected from the consequences, for example, by insurance. This often leads to a principal–agent conflict, where the principal has to be compensated via higher payments because of the potential for agent underperformance.

entirely disappears. At certain times and places, entrepreneurs have claimed this to be true for their projects.

Asymmetric information problems can be reduced by increasing the amount of detail supplied to the potential investor, but this strategy encounters the problem of appropriability: If the innovative idea is completely revealed, it can be imitated and the entrepreneur will not receive the appropriate returns, which limits their willingness to supply information. There are at least two solutions to the problem: nondisclosure agreements (NDAs), which are widely used by venture capitalists (VCs) and entrepreneurs when considering whether innovative startups should be funded, and patent applications early in the life cycle of the innovation development so that ownership of the idea is established early. For example, patent applications for potential drugs are filed by pharmaceutical firms after research has identified promising targets and before the bulk of the R&D spending (which is spending on clinical trials) is incurred.

The moral hazard problem is the existence of a potential conflict between financier and entrepreneur or between investors and the management of a firm. Investors prefer that the entrepreneur or firm managers maximize the value of their investment, while those who undertake the innovation may prefer less effort and an easier life than that needed to ensure the investment gains' maximal returns. Alternatively, a diversified investor may prefer that the firm undertake riskier investment with potentially high payoffs, whereas a manager prefers less risk because they are unable to diversify effectively to reduce their risk of failure.

Mitigating moral hazard takes a number of forms. In the case of startups and early-stage firms where the information asymmetry is greatest, VC financiers undertake substantial monitoring and stage the supply of finance over several "tranches" so that they can terminate the project if they perceive it to have limited chances of success (Gompers and Lerner 2001). Another advantage of VC financing is that VC firms are structured to pool risk by investing in a number of startups at the same time. Although numbers vary, typically only 1 in 5 or 10 startups is successful.[11]

For established firms, one strategy for reducing moral hazard behavior is to limit the freedom of managers by leveraging the firm, which reduces the free cash flow available to them (Jensen and Meckling 1976). In the case of innovative firms, this approach is somewhat problematic, as debt is a less favored form of finance due to the fact that innovation investments generate knowledge and other intangibles that are not generally suitable as security for loans.[12]

In principle, publicly traded firms should be able to undertake risky and uncertain innovation investments due to their ownership by diversified investors who can mitigate their risk by holding a portfolio of such firms. However, there is a view widely held by managers and others that the focus of the market participants on quarterly earnings reports discourages longer-term investments. Empirical research on the question of whether this focus reduces innovation investments has produced somewhat ambiguous results, although the majority of studies lean toward a rejection of this hypothesis.

---

[11] For a survey of the advantages and disadvantages of the VC financing system, see Lerner and Nanda (2020).

[12] For a review of the role of patents in creating securable assets for innovative firms, see Hall (2019).

Nevertheless, a considerable amount of empirical work has confirmed that the factors listed earlier do mean that innovative firms face higher costs of financing, especially if they are new or small (Hall and Lerner 2010). Although VC financing mitigates this to some extent, such capital is not widely available and tends to concentrate on a few sectors and geographic areas at a time. For example, van den Heuvel and Popp (2022) use evidence from the first wave of VC financing of green technologies directed toward climate change mitigation in the early 2010s to argue that insufficient demand and a lower potential for outsized returns make clean energy firms less attractive to VCs than startups in information and communications technologies (ICT) or biotech.

There are other alternatives to the VC solution, many of which rely on close relationships between the investor and the entrepreneur. These include friends and family investing, angel investing, and some forms of crowdfunding. Friends and family investing is just what it says––relying on friends and family members for the necessary loans or gifts to make the innovation possible. Obviously, this avenue is one where those at higher income levels find financial assistance easier to obtain, contributing to the findings cited in Section 3.2.1 on missing inventors.

Angel investors are high-net-worth individuals who invest their own capital into startup companies during early stages of development, receiving an ownership stake in return. The appeal is the possibility of high returns accompanied by considerable risk. It is distinguished from VC investing, where VCs invest a pool of money from other individuals in new ventures. Around the world, angel financing represents a larger share of startup financing than VC financing (OECD 2011). Table 3.1 shows that the amounts are roughly comparable in the United States.

Recently, a new source of financing for startup firms has arisen: crowdfunding via the internet. Hervé and Schwienbacher (2018) review the literature on crowdfunding and innovation, highlighting two ways crowdfunding can contribute to innovation: (1) by funding worthwhile projects that might not otherwise be funded; and (2) by "crowdsourcing," that is, by participating in shaping the project to satisfy more consumer demand. The authors conclude that both effects are present, although the

Table 3.1 Source of Funding for US Startups in 2004

Source of Finance	Millions of 2004US$	Share of Finance (%)
Self-financed	145.6	33.0
Friends and family	28.3	6.4
Angel financing	34.2	7.8
Government	9.2	2.1
VC	30.2	6.9
Corporate	19.5	4.4
Bank loans	173.6	39.4
Total	440.6	100.0

Source: Robb and Robinson (2012), Table 4.

need to reveal the idea publicly may affect the types of innovative projects suitable for crowdfunding.

Finding a comprehensive source of data on the funding of entrepreneurial startups is challenging. Robb and Richardson (2014) report on a survey of US startups during the 2004 period that were eventually followed through to 2011, although their study ends in 2007. Among other variables, they were asked about the sources of their initial funding. The results, for the 4,000 firms that were tracked until exit or 2007, whichever came first, are shown in Table 3.1. It is important to note that in a random sample of startups like this, the modal startup is a home-based sole proprietorship with zero employees that shows a loss in the first few years. Firms that expect to grow in the future will be a small subset of the sample (Guzman and Stern 2017).

Table 3.1 shows that a third of the financing of these startups was from the owners via credit cards, personal loans, and equity stakes, and 39% derived from bank loans and credit lines. Given the finding in Guzman and Stern (2017) that most future firm growth in startups comes from 5% of the sample, it is not surprising to find that only 6.9% of the firms received VC funding, and similarly for angel financing, government financing, and financing from established corporations.

3.3 Demand for Innovation

Where does the demand for innovation come from? We can divide the agents that express their desire for new and improved goods and services into three groups: consumers, firms, and governments. First on the list are consumer wants and needs, although many innovations will arrive without there being a clear signal of desire for them, at least at first. An example is the internet itself, which may have been perceived as a useful way to communicate among scientists, but certainly consumers in general were not clamoring for access to cat videos, much as they might enjoy them once they were provided. Seriously, the idea that one could manage much of one's financial and bureaucratic life remotely was probably not on the list of most consumers' wants 50 years ago. Similarly, if such a consumer had contemplated lower cost for international communication, it probably would have been in the expectation that telephone costs would continue to decline, rather than the idea that free worldwide voice communication would be available via the internet.

In contrast, one can point to a number of inventions or innovations where consumer demand was and is very clear, such as many pharmaceuticals and vaccines, improvements to internet speed and batteries, or larger screens for televisions. Thus, it is neither true that all innovations are completely demand-driven, nor is it true that demand plays no role. It is clearly one of the factors that motivates some kinds of innovation. In many cases, if not all, consumer demand will focus on incremental innovations to technologies with which they are already familiar, as in most of the examples just given.

In general, consumer demand is assessed and filtered through the medium of commercial firms including startups. Firms also have their own desires for innovation. For example, the development of the internet and international networking improvements greatly facilitated passenger management for international airlines and reduced their costs. Many of the most important patents are for inventions that are or were widely used in industry, for example, patents on methods for manufacturing semiconductor devices and for chemical reaction catalysts.

Firms' responses to the various demands for innovation will depend on the profit they expect to earn from their investments and innovation choices. Broadly speaking, expected profit will depend on the following demand factors:

- The size of the market or potential market that can be served. Because the costs of the innovation can be spread across as many customers as are in the market, firms will prefer larger to smaller markets, other things equal. Of course, the innovation itself may expand the market and related markets. For example, the wide availability of high-speed internet expanded the market for live streaming of video.
- Per capita income in the relevant market, which will affect the willingness to pay for the innovation.
- In the case of process innovation, the amount of cost reduction that can be achieved by the potential innovation.
- In the case of product innovation, the benefit to the buyer, whether it is a consumer or other firm. This benefit could be improved product quality, or the solution to a problem faced by the buyer, or something completely new that the customer perceives as valuable. The buyer's perception will also affect the willingness to pay and hence the price that can be charged.

Schmookler (1966) was probably the first to study the role of demand in eliciting innovation. He argued that although the supply of science and technology was important, their potential applications were many and that the larger a potential or actual market was, the more inventive activity would be directed to that market. Using patent data classified by industrial end use during the 1936–1950 period, he showed that the greater the capital investment in an industry, the higher the patenting rate for capital goods used in that industry.

Scherer (1982) repeated Schmookler's analysis with a much larger and improved dataset based on the US Federal Trade Commission 1974–1976 line of business data and confirmed Schmookler's basic result that capital investment in an industry elicited patenting activity in capital goods used by that industry. However, he also found that differences in technological opportunity (measured as differences across industries in whether they relied on chemical, electric, etc., technologies) also mattered a great deal in explaining patenting levels across industrial sectors. Not surprisingly, the conclusion is that demand and supply both stimulate inventive activity.

Demand may also be signaled by governments via public procurement of various kinds. The most obvious demand signals are the various requests for proposal (RFPs) issued by government departments, with detailed specifications that may involve inventing something new, or improving an input or output. In addition, we are all familiar with the role of government mandates such as fuel efficiency targets for automobiles, which have clearly required innovation investments on the part of auto manufacturers.

For another example, in 2010 the State of California's Public Utility Commission adopted the Lighting Chapter of the Long-Term Energy Efficient Strategic Plan, including mandated lighting standards that could be satisfied by fluorescent bulbs but not by traditional incandescent bulbs.[13] Other jurisdictions have issued similar mandates. Consumer dissatisfaction with fluorescent technology, coupled with these mandates, has led to a wave of innovation in LED bulb technology, with the result that there has been a nine-fold increase in energy efficiency and the new bulbs have a lifetime at least 20 times longer than that of incandescent bulbs.[14] Because the upfront costs of an incandescent bulb are about one-quarter those of an LED bulb, it is unlikely that builders and contractors would have made this shift without the mandate, as they were unlikely to be able to recover the costs, given consumer myopia.

The role of demand in eliciting innovation is influenced by the appropriability of the contemplated innovation. For example, in pharmaceuticals there are a number of old drugs that are off-patent, but that could be useful for diseases or other indications that were not originally contemplated when the patent(s) were obtained. Firms may not be willing to invest in costly clinical trials to validate their potential new use in the absence of patent protection, as the (off-patent) drug might be easily imitated once it has been approved by the regulatory authority. Thus even in the presence of demand for what appears to be a useful drug, the full innovation will not take place due to lack of appropriability.[15] Shaughnessy (2011) gives many examples of such drugs, like sildenafil, which was originally for angina and repurposed for erectile dysfunction. We further explore this and related topics in Chapter 16.

3.3.1 War and Demand for Innovation

In addition to its impact on raw material supply, historians have pointed to war as the impetus behind many important innovations, possibly not all beneficial. Examples include the boring machine of Wilkinson, designed for the production of cannon, but important in the development of the steam engine by Watt and Boulton (Mokyr 1990) as well as spillovers from the invention of firearms to metalworking technology. The technology historian Lynn White (1962) argued that the development of the stirrup enabled effective warfare on horseback using armor during the medieval period.

In our own time, the experience of the United States and other countries during World War II highlighted the importance of science and technology in enabling many innovations that clearly happened because of military demand. The most visible was the atom bomb, of course, which depended on developments in physics during the preceding half century. But there are many other examples, such as radar, microwaves, and medical treatment improvements in blood transfusion, skin grafts, and trauma.[16] Another interesting example was the development of penicillin, the first antibiotic, which was discovered by Alexander Fleming in 1928 by accident. Although its potential was obvious, it proved extremely difficult to produce in the laboratory and it was not until the US government together with major pharmaceutical companies accelerated

---

[13] https://www.energy.ca.gov/programs-and-topics/programs/building-energy-efficiency-standards.

[14] https://www.viribright.com/lumen-output-comparing-led-vs-cfl-vs-incandescent-wattage.

[15] Of course, the drug may still be prescribed for "off-label" use, but lack of the relevant testing will inhibit marketing and diffusion.

[16] https://www.nationalww2museum.org/war/articles/scientific-and-technological-advances-world-war-ii.

research on its production that sufficient quantities were available to supply the Allies armed forces by 1943, after the United States entered World War II.

The importance of science and technology during World War II together with his experience directing the US Office of Science, Research, and Development during the war led Vannevar Bush to issue a well-known report to President Franklin Roosevelt in 1945, entitled *Science, the Endless Frontier*. In this report, he argued for a national science policy and for the creation of the National Science Foundation (NSF). This led ultimately to the creation of this foundation in 1950 under President Harry S. Truman. Initially, the NSF was the primary funder of basic scientific research in the United States, as well as the body responsible for collecting data about all US R&D activities. With the increase in federal funding of research in medical science, the National Institutes of Health (NIH) is now the largest federal funder of basic research. Many other developed countries such as France, Italy, the United Kingdom, Sweden, and Australia also introduced such an R&D funding system during the second half of the 20th century. In Chapter 10, we discuss the direction and results of government R&D funding.[17]

Another outcome of World War II in the United States was the creation of the US Atomic Energy Commission (AEC) in 1946 to research nuclear technologies, encourage the use of nuclear power, and regulate its safety. The creation of this agency was partly a response to the successful creation of an atomic bomb during the war, as well as a desire to continue weapons development during the Cold War. The AEC was also responsible for funding basic high-energy physics research until 1974, another example of technology feeding back to scientific research, this time financially.

3.4 The Direction of Innovation

What do we mean by the direction of innovation? Generally, there are (infinitely) many paths in different directions that might be pursued at a given point in time. Which ones are attractive will be determined by the same factors that determine the overall level of innovation: the science base, expected innovation cost, expected profit from the innovation, risk and uncertainty, and so forth. Innovation researchers have attempted to classify the different paths in multiple ways: (1) by broad science/technology field, (2) as process-oriented versus product-oriented, or (3) as incremental versus radical. The science or technology field is largely a supply influence on the direction of innovation in that the availability of scientific knowledge will often encourage an inventor in a particular direction. For example, advances in neural network algorithms have encouraged the innovation of new uses for AI technologies such as translation and face recognition.

The process/product or radical/incremental choices, which we discussed in Chapter 2, are often determined by market structure, demand, and the size of the firm undertaking them. Cohen and Klepper (1996) present evidence that larger established firms will invest more in process than product R&D. The argument is that process R&D generates cost savings that are greater, the greater the output over which these savings can be spread, whereas product R&D generates new markets and future output even if the firm has little or no current output. Product R&D also generates innovations that

---

[17] See also Gross and Sampat (2020).

are not necessarily embedded in the existing firm and are therefore more easily salable or licensable to another firm. They develop a model of these differences and apply it to business units in 36 industrial sectors for the United States, 1974–1976.[18]

Using patents to classify the business unit's R&D as process versus product, Cohen and Klepper find that business units with larger sales have a higher share of process R&D, but that the effect diminishes for the largest units. They also show that industries where innovations are more salable (as evidenced by rapid growth rates of new entrants within the industries) have a higher share of process R&D on average, but that the share also increases more rapidly with the sales of the unit, confirming that the salability of the output of product R&D makes it more attractive for smaller firms. But as we showed in Chapter 2, product R&D is often accompanied by the process R&D necessary for manufacturing a new product, which probably weakens the observed effect of business unit size on the choice of R&D.

The choice of incremental or radical innovation has been widely studied. Incremental innovation is that which improves an existing good or service, probably leaving it still in competition with older less improved versions. Radical innovation creates a new market and causes the competing goods or services to become no longer viable. As in the case of process versus product innovation, we would expect incremental innovation to be the dominant type pursued by established firms, and radical innovation to be more likely to come from new entrants. We pursue this topic further in Chapter 5.

3.4.1 Influence of Supply on the Direction of Innovation

The key supply influence on the choice of which inventions to pursue is the current state of scientific or technological knowledge. There may be innovations that are perceived as desirable but are not undertaken over long periods of time because the necessary science is not ready. There are many examples: cures for cancer and AIDS, vaccines for malaria, powerful lightweight electric batteries. Rosenberg (1976d) cites the treatment of diabetes, which was held up by the complexity of understanding insulin so that the development of crystallography was needed in order to understand complex organic molecules. In contrast to organic chemistry, inorganic chemistry is simpler and so innovations in metals proceeded much more quickly.

More broadly, Rosenberg points to the state of mathematics and astronomy in the 16th and 17th centuries as sufficient for great advances in ship navigation, whereas equally desired health and medical improvements had to wait until the 19th-century development of bacteriology.[19] In our own time, advances in deep learning algorithms and computational science are needed if we are to continue to develop AI applications, as the limits of computing power are the binding constraint (Thompson et al. 2021).

Another supply determinant of innovation choice that has recently been shown to matter is the composition of potential innovators. Einiö et al. (2019) use data on

---

[18] These data, collected by the FTC in a short-lived project, contain a great deal of information that is unobtainable elsewhere because the unit of observation was a coherent business unit in a firm, rather than the entire firm. Unfortunately, similar data for more recent periods do not exist, although the US NSF has recently begun collecting data on R&D by line of business rather than solely at the firm level.

[19] Rosenberg (1976d), pp. 267–268.

individual entrepreneurs in the United States and Finland to show that innovators tend to create new products for people who are similar to them in gender, age, and socioeconomic status. That is, the information available to an innovator about consumer demand tends to come from people who are similar to them or whom they know and with whom they communicate, and this has an influence on their choice of innovation direction.

3.4.2 Influence of Demand on the Direction of Innovation

Rosenberg (1976e) emphasized the role of "inducement mechanisms and focusing devices" in determining the direction of innovation. He suggested that many times the direction of innovation was dictated by a technological bottleneck or imperative need (demand) for improvement. He cited the development of the oil tube drill, used for the inside of bicycle hubs to speed up drilling so it was in step with the outside forming tool. Prior to this invention, the manufacturing of the hubs was slowed by lack of compatibility between the two processes (shaping inside and outside of the hubs). He emphasized here also the feedback from manufacturing experience to innovation. His article contains many such examples.

Other examples can be seen in the development of the laptop computer. As the chips to run these computers got progressively smaller and more powerful, it led innovators to focus on the development and improvement of color screens to be cheaper and lighter. PC developers also demanded smaller, lighter rechargeable batteries with longer lives, and that also generated less heat as the computers got more powerful. A similar innovation direction in batteries is now targeted toward automobile batteries for electric cars and trucks. Lighter batteries are especially needed for trucks, as the weight of the current batteries required is too heavy for the largest truckloads. In our own time, we can see the acceleration of innovation in ventilators, and even touchless technologies due to COVID.

Economists in the past have argued that relative factor prices may dictate the direction of innovation, on the grounds that effort will be spent to economize on "expensive" factors. This argument fails under classical economic assumptions about production. If each factor (labor, capital, etc.) is paid its marginal product, then the firm has already optimized its production so that all factors appear equally "dear" or "cheap." The relevant question is how costly the innovation in the different types of factor-saving inventions may be relative to the potential savings in reducing the use of that factor. However, because production processes do not always allow smooth adjustment of inputs in response to price changes, sharp changes in relative prices will focus attention on particular costs.

There are many examples of inventions that were a response to increases in the cost of an input, or shortages in supply of that input. Rosenberg (1976e) cites a number of such cases. A leading example is labor cost, the threat or actual withdrawal of labor due to strikes. Karl Marx himself cited the self-acting mule, an automatic cotton-spinning device, as created in response to a strike by mule-spinners in 1825. As employee costs have risen over the past 200 years, partly because of social taxes and legal requirements, the process of using improvements in capital to save on labor has continued. Manufacturing robots are the latest indicator of this trend. Another more trivial example is the use of remote sensors and license plate readers to replace toll collectors on bridges and roads.

A second powerful influence on the direction of innovation via the demand channel is the interruption of the source of supply of a key raw material, often because of war. During World War I, Germany developed the nitrogen fixation process in response to its inability to obtain nitrates from Chile, and the United States developed its dye industry due to interruption in its access to German dyes. The American synthetic rubber industry arose as a response to the cutoff in supply of Southeast Asian natural rubber during World War II. Hanlon (2015) studied the cotton industry during the American Civil War. The interruption in cotton supply from the United States forced British firms to use lower-quality Indian cotton, which, in turn, induced technical change in cleaning and spinning cotton.

3.5 Simultaneous Invention

Many researchers have pointed out that invention is often nearly simultaneous. That is, two or more individuals who may or may not be in contact with each other come up with the same or very similar ideas at almost the same time. Ogburn and Thomas (1922) list 148 such inventions that were made during the 17th, 18th, and 19th centuries. They include well-known discoveries in science such as calculus (Isaac Newton in 1671; Gottfried Wilhelm Leibniz in 1676), the theory of natural selection (Charles Darwin and Alfred Russel Wallace in 1858), and the principle of least squares (Adrien-Marie Legendre in 1806; Carl Friedrich Gauss in 1809). They also include more technological discoveries such as the telephone (Alexander Bell and Elisha Gray in 1876); flying machines (Orville and Wilbur Wright in 1895–1901, Samuel Pierpoint Langley in 1893–1897, and others); photography (Nicéphore Niépce, Louis Daguerre, and Henry Fox Talbot in 1839); and the telegraph (Joseph Henry in 1831, Samuel Morse in 1837, William Fothergill Cooke and Charles Wheatstone in 1837, and Carl August Steinheil in 1837).

In our own day, we have the work on the CRISPR gene-editing technology of Doudna and Charpentier at the University of California, Berkeley, and the Broad Institute, MIT, which has led to patent disputes in the United States and Europe. This is a case where both research groups were working along the same lines but applied for slightly different patents about 6 months apart. UC Berkeley's patent was general and covered the use of CRISPR-Cas9 technology in any cell, while the Broad Institute's patent covered its use in plant and animal cells.[20] This is essentially a case of simultaneous invention with variations, which is typical of most of the simultaneous inventions listed earlier.

Why is simultaneous invention apparently common? When one examines the factors affecting supply and demand that we have discussed earlier, it is fairly obvious that most of them are characteristics of an economy or society rather than of an individual: risk

[20] The dispute over priority in this case is complicated by the fact that UC Berkeley filed first and was granted second, at the same time that the US Patent Office switched form a first-to-file to a first-inventor-to-file system (Chapters 4 and 11 explain this switch). For more on this patent dispute, see https://www.science.org/content/article/latest-round-crispr-patent-battle-has-apparent-victor-fight-continues, https://www.science.org/content/article/new-crispr-patent-hearing-continues-high-stakes-legal-battle, https://www.law.upenn.edu/live/news/15802-crispr-technology-and-patent-ownership.

bearing, financing availability, the state of scientific knowledge, the size of the market, and so forth. Thus, it is perhaps not surprising that more than one individual perceives the opportunity to make a technological invention that satisfies consumer or other needs and where the cost of the invention is recoverable via potential profit. Later on, when we study patents, we will explore the implications of this fact for the patent system, its operation and design.

3.6 Summary

In this chapter, we have presented innovation as determined by the usual economic factors, that is, as a quantity that results from the interaction of supply with demand for innovation. Although this is perhaps an oversimplified lens through which to examine the determinants of innovation, it is helpful as a method of organizing them for analysis. There is no doubt that noneconomic factors and chance also matter, but these factors are less subject to policy targeting or indeed to conscious strategy by individuals and firms.

The supply factors we have identified are the current science and technology base, individuals and institutions with the relevant knowledge, the availability of finance, cultural attitudes such as those toward risk, newness, and societal values. Demand factors include consumer needs and willingness to pay, market size, shocks to relative input costs, regulatory mandates, and the perceived benefit of the potential innovation.

From the review of these determinants, we have also drawn two conclusions. (1) Supply and demand factors also determine the direction of innovation, with market structure and potential market entry playing a somewhat larger role in this case. (2) Because many of the factors determining innovation are economy- or society-wide, it is not surprising that many inventions and scientific discoveries are apparently simultaneous, made by different individuals possibly in slightly different ways at almost the same time.

4

Appropriation Mechanisms

Learning Objectives

After reading this chapter, you will be able to understand and explain the following
concepts:

- The basic structure and purpose of intellectual property (IP) rights
- The main features and laws associated with each type of IP right:
  - patents including utility models, design rights, and plant patents
  - copyright
  - geographical indications
  - trademarks
  - *sui generis* IP rights
  - trade secrecy
- How to compare and combine these different IP rights

4.1 Introduction

In Chapter 2, we discussed the fact that innovation is a quasi-public good, in the sense
that it creates knowledge that can be used by others who do not bear the costs of its
creation. One implication of this characteristic is that methods by which firms and
individuals can secure the returns to their innovative efforts become important if we
wish to encourage innovation. Such methods can be either informal (based on actions
undertaken by the innovator without recourse to legal protection) or formal (defined
by the legal system, often requiring some kind of registration) or even a hybrid of the
two methods. Generally, we refer to the ability to secure returns via such methods as
appropriability (of an invention or innovation).

In this chapter, we briefly overview the formal and informal methods used
by individuals and firms to protect their innovations from being freely imitated.
Understanding the legal framework within which firms are operating is essential when
studying their innovation strategies. In later chapters, we will look much more closely
at the most important of these rights, focusing on the ways they are used in practice: patents and related methods (Chapter 11), trademarks (Chapter 12), copyright
(Chapter 13), and alternatives to IP protection (Chapter 14). In this chapter, we provide
an introduction for those who are unfamiliar with intellectual property rights (IPRs)
or would like a review of the types available in most countries. However, keep in mind

The Economics of Innovation and Intellectual Property. Bronwyn H. Hall and Christian Helmers, Oxford University Press.
© Oxford University Press 2024. DOI: 10.1093/oso/9780197630914.003.0004

that this is only a broad overview and that the legal landscape for any particular IPR in a country may be more complex than described here.

4.2 Intellectual Property

The term *intellectual property* is commonly understood to refer to the intangible products of human creativity. Such products include the following:

- The knowledge of how to make or do something
- Creative works such as books, movies, musical recordings, photographs, and the like
- New designs for commercial use
- Original product markings and trade names
- New plant varieties

As we learned in previous chapters, goods like these are often both *non-rival* (the good can be used by more than one individual at the same time) and *non-excludable* (it is not possible for the "owner" to exclude others from using the good, unless there are specific legal and enforceable prohibitions). Given these characteristics, the term *property* is somewhat misleading, because without legal protection of some kind, they are not really property in the traditional sense. That is, absent some kind of legal protection, the creator (or owner) cannot exclude others from using the idea, even if they are able to exclude them from any specific physical object that results from its application.

For example, without special legal provisions such as the US Digital Millennium Copyright Act of 1998 (DMCA), it is not possible to exclude others from copying the contents of a book, although the physical book itself is conventional property.[1] Even in the absence of the DMCA, copyright laws would make such copying illegal, although perhaps not preventing it. Similarly, without legal restrictions, one cannot exclude others from imitating a new invention, even though any individual product containing that invention will also be conventional property.

Currently, legally defined IPRs include the following:

- Patents including plant patents
- Copyrights
- Trademarks
- Design rights
- Geographical designations
- Semiconductor mask protection
- Trade secrets (a special case, which might be considered informal also)

These various rights differ in the length of term, whether prior registration or examination is required for enforcement, their effectiveness, and in many other respects. In this chapter, we give a brief overview of the different types, while in Parts II and III of this

---

[1] If you are reading an electronic copy of this book in the United States, you may point out that the DMCA criminalizes the act of violating access control in order to copy the book electronically. However, this does not prevent you from printing it out and copying it manually.

book, we provide more detail as well as extensive coverage of the contemporary use of the most important right for innovation, patents.[2]

From an economic perspective, IPRs are generally a response to the problem created by non-excludability, which is that incentives for producing information and ideas are weak if they are shared freely with all comers. However, there are other arguments for the creation of IPRs. For example, many countries confer moral rights to the creator in the case of artistic creations, granting the creator the right to control their work (Box 4.1). In some cases, it is not possible to assign away some of these rights. We discuss these rights in the copyright section of this chapter. In contrast, the rationale for trademark protection is usually to protect consumers from confusion and potential fraud, although trademarks also create value for their owners in the sense that they help to build a reputation for the owner and their products. In the case of patents, there are a number of theories that justify their existence that we address in the relevant section of this chapter.

Box 4.1 Moral Rights

Moral rights are the rights "to claim authorship of the work and to object to any distortion, mutilation or other modification of, or other derogatory action in relation to, the said work, which would be prejudicial to his honor or reputation" (definition from the Berne Convention for the Protection of Literary and Artistic Works (1886), Article 6).

The coverage of the legal forms of IP protection is generally restricted to the country that grants them. However, IP protection is one of the areas where international cooperation is fairly advanced, which has both good and bad implications as we discuss later in Chapter 15. There exist a number of treaties that specify minimum standards of protection that must be observed by the states that are party to the treaties. These treaties are generally administered by the World Intellectual Property Organization (WIPO) in Geneva, Switzerland, and are summarized on their website.[3] The number of contracting parties varies across the treaties and conventions, but the most important of these, the Paris Convention of 1883 (patents and related instruments) and the Berne Convention of 1886 (copyright), have almost 180 contracting states, which covers most of the world. For comparison, the United Nations has 193 member states, which implies that WIPO has 193 potential members of these conventions.[4]

An important example of one of these treaties is the Paris Convention, which specifies the minimum level of protection for industrial property in the widest sense, including patents, trademarks, industrial designs, utility models, service marks, trade names, and geographical indications. In addition, this treaty requires national treatment of all patenting entities (Box 4.2). This international treaty initially had 11 signatories, mostly European countries, and there are 180 contracting countries as of

---

[2] We caution the reader that while the description of the specifics of these IPRs is correct at time of writing, it is advisable to check the relevant websites cited in this document for the latest information on the precise legal provisions.

[3] https://www.wipo.int/treaties/en.

[4] Nonmembers of the Paris Convention include Eritrea, Ethiopia, Somalia, South Sudan, Timor-Leste, and a number of small island nations.

Box 4.2   National Treatment

This is the principle that countries should treat intellectual property applicants and holders from other countries in the same way they treat their own IP applicants and owners.

April 2024. It has been revised several times, the last time in 1979. Although it is still in force, in many ways it has been superseded by the TRIPS (Trade-Related Aspects of International Property Rights) agreement of the World Trade Organization (WTO), which sets minimum standards for copyright, trademarks, geographical indications, industrial designs, patents, integrated circuit layouts, trade secrets, and anti-competitive licensing practices.[5] The TRIPS agreement also contains enforcement and dispute resolution provisions, as well as some administrative requirements for timely registration/grant. As of April 2024, 164 countries are members of the WTO and 28 additional countries are designated as "observers," mostly in the Middle East and North Africa.

4.3   Patent

A *patent* confers the right to exclude others during a limited period from the use of an invention. The patentholder may or may not be actively using the invention. Patents are generally national rights, and we give the definition of a patentable invention for the United States, Europe, Japan, and China in Box 4.3. Definitions at other patent offices are similar. Although the requirements we show are worded somewhat differently, they are substantively the same. Briefly, they require that the invention be novel, non-obvious, and useful.

The novelty requirement is just what it says: The invention must be new, which is interpreted as new to the world, that is, not already invented in any other country. This requirement also means that the applicant should not have exhibited publicly or published the invention before making the application for a patent.[6] The utility or usefulness requirement stipulates that the invention actually work as claimed and excludes such impossibilities as a perpetual motion machine and other products of science fiction. Non-obviousness is more difficult to define, as what is obvious to one person may not be so to another. It is usually defined as not obvious to a person skilled in the art (PHOSITA; see Box 4.4), that is, to someone who has experience in the relevant field of technology.

Although the process for granting a patent varies slightly according to the jurisdiction for which protection is desired, the adoption of the TRIPS agreement in 1995 ensures that it is at least approximately the same everywhere in the world. As we discuss in Chapter 15, standardization around the world has some drawbacks, especially for

---

[5] https://www.wto.org/english/docs_e/legal_e/27-trips_01_e.htm.

[6] This point can be controversial—in the United States, there is a grace period of 12 months prior to the first filing of the patent application worldwide during which disclosures by the inventor do not count as prior art. In some other patent systems, there is a 6-month grace period, while in many European countries, there is no grace period. The exact rules surrounding disclosure also vary by jurisdiction.

Box 4.3 Patentability

US Patent and Trademark Office (USPTO): any new and useful process, machine, manufacture, or composition of matter, or any new and useful improvement thereof. This excludes laws of nature, physical phenomena, and abstract ideas. (https://www.uspto.gov/patents/basics/general-informationpatents)

European Patent Office (EPO): an invention in any field of technology. The invention must be new, susceptible of industrial application, and involve an inventive step. Excluded are discoveries, scientific theories and mathematical methods, aesthetic creations, schemes, rules and methods for performing mental acts, playing games or doing business, and programs for computers, and presentations of information. (https://www.epo.org/lawpractice/legal-texts/html/guidelines/e/g_i_1.htm)

Japan Patent Office (JPO): an invention that is industrially applicable, not previously publicly known or described, and not obvious to one skilled in the relevant art. (https://www.jpo.go.jp/e/system/laws/rule/guideline/patent/tukujitu_kijun/document/index/03_9900_e.pdf)

Chinese National Intellectual Property Administration (CNIPA): an invention patent is granted for new technical solutions or improvements to a product or process, provided that the technical solutions have a practical applicability. (https://www.chinaiprhelpdesk.eu/sites/all/docs/publications/China_IPR_Guide-Guide_to_Patent_Protection_in_China_EN-2013.pdf

---

Box 4.4 PHOSITA

Meaning a "person having ordinary skill in the art," the term PHOSITA is used regularly in US courts. It describes a person with average vocational or (more likely) professional knowledge in the field of a particular patent or invention.

---

countries at widely differing levels of development, because it has the potential to rule out some kinds of learning by imitation.

The TRIPS agreement also requires its member countries to make patent protection available for any product or process invention in any field of technology with only a few specified exceptions. For example, it allows countries to exclude diagnostic, therapeutic, and surgical methods for the treatment of humans or animals from the scope of patentable subject matter. The agreement specifies that the term of patent protection available to inventors be not less than a period of 20 years from the date of filing the patent application. Prior to this agreement, the US patent term was 17 years from the date of granting, although most other countries have always counted the term from the date of filing.[7]

As we observed in Chapter 3, many discoveries and inventions are made almost simultaneously. This fact requires some kind of rule to define who receives the patent if

---

[7] The United States changed the patent term with the Uruguay Round Agreements Act in 1995. The surge in US filings prior to this change suggests that such a change was viewed as an effective shortening of patent term, especially by pharmaceutical firms.

both parties apply for one on a similar invention. Most countries in the world use the "first-to-file" system, whereby priority goes to the first applicant that files for a patent on an invention. Until 2013, the United States was the exception, with a "first-to-invent" rule, whereby priority went to the inventor that could prove the earliest invention date. With the America Invents Act (AIA) of 2011, the United States switched to a "first-inventor-to-file" system (with an 18-month delay to March 16, 2013). The advantage of this switch was both international harmonization as well as a reduction in court disputes over invention timing. The disadvantage is that such a change may favor larger firms with in-house patent departments, although this problem has been somewhat mitigated by reductions in filing costs for small firms and independent inventors (Abrams and Wagner 2013; Mossinghoff 2005).

In general, a patent right extends only within the border of the jurisdiction that has granted it (usually but not always a country). An important exception to this rule is the European system, where it is possible to file a patent application at the EPO that will become a set of national patent rights in several European countries at the time of issue (EPO, 2024). A similar situation exists with respect to the African Regional Intellectual Property Organization (ARIPO, with 19 African member states); the Organisation Africaine de la Propriété Intellectuelle (OAPI, with 17 Francophone African member states); and EAPO (Eurasian Patent Organization, with 9 member states from the former USSR).

In June 2023, the European Union (EU) introduced the first truly transnational patent, the European Unitary Patent.[8] This patent is examined and issued by the EPO, but provides coverage for the participating member states (currently 18 and up to 25 when the remaining 7 states who have agreed to enhanced cooperation ratify the agreement). Enforcement is the province of the newly created Unified Patent Court (UPC), with courts of first instance in several European cities, and a Court of Appeal in Luxembourg. The patent has a single fee payable to the EPO that potentially covers all 25 countries.[9]

In spite of the TRIPS requirement that patent protection be available in any field of technology, in practice the various patent offices do differ somewhat in the subject matter for which they allow patents. The EPO explicitly excludes a number of areas that have been the subject of debate in the United States during the past half century, notably business methods and computer programs as such. This reflects disagreement among patent offices over what qualifies as a field of technology. We will discuss the nuances of these subject matter differences and how they have changed over time more fully in Chapters 11 and 17.

The filing and examination process for a patent in most countries follows a similar course. Once the relevant office has received an application, it is examined for the three patentability criteria. Most importantly, novelty and non-obviousness are determined via a search of "prior art" (Box 4.5). Usually, there are requirements of adequacy of disclosure and clarity of the language in addition. If no relevant prior art can be found

---

[8] https://www.epo.org/applying/european/unitary.html.

[9] The EU has 27 members currently (following the withdrawal of the United Kingdom after the Brexit vote). Only two countries have not yet signed up to at least enhanced cooperation with respect to the unitary patent at the time of writing: Croatia because it joined the EU after the UPC agreement was signed, and Spain because of unhappiness with the linguistic regime, which requires applications and other patent business to be conducted in English, French, or German.

Box 4.5 Prior Art

At the USPTO, **prior art** constitutes those references or documents that may be used to determine the novelty and/or non-obviousness of claimed subject matter in a patent application. It includes patents and published patent applications (domestic and foreign) as well as non-patent literature: magazine articles, newspaper articles, electronic publications, online databases, or websites. It also includes any item that was once on sale or presented at a seminar or trade show. At the EPO, the definition of prior art is "any evidence that the claimed invention is already known."

---

and the invention satisfies patentability requirements, the patent will be granted. Most jurisdictions charge fees at regular intervals to keep the patent in force until its statutory term.

A patent is generally nonrenewable beyond 20 years from its filing date and can be allowed to lapse earlier than its statutory term if renewal fees are not paid. A patent may be licensed or ownership transferred to another party, who/which will have the same rights as the original patent holder. A patent holder can sue to enforce the patent and a potential infringer can countersue by challenging validity. In Chapter 19, we discuss patent enforcement more fully.

The fact that a patent is only valid within a particular jurisdiction clearly creates substantial costs for an inventor who wishes protection around the world, even if they confine such protection to developed or high-income countries, that is, those where imitation is feasible or the potential market is attractive. This fact has led to various cooperative agreements among patent agencies to reduce the cost of application and search for prior art. The most important cooperative agreement is the Patent Cooperation Treaty (PCT), which came into existence in 1978, and has 157 countries as contracting signatories as of April 2024. Any resident or national of a contracting state of the PCT may file an international application under the PCT that specifies the office which should conduct the search.

The PCT application serves as an application filed in each designated contracting state. However, in order to obtain patent protection in a particular state, a patent needs to be granted by that state to the claimed invention contained in the international application. The advantage of a PCT application is that fewer searches need to be conducted and the process is therefore less expensive. Thus, although application and search are to some extent standardized across offices, grants are not. In fact, 95% of the PCT applications go to one of five patent offices for search: those in Europe (31%), China (27%), Japan (18%), Korea (11%), and the United States (8%) (WIPO 2023). Most of the other systems rely on these offices for the search process and follow them in a number of other areas. For example, PCT applications and patent applications from most other offices are published (revealed to the public) 18 months after the earliest priority filing for the patent (Box 4.6).[10]

---

[10] In the United States, exceptions to this are provisional patent applications and those where the applicant has opted out of publication. Graham et al. (2017) report that published applications are fairly representative of all applications and that unpublished applications are fewer than 10% of the total (excluding provisionals).

Box 4.6 Patent Priority Date

This term refers to the date of the earliest patent application filing anywhere in the world to which priority is claimed. The importance of the priority date is that novelty is measured at that point in time. That is, no publications or other information dated later than the priority date are considered **prior art** or can be used to argue that the invention is not novel. There are some exceptions to this novelty rule in countries like the United States that have a grace period.

What is the economic justification for the existence of a patent system? Mazzoleni and Nelson (1998) suggest four related economic theories that justify patent rights to invention:

1. *Invention motivation.* The right to exclude others from using the invention creates an incentive to invent.
2. *Invention dissemination.* Patents disclose an invention and therefore facilitate knowledge diffusion (in contrast to trade secrecy).
3. *Induce commercialization.* Patents also provide incentives to develop and commercialize an invention by excluding others from this activity for a time.
4. *Exploration control.* Also known as *prospect theory* (Kitch 1977), this justification is that ownership of a broad patent on an initial breakthrough allows for orderly exploration and development or in a number of directions without the wasteful effort that would occur if anyone could enter the area.

Clearly, there is substantial overlap among Theories 1, 3, and 4, all of which use the right to exclude to guarantee an incentive to invent and develop an invention. Theory 2 is different, in that it emphasizes the role of the patent system in encouraging the disclosure of inventions. Spulber (2015) provides a related set of views, emphasizing the role of patents in facilitating a more efficient market for technology and its development.

In practice, patents are often used by firms as part of a complex strategy to secure returns to their innovations. The complexity arises from a number of factors, of which the most important is probably the fact that a patent covers only a single invention, and many of the products produced by firms comprise and rely on a number of inventions, not all of which will be the property of that particular firm. Coupled with the fact that patent protection can be quite valuable in some cases, this leads other parties and their legal advisors to attempt to extract some of that value. In turn, firms adopt a number of patenting strategies for their defense against these attempts. We explore many of the strategic questions and issues that arise later in Part III of this textbook.

Another feature of patents that deserves mention is their public nature. Unlike many firm strategies and actions, patents are explicitly designed to be public information. Even if they may not be easily used by others to put the invention into practice without additional information, because they contain technical information in a standardized format and are classified by the patent offices in detailed technology categories, they provide a window into a firm's technology strategy that is observable by others, in-cluding economic researchers.[11]

There is a great deal more that is useful to understanding the operation of the patent system, such as the details of what the application contains and the ways in which a patent can be enforced. We refer the reader to a fuller discussion in Chapter 11 of this textbook.

4.3.1 Utility Models

Some IP systems also include utility models, a weaker form of patent that has less strin-gent requirements for patentability. In many patent systems, these are referred to as utility patents, in contrast to true invention patents. However, the US patent system uses the term utility patent for invention patents, which can lead to confusion.[12] In this text-book, we will follow the usage at WIPO, which refers to the type of patent obtainable in some jurisdictions on minor inventions as utility models, reserving the term patent or utility patent for invention patents.[13]

Compared to patents, *utility models* are generally cheaper to obtain and maintain, have a shorter term (generally 6–15 years), and take less time to receive a grant. In some countries, utility models do not require substantive examination. Utility models are considered particularly suited for protecting inventions that make small improvements to, and adaptations of, existing products or that have a short commercial life.[14] About 75 countries plus OAPI and ARIPO offer a utility model patent. This type of patent is not governed by an international convention other than the Paris Convention.

Utility models are often used by local inventors in developing countries, especially in Asia (Prud'homme 2017). For example, they are heavily used in China, where they are growing faster than invention patent applications since 2016, presumably because China does not require examination before grant. Another example of the use of utility models during economic development is that of South Korea: During this country's rapid de-velopment, the ratio of utility model applications to invention patent applications fell from about 0.38 in 2000 to 0.025 in 2019, a decline of over 90%. Historically, Japan used the utility model patent, introduced originally in 1905, as a path for development from a craft-oriented industrial model to the modern industrial sector of today.

4.3.2 Plant Patents

IP protection for new plant varieties is a relatively recent development. The United States introduced the first IPRs in 1930 with the PPA, which was an effort to give the agriculture sector the same incentives for innovation as industry. To some extent,

---

[11] In Appendix C: Data, we discuss briefly how to access and use patent data. The international patent clas-sification (IPC) system is available at https://www.wipo.int/classifications/ipc/en.

[12] That is, the *utility model patent* is not be confused with the term *utility patent* in the United States, which is used to describe the ordinary invention patent.

[13] https://www.wipo.int/patents/en/topics/utility_models.html.

[14] https://www.wipo.int/patents/en/topics/utility_models.html.

this argument for protection arose from food shortages that occurred during World War I (Moser and Rohde 2012). The act allowed protection of new varieties created asexually, that is, via cuttings and roots rather than seeds. It was not until 1961 that the International Union for the Protection of New Varieties of Plants or UPOV was created in Geneva. Unlike WIPO, UPOV is not a United Nations member organization. After revision in 1972, 1978, and 1991, the UPOV Convention currently creates plant breeder's rights for a new plant variety however it has been obtained, for example, whether through conventional breeding techniques or genetic engineering. The requirements specified are the following:

- The new plant must be novel, which means that it must not have been previously marketed in the country where rights are applied for.
- The new plant must be distinct from other available varieties.
- The plants must display homogeneity.
- The trait or traits unique to the new variety must be stable so that the plant remains true to type after repeated cycles of propagation.

As in the case of patents, trademarks, and industrial designs, prior examination and granting by the relevant authority are required to establish the breeder's right. At the present time (April 2024), there are 79 members of UPOV, of which 17 countries have not signed up to the 1991 revision, probably because of the expansion of methods of creation to include genetic engineering. This expansion has proved to be controversial given the potential for genetic use restriction technology, otherwise known as terminator genes, which render the seeds produced by the plant infertile and prevent reuse.[15] Member countries tend to be either highly developed (e.g., the US and Europe) or large agricultural countries (e.g., Ukraine and the Russian Federation).

Another indication of the controversy over living organism patenting is contained in TRIPS Article 27.3(b), which states the allowed subject matter restrictions by members:[16]

plants and animals other than micro-organisms, and essentially biological processes for the production of plants or animals other than non-biological and microbiological processes. However, Members shall provide for the protection of plant varieties either by patents or by an effective *sui generis* system or by any combination thereof. The provisions of this subparagraph shall be reviewed four years after the date of entry into force of the WTO Agreement.

As of April 2024, this review does not seem to have yielded any agreement on revisions to Article 27.3(b). One of the complications is concern expressed by many countries over the way such protection may interact with the protection guaranteed to

---

[15] Monsanto owned the patent (US 5,723,765) on the method of rendering a seed sterile via genetic modification, but promised never to use the technique. The patent has now expired.

[16] For further information on the TRIPS agreement and the text, see the WTO website: https://www.wto.org/english/tratop_e/trips_e/trips_e.htm.

Box 4.7 *Sui generis*

The literal translation of this term from Latin means "of its own kind." In legal contexts, *sui generis* denotes an independent legal classification.

---

geographical indications and the commercial use of traditional knowledge and plants (see Section 4.4).[17]

Today, the United States has three types of IP protection available for plants:[18]

- Plant variety protection (PVP) for seeds, tubers, and asexually reproduced plants (issued by the PVP Office of the Department of Agriculture). Term is 20 years (25 for trees and vines). This IP right is subject to a research exemption for the purpose of breeding new varieties as well as a farmer's exception to allow for the saving of seed to replant. The novelty requirement is much weaker than that for plant patents or utility patents.
- Plant patents for asexually reproduced plants (issued by the US Patent and Trademark Office (USPTO)). Term is 20 years from filing date. Unlike the case of utility patents, enforcement of a plant patent requires proof that the copy is the progeny of the patented plant.
- Utility (invention) patents for genes, traits, methods, plant parts, or varieties (issued by the USPTO). Term is 20 years from filing date.

Note that it is possible to use more than one of these to protect a new plant variety. For example, a plant patent could protect the new variety, while a utility patent might protect the method of propagation. In addition, a PVP might be used to protect later off-shoot varieties related to the original utility patent.

In line with TRIPS and the UPOV 1991 Convention, the EU has established a system that grants IPRs to new plant varieties called the Community Plant Variety Right (CPVR). It is similar to a plant patent and, once given, is valid throughout the EU. The situation at the EPO with respect to utility patents on plants is somewhat complex. Currently and as of 2017, EPO policy is not to grant patents for animals, plants, or plant parts obtained exclusively by means of essentially biological processes, but apparently they have granted many such patents in the past and these are still valid patents.

4.3.3 Design Rights

Design rights are intellectual property protection for industrial designs that constitute the ornamental aspect of an article. They can cover the shape, pattern, color, and so on of an article. Unlike utility patents, the scope of a design patent or right is generally

---

[17] See https://www.wto.org/english/tratop_e/trips_e/art27_3b_background_e.htm.
[18] See Knauss et al. (2019) for details.

given by an image rather than text. The owner of a registered industrial design or of a design patent has the right to prevent third parties from making, selling, or importing articles bearing or embodying a design that is a copy, or substantially a copy, of the protected design, when such acts are undertaken for commercial purposes. In some countries, notably the United Kingdom and member states of the EU, registration is not necessarily required, although the term of protection is much shorter in that case. In some other countries, designs may be protected as works of art under copyright law (Section 4.5), which presumably means there is no examination requirement for a grant. They may also be protected as "trade dress" via the trademark system in some countries.

Industrial designs are governed by the Hague Agreement, administered by WIPO. This agreement was first adopted in 1925 and has been revised several times since. It establishes an international system that allows industrial designs to be protected in multiple countries or regions with minimal formalities. There are 79 signatories to the agreement, including most developed countries as well as the EU and OAPI. Signatories to the agreement can register industrial designs at WIPO and receive protection after minimal examination for 5 years, renewable up to the individual country's terms. Such registrations can be refused by any of the contracting member states, leaving them valid in some countries and not in others, similarly to patents.

In the United States, industrial designs may also be protected by the design patent system, which, in principle, means that they are subject to more rigorous examination. The requirements are similar to those for patents in general: novelty, non-obviousness, originality, ornamentality, and the subject matter must be an article of manufacture. The term of a US design patent is 14 years from date of issue and there are no maintenance fees payable.

Although design patents have been relatively unimportant in the past, the recent litigation between Samsung and Apple over the design of mobile phones has demonstrated that such rights can be quite valuable. Apple and Samsung have engaged in substantial cross-litigation involving both invention and design patents since 2011. There were four design patents involved in these suits, covering such things as the rounded corners, the uniform bezel, the home button, and even the icon layout. After some back-and-forth, in a May 2018 trial, Apple was awarded US$533.3million for Samsung's design patent infringement and $5.3million for utility patent infringement, demonstrating the importance of Apple's design patents (see Chapter 11).

4.4 Geographical Indications

A *geographical indication* (GI) is an indication or designation that a particular product is produced in a specific region, excluding similar products produced elsewhere by claiming they come from the region or using a trademark that suggests they do. Classic examples are wine, such as champagne from the Champagne region in France, or various kinds of cheese. A well-publicized recent dispute over the right to a GI is that between India and Pakistan over the rights to the basmati rice designation in the EU.[19] GIs are similar to trademarks (Chapter 12), although they are more restrictive in that they must be connected to a specific place. They are also less standardized around the world.

Article 22.1 of the TRIPS agreement defines GIs as "indications which identify a good as originating in the territory of a Member, or a region or locality in that territory, where a given quality, reputation or other characteristic of the good is essentially attributable to its geographical origin." The article specifies that individuals should have legal redress for the misuse of a geographical origin or trademark. However as written, the current article pertains only to wine and spirits, although individual countries and the EU have often extended GIs to cover all agricultural products, foodstuffs, handicrafts, and industrial products.

The Lisbon System at WIPO, introduced in 1966, allows the owners of GIs (termed Appellations of Origin by the agreement) in their home country to apply for simplified registration of the GI across the 55 country members of the system. The members include the EU and a number of countries in Asia and Latin America, but does not include several large or developed countries such as Canada, China, Japan, Korea, and the United States. A major stumbling block for developed countries is that the Lisbon agreement does not provide safeguards for the prior use of the GI as a generic term (one example is Camembert that is considered generic for Camembert-type cheese) or a previous trademark involving a GI.

One difference between the use of GIs and trademarks for identifying a product is that GIs tend to be bound up with the cultural and historical identity of a place and may therefore be highly valued by residents for noneconomic as well as economic reasons. For example, see DeSoucey (2010), who studies the use of EU geographical and traditional food labeling as an important exception to the standardization of food processes required by the EU's Common Agricultural Policy. Another example is the dispute over the rights to a GI on the brandy Pisco between Chile and Peru.[20] Most importing countries allow the name to be used for Pisco from either Chile or Peru, but Mitchell and Terry (2011) argue that the dispute is grounded in the traditional and historical memories of individuals in both countries.

4.5 Copyright

Copyright (usually indicated by a © symbol) covers original works of authorship that are fixed in tangible form, such as books, artworks, prints, photographs, films, recordings. A copyrighted work must involve some original creation and may not simply be an idea. Copyright grants the creator exclusive control over their creation: the rights to reproduce the work, to produce derivative work including audiovisual adaptation, to perform or record the work, to distribute the work, or to display the work. Exceptions are made for parody and fair use, including copying for academic uses; the latter may require

---

[19] See https://www.scmp.com/week-asia/politics/article/3141287/battle-over-basmati-rice-why-india-and-pakistan-may-both-claim. The central problem is that prior to the Partition of India and Pakistan in 1947, basmati rice was historically grown on both sides of the border in the Himalayan foothills, giving both countries a claim to the GI. In addition, both countries have substantial sales shares of basmati rice in the EU.

[20] https://www.cnn.com/travel/article/pisco-sour-chile-peru/index.html.

payment of a fee to the author. Registration of a copyright is generally not required, although it is usually necessary before litigation over ownership or infringement.

In the United States, registration is done at the Copyright Office and requires depositing a copy of the work. In the EU, registration is not required before enforcement via litigation. However, if registration occurs within 5 years of publication, it is considered prima facie evidence in a court of law. There is no registration requirement in the United Kingdom. In Japan, works other than computer programs are registered by the Agency for Cultural Affairs and those concerning computer programs by the Software Information Center. Japan requires registration before litigation.[21]

In the United States, the length of term has varied over the long history of copyright in that country. The initial Copyright Act of 1790 specified 14 years, renewable for another 14 years, and the amendment of 1831 replaced this with a simple 28 years. Since 1976, the term has been life of the creator plus 50 years, but this was changed to the life of the creator plus 70 years in 1998. The member states of the EU abide by the same term, and most other countries have similar terms, from life plus 50 years to life plus 70 years.[22] There are often special provisions for anonymous or pseudonymous creations and for cases where first publication takes place 50+ years after the death of the creator. Copyrights are generally not renewable, but since they are normally free and have a very long term, this is not much of a constraint.

The Berne Convention of 1886, which has 179 countries as signatories, specifies moral or authors' rights (WIPO 2021a; see Table 4.4). It requires national treatment and that formality (legal registration of ownership) not be required in order to hold a copyright. In the United States, 17 USC. §106A, known as the Visual Artists Rights Act of 1990 (VARA), grants the creator of a painting, drawing, limited edition print, sculpture, or photograph the right to its integrity and attribution as the creator.

We discuss copyrights and their use in more detail in Chapter 13 of this book. In particular, we discuss their changing nature and increased importance in the digital world, where copying of some types of work is very cheap (nearly zero), making infringement low-cost.

4.6 Trademark

A *trademark* (often indicated by a superscripted TM or R symbol) is a sign capable of distinguishing the goods or services of one enterprise from those of other enterprises. A trademark can also be issued for the design or packaging of a good or service. A trademark can be a phrase, word, symbol, device, or even a color that distinguishes the goods of one party or company from another. Depending on the jurisdiction, protection is available in the form of registered and unregistered trademarks. In most countries, the term of trademark registration is 10 years, renewable indefinitely. A trademark is a right to exclude others from using the mark or one that is substantially similar, unless it is licensed to them by the owner of the trademark.

Trademarks have their origin in common law, as they have been used even in ancient times to mark goods with the identity of the maker (Diamond 1983, VerSteeg 2018,

[21] http://www.seto-office.com/copyrightregistration.htmA.
[22] TRIPS mandates life plus 50 years, except for photographs or applied art, that may have shorter lengths.

Johnston 1974). We have a great deal of pottery from ancient Rome, Greece, Egypt, and China that is marked in this way. However, for much of the evidence from an-cient civilizations, it is difficult to distinguish the use of identifying marks simply to denote ownership from use intended to indicate the producer of the good to others. That is, a mark incised on ancient pottery is not always easy to interpret as branding per se. Indeed, the word *brand* itself contains this ambiguity, as it can denote both a trademarkable feature of a firm's output as well as the physical sign placed on an animal's back to denote the ownership of a herd.

Unlike the case of patents and copyrights, the principal justification for trademarks is consumer protection, that is, to ensure the consumer obtains the good or service that they think they have purchased. The owner of a trademark can challenge others' use via a civil suit by proving that confusion is likely to result in the marketplace, and requesting injunctions and/or damages. In the United States, the customs agency can stop entry of goods that are deemed to violate US trademarks, and egregious trademark counterfeiting can also lead to criminal penalties.

The Trademark Law Treaty (TLT) of 1994 standardizes trademark law internation-ally to some extent.[23] It has 54 contracting parties, including the United States, Japan, Korea, China, and most of Europe. This treaty specifies the 10-year term, renewable in 10-year increments, and mandates relatively simple application procedures. The Singapore Treaty of 2009 extended the TLT in several ways to accommodate changes due to the evolution of digital and internet technology. It expanded the types of marks to include nontraditional visible (e.g., holograms) and nonvisible marks (e.g., smell and sound). This treaty explicitly allowed for trademark registration to be operated digitally. This treaty has the same contracting parties as the TLT.

TRIPS (following the Paris Convention to some extent) specified trademarks as any sign, or any combination of signs, capable of distinguishing the goods and services of one "undertaking" from those of other undertakings These signs could be words, in-cluding personal names, letters, numerals, figurative elements, and combinations of colors, as well as any combination of signs. They also may include smells and sounds. Applicants must publish a trademark either before, or promptly after, it is registered. Contracting member states must provide for a reasonable opportunity to request the cancellation of the trademark so that interested parties can challenge a registration. In addition, members may allow for trademark opposition, a procedure whereby a trade-mark can be challenged after it is accepted by the trademark office, but before it is reg-istered. TRIPS also specifies that the initial term of a registered trademark should be no less than 7 years, renewable in 7-year increments, although most jurisdictions use 10 years rather than 7.

These various treaties also specify that the marks filed should have their relevant classes of goods and services specified according to the classification of the 1957 Nice Agreement.[24] There are currently 34 such classes for goods and 11 for services.

[23] https://www.wipo.int/treaties/en/ip/tlt.
[24] https://www.wipo.int/treaties/en/classification/nice/summary_nice.html. This agreement establishes a classification of goods and services for the purposes of registering trademarks and service marks (the Nice Classification). The trademark offices of the 93 contracting states must indicate, in official documents and publications in connection with each registration, the numbers of the classes of the classification to which the goods or services for which the mark is registered belong.

Examples of these classes are such things as pharmaceuticals including veterinary, nonmedicated toiletries and cleaning substances, telecom services, and a broad goods class that includes scientific instruments and computer software.

Fifty-five countries, not including the United States and the United Kingdom, have also signed on to the Madrid Protocol of 1989, which makes it possible to protect a mark in all the contracting countries by obtaining an international registration of that mark. This system evolved from a much older treaty, the Madrid Agreement of 1891, an agreement among seven European countries and Guatemala.

4.7 *Sui generis* IP Rights

In some jurisdictions, specialized IP rights have been introduced that apply only to a single type of invention. For example, these include semiconductor mask protection in the United States and Japan, vessel hull designs in the United States, database protection in the EU, and traditional knowledge protection in several developing countries. We discuss these examples briefly in this section.

The Vessel Hull Design Protection (VHDP) Act, Title 17, Chapter 13 of the United States Code, was signed into law on October 28, 1998, providing protection for the original designs of vessel hulls. This right grants an owner of an original vessel design the exclusive right to make, have made, or import, for sale or for use in trade, any useful article embodying that design; and to sell or distribute for sale or for use in trade any useful article embodying that design. The right is distinct from design patents and looks more like a copyright, although it requires formal registration.[25] It is weaker than a patent but can be obtained earlier during the design of the vessel; if a design patent is issued later covers the same vessel, the VHDP right terminates.

The EU provides a *sui generis* database protection right to its citizens and residents that protects the contents of the database as a whole, although it allows the copying of individual entries or a small selection. In order to enforce this right, the owner of the database must prove that substantial investment was involved in its creation. In addition, the structure of a database may be protected via copyright. Maurer et al. (2001) discuss some of the practicalities of this database right. Although the United Kingdom, France, and Germany saw a one-time surge in database creation following the implementation of the database directive in 1998, they concluded that the introduction of the right also "eroded the public domain, overprotected 'synthetic value' of doubtful worth, and raised new barriers to data aggregation." By synthetic value, they refer to the value of a collection of synthetic data such as telephone numbers.

In most of the world, the *sui generis* right of greatest interest is the right associated with traditional knowledge and cultural expression. Many countries have rights like this incorporated into their IP laws. The WIPO compilation of 2022 lists 28 countries with such legislation.[26] Geographical indications are sometimes considered a type of *sui generis* traditional knowledge protection.

---

[25] See this website for the details of the right: https://www.uspto.gov/ip-policy/copyright-policy/vessel-hull-designs#:~:text=The%20Vessel%20Hull%20Design%20Protection,original%20designs%20of%20vessel%20hulls.

[26] https://www.wipo.int/export/sites/www/tk/en/resources/pdf/compilation_sui_generis_regimes.pdf.

4.7.1 Semiconductor Mask Protection

A *sui generis* IPR for semiconductor masks was introduced in the United States by the Semiconductor Chip Protection Act (SCPA) of 1984, 17 USC. §§ 901–914. A semiconductor mask or *mask work* is defined as follows:

> a series of related images, however fixed or encoded––(A) having or representing the predetermined, three-dimensional pattern of metallic, insulating, or semiconductor material present or removed from the layers of a semiconductor chip product; and (B) in which series the relation of the images to one another is that each image has the pattern of the surface of one form of the semiconductor chip product." (17 US Code § 901 (a)(2))

This legislation was essentially a response to Japanese competition in the semiconductor sector, and was soon followed by the Japanese Act Concerning the Circuit Layout of a Semiconductor Integrated Circuit, which was very similar to the US Act (Curtin 1992).

Semiconductor mask protection was originally a response to the threat of foreign competition via imitation because neither copyright nor patents provided appropriate coverage. It is essentially a part of copyright law, as it only protects the exact expression of the logic on the chip and allows reverse engineering. It probably does require slightly more originality than copyright itself.

In practice, there has been relatively little take-up of semiconductor mask protection and little litigation of those that have been registered. During the late 1990s, Ziedonis (2003) interviewed semiconductor manufacturing and design firms and found that although mask protection was easy to obtain, effective at preventing pure copying, and quite cheap, the bulk of these firms' time and money was devoted to patents, especially since the patent reforms of the early 1980s. The reasons for this are probably technical change in the industry, which made direct copying much more difficult, as well as the evolution of the importance of patent use in the industry (Ziedonis and Hall 2001).

An interesting feature of semiconductor mask protection is that it generally did not require national treatment, but instead has relied on reciprocal arrangements between countries that mutually recognize the rights of the others' mask layouts. An international treaty, the Washington Treaty on Intellectual Property in Respect of Integrated Circuits, was adopted at WIPO in 1989. This treaty has been ratified by only 10 countries, including China and India as well as places such as Ghana, Egypt, and Santa Lucia, and has not come into force. Nevertheless, its provisions were incorporated into Article 35 of TRIPS and therefore apply to all signatories of that treaty.[27]

4.8 Trade Secret

Trade secret protection is rather different from the types of IP rights we have discussed earlier, in that it is not registered, has an indefinite term, and only offers protection from misappropriation. A *trade secret* is information kept within the firm, where the firm has made

---

[27] See https://www.wto.org/english/tratop_e/trips_e/intel2_e.htm#layoutdesigns.

an effort not to reveal it to the public, and where the information is not already generally known. Trade secrets can include any business information that has economic value and where there is an attempt to keep the information secret. Such things can include customer lists, formulas, pharmaceutical test data, methods of production, advertising strategies and marketing plans, and any other information within the firm that is not generally known. Clearly, the essence of trade secrecy is non-disclosure, which also makes it different from other IP rights, especially patents. It also differs in that only actual misappropriation is grounds for enforcement. Successful imitation without misappropriation is allowed. Thus, the firm is generally expected to exert efforts to keep the relevant information secret.

Trade secrets can be enforced by litigation; often this takes the form of litigation over non-disclosure agreements signed by former employees. US courts can protect a trade secret by (1) ordering that the misappropriation stop; (2) that the secret be protected from public exposure; and (3) in extraordinary circumstances, ordering the seizure of the misappropriated trade secret. A particularly visible recent case of this kind was the prosecution of Anthony Levandowski for the theft of trade secrets when he left Google to found his own autonomous trucking company, which was later sold to Uber.[28]

Because the legal protection of trade secrets arose from common law, in the past, trade secrets have generally been regulated by state law in the United States. In 1979 (revised 1985), trade secret protection at the federal level was formalized in legislation under the Uniform Trade Secrets Act (UTSA). The USTA created a "model" state law, a version of which has been enacted by 48 US states, Puerto Rico, the District of Columbia, and the US Virgin Islands as of 2019. Enforcement under these laws is civil courts at the state level. In addition, there are US federal trade secret laws from 1996 (the Economic Espionage Act) and 2006 (the Defend Trade Secrets Act), which is similar to the USTA, but at the federal level. The former act allows for criminal prosecution.

Trade secret protection is included in the Paris Convention and TRIPS, but enforcement internationally varies depending on the legal system. Trade secret violation may be considered unfair competition, or subject to specific provisions in the law covering industrial or commercial espionage, breach of contract, and breach of confidence.

4.9 Comparing IP Rights

In practice, innovators use the different types of IP rights both as complements and as substitutes. We discuss the most common substitution, trade secrecy versus patents, in Section 4.9.1. However, most commercialized innovations are protected by a bundle of IP rights. For example, a software program might be copyrighted to protect the code and also have patents if there is an original method involved. In addition, its unique name would be trademarked, and there might also be some trade secret protection for the customer list of the firm that sells the software. A new drug would almost certainly be covered by patents, and the proprietary name also trademarked. The production process for the drug as well as the test data would probably have some trade secret protection.

---

[28] Levandowski was indicted on 33 federal charges of trade secret theft; he admitted downloading documents from Google before leaving and pleaded guilty to one charge. See Chapter 14.

Table 4.1 IP Use by the Top 2,000 R&D Performers, 2010–2012

Office	USPTO	EPO and EUIPO	JPO
Share of firms using TMs only	69%	56%	28%
Share of firms using patents only	10%	20%	13%
Share of firms using both	12%	10%	16%
Total share using either TM or patent	91%	86%	57%

Source: Dernis et al. (2015), Figure 5.1.

Dernis et al. (2015) look at the use of patents and trademarks by the top 2,000 R&D performers in the world in the United States, Europe, and Japan. The data they use come from the USPTO, the EPO, the European Intellectual Property Office (EUIPO), and the Japan Patent Office (JPO, which also handles trademarks). For 10–15% of these companies, they find joint use of patents and trademarks. Although this does not necessarily imply that joint use is for the same product, in many cases, this is likely. Also note that these are shares that such firms file at each office, which explains why the JPO shares are rather low. Many multinationals do not bother to file in Japan, especially in the publishing, IT services, telecommunications, other services, and pharmaceutical sectors.

A similar study by the EUIPO found that 8.3% of a very large sample of EU firms applied for more than one type of IPR during 2014–2015, but that these firms accounted for 35.7% of IPRs, 35.5% of turnover, and 31.9% of employment among the sample. That is, multi-IPR firms are generally much larger than other firms and are also more likely to be in manufacturing than in services, broadly defined.

In two important US surveys (Levin et al. 1987, Cohen et al. 2000), researchers at Yale and Carnegie Mellon asked firms about the importance of the methods they used to secure returns to their innovations, both product and process. In Table 4.2 (product) and Table 4.3 (process), we summarize the results, aggregated to the three-digit industry level. The table shows the number of industries ranking each of the appropriation methods first, second, and so forth. For example, in the Yale survey of 1983, 4 of the industries ranked patents first, while 24 industries ranked the accompanying sales and service first.[29] Most of the industries ranked patents third or fourth. In the Carnegie Mellon Survey of 1994, patents were ranked even lower.[30]

The interesting feature of these survey results is their variability, both within industry and across industries. In general, the few industries where patents are effective for product innovation are drugs, specialty chemicals, medical devices, special-purpose machinery, and auto parts. That is, they are effective either for new chemical formulas

[29] The term *accompanying sales and service* means that the firm viewed its competitive advantage from innovative products or processes as secured at least partly by the fact that it did a good job of making the sale easier for the customer and provided servicing in case of problems. For example, think of Apple Stores and the Genius Bar.

[30] In the Carnegie Mellon Survey, firms were also asked whether complementary manufacturing and know-how were helpful in protecting their competitive advantage from innovation. Firms usually ranked this means second or third, indicating that they believed their experience and knowledge gave them an advantage over competitors.

Table 4.2 Effectiveness of Appropriability Mechanisms for Product Innovations

Mechanism	1st	2nd	3rd	4th	5th
Yale Survey 1983					
Patents	4	1	30	10	
Secrecy	0	0	12	33	
Lead time	20	22	3	0	
Sales and service	24	20	1	0	
Carnegie Mellon Survey 1994					
Patents	3	4	5	12	20
Secrecy	14	14	7	8	1
Lead time	22	6	10	4	2
Sales and service	3	9	11	15	6
Manufacturing	4	14	13	7	6

Sources: Levin et al. (1987); Cohen et al. (2000); authors' computations.

and uses, or for smaller physical (tangible) devices. In both cases, it is possible to define the scope of the patent fairly clearly and completely so that its boundaries are clear, making it easier to enforce against imitators. In contrast, for process innovations, patents are almost never preferred to secrecy and other means except in drugs and some other chemicals, including oil products.

Table 4.3 Effectiveness of Appropriability Mechanisms for Process Innovations

Mechanism	1st	2nd	3rd	4th	5th
Yale Survey 1983					
Patents	2	4	11	28	
Secrecy	3	17	20	5	
Lead time	35	8	2	0	
Sales and service	6	19	11	9	
Carnegie Mellon Survey 1994					
Patents	0	5	4	14	21
Secrecy	28	8	6	1	1
Lead time	6	10	19	7	2
Sales and service	1	2	10	21	10
Manufacturing	12	22	8	2	0

Sources: Levin et al. (1987); Cohen et al. (2000); authors' computations.

4.9.1   Trade Secrets versus Patents

Many inventions can be protected either by trade secrecy or by patents, so the innovating firm faces a choice. They will choose trade secret protection over patenting when patent protection is too costly relative to the invention value, the innovation or information is not patentable, the patent term is insufficient, or there is no patent system available (historically, although rarer today).[31] They will also be more likely to choose trade secrecy when the enforcement of trade secrets is strengthened.

An example of when trade secrecy would be preferred is the development of a new manufacturing process, one that is fairly easy to keep secret within the firm. The advantage of trade secrecy in this case is its relatively lower cost and the fact that, in principle, it lasts forever. Of course, the firm cannot prevent others from discovering and using the process independently, whereas if it were patented, it might be possible to sue for infringement. In contrast, an easily reverse-engineered product will usually be protected by patents because it is not possible to keep it secret.

Png (2017) used the staggered enactment of state laws following the UTSA across US states between 1981 and 2010 to show that patenting declined an average of 39% in the first year when a state introduced the act. Ganglmair and Reimers (2019) extend their work to states adopting the act through 2018 and found the bias toward process secrecy to be true empirically. Adopting this act, which strengthened trade secret protection, led to a reduction in process patents versus product patents. This suggests that more processes were being protected as trade secrets.

Note that nothing prevents the patent–secrecy mechanisms from being used as complements rather than substitutes, given that there may be some tacit knowledge necessary in order to implement a patented invention.[32] Such knowledge can be protected via trade secrecy, giving the inventor the best of both worlds. Another way the two, patents and secrecy, can complement each other is that secrecy can be and often is used to protect R&D in progress, while the ultimate output (an invention of some kind) will be patented.

4.10 Summary

The creators of ideas and intangible products are motivated by a number of factors, and an important one is the ability to capture some returns from their activities. In this chapter, we reviewed the methods they use, both formal and informal, and how they might interact or be used jointly. Along the way, we noted some related ways in which these various IP rights might also serve useful functions: (1) ensuring the development of future prospects from an invention; (2) providing disclosure of technical information that might otherwise be kept secret; (3) enabling trade in technology; (4) ensuring "moral rights" for creators even if they make no effort to claim ownership; and (5) providing protection via geographical indications to those whose traditional

---

[31] For evidence on the impact the existence of a patent system has on the direction of innovation, see Moser (2005). Using data form the 19th century, she shows that in the absence of a patent system, firms and individuals turn to innovation that can be protected by secrecy.

[32] In principle, the patent document should allow a the PHOSITA to implement the invention, but this is not always the case. See Ouellette (2012) for evidence on this point.

inventions do not rise to patentability or other modern IP protection due to their historical development.

Obviously, all this comes at a cost, legal and otherwise. In subsequent chapters, we will explore more precisely the trade-offs inherent in designing and using an IP system.

We conclude this chapter with a pair of tables that summarize the key features of international IP agreements and the various IP protections available. Table 4.4 lists the various international conventions and which types of IP to which they apply. In Table 4.5, we summarize the features of the most important IP rights as specified in

Table 4.4 Major International IP Agreements

Agreement	Origin Date	Number of Members*	Coverage	Features
Paris Convention	1883	177	Industrial property, including patents, trademarks, industrial designs, utility models, service marks, trade names, and geographical indications	Requires national treatment, much else superseded by TRIPS
Berne Convention	1886	179	Provides creators such as authors, musicians, poets, painters, etc. with the means to control how their works are used, by whom, and on what terms	Requires national treatment, no formal registration, and still applies even if work was created outside the contracting state
Trademark Law Treaty, Singapore Treaty	1994, 2009	54	A phrase, word, symbol, device, or even a color that distinguishes the goods of one party or company from another; also holograms, and marks involving smell and sound	10-year term, renewable in 10-year increments, relatively simple application
Madrid Protocol	1989	55	Unified international trademark application	Allows a single application to cover multiple countries
Hague Agreement	1925	79	Industrial designs	Allows obtaining design rights in multiple countries with minimal formalities
Lisbon System	1958, revised 2015	71	Appellations of Origin (AOs) and GIs	Allows a single registration procedure with WIPO, in one language, and with only one set of fees
TRIPS	1995	164	Industrial property, including patents, trademarks, industrial designs, utility models, plant variety, service marks, trade names, and geographical indications	Provides for minimal standards of IP protection in all signatory countries; enforcement via WTO processes

*The number of members is the number of countries covered, which may be slightly more or less than the number of signatories to the agreement.

Table 4.5 IP rights summary

	Trademark	Copyright	Patent	Trade Secret
International convention*	Trademark Law Treaty (1994); Madrid agreement (1901)	Berne Convention (1886)	Paris Convention (1883)	Paris Convention (1883)
Subject matter	Word, phrase, symbol, logo, design, etc. used in commerce to identify the source of goods and services	Creative works—e.g., books, songs, music, photos, movies, computer programs	Inventions— new and useful processes, machines, manufactured articles, compositions of matter	Any confidential business information that provides an enterprise with a competitive edge and is unknown to others
Requirements for eligibility	Identifies source of product or service used in commerce	Original and creative expression, fixed in material form	Useful, novel, and non-obvious to a PHOSITA (and adequately disclosed to the public)	Commercially valuable; known only to a limited group of persons; subject to reasonable steps to keep it secret, including the use of confidentiality agreements
Rights	Basic trademark right only vis-à-vis a particular good or service; prevents others from using similar trademarks; for famous marks, prevents others from "diluting" the mark	Exclusive rights to copy, distribute, make "derivative works," publicly perform, and publicly display	Exclude others from making, using, selling, or importing invention	Exclude others from using or disclosing the information acquired in an unauthorized manner
Duration	If renewed and continually used in commerce, can be perpetual	Life plus 70 years; 95 years after publication for corporate works	20 years for utility (invention) patents	Perpetual, although may be discovered independently or reverse-engineered
How rights are procured	Trademark registration process, though common law rights are recognized absent registration	Creation and fixation in tangible medium; registration not required (except for suit to enforce)	Patent application process at the relevant office	By taking reasonable steps to keep the information secret

*The Paris Convention of 1883 and the TRIPS agreement cover all these rights. In addition, there are many specialized conventions and treaties administered by WIPO and available on their website: https://www. wipo.int/about-ip/en.

international treaties, those that have broad subject matter coverage and are the most widely used. Keep in mind that for any given country, the precise features of its IP system will be given by national legislation. The international treaties define a minimum level of protection and administration to which its signatories should adhere.

5

Innovation and Competition in Firms

Learning Objectives

After reading this chapter, you will be able to understand and explain the following concepts:

- How innovative activity varies with industry and firm size
- The relationship between market structure and innovation
- "Patent races" and the timing of innovation
- The role of innovation in the evolution of industries and their structure

---

5.1 Introduction

In this chapter, we look at the major innovative actors today, both established firms and startups, and their interactions in the market. In order to set the stage, we begin by presenting some facts about observed innovative activity by industry and firm size in the United States and elsewhere. We focus on the best measured indicator of innovative performance, R&D spending. Not all innovation comes from R&D, but the other indicators available are either less precise (patent counts), badly measured (innovation survey measures), or not available consistently over long time periods.[1]

Then we review the advantages of monopoly and competitive industry structures for innovation and introduce some simple models that are useful for static analysis of the relationship between innovation and competition/market structure. Following Schumpeter (1960) and because innovation has the potential to change everything, including market structure, it is important to introduce dynamic considerations into its analysis, as more recent models do. As we have seen, there is considerable uncertainty involved when undertaking innovation, which complicates the decision making of firms making such investments. We follow the discussion of the theoretical relationship between innovation and competition with a summary of the empirical evidence.

As firms innovate and new products are introduced, industries develop and evolve: New industries are created and old ones sometimes disappear. The final section of the chapter presents some historical evidence and empirical regularities about the

---

[1] Patents do track R&D, but simple counts are much noisier than R&D with a signal-to-noise ratio of about 2% (Griliches et al. 1987). Innovation survey measures are generally based on a yes/no answer to a question of the form "Did you introduce an innovation in the past three years?," regardless of firm size. See Appendix C: Data for more information on innovation measurement.

The Economics of Innovation and Intellectual Property. Bronwyn H. Hall and Christian Helmers, Oxford University Press.
© Oxford University Press 2024. DOI: 10.1093/oso/9780197630914.003.0005

evolution of industries and their structure. The rise of the internet and Web-based services has recently led to the creation of new industries and new ways of delivering services. In turn, this has raised new antitrust concerns, which we discuss in Chapter 7, when we present the economics of network industries.

5.2 Industrial R&D

We begin this discussion of innovation in firms by looking at the basic facts about a major indicator of innovative activity by firms, their R&D spending. Recall that Figure 1.3 in the introductory chapter showed that R&D intensity had risen between 1981 and the present time in five of the seven major R&D-producing countries (United States, South Korea, China, Japan, and Germany). Figure 5.1 shows the ratio of R&D spending to GDP over more than half a century for the United States, broken down into spending by the federal government, industry, and others (nonprofits and state governments). There is a clear increase in the total during the 1950s, but after that the ratio is roughly flat with a dip during the 1970s and a slow increase after about 1993. Looking at the components of this spending, beginning in 1980 there is a substantial increase in spending funded by industry coupled with a somewhat later decline in federal spending. As much of the federal spending on R&D reflects defense R&D spending, this decline is mostly associated with the gradual decline in importance of the Cold War arms race. However, the most noteworthy fact about these trends is that business funded R&D in the United States increased from 0.5 to 1.8% of GDP in the past 50 years, a more than three-fold increase.

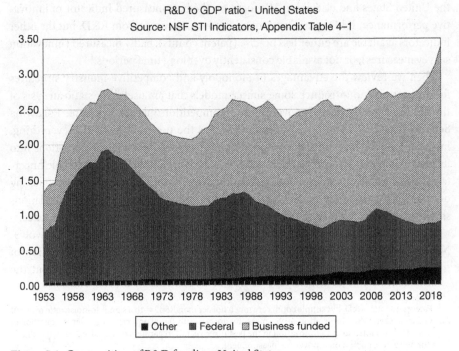

Figure 5.1 Composition of R&D funding: United States.

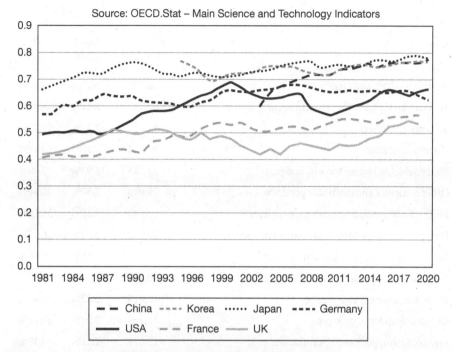

Figure 5.2 Business R&D share for the seven largest R&D spenders.

The data for R&D spending in other major economies are only available back to 1981, but they, too, show an increasing share for business R&D in total R&D spending, with the possible exception of the United Kingdom, where the share fluctuates between 0.4 and 0.5. [Figure 5.2 shows the share of business R&D in the total for the seven largest R&D spending countries. These countries account for about 80% of total spending on R&D in the world. By the end of the period, the three Asian countries have a business-financed R&D share of roughly 78%, while the United States and Germany have shares of about 65% and the United Kingdom and France about 55%. In all these countries, the remainder will be primarily R&D financed by the government. In the United States, France, the United Kingdom, and increasingly China, much of this government R&D is defense-related R&D.

Why has industry R&D spending increased during the past 50 years? The primary reasons are likely to be increases in technological opportunity and the market demand for new products, along with increases in market size due to globalization. However, Bloom et al. (2020) argue that this increase has not led to as much increased productivity and economic growth as might have been expected. That is, firms and countries are running faster to stay in place, sometimes called the "red queen" effect, after a character in *Alice in Wonderland*.[2]

The first important feature of industrial R&D is that it varies considerably across industries. Table 5.1 shows the total R&D spending accounted for by US

---

[2] The "red queen hypothesis" was introduced in evolutionary biology by Leigh Van Valen in an unpublished paper dated 1973. It describes the need of a species to continuously evolve to remain fit for the environment as other species evolve around it. It refers to a quote by the Red Queen in Lewis Carroll's *Through the Looking Glass*: "It takes all the running you can do, to keep in the same place."

Table 5.1 Worldwide R&D-to-Sales Ratio for US-Based Firms in 2018 by Industry

Industry	R&D 2018 (MUS$)*	Share R&D	R&D to sales
Pharmaceuticals and medicines	88,537	16.35%	10.46%
Semiconductor and other electronic components	45,540	8.41%	8.94%
Software publishers	39,815	7.35%	12.22%
Other information	39,814	7.35%	10.17%
Motor vehicles, bodies, trailers, and parts	32,125	5.93%	3.00%
Other computer and electronic products	29,099	5.37%	5.31%
R&D services, including leasing intangibles	28,566	5.28%	31.19%
Data processing, hosting, and related services	28,045	5.18%	6.15%
Aircraft, aircraft engine, and aircraft parts	23,691	4.38%	5.80%
Computer systems' design and related services	20,287	3.75%	8.00%
Medical equipment and supplies	17,415	3.22%	5.62%
Communications equipment	16,483	3.04%	12.72%
Electronic shopping and electronic auctions	13,615	2.51%	5.39%
Search, detection, navigation, guidance, aeronautical, nautical instruments	9,997	1.85%	9.04%
Finance and insurance	8,356	1.54%	0.80%
Other machinery	8,083	1.49%	2.12%
Other measuring and controlling device	6,524	1.20%	5.93%
Electrical equipment, appliances, and components	6,180	1.14%	2.92%
Food	5,518	1.02%	0.74%
Other professional, scientific, and technical services	5,298	0.98%	3.67%
Semiconductor machinery	5,077	0.94%	11.14%
Electromedical, electrotherapeutic, and irradiation apparatus	4,378	0.81%	9.20%
Architectural, engineering, and related services	4,022	0.74%	3.18%
Other nonmanufacturing	4,001	0.74%	0.41%
Telecommunications	3,830	0.71%	0.78%
Soap, cleaning compound, and toilet preparation	3,557	0.66%	1.74%
Engine, turbine, and power transmission equipment	3,429	0.63%	3.04%
Plastics and rubber products	3,179	0.59%	1.50%
Other miscellaneous manufacturing	3,067	0.57%	2.02%
Basic chemicals	3,046	0.56%	1.29%
Other transportation	2,960	0.55%	3.41%
Agricultural implement	2,730	0.50%	3.38%
Fabricated metal products	2,544	0.47%	1.53%

Table 5.1 Continued

Industry	R&D 2018 (MUS$)*	Share R&D	R&D to sales
Resin, synthetic rubber, and artificial synthetic fibers and filaments	2,434	0.45%	2.08%
Mining, quarrying, oil and gas extraction, and support activities	2,068	0.38%	0.55%
Pesticide, fertilizer, and other agricultural chemicals	1,792	0.33%	1.54%
Beverage and tobacco products	1,629	0.30%	0.65%
Nonmetallic mineral products	1,567	0.29%	2.06%
Paint, coating, adhesive, and other chemicals	1,521	0.28%	1.45%
Health care services	1,498	0.28%	1.49%
Petroleum and coal products	1,462	0.27%	0.22%
Guided missile, space vehicle, and related parts	1,323	0.24%	5.25%
Textile, apparel, and leather products	1,205	0.22%	1.17%
Other real estate and rental and leasing	1,067	0.20%	11.95%
Paper	1,014	0.19%	0.87%
Primary metals	990	0.18%	0.58%
Transportation and warehousing	956	0.18%	0.31%
Wholesale trade	938	0.17%	0.52%
Furniture and related products	435	0.08%	0.97%
Utilities	283	0.05%	0.08%
Printing and related support activities	246	0.05%	0.73%
Wood products	206	0.04%	0.65%
All industries	**541,412**		**3.74%**

*Worldwide R&D performed by US company and paid for by company and others.
Source: Authors' computations from NSF S&E Indicators for 2018.

firms in each industry, the corresponding R&D intensity of the sector, and the share of business R&D accounted for by each sector. Six sectors account for half of all R&D spending by US-based firms: pharmaceuticals, semiconductors, software, other information industries, motor vehicles, and computers. Some but not all of these sectors are also very R&D-intensive, with an R&D-to-sales ratio above 10%. Other sectors with R&D intensities above 10%, but with less total R&D, are R&D services, communication equipment, and semiconductor manufacturing machinery. There are also a number of sectors with R&D intensities above 5%. It is noteworthy that half of the six highly R&D-intensive sectors are nonmanufacturing industries, something that would not have been true 40 years ago and reflects the evolution of an advanced economy.

Table 5.1 illustrates one of the stylized facts about R&D activity: One of the most if not the most important predictors of how much a firm will invest in innovation is

Table 5.2 Worldwide R&D-to-Sales Ratio for US-Based Firms in 2018 by Firm Size

Size (number employees)	R&D (MUS$)*	Share doing R&D	R&D to sales for R&D performers
10–19	4,518	0.8%	21.42%
20–49	11,821	2.2%	16.04%
50–99	13,013	2.4%	9.51%
100–249	20,420	3.8%	5.78%
250–499	21,824	4.0%	6.70%
500–999	20,214	3.7%	3.96%
1,000–4,999	83,761	15.5%	4.26%
5,000–9,999	60,875	11.2%	4.43%
10,000–24,999	106,777	19.7%	3.25%
25,000 or more	198,190	36.6%	3.09%
All	**541,413**		**3.74%**

*Worldwide R&D performed by US company and paid for by company and others.
Source: Authors' computations from NSF S&E Indicators for 2018.

its industry, regardless of industry size. Later in this chapter, we will present a simple static model of how variations in R&D intensity relate to the competitive structure of the industry.

A long-debated question is whether R&D intensities are related to the size of firms, and if so, how? As a general rule, present-day large samples of firms in many countries usually have R&D rising slightly less than proportionally with size measured as sales or employees. But this has not always been true. Earlier research reviewed in Cohen (2010) tended to find proportionality at larger firm sizes. Table 5.2 shows the situation in the United States as of 2018.[3] Two conclusions can be drawn: (1) The majority of R&D (83%) is performed by large firms with more than 1,000 employees; (2) when small- and medium-sized firms perform R&D, their intensity is much higher. However, far fewer of them do R&D, as is shown in both Table 5.2 and Figure 5.3.

Like innovation input, innovation output, whether measured by patents or the sales of new products, increases less than proportionately with firm size. However, in general, measuring R&D or innovation across firms relies on surviving samples of firms or samples of firms based on public financial markets rather than true "random" samples. For smaller firms and new entrants, failure to innovate successfully means that they disappear quickly, whereas the same is not true of larger firms with an established market.

Another factor that helps to explain the relative propensity of smaller firms to be more innovative if they engage in innovation at all is the typical breadth of activity undertaken by large firms versus small firms. Industries tend to have a fairly stable skew size distribution covering a wide range, which suggests that the firms within them

---

[3] 2018 is the latest year with the most detailed complete data from the NSF at the time of writing.

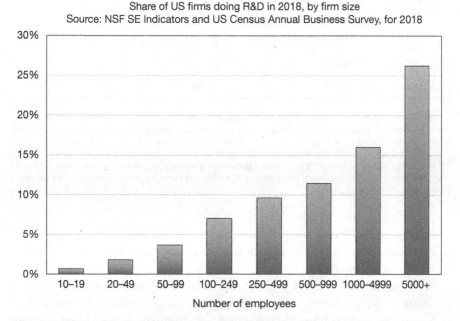

Figure 5.3 Share of R&D performers in 2018 by firm size.

are not identical, nor are they likely to be producing identical output. For example, in pharmaceuticals, the largest firms conduct R&D, but also manufacture drugs, market and distribute them. Smaller firms in the sector are often biotechnology firms that specialize in finding new drug candidates, and then license them to larger firms for development and manufacture. Thus, even though these firms are in the same industry, they are doing different things and the small ones are more specialized in research.

The same features characterize many other industries. Smaller firms tend to be more specialized in their activities, and one of the ways they specialize is in innovation, leading to a finding that smaller firms have higher innovative activity if they are engaged in any innovative activity. Pavitt (1984) highlighted this feature of the size distribution for firms by classifying manufacturing industries into four categories of technology trajectories:

1. *Supplier-dominated.* Industries such as textiles where innovations come from their equipment suppliers and firms therefore tend to be relatively small and not R&D-intensive.
2. *Production-intensive with scale economies.* Industries such as steel or automobiles with large firms that innovate internally, focusing on cost-reducing process innovation. These industries tend to integrate vertically.
3. *Production equipment suppliers.* Industries such as machinery and instruments that innovate their products, and tend to have relatively smaller firms that supply various other sectors.
4. *Science-based firms.* Industries such as electronics and pharmaceuticals that are very R&D-intensive and tend toward larger firms to spread the cost of R&D. Innovation in these industries often leads to horizontal diversification.

Table 5.3 Share of Firms with Different Types of Innovation (among innovators)

	Process and Product	Process Only	Product Only
United States	35.2%	39.0%	25.8%
European Union	43.2%	30.9%	25.9%

Source: Authors' computations from Kindlon and Jankowski (2017).
Note: Kindlon and Jankowski (2017) chose the two samples (EU and US) to be as comparable as possible in industry and firm size coverage, but the comparability by industry is not exact, due to differences in the way industries are defined by the various statistical agencies. The overall innovation rate is higher in the EU (27% vs. 17%), reflecting the fact that the EU contains separate countries rather than states, and "new to the country" innovations are therefore more common. Therefore, we have chosen to normalize by the overall innovation rate in the two regions.

Although this classification is slightly dated, it is still useful for understanding why firms in a particular sector tend to be large or small, and how that is driven by the nature of their innovative trajectory.[4]

The specialization inherent in small firm innovation has its downsides in terms of ability to capture returns to innovation. Cohen et al. (2023) show using patent indicators that average invention value rises with firm size, while average invention quality declines. This suggests that the higher invention value in large firms is not due to superior inventive capability, but due to their superior ability to extract value. They argue that this superior ability to extract value is due to the greater commercialization capabilities of larger firms.

As we discussed in Chapter 2, innovative activity can often be characterized as either process- or product-oriented. We can ask which is more important in practice: process or product innovation? That is, are firms more likely to innovate to reduce cost, or in order to introduce a new product to the market? There is some evidence on this question from the various innovation surveys that have been conducted by many countries. Table 5.3 shows the breakdown between different types of innovation. Overall, a slightly larger share of firms innovates processes than products, but the more common pattern is to do both if doing any, which suggests that innovative products are often accompanied by innovative ways of making them.

5.3 Market Structure and Innovation

The relationship between innovative activity and the competitive structure of the market has a long history, going back at least to Schumpeter (1942). Chapters 7 and 8 of his well-known book discuss the innovative performance of monopolistic and competitive firms extensively. Schumpeter argued that large firms, including industry monopolists, were important sources of innovation, including "radical" innovation. The debates surrounding monopolies and innovation have resurfaced with the rise

---

[4] For an example of how things are changing since Pavitt wrote his study, the production and scale intensive industries in developed economies have faced considerable competition from lower cost producers over the past decades and have therefore shifted towards greater product innovation.

of technology giants such as IBM, Microsoft, Google, and the social media giants. Schumpeter also argued that competition primarily takes place via creative destruction, where a new innovating firm displaces an older firm, rather than via static price competition. The implication was that monopolies do not last, given the constant entry of new innovators. To quote Schumpeter:

> [T]he problem that is usually being visualized is how capitalism administers existing structures, whereas the relevant problem is how it creates and destroys them. (Schumpeter 1942, 1960 ed., p. 84)

His arguments are highly relevant to antitrust and merger policy, as they suggest that the impact of firm behavior and mergers on future innovation in the industry should be weighed at least as strongly as their impact on prices.

Over time, Schumpeter's views have influenced the approach of economists to the analysis of antitrust and mergers. Much of the industry economics research during the past couple of decades has addressed competition and innovation performance. This research has been to some extent both inspired by and caused changes in the views of antitrust authorities, which have come to recognize that evaluating the dynamic efficiency of a merger may be just as important as evaluating the static efficiency (Katz and Shelanski 2005). Researchers have asked which existing market structures are favorable to innovation, monopolistic or competitive. They have also explored questions related to the evolution of market structure given innovation. Multiple approaches have been used: theoretic, empirical, and historical. The topic turns out to be very complex, and strong conclusions are difficult to come by. Here, we provide only a basic introduction to the topic.[5]

In this section of the chapter, we summarize the basic differences between monopoly/oligopoly and competition as innovation generators and then present some simple stylized models of R&D competition that illustrate the innovation pressures that derive from both market structures.

The advantages of monopoly and large firm size for innovation come primarily from economies of scale and scope. Because R&D is a fixed cost, spreading over more units is cost-efficient. Because R&D in one area often generates spillovers to another area, a multiproduct firm more efficiently internalizes these spillovers, increasing their incentive to innovate. A pure monopoly reduces redundant research and therefore the number of wasteful patent races. In some circumstances, monopolists face greater incentives to innovate because they will lose market power if they fail to innovate. That is, Gilbert and Newberry (1982) showed that the incentive to remain a monopolist is greater than an entrant's incentive to become a duopolist. A final advantage of larger firm size and/or concentration for innovation is that such firms may find it easier to finance innovation, either because of their existing profits, or because they face lower costs in the capital market.

The advantages of competition for innovation are basically the fact that "creative destruction" (in Schumpeter's words) can be a spur to innovation. In Andy Grove's famous

---

[5] Those interested in going deeper should see, for example, Gilbert (2006) and Cohen (2010).

quote about competition in the semiconductor industry, "Only the paranoid survive," which he used as the title to his book about his experiences as CEO of Intel (Grove 1988). Under competition, pressure to innovate comes from the fear that others will do it if you don't. In addition, innovation is uncertain, and having more than one firm in the market makes it easier to achieve a diversity of approaches. As discussed below, one can show that firms in a competitive market have a greater incentive for innovation than monopolists in some situations.

5.3.1 Static Theory

The first set of models we discuss are static models, that is, models that describe the status quo and are essentially timeless, even though they may consist of two periods rather than a single period. These models were created partly because economists wished to make policy or welfare statements concerning the market structures that would encourage the optimal level of innovation.

We will examine the dynamics of industry evolution later in this chapter, but for the moment we consider static models, where market structure is taken as given. Following this, we look at equilibrium models where market structure and innovative activity are jointly determined.

From the perspective of economic welfare, the first best solution to the provision of innovation is to cover the fixed cost of an invention and its development with a lump sum tax and let competition bring down the price of the product to marginal cost. For a number of reasons related to uncertainty and incomplete information, this is obviously not feasible.

Therefore, we turn to the property rights solution, allowing patent protection for an invention, which grants the inventor a short-term monopoly. In this case, the inventor/ innovator will do all projects whose profits cover the fixed costs of the R&D needed for completion and there will be deadweight loss (DWL) due to monopoly pricing above marginal cost.

If patent protection is not available but the innovator is able to protect their invention briefly via the first mover advantage, there will be imitation. As successive imitators enter, consumer surplus grows, and profits and DWL shrink. However, firms will not enter past the point where profits cover the fixed cost of R&D (innovation or imitation cost).

The conclusions from this verbal analysis are: (1) Other things equal, there will be more innovation with patents, at the cost of DWL, because there will be higher profits to cover costs. (2) With no patent protection, the number of firms in the market depends on the relative costs of imitation (appropriability conditions). If imitation costs are large, few additional firms will find it profitable to enter, whereas if they are small, many firms will. If there is no first mover advantage (imitation is instant), in equilibrium no one will enter if innovation cost is greater than imitation cost.

5.3.2 Drastic versus Nondrastic Innovation

The first formal model of the incentive for innovation under different market structures was due to Arrow (1962b). His analysis considered a single cost-saving innovation that was perfectly appropriable in the sense that it could not be imitated by the other firms in the (possibly) competitive market. Because the innovation he had in mind only affects the cost of production, there is no change in the demand curve after innovation in this model. The model made the important distinction between drastic (major or radical) innovations and nondrastic (minor or incremental) innovations, a distinction that has proved useful in the more complex theoretical models that followed his. A drastic innovation is one whose monopoly price is below the marginal cost of the previous technology and that will therefore take the entire market when it is introduced. In contrast, a nondrastic innovation is one that allows the previous technology to co-exist with the new technology, albeit at a lower price. The notation for this model is shown in Table 5.4,

$D(x)$ denotes the demand curve as a function of quantity and $R(x)$ the monopolist's marginal revenue curve. Using this notation, we can define the type of innovation:

Minor (nondrastic): $p_M' > c$. The potential post-innovation monopoly price is above the pre-innovation unit cost, which limits the market power of the innovator.

Major (drastic): $p_M' < c$. The post-innovation monopoly price is below the pre-innovation unit cost, so the innovator drives everyone else out of the market.

Figure 5.4 illustrates the difference between minor and major innovations. In the second panel, the marginal cost and price intersect the demand curve at A, and the firms supply x_c at price p. Innovation by one firm (a potential monopolist) reduces cost to c' after the innovation, and the monopoly price for the innovator is determined by the point on the demand curve B that corresponds to the point where the new marginal cost intersects the marginal revenue curve. But because the new monopoly price is above the competitive price, the innovating monopolist will only be able to charge the old competitive

Table 5.4 Definitions for Arrow's Model

	Before Innovation	*After Innovation*
Marginal cost	c	c'
Monopoly price	p_m	p_m'
Monopoly profits	Π_m	Π_m'
Demand at monopoly price	x_m	x_m'
Competitive price	p_c	
Demand at competitive price	x_c	

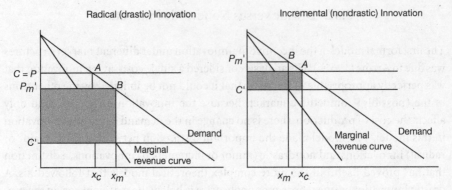

Figure 5.4 Drastic versus nondrastic innovation.

price c. Their pricing power is limited by the presence of other firms in the market, even if the other firms have higher costs. Of course, they will capture the shaded rectangle as profits, unlike the other firms, because their costs are lower.

In the first panel of Figure 5.4, the innovation reduces marginal cost by a much larger amount. In this case, the implied monopoly price at B is less than the previous competitive price, and the innovating monopolist obtains all of the market and is able to sell a larger quantity x'_m, while retaining the shaded rectangle as profit.

Now consider the incentives for innovation under two extreme market structures: perfect competition and monopoly. Under perfect competition, price before the innovation is marginal cost c, quantity is x_c, and profits are zero. If one of the competitive firms innovates (and obtains patent protection), we have the following two possibilities:

Drastic innovation. The firm becomes a monopolist, so price and quantity are p'_m and x'_m. Profits are Π'_m.

Nondrastic innovation. The firm cannot price higher than c, due to competition from the old technology. Therefore, the quantity is still x_c, but costs have fallen to c' and profits are $x_c (c - c')$.

Now consider the behavior of a monopolist: Before the innovation, they price using the marginal revenue curve, so $R(x_m) = c$ and price p_m is chosen to achieve demand x_m. Profits Π_m are $x_m (p_m - c)$. After the innovation, the monopolist again prices using the marginal revenue curve $R(x'_m) = c'$ at the new lower cost level, and price $p'_m < p_m$ is chosen to achieve demand $x'_m > x_m$ and profits $\Pi'_m = x'_m (p'_m - c')$.

Table 5.5 shows a summary of the results of a comparison between profits from innovation under perfect competition and under monopoly.

It is thus easy to show that under the assumptions of the model, a monopolist has less incentive than a competitive firm for major or drastic innovation. This fact is known as the *replacement effect*: The monopolist only gets the increase in profit from the new technology, while the competitive firm gets the whole profit.

Showing that competition generates more innovation than monopoly in the nondrastic case is much more complicated. We have to show that the change in a

Table 5.5 Comparing Competition and Monopoly in Arrow's Model

	Competition	Monopoly	Compare
Nondrastic innovation	$x_c(c-c')-0$	$\Pi'_m - \Pi_m$	$M < C$ (difficult to show)
Drastic innovation	$\Pi'_m - 0$	$\Pi'_m - \Pi_m$	$M < C \Leftrightarrow \Pi_m > 0$

monopolist's profits is less than the increase in revenue achieved by the cost reduction in the competitive case:

$$\Pi'_m - \Pi_m < x_c(c-c')$$
$$\Leftrightarrow \Delta revenue - \Delta \cos ts < x_c(c-c')$$
$$\Leftrightarrow \int_{x_m}^{x'_m} R(x)dx - (c'x'_m - cx_m) < x_c(c-c')$$

Now recall that the monopolist's marginal revenue curve is downward-sloping and lies below the pre-innovation marginal cost when quantity is greater than x_m. This implies the following inequality:

$$\int_{x_m}^{x'_m} R(x)dx < \int_{x_m}^{x'_m} cdx = c(x'_m - x_m)$$

And therefore, we have the following (after some algebra), which shows that even in the nondrastic case, the profits from innovation are greater for the competitive firm than for the monopolist:

$$\Rightarrow \int_{x_m}^{x'_m} R(x)dx - (c'x'_m - cx_m) < c(x'_m - x_m) - (c'x'_m - cx_m) = cx'_m - c'x'_m$$
$$= x'_m(c-c') < x_c(c-c').$$

This static model shows that a monopolist has less incentive to innovate in general because they already have some profit, and the cost reduction benefit is spread over smaller output than under competition. The model also shows that a monopolist has relatively more incentive for minor than for major innovations.

Note that first best (price post-innovation equal to marginal cost, $p'_c = MC = c'$) is not achieved because we assumed that preventing imitation was feasible via a patent or other means, and so the innovating firm has some market power. In the case of nondrastic innovation, the innovator gets all the surplus and second best is achieved. However, in the case of drastic innovation, the innovator gets the monopoly markup, but this is less than the full consumer surplus (the difference between pricing at c and c'), so will undersupply innovation for the usual monopoly reasons.

Arrow's model assumes that there is no entry in the monopoly case, which is an extreme assumption. Gilbert and Newberry (1982) allow entry and reverse his conclusion, showing that the monopolist will have a greater incentive to introduce a new patented technology than an entrant because their profits from preempting a potential entrant are greater than the profits they would earn if they compete (or collude as duopolists) after entry. Thus, the answer to the simple question of which is better for innovation, competitive or monopolistic market structure, turns on what we assume about potential entry threats. Later in this chapter, we look at a model due to Aghion et al. (2005) that incorporates variations in "entry" threat directly.

5.3.3 Dasgupta-Stiglitz Model

The Dasgupta-Stiglitz (DS, 1980) model relaxes some of the simplifying assumptions in the previous analyses: (1) It allows supply and demand conditions to vary, in order to derive the implications of these variations. (2) It allows for imperfect patent protection. The resulting model results in an equilibrium between market structure and R&D intensity, given particular supply and demand conditions. It is essentially a static model suitable for describing the variations across industries in innovative behavior that we observe at a point in time. The advantage of the model is that it allows for causality to flow two ways: from innovation to market structure and from market structure to innovation. Looking at the equilibrium between the competitive structure of an industry and its innovative activity is preferable to examining only the unidirectional channel from market structure to innovation.

The parameters of the DS model are the following:

- Elasticity of demand ε
- Market size σ
- Innovation elasticity: the productivity of R&D in reducing unit cost α
- Scale between R&D and its cost β

DS assumes that both the demand function and cost function have the constant elasticity form:[6]

$$P(Q) = \sigma Q^{-1/\varepsilon}$$
$$c(x) = \beta x^{-\alpha}$$

where P is market price, Q is the total quantity produced in the market, and c is the unit cost of production. At first, c is treated as a constant, and then later we introduce a cost shifter x that we identify as R&D spending. In this model, a cost shifter is a fixed cost (x) that shifts the constant marginal cost downward so that the new marginal cost is $c(x)$. DS assumes that firms make Cournot conjectures about both the output and R&D of other firms. That is, they assume that each firm chooses its profit-maximizing output

---

[6] Constant elasticity means that if the variable x increases by 1%, the cost $c(x)$ declines by $-\alpha$%. Such functions are often plausible simplifications and have the advantage that they are independent of the units in which x and c are measured. See Appendix A: Mathematics and Statistics for further discussion of elasticities.

Box 5.1 Models of Competition

Cournot competition: model of industry competition where each firm chooses its profit-maximizing quantity expecting that the other firms will choose their profit-maximizing quantities. With a finite number of homogeneous firms, the equilibrium solution is a Nash equilibrium with price above marginal cost, so there are nonzero profits.

Bertrand competition: model of industry competition where firms compete on price. In the absence of fixed costs, each additional unit they sell above marginal cost gains profits, so the competing firms will drive the price down to marginal cost, unlike Cournot competition.

Free entry zero profit equilibrium: an equilibrium where firms enter a market until the next firm to enter would earn negative profits. Thus, the number of firms in the market is determined by the model, rather than given. It is a useful solution concept when there are fixed costs to be covered.

---

and R&D assuming that the other firms are doing the same. The first is a conventional Cournot assumption, and the second allows the R&D equilibrium to be computed. These assumptions imply that all firms will make the same choices and can be treated as identical. DS then computes a free entry zero profit equilibrium (see Box 5.1 for a definition).

Note that the presence of the fixed cost (R&D) means that the market can only support a finite number of firms with markups above marginal cost if the fixed cost is to be covered. See Box 5.2 for the definition of the markup. When it is measured relative to price, we obtain the well-known Lerner index, which is often used to measure the level of competition faced by a firm.

The model solution strategy is as follows: (1) Derive the equilibrium output given demand parameters, number of firms n, assuming no entry and constant unit (variable) cost. (2) Assume that each firm pays a fixed cost x to enter and compute the equilibrium number of firms as a function of demand and cost. (3) Next, assume the only fixed cost (x) is R&D and that firms can choose the level of x to reduce their production cost. Using these assumptions, compute a new equilibrium that gives the number of

---

Box 5.2 Measuring Competition

Markup: price less marginal cost.
Lerner index: the ratio of price less marginal cost (the markup) divided by price:

$$L = (P - MC)/P$$

For a profit-maximizing firm, one can show that L is equal to minus the inverse of the demand elasticity faced by the firm: $L = -1/\varepsilon$. For a profit-maximizing firm, the Lerner index is bounded by zero (perfect competition) and 1 (elasticity equal to -1). A profit-maximizing firm will never face inelastic demand ($|\varepsilon| < 1$).

---

firms, output, and the level of R&D as a function of the model's supply and demand parameters.

The solution to the first step is well known:

$$markup = \frac{P-c}{P} = \frac{1}{n\varepsilon}$$

Given n firms, Cournot equilibrium determines the price P given marginal cost c and the demand elasticity ε. The implications are that lower markups are associated both with a higher number of firms n and higher demand elasticity, which concords with our intuition.

To solve the second step, introduce a profit equation for the firms that includes fixed costs. Note that Q denotes aggregate output and q the output of an individual (identical) firm:

$$profits \ \pi = \text{variable profits - fixed costs} = 0$$
$$\pi = (P(Q) - c)q - x$$
$$\Rightarrow n = \frac{(P(Q) - c)q}{x} = \frac{(\sigma Q^{-1/\varepsilon} - c)q}{x}$$

The above simply says that the equilibrium number of firms in the market is the number for which variable profits can cover their fixed costs.[7] It also shows that a larger market (σ) increases the equilibrium number of firms n, while higher fixed costs reduce n for a given markup, as expected, and increase the markup holding n constant.

To compute the equilibrium of interest (the third step in solving the model), assume that fixed costs x are R&D spending and firms can choose the level of x as well as output q. The choice of x reduces unit cost according to the constant elasticity formulation βx^α (i.e., R&D is treated as cost-reducing). For example, if a firm increases R&D by 10%, then its unit cost goes down by α10%.

Each firm chooses output q and R&D x to maximize its profit:

$$\pi = [P(Q) - c(x)]q - x$$

The solution is obtained using three equations: the first-order conditions for output and R&D plus the zero profit condition. These equations yield values for n, Q, and x:

$$\text{zero profit } [P(Q) - c(x)]q - x = 0$$
$$\text{FOC for output } \quad \frac{P(Q) - c}{P(Q)} = \frac{1}{n\varepsilon}$$
$$\text{FOC for R\&D} \quad x = \frac{\alpha c Q}{n}$$

---

[7] Note that the resulting n is not necessarily an integer. Because these models are very stylized, we ignore this problem, as it does not affect the qualitative results.

Using these equations, one can show the following:

$$n = \frac{(1+\alpha)}{\alpha\varepsilon}$$

$$\text{Industry R\&D intensity} = \frac{nx}{PQ} = \frac{\alpha}{1+\alpha}$$

The equilibrium number of firms therefore depends on the demand elasticity ε (if higher, then there are fewer firms in the industry holding α constant) and technological opportunity α (if higher, then there will be fewer firms in the industry and the R&D intensity will be higher). Thus, the conclusion of the model is that in equilibrium, comparing across industries, those with high technological opportunity will have higher R&D intensities, fewer firms, and high markups. This seems like a good description of the pharmaceutical industry, for example. However, it is generally challenging to verify because the typical industry is very heterogeneous and produces a great variety of products, making the assumption of (nearly) identical firms hard to sustain.

Note that because we assumed constant elasticity of demand and unit cost reduction, the DS result is independent of scale (market size). In larger markets, each firm will be larger and do more R&D, but the number of firms will remain unchanged. Testing this conclusion is also difficult, given the problem of market definition. To a certain extent, it is approximately true when we look across countries, in the sense that larger countries have larger firms on average. However, R&D-intensive firms are precisely those that look beyond country boundaries for their market and can therefore survive in smaller countries while marketing to the world, such as the Netherlands (Shell, Unilever), Sweden (Spotify), or even Estonia (Skype, formerly).

The DS model is a good starting point, but it omits some things that we might think are important. First are spillovers, either positive or negative, as the choice of R&D is not affected by the other firms' choice of R&D. That is, one firm's R&D does not make another firm's R&D more or less productive. Second, the model considers only process R&D, not product R&D, which is more likely to shift the demand curve than to lower costs. Because most estimates of the composition of R&D suggest that product R&D accounts for roughly two-thirds of R&D, this is an important omission, albeit one that is difficult to deal with empirically, given the absence of the appropriate data for the R&D breakdown.

Levin and Reiss (1988) show that if both types of R&D and spillovers are allowed, the conclusions about the relationship between R&D and market structure become more ambiguous than implied by Dasgupta-Stiglitz. Using empirical data, they show that the estimated parameters in the model occur in regions where concentration and R&D intensity fall with increased spillovers, although increases in the productivity of such spillovers increase their own R&D and reduce the number of firms. They also find large variations across industries consistent with the importance of technological opportunity in R&D strategy. Unfortunately, their empirical analysis is hampered by the lack of appropriate data in many places, so the tests for spillover effects are rather weak.

5.3.4 Aghion et al. Model

Aghion et al. (2005) takes a first step toward a model that captures the inherent dynamism in innovative competition, deriving the implications of this dynamism for the relationship between innovation and market structure. They begin by observing that the
relationship between the firm markup (measured as 1 minus the Lerner index, see Box
5.2) and innovation (measured as citation-weighted patents, see Box 5.3) has a rough
inverted U shape, implying that as a firm's market power increases, it first becomes
more innovative, and after a certain point, its innovative activity declines. They use a
series of policy changes that affected market power as instruments to ensure that they
identify the impact of market power on innovation (rather than the reverse).

The model is complex and will only be sketched here. The key idea is that firms innovate to climb a "quality ladder," moving up one step at a time. They spend R&D to try
to move up the ladder, and succeed with a probability determined by the level of R&D.
This feature of the model captures the fact that there is uncertainty in the R&D process.
A simplified version of R&D competition exists between firms: They are either neck-
and-neck (at the same point on the quality ladder) or there is a leader and a follower
(one step behind on the quality ladder). The follower is assumed to imitate the leader
and move up a step on the ladder with a small probability. The competitive structure is
similar to that in Arrow's model when the firms are on different steps: zero profit for the
follower and a profit determined by the size of the step for the leader. When the firms are
even, product market competition is either Bertrand (zero profit for both) or collusive
to a varying degree.

With this setup, the authors are able to show a series of propositions: (1) The research
intensity of neck-and-neck firms increases if there is less collusion (*escape competition
effect*), and the research intensity of the laggard firm declines with less collusion (which
they call the *Schumpeterian* effect). Thus, competition is good for innovation if firms are
on a level, but discourages innovative activity in the firm that is behind. (2) As long as the
imitation probability of success is high enough, the aggregate innovation rate follows an
inverted-U pattern, first increasing with increases in competition and then decreasing.
(3) The technological gap between leader and follower increases as product market competition increases. (4) The peak of the inverted U is larger and occurs at a higher level of
the competition index in industries where competition is more neck-and-neck.

Box 5.3 Citation-Weighted Patents

Patents by date of application or priority date are a frequently used measure of innovative activity (see Chapter 11). However, most patents turn out not to be very useful
or valuable, while some are worth a lot. Citations are references to a patent made
in subsequent patents, and the number of such later references has been shown to
approximately reflect the value of the invention described by the patent. Therefore,
when measuring innovation, it is common to weight the relevant patent counts by
the number of citations they receive in subsequent patents. This measure has been
shown to correlate more highly with firm value and profits than simple patent counts.

The conclusions of this model are supported by the data and regressions Aghion et al. present. As market structure increases toward perfectly competitive, innovation increases at first and then declines when the Lerner index is equal to about 0.05 (a 5% markup). For an industry that is more neck-and-neck in innovation (measured as the productivity gap between the leader and other firms), the slope of the curve is steeper, as predicted. However, the difference between neck-and-neck industries and others is not very precisely measured, so precise conclusions are not warranted.

5.3.5 Bounds Theory

The central problem that confronts any attempt to empirically examine the concentration–innovation relationship is the range of activities encompassed by an "industry," not all of which will be directly in competition with each other. In fact, each firm will be pursuing a strategy designed to differentiate them from the others, as this allows them to price above marginal cost and generate economic rents. For example, see the pharmaceutical industry referred to previously. This industry is composed of large manufacturers and smaller research firms, where one type is the customer of the other and where, even among firms of the same type, the products are not necessarily substitutes.

Sutton (1998) confronted this problem and developed a model that incorporates the idea of submarkets within an industry's market. His submarkets are assumed to be doing related things (that's why they are in the same market), and the products in the submarket will be substitutes, but perhaps not very close substitutes. His model delivers lower bounds to concentration, one that rests on three relatively simple assumptions:

1. Firms do not pursue loss-making strategies. That is, the set of products entered by each firm covers its fixed (and sunk) costs.
2. If a profitable opportunity emerges, some firm will take it. That is, there is no gap in the configuration of products in the sense that no set of products can be added that will cover its fixed (and sunk) costs in equilibrium.
3. All potential entrants to a new submarket are equally advantaged.

Sutton sets up the game as two-stage, where the first stage involves choosing R&D, advertising, and other sunk costs, and the second stage is the price/quantity competition stage. He does not constrain the types of equilibrium that might be computed, allowing Cournot, Bertrand, and the like (see Box 5.1).

The key parameter used to characterize an industry (labeled *alpha* or α) is a kind of R&D productivity. It specifies "the extent to which an industry consisting of many small firms can be destabilized by a firm that outspends [on R&D] its many small rivals" (Sutton 1998, p. 10). Unfortunately, α is not measurable, although its implications for concentration and R&D intensity can be derived. Sutton shows that α will be high under two industry configurations: (1) R&D is productive, and the goods in the submarkets are close substitutes so spending more can easily attract customers from competitors; and (2) R&D is productive, and the goods in the submarkets are poor substitutes. In both cases, R&D intensity will be high, but in the first case concentration will be high, whereas in the second case concentration may be quite low because each firm has a niche that it can protect.

This result, which seems plausible, is subjected to analysis by a series of case studies of various industries, classifying them as high (e.g., color film) or low (e.g., flow meters) α. The advantage of Sutton's analysis is that it uses fewer assumptions and does not constrain the form of the game. It also provides an explanation of why the simple R&D intensity–concentration correlation may not be informative. The disadvantage is that it does not yield precise predictions but only bounds the relationship between R&D intensity and concentration.

5.4 Timing of Innovation and Patent Races

The question of innovation timing is a large one. Sometimes timing is determined by the availability of complementary inputs. Sometimes it depends on a new and compelling need arising, as in the case of COVID vaccines. Sometimes an innovation arises not from a conscious search with a well-defined goal but from an accident. The last is especially true of major innovations, as we saw in Chapter 2. This means that the timing of the invention is also fairly random. One example is the invention of the Post-it note by Spencer Silver, a scientist at 3M, in 1968. While attempting to develop a super-strong adhesive, he accidentally created a "low-tack," reusable, pressure-sensitive adhesive.[8]

Theorists have explored the question of whether firms will choose the socially optimal date of an innovation. The answer is generally no. The only case of optimality occurs when there is a single firm that gets all the surplus (consumer and producer), thus internalizing the process. Such a firm will choose the optimal timing, but, of course, being a monopolist, it will also restrict output embodying the innovation.

Monopolies that do not get all the surplus from their innovation tend to be too slow, while competition can be either too fast or too slow. If there is Cournot competition in R&D, the more firms are in the race, the sooner innovation will occur. Using a game theoretic model of R&D competition, Reinganum (1982) showed that the speed with which innovation occurs and the resources devoted to it depend on appropriability of the returns. With perfect patent protection, innovation will happen too quickly compared to the social optimum. As in many models of "racing for a prize," that is, settings where more than one firm is investing in R&D to be first to successfully innovate, there will be wasteful duplicative effort. However, if appropriability is difficult, innovation will be too slow, other things equal (i.e., holding constant rate of the exogenous fall in innovation cost over time and the interest rate).

Reinganum's model incorporated uncertainty over success and allowed firms to adjust their strategy over time as they learned about the probability of success and their rivals' strategies. However, it did not incorporate the potential spillovers from the rivals' R&D. Subsequent work by Reinganum and other researchers added this feature to the model, showing that such spillovers might reduce the amount of wasteful investment while speeding the innovation.[9]

---

[8] For some more examples, see Yonatan (2017).
[9] For more on the theory of patent races, see Tirole (1988), Chapter 10.

We have very little empirical evidence available to test these models of racing for an innovation as it is difficult to collect the detailed data one would need to look closely at racing behavior. One effort was that of Cockburn and Henderson (1994), who looked at racing in approximately 40 individual drug discovery areas by 10 major pharmaceutical firms over 30 years. They found little evidence of racing. R&D in each area was only weakly correlated across firms, suggesting a lack of strategic reaction. They also found positive correlation between own and rivals patenting in particular areas, suggesting that rivals' success helped the firm's R&D productivity rather than hindering it. This, in turn, implies that spillovers of knowledge among firms are more important for drug discovery than patent racing per se. This finding is confirmed by Austin (2000), who found that issuance of a successful high value patent by one firm generated a positive market value response for its direct competitors that was positive and 15–45% of the firm's own positive response to the patent issue.

5.5 Empirical Evidence

5.5.1 Firm Size and Innovation

Earlier we presented a few basic facts about firm size and innovative activity. Innovation input in the form of R&D has been found to be roughly proportional to firm size, at least for larger firms, although more recent data that include more smaller firms and new entrants present a more nuanced picture: Smaller firms are less likely to perform R&D, but when they do, their R&D intensity is higher. Innovation output in the form of patents or new product counts is somewhat higher as a proportion of firm size for smaller firms, both because the observed samples of small firms tend to be selected for innovation success and because of greater specialization at smaller firm sizes.

Although the relationship between R&D and firm size is of interest, Fisher and Temin (1973) showed that measuring this relationship cannot confirm or deny the Schumpeterian hypothesis that large firms are "better" at innovation and that combining small firms into a single large firm will produce more innovation.[10] They assume a firm is composed of two types of workers: R&D workers R and production workers N, with firm size S given by $R + N$. They then posit two functions that describe the performance of an R&D firm:

$$\textit{Value added per worker from R\&D workers } R = F(R, N)$$
$$\textit{Total R\&D output of the firm} = RF(R, N)$$

The first equation describes the productivity of a single R&D worker in adding to the firm's profits, while the second is the total profit derived from the size of the R&D labor force. To clarify, F is defined in their model as the dollar value generated by an R&D worker above and beyond the value generated by a firm without R&D workers. They

---

[10] Fisher and Temin explicitly address the R&D-size relationship, but the model can easily be applied to innovative activity more broadly if such measures are available.

argue that the tests of the Schumpeterian hypothesis in the literature are based on the following elasticity:

$$\eta = \frac{S}{R}\frac{\partial R}{\partial S} > 1$$

That is, does the size of the firm (measured as employment) rise more than proportionately with increases in R&D (measured as number of R&D workers)?

However, the true test of this hypothesis is a test of whether the total R&D output of the firm rises more than proportionately with increases in R&D:

$$\varepsilon \equiv \frac{S}{RF}\frac{\partial(RF)}{\partial S} = \eta + \frac{S}{F}\frac{\partial F}{\partial S} > 1$$

Fisher and Temin (1973, 1979) show that a finding that η is greater than or less than unity has no particular implications for the magnitude of ε. The intuition is that the relevant test is a test for the total impact of R&D on firm size, which combines two effects: the impact of firm size on R&D productivity together with the impact of the size of the R&D program on total firm size. Because the impact of firm size on R&D productivity is difficult to measure, this test has rarely been done.[11]

One possible test treats patents as a measure of R&D productivity, although patents are a very noisy and possibly biased measure. The value of an individual patent varies considerably and not all innovation is patentable. Nevertheless, researchers usually find that smaller firms obtain more patents per R&D than larger ones do, although there are some caveats to this finding: (1) Selectivity in the sense that unsuccessful innovators disappear if they are also small; and (2) smaller firms are less likely to have formal R&D programs that are covered by data collection, although they may do something that looks like R&D. Using a large sample of publicly traded US firms from 1976, Bound et al. (1984) found that the patents–R&D relationship was mostly linear with an elasticity considerably less than 1, implying that smaller firms had higher patent productivity than larger firms.

5.5.2 Concentration and Innovation

When industry concentration is simply correlated with R&D or innovation count intensity across industries, one finds a fairly weak or nonexistent relationship. The industry of the firm is a much stronger predictor of R&D intensity than the market structure of the industry, which highlights the importance of technological opportunity as a driver of innovation. To the extent that there is a relationship, it looks like the theoretical one of Aghion et al. (2005): an inverted u-shaped curve, with the most

---

[11] The econometric difficulty in measuring the impact of firm size on R&D productivity is beyond the scope of this book. Briefly, the problem is that size is an outgrowth of past R&D spending, so we do not have the appropriate experiment, which would involve random assignment of firm size, and then observing R&D productivity. A second problem is measuring R&D productivity (as opposed to firm productivity) without good measures of R&D output.

innovation going on at medium to high levels of concentration. Very monopolized industries usually have less innovation, and industries with many small firms also have less.

Many of these early empirical studies were critiqued because the causality in the relationship is unclear. It was not clear whether innovation causes successful firms to grow and an industry to become concentrated or whether an industry with several large firms does more innovation because it is optimally concentrated. Another problem with the raw correlations is that they fail to hold constant the "exogenous" determinants of innovation:

1. The potential size of the market (demand)
2. Technological opportunity (the science and knowledge base available in the industry)
3. Appropriability conditions (the ability to capture the returns to innovation in the industry)

Controlling for the variation across industry in these factors by including industry dummies is sometimes done, but this obscures much that might be of interest.[12] In addition, it is not feasible to include industry dummies in this way in a simple cross-section regression of innovation on some kind of competition or concentration measure, as that also varies only by industry.

Like Dasgupta and Stiglitz (1980), Sutton (1998) looks at the relationship of concentration and R&D intensity in a static equilibrium framework and obtains weaker predictions with a much less restrictive and more realistic model. Empirically, he considers three variables: (1) whether or not the industry is R&D-intensive; 2) C4, industry concentration as the four-firm concentration ratio; 3) h, industry homogeneity measured as the largest seven-digit product share in the five-digit industry. He shows that the lower bound to concentration increases with the homogeneity of the industry for R&D-intensive sectors, but not for sectors where R&D fixed costs are not important. This prediction is confirmed by Sutton's use of US data for 1977.

The other difficulty with earlier empirical work on the concentration–innovation relationship is that concentration measures at the industry level do not quite capture the relevant competitive environment. This is related to the problem of industry definition, which is not the same as market definition, as Sutton (1998) emphasized. Firms defined as within the same industry may be competing heavily with each other with close substitutes, or they may, in fact, be producing complements or unrelated items. For example, consider biotechnology research firms, whose market is pharmaceutical firms in the same industry, and who may even have contracts or joint ventures with such firms. Another example is the automobile sector that includes automobiles but also automobile parts, which certainly do not compete with automobiles. Accordingly, more recent work such as Aghion et al. (2005) has shifted to the use of a direct measure of market

---

[12] Including industry dummies means that we allow each industry to have a different overall mean R&D intensity, which removes much of the variation across industries that we might find interesting and that may be related to the concentration variable in the longer run.

power, the markup of price over marginal cost, which can be shown to be the inverse of the demand elasticity of a profit-maximizing firm. As we saw in Section 5.3.4, the central prediction of their model, an inverse U-shaped relationship between R&D intensity and market power, was confirmed in their data.

5.5.3 Structural Models of Competition and Innovation

Evaluating the competition–innovation relationship is complicated by the fact that not only does one wish to know the impact of the competitiveness of a market on innovation, but also whether the level of innovation is too low or too high from a consumer welfare perspective. Determining the optimal level requires knowledge of consumer demand and willingness to pay. Recently, a number of economists have developed dynamic game theoretic models of the competition–innovation interaction among firms that incorporate demand. Innovations in estimation methods have allowed such models to be successfully estimated. The idea here is to describe the sequential interaction of firms that both compete in a sector and also innovate to improve their competitive position. By restricting the study to a specific technology sector like airframes, hard drive production, or semiconductors, such studies are able to tailor the model to a specific setting, and assume some homogeneity of the product being considered. Homogeneity allows simple specifications for price and quantity of the product. For example, hard disks are measured by the number of bytes they can hold.

The empirical models used here are fully structural and require estimation of the demand function and marginal cost functions at each point in time as well as the quality evolution (innovation) over time.[13] The advantage of this approach is that the results can be used for counterfactual simulation in order to estimate welfare and examine the trade-off between concentration leading to higher prices versus concentration leading to more innovation. This question is at the center of modern antitrust enforcement. The estimation of a demand curve for the innovative products allows one to use willingness to pay to evaluate welfare. A full discussion of this modeling approach is beyond the scope of this book, but interested readers should look at Benkard (2004), Goettler and Gordon (2011), Igami (2017), and Igami and Uetake (2020).

Goettler and Gordon (2011) simulate competition between Intel and Advanced Micro Devices (AMD), the principal producers of semiconductor chips during the 1993–2005 period (95% of all sales), allowing for dynamic decisions by the two firms on pricing and investment, as well as for forward-looking consumers responding to pricing and quality improvements when upgrading. They find that for this duopoly, the rate of innovation in chips would have been 4.2% higher without AMD present, and that these higher prices would have reduced consumer surplus by US$12billion per year. So competition between duopolists reduces innovation in this case and has the benefit of reducing price below monopoly price, so there is probably too much innovation under monopoly. They are also able to show that the conclusions about competition and innovation depend on industry characteristics such as price sensitivity of

---

[13] "Structural" means that explicit economic theory is used to directly inform the corresponding empirical analysis, allowing out-of-sample predictions, assuming the model is reasonably accurate.

consumers, innovation spillovers, and substitutability among different generations of the chip, making broad conclusions difficult to achieve.

Igami has undertaken an extensive study of the hard disk industry sector, covering the years 1981–2016 (Igami 2017, Igami and Uetake 2020). During this period, the industry evolved in some of the ways described in the next section, from a fragmented industry with many innovating entrants to a consolidated industry achieved via several mergers. Igami (2017) shows that fear of cannibalization of their existing lines discouraged incumbents from innovating during the 1980s and early 1990s, leaving room for entrants in the sector. Cannibalization refers to a phenomenon whereby the introduction of an improved product by a company leads to a reduction in sales of the company's older similar products. In this case, it was fear of losing sales of their 5.25-inch hard drives if they transitioned to 3.5-inch drives, evidence of Arrow's (1962b) prediction that successful firms with market power have a lower incentive to innovate because they will simply replace existing profits.

Igami and Uetake (2020) study the hard disk drive industry during a later period (1996–2016), when substantial consolidation via merger and acquisition took place. Their model incorporates entry, exit, and merger choice. They find that incentives to innovate increase sharply as the industry evolves from one firm to three firms, and that innovation plateaus after that. Counterfactual simulations show that blocking mergers that leave the industry with fewer than three firms is nearly optimal from a social welfare perspective. They argue that this concords roughly with the current rule-of-thumb policies of antitrust agencies.

5.6 Innovation and Industry Evolution

Schumpeter (1942) was the first to emphasize the role of creative destruction in the generation of new goods and methods that lead to increases in the standard of living and reduction in production costs. He was concerned to some extent about the role of monopolies in the economy, arguing that they were not necessarily inimical to consumer welfare if they generated innovations and were (or had the potential to be) replaced by new innovating monopolies. He believed strongly that static price competition was less important for welfare than competition from "new goods." The key idea was that industries are observed over the long sweep of history to evolve continuously, making antitrust policy addressed to a static point in time misguided.

We are all familiar with the fact that major innovations can create entire new industries: for example, steam engines leading to railroads, the automobile and aircraft sectors, internet commerce following the development of the Web. Many of these industries today are highly concentrated, but it was not always so in their early development.

In a series of sector studies, Klepper (2016) showed that these new industries exhibit two common patterns as they develop. The first and most common occurs in three phases: (1) When the technology is new and continuously evolving, with uncertainty about exactly which version will dominate, the industry experiences high entry rates and a growth in the number of firms; that is a number of "experiments" in the business models and technology take place. (2) After rough agreement in the market on the technological features and any necessary standards to implement them, exit from the industry increases and entry declines along with the number of firms. This evolutionary process is helped along by the fact that successful firms have larger market shares, which, in turn, may mean they have a greater incentive to innovate, thus becoming even larger, a self-reinforcing process. Klepper refers to this phase as the industry *shakeout*. (3) After the shakeout, only a few firms survive and the industry becomes concentrated and innovation stagnates. Ultimately, possibly after considerable time, the industry is ripe for disruption as the world around it changes.

Building on work by Utterback and Abernathy (1975), Suárez and Utterback (1995) describe this industry life cycle as the emergence of a dominant design and supply six examples: the typewriter, automobile, TV, picture tube, transistor, and electronic calculator. They argue that four factors influence the emergence of a dominant design: (1) the possession of collateral assets such as market channels and brand image; (2) industry regulation and government intervention; (3) strategic maneuvering at the firm level; and (4) the existence of bandwagon effects or network externalities in the industry (see Chapter 7 for the role of networks). In their data, the peak number of firms in an industry occurs precisely as the dominant design emerges and declines steeply thereafter. They also show that survival after entry is more difficult for firms entering after the dominant design has emerged.

As examples of the kind of industry evolution he has in mind, Klepper presents automobiles, tires, TV receivers, and penicillin, all of which exhibited this kind of behavior over periods of roughly 50–70 years during the 20th century. See Figure 5.5 for the evolution of the automobile industry.

The other evolutionary pattern observed by Klepper was quite different: In the third phase, firms continue to enter, opening up new submarkets with new products in the broad industry. This picture is characteristic of the laser and semiconductor sectors. One way to view this kind of third phase is that it characterizes industries where the early innovation process has created a set of technological standards that allow vertical disintegration to take place. That is, firms are able to specialize in a particular stage of production because the features of design needed for a subsequent stage are well defined due to the existence of technological standards. Ziedonis and Hall (2001) show that in

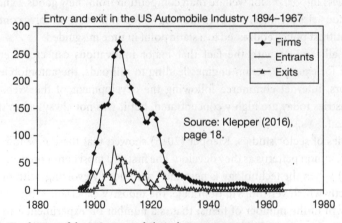

Figure 5.5 Evolution of the US automobile industry, 1894–1967.

the semiconductor sector, the rise of the complementary metal-oxide semiconductor (CMOS) standard and the strengthening of patent protection led to the development of specialized firms that only did chip design and contracted out their manufacture.

A second feature of industries like lasers and semiconductors is that the technology involved has many diverse and specialized applications requiring specialized technology, which delayed the inevitable shakeout. For example, Klepper (2016) argues that the introduction of solid-state lasers in the 1980s ultimately drove out firms using gas and chemical dye-based lasers, leading to a delayed shakeout in the sector. A third driver of both industries was demand and procurement by the US Department of Defense, which defined and opened up new markets in specific applications over time (Langlois and Steinmueller 1999, Bhaskarabhatla and Klepper 2014).

Using historical analysis of the machine tool industry, Rosenberg (1976b) comes to similar conclusions about the evolution of industries. When industries are young, they tend to use specialized and nonstandardized inputs made in-house, meaning that they are vertically integrated, and also that there may be many firms pursuing different technological strategies. As the industry matures, typically a dominant variant of the technology emerges, leading to *technological convergence*. In the case of the machine tool industry, common processes throughout machinery and metal-using sectors developed over time.

As the technology becomes more standardized, diffusion is facilitated and the standardization allows for greater specialization. This leads to what Rosenberg called *vertical disintegration* of the industry. We have already mentioned the semiconductor industry example of this phenomenon. In a maturing industry, standardization may also lead to greater concentration in some sectors of the vertically disintegrated industry. In the previously discussed hard disk drive study, Igami and Uetake (2020) find that merger incentives increased as the industry matured and the 3.5-inch form-factor became the standard.

5.7 Summary

What are the determinants of innovation by firms? First, we have seen that firm size has a fairly weak and somewhat unstable connection to innovative activity, depending on where and how this is measured. Unpacking the implications of this relationship, we saw that it measures the combination of firm efficiency in innovation together with innovation scale effects. Empirical work suggested that firm efficiency has a negative elasticity with size, while the elasticity of R&D with respect to size was about unity. The implication of these findings is that the elasticity of total R&D output with respect to firm size is somewhat less than 1, but with several caveats based on the difficulty of such measurements.

In contrast to the size–innovation relationship, a firm's industry is highly correlated with its innovative effort, and within industry, concentration tends to be higher if innovative effort is higher. The strong variation across industries suggests that the most important determinants of innovative activity may be demand for the industry's products as well as what we have termed *technological opportunity*, that is, the availability of potential innovations arising from various scientific and technological breakthroughs.

This chapter also reviewed a number of efforts to model the behavior of innovative firms in order to understand the bidirectional relationship between innovation and market structure. Although much progress has been made, it is a complex problem for at least two main reasons: (1) Realistic models are so complex that analytic solutions are usually not feasible, so more advanced computational techniques are needed to solve them. (2) Although we have fairly good measures of innovative input in the form of R&D expenditures, our measures of innovative output are quite coarse and rarely denominated in ways that make them easy to use and compare. That is, the actual value to a firm or to society of a patented invention or a count of innovations is highly variable across innovations and inventions, in contrast to firm R&D spending.

6

Returns to R&D and Innovation

Learning Objectives

After reading this chapter, you will be able to understand and explain the following concepts:

- Theory behind the measurement of returns to R&D investment and innovation
- Estimation of returns to R&D using the production function approach
- Estimation of returns to R&D using the rate-of-return formulation
- Challenges in the econometric estimation of returns to R&D
- The importance of price deflation for measuring returns to R&D
- Using firm market value to measure returns to R&D investment and patenting

---

6.1 Introduction

When individuals, firms, and even governments undertake investments for which they expect some return in the future, they often want a measure of the returns they expect from the investment. *Ex ante*, that is, before the investment is undertaken, they evaluate its expected return. *Ex post*, that is, after the investment and its results have been realized, they would like to measure the return on the investment, as a guide for undertaking such investments in the future. Because R&D and innovation have the characteristics of an investment (spending today to achieve returns in the future), they will wish to measure the returns to these investments for many of the same reasons cited above.

However, R&D and innovation differ from many other types of investment in an important way––because they often generate spillovers to others than those who undertake them, the returns that are of interest depend on who is asking the question. For example, a pharmaceutical firm that undertakes an R&D project that is expected to generate a new drug will be concerned about the increased profit from the sales of the drug less the cost of the project. They will ignore the possible knowledge spillovers to other firms from their success or failure in the project, but society may care about these, as the knowledge thus acquired can contribute to others' R&D productivity in the future. For an example of the benefits of failures, see the contribution of failed HIV vaccine research to the creation of SARS-Cov-2 vaccines (Harris 2021). In addition, there also may be *pecuniary spillovers* to consumers in the form of lower prices or improved products (see Box 6.1 for definitions).

Most of the literature on innovation returns focuses on the returns to R&D investment. This is partly for historical and data availability reasons, because until very

The Economics of Innovation and Intellectual Property. Bronwyn H. Hall and Christian Helmers, Oxford University Press.
© Oxford University Press 2024. DOI: 10.1093/oso/9780197630914.003.0006

Box 6.1 Externalities

Pecuniary externality: a change in the price faced by a firm or individual due to the actions of others in the market. For example, a fall in gas prices from reduced demand due to increases in electric-powered autos.

Real or technological externality: actions by one agent that affect another but do not go through the price system. For example, pollution from a local factory that has negative effects on those living nearby.

---

recently data on the full set of investments necessary to bring a new or improved product to market were not available. These other components of innovation spending usually consist of the following:

- Purchase of external knowledge and IP (patents, trademarks, know-how, etc.)
- Purchase, installation, and use of new (technologically advanced) equipment
- Training of employees in new processes, or in supporting new products
- Marketing new goods and services

Compared to R&D, most of these components have less associated uncertainty once undertaken, and also pay off to the firm in a shorter length of time. These factors make returns somewhat easier to compute. But their existence implies that any R&D-driven innovation project will include other costs if it is successful. As Brynjolfsson et al. (2002) found for investments in computer hardware, the presence of necessary complementary investment accompanying R&D may make the valuation of R&D seem high if other related spending is unobserved or not accounted for. In this chapter, we will discuss returns measurement for R&D but keep in mind that there may be necessary complementary innovation investments also undertaken by firms.

Estimates in the economic literature are usually reported for two quantities: private returns and social returns. Private returns are based on the average profits above costs made by individual firms and individuals that invest in R&D. In general, given the usual optimizing calculus of the firm, these returns will be somewhere in the neighborhood of the cost of capital needed to undertake the investment. Social returns are the benefit (usually in GDP terms) achieved by R&D investment at the economywide level relative to its cost. These returns may also be measured at the industry level (which excludes spillovers to other industries) or even the regional level (excluding spillovers to other regions). Social returns are ordinarily higher than private returns, but there is no reason that they must be. If there is intense competition among firms in R&D toward similar ends, social returns could be lower than private, rather than higher. But in practice, most measured social returns have proven to be substantially higher than private returns.

Measured returns to R&D are used for a number of purposes. Private returns to past R&D may serve as a guide to firms deciding to invest in particular areas, or as a benchmark against which to compare themselves to their competitors or other similar firms. They may also guide policymakers who perceive a lack of competitiveness in an economy's innovative effort. In such a setting, if returns are high, that suggests firms are behaving as though the cost of investment capital is high because they are not able to access sufficient capital for their investments. If returns are low, there are alternative explanations, such as lack of an environment (regulatory, availability of human capital, risk of expropriation by government or others, etc.) conducive to innovation, lack of demand, or weak management.

Social returns and the gap between private and social returns serve as guides to government policymakers designing or targeting R&D subsidies (see Chapter 10). The need for an R&D subsidy is greater when the gap between private and social returns is larger, that is, when the externalities discussed in Chapter 3 are greater. Accordingly, there has been considerable policy interest in estimating both social and private returns to R&D. Unfortunately, social returns are much harder to measure, because instead of having a set of firms from which we can construct econometric estimates, we have a single economy (or set of economies with very different characteristics and institutions that cannot be completely controlled for) for which R&D tends to grow in parallel with the other components of the economy, making distinguishing its impact separately difficult.[1]

Often addressing social returns is more effectively done via case studies. This is particularly true for innovations that pay off over a long period. For example, Bayesian probability theory, as formalized and developed by Laplace in the early 19th century, is in use everywhere today and, in particular, lies behind some machine learning models. It is not possible to measure precisely the returns to the time devoted by Laplace and others to this theory, but it is very clear that they are large.

For another example, consider investment by the US Department of Defense in packet-switched computer networks (ARPANET) during the 1960s and 1970s, which lie behind the internet we use today. Quantifying these examples is difficult because other developments were needed along the way, and there may have also been research costs in the form of "dry holes," that is, research that yields nothing usable, but it seems fairly clear that the payoff to the original investment was still quite large.

In this chapter, we mainly study private returns' measurement, and we defer further discussion of the measurement of social returns to Chapter 9. The following sections present the basic theory behind investment project choice, and two methods of estimating private returns or value of R&D investment. We also spend some time on the hedonic method of valuing heterogeneous goods in terms of their characteristics and adjusting for quality change in goods. These methods are essential for a full measurement of the benefits of innovation for product improvement.

6.2 Theory

Economic theory is a useful guide for thinking about how to estimate returns to an investment and how to understand the results. A firm deciding to undertake an investment project will typically compare its expected returns or the net present value of the project to the cost of the capital needed to finance it. This approach leads to a ranking of

[1] See Guellec and van Pottelsberghe (2004) for an example of this kind of cross-country study that uses modern time-series methods.

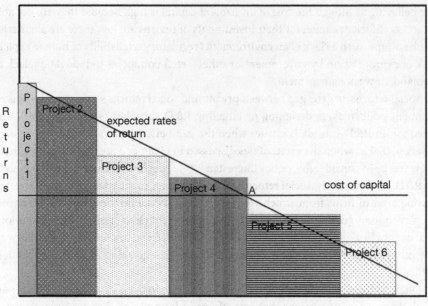

Figure 6.1 Choosing R&D projects.

projects from those whose returns are well above the cost of capital to those that are well below. Those projects whose expected returns are greater than the cost of capital will be chosen. Given the risk inherent in R&D and innovation projects, the comparison cost of capital may be somewhat higher than the usual risk-free rate. We illustrate this choice with a stylized supply-demand graph in Figure 6.1.

The figure shows a series of six R&D projects arrayed by the size of their return. The projects vary in total size. The cost of capital is assumed to be constant in the region of interest.[2] In this example, the firm will choose to do Projects 1 through 4, which have higher expected returns than the cost of financing them, but will forego Projects 5 and 6. Thus, the total level of R&D investment will be that shown at point A. In our analysis, we usually ignore the discreteness of the projects and treat the returns to R&D as though they follow the smooth downward-sloping line. For large firms with many projects, this is a reasonable approximation.

Before going further into the analysis of returns, we need to define the concept of R&D or knowledge capital. When a firm invests in R&D, it creates a kind of capital or intangible assets that it expects will yield a flow of returns over several years (Box 6.2), in a way similar to that generated by other investments. That's why it's called R&D *investment*. For example, the flow of spending by Google on improved search algorithms has generated knowledge within the firm that continues to yield a flow of profits into the

2 Most economists and managers would argue that the cost of capital increases when the firm is forced to go outside its current cash flow to finance investment. This issue has been the subject of considerable research in the past, mostly confirming the fact that costs are higher for external financing of R&D (Hall and Lerner 2010). The analysis here would be substantively the same if the cost curve was increasing instead of flat.

Box 6.2 R&D Capital

R&D capital is a measure of the stock of knowledge generated by past R&D investments of the firm (or country). This concept goes by various names in the literature: R&D assets, knowledge capital, knowledge or R&D stock. It is also referred to as an intangible asset or capital, of which there may be others within a firm such as a customer list or brand name recognition.

---

future. But such knowledge depreciates over time as others replicate it or improve on it, unless investment in improvements to replace the depreciated knowledge continues to take place. Although this is analogous to the ways we think about ordinary tangible investment, there is an important difference. Within the firm, depreciation of the knowledge asset means depreciation in its ability to earn private returns, whereas the knowledge itself may continue to be useful to others, implying that the social rate of depreciation may be much lower.

We will return to the topic of the correct depreciation rate in Section 6.3.3.1. For the moment, treating depreciation δ as a parameter, the conventional definition of knowledge capital K at the firm level is given by a perpetual inventory formula:

$$K_t = (1 - \delta)K_{t-1} + R_t$$

That is, knowledge capital K at time t is the depreciated knowledge capital from the previous period plus the current R&D investment R, by analogy to ordinary investment. One feature of this equation that can be useful in simplifying analysis is that if we assume the knowledge accumulation process has gone on a long time (in practice, 20 years or so to ensure minimal approximation error) and that real R&D spending is constant over that period, we can show that K is approximately equal to R/δ.[3] Using the common assumption that the depreciation rate for R&D is 15%, this implies that K is about $6.6R$ for an ongoing firm with stable R&D investment. If instead R&D has grown at a constant rate g over time, we can show that K is approximately equal to $R/(\delta + g)$. These benchmarks are useful when thinking about R&D investment in large established firms, where R&D spending tends to be rather smooth over time. They are obviously less applicable to startups and more volatile firms.

With R&D investment treated as creating an intangible asset or knowledge capital, we can use standard investment theory to tell us that point A in Figure 6.1 can be characterized by the following equation:[4]

$$c = r + \delta - \dot{p}/p$$

where c is the cost of capital, r is the current net return from R&D investment, δ is the depreciation of the knowledge capital created by the R&D, and $\dot{p}/p$ is the percent

---

[3] This computation makes use of the well-known relationship $\sum_{s=0}^{\infty} x^s = \dfrac{1}{1-x}$ for $-1 < x < 1$. See Appendix A: Mathematics and Statistics for further detail.

[4] For example, R. E. Hall and Jorgenson (1967).

increase or decrease in the price of such investment over time.[5] This equation says that the cost or rental price of investment during a period is composed of three terms: (1) the net return it can earn each period in use; (2) the cost of depreciation this period that renders the capital less useful in the future; (3) the rate of capital gain (or loss) on its price during the period, which reduces (or increases) the investment cost today relative to the future. Of course, all these items are highly uncertain at the time the investment choice is made, so realized returns may be quite different.

If there are corporate taxes and tax credits for R&D and R&D is expensed, all of which are now common in many countries, this expression becomes the following:[6]

$$c = \left(\frac{1-\tau-A^c}{1-\tau}\right)(r+\delta) = \left(1-\frac{A^c}{1-\tau}\right)(r+\delta)$$

where τ is the corporate tax rate and A^c is the net present value of the tax credit for R&D investment.[7] This equation shows us two things: (1) For a given net rate of return r, R&D tax credits will tend to lower the cost of capital. (2) If there is no R&D tax credit ($A^c = 0$) and R&D is fully expensable, the corporate tax rate drops out of this equation and corporate taxes do not affect the choice of R&D on the margin.

There are at least two important takeaways from the standard theory that have implications for our interpretation of the measurement of the returns to R&D. First, the interpretation of measured returns depends on how quickly one thinks that the knowledge and innovation produced by the R&D depreciate. From the perspective of the firm, depreciation takes place when the "asset" becomes less productive. In the case of R&D capital, its productivity can depend very much on changes in the competitive environment. For example, when Apple introduced the iPod in 2001, the R&D of previous manufacturers of portable MP3 players became suddenly less valuable, and many exited the sector over time. The fact that competitors matter for the productivity of own R&D means that measured or realized returns can be quite volatile, even when they are approximately equal to the cost of capital on average.

This feature of R&D investment can be contrasted to ordinary tangible investment. In general, with the exception of very specialized equipment, the results of tangible investment (e.g., machines, manufacturing plants, trucks) have a secondary market in which they can be sold. Their economic value tends to depreciate because of wear and tear over time, but less often because of the actions of their competitors. Even though the business model of a particular firm may fail, its tangible assets can usually find a market that realizes their depreciated value. The intangible asset created by R&D investment is not as easy to sell, and the private value is often reduced significantly by competition, so it is more subject to economic depreciation that is endogenous to competition.[8]

---

[5] The notation $\dot{p}$ is short for the time derivative of p, dp/dt.

[6] See the appendix in Hall and Van Reenen (2000) for details. We have omitted the capital gains term. Also see Chapter 10 for more information on the tax treatment of R&D.

[7] Note that we have assumed the price change for R&D investment from year to year is zero in deriving this formula. This is unavoidable in the case of R&D because we do not have an estimate of its real quantity that is separate from the total spending. In fact, it is not even obvious how such a thing could be defined.

[8] Some efforts to create a market for intangible R&D assets via patent sale do exist, but are not always successful. We discuss this topic further in Chapter 20.

Second, the derivation of the above relationship relied on the assumption that the firm was choosing inputs and R&D to maximize the present discounted value (PDV) of its profits. This means that, on average, the marginal after-tax gross return to R&D (the right-hand side of the equation) should be approximately equal to the cost of capital, possibly with a risk premium added. Thus, we expect measured private rates of return to be disciplined by financial markets toward a particular level. In contrast, social rates of return (the return to an industry or an economy) are not constrained in this way. When the firm undertakes investment, it focuses on its own return, ignoring the spillovers to other firms unless they turn out to benefit the firm itself in the future.[9] An implication is that measured social rates of return to R&D may be even more variable than private rates of return as there is little to attract them to a particular value.

6.3 Econometric Method

Our presentation of the empirical methods that have been used to estimate the returns to R&D focuses on the private returns to the firm. We will discuss the extensions to other units such as regions, industries, or countries in Chapter 9. The usual econometric method for measuring the returns to R&D begins by recognizing that expenditure on R&D creates a kind of intangible capital within the firm that we call knowledge capital, as described in Section 6.2. This computation of R&D capital is an important building block in almost all of the econometric studies that attempt to estimate the returns to R&D investment.

Therefore, in order to form a reasonably accurate estimate of R&D capital at the firm, industry, or country level, one needs an adequate time series of R&D spending, one that is consistently measured over time. This is not always easy to come by, although with advances in data collection in the recent past, it is considerably more straightforward to construct than any other potential measure of knowledge assets, such as one based on patent or publication counts. It also has the advantage of being denominated in currency units, which allows the computation of returns. In the estimation of R&D returns or values discussed below, this measure of R&D capital will be used as a proxy for the knowledge assets of a firm.

6.3.1 Estimation Using the Production Function

Using the above concept for R&D or knowledge capital, we can measure the private firm returns to R&D in the current period using the (revenue) production function.[10] We write output or sales S as a function of the inputs C (capital), L (labor), and R&D capital K:

$$S = F(C, L, K)$$

---

[9] See Belenzon (2012) for evidence that knowledge spillovers to others can result in future benefits for the firm spilling the knowledge.

[10] The revenue production function uses sales as a measure of output, which incorporates the prices the firm charges as well as the quantity it produces. The increase in sales from additional R&D is the relevant quantity for private returns measurement, as it encompasses both increases in production due to R&D as well as increases or decreases in the prices the firm can charge given product improvement and cost reduction.

Then the derivative of S with respect to K is the amount of additional output per one unit of K, holding capital and labor fixed. Using data on firms, we can measure this derivative using a regression in a couple of ways. The first method uses conventional production function estimation of the Cobb-Douglas form. Using lowercase to indicate the logarithm of the variables, the subscript i to indicate each of N individual firms, t to indicate the time period (usually a year), and adding an error term ε, we have the following:

$$S_{it} = A_t C_{it}^{\alpha} L_{it}^{\beta} K_{it}^{\gamma} e^{\varepsilon_{it}} \qquad i = 1, \ldots, N \quad t = 1, \ldots, T$$
$$s_{it} = a_t + \alpha c_{it} + \beta l_{it} + \gamma k_{it} + \varepsilon_{it}$$

A_t represents the trend in productivity change over time that is not accounted for by changes in the level of inputs. Because this is a logarithmic relationship, the estimated parameter γ measures the elasticity of output with respect to knowledge capital. To extract the returns to R&D capital, which is the derivative of output with respect to K, we use the formula for an elasticity:

$$\hat{\gamma} = \frac{\partial s}{\partial k} = \frac{K}{S} \frac{\partial S}{\partial K}$$

So that returns are given by

$$\frac{\partial S}{\partial K} = \hat{\gamma} \frac{S}{K} = \hat{\gamma} \left(\frac{K}{S} \right)^{-1}$$

Table 6.1 shows some estimates of the production function with knowledge capital included. Before looking at the table, we note that estimation has been performed on an equation that was transformed by subtracting the log of labor from both sides of the equal sign:

$$s_{it} - l_{it} = a + \alpha(c_{it} - l_{it}) + \gamma(k_{it} - l_{it}) + (\beta + \alpha + \gamma - 1)l_{it} + \varepsilon_{it}$$

This transformation does not affect the results for the coefficients of the two capitals. It has the advantage that the coefficient of labor is now a test for constant returns to scale in production, which is what we expect to find, so it is a useful check on the data and the estimation. Constant returns to scale means that if we increase all three inputs by the same amount θ, output will also increase by θ:

$$A\left[C(1+\theta)\right]^{\alpha} \left[L(1+\theta)\right]^{\beta} \left[K(1+\theta)\right]^{\gamma} = AC^{\alpha}L^{\beta}K^{\gamma}(1+\theta)^{\alpha+\beta+\gamma}$$
$$= AC^{\alpha}L^{\beta}K^{\gamma}(1+\theta) = S(1+\theta) \Leftrightarrow \alpha + \beta + \gamma = 1$$

In a cross section of firms such as would be used here, large deviations from constant returns are unlikely. We define the scale coefficient $\sigma = \alpha + \beta + \gamma$. Then a simple t-test on the coefficient of labor is a test for constant returns, that is, $\sigma = 1$. Negative estimates imply decreasing returns or $\sigma < 1$. In the decreasing returns case, increasing inputs proportionally results in less than proportional output.

Table 6.1 Estimates of the Production Function with R&D

Sample	French Manufacturing	US Manufacturing
No. of firms and years	197 firms; 1980–1987	1,073 firms; 1981–1989
Dependent variable	Log (value added/employee)	Log (sales/employee)
Log (capital/employee)	0.199 (0.013)	0.289 (0.008)
Log (R&D capital/employee)	0.252 (0.008)	0.035 (0.005)
Log (employees)	−0.035 (0007)	0.010 (0.010)
R-squared (standard error)	0.966 (0.344)	0.936 (0.360)
Source	Hall and Mairesse (1995), Table 3	Hall and Mairesse (1995), Table 3 (The estimates are transformed from the original as described above, in order to show the scale coefficient as the coefficient of labor.)

The results for the French manufacturing firms below indicate that there are very slight decreasing returns in this sample of firms, whereas the US firms show constant returns. The labor coefficient itself can be recovered from the scale coefficient σ as $\sigma + 1 - \alpha - \gamma$, which in this case yields -0.035 + 1.000 - 0.199 - 0.252 = 0.514 for the French estimates.

There are a number of econometric issues that arise with such an approach, many of which have at least partial solutions.[11] Probably the most important substantive issue is the assumption that γ is a constant parameter, invariant across firms in different industries. Clearly, the importance of knowledge capital in the production function will be different in the pharmaceutical industry when compared with the textile or food sectors. This has implications for the estimated γ in these sectors. Under some simple assumptions about returns to scale and imperfect competition, one can show that the elasticity of output with respect to an input is equal to the share of the input in the costs of production. This means that γ is expected to be higher in sectors with greater R&D intensity. Table 6.2 shows some estimated R&D capital elasticities γ together with the average R&D intensity for firms in a few selected US industries during the 1980–2018 period.[12]

We show two R&D intensities. The first is the average across all firms and years in the industry, and the second is the average over time of the ratio of industry R&D to industry sales. One can show that the ratio of industry R&D to industry sales is a weighted average of the firm R&D-to-sales ratios with industry sales shares as weights:

$$\frac{\sum_i R_i}{\sum_i S_i} = \frac{\sum_i \frac{R_i}{S_i} S_i}{\sum_i S_i} = \sum_i \frac{R_i}{S_i} \frac{S_i}{\sum_i S_i}$$

[11] We refer the interested reader to Hall and Mairesse (1995) and Blundell and Bond (2000) for further information on the econometric estimation of this relationship.

[12] The sample here has been restricted to those firms that actually do R&D. In some sectors, such as textiles, there are relatively few such firms, while in others, such as pharmaceuticals, almost all firms report R&D. The data are from Standard and Poor's Compustat annual industrial files.

Table 6.2 R&D Intensity versus the Estimated R&D Elasticity

Industry	Average R&D-to-Sales Ratio	Aggregate R&D to Aggregate Sales	R&D Capital Coefficient (elasticity)	Returns to R&D (derived)
Pharmaceuticals	6.9%	11.1%	0.097	27.6%
Computing equipment	8.8%	8.0%	0.128	30.5%
Software	10.1%	2.1%	0.102	21.0%
Chemical products	3.1%	2.9%	0.055	31.7%
Textiles and apparel	1.5%	1.2%	0.016	20.6%

In the above equation, R denotes R&D, S denotes sales, and i is the index of firms in the industry. Using this formula, one can see that the aggregate R&D intensity is usually lower than the average R&D intensity because larger firms (with higher sales shares and therefore higher weight in the aggregate) typically have lower R&D intensities. They are more likely to be established rather than growing and also to be vertically integrated with many non-R&D-oriented functions. Pharmaceuticals is an exception to this rule because the development portion of R&D is largely the cost of clinical trials. These are conducted primarily by the large established pharmaceutical firms that are household names, not by the new research-intensive firms in the sector.

The main takeaway from Table 6.2 is that the estimated R&D capital elasticity in a production function is not a constant parameter, but tends to be higher when the industry is more R&D-intensive and lower when the industry does not do much R&D. The correlation across 25 industries between R&D intensity and the estimated R&D elasticity for this sample of US manufacturing firms is above 0.6. Obviously, the relationship is not perfect, for a number of reasons. The most important is the presence of dynamics in the relationship. That is, the regression asked how much past investment in R&D affected sales during this period. But if the firm is growing and investing with an eye to profits in the future, as will be the case for many startups and young firms, current year sales may not be a good proxy for the future returns to the R&D. For example, one reason the pharmaceutical elasticity seems low given its high R&D intensity is that the sector contains many biotechnology firms that are far from having a product, so the expected sales increase from their past R&D has not yet materialized.

The fact that the estimated R&D elasticity varies with the R&D intensity is precisely what we would expect if returns to R&D are roughly constant across firms and industries. Recall the equation for the marginal product of R&D that we gave above, where the increase in sales due to an increase in R&D capital is given by the product of the estimated elasticity γ with the inverse of the R&D capital-sales ratio. Economic theory suggests that this would be the case: Firms would tend to invest in R&D up to the point where the returns are equal to the cost of R&D capital. Obviously, this is an oversimplification, as there may be variations in risk adjustment depending on industry, and investments are made using expected returns, which may not be the same as realized returns. Nevertheless, the assumption of equalized rates of return across sectors is a better benchmark than equalized elasticities, as this assumption is grounded in economic theory. In Table 6.2, the last column shows the rates of return computed by multiplying the estimated elasticity γ by the inverse of the R&D capital-sales ratio. From this, one can see that the rates of return are more equalized across industry than the elasticities, as they range from 20% to 30%, whereas the elasticities vary by a factor of almost 10.

6.3.2 Estimation Using the Rate-of-Return Formulation

The fact that theory says the rates of return should be approximately the same in all industries has led several researchers in the past to use a different version of the above model for estimation, one that treats the rate of return to R&D as a constant parameter. Estimating this version of the model requires more than 1 year of data for each economic unit in the sample (firm, industry, or economy) because it is based on growth rates. We start with the differenced version of the production function, obtained by subtracting the previous time period's equation from the current period:[13]

$$\Delta s_{it} = \alpha \Delta c_{it} + \beta \Delta l_{it} + \gamma \Delta k_{it} + \Delta e_{it}$$

We then transform $\gamma \Delta k$ so that it is written in terms of the gross rate of return ρ:[14]

$$\gamma \Delta k = \gamma \frac{\Delta K}{K_{-1}} = \gamma \frac{\Delta K}{K_{-1}} \frac{S_{-1}}{S_{-1}} = \left(\gamma \frac{S_{-1}}{K_{-1}} \right) \frac{\Delta K}{S_{-1}} = \rho \frac{\Delta K}{S_{-1}}$$

The new estimating equation is the following:

$$\Delta s_{it} = \alpha \Delta c_{it} + \beta \Delta l_{it} + \rho \frac{\Delta K_{it}}{S_{i,t-1}} + \Delta e_{it}$$

Recall that $\Delta K = R - \delta K_{-1}$. To estimate, one can either compute $\Delta K/S(-1)$ with a suitable assumption on δ, or assume that depreciation is zero and simply include the R&D intensity R/S in the equation. Many analysts using data at the economywide level have chosen to use zero depreciation on the grounds that the knowledge created by R&D is always available to the economy even after it stops generating profits for the firm. Some sample results using this method and the same data as was used for Table 6.2 are shown in Table 6.3.

With the exception of textiles and apparel, where over half the firms do no R&D, these estimates are quite high and do not vary as much across sectors as the R&D-to-sales ratio. Recall that this is an estimate of the gross rate of return to R&D, the sum of the net rate of return r and depreciation δ.

---

[13] Recall that $\Delta x = x - x(-1) = \log X - \log X(-1) = \log(X/X(-1)) = \log((X(-1) + \Delta X)/X(-1)) = \log(1 + \Delta X/X(-1))$ $\approx \Delta X/X(-1)$ for small growth rates $\Delta X/X(-1)$. That is, the difference of the logarithms of X between two periods is approximately the same as the growth rate of X. As a rough rule of thumb, the approximation is pretty good up to a growth rate of about 15%.

[14] Note that the use of the lagged R&D capital-output ratio instead of the current R&D capital-output ratio is helpful here as it is predetermined with respect to the disturbance.

Table 6.3 Estimated Rate of Return to R&D

Industry	Average R&D-to-Sales Ratio	R&D Intensity Coefficient (zero depreciation)	R&D Intensity Coefficient (15% depreciation)	Lagged R&D Intensity Coefficient (zero depreciation)
Pharmaceuticals	6.5%	55.5%	58.8%	45.4%
Computing equipment	8.6%	51.3%	76.2%	25.8%
Software	9.2%	54.5%	58.8%	38.9%
Chemical products	3.0%	51.4%	72.1%	42.9%
Textiles and apparel	0.9%	17.5%	29.6%	-38.1%

One possible explanation for these high rates of return is econometric: There is undoubtedly simultaneity in the relationship. When the firm has high sales growth in a period, it generally has positive cash flow, which both signals future demand and makes cheaper funds available for investment; this can cause feedback to current R&D investment, which responds to the prospect of increased future returns. The last column of Table 6.3 shows estimates based on R&D intensity in the previous year, which avoids the feedback effect to some extent. In this case, the estimates are 10 to 15 percentage points lower, confirming such an interpretation. However, with the exception of textiles, they are still fairly high.

6.3.3 Some Issues in Estimating Returns to R&D

A number of other issues arise in attempting to estimate the returns to R&D. Many of these also apply to estimation at the economywide or country level and concern issues also faced by government statisticians who construct the national income accounts (NIAs). They include the following:

- Choice of depreciation rate
- Double counting of R&D inputs
- Implications of omitting others' R&D in estimation
- Definition and scope of output
- Output measurement for services
- Price measurement (to get real output, nominal output needs to be deflated by its price; some R&D raises quality, therefore lowering the price of a constant quality good, presumably increasing demand)

The measurement of quality-adjusted prices and its implications is covered in Section 6.4 of this chapter and the issues related to output measurement are deferred to Chapter 9, where we discuss including R&D in the NIAs. We explore the remaining issues in this section of the chapter.

6.3.3.1 Choice of Depreciation Rate

As we discussed earlier, because the returns to R&D are intertemporal and estimation therefore relies on the construction of a "stock" of R&D knowledge, we need to choose a depreciation rate to construct such a stock. In their exploration of the impact of the choice of R&D depreciation rate in the production function, Griliches and Mairesse (1984, for US firms) and Hall and Mairesse (1995, for French firms) found little difference in the estimated elasticity when varying levels of the depreciation rate were used. However, as Hall (2005) showed, when the rate of return to R&D is computed from the elasticity, the choice of depreciation rate will still matter because estimated return is the product of the elasticity with the output-R&D capital ratio, and the R&D capital estimate depends inversely on depreciation.

It is fairly easy to see why estimates of the elasticity using relatively short panels of large manufacturing firms are not sensitive to the choice of depreciation rate. Recall that for firms with a roughly constant depreciation rate and growth rate of R&D, $K \cong R/(\delta + g)$. When we write the production function from Section 6.3.1 incorporating this approximation, we obtain the following:

$$q_{it} = a + \alpha c_{it} + \beta l_{it} + \gamma r_{it} + \gamma \log(\delta_i + g_i) + e_{it}$$

Here, we have assumed that the depreciation rate and growth rate of R&D are constant over time within the firm, but may vary across firms.[15] If a fixed firm effect a_i is included in the estimation, the $\log(\delta + g)$ term will be subsumed in that, and the estimate of γ will be approximately equal to the estimated coefficient of current R&D, no matter what depreciation rate we have chosen for K. Of course, this approximation is only suitable for situations where the firms being analyzed are relatively stable and not subject to sudden obsolescence of their past R&D or large fluctuations in R&D growth.

Some researchers have tried to develop estimates of R&D depreciation using external information or surveys. For example, Hall (2005) uses two slightly different but related assumptions implied by economic theory to derive implications for the relationship between R&D investment and depreciation:

1. R&D investment is chosen to satisfy the user cost equation given above so that depreciation is equal to normal user cost less net return, as measured by a production function with R&D. This approach gave implausible estimates of negative depreciation, which implies that firms were investing as though returns and/or the cost of R&D were expected to rise in the future. A similar assumption is used by Chinloy et al. (2020) to measure time-varying depreciation rates. In the same spirit, Li and Hall (2020) estimate depreciation using a simple model of the relationship of industry sales or output with R&D.

2. R&D investment is undertaken so that the marginal value of R&D capital is equal to its cost. This implies that Tobin's q (the ratio of the value of an asset to its replacement cost) should be equal to 1 in equilibrium, as discussed later in this chapter (Section 6.6). An implication of this assumption is that depreciation can

---

[15] This is a reasonable assumption for fairly short panels of firms, which is typical of those used for past estimates.

be derived from the measured valuation of R&D capital. This method was also used by Hirschey and Weygandt (1985).[16]

An alternative method of estimating R&D depreciation is to use survey evidence, asking firms to estimate the rate at which profits from R&D erode. De Rassenfosse and Jaffe (2018) surveyed the holders of Australian patents, asking about the valuation of their inventions. They make the important point that depreciation based on the value of successful inventions may be lower than that based on R&D expenditure, as the latter includes unsuccessful R&D, which presumably depreciates faster. Their estimates are considerably lower than those from the market value and profit function estimates, which may be due to the omission of unsuccessful R&D, but also to the restriction to the returns from patented inventions, which can be expected to generate profits over a longer period due to the ability to exclude direct competitors. They do find that the value of inventions whose patent applications are unsuccessful does depreciate somewhat faster (1–2%).

Table 6.4 presents a selection of the estimates of R&D depreciation from the literature. They are somewhat dispersed, and the more detailed results in the literature also vary over time. With the exception of de Rassenfosse and Jaffe (2018), they are largely based on data for the United States. Nevertheless, a couple of conclusions about R&D depreciation can be drawn from these estimates. First, they tend to be somewhat higher than the usual 15% used for R&D depreciation when constructing knowledge stocks in the literature. Second, depreciation of R&D in the various computing-related sectors is much higher than that in pharmaceuticals, reflecting differences in the innovation process in the two sectors. The pharmaceutical sector tends to move at a slower pace and the effectiveness of patent protection means that profits from R&D last for a longer period. In computing, new models arrive almost every year, and past R&D more quickly becomes obsolete. Although patents are heavily used, they are less successful at preventing profit erosion.

6.3.3.2 Double Counting

Double counting of R&D inputs refers to the fact that the labor and capital expense in R&D expenditure is also included in labor and capital itself. The main problem is labor because the share of R&D spending devoted to tangible capital is small (about 10%), and such capital is generally expensed directly and not included in the firm's capital stock. The majority of R&D spending is labor-related, and the R&D employees tend to be well paid compared to the rest of the firm. Schankerman (1981) identified this problem and found that the downward bias in the estimated R&D coefficient was of the order of 25–85% of the true coefficient and higher when R&D intensity was higher. Hall and Mairesse (1995) uses data on French manufacturing firms to find a downward bias in the elasticity of approximately 28%.

6.3.3.3 Bias from Omission of Spillover Variables

Within industries and even within the whole economy, R&D intensities across firms tend to be modestly correlated over time. One implication of this fact is that if there are

---

[16] See Hall (2005) for details.

Table 6.4 Some Estimates of R&D Depreciation

Authors	Sample	Years	Method	Estimates (s.e.)
Hirschey and Weygandt (1985)	Fortune 500 US	1977	Market value	6–15%
Hall (2005)	Compustat, pharma and medical instruments firms	1974–2003	Market value	14.9% (1.7%)
Hall (2005)	Compustat, computers and software	1974–2003	Market value	31.5% (3.5%)
Huang and Diewert (2011)	BLS/NSF, US manufacturing	1953–2001	Production function	29% (2.8%)
Li and Hall (2020)	BEA/NSF, computers and peripheral eq. industries	1987–2007	Profit function	36.3% (3.8%)
Li and Hall (2020)	BEA-NSF, software industry	1987–2007	Profit function	30.8% (0.5%)
Li and Hall (2020)	BEA/NSF, pharma industry	1987–2007	Profit function	11.2% (4.8%)
De Rassenfosse and Jaffe (2018)	Australian patent holders	1986–2005	Patent revenue	2–7%

R&D spillovers from one firm to another, a productivity regression that includes only a firm's own R&D will overestimate the returns to that R&D. That is, the estimated coefficient of own R&D is biased upward due to an omitted variable in the equation.[17]

Eberhardt et al. (2013) suggested using a common factor approach when estimating the R&D productivity equation and apply their approach to a 10 country–12 industry panel dataset for the years 1980–2005. This approach amounts to including the mean across time of the dependent and independent variables in each country–industry equation. The advantage of their approach is that it does not require a specific model for the measurement of spillovers, and also that it can accommodate the double counting discussed in the previous section. The disadvantage is that including a common factor with industry-specific coefficients may overcorrect, in the sense that it also accounts for any other industry characteristics that might be correlated with R&D.

The preferred estimates of Eberhardt et al. do indeed show that own R&D is insignificant in the productivity equation once industry–country variation in R&D is removed. Should we infer from this that R&D is unproductive for the firm? Given the amount firms spend in R&D, this seems unlikely. A more likely explanation is that firm ·

[17] For the econometrics of omitted variable bias, see Wooldridge (2000), pp. 87–90; Greene (2008), pp. 133–134; or Angrist and Pischke, pp. 59–60.

R&D and its industry R&D are correlated over time, and if firm R&D is measured with greater error than the aggregate, the aggregate industry R&D will dominate in explanatory power. The problem here is lack of the right experiment to truly identify the productivity of R&D. As Eberhardt et al. point out, the way out is to develop a more explicit model of how spillovers contribute to firm's own R&D.

6.4 Price Deflation

In the regressions in the previous section, output is often simply sales or GDP, possibly deflated by a single deflator that does not incorporate much quality change. To understand the implications of this fact for our measurements, we define Y as the quantity of real output and P as the price of each unit. For example, Y is the number of computers sold and P is the price of each computer.[18] Sales S is the product of price and quantity, $S = PY$. The consequence is that our logarithmic equation becomes the following:

$$s_i = p_i + y_i = a + \alpha c_i + \beta l_i + \gamma k_i + \varepsilon_i$$

And the estimated coefficient γ is the sum of two effects: the elasticity of real output with respect to R&D plus the elasticity of price with respect to R&D:

$$\hat{\gamma} = \frac{\partial s_i}{\partial k_i} = \frac{\partial y_i}{\partial k_i} + \frac{\partial p_i}{\partial k_i}$$

We might expect that this latter elasticity is negative. That is, that R&D lowers the price of a constant quality output. But this presumes that we have very good constant quality measures of output, which may be unrealistic. However, understanding this relationship helps us to understand the impact of R&D at the firm level as it affects consumers as well as the firm. If R&D produces new and improved products whose benefits to consumers are not fully captured in their prices (think of the improvements in personal computers or mobile telephones over time that are not fully reflected in price), then the impact of R&D on price generates a positive *pecuniary* spillover or externality to consumers (Box 6.1).

Thus if we have quality-adjusted prices, we can interpret the response of sales to R&D estimated via the methods above as follows:

$$\frac{\partial s}{\partial k} = \text{sales impact} = \text{return to the firm}$$

$$\frac{\partial y}{\partial k} = \text{real output impact} = \text{partial "social" return}$$

$$\frac{\partial p}{\partial k} = \text{price impact (presumed negative)} = \text{benefit to consumers}$$

---

[18] As the example makes clear, it is almost never this simple. All firms have more than one product with more than one price. The usual approach is to construct an index of prices and quantities that can be combined to generate output.

This breakdown at the firm level does not measure true social returns because it ignores the potential spillovers of the knowledge produced by the R&D on other actors in the economy. These latter spillovers are generally called real or technological externalities (see Box 6.1).

In the next section, we explain briefly how quality change is measured by statistical agencies and give some examples.

6.4.1 Hedonic Prices and Welfare

Hedonic prices are the prices of characteristics that customers actually care about when they purchase a good or service. For example, consumer willingness to pay for a personal computer is determined by a combination of characteristics such as speed, memory, weight, and so forth. In the market, each of these characteristics has a price that is the result of a market equilibrium between demand by heterogeneous customers and the cost of supplying each characteristic. Hedonic prices are often determined using econometric regression, where the prices of various goods are regressed on their characteristics. The estimated coefficients from such a regression are the implicit price of the characteristic in the market.

These coefficients allow us to predict the price of a newly introduced good using its characteristics. A price index can be constructed by observing the change in prices of the same characteristics from period to period and aggregating them using weights that reflect the shares of the individual goods in the market. This kind of computation is done by the US statistical agencies for a range of goods including apparel, computers, other electronics, phones, household appliances, automobiles, and photographic equipment. For details see Griliches (1961) and the US Bureau of Labor Statistics (BLS) website.[19]

Other important applications of hedonic pricing are in real estate, especially residential real estate, where each residence has a fairly unique combination of characteristics such as number of rooms, square footage, bathrooms, acreage, location, quality of maintenance, and so forth. Websites such as Zillow make use of hedonic regression combined with machine learning in a proprietary methodology to estimate the market price of individual residences. A second application of hedonic pricing, pioneered by Griliches (1981), is to the market valuation of firms as a function of their assets. We discuss this application to innovation assets in the next section of this chapter.

Here, we give a simple example of the use of a hedonic measure of quality change due to Nordhaus (1996). His example was intended to be representative of the long-term growth consequences of using a price index that accounts for the utility or benefit to consumers of a product. He chose a good that has been used for thousands of years for essentially the same purpose but with very different technologies: lighting.

A conventional light and heating price index is a weighted average of the prices of various inputs, with weights w that add up to 1:

$$p(t) = p_1(t)w_1(t) + p_2(t)w_2(t) + \ldots\ldots + p_n(t)w_n(t)$$

---

[19] https://www.bls.gov/cpi/quality-adjustment/questions-and-answers.htm.

The n prices p in this formula include such things as the following:

- Per gallon fuel price (weighted by the share of heating in a typical consumer light and heating budget)
- An electricity Kwh price (the price of a kilowatt hour, weighted by the share of electricity)
- The price of a 60-watt light bulb (weighted by the share of light bulbs in the budget)

A hedonic (quality-adjusted) light and heating index has the same form, with weights s:

$$q(t) = q_1(t)s_1(t) + q_2(t)s_2(t) + \ldots\ldots + q_m(t)s_m(t)$$

The m prices q are the prices of such things as the following:

- Raising the temperature in the house 1 degree (or cooling it 1 degree in the summer)
- 1,000 lumen-hours of light
- operating a TV or other viewing device 2 hours a day

That is, they are the prices of the characteristics that consumers actually care about, and whose quality is constant over time, although, of course, the share of these in the budget may change over time.

Nordhaus (1996) focused on the lighting portion of this price index. He assumed a single characteristic of light that humans care about: brightness per hour. He then chose a unit of a 1,000 lumen-hours of light as his standard. By choosing a single characteristic, he avoided the problem of needing weights to construct the price index for lighting. He argued that the official price indices miss much of the output growth in this industry as it shifted from oil to candles to gas to electric light. Although his research went back to the oil lamps of Babylonian times, he focused on the period from 1800 to 1992, given measurement difficulties for data prior to the 19th century. He estimated the price of light using only the fuel input and ignoring the purchase of a bulb, infrastructure, and the like; this is also the way the price is estimated in official statistics.

Figure 6.2 shows the results of his measurements together with the official price index of light for comparison. The scale is logarithmic to show the detail for recent years, when the price index falls substantially. Because the data are drawn from different sources and fairly approximate, the new price index fluctuates quite a bit, but the main message is that after 1860, the cost of 1,000 lumen-hours of light fell precipitously by a factor of about 1,000. After about 1880, much of this fall is due to the replacement of gas with electricity as a source of fuel for lighting.

Nordhaus uses his new hedonic price index to show that if lighting was 1% of the household budget over the 192 years, real wage and output growth have been underestimated by 0.036% per year. This seems small but over the whole period it is a factor of 1.036 raised to the power of 192, which is about 900. When multiplied by the 1% share, this adds about 9% to real wage or real productivity growth over the whole period. He goes on to speculate about how much the growth in real wages would be if we tried to do the same adjustments for all goods. Conventional measurement finds a 13-fold increase in

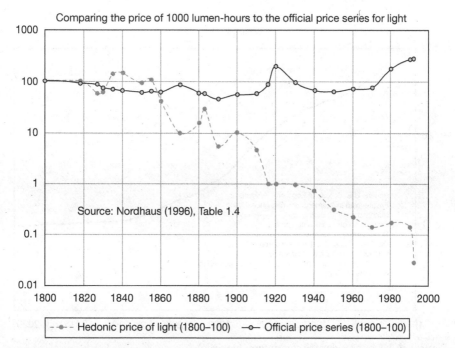

Figure 6.2 The price of light.

real wages between 1800 and 1992, whereas he finds the growth to be between 40- and 190-fold if prices properly reflected the true quality of the good purchased.

For a more mundane example using the price of nails, a product whose basic form has not changed in over three centuries, see Sichel (2022). He finds that the real price of nails fell between 1695 and the 1930s due to decreases in manufacturing cost, but began to increase again afterward due to a rise in the materials cost (iron) and a shift of US manufacturing toward specialty nails as foreign competition increased.

Here is another example using the computing equipment sector we studied earlier. For a number of years, the US BLS has produced a quality-adjusted price index for computing equipment that takes into account the vast improvement in computers over time.[20] Figure 6.3 shows a graph of this index from 1980 to 2020, again on a logarithmic scale. The main decline in price occurs between 1980 and 2010, when the index falls to one-hundredth of its 1980 level. After 2010, the slowdown in price declines is associated with the slowdown in semiconductor improvement, often described by the so-called Moore's law.[21] This law describes the historical evolution in the cost and size of semiconductor microprocessors, and it is widely believed that the rate of improvement has slowed considerably due to the challenges of further miniaturization and the associated heating problems.

The computer price index is based on computer attributes such as clock speed of the processor and memory capacity, which are only proxies for what the consumer cares about. The need for faster processors and larger memories is driven partly by increases

[20] For further information, see https://www.bls.gov/cpi/factsheets/personal-computers.htm.
[21] See Flamm (2021) for a full discussion of the price and cost trends in semiconductors.

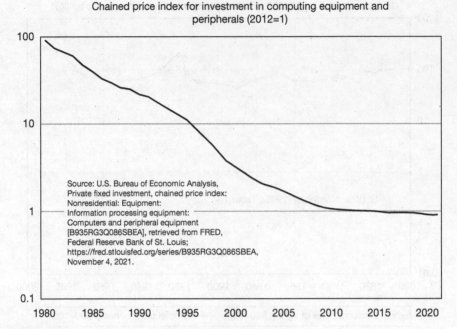

Figure 6.3 US price index for computers (log scale).

in software complexity due to security and privacy concerns, regulatory changes to deal with these, and the need to support many new types of hardware peripherals. Although there is no doubt that greater speed and memory are welcome for some applications, many applications function only slightly better with these enhancements. In addition, making use of the cheaper hardware requires complementary goods in the form of software and user support. All this is to say that the steep decline shown in Figure 6.3 may overstate the actual benefit to consumers.

6.5 Using Market Value to Value R&D

As we discussed earlier, the challenge in measuring the returns to R&D is that they are both uncertain and in the future. Beginning with Griliches (1981), this problem has led a number of researchers to turn to financial market theory to construct a valuation method based on the stock market value of the firms that invest in R&D. Financial economic theory tells us that the price at which a firm trades is the market's estimate of the PDV of the dividends that will be generated by its current assets, both tangible and intangible. If one knows the quantity of these assets held by the firm, one can infer the marginal value or shadow price placed on each of the asset types using a hedonic regression of stock market value as a function of the quantity of the various assets held by a set of firms.

Tobin (1969) presented a GE model of the capital account for the economy that showed the shadow price for tangible assets (physical capital) was unity in equilibrium. He also showed that this shadow price, which he called *q*, was a signal for investment: When q is greater than unity, the value of assets is higher than their cost, and firms should invest to bring q toward unity. When q is less than unity, the value of assets is lower than their cost, and firms should disinvest. This interpretation can be extended to firms with more than one type of asset, as shown by Hayashi and Inoue (1991).

Beginning with the 1981 paper by Griliches, a number of authors have used this approach to estimate the marginal value of innovation assets such as R&D capital and the stock of patents. The usual model is a simple additive one in logs, although it could be generalized to include interactions among the assets. Denoting market value by V, physical capital by A, and R&D capital by K, a typical model is of the following form:

$$V = q(A + \gamma K)^{\sigma}$$

σ is a scale coefficient that should be near unity, and γ is a premium or discount that is applied to knowledge assets. With properly measured A and K, γ should also be near unity, but there are many reasons why measured γ may diverge: higher risk for R&D, incorrect depreciation used in constructing K, correlation of A and K combined with differing measurement errors in the two, which means that their estimated coefficients may suffer from bias of different magnitudes, and so forth. Taking logarithms of both sides and adding a disturbance to accommodate any errors in the relationship, we obtain the following:

$$\begin{aligned} \log V_i &= \log q + \sigma \log\left(A_i + \gamma K_i\right) + \varepsilon_i \\ &= \log q + \sigma \log A_i + \sigma \log\left(1 + \gamma K_i / A_i\right) + \varepsilon_i \\ &\approx \log q + \sigma \log A_i + \sigma \gamma K_i / A_i + \varepsilon_i \end{aligned}$$

The last equation makes use of the approximation $\log(1 + x) = x$, where $|x|$ is small.[22]

Frequently, the assumption of constant proportionality between market value and size measured by capital stock is tested by subtracting the log of tangible capital from both sides of the equation:

$$\log Q_i = \log(V_i / A_i) \approx \log q + (\sigma - 1)\log A_i + \sigma \gamma K_i / A_i + \varepsilon_i$$

In this version of the equation, the coefficient of $\log A$ will be zero if V and A vary proportionally across firms, and it is easy to test for proportionality using the estimated coefficient of $\log A$. Q is measured as the empirical ratio of the total market value of the firm V to the estimated replacement value of its tangible assets A.

Figure 6.4 shows the evolution of median $Q = V/A$ for US publicly traded firms, all firms, and then only those that have nonzero R&D capital. Both curves show the various macro shocks during the period that caused market value to fluctuate (oil price shock in 1973–1974, 2008 financial crisis, etc.). In the early 1970s, the curves coincide,

---

[22] This approximation was adequate 40 years ago, but over time, the importance of investments in intangibles such as R&D has grown and the approximation is no longer appropriate for many firms. In fact, a small number of publicly traded firms in pharmaceuticals and instruments have essentially no physical capital compared to their R&D capital. More recent estimates of the model sometimes rely on the nonlinear formulation in the second line of this equation or even on semiparametric estimation for this reason.

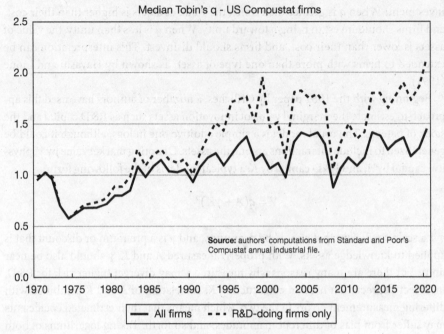

Median Tobin's q - US Compustat firms

Source: authors' computations from Standard and Poor's Compustat annual industrial file.

— All firms   - - - R&D-doing firms only

Figure 6.4 Evolution of median Tobin's q: US publicly traded firms.

but they increasingly diverge as time passes, reflecting the increasing importance of R&D in firm assets. The value of R&D capital is included in the numerator of Q (market value), but its replacement cost is not contained in the denominator (tangible assets).

Figure 6.5 shows the increase in relative importance of R&D capital in publicly traded US firms over the past 50 years. This figure is based on all R&D-performing firms that are headquartered in the United States and traded on a public stock exchange. The number of such firms grew until the late 1990s and then began to decline, as entry fell and concentration increased.[23] The two curves show the R&D capital-physical capital ratio for these firms as it evolves from 1981 to 2022.[24] The top curve is the median ratio, and the bottom is the ratio of aggregate R&D capital to aggregate physical capital. The aggregate R&D capital-physical capital ratio for R&D-doing firms in the United States has increased from 0.3 to 1.0 over the past 40 years. The curves roughly coincide in the early 1980s and then diverge substantially. The fact that the median is higher than the aggregate implies that the smaller (and presumably newer) firms are increasingly R&D-intensive. We confirm this fact in Figure 6.6, which shows the median ratio by age of firm. R&D stock is 250% of physical capital for the youngest firms and falls to about 100% by age 30.

---

[23] The basic facts about declining US business dynamism have been summarized in Akcigit and Ates (2021).

[24] R&D capital is measured as described earlier, using a 15% depreciation rate and capitalizing the initial period R&D using 0.15 plus a suitable growth rate, as in the equation $R/(\delta + g)$. Physical capital is the replacement value of net plant and equipment, as computed in Lewellen and Badrinath (1997) and Hall (2005).

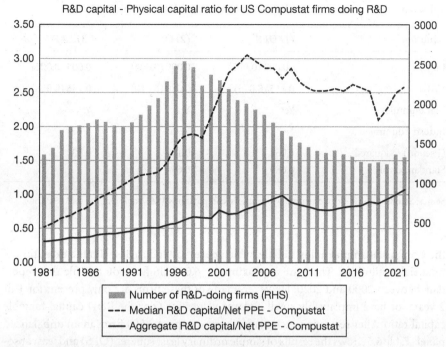

Figure 6.5 R&D capital-to-physical-capital ratio for US public firms.

The main message of these figures is that R&D capital has become increasingly important for publicly traded firms and especially for smaller and newer firms. How does this growth compare to the market valuation of R&D capital? To answer this question, we estimate the regression described in the equation for log Q above, using data from

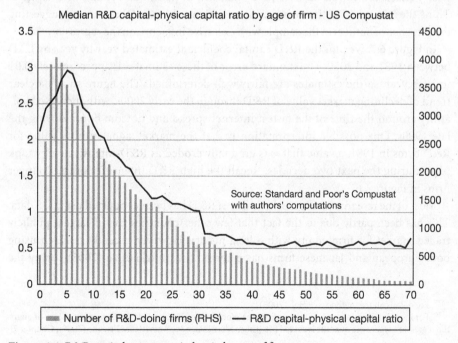

Figure 6.6 R&D capital-to-net-capital ratio by age of firm.

Table 6.5 Estimates of a Market Value Equation for US Firms, 2000–2020

Equation	(1) OLS	(2) OLS	(3) LAD
Log A	−0.002 (0.005)	0.009 (0.004)	0.005 (0.002)
K/A	0.115 (0.015)	0.080 (0.010)	0.156 (0.008)
Year dummies	Yes	Yes	Yes
Industry dummies	No	Yes	No
(Pseudo) R-squared	0.068	0.137	0.039
Standard error	0.689	0.664	

Source: Standard and Poor's Compustat with authors' computations 33,858 observations on 3,834 firms.

the Compustat annual industrial file, which covers all industries with the exception of financial institutions. There are approximately 6,000 US firms on this file that report data between 2000 and 2020. However, many of these firms are only present for 1 or 2 years, or have implausibly small or large values for Q or the R&D capital-tangible capital ratio. After removing such firms, there are about 3,500 firms in an unbalanced panel. Table 6.5 shows the results of simple ordinary least squares (OLS) and least absolute deviation (LAD) estimation applied to the log Q equation.[25]

From Table 6.5, one can draw several conclusions: First, the assumption of constant returns to tangible capital ($\sigma = 1$) is clearly accepted because tangible capital (A) does not enter the equation when market value is normalized by tangible capital. Second, R&D capital enters significantly and has a coefficient equal to 0.08–0.16. This coefficient is somewhat reduced when we control for differences across industries because the industry effects are correlated with R&D intensity, as we saw earlier and in Chapter 5. Third, the robust LAD estimate is significantly higher than the OLS estimate, suggesting the presence of outliers in the sample with excessive influence on the regression.[26]

In Figure 6.7, we plot the R&D capital coefficient estimated year by year by LAD between 1981 and 2020. The standard error of these estimates is approximately 0.01 in each year, so the estimates are fairly well determined. The figure shows a clear trend of declining market value of R&D through the early 2000s, with increased volatility around the time of the fastest internet spread and dotcom boom during the late 1990s. One possible interpretation is that the market signaled high value for R&D firms in 1981, a value that was gradually eroded as R&D-intensive entry took place during the next two decades. Recall the high R&D intensities of the younger firms in Figure 6.6.

Most of the research on the market value of R&D has been conducted using US data. This has been partly due to the fact that few other countries had as large a publicly traded market for firm equity with a long history. However, recently research using both European and Japanese firms has emerged. Czarnitzki et al. (2006) survey the

[25] For details on the method, see Hall (2005).
[26] For more information on LAD estimation, see Wooldridge (2000), p. 304. LAD is a special case of quantile regression where the quantile is set to 50% (the median). Also see Angrist and Pischke (2009), Chapter 7.

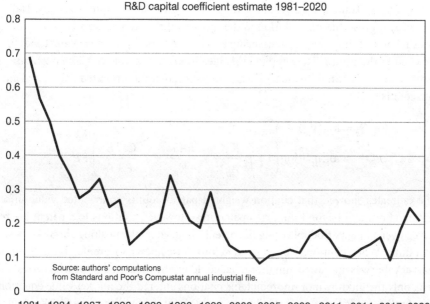

Figure 6.7 Historical evolution of the R&D capital value in the United States.

research and conclude that "in most countries one dollar of additional R&D spending adds slightly less than a dollar to market value."

6.6 Returns to Other Innovation Measures

Economists, managers, and policymakers focus on measuring returns to R&D for two reasons. The first is that R&D investment is an input choice made by the firm or government, and is therefore subject to direct manipulation and policy intervention, unlike innovation outcomes. Clearly, the choice of R&D will affect outcomes, but only indirectly, as many other factors, including luck, intervene. Second, data on R&D spending are widely available, and the unit of measurement is currency units rather than innovation, patent, or publication counts. When the latter are used as a measure of innovative activity, one must confront the problem that individually they vary enormously in importance or value so that mere counts are a poor indicator of the actual value of a set of innovations, patents, or publications.

In spite of these drawbacks, there is interest in measuring returns or values of innovation using patents or other counts as proxies for innovation output, beginning with Griliches' original 1981 paper, where he showed that patents contributed to firm market value above and beyond R&D spending, suggesting that they could proxy for success in R&D. However, it is worth recalling that patents are more likely associated with successful inventions rather than successful innovation per se, although they are clearly related to ultimate success. Pakes (1985) and Hall et al. (1986) show that within firms, the timing of R&D and patents tends to be simultaneous, suggesting that patents are actually an intermediate output during the R&D process.

Inspired by Trajtenberg's (1990) study of computed tomography scanners, Hall et al. (2005) suggest that one solution to the problem that patent counts are a very noisy measure of the things they are measuring is to weight them by the number of times they are cited in the future. They applied this idea to a large sample of US manufacturing firms, using a version of the market value equation that incorporated patent and citation counts:[27]

$$\log Q_{it} = \log(V_{it} / A_{it})$$
$$= \log q_t + \log\left(1 + \gamma_1 \frac{K_{it}}{A_{it}} + \gamma_2 \frac{PAT_{it}}{K_{it}} + \gamma_3 \frac{CITE_{it}}{PAT_{it}}\right) + \varepsilon_i$$

The estimates showed that citation-weighted patent counts contributed value information above and beyond the firm's patenting. However, citations to a patent are received over a long period following the patent filing, generally peaking about 4–5 years after filing. When citations were separated into those known or predictable at the time market value was measured and those that could not be predicted by past history of the firm, only the unknown or unpredictable citations entered the market value equation. The implication is that the market knows more about the quality of the firm's patented inventions than is captured by current R&D, patents, and cites to date. Therefore, because cites are only revealed slowly over time, they are not very useful as a future value predictor.

An influential paper by Kogan et al. (2017, hereafter KPSS) takes this idea further, using the market value response to the issuance of a patent as a measure of the patent value. They use a version of a stock market event study to estimate the distribution of patent values. An event study is a statistical method of estimating the value associated with an event that affects the firm, by measuring the abnormal return to its stock over a short period that includes the event.[28] An event study relies on the assumption that in a rational market, all information about the consequences of an event for the firm is immediately incorporated into its stock price.

In the implementation in KPSS, it is assumed that the market knows the value of the patented invention to the firm as well as the average probability π that a patent is granted. When the patent issues, the probability of grant is revised to unity so that the observed change in market value ΔV_i of the firm is equal to the following if there is no other news affecting the firm at the same time:

$$\Delta V_i = v_i = (1 - \pi)\xi_i$$

ξ_i is the value of the patent, which they wish to estimate. In practice, the problem is to extract the market value change due to the patent from the observed market value change, which will contain responses to other news as well. KPSS assume that the observed

---

[27] The use of ratios roughly orthogonalizes the three variables, which are highly correlated across the firms. That is, we measure patents relative to R&D spending (which is expected to yield patents) and total citations relative to the number of patents that can receive citations.

[28] The many details and considerations involved in doing such a study are beyond the scope of this textbook. See MacKinlay (1997) or Chapter 4 of Campbell et al. (1997) for full information on financial market event studies.

market return R_i can be decomposed into $v_i + \varepsilon_i$, the sum of the return associated with the patent issuance and the return due to any other news uncorrelated with the patent issuance. Under some assumptions about the distribution of v and ε, they derive an expression for $E[v_i|R_i]$ that is a linear function of R_i.[29] This, in turn, allows them to extract an estimate of the private patent value ξ_i:

$$\widehat{\xi}_i = (1 - \pi)^{-1} E[v_i \mid R_i] M_i$$

M_i is the market capitalization of the firm, which is needed to convert the return v into the market response in dollars.

The above procedure yields a median patent value of 1982 US\$5.45 million, which is somewhat higher than previous estimates, but not unreasonably so. Using a patent-level value equation with citations to the patent, they find results similar to Hall et al (2005): At the median level of citations, adding one cite to each of its patents increases the firm value by about 3% without controls beyond technology and time effects. This method of determining the private value of patents seems promising and has already been used by other researchers (Arora et al. 2022). It also involves a number of assumptions that are continuing to be tested.

Beyond patents, a few researchers have also explored the impact on market value of the production and use of scientific literature. For example, Deng et al. (1999) find a positive impact from a firm's use of scientific publication on their market value. Arora et al. (2023) use the KPSS methodology to measure the value to a firm of being the first to make use of a particular public science input.

6.7 Summary

Measuring the returns to R&D and innovation has proved challenging, not least because the analogy to ordinary physical investment is imperfect. R&D generates a knowledge capital that benefits others besides those who own it, and whose productivity is more affected by the actions of competitors. In addition, some of the knowledge generated is tacit and held by the employees of the firm, which may allow them to capture some of the returns in the form of higher wages. Lack of robust secondary markets for the output of R&D investment means that measuring depreciation is very challenging and efforts to date have yielded widely varying estimates. Yet deriving the net rate of return to R&D requires such an estimate, regardless of the methodology used.

In this chapter, we considered the usual methods for measuring R&D and discussed the complications that can arise: measuring R&D depreciation, double counting of R&D inputs in the production function, proper measure of output that accounts for improved quality from innovative activity, and accounting for spillovers in estimates at the level of the firm. To the extent possible, we reported on attempts to incorporate these issues in the methodology or to assess their importance.

The final sections of this chapter discussed a widely used method of assessing the value of innovation at the firm (company) level, the market value approach. This

---

[29] They use a number of different assumptions, most of which yield similar results. See the paper for details.

method has the advantage of being forward-looking, in that it relies on the market's ability to forecast future success or failure and relate this forecast to observable innovative activity (R&D and patenting). The drawback of the method is that its applicability is restricted to publicly traded firms in thick financial markets.

There are major differences between social and private rates of return. The most important is that although private rates of return are subject to the discipline of financial markets and the cost of capital, the same is not true of social rates of return, which can take on widely varying values depending on the nature of the innovation. We will address this question more thoroughly, along with the implications for the macro economy, in Chapter 9.

7

Diffusion

Learning Objectives

After reading this chapter, you will be able to understand and explain the following concepts:

- The s-curve model of innovation diffusion
- Factors affecting the diffusion of innovation
- Diffusion of network goods
- The role of network externalities in diffusion of innovation
- Empirical estimation of diffusion processes

[I]n the history of diffusion of many innovations, one cannot help being struck by two characteristics of the diffusion process: its apparent overall slowness on the one hand, and the wide variations in the rates of acceptance of different inventions, on the other. (Rosenberg, 1976, p. 191)

7.1 Introduction

For an innovation to have an impact on economic growth and welfare, it must be adopted by enough of the relevant users. We refer to this process as diffusion, and in some ways, it is the most important step in the path from an idea to the realization of its full benefits.

In this chapter, we first present some stylized facts about the adoption of innovations during the past 100 years. Most of these display behavior that resembles an s-curve when the cumulative share of adopters is plotted versus time. This leads to the development of a couple of widely used simple models that generate such a curve and can be used to estimate the determinants of diffusion.

We then review the many factors affecting the rate and extent of diffusion, focusing on economic factors. We provide a number of examples from the introduction of hybrid corn, the spread of ATM machines, and the use of manufacturing robots.

Network technologies are a particularly difficult case for diffusion because they require coordination among adopters in many cases. Without coordination and without an organization or firm sponsoring the technology, diffusion tends to be quite slow and may end up settling on an inferior technology. We discuss some examples, beginning with the dynamo (electric generator) and continuing to modern-day computing and the

The Economics of Innovation and Intellectual Property. Bronwyn H. Hall and Christian Helmers, Oxford University Press.
© Oxford University Press 2024. DOI: 10.1093/oso/9780197630914.003.0007

Box 7.1 Diffusion and Adoption

Diffusion: the spread of an innovation throughout the economy or the relevant set of potential users.
Technology adoption: the choice to acquire and use a new invention or innovation.

---

internet. We also provide a simple model that mimics the behavior of diffusion under increasing returns from adoption that are usually characteristic of network technologies.

The final section of the chapter reviews some empirical work that tests for the various factors affecting diffusion, introducing the main econometric model for such estimation, the failure time or hazard rate model.

Before moving on, a quick note about vocabulary: *Diffusion* refers to the process of spread of an innovation throughout the economy or the relevant set of potential users. When looking from the point of view of individual choice by economic agents to use a new innovation or technology, we tend to use the term *(technology) adoption* (Box 7.1).

7.2 The s-Curve for Diffusion

The usual way to display the speed of diffusion of a particular technology in a population of potential adopters is the s-curve. This curve shows the share of the population of potential adopters that have adopted the new technology versus the time since the introduction of the technology. The typical pattern observed is an s-curve that begins by trending upward slowly, gradually becoming steeper as the technology spreads rapidly, and eventually flattening out because there are fewer and fewer potential users that have not already adopted the new technology. Often diffusion is less than complete, implying that the curve reaches its limit somewhere below 100% adoption.

Figure 7.1 shows the diffusion of some major consumer inventions in the United States during the past 100 years.

7.2.1 Models of the s-Curve

The simple s-curve model can be derived in two different ways. The first assumes that the benefits of the new technology vary across potential adopters (consumers). The second is based on an epidemic model of information spread among potential adopters.

For the first model, suppose that potential adopters will receive benefits from adoption that vary, but these benefits have a unimodal distribution (a single-peaked distribution like the normal bell curve). Assume that the costs of adoption decline monotonically over time and are the same for all potential adopters (this assumption can be relaxed). Consumers will adopt when their benefit is greater than the cost of adoption. With a unimodal benefit distribution, this yields a curve where the share of adopters is low at first, accelerates as the center of the distribution adopts, and then slows down again when there are fewer people left who have not adopted.

To make this precise, assume that the benefits B of adoption have a normal distribution, and that cost declines at a rate b over time according to $C(t) = a - bt$. At any

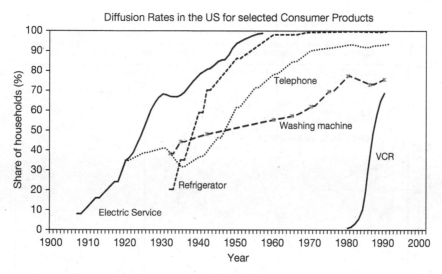

Figure 7.1 Diffusion of major inventions in the United States.

time t, the share of those that have already adopted are those with $B > a - bt$, shown in Figure 7.2 as a shaded area. This area under the curve shown by the hatched lines is clearly 1 minus the cumulative normal distribution evaluated at $B^* = a - bt$, which is often written as $1 - \Phi(a - bt)$, where $\Phi(.)$ denotes the cumulative normal distribution function. Because $a - bt$ is a monotone decreasing function of t, a simple change of variables allows us to write the share of adopters at any time t^* as $\Phi(t^*)$, where t^* is equal to $(a - B^*)/b$. Thus, normally distributed benefits and declining costs will imply an s-curve that has the shape of the cumulative normal distribution. The s-curve will also result from most unimodal distributions of benefits such as the logistic, chi-squared, or t-distributions, and will take the shape of their cumulative distribution functions. It is also not necessary that costs decline linearly, so long as they decrease monotonically over time. Costs that stop declining or increase will bring the diffusion process to a halt because all the potential adopters at same or higher costs will have already adopted.

Obviously for this to be relevant, the support of the benefit and cost distributions must overlap. If the benefit distribution lies below the minimum cost, no one will adopt. Alternatively, if the benefit distribution lies entirely above the maximum cost, everyone will adopt instantaneously. Truncated results are also possible. If there are some consumers whose benefit never exceeds even the lowest cost, full adoption will not take place and the s-curve will asymptote at a value less than 1. If the technology is introduced at a cost that is below benefits for a share of consumers, the s-curve will not start at zero, but at some higher value, assuming adoption by such consumers is nearly instantaneous.

In contrast, the epidemic model does not rely on heterogeneous consumer tastes or willingness to pay. Rather, it assumes that adoption spreads throughout the population as consumers encounter those who have already adopted and learn of the advantages of the new technology. It is initiated by a small number of consumers who adopt early and then encounter the remainder randomly. All (or a share) of those contacted adopt. Eventually, enough people have adopted so that few of those contacted randomly have not already adopted, and the process ends. This model can be modified so that the encounters are not random, which will generally slow the process.

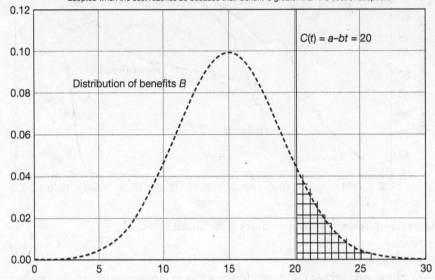

Figure 7.2

Benefits and cost of technology adoption

The dashed line in the figure is the distribution of benefits for potential adopters and the solid vertical line is the cost of adoption at a particular time t when $C(t) = 20$. The shaded area shows those who have adopted when the cost reaches 20 because their benefit is greater than the cost of adoption.

$C(t) = a–bt = 20$

Distribution of benefits B

Figure 7.2 Generating a diffusion curve with heterogeneous adopters.

Assume there are N potential users of a new technology, and at any time t, n_t users have already adopted the technology. The $N - n_t$ that have not yet been informed and have not adopted encounter the users and learn about the technology with a probability equal to a constant β times the share of users that have already adopted n_t/N. Assuming they adopt as soon as they learn about the new technology, the rate of change of adoption is given by the following equations:

$$dn_t = \beta\left(\frac{n_t}{N}\right)(N - n_t)dt$$

$$or \ \frac{dn_t}{N} = \beta\left(\frac{n_t}{N}\right)\left(\frac{N - n_t}{N}\right)dt$$

which is a differential equation with the solution[1]

$$\frac{n_t}{N} = \frac{1}{1 + \exp(-(\alpha + \beta t))}$$

The above equation has the cumulative share of adopters at time t on the left-hand side and a version of the cumulative logistic function on the right-hand side. α is a constant of integration whose value can be determined by the initial (presumably small) number of users. That is, setting t to zero, we have the following:

[1] You are not expected to solve this differential equation, but you may wish to check its validity by taking the time derivative of the solution, as an exercise. (*Hint*: You will need to substitute the solution into the derivative to obtain the expression for dn_t/N given above.)

$$\alpha = \log\left(\frac{n_0}{N - n_0}\right)$$

which will be quite small in most cases and is always negative when $n_0 < N - n_0$.

This interpretation allows us to obtain the mean and variance of t, the time of adoption, using the known characteristics of the logistic:

$$Mean(t) = -\alpha / \beta$$
$$Var(t) = \pi^2 / 3\beta^2$$

Thus, β describes the dispersion of the time of adoption, with lower β implying greater dispersion and higher variance (spread) in the time of adoption. The mean is proportional to α, scaled by the dispersion parameter β.

Figure 7.3 illustrates the logistic curve for a range of mean adoption times and their dispersion (shown as the standard deviation). Note that because the logistic is a symmetric distribution, the mean and the median coincide and the curves always cross 0.5 at the mean, when half of the potential adopters have adopted. Empirically, this may not be true generally (see Figure 7.1). In Figure 7.3, curves 1 and 2 are for a diffusion process with a standard deviation of about 11 years and two different means (10 years and 15 years); the curve with the larger mean is simply shifted to the right 5 years. The initial condition for both is very small (0.01 and 0.001), and both reach their asymptote (upper limit) by 30 years. In contrast, curve 3, with a standard deviation of 22 years, shows a case where there is significant adoption already at time zero (0.08), while curve 4, which has a much higher mean, shows incomplete adoption at 30 years past introduction.

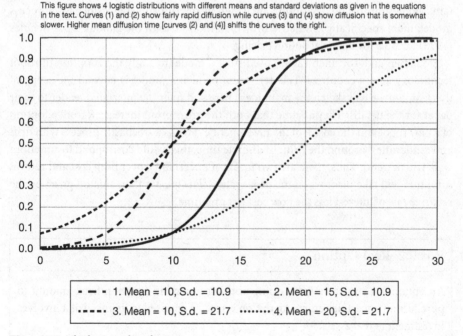

This figure shows 4 logistic distributions with different means and standard deviations as given in the equations in the text. Curves (1) and (2) show fairly rapid diffusion while curves (3) and (4) show diffusion that is somewhat slower. Higher mean diffusion time [curves (2) and (4)] shifts the curves to the right.

- - - 1. Mean = 10, S.d. = 10.9   ——— 2. Mean = 15, S.d. = 10.9
······ 3. Mean = 10, S.d. = 21.7   ········ 4. Mean = 20, S.d. = 21.7

Figure 7.3 The logistic distribution.

Both of the simple models presented above imply an s-shaped curve for diffusion and choosing between them is more of an interpretive question. They can also be combined of course, and a realistic model would doubtless have elements of both.

One variant of the logistic model that has been very successful in practical applications such as forecasting associated with marketing a new product is the Bass model (Bass 1969), which expresses the probability of adopting as a function of the number of previous adopters. See Section 7.6 for an example.

7.2.2 Adoption as Investment under Uncertainty

As suggested earlier, the decision to adopt involves some uncertainty, as the potential adopter compares an upfront cost with an uncertain stream of future benefits. Adoption is an absorbing state in the sense that once the upfront costs are incurred, they are sunk, and as a general rule, the decision cannot be reversed without additional cost. Thus, the decision is not "adopt or do not adopt" but instead "adopt now or wait to decide whether to adopt later." Given the uncertainty surrounding the costs and benefits of adoption, this characterization suggests analysis using a real options model, like the ones proposed by Dixit and Pindyck (1994) for investment under uncertainty (see Box 7.2).

A financial option is a contract that grants its owner the right to buy or sell an underlying asset at a specified strike price on or before a specified date. There is no requirement that the owner exercise this right. Real options are those where the asset is real, that is, some kind of tangible investment. In the adoption setting, there is no contract, simply the option to invest in adopting a new technology at any point in time at a price that is uncertain, and whose payoff (which depends on the cost of adoption) is uncertain. Models for this type of option are generally developed using a stochastic process model, more specifically geometric Brownian motion, as in the famous Black-Scholes (1973) formula for financial option pricing.

Stoneman and Toivanen (2006) used such a model to study the adoption of robot technology across countries. The derivation of such a model is beyond the scope of this text, but we will sketch the main ideas here and refer the interested reader to their paper for the details. They assume that both the gross profit increase R from adoption of a new robot and the cost P of the investment evolve as a stochastic process with drift and randomness around the drift. In discrete time, this would correspond to a random walk with a trend. Thus, there are two forms of uncertainty, over both cost and return. Adoption will take place when the profit rate R/P is greater than a cutoff given by the risk-free rate of interest less the flow cost per unit time.

Box 7.2 Real Option

An option is a choice between doing nothing or paying a certain fixed amount to purchase an uncertain return. An option is real, as opposed to financial, if it involves investment in real assets.

Stoneman and Toivanen show that with uncertainty in both return and cost of adoption, it is not possible to predict whether these uncertainties slow or speed up the rate of adoption, although they will certainly affect it. In the empirical work, they find that the diffusion of robots across countries and over time is negatively related to their four proxies for uncertainty in returns and cost.

7.3 Factors Affecting Diffusion

The diffusion of innovation has the same broad determinants as innovation itself: demand for the new technology or good (benefit); the cost of adopting the new technology; the level of uncertainty about both these features as well as the availability of information about them; and the market and regulatory environment in which the adoption takes place, which affect all of these.

The benefits of adoption of a specific new technology depend on the perceived improvements it offers in consumption or industrial use as well as the closeness of potential substitute technologies, either new or those in prior use. Another important determinant in many cases is the extent to which the new technology is supported by a network. For different technologies, the type of network will vary and may depend on the number of other users, the availability of complementary goods, or maintenance services. Later in the chapter, we will discuss this topic in detail, as it is probably one of the most important determinants of adoption in today's world.

The costs depend first on the price of the new technology and the cost of financing the investment necessary. In addition, some investment in complements to the new technology may be necessary, raising its cost. For example, the introduction of new technology to a workplace generally requires training of workers and possibly the hiring of workers with specific skills. Such costs are often referred to as *switching costs*. Another example is the purchase of an electric car, which may require the installation of a convenient charging station in or adjacent to one's dwelling, which can be expensive. Because technology adoption is largely a fixed cost, the decision to adopt will also be affected by the scale of the potential use of the new technology. In the case of firms, larger firms may be more willing to pay the costs of adoption.

The presence of patents covering the new technology may slow its diffusion, both because they can raise its price due to the market power patents convey and because the need to access the inventions covered by the patents may inhibit the contributions of others to its development and improvement. For example, there is considerable debate over whether Watt's steam engine patents slowed the diffusion and development of steam engines. Boldrin and Levine (2013) argue that Watt's patents and their success in enforcing and extending them delayed the Industrial Revolution by one or two decades. However, this conclusion is strongly critiqued on factual grounds by Selgin and Turner (2006), who also argue that the expectation of returns from holding a patent on his steam engine motivated Watt's efforts at its development.

As the Rosenberg quote at the beginning of this chapter suggests, diffusion is often slow, especially for major inventions. He goes on to argue that during the diffusion process, much invention in the form of tweaking and adaptation also takes place, offering as examples coal-using technology in England, steamboat technology, and petroleum refining. In all these cases, costs fell faster during the period of diffusion than during the initial period of the technology's introduction.

Rosenberg also emphasized the role of necessary complementarities in slowing the rates of adoption. For example, he cites the importance of John Wilkinson's invention of the first machine tool (a boring tool for cylinders) in 1774 for making James Watt's steam engine practicable for a much wider range of uses than just mining. Improvements in machine tools throughout the 19th century were essential in the later manufacture of bicycles and sewing machines. During the same century, growth in the productivity of railroads was greatly facilitated by inventions in block signaling, air brakes, automatic couplers, and the telegraph, increasing the benefits of adoption.

Another complementary asset that is essential if a technology is going to diffuse successfully is the knowledge and skill of the workers that use the technology. Many of the necessary skills are acquired by the use of the technology and therefore develop along with it. As workers and managers learn about the technology via use, they may also suggest and implement ways in which its performance can be improved. A simple example is your own experience with a new software app, which can easily throw up ideas for improvement as you develop skills using it. This example suggests that another factor affecting the diffusion and use of new products is the need for potential users to develop skills in their use.

In some cases, the complementary asset required for effective use of a new technology is the complete reorganization of production. Brynjolfsson and co-authors (Bresnahan et al. 2002, Brynjolfsson et al. 2021) have provided evidence that the effective use of computing and the internet in firms has required substantial investments in organizational capital to rearrange the workflows within firms, in many cases reducing the need for many middle management jobs and flattening the management structure. Similarly, David (1990) argues that the full benefits of electric motors in a factory were not realized until the factory itself was radically redesigned and the heavy bracing and multiple floors required for steam and water power eliminated.

Uncertainty and the availability of information that might reduce that uncertainty will clearly affect the decision to adopt a new technology. This uncertainty can be both about how well the technology works and also about whether the technology will be successful enough that others also adopt it. As we will discuss below, use by others is very important in the case of technologies with network effects. Because of uncertainty, there is an option to delay the decision in order to acquire more information. In addition, in many cases, the technology is continually improving, so users wait for improved versions. Both of these factors may cause a delay in adoption and also suggest the use of option theory to analyze the choice of when to adopt.

A second form of uncertainty that affects the diffusion of new technologies is the inability to anticipate the uses to which a new technology can be put. In Chapter 2, we mentioned the fact that radio technology was originally developed for narrowcasting between ships but went on to have wide applicability for broadcasting. Another example cited was that the builder of the first laser was unable to anticipate the full range of applications of his invention; in fact, he thought there were none.

The market structure of an industry will affect both the diffusion of production technology and diffusion to consumers of the goods produced. The size and market power of a firm affect its adoption of new technology in the same ways it affects innovation as described in Chapter 5. In concentrated markets, adoption may be faster due to cost spreading and easier financing, or slower because there is less fear of market share loss to entry if the firm fails to adopt new technology. A good example of how this strategy can fail is the delay in introduction of lower-cost long-distance telephony by ATT in the 1960s. MCI Communications eventually succeeded in introducing microwave relay technology in this market, ultimately leading to the breakup of the ATT telecommunications monopoly.

A firm with a large market share can facilitate consumer adoption of new technology in settings where there are competing standards and uncertainty over its performance. An example of this phenomenon is the entry of IBM into the PC business, which was more of a hobby activity prior to their entry in 1981. Bresnahan et al. (2012) argue that the corporate customers of IBM were familiar with and had confidence with the firm's technology and support, which encouraged the diffusion of the PC once IBM entered the marketplace. Figure 7.4 shows the early evolution of the PC market until 1995. With the passage of time since then, IBM became less dominant, but the Microsoft operating system that was introduced with that PC is still the dominant operating system for PCs.

The regulatory and institutional environment also influences diffusion, both positively and negatively. For example, the diffusion of LED bulbs has been greatly encouraged by regulations that restrict the use of incandescent bulbs. Electric car diffusion has been encouraged both by subsidies for their purchase and by fleet gas efficiency requirements, which are easier to satisfy if a share of the fleet is electric. Mandated pollution or safety standards can also encourage the diffusion of new technologies that satisfy them.

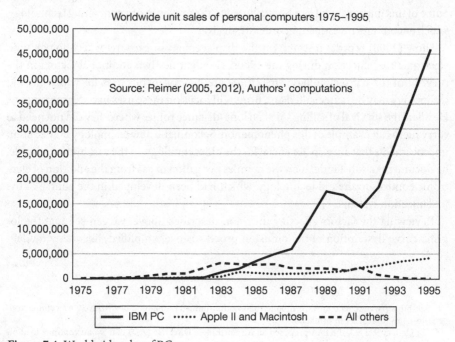

Figure 7.4 Worldwide sales of PCs.

In contrast, safety regulation of such things as new pharmaceuticals and new surgical procedures can delay their adoption. In the case of technologies that require standard setting, regulatory delay in setting standards will delay diffusion. For an example, see the allocation or reallocation of spectrum for communication use. At one time, this was done in the United States and elsewhere by choosing among comparative proposals presented to a hearing, but recently an auction methodology has been used. When the US Federal Communications Commission (FCC) proposed to release the 3.7 to 4.2 GHz band in the spectrum for 5G cellular use near airports in early 2022, the Federal Aviation Commission (FAA) and the airlines complained that this would interfere with landing technology on planes that is used in bad weather.[2] This has led to a battle of regulatory agencies that was resolved in January 2023, but it did slow the diffusion of 5G near airports temporarily.[3]

A classic example of slow diffusion due to the institutional environment is the case of the Dutch flute, which was a speedy sailing vessel invented in the 1600s, highly suited to shipping due to enhanced cargo space. Unfortunately, the speed was achieved by not providing the weight and space to allow it to be converted to a warship, which required space for very heavy cannons and ammunition. North (1968) points out that although this type of ship quickly took over the English coal trade and Baltic routes, it took a century for it to be used on the Atlantic routes and elsewhere because of the dangers of piracy and privateering there and the lack of armaments on the ship.

A final factor slowing the adoption of new technologies is the competition from old technologies, which may be improving at the same time the new technology is being improved and enhanced. A classic example is the survival of wooden sailing ships in the second half of the 19th century after the introduction of iron hull steamships, thanks to many improvements in their design and the addition of labor-saving machinery. Some of this improvement can be attributed to the existence of a competing technology, which encourages investment in order to survive.

Snow (2008) reports research on the displacement of carburetor technology with electronic fuel injection during the 1980s. He identifies two additional factors in the survival of the old technology. First, there are heterogeneous uses for which the old technology may be better suited and firms will focus on these uses in order to compete. He offers the survival of sailing ships on long-distance routes where they did not need to carry fuel as an example of this phenomenon. Second, the new technology may contain improvements that are also beneficial for the old technology. In the carburetor example, he documents a substantial increase in miles per gallon of gas from the addition of electronic controls to the old technology, which had been developed in the course of the fuel injection systems.

Reviewing the factors affecting diffusion described above, we can see that the logistic curve description of the diffusion process is oversimplified, like many models.

---

[2] See https://www.cnet.com/tech/mobile/the-aviation-industrys-ongoing-beef-with-5g-everything-you-need-to-know for further information.

[3] On January 9, 2023, the FAA proposed an Airworthiness Directive (AD) that would continue to allow aviation and 5G C-Band to safely coexist. See https://www.faa.gov/5g.

Innovations rarely have a simple distribution of benefits and costs that are the same for all potential adopters, nor is the process of learning about a new innovation and its benefits completely random as assumed by the epidemic model. Nevertheless, the logistic curve is a useful starting point, and we illustrate its use in a setting with heterogenous users in Section 7.6.

7.3.1 Issues with the Diffusion of Some New Technologies

At the present time, two sets of technologies have the potential for substantial impact if they can be fully and safely diffused: (1) various types of clean technologies such as electric vehicles, and (2) AI applications.

For clean technologies, the primary difficulty is one we have met before and will discuss in the next section. Many of the most important of these technologies, especially those relating to reducing carbon consumption, require considerable investment in infrastructure and realignment of the end-user delivery. This implies that coordination is necessary and that there will be stranded assets that must be written off at a cost to someone (often the utility customers). In addition, clean technology development and diffusion face a double externality problem in that there are the usual positive externalities from R&D in this area as well as positive externalities from their diffusion in the form of less pollution and global warming. This suggests an even greater role for government policy toward increasing adoption.

Despite its obvious benefits (consider the improvements in machine translation), AI faces greater headwinds for reasons articulated by Agrawal et al. (2019). The first is consumer concern about privacy. The machine learning that lies behind AI requires a large amount of data to be effective and accurate, and this inevitably means that even anonymized data on an individual could conceivably be linked to an identifier. Privacy concerns have already been shown to delay and discourage an important innovation, the digitization and portability of medical records.

A second major unsolved problem in the diffusion of AI technologies is the issue of who is liable when things go wrong. This issue has become particularly salient in the case of autonomous driving. With no driver, is the auto manufacturer liable in the case of accidents? Or is it the software programmer? Or the provider of telecommunications to the auto? Worries of this kind may make some reluctant to develop technologies, but also may lead to greater regulation that discourages diffusion.

7.4 Network Goods and Standards

An important class of technologies whose characteristics affect diffusion are those termed network goods. These are systems of technology whose value to one user depends somewhat on use by others. To some extent, this is true of almost all technologies, but for network goods it is particularly salient in the adoption decision. Network goods are those that usually require standards and coordination to make them useful. In Chapter 21, we will study standards in more detail along with their interaction with the patent system and the strategic use of patents in this area.

There are two general classes of such goods:

- *Direct networks.* In communications networks such as the telephone, fax, email, messaging systems, the value to a user depends on with whom they can communicate.
- *Indirect networks,* In virtual networks created by "hardware/software" systems, the value depends on the number of other users because the existence of more users means more software available due to economies of scale in providing such software.

In the case of direct networks, the network externality is immediate and obvious. When a user joins, they compare the value of the network to themself with the cost of joining, but do not take into account the benefit to others of having one additional member of the network. These networks are also those where the identities of the members matter a great deal to potential users because users have strong preferences over the people and firms with which they want to communicate.

Indirect networks differ in that the adoption decision is usually the choice to purchase a particular type of hardware and then a series of decisions to purchase compatible software. This fact implies that more complex strategies are available to sponsoring firms and also that compatibility across hardware types becomes a factor. The fact that purchase decisions are made over time means that network effects arise from the adoption decision by one purchaser through its impact on future prices or variety of software.

Table 7.1 contains a number of examples of network goods, not all of which are technologies per se. These networks may rely on some form of physical connection

Table 7.1 Hardware/Software/Wetware Networks

Hardware standard or network	Hardware/software (or "wetware")
Video/audio player	Video or audio tape, CD, DVD format
Voice-activated home controller	Heating, locks, windows controlled
Computer	Operating system, applications software
Durable equipment including autos	Repairs and parts
Mobile telephone	3G, 5G, LTE, etc., standards
Language	Ability to speak it
Typewriter	Experience on the keyboard layout
ATM network	ATM card and bank account
POS terminal/merchant acceptance	Credit or debit cards accepted; method
Money (e.g., dollar, bitcoin, euro, etc.)	Places accepting this form of payment
Railroad gauge	Railroad rolling stock
Electrical network (AC vs. DC)	Electrical equipment
Color television standard (RCA vs. CBS)	Broadcast equipment and televisions

Source: Authors' compilation.

(think electric plugs in the United States vs. Europe), or on compatibility of software with the equipment it runs. They may also depend on "wetware," that is, the experience and training of a human with a technology, such as a language. It is apparent that many if not most of these technologies rely on interface standards for the ability to communicate with others. For example, every new peripheral you wish to attach to a computer comes with one or more drivers that need compatibility in two dimensions: to interface with the operating system and to operate the peripheral, leading to a need for software standards. In the next section, we discuss standards for network goods more thoroughly, as they are central to the understanding of diffusion.

Although competing networks and standards have become more important in the digital age, there are a number of historical examples shown in Table 7.1, which illustrate that network standards competition has been with us for a long time. For example, early railroads typically had a number of competing gauges (track widths). Because the railroad cars had to be designed with tires a certain width apart, it was difficult to move them between gauges. By 1860, there were seven different gauges in use in the United States (Shapiro and Varian 1999a, b). The two most popular were concentrated: one in the North and one in the South; the standard of the North eventually prevailed, partly because of their Civil War victory and partly because of westward expansion of the railroads from the Northeast, for which the Northern gauge was more suitable.

7.4.1 General-Purpose Technologies and Standards

Many scholars of diffusion have emphasized the fact that the diffusion of GPTs can be slowed by the need for complementary investments by users, some of which may be quite costly and disruptive. Many of these potential adopters will also delay their investment until the standards necessary for use of the technology emerge or until it becomes evident which of the competing standards will be dominant.

David (1990) reported on the historical case of the electric dynamo as a component of a GPT, comparing it to computer and computer network diffusion during the 1980s. An electric dynamo is what is now called an electric generator; it converts some form of energy (usually mechanical) into electrical, often using magnetism as in Faraday's original invention. The argument is that use of the electricity this generated required investment in complementary assets. In the case of electrified factory power, these investments included reorganizing the entire layout of a factory, as well as raising the skills of the workers in order to take full advantage of the innovation.

Table 7.2 gives the timeline for the diffusion of electricity in the United States. Use of electricity in homes needed even further investments, both in the construction of a network to deliver the electricity as well as education of the consumer, given the apparent new danger of electrocution when misused.

In the first few decades after the invention of the dynamo, the primary use was stand-alone in factories; diffusion of central power stations and networks did not take off until the electric light invention. A similar phenomenon occurred with computers

Table 7.2 Timeline for the Diffusion of Electricity in the United States

Year	Event
1832	Electric dynamo invented by Michael Faraday (UK) and Joseph Henry (US) independently
1879	Electric lamp invented by Thomas Edison and Joseph Swan
1892	First alternating current generator (US)
1899	Electric light in 3% of US homes and 5% of factories
1902	Five-megawatt turbine installed at Fisk St. Station, Chicago
1920	Electricity use diffused only to 50% level in over 20 years
1922	Connecticut Valley Power Exchange (CONVEX) starts up, pioneering interconnection between utilities

that were initially the province of large firms, government, and research institutions, and were networked locally if at all. The trends in development of the technologies can be seen in Figure 7.5, which shows the evolution of US patenting in electrical and computing/communication technologies, on a log scale because of the rapid growth in both. The growth in computing and communication technologies tracks that of electricity with about a 30-year lag until changes in the US patent system in the early to mid-1980s, at which point the growth rate in these technologies increases and overtakes electricity.[4]

David argues that there are similarities between the slow diffusion of electricity and networked computing. Both the dynamo and the computer are nodal elements of a distribution/transmission network for which compatibility standards are required. This fact creates a web of complementary technical relationships and an extended trajectory of improvements to the technology during its diffusion. In addition, such diffusion is slowed by lack of skills and by the difficulty of appropriating returns to investments in improvements of the necessary capital goods. The latter appears to be less of a problem for computing, and the patent statistics support this, given their recent growth.

7.4.2 Slow Diffusion and Productivity Slowdown

One of the consequences of the slow diffusion of new GPTs that essentially create new techno-economic paradigms (in the words of Dosi 1982 and Perez 1983) is a corresponding slow rate of productivity growth as firms and individuals adjust and reorganize for the new ways of doing things. The diffusion of major new systems leads to a number of changes, some of which are not always reflected in conventional productivity statistics.

---

[4] Later in Chapters 11 and 18, we will discuss the nature of these changes, which were both due to legal changes and shifts in firm IP strategy in the sector.

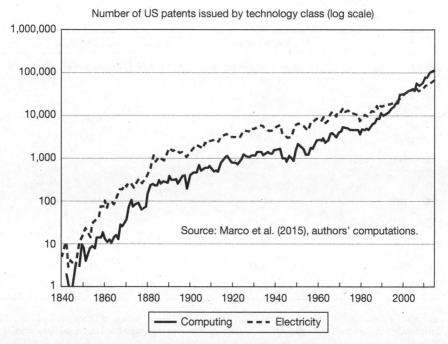

Figure 7.5 Trends in electrical and computing patenting, 1840–2014.

For example, both electricity and computing have expanded the number of goods and services available to the consumer and improved their quality. Think of lighting and transportation alternatives made available by electricity, or the expansion of communication and remote working from the PC and the internet. Neither expansion of available goods and services nor their quality are completely captured by productivity measures, as we suggested in Chapter 6.

Nevertheless, there are good reasons to think that some of the observed slow productivity growth during the transition to a new techno-economic paradigm is real. These shifts lead to productivity improvements only slowly as networks are built and factories are restructured to take advantage of the new technology. As discussed earlier, work by Brynjolfsson and others suggests that in the case of computer technology, a new organizational structure within the firm was also necessary to achieve the productivity benefits of networked computer technology.

Table 7.3 shows measured productivity growth for a number of decades in the 20th and beginning of the 21st century. Sluggish productivity growth in both the United States and the United Kingdom is visible during the first two decades of the 20th century when electric lighting and transportation improvements were diffusing. As we saw in Figure 7.1, electricity and the automobile had diffused to over 50% of the population in the United States by 1925. Similarly, low productivity growth in the United States during the PC–internet transition is visible during the 1973–2000 periods, although less so in the United Kingdom. By 1995, the computer had diffused to 40% of US households and, by 2004, internet use per capita in the United States was 45% and growing (Andrés et al. 2007).

Table 7.3 Productivity Growth in the United States and United Kingdom

Period	United States TFP (percent per annum)	United Kingdom TFP (percent per annum)
1899–1909	0.93	−0.10
1909–1919	0.64	1.15
1919–1929	1.63	1.28
1929–1941	1.86	1.96
1948–1960	1.98	2.33
1960–1973	2.21	2.49
1973–1989	0.48	1.23
1989–2000	0.97	1.02
2000–2007	1.44	1.17

Sources of US data: Bakker et al. 2019, Table 3, and BLS (2014); National Bureau of Economic Research; US Business Cycle Expansions and Contractions. See http://www.nber.org/cycles.html (accessed November 28, 2015).

Source of UK data: Authors' computations from Bank of England data. See https://www.bankofengland.co.uk/statistics/research-datasets.

7.5 Network Externalities and Diffusion

The rise of the internet and the increased importance of goods and services delivered digitally mean that networks, network platforms, and network standards have become very important to our understanding the diffusion of new technologies. The basic idea here is that the choice to adopt a new network technology depends on the potential adopter's view of the likelihood of its success. This fact feeds back to the strategic behavior of the producer of the new technology, generating a complex intertemporal game in which competing producers have strong incentives to price low initially in order to build their market share. We are all familiar with this phenomenon, which generates extended loss-making periods in technology startups.

The essential fact that one person's preference for a particular network depends on the presence and identities of the other users creates network externalities, and leads to increasing returns for the adopters of a network. In the discussion that follows, we first review the implications for welfare of network competition and then present a simple model that can illuminate the potential outcomes of such competition.

7.5.1 Welfare with Network Competition

In many cases, where there are competing technologies with network characteristics, an early adopter may find themselves stranded if their choice turns out to be the loser in a systems competition. This fact, in turn, may lead to delayed adoption and slow diffusion. Alternatively, from a consumer welfare perspective, diffusion of a new technology might be too rapid in some cases.

Adoption rates for Pareto-improving standards (technologies) can be too slow (excess inertia) for these reasons:

- One technology has a large installed base, and early adopters of the other bear too large a share of the switching costs.
- A new technology is unattractive with few users.
- A new technology's advantage is positive but relatively small.

Alternatively, adoption rates might be too fast (excess momentum) for these reasons:

- If users are heterogeneous, the first adopters are those who like the new technology and ignore their negative effects on the users of the old technology.
- The network advantage is not that large, so both technologies survive.
- The older technology has a small installed base, so switching costs are low.

If there is network competition, it is not always assured that the better technology wins. Small historical accidents at the outset can tip adopters to choose a standard that later users perceive as non-optimal. One widely cited historical example is the QWERTY keyboard, which is probably a non-optimal layout, but did help early typewriters avoid jamming (David 1985). Other well-known examples are VHS versus Betamax and HD-DVD versus Blu-ray. Some would argue that in the first case, the technically superior technology was not the dominant technology (VHS), but of course, all these technologies lost eventually to video streaming.

Japan invested heavily in analog HDTV during the 1980s but by 1994 was forced to admit that the US digital standard was much better and abandoned their analog strategy. A well-known historical standards war was that between Thomas Edison, who favored DC (direct current) current for electricity delivery, and George Westinghouse, who promoted AC (alternating current) and was eventually joined by Nikola Tesla in this promotion. Although DC was suitable for running machines and had an initial head start, it was poor at transmission over distances, requiring power plants every mile or so, and ultimately AC technology won out.[5]

In spite of these examples, the view that network competition can lead to non-optimal outcomes has been heavily critiqued by Liebowitz and Margolis (1995). Their arguments are first that the technical differences in these examples were not all that clear-cut, either at the outset of the process or as the technology evolved. Second, even where such differences exist, they can be internalized via ownership or sponsorship of the technology, which, of course, implies some monopoly behavior.

Third, if the standard is obviously inferior, users can coordinate to switch even after it is established. Nevertheless, in some cases the required benefit from switching will have to be very large to overcome both the switching and the coordination costs. For an example of high switching and coordination costs, consider the cost of switching from

---

[5] King (2011). This story has been dramatized fairly accurately in a 2017 Hollywood movie entitled *The Current War*.

Box 7.3 Sweden's Switch to Right-Hand-Side Driving

On September, 3, 1967, Sweden switched the entire country from left-hand-side driving to right-hand-side driving (a switch called *Högertrafikomläggningen*). We can get some idea of the benefits and cost of such a switch from their experience. It was a massive undertaking involving thousands of volunteers, police, soldiers, and school police, as well as the changing of 350,000 street signs during the night before the change. But the change went fairly smoothly, thanks to careful planning. The full cost (direct and indirect) was estimated at 1 billion Swedish kroner, about 1 billion US dollars in today's prices. Unlike the two island countries that still drive on the left, Sweden borders two countries that drive on the right (Norway and Finland), and most of the cars in Sweden at the time were already manufactured for left-hand driving. Thus, the benefits in terms of reduced accidents were presumably quite large, although they have not been estimated.

The *Guardian* newspaper reprinted their 1967 article describing the switch in 2022: https://www.theguardian.com/world/2022/sep/07/dagen-h-sweden-switc hes-to-driving-on-the-right-1967.

---

driving on the left to driving on the right in the United Kingdom or Japan. The benefit might be that the risk of accidents for drivers who drive in the two different (left- and right-side) systems would be lower, and potentially lower prices of automobiles, because the steering mechanisms could now be on the most common (left-hand) side. But clearly, the coordination costs would be quite high (see Box 7.3).

7.5.2 Modeling Competing Networks

Arthur (1989) and David (1985) were among the first to point out that the presence of network externalities implies an adoption process that may result in a non-optimal choice of the network standard that prevails. Here, we follow Arthur in presenting a simple stylized model of the adoption process and its possible outcomes. Assume two technologies (*A* and *B*) and two groups of potential adopters (indexed by *R* and *S*), where the *R*-agents prefer *A* and the *S*-agents prefer *B*. In addition, these agents care about the number of prior adopters of a technology when they make their choice. Choices are made in sequence, one at a time. This leads to the payoff matrix in Table 7.4. The preference assumptions mean that $a_R > b_R$ and $a_S < b_S$. By allowing r and s to be positive, zero, or negative, Arthur allows for increasing, constant, or diminishing returns to adoption.

Table 7.4 Payoff Matrix for Network Competition

	Technology A	Technology B
R-agent	$a_R + rn_A$	$b_R + rn_B$
S-agent	$a_S + sn_A$	$b_S + sn_B$

To analyze this setup, assume that R- and S-agents arrive in a random sequence with a probability that the next agent will be an R equal to 50% (i.e., a sequence like that for a heads or tails coin toss). For example, when an R-agent is the next to choose a technology, they choose A if $a_R - b_R + r(n_A - n_B) > 0$. The first term is positive by assumption, so the decision turns on whether the number of A-adopters is greater than or, if less than that number, close enough to the number of B-adopters. A similar argument applies for the S-agent. Note that if $r = s = 0$ (constant returns), R will always choose the A technology and S will always choose B. Given a choice order probability of 0.5, this implies that in the long run, both A and B technologies survive with 50% market share each.

We are interested in the increasing returns case where both r and s are positive. Define $n = n_A + n_B$ to be the number of choices already made and $d_n = n_A - n_B$ to be the difference between A and B choice given n. A newly arrived R-agent will choose B even though they prefer A under the following condition:

$$d_n < \frac{b_R - a_R}{r} < 0$$

Similarly, if the new arrival is an S-agent, they will choose A over B if the numbers already adopting B are large enough:

$$d_n > \frac{b_S - a_S}{s} > 0$$

Arthur shows that with this setup and increasing returns to adoption (i.e., heterogeneous adopters prefer to join the network with a greater number of users once it has a large enough lead), eventually a tipping point will be reached after which everyone will choose one of the two technology alternatives. It is not possible, in general, to predict which technology will prevail and the outcome will depend on the arrival rates of agents with different preferences. Figure 7.6 plots d_n versus n, showing a typical adoption path under this model, one that leads to lock-in (see Box 7.4) on technology B.

There are three regions divided horizontally: In the top region, all adopters choose A; in the middle region, either choice can happen depending on agent type; and in the bottom region, all adopters choose B. Once the path crosses one of the two boundaries, lock-in happens because the advantage of the preferred technology is not enough to

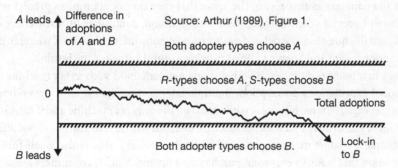

Figure 7.6 Increasing returns adoption.

Box 7.4 Path Dependence and Lock-In

Path dependence: the dependence of economic outcomes on the path of previous outcomes, rather than simply on current conditions, leading to situations where "history matters"

Lock-in: a form of economic path dependence whereby the market selects a technological standard and because of network effects the market gets stuck with that standard even though market participants may have been better off with an alternative

---

overcome the advantage of the large installed base. The bounds are given by expressions involving the technology advantage and the value placed on the network size:

$$\text{upper bound(A preferred): } (b_S - a_S)/s$$
$$\text{lower bound (B preferred): } (b_R - a_R)/r$$

Clearly, the first is positive and the second is negative. The higher the value placed on network size by the potential adopters, the tighter are the bounds and the sooner tipping into lock-in will happen.

This model can be made more realistic by changing the assumptions about arrival times, increasing the heterogeneity of adopters, giving one technology a greater advantage than the other, and so forth, but the essential conclusion that increasing returns in technology adoption can lead to lock-in on a technology over time remains. Note that nothing says that the winner will be the better technology. However, if A is enough better, for example, both the upper bound and the lower bound will be lower, increasing the likelihood that A wins. This situation might be a good characterization of the AC/DC competition, where AC ultimately won in spite of a late start.

7.5.3 Systems Competition

Although useful for understanding the impact of dynamic increasing returns on technology adoption, Arthur's approach to modeling network competition assumes away the behavior of firms that compete in offering their systems to consumers, ignoring the potential for strategic pricing behavior to induce consumers to adopt a system. It also treats the adopters as myopic, in the sense that they do not attempt to predict which system will prevail when making their own decision. A number of researchers have addressed the questions associated with firm and consumer behavior if we relax these assumptions. Katz and Shapiro (1994) provide a useful survey of the results.

They first point out that even with a single network good such as fax machines and a rational expectations assumption, multiple adoption equilibria exist depending on consumer expectations. No one is willing to own the only fax machine and if consumers assume they all behave that way, fax machine demand will be zero and it will not diffuse. If consumers assume that everyone will be on the network, that is also a self-fulfilling expectation that leads to everyone purchasing a fax machine. If consumers are able to coordinate, for example, by being part of a large multinational adopting all at once in their offices, the adoption process might be kicked off in that way.

Box 7.5 Two-Sided Platform

A **two-sided platform** is a marketplace (usually implemented on the internet) that brings together buyers and sellers to create and exchange value. Examples are services like Airbnb, eBay, and Uber. They are sometimes referred to as peer-to-peer (P2P) markets. Other possible terms are business-to-business (B2B) or business-to-consumer (B2C).

An important business model innovation that has arisen with the spread of the internet and that clearly exhibits network effects is the two-sided platform (see Box 7.5). Such platforms are typically websites that bring together the sellers and buyers of a particular type of good. Of course, these markets have predecessors in the form of auctions and any market that functions with intermediaries. Spulber (2019a) has emphasized the fact that platforms are simply markets where the transactions are more visible and can therefore be used to study the operation of markets more broadly.

The internet has facilitated the creation of these platform markets and made transactions between participants who have no knowledge of each other easier and safer, as well as lowering the cost of obtaining information on availability. Such platforms provide payment protection to both sides as well as information about the quality of the participant, based on ratings and prior customer experience with delivery, and so on. They may also set pricing rules (as in the case of providers of generic goods like Uber or Lyft) or allow the seller to do so (as in the case of heterogeneous goods like those rented by Airbnb or jobs provided by TaskRabbit).

Given the fixed cost for a supplier working with a particular platform or the desire of the consumer to have a wide choice of products/possibilities, platforms exhibit network externalities in both directions. Their diffusion is therefore affected in two dimensions: They need to attract participants on both sides of the market. Both sides will exhibit increasing returns to adoption.

When there are multiple competing networks or multisided platforms, a range of strategies over pricing and compatibility are available, and their choice will depend on the precise market structure and regulatory environment. We defer discussion of the strategic interaction of firms offering networks or platforms to Chapter 8.

7.6 Empirical Estimation

A substantial amount of empirical research has been conducted that explores the factors affecting the diffusion of new technology. We summarize some of these papers in Table 7.5. They cover a range of technologies all the way from mechanical reapers to on-board IT technology for trucking and mobile telephones to fantasy sports participation. Some are producer technologies (such as machine tools) and some consumer technologies (ATMs). Many of the factors identified in the previous section are confirmed, such as scale and market concentration, financing, network size, and learning by consumers. An interesting result is that the size of the local network matters for the diffusion of fantasy sports use.

Table 7.5 Some Empirical Research on Factors Affecting Diffusion

Date	Author(s)	Technology	Observations	Factors
1957	Griliches	Hybrid corn	Midwest farms	Profitability; need to specialize product
1961	Mansfield	12 manufacturing innovations	US firms	Profitability; cost
1968	Mansfield	Diesel locomotives	US railways	Liquidity (financial factors)
1975	David	Mechanical reaper	US, UK farms	Minimum efficient scale
1984	Hannan and MacDowell	ATMs	US banks	Reputation; concentration; firm size; holding co. structure (risk)
1995	Saloner and Shepard	ATMs	US banks	Network size; customer deposits (size)
1995	Helper	CNC machine tools	US auto component firms	Production worker wage; tech complexity; size; stable customer relationship
1997	Kennickell and Kwast	Electronic banking	US consumers	Education; assets; learning
1998	Majumdar and Vankataraman	Electronic switching	US telecoms	Network and scale effects (weaker over time)
1998	Gray and Shadbegian	New paper technology	US paper plants	Environmental regulation
1998	Hubbard	On-board IT	US trucking	On-time benefits; stable customer relationship; monitoring
2000	Stoneman and Toivanen	Robot technology	Firms, cross-country	Real options; volatility in uncertain investments
2001	Caselli and Coleman	Computers	OECD countries	Education level of workers; openness; overall investment rate
2001	Gruber and Verhoven	Mobile telephones	European consumers	Concentration of providers; technology improvements
2011	Suri	Hybrid corn	Kenya households	Profitability; infrastructure; adoption costs
2018	Van der Kam et al.	Solar photovoltaic; electric vehicles	Dutch households	PV: education; HH and building size; low density. EV: No. of vehicles; charging stations; income
2022	Kim, Newberry, Wagman, and Wolff	Fantasy sports	US counties	Number of users in country: local network effects

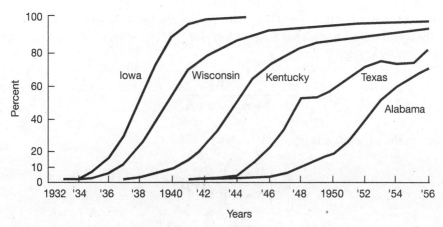

Figure 7.7 Percentage of total corn acreage planted with hybrid seed.

The pioneering work in this area was done by Griliches (1957), studying the diffusion of hybrid corn technology in the US Midwest during the 1930s to the early 1950s. Hybrid corn was an improved way of breeding corn for characteristics such as drought and insect tolerance, a shorter growing season, and greater yields. Figure 7.7, taken from his paper, shows the diffusion curves for hybrid corn in several US states. The puzzle was to explain why these curves started at different times and also indicate adoption at different rates. Using pre-computer methods, he explained the different rates of takeoff using several explanatory variables.

Griliches argued that the hybrid corn invention was a "method of inventing" and that each new hybrid had to be specialized to the region where it was to be used. Therefore, the problem was to explain the incentives to invent for a particular region and then the adoption of the new hybrid in that region. He chose to use the logistic curve we described in Section 7.1.1 to model diffusion as this was the easiest to work with in a pre-computer age.[6] Using more detailed data than states (132 crop-reporting districts), he estimated the origin date, slope (speed of adoption), and ceiling for each one. He then explained the variation in these across districts by supply factors (the origin date), factors affecting acceptance by farmers (the slope), and aggregate demand factors (the ceiling). The supply factors were measured by potential market size and proxies for invention and marketing cost, while the acceptance rate was measured by the expected profitability of a switch to hybrid corn. The measured ceiling also responded to profitability but to the pre-hybrid yield and average corn acres per farm in addition. The argument was that in marginal corn areas where corn was mainly grown for the farm's own use adoption of the new technology would never take place, as it would not be profitable.

With the exception of Mansfield (1961), the earliest papers in Table 7.5 used quantitative methods but stopped short of actual multivariate regressions. Mansfield used a property of the logistic function described above to derive a linear equation for the

---

[6] Computers did exist but were largely used by large firms and government institutions, rarely by researchers in economics.

share of adopters as a function of time, which he could estimate using manual methods. If the equation for adoption has a logistic form for n_t/N (the share of firms at time t that have already adopted):

$$\frac{n_t}{N} = \frac{1}{1+\exp(-(\alpha+\beta t))}$$

one can show the following:

$$\log\left[\frac{n_t}{N-n_t}\right] = \alpha+\beta t$$

That is, the log ratio of adopters to those who have not yet adopted is a linear function of the time trend t. Adding a disturbance to allow for estimation error, Mansfield implemented this equation across 12 different technologies, allowing the α and β coefficients to differ across technologies. He then related β, the speed of diffusion, to expected profitability and the cost of investment, finding a fairly good fit to the data and the expected signs.

If one has individual adoption data and access to a computer, unlike these pioneering researchers, the natural model for estimating the determinants of adoption is a failure time or hazard rate model. This model describes the probability at a point in time that an agent will adopt the new technology, given that they have not yet adopted it.[7] A typical example is the following, where f is a density function of t and F is the corresponding cumulative function:

$$h(t) = \frac{f(t)}{(1-F(t))} = \frac{\text{\# adopt at t}}{\text{\# not yet adopted}} = \text{hazard rate}$$

The most widely used version of the model is the Weibull, which allows for an increasing ($\alpha > 1$), constant ($\alpha = 1$), or decreasing ($\alpha < 1$) hazard rate:

$$F(t) = 1 - \exp(-\gamma t^\alpha)$$
$$h(t) = \gamma \alpha t^{\alpha-1}$$

A typical estimation approach is to parametrize γ as a regression function of the determinants of adoption or diffusion.

Hannan and McDowell (1984) were probably the first to use a version of the hazard rate model to estimate the adoption of ATM networks by banks. They found that the usual variables such as size and potential customer demand were predictive of adoption.

An interesting line of research in this area is that which tests for the presence of network externalities via their impact on diffusion. We summarize some of the empirical work in Table 7.6. Three strands of literature can be observed. One tests for network

---

[7] For a full treatment of hazard rate models, see Lancaster (1990).

Table 7.6 Empirical Papers That Test for Network Externalities

Authors	Primary Question	Industry/ Technology	Methodology	Unit of Observation	Dependent Variable.	Independent Variables	Conclusions
Greenstein 1993	Does being an incumbent confer an advantage in hardware sales?	Mainframe computers	Logit model	Buyer (government agency)	Choice of computer vendor	Buyer characteristics; previous choice	Yes, for IBM 360 series, but not for other IBM computers
Gandal 1994	Do proxies for network externalities enter price equation?	PC software/ spreadsheets	Hedonic regression	Product	Price	Characteristics of product	Lotus compatibility: 66% increase in price
Gandal 1995	Do users value file compatibility across platforms?	Spreadsheets/ database managers	Hedonic regression	Product	Price	Characteristics of product	Yes, but only Lotus file standard, for both spreadsheet and database
Salomer and Shepard 1995	Do consumers value network size?	ATM networks	Hazard rate estimation	Bank over time	Time until adoption	No. of branches; value of deposits	Increasing hazard due to fall in costs, value higher with more branches
Brynjolfsson and Kemerer 1994	Do consumers value installed base and compatibility?	Spreadsheets	Hedonic regression	Product	List price; market price	Product characteristics; market share; time	Yes, price elasticity to installed base is 1; Lotus compatibility = 46% higher price
Park 1997	What is the relative effect of installed base and expected future sales?	Video recorders (VHS/Beta)	Structural model: hedonic/logit	Product year	List price; market share	Product characteristics; time	Both matter, and installed base matters more over time
Economides and Himmelberg 1995	What is consumer valuation of installed base?	Fax machines	Theory and calibration	Aggregate US time series	Nonlinear function of price	Price; lagged network size	Expected future rate of price decline: when slow, demand falls
Gandal, Kende, and Rob 2000	Interdependence between demand for hardware and supply of software?	CD players and CDs	Structural model estimated by IV	Quarterly series of CD player sales and CD title variety	Player's sales; no. of titles	Installed base; price; variety; entry cost	Cross elasticity of CD demand (p) and CD title variety significant determinant of diffusion
Stavins 2003	Are there network externalities in electronic check services (ECS)?	Banking/ ECS	Logit for adoption; least squares and IV for use	Quarterly: bank level series	Adoption (0/ 1); volume of use	Local concentration; market share; size	Little evidence of network externalities affecting bank adoption of ECS

effects in diffusion, as exemplified in the two papers by Gandal and the Saloner and Shepard (1995) paper that we discuss below. Another tests for the existence of switching costs, which should lower consumers' willingness to pay for new noncompatible technology. Greenstein (1993), and Brynjolfsson and Kemerer (1994) confirm their existence for mainframe computers and PC software. A third set of papers develops and estimates a full structural model of supply and demand in the presence of network effects (Park 1997, Gandal et al. 2000).

One example of testing for network effects in the adoption choice is the Saloner and Shepard (1995) paper, which studied the diffusion of ATM networks, assuming that banks internalize the tastes of consumers for larger networks when making a decision to adopt.[8] They model the consumer benefits as increasing both in the number of ATMs in a network N and in the number of depositors at the bank n. The costs of installing a network are modeled as a linear function of the number of ATMs to be installed and declines over time. They show that a bank will adopt an ATM network of size N when the following condition holds:

$$\lambda n[a+b(N)]g^t > C(N,t) - \delta C(N,t+1)$$

g represents the growth in benefits to each consumer over time (assumed to be positive), and $a + b(N)$ are the benefits per consumer in the initial period. This condition specifies that the per period benefit and hence profit increase at time t should be greater than the cost of adopting now less the discounted cost of waiting one period.

With this equation, they show that there is a problem identifying the consumer network effect because network size increases both the benefit to consumers and the cost to the firm. Because these effects will have opposite signs on the time to adopt, they are able to bound the estimate of the network effect. They show that the test for network effects holding n constant will understate the effect and the test holding n/N constant will overstate the effect. The empirical results support the idea that firms adopt earlier when they have many branches and therefore the possibility of a larger network of ATMs. The estimated bounds on the network effect are an increase in the hazard between 6% and 11%, with a cumulative 9-year increase of between 0.9 and 1.7 percentage points on the probability of introducing a network if its expected size is one node larger.

Given the importance of clean technology diffusion in the presence of climate change, van der Kam et al. (2018) analyze the diffusion of photovoltaic rooftop cells and electric vehicles across regions of the Netherlands with different household configurations, education and income levels, Green voter shares, and availability of charging stations. Electric vehicles are expected to contribute to energy storage from solar cells while also drawing on them so there is interest in the geographic distribution of these technologies because it affects the grid necessary to use them efficiently.

Van der Kam et al. use the Bass (1969) model of diffusion to forecast future adoption of these technologies; this widely used model has the following form of the hazard rate:

$$h(t) = p + qF(t)$$

[8] The data used in this paper come from a period when there was very little use of networking ATMs between different banks, so the network size was determined by the bank's choice.

where p is a measure of "innovators" and q a measure of "imitators." When $p = 0$, the model reduces to the logistic curve we described above. The idea of the model is that some agents spontaneously adopt a new technology (innovators), while others adopt when those around them adopt (imitators). The paper concludes that the determinants of adoption of these two technologies are quite different, suggesting that a nationwide grid is necessary for their efficient use together.

The estimation approaches we have discussed here generally do not take into account the uncertainty in future benefits and costs from adoption, something that may loom large in the eyes of those making the decision. As we discussed earlier, this suggests the use of real options models of investment to analyze the diffusion process, as used by the Stoneman and Toivanen (2006) paper discussed earlier.

7.7 Summary

Diffusion is the way the benefits of new technology reach society. Nevertheless, it can often be quite slow due to a number of factors: (1) uncertainty over the benefits and costs; (2) the need for complementary investments by the adopter; (3) the need for standards to make it useful if there are network effects.

Empirical work studying the factors affecting diffusion has confirmed that profitability and other financial factors, firm concentration and size, complexity, customer relationships, worker skill and education, uncertainty, and the network nature of the technology all affect its diffusion. Looking forward, we can identify some issues that will arise in the diffusion of clean technologies and AI-based technologies.

Technological standards are specifications (of measures or a measurement system) of functions and the way they must be performed, or of the input/output parameters. These make it possible for different components of a system to work together successfully. General-purpose technologies such as electricity and the internet require technological standards if they are to diffuse widely.

Network goods are goods whose value to one user depends on use by others. They usually involve some use of standards, as the ability to communicate between nodes is essential. Network externalities are the benefit or cost conferred on others when an individual chooses to purchase a network good. A positive externality arises from the fact that other people's utility is increased when someone joins a network, while a negative externality exists if there is another competing network good. When an individual adopts the first one, the decision is negative for the users of the second.

8

Innovation Strategy

Learning Objectives

After reading this chapter, you will be able to understand and explain the following concepts:

- How firms create and capture value from innovation
- The role of strategic goals for value creation and appropriation
- Characteristics of different research strategies
- The impact of network effects on innovation strategy
- Strategies for network competition

8.1 Introduction

Given what we know about innovation, how should innovative firms and individuals respond? That is, what does our knowledge tell us about the best innovation strategy to pursue in particular cases? In this chapter, we draw a few conclusions from what we know about innovation and diffusion, but we leave the more detailed advice to strategy specialists such as Shapiro and Varian (1999a) or textbooks such as those by Schilling (2020).

Most management scholars would define the goal of a firm's management as the creation of value for the firm. Here, we discuss the strategies that might help create that value in the innovation context. We explore how the difference in the skills of established firms and startups means that they are to some extent suited to different types of innovation: incremental, which builds closely on prior technology, and radical, which calls for entirely new combinations of knowledge. Another type of innovation, architectural, lies somewhere between the two, but like radical innovation, it also destroys existing competencies.

One of the major questions facing an innovative firm is how to structure its R&D efforts. Accessing and using basic research and science are important, but the ways in which both are done have evolved over time, due to other changes in the industrial landscape. The open innovation strategy involving forward and backward links to customers, suppliers, and other specialists has become more prevalent, although it has always been used to some extent by innovating firms. This strategy is part of a larger decision, the make or buy decision with respect to innovative assets. We use the lens of transaction costs economics to analyze this choice.

With the rise of the digital economy, hardware–software and platform technologies, including two-sided platforms, have risen in importance. Competition strategy in these

The Economics of Innovation and Intellectual Property. Bronwyn H. Hall and Christian Helmers, Oxford University Press.
© Oxford University Press 2024. DOI: 10.1093/oso/9780197630914.003.0008

areas is complex, depending both on technology and market structure. An important question is whether it is better to cooperate with other firms to achieve compatibility when introducing a new system or whether incompatibility is the better strategy. We discuss some examples and some very simple game theoretic models of systems competition that illustrate the costs and benefits of the two approaches.

8.2 Value Creation and Strategic Goals

In order to define the amount and direction of a firm's innovative activity, it is first necessary to understand what the goals of such activity might be. The overarching goal will generally be value creation and the ability to capture the returns to such creation. In our context, value creation is the act of innovating a product or service that provides benefits to current or new customers large enough that at least some of them are willing to pay more for the innovative good than it costs to make it (where the costs include the innovation investment).

For established firms, there are a number of factors to consider when thinking about their innovation strategy. The first step is to examine the threats and opportunities in the firm's environment that seem most important. Threats to the innovating firm may include new entrants to the sector or the presence of a particular competitor whose product has a technological edge. They may even include a looming paradigm shift (see Box 8.1), such as that facing oil and coal-fired power plants or gasoline-powered automobiles. You may be able to think of other examples from your experience.

One example of a compelling threat to firms in the transportation sector is the potential for unexpected accidents from failures of driverless automotive technologies. This problem clearly focuses the attention of firms like Tesla and Waymo as well as the traditional automakers on the quality of the sensors and the associated AI technology needed to interpret them. These technologies already exist and are fairly sophisticated, but these firms are heavily engaged in their further refinement in order to reduce the probability of accidents further. The threat is that their products will not be approved for general use nor will people be willing to use them without improved technology.

Especially for existing firms, opportunities may include the next steps along the technological trajectory with which they are engaged. These opportunities are for

---

Box 8.1 Technological Paradigm

Technological paradigm: a model of the particular technology (e.g., the basic structure of a microprocessor) and the specific technological problems posed by such model (e.g., increasing computational capacity, reducing dimensions). "An outlook, a set of procedures, a definition of the relevant problems, and of the specific knowledge related to their solution" (Dosi 1982).

Paradigm shift: a move from one technological paradigm to another in the market. Examples include gasoline-powered vehicles from horse-drawn vehicles, the internet for communication and the distribution of digital products, the assembly line from traditional craft production.

evolutionary rather than radical innovation. For example, recall Rosenberg's "induce-ment mechanisms and focusing devices" (Chapter 3) that send signals on technological imbalance that determine the direction of innovation. His examples included the oil tube drill for machining that was developed to match the speed of the outside forming tool in making bicycle hubs. The oil tube drill made it possible to smooth edges and remove chips on the inside of the hub, while forming the outside of the hub. This was an immediate opportunity that arose from a manufacturing bottleneck, and one that is typical of incremental innovation.

Today, the signals are no less clear in some areas. For example, blockchain and bitcoin technologies suffer from the fact that ever-increasing computing power will be needed to implement them for recording contracts, financial transactions, gaming, non-fungible tokens (NFTs; see Box 8.2), and other applications. Verifying such transactions is already slower than with a centralized database in some cases and could get worse as blockchains lengthen. Solving the "scalability" problem in blockchain technology is a pressing need to make it really useful.[1]

Box 8.2 NFTs and Blockchains

Non-fungible token (NFT): a unique digital identifier that cannot be copied, substituted, or subdivided, that is, recorded in a blockchain, and that is used to certify authenticity and ownership

Blockchain technology: a shared, immutable ledger for recording transactions, tracking assets, and building trust

---

A second question for the innovative firm is whether it possesses any sources of sus-tainable competitive advantage. In effect, this is asking whether there are any long-run sources of economic rent for the firm. If so, these may serve as a guide to the direction of innovation. Besides obvious physical assets such as a diamond mine or ownership of the source of a rare mineral, rent sources might include a significant brand name (such as Coca-Cola or Apple), a well-developed distribution network (e.g., Walmart or Amazon), a customer list for a specialized service (such as held by investment brokers or even law firms), and so forth. The test is how much it would cost for a competitor or new entrant to imitate the asset that creates the competitive advantage.

Possession of such an asset may inform the firm about the direction its innovation might take. For example, Amazon's successful innovation in the delivery of books, with an emphasis on the ability to allow search and purchase of less-demanded titles, clearly suggested that expansion into the delivery of other products such as CDs and DVDs using their existing shipping system and expertise might be a good innovation. Invention of the Kindle and digital book delivery was less obviously driven by their ex-isting assets, with the exception of the search engine targeted to books. However, when Sony introduced an e-Ink reader in 2004, it was already clear that the physical book busi-ness would be threatened by e-books. Amazon followed suit with the introduction of the

---

[1] See   https://www.techtarget.com/searchcio/tip/6-potential-blockchain-limitations-for-enterprise-use for discussion of these issues.

Kindle in 2007. This looks like a case of radical innovation undertaken by an established firm. However, it turned out not to upset their existing business model, but to augment it.

In spite of arguably superior technology, Sony eventually exited the sector in 2014, and Amazon is now estimated to have two-thirds of the market share of e-books. There are a couple of lessons from this outcome. First, the crucial ingredient to make an e-reader useful is a supply of reading material. It turned out that Amazon's experience selling large numbers of physical books gave them an advantage in understanding the concerns of the book publishers, whose business models were threatened by the circulation of electronic editions. Accordingly, they used digital rights management (DRM) to protect their proprietary format and offered the publishers an attractive deal where they earned the same royalty on e-books as physical books, at least at first. This made them much more willing to supply books to the platform. Second, Sony's first-mover advantage was dissipated by a failure to continue marketing at the right level and, more importantly, a failure to acquire a sufficient variety and supply of reading material.

An important example of sustainable competitive advantage exists in platform and software competition, where a major source of advantage is the installed base of users that is already familiar with the use of the software interface. In addition to lowering the cost of serving additional customers, diffusion to new customers is facilitated by existing customer familiarity with the interface and use. We expand on strategies for this form of competition later in the chapter. For fast-food franchises or hotel chains, it can be the familiarity of the customers with their food and the availability of standardized offerings whenever they travel to new locations. For airlines, the management of frequent flyer programs is important for sustaining their competitive advantage when low-cost entry takes place on their routes.

8.2.1 Startups

Thinking about innovation in startups will have slightly different emphases. They are not normally already in possession of a competitive advantage although they are searching for one. Their main possession may be an idea, which they protect with patent application(s) and trade secret/non-disclosure agreements as they search for financing. Startups are more likely to either be trying to create a new industry (somewhat rare), a new niche for themselves in an existing industry, or to replace existing firms with better technology.

The innovation management literature suggests that startups are more likely to have success over existing firms when their innovations are radical or upset the existing architecture and business models. In contrast, incremental innovation tends to reinforce the existing core competencies of established firms. Chesbrough (1999) emphasizes that this simple dichotomy can be modified by the institutions and market structure of the economy in which the firms are embedded. He studied the evolution of the hard disk industry during 1973–1996, a period of rapid technical change with reduced form factors (i.e., the size of the disk), increased storage capacity, and rapidly declining prices per unit of storage. During these changes, in the United States startups replaced incumbent firms repeatedly, whereas in Japan incumbent firms remained the dominant producers, while most startups failed. Europe had the worst of both worlds, with its worldwide share of hard disk sales dropping to 0.2% by the end of the period.

The Japanese experience suggests that at least in some sectors and economies incumbency is not always an obstacle to innovation that is somewhere between incremental and radical. Chesbrough attributes the US startup success to the mobility of key engineers, something that was not accepted or feasible in Japan and Europe. It is probably also worth pointing out that IBM, which made many of the basic inventions that underpin the evolution of the hard disk industry, tied its own hands by refusing to supply any but its own systems manufacturers, which effectively left room for the entry of new disk drive producers as the demand for PCs produced by companies other than IBM grew.

Work by Henderson and Clark (1990) on systems innovation suggests that architectural innovation, which they describe as "reconfiguration of an existing system to link components in a new way," is as much of a challenge to existing firms as radical innovation, which may make the entire system obsolete. The idea is that adapting to architectural innovation is difficult for existing firms because some of what they know may actually hamper such adaptation, even if they have expertise in building the components of the system. They may also have difficulty even recognizing that an innovation is architectural in nature and requires reconfiguration of the ways in which they are producing.

These authors offer several examples, the most extensive of which is the evolution of photolithographic alignment equipment in the semiconductor industry during the 1980s. The original innovation that applied photolithography to semiconductor manufacturing in the 1950s was radical. Then this sector experienced four waves of architectural innovation during the 1970s and 1980s, during each of which there was a different dominant firm, in spite of the facts that the basic technology remained the same and that the incumbent firm invested heavily in the new technology. Table 8.1 summarizes these changes.

In a follow-up paper, Henderson explores the failures of the existing market leader to make the transition to the newer technology in the four transitions documented in the table above. She argues that the architectural innovation led to changes in the way that components linked together, rendering existing firm knowledge of the linking technologies obsolete. Like the rest of us, engineers have bounded rationality and are accustomed to the current dominant design. Accordingly, they have built their knowledge on how the parts currently fit together and the firm and its employees have developed routines, communication channels, and information filters based on this architecture. Such routines reduce the cost of processing information while possibly blinding the firm to radical changes in their technological area.

For these reasons, it is very difficult for the established firm to adapt to the new architecture. In part, this is because communication channels within the firm are adapted to the old architecture, suggesting that architectural innovation may require organizational innovation. The same arguments will apply to radical innovation more broadly, where both the components and the methods by which they are put together change. All of this will reduce the established firm's innovation production advantage over startup firms when confronted with radical or architectural innovation.

Table 8.1 Architectural Innovation in Photolithographic Alignment Technology in the 1970–1980s

Equipment	Technology	Critical Component Relationship	Dominant Firm (market share)	Approximate Date of Introduction
Contact	Previous technology		Cobit (44%)	Pre-1974
Proximity aligner	Mask and wafer separated	Accuracy and stability of gap between mask and wafer dependent on links between gap setting and other components	Canon (67%)	Late 1970s
Scanning projection	Mask projected onto wafer using reflective optics	Interaction between optical lens and other components critical	Perkin-Elmer (78%)	Late 1970s
First-generation stepper	Image of mask projected through refractive lens; stepped across wafer	Lens field size–source energy link, depth of focus, stage–alignment links critical to throughput of process	GCA (55%)	Early 1980s
Second-generation stepper	Intro of section-by-section mask projection on wafer, larger lenses	Calibration-stepper stability drives throughput; lens–mechanical system link crucial for controlling distortion	Nikon (70%)	Mid-1980s

Source: Henderson and Clark (1990), Tables 1 and 2. See their paper for more details on the technology.

8.2.2 Some Empirical Evidence on Innovation and Value Creation

The importance of technological differentiation as a creator of value and economic rents has been documented empirically in the economic literature. Jaffe (1986) used technological closeness as measured by the correlation of technology class-based patenting profiles among firms to show that firms benefited by spillovers from those close to them but had lower profits if their technology neighbors were more R&D-intensive. Jaffe measured closeness by constructing a technology profile for each firm using their patent classified in each of K patent classes. Thus, each firm i is characterized by a vector of patent counts (generally, those patents taken out over the last 5 or 10 years by the firm):

$$F_i = (F_{i1}, F_{i2}, ..., F_{iK})$$

where many of the F_{ik} will be zeros for any given firm. The proximity of one firm i to another firm j in technology space is given by the following:

$$P_{ij} = \frac{\sum_{k=1}^{K} F_{ik} F_{jk}}{\left(\sum_{k=1}^{K} F_{ik}^2 \sum_{k=1}^{K} F_{jk}^2 \right)^{1/2}}$$

This formula can be recognized as the cosine of the angle between the two vectors F_i and F_j or, equivalently, their dot product normalized by their lengths. This idea has proved useful, and variations have been used in many subsequent papers.

Bloom et al. (2013) distinguish the effects of product market and technology competition, finding that firms benefit from the R&D spillovers from those close in technology space, but that their market value is lower if they have close neighbors in product market space. This paper uses a Malahanobis measure of distance (proximity) in addition to Jaffe's measure in an attempt to account for the fact that some technology classes are more similar to each other than others.[2]

Arts et al. (2023) use a methodology similar to Jaffe but with greatly refined technology measures based on patent texts. Their work shows that market value and return on assets are strongly positively associated with the technological differentiation of the firm from other firms. This supports the idea that greater value is available to innovative firms that successfully differentiate their technology from that of other firms.

8.2.3 Lessons from Industry Evolution

As we described in Chapter 4, the history of industry evolution suggests that startups are very active early in the development of an industry, when there is no dominant design and firms are experimenting with ways to produce a new good or service. Klepper described the evolution of industry as a life cycle with many innovating startups at the beginning, gradually leading to a shakeout with the successful growth of a few firms producing products with the dominant design. During this phase, there is continuous incremental innovation and diffusion, both of which mean that the productivity gains are greater during this phase than earlier. Finally, the innovation slows down until another radical innovation arrives to replace the dominant design.

Dosi (1982) described the same kind of evolution from the perspective of technological change. He referred to the dominant design as the technological paradigm and argued that once such a paradigm was commonly agreed on, the technological trajectory of incremental innovation was in some respects chosen and inevitable in the ways described by Rosenberg. Table 8.2 shows some examples of the transformation of a generic need for innovation to a specific paradigm.

Abernathy and Utterback (1978) make similar arguments, giving the Ford Model-T as an example of finding a dominant design within a single firm. Prior to the introduction of this model, Henry Ford spent 4 years trying five different engines with different configurations, ultimately settling on the one used in the Model-T. After another 15 years of incremental innovation to this dominant design, 2 million of these cars were being sold each year and the basic design of the gasoline-powered automobile had been established.

This picture of industry evolution suggests that during periods following a radical innovation, a lot of experimentation will take place, much of it by startups, trying various ways of approaching the problem of commercializing the invention. Ultimately,

---

[2] See the appendices to Bloom et al. for details.

Table 8.2 Technological Paradigms

Generic Need	Specific Paradigm
Transportation of people and commodities	Internal combustion engine
Producing chemical compounds with certain properties	Petrochemical processes
Switching and amplifying electrical signals	Basic semiconductor design
Transportation of people and commodities by air	Douglas DC-3 for extended period
Ability to communicate over distance without wires	"Smart" mobile phone, with no physical keyboard, high-quality camera, large screen

Source: Dosi (1982), Teece (1986), and authors' additions.

a dominant design or paradigm will emerge, at which point incremental innovation to improve it will take off because the technological trajectory has become clearer. Therefore, understanding which phase of industry evolution a firm is in is important for seeing how to profit from innovation.

One recent example of a radical innovation followed by considerable experimentation on the part of firms, much of it directed toward learning about the services desired by the consumer and by users of the technology themselves, is the development of the internet. The basic technology was in place already by 1991, when Tim Berners-Lee combined hypertext with the Web to allow the linking of information without sending it. The takeoff in use began in 1995, and by 1998 increased entry by firms hoping to profit from the internet was accompanied by a rise in market valuations of technology stocks, leading ultimately to the "dotcom bubble." Wang (2007) reports that 7,000–10,000 dotcom firms were created in the late 1990s and that by the spring of 2003 more than half had exited. This is illustrated by the rise and fall of the National Association of Securities Dealers Automated Quotations (NASDAQ) index between about 1995 and 2002 in Figure 8.1. The NASDAQ index (Box 8.3) did not recover until about 2015. Ironically, the index has recently eclipsed its 2000 boom threefold, so the 2000 "bubble" can be seen as premature rather than mistaken.

The earlier 1995–2002 period can be viewed as a period of learning how the consumer wants to use the internet and which services are best delivered in that way. It was also a period when the potential for security flaws became clear and considerable effort was devoted to increasing protections, an effort that is ongoing today. Post-2000, the basic architecture of use and browser technology was more or less stable and the main players such as Amazon and Google had begun to emerge. In addition, hardware improvements to network technology, computers, mobile telephones, and other electronics such as TVs meant that widespread streaming of video became feasible. We could say that now there are several dominant designs in use on the Web: search engines, video delivery, social media, retail sales, and so forth. Each of these has multiple suppliers whose interfaces operate in similar ways.

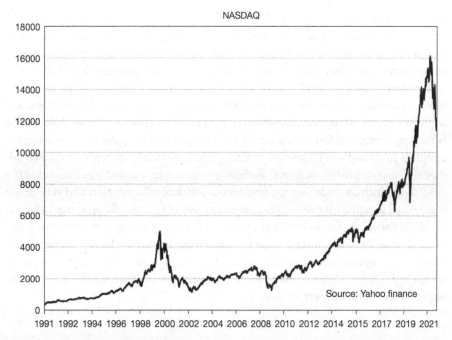

Figure 8.1 NASDAQ composite index.

8.3 Value Capture

For the firm, value creation is not worth much unless at least some of it is captured as profits. Value capture is the ability of the firm to obtain at least some of the benefits of the innovation via pricing above cost. This is usually known as appropriability, as we saw earlier in the book. Methods for value capture include the usual IP protections, both formal and informal, discussed in Chapter 4. Traditionally, these are mostly used to exclude entry by competitors that threatens the profits of the innovating firm by providing substitute goods and services to the market via imitation. In Chapter 18, we will learn how the use of IP has expanded to serve many strategic purposes of the firm.

In Chapters 4 and 14, we discuss the contrast between formal methods such as patents and more informal methods such as trade secrecy and point out that they are often used in combination. The formal methods typically are term-limited, which makes them unsuitable for situations where there is a long time between invention and

---

Box 8.3 NASDAQ

NASDAQ (National Association of Securities Dealers Automated Quotations) is an American stock exchange based in New York City. The NASDAQ index has a high concentration of companies in the technology sector, especially newer firms, so it is often viewed as a barometer of sentiment in this sector.

successful commercialization.[3] Such situations are fairly rare but do exist, such as in the case of new uses for old drugs, so-called second-use drugs. In the cases where the invention can be clearly articulated, formal methods provide a more secure protection from imitation, although they may be costly to enforce against an aggressive imitator.

The main formal method of protection for innovation is the use of patents, with lesser or more specialized roles for copyright, trademarks, geographical indications, and semiconductor mask protection. However, with a few exceptions, patents alone can be fairly weak protection from imitation via inventing around the patents. Enforcement of patents is costly and also distracting to management, especially in startup firms. For this reason, firms often turn to informal methods of value capture as well (see Chapter 14).

Methods such as trade secrecy, first-mover advantage, better sales and service are widely used to capture the returns to innovation and, in fact, may be preferred to formal methods. Especially for process innovation, trade secrecy can be very attractive if feasible. Most of these less formal IP protection methods are members of an important class of value capture methods: the creation of complementary assets that are necessary for full exploitation of the innovation and are costly to reproduce. We discuss these assets and their use in the next section.

8.3.1 Complementary Assets

Complementary assets are assets whose value when combined with an innovation is greater than their stand-alone value. In the case of social media firms, for example, the database of user information is a complementary asset useful in adding value via advertising, and also hard for a new entrant to replicate. For many technical products, a service network like the Apple Genius Bar creates a barrier to entry for products from other firms that compete with Apple's.

The concept of complementary assets and their relevance for innovation value capture was introduced in an influential paper by Teece (1986). This paper was motivated by the fact that the firm that was most successful with an innovation was not the original innovator, but an imitator. In seeking to understand why, Teece posited that in areas with weak appropriability, the possession or development of specialized assets that were necessary for exploiting the innovation often enabled a second or subsequent entrant to capture the value of the innovation.

As we have discussed before, industries such as chemicals and pharmaceuticals as well as those with simple devices that are either not part of a system or have generic interfaces are those where patents provide high appropriability, at least for a time. But in most industries, the various methods of IP protection provide relatively weak protection. In this situation, being the first mover may not be an advantage, especially since the first mover enters during the early development of an industry where the dominant design or technological paradigm has not been settled.

Most innovations require other investments if they are to be commercialized: manufacturing, marketing and distribution, after-sales service, and possibly other complementary technologies. The decision a firm faces is which of these to own and which

---

[3] One exception to this is trademarks, where continuous use usually permits an indefinite term.

to contract over with external suppliers. To some extent, this will depend on the type of asset that is created by investment in any of these activities. Teece distinguishes complementary assets between those that are generic, those that are specialized, and those that are cospecialized with each other. As examples of specialized assets, he offers a drug distribution system, which is particular to drugs given the specialized information they require, but can be used by any drug innovator. In contrast, an example of cospecialized assets is containerized shipping, where both the container ships and the ports that receive them must be customized to make such shipping feasible (Rua 2014). An example of a generic asset is a manufacturing establishment for running shoes, which can easily be retooled to supply a different running shoe company or even another product with similar manufacturing requirements.

In weak appropriability contexts when the industry has at least partially agreed on a dominant design, whether (co-)specialized or generic assets are needed for commercialization will affect the innovator's ability to capture value from their innovation. Generic asset investments are reversible and easily imitated, so no rents can be created with those. In contrast, those who control specialized assets are in a position to earn the returns from the innovation if those assets are necessary for its exploitation.

One example of this situation is the licensing of patents and technology from the university. The specialized assets are the knowledge and ability of how to commercialize the invention, whereas the main asset possessed by the university is the patent and some tacit know-how. This may perhaps explain the fact that the most successful commercialization from university technology transfer offices (TTOs) is in biotechnology and agricultural new varieties, which are characterized by strong patents. Mowery et al. (2004) report that the biotechnology share of technology license agreements at Stanford University, Columbia University, and the University of California ranges from 70% to 100% during the 1980–1994 period. In other technologies, TTOs have considerable difficulty reaching agreement on profit sharing with industry. Universities often feel that they are being undercompensated for their inventions, but if costly specialized assets are needed for commercialization and the patents associated are relatively weak, this is not surprising.

Other cases of the value disconnect between a knowledge producer and the entity that commercializes the invention occur in the case of independent inventors. A well-known example of this kind of problem is the history of variable speed windshield washers, recounted in a *New Yorker* article and the 2008 film *Flash of Genius*.[4] The inventor Robert Kearns disclosed his invention to Ford employees in detail in 1963 and was encouraged to develop, test, and manufacture the washer blades for them. However, in the end Ford released autos containing intermittent windshield wipers produced in-house. They and other auto manufacturers used the invention without licensing his patent, arguing that the invention was obvious and should not have been patented. Litigation between Kearns and the auto manufacturers took 30 years, and he eventually prevailed at the end of his life, at considerable cost to himself and his family. The value disconnect is revealed by the fact that he sued Ford for US$350million in 1978 and turned down a settlement offer of $30million. His experience is not unusual in

[4] https://www.imdb.com/title/tt1054588. The account was drawn from a *New Yorker* article (Seabrook 1993).

the independent invention field, where litigation with large established firms is fraught with cost and delays that make it unprofitable to pursue.

8.4 Research Strategy

Given the existence of spillovers from research, especially research of the kind with wide and uncertain application, one question that firms face is how much, if any, of this type of research they should undertake. There is clear evidence in the past that large multiproduct firms have undertaken basic research, not all of which was solely for their immediate purposes. Rosenberg (1990) asked why this was the case and came up with a number of reasons why firms should perform such research in spite of the fact that the spillovers might be large and the returns difficult to appropriate.

First, the majority of firms conducting basic research at the time were large established firms with market power (IBM, AT&T before divestiture, DuPont, Dow Chemical, Eastman Kodak, etc.). This means that they expected to be around in the future to capture returns to research that may have long-term payoffs, which is characteristic of basic scientific research. Large multiproduct firms that are diversified are also more likely to find a use for the results of their research within the firm. The biotechnology sector is an exception to this rule since discoveries there are closer to commercialization and patents on basic discoveries are very effective protection from imitation. Consequently, patents can be used for contracting with the larger firms that will commercialize the discovery. In fact, the pharmaceutical biotechnology industry grew up as a web of network connections where pharmaceutical firms finance a number of biotechnology firms and biotechnology firms have agreements with a number of pharmaceutical firms for potential exploitation of their technologies.

Second, even though the information generated by such research may spill easily to others, there is a first-mover advantage that accrues to those who generate it. Third, the results of such research are highly uncertain, and some of the results of research conducted by firms to solve specific problems have turned out to be very basic indeed (recall Pasteur and other examples in Chapter 2). The reverse, of course, is also true in the sense that basic research may be undertaken in an industrial laboratory in order to understand an applied problem. All this suggests that doing basic research is a way to participate in an information network that connects the firm to scientific research done elsewhere that might be significant for their own R&D. In short, doing such research builds the firm's absorptive capacity. All these arguments point to a productive role for a basic scientific research laboratory within a large multiproduct firm that may also serve as one of the barriers to entry from startups and new firms.

However, in spite of these arguments and the historical experience of US firms during the 1950s to 1970s, Arora et al. (2018) point out that circumstances have changed considerably since then. NSF statistics on corporate R&D in the United States show a decline in the share of basic and applied research in R&D from 28% in 1985 to 21% in 2009, the level at which it has remained at least until 2019. There has also been a decline in the number of papers by corporate researchers published in academic journals during the same period. Because the share of basic and applied research in R&D is unavailable easily at the individual firm level, Arora and coauthors constructed a proxy measure for a firm's activity in scientific research using the number of papers published by researchers of a firm in scientific journals.

Using these numbers along with the market value of the firm in a regression like that we discussed in Chapter 6.5, they were able to show that the net returns expected from scientific research have declined between 1980 and 2006. This was accompanied by a decline in scientific publication on the part of corporations, as suggested by the NSF statistics. The exception to this was the pharmaceutical sector, which has remained close to science. Another finding from these data was the patent citations to scientific literature increased for those firms that also published in scientific journals, reinforcing the idea that absorptive capacity matters and also suggesting that some firms at least are better able to exploit research done elsewhere.

Why have returns to corporate research fallen overall in the past three decades? The private returns to corporate research depend on the balance between own downstream use and costs of spillovers to rivals. Arora et al. (2021a) present evidence that this is true, in the sense that firms reduce their own research when more is spilling over to rivals. Downstream use of own research is increased by the closeness of the industry to science, the ability to use the potential output of the research in multiple areas, and the ability to sustain the firm's position in the market over long periods. The first two requirements seem to have weakened over time. There is less reliance on science in IT and software than in chemicals, and fewer firms are widely diversified.

However, one could argue that recently there has been an increase in firms with fairly long-run market dominance. There are now some superstar firms, including such well-known names as Apple, Alphabet, and so forth. These firms have solidified their market shares, productivity, and stability as documented in Autor et al. (2020) and Andrews et al. (2016), among others. In addition, these firms do seem to have developed some interest in applied research, at least as it relates to their interests. However, much of this research is not in traditional fields, but in computer science and social science. It remains to be seen whether this strategy will be as fruitful in the future as that of AT&T's Bell Laboratories was in the past.

8.4.1 Open Innovation

The fact that firms are no longer relying as heavily on their own basic and applied research has been accompanied by a shift toward the use of knowledge external to the firm. This strategy has come to be known as *open innovation*. Open innovation is a term pioneered by Chesbrough (2006), who defined it as "a paradigm that assumes that firms can and should use external ideas as well as internal ideas, and internal and external paths to market, as the firms look to advance their technology."

In a revealing survey of manufacturing firms described in Arora et al. (2016), half of innovating manufacturing firms reported that their most important new product originated from external sources: customers, suppliers, or outside technology specialists such as universities, independent inventors, and R&D contractors. There was little variation in this share across industries, although the relative importance of the different external sources varied. A range of their evidence points to the conclusion that customer-sourced innovations are more incremental and less valuable, and that the innovations sourced from specialists are the most valuable and require the greatest further investment.

Thus, the evidence suggests that innovation from external sources is of significant importance for innovating firms. Nevertheless, assimilating such ideas and inventions does require effort and management on the part of the firm. In fact, for firms such as Oracle and Cisco, which have obtained considerable innovative knowledge via acquisition of other firms, the ability to make use of the knowledge thus acquired is a core competence that took time and conscious effort to build.

Chesbrough argues that the old model of industrial R&D operating within a firm from initial project to commercialization broke down partly because of the rise of venture capital (VC) financing. This meant that engineers with ideas and inventions that their employers refused to support adequately or for which they feel undercompensated could leave the company and start a new one, given the potential availability of financing. The pitfalls of being an independent startup are mitigated both by the experience, size, and advice of the venture capitalist, and by the fact that their prior firm has shown little interest in the idea they are exploiting. In turn, if the idea was successful, they might end up selling their startup to another larger firm or be the subject of an initial public offering (IPO). These possibilities mean that some large established firms conduct relatively little research and rely on the ecosystem around them for some of their innovation.

The industry that is particularly emblematic of this structure is the electronics and semiconductor industry centered in Silicon Valley, but there are others elsewhere. For example, the Hollywood film sector has long operated as a network of workers and companies with varying skills that come together for particular film projects. Chesbrough also points out that some sectors, such as the nuclear reactor and aircraft sectors, still conduct R&D to a great extent within the firm. However, the recent development of the Boeing 787 Dreamliner drew components from all over the globe, without detailed specifications for each, suggesting some spreading out of at least the development part of R&D to other firms. However, this "experiment" with open innovation development was a mixed success with many delays and performance problems, even though ultimately the Dreamliner was successful (Shenhar et al. 2016).

Although superficially the term *open* suggests such things as "open source" in software or "open access" in Web publications, open innovation is often managed via the use of proprietary systems, namely, patents (see Chapter 17.4 for a discussion of the role that patents play in the context of OSS). Acquisition of innovative firms specifically includes their IP portfolio. Licensing of IP associated with innovative ideas is widespread. Firms still choose to patent discoveries that are part of their core technologies. However, firms such as IBM and Intel also maintain in-house technical journals that publish discoveries that either may not be patentable or are part of the technology knowledge base that they know will become generally known anyway. By publishing these discoveries, they preclude other firms from trying to patent them, and at the same time reduce their own patenting costs.

8.4.2 Make or Buy?

One decision that confronts many innovative firms, especially those in the open innovation setting, is the question of whether to make or buy new technology that is needed to pursue their particular strategic choices. Many factors will influence their choice. Purchase of new technology often takes the form of purchase of the firm that owns it, or one of its subsidiaries. Such acquisitions are often difficult to assimilate within an existing firm and sometimes risk the loss of human capital from the acquired firm via the exit of key employees, reducing its value. The decision will depend on the importance of speed if the technology already exists externally but would have to be developed in-house. It will also depend on how closely linked it is to the firm's own core competencies (see Box 8.4): if close, it may be better to develop internally given the knowledge base of the firm and the cost of absorbing an external acquisition.

Another issue is the IP right that is already associated with the technology. Is it owned by another firm and impossible to invent around? Then the firm will have to license the technology or acquire the owner. Depending on the technology, the latter may be preferable if an exclusive license is not available.

For the electronics and electrical equipment industry, Blonigen and Taylor (2000) show that a firm's own R&D intensity and its acquisition activity are negatively correlated, suggesting that in this sector at least, making and buying knowledge assets are substitutes to some extent. Nevertheless, even a firm like Oracle, which is skilled at acquiring and assimilating other technology firms, has its own internal R&D program to support the activity of managing the technology from acquisitions. Cassiman and Veugelers (2002) used a sample of Belgian manufacturing firms in many industries to show that large firms tend to combine external and internal knowledge acquisition strategies, whereas small firms tended to specialize in one or the other.

Pisano (1990) found that about half of the R&D projects conducted by the 50 largest pharmaceutical firms during the mid-1980s were external to the firm. He then studied this make or buy choice for R&D in drug development using transaction cost theory (Williamson 1979). This theory posits that the costs surrounding a transaction will determine whether it takes place within the firm or is transacted in the market. Determining factors include the level of uncertainty surrounding the transaction process and outcome and whether it requires one of the parties to invest in transaction-specific assets. The idea is that uncertainty means that contracts are incomplete, and because many transactions take place over time, new information will be revealed that may require some change in terms. The fact that contracts must be adjusted during the transaction means that opportunistic conduct on the part of one or more of the parties may occur. If one party has sunk costs in transaction-specific assets, they are vulnerable to renegotiation at worse terms. Such transactions will tend to move inside the firm so that the interests of both parties are aligned because they are the same party.

The application to innovative activity is clear, as it is both highly uncertain and requires very specific investments. This suggests that much research and product

---

Box 8.4 Core Competency

Core competency (Prahalad and Hamel 1990) refers to the capabilities, knowledge, skills, and resources that are distinct to the firm and therefore not easily replicated by other organizations, whether they are existing competitors or new entrants into its market.

development will reside within the firm, and only a limited amount will be contracted out. Nevertheless, a number of firms do contract out some R&D. In 2019, about 5% of US business-funded R&D was performed by R&D service establishments and another 3% by other companies. In addition, about 8% of the total R&D performed by business was paid for by companies that did not perform the R&D themselves.[5] For pharmaceuticals, this number is much higher: 25% of pharmaceutical R&D is done by companies that did not fund it. This does suggest that the sector finds it somewhat easier, in general, to contract out for R&D, perhaps because patent protection is more secure in this area of technology.

Pisano focuses on two sources of transaction costs that are characteristic of R&D contracts: small numbers bargaining and concerns about the ability to appropriate returns to the R&D. The typical R&D contract in the pharmaceutical sector is a contract between a large pharmaceutical with some internal research capability as well as experience with clinical trials and a biotechnology firm with specialized knowledge about research in a particular therapeutic class or using a specific technology. The pharma firm supplies the funds and the biotech firm does the research, the results of which will be developed and marketed by the pharma firm. The contract is over a fairly long period (5–7 years) and is subject to renegotiation during that period as new information is revealed.

The small numbers problem is due to the fact that the research investment by the pharma firm is sunk when it wishes to switch to a different supplier, unless there are multiple other biotech firms with the relevant experience. Pisano shows that the decision to invest in an R&D project in-house rather than via external contract does indeed depend negatively on the number of potential biotechnology partners in the relevant therapeutic class. The appropriability problem arises because not all of the knowledge created by the biotech partner but paid for by the pharma firm can be reliably protected with IP, and therefore the pharma firm is concerned that they can be expropriated if the biotech firm decides to partner with another pharma firm. Pisano shows that the number of competitors in the therapeutic class is associated positively but not significantly with the decision to do an R&D project in house.

Before leaving this topic, it is worth mentioning that not all acquisitions of smaller technology firms are benign. Cunningham et al. (2020) study acquisitions in the pharmaceutical sector, arguing that one way out of Arrow's incumbent's dilemma is to acquire the firm that might replace the incumbent (acquiring firm). Their model shows that acquired drug projects are less likely to be developed when they overlap with the acquirer's existing product portfolio, especially when the acquirer's market power is large. They find empirically that a relatively small share (5.3–7.4%) of pharmaceutical acquisitions appears to be of this kind.

8.4.3 Or Collaborate?

Another option for accessing research that a firm needs but for which it may not have the requisite skills is collaborating with a partner or partners via a strategic alliance,

---

[5] https://ncses.nsf.gov/pubs/nsb20225/u-s-business-r-d#key-characteristics-of-domestic-business-r-d-performance.

joint venture, technology licensing, or a collective research organization. We have already touched on this topic in our discussion of the pharmaceutical-biotechnology research contracts, and collaboration for a finite time is one of the outcomes of an open innovation strategy. Also see Section 20.6 of this book for more on the use of patents in collaborative agreements.

There are advantages and disadvantages to collaboration. The advantages include increased flexibility, speed, and the sharing of risk. The firm does not have to develop research assets in-house that are already available externally and are not committed to the ownership of specialized assets if the project fails to succeed or goes in a different direction. Collaboration also allows the firms involved to learn from each other and create new knowledge that would have been difficult to create solo.

If the innovation project requires the creation of a new or improved standard, collaborating on the definition of that standard may benefit all the firms involved. For example of the latter, there are multiple standards for high-speed (Level 3) charging of electric vehicles, two of which are those from consortia. The first, CHAdeMO, was developed by a coalition of Japanese automakers (Toyota, Mitsubishi, Subaru, and Nissan). The second, CCS, was developed by a collaboration between BMW, Ford, Jaguar, General Motors, Polestar, and Volkswagen.[6]

The disadvantages of collaboration center on the problem of value capture. Firms can be reluctant to reveal their knowledge to other firms, which may reduce the potential productivity of the collaboration. There can be disagreement over who owns the IP generated by the alliance. Firms often wish to control all of the resulting IP themselves to facilitate further moves, so this can be the most difficult part of the contract negotiation. At the same time, firms would like to maximize their ability to receive R&D spillovers from their partner.

The different collaborative structures face slightly different trade-offs, of course. The most integrated is a joint venture, where a new business entity may be created with equity stakes from the partners, and the venture may own the resulting IP itself. A joint venture may last indefinitely or at least for a fairly long time. A strategic alliance is a step down from this, being temporary and generally not involving the creation of a new entity. Many of the large pharma firm–biotechnology firm alliances are of this type. This is where complete specification of IP rights and other ownership rights at the beginning of the relationship will be helpful, to prevent opportunistic behavior by one of the partners.

Licensing technology in or out is a more arm's length transaction, although the transfer will often include some tacit knowhow in addition to whatever IP is involved. Licensing is often used in situations where the firm does not have the time to develop the technology in-house. A famous example of the failure to capture value from licensing is when IBM's PC development division licensed the operating system for its new PC from Microsoft in 1981, renaming it PC-DOS from MS-DOS. Unfortunately for them, they signed a non-exclusive license, enabling Microsoft to license its operating systems to other computer manufacturers. Because the IBM PC had an open architecture, imitators found it easy to enter the sector. In this case, once there was a dominant design (the IBM PC and its PC-compatible imitators), the value turned out to lie in the

---

[6] Tesla has gone its own way, but on several models and in some markets, it offers connector adaptors for CCS and CHAdeMO. This is an example of the use of a gateway technology, as described later in the chapter.

operating system standard rather than the hardware, owing to the many network effects arising from software provision for the computer. See Box 8.5 for more on the evolution of the Microsoft–IBM operating system relationship.

Box 8.5 IBM's OS/2 versus MS Windows

This is an example of the power of network effects and also of openness. In an effort to free itself from its contracts with Microsoft for operating systems and in response to Microsoft's development of Windows 3.0, in 1991 IBM released OS/2. It was expressly tailored to IBM's PC, while Microsoft's Windows had a broader market in mind. In addition, Windows supported more device drivers than OS/2, although OS/2 was technically superior, being a 32-bit operating system, something not available from Microsoft until Windows 95.

By 2001, it was clear that Windows was the dominant operating system for PCs, and OS/2 development was discontinued by IBM, with support discontinued by 2006. It was licensed to third-party suppliers, as there remained a few niche users. In spite of support from a large incumbent firm with deep pockets, OS/2 failed to take off partly because there was a lack of complementary software applications and hardware, unlike the existing installed base of MS-DOS and then Windows.

The final type of research collaboration is the collective research organization. These can be organized by the industry itself or may be joint with government or university-provided research centers. They tend to arise in environments where there is a dominant design or common technology that is somewhat stable, or where the industry is a public utility so that concerns over IP are minimized. They also often target the basic end of industry research that has the largest spillovers and is the furthest from commercialization (so that value capture issues are less important). They may also be the result of targeted government or regulated utility policy, such as Sematech and the Electric Power Research Institute in the United States.

An example of a private collective research organization is the Interuniversity Microelectronics Centre (IMEC), founded in 1984 by the Flemish government with headquarters in Belgium, and offices in Taiwan, Japan, the United States, China, the Netherlands, and India. Although it concentrates on Flemish firms, IMEC has more than 600 industry partners around the world, each of which pays for access to the researchers at IMEC, which include many university researchers who are there for temporary assignments. Cassiman et al. (2018) describe the careful crafting of their IP policy, with basic platform technologies held by IMEC and other IP held by the individual firm that develops it. They also show that the most valuable patented inventions are produced by collaboration between inventors that have left IMEC (and are presumably academic in origin) and the firms with which they patented, suggesting the importance of tacit knowledge transfer generated by coworking on innovation.[7]

---

[7] Because of data limitations, value is measured as the number of forward citations to the relevant patent. Profits due to a patented invention have been shown to be related to its citations, but it is worth remembering that the relationship is fairly noisy and influenced by other factors.

8.5 Goods with Network Effects

What about a strategy for markets with network externalities, which have become increasingly important in the digital age? Static analysis of a market that potentially has network effects shows that these effects do not rise to the level of creating a network externality as discussed in Chapter 7. Assume a set of nonintegrated firms competitively supplying hardware and software. If customers are myopic, that is, they do not attempt to evaluate the future supply of software for their hardware choice, this is a normal market with complementary goods. One person's purchase decision has no effect on another person's welfare so there is no network externality. With sufficient competition among hardware and software suppliers, the market equilibrium will be first best.

In this type of market, if a monopolist supplies both hardware and software, there may be a DWL from the usual monopoly pricing. If there is consumer heterogeneity, for example, some consumers demand more software than others, the monopolist can use two-part pricing to extract more consumer surplus, which means lower DWL but with the monopolist capturing the increased surplus. There will still be no network externalities. For these to matter, we must move to a dynamic analysis where firms and consumers are forward-looking.

8.5.1 Dynamic Analysis

Dynamic analysis of this type of market changes everything. Now the adoption decision depends on expectations about other people's future decisions because the value of the system is determined by expected future software availability--therefore, there is a network externality where one person's demand increases if another person purchases the system. If firms and consumers are forward-looking, firms cannot commit to software prices in advance, and the consumers' expectations of ultimate network size will matter. This creates a link between the installed base of hardware and the variety of software available. The elasticity of demand for hardware will be increased by this positive network externality.

The consumer now has a two- (or multi-) period purchase decision: first hardware and then software, potentially over several future periods and of varying quantities across consumers. They choose hardware in the first period and are then "locked in" via the sunk costs they have expended. The quantity of hardware sold in the first period signals the future price of software because a larger hardware base implies lower marginal cost, lower price, and greater variety of software, given economies of scale in software. This linkage increases the elasticity of demand for hardware, and the result is an indirect network externality.

The conclusion is that network externalities in systems competition could lead to underutilization and delayed adoption in some situations if consumers fear lock-in and wait for the winning hardware to emerge. A subsidy to hardware buyers in the form of initially pricing below cost can increase welfare in this situation. Of course in other contexts, this would be predatory pricing, which is a controversial practice from the perspective of antitrust regulation (Bolton et al. 1999).

Ex post, such a market is subject to consumer lock-in, which can be reinforced via producer strategies. Lock-in can arise from familiarity with a particular hardware platform, which makes learning to use a new system costly. Incompatible software or even plug incompatibility can create lock-in whose cost varies from not much to a lot. For example, the survival of antiquated computer languages such as Cobol and Fortran in mission-critical applications is due to lock-in, primarily created by years of robustness testing due to use in practice. Conversion to new languages would create the risk of errors and unexpected consequences due to software changes. Lock-in also arises from the simple search costs of looking for and evaluating a new system. We discuss methods to increase or reduce lock-in in Section 8.6.

8.5.2 Competition among Systems

When standards are important to consumers, competing systems with different standards behave like network goods. As we saw in Chapter 7, when the market share of any one competing system gets large, there is an increasing returns effect from increased consumer demand due to preference for software variety that tends toward dominance by one system. This phenomenon leads to intense competition among systems manufacturers.

This has several implications for competition among network system suppliers. Success of any system is strongly influenced by consumers' adoption decisions, which depend on their expectations of which system will win. However, consumer heterogeneity of tastes will limit standardization. A good example of this is the survival of two main personal computer and, more recently, mobile telephony systems: one closed (Apple) and one open (Windows computers and Android phones).[8]

This survival is obviously partly attributable to consumer inertia, in the sense that once a system is being used, it is difficult to switch from one to the other. Initially, the Apple family of PCs was also preferred in some industry sectors such as graphic design. But the survival of the two systems is also due to differing customer tastes for flexibility in use and a willingness to interact with the details of software maintenance. A closed system greatly reduces the number of unexpected problems that can arise when new hardware or software is connected to it. As a consequence, such a system also limits the kinds of hardware and software that can be installed on the system to some extent.

In some situations, where customer demand for compatibility standards is strong enough, firms can coordinate to achieve compatibility. They may also choose to supply gateways such as file conversion methods or telecommunication gateways that facilitate communication among different systems.

---

[8] As of June 2023, Windows and OS X had over 90% of the PC operating system market worldwide. The remainder was held by Linux, Chrome OS, and others. The mobile telephony market was shared between Apple and Android, with over 99% between them. https://arstechnica.com/gadgets/2023/07/report-linux-desktops-hit-3-global-market-share-but-are-declining-in-us.

8.5.3 Game Theoretic Analysis

In order to highlight the potential results of standards or system competition, we analyze a simple two-player game between the producers of a network good that requires standards. We consider two different forms of the payoff matrix: one that leads to incompatibility and one that leads to compatibility.

In the incompatible game, the payoff matrices are such that choosing compatibility leads to lower payoffs for both players than incompatibility. This kind of situation could arise when consumer taste is sufficiently differentiated or lock-in is sufficiently strong so that when standards are incompatible, each producer is able to earn a higher markup. Compatible standards would limit their market power.

Table 8.3 shows a simple payoff matrix with the property described above. Each player has two action or strategy choices, which involve choosing Standard 1 or Standard 2, and there are different payoffs for each combination of choices. The table shows one version of a payoff matrix where Player (firm) 1 prefers Standard 1 and Player 2 prefers Standard 2, although both receive positive payoffs from choosing the other standard, too. For example, we might imagine that Player 1 has some technical advantage in producing goods with Standard 1, such as some R&D sunk costs in that direction or the ownership of some standard essential patents (SEPs).

Table 8.3 Sample Payoff Matrix (incompatibility)

Player 1	Player 2			
	Standard 1		Standard 2	
Standard 1	100	100	150	150
Standard 2	150	150	100	100

For the game in Table 8.3, there is no dominant strategy (see Box 8.6). If Player 1 chooses Standard 2, Player 2's best response is Standard 1. If Player 2 chooses Standard 1, Player 1's best response is Standard 2. So there are two Nash equilibria, both of which are incompatible standards: (1, 2) and (2, 1). An example of this might be messaging networks such as Apple, Facebook, and the like, especially in their early incarnations. As time passed, networks such as WhatsApp have grown relative to these partly because of their compatibility with multiple platforms.

Box 8.6 Game Theory Concepts

Dominant strategy: a strategic choice that is best regardless of what the other player does

Nash equilibrium: a combination of both players' strategies where neither player finds it beneficial to deviate on their own (given the other player's choice)

Table 8.4 shows a different situation where incompatibility is quite costly. In this case, if the firms choose incompatible standards, they both receive zero. This creates a

Table 8.4 Sample Payoff Matrix (compatibility)

Player 1	Player 2			
	Standard 1		Standard 2	
Standard 1	200	100	0	0
Standard 2	0	0	100	200

coordination game, where the best response depends on what the other player does and there is no dominant strategy. However, there are two possible Nash equilibria: (1, 1) and (2, 2).

Most communication networks such as the telephone, email, and fax are like this example. If the two firms choose different standards, customers of one firm cannot communicate with customers of the other firm, and demand for either system is greatly reduced (possibly not to zero in the real world).

To summarize, when there are competing standards, the outcome of competition between two competing standards (systems) depends on whether firms prefer incompatibility or compatibility. Incompatibility is more likely when firms are similar in size and market share, when the standards battle does not delay adoption too much, and when product differentiation gives each one some market power.

Compatibility is more likely when demand depends greatly on having a single standard, as in communications technology with direct network effects, and when a standards battle will dissipate too much in the way of profits.

8.6 Strategies for Network Competition

In the presence of network competition, there are a number of strategies available to firms for successful competition in this kind of market. We review some here under three headings: (1) how to induce new customers to adopt a standard or network; (2) how to create or reinforce lock-in of existing customers; and (3) how to enter a network competition and attract locked-in customers.

8.6.1 To Induce Adoption

The problem here is to override the customer's fear that they will choose a system that is later abandoned either by the current supplier or because a better incompatible system supersedes it. Firms have a number of strategies available by which they can signal to the consumers that they will not be stranded with a defunct network. For example, if the firm owns both hardware and software, the network effects are internalized and the hardware price can be lowered to induce purchase, although commitment to future software prices is difficult. Examples of this strategy are computer games such as Nintendo, Sega, and Atari.

A hardware-only firm can use penetration pricing for hardware with discounts to early adopters, or rent the hardware rather than selling it, which means that they, rather than their customers, suffer the loss if the system exits prematurely before the benefits to owning the hardware have been exhausted. This also protects the customer who may choose to abandon the system because of high software costs in the future.

The producer of a new system might signal its survival by means of its own reputation, advertising, and sunk costs of investment in the system. Many view IBM's successful entry into the production of PCs as critical to the early development of the industry. Prior to IBM's entry, most of the producers were small, producing a range of hardware with primitive operating systems. It is clear that having the IBM name on the PC attracted many corporate customers and ensured its survival.

Second sourcing is also an option that may help to reassure customers. For example, opening the market to independent software suppliers can attract users by committing to a lower price path for software. An extreme version of second sourcing in the computer industry is the use of OSS such as Linux.

During the early phase of its supplying microprocessors to the PC industry, notably to IBM, in 1982 Intel licensed AMD to produce the 8086 and X86 microprocessor to provide a second source for these chips. However, as the PC business and Intel's strength in the business grew, this agreement led ultimately to considerable litigation over the terms of the agreement between the two when the 386 microprocessor was introduced after Intel terminated the agreement in 1987. Ultimately, AMD prevailed in this suit.

8.6.2 To Create Lock-In

Methods by which a producer can create additional lock-in by increasing switching costs include contracts for service or parts, as in the case of equipment for the use of mobile telephone networks ("locked" phones).

Another method of increasing switching costs often used by both hardware and software producers is the cost of data conversion. By using proprietary formats that are costly or difficult to translate, it is possible to discourage customers from switching to a new medium. In the case of physical networks such as audio, video, and gaming systems, lock-in is easy to create via incompatible form factors for the "software."

Loyalty and preferred customer programs are very widely used in settings where switching is otherwise cheap, such as retail shopping or travel service suppliers. Such programs tend to increase their awards in a nonlinear way as a customer's usage grows, which ensures that the customer has stronger incentives to continue to purchase from the supplier, and also means that the more valuable customers (those who purchase more) are more strongly incentivized.

8.6.3 To Break Lock-In

Many of the strategies used to encourage adoption of a new system are useful also for entry of a new system where some lock-in of customers to the old system already exists. For example, if there are enough new customers, they will ignore the negative externality on old customers of their decision to choose a new (incompatible) standard.

Firms attempting to establish new standards could offer rebates to buyers turning in old equipment or competitive upgrades for software. They might also offer free training in the new standard or system. A strategy pursued by almost all cable, telephone service, and internet service firms is to offer the first year or two at a much lower price to attract users from other systems. This strategy attempts to overcome consumer inertia as well as compensate them for switching costs.

An important method for ensuring that a new otherwise incompatible technology can interact with an older technology is the provision of a *gateway technology*. Many of us are familiar with the use of electrical conversion plugs that allow our electronic systems to plug in and operate where the sockets in the wall provide different voltages and are also shaped differently. On the software side, there are a number of programs providing file format conversions from one standard to another. Apple even provides a way to install Windows on an Apple Mac computer, allowing the use of otherwise incompatible Windows software on a Mac.[9] For e-readers, software services such as Calibre can convert books from one format to another.

Gateway technologies are now widespread on networks. For example, home WiFi networks with multiple systems from different manufacturers (computers, printers, audio, phones, etc.) use gateway technology to allow them all to communicate. The same type of system can be used by IoT (internet of things), which prevents some lock-in, although this still seems to be an evolving area. This is typical of technology evolution in the area of digital innovations. They frequently begin with proprietary formats and interfaces, and ultimately transition to functioning with gateway technologies if they are successful, simply because there is market demand for innovation in gateways when a product is widely used. See the Tesla charging example described earlier.

8.7 Summary

The goal of firm-level innovation is usually value creation and its capture. This is easily stated but difficult to achieve in light of the uncertainty that surrounds innovative activity and the appropriation of its returns. Thinking about strategy involves understanding where the industry is in its life cycle, and will depend on whether a firm is a startup, young, or established.

Established firms that wish to survive and remain innovative will need to learn to adapt to radical and architectural inventions and to understand their implications for the organization of their own research. They will already possess a number of assets that will help them capture returns to their innovation, and identifying those that are hard to replicate will be important.

Startups, in particular, will look to formal IP protection and the development of complementary assets to go along with their innovations if they wish to capture their value.

Different technologies may favor different market structures. When large amounts of investment that is very specific to a particular innovation are to be undertaken, such may be best done in-house, rather than contracted out, to avoid opportunistic behavior.

---

[9] https://support.apple.com/en-us/HT201468.

Industries using technologies that are well protected by patents and other formal means will find it feasible to vertically disintegrate, with firms specializing at different stages of the value chain. Temporary technology-based collaborations are widespread, especially in high-technology industries where speed is of the essence, compatibility standards are important, and no single firm has the expertise to undertake all the needed pieces of the innovation.

Platform technologies introduce new questions for the innovating firm: What level of compatibility with other platforms is appropriate, and how should they ensure that their platform survives? Here, the heterogeneity of customer demand and the desire of customers to communicate with others on the system will matter. If customers are very heterogeneous, differentiation may provide market power to the owners of incompatible systems. If the desire for communication (direct or indirect via common software demands) is great, compatibility will be the outcome.

9

Innovation and Economic Growth

Learning Objectives

After reading this chapter, you will be able to understand and explain the following concepts:

- The basic Solow-Swan economic growth model
- Modern growth models that allow for changes in knowledge over time
- Total factor productivity (TFP) decomposition and growth accounting
- The empirical measurement of knowledge spillovers
- The empirical measurement of social returns to innovation
- R&D in the national income accounts (NIA)

9.1 Introduction

Ultimately, the goal of innovative activity is to increase the standard of living and welfare of society. Economists therefore have had a long-term interest in the relationship between innovation and economic growth. This interest was reinforced by the discovery that when one tried to explain US output growth during the first half of the 20th century using the growth of capital and labor inputs, most of the growth remained unexplained and was conjectured to be the result of technical change (Solow 1957).

In this chapter, we present and review the various growth models that have been developed since the publication of Solow's article, with an emphasis on those that incorporate the roles of human capital and knowledge in development. These models include the original model of Solow, as well as the endogenous growth models of P. Romer, Jones, and Aghion and Howitt. Given the relatively complex mathematics of some of these models, our emphasis is on their assumptions and conclusions rather than detailed derivations.

The basic growth model serves as a guide both for estimating the productivity of R&D and for the inclusion of R&D and other intangible investments in the national income accounts (NIA), a recent innovation at a number of government statistical agencies. This follows from the increasing evidence of the importance of R&D and knowledge capital in modern economies that we saw in Chapter 6. We therefore spend some time reviewing the results from the inclusion of intangible capital in our measures of capital.

Growth models also highlight the importance of R&D spillovers or externalities, so we look at methods for the measurement of spillovers. We review the empirical

The Economics of Innovation and Intellectual Property. Bronwyn H. Hall and Christian Helmers, Oxford University Press.
© Oxford University Press 2024. DOI: 10.1093/oso/9780197630914.003.0009

literature, both case study and econometric, and also discuss how growth models can be a guide to the estimation of the social returns to R&D and innovation.

9.2 The Basic Growth Model

Interest in the empirical economics of technical change and innovation can probably be traced back to the seminal work of Solow, Abramovitz, and Swan, who developed and estimated the first models of economic growth along with the necessary data for its estimation. In this section, we present Solow's (1957) version of the model and discuss the results of its estimation using historical US data. The ideas here form the basis for modern growth accounting and are easier to see in a simple model.

9.2.1 Solow-Swan Growth Model

This model of economic growth was developed independently by Robert Solow (1957) and Trevor Swan (1956). We follow Solow's presentation of the model. He posited an aggregate production function, using the simplest Cobb-Douglas form with constant returns to scale. There are only two inputs, capital and labor, that combine to produce output:

$$Y = F(K,L) = AK^{\alpha}L^{1-\alpha}$$

A is a scale factor that converts capital and labor into output; later on, A will be identified with technical change or innovation so that it grows over time and more output is produced for the same levels of capital and labor. The model imposes constant returns to scale because the sum of the input coefficients α and $1 - \alpha$ is equal to 1.

Assume profit maximization with respect to K and L given the relative real wage w and the real return to capital r. The first-order conditions are given below:

$$\max_{K,L} F(K,L) - rK - wL$$

$$w = \frac{\partial F}{\partial L} = (1-\alpha)\frac{Y}{L}$$

$$r = \frac{\partial F}{\partial K} = \alpha\frac{Y}{K}$$

At the solution, α is equal to capital's share rK/Y and $(1 - \alpha)$ is equal to labor's share wL/Y. Note also that α and $1 - \alpha$ correspond to elasticities of output with respect to capital and labor, respectively:

$$\alpha = \frac{K}{Y}\frac{\partial F}{\partial K}$$

$$1-\alpha = \frac{L}{Y}\frac{\partial F}{\partial L}$$

Another implication of this constant returns framework is that there are zero profits at the maximized profits solution since capital and labor account for all the revenue:

$$Y = wL + rK = (1-\alpha)\frac{Y}{L}L + \alpha\frac{Y}{K}K = (1-\alpha)Y + \alpha Y$$

From the perspective of innovation economics, the scale factor A in the production function is the key point of analysis in many of the models that follow this one. A is generally assumed to grow over time, meaning that aggregate output is growing relative to aggregate capital and labor.

Solow used this model to derive the implications for growth with a few simple assumptions:

- A constant savings rate over time s
- A constant depreciation rate δ of capital K
- Constant population and labor growth equal to n
- A closed economy (no trade or investment in or out of the country)

Given these assumptions, net investment (the change in capital stock) is equal to savings less depreciation of existing capital:

$$\frac{dK}{dt} \equiv \dot{K} = sY - \delta K$$

The next step is to redefine labor to incorporate A, so in effect we are assuming that the growth in productive efficiency over time is a growth in the effectiveness of labor:

$$A = \tilde{A}^{1-\alpha}$$
$$Y = K^{\alpha}(\tilde{A}L)^{1-\alpha}$$

Following Mankiw et al. (1992), we add an exogenous growth in A (technical efficiency or productivity) of g_A. Thus, $\tilde{A}L$ has growth rate $n + g_A$.

We make the following notational definition:

$$\frac{\dot{X}}{X} = \frac{1}{X}\frac{dX}{dt} = \frac{d\log X}{dt} \cong g_X, \text{ the growth rate of X at time t}$$

where X stands for any variable. Also define k as the effective capital-labor ratio $K/\tilde{A}L$. Then the equilibrium growth in capital and output per effective labor can be derived as follows:

$$\frac{\dot{k}}{k} = \frac{\dot{K}}{K} - \frac{\dot{L}}{L} - \frac{\dot{\tilde{A}}}{\tilde{A}} = \frac{sY - \delta K}{K} - n - g_A$$
$$= s\frac{Y}{K} - \delta - n - g_A$$
$$\Rightarrow \dot{k} = sy - (\delta + n + g_A)k$$
$$\text{Also } \frac{\dot{y}}{y} = \frac{1}{\alpha}\left[s\frac{Y}{K} - (\delta + n + g_A)\right]$$

where $y = Y / \tilde{A}L$ is the effective output-labor ratio or labor productivity. We draw two conclusions from this simple model:

- The growth in the capital-labor ratio depends positively on the savings rate and negatively on depreciation, labor growth, and the current capital-labor ratio.
- The growth in output per labor (labor productivity) depends positively on the savings rate and the output-capital ratio, and negatively on depreciation and labor growth. Other things equal, growth is lower when the capital share is higher.

Assuming a developing economy with relatively low capital, labor productivity growth will decline as the capital-labor ratio grows, until a steady state is reached. Because $y = k^\alpha$, the equations for the steady state can be derived from the equation for the rate of change of the capital-effective labor ratio:

$$\dot{k} = sy - (\delta + n + g_A)k = sk^\alpha - (\delta + n + g_A)k$$

Setting the rate of change of the effective capital-labor ratio to zero, we can derive the equilibrium value of capital and output per worker:

$$k^* = \left(\frac{s}{\delta + n + g_A} \right)^{1/(1-\alpha)}$$

$$y^* = \left(\frac{s}{\delta + n + g_A} \right)^{\alpha/(1-\alpha)}$$

Because $0 < \alpha < 1$, in both cases the superscripts are positive. The central prediction of the Solow-Swan growth model is that the equilibrium capital-labor ratio and labor productivity are higher when the savings rate is higher and lower when depreciation and labor growth are higher. The model also predicts diminishing returns to both capital and labor inputs and that labor productivity growth depends only on exogenous population growth n and exogenous technical change g_A.

9.2.2 Empirical Growth Accounting

The importance of the basic Solow-Swan model derives from its ability to define a framework for growth analysis and to identify empirical puzzles via deviations from its predictions. Across countries, the main predictions are the long-run convergence to the same productivity levels conditional on population growth, capital depreciation, and the savings rate. In addition and assuming that capital intensity is below its equilibrium level, there should be a positive relationship between savings rate and growth of output per capita, and a negative one between population growth and growth of output per capita, looking across countries. But from our innovation perspective here, the most important implication of the framework is the role of the efficiency term A.

The first test of this model used US growth accounting data and identified the importance of changes in A in explaining the data. Solow used a growth accounting approach that was based on his model to estimate A, which he labeled technical change. We present this approach here, as it is the basis for growth accounting measures used until the present day.

Begin with the aggregate production function presented above but without the Cobb-Douglas functional form assumption. We index by time t to represent the changes over time. As before, efficiency or technical progress is represented by $A(t)$ and there are two inputs, capital $K(t)$ and labor $L(t)$:[1]

$$Y(t) = A(t) F\big[K(t), L(t)\big]$$

$Y(t)$ is aggregate output (GDP) in year t. Labor $L(t)$ is measured in person-hours or number of workers. We will compute the growth of output over time as a function of the growth of labor and capital by differentiating this expression.

Differentiate output $Y(t)$ with respect to time t, using the chain rule:

$$\frac{dY}{dt} = \frac{dA}{dt} F[K(t), L(t)] + A(t) \frac{dF[K(t), L(t)]}{dt}$$

$$\frac{dY}{dt} = \frac{dA}{dt} \frac{Y(t)}{A(t)} + \frac{Y(t)}{F[K,L]} \left(\frac{dF(K,L)}{dK} \frac{dK}{dt} + \frac{dF(K,L)}{dL} \frac{dL}{dt} \right)$$

In order to express this in terms of the growth rates, we divide by $Y(t)$ and we multiply the second term by K/K (=1) and the third term by L/L (=1):

$$\frac{1}{Y} \frac{dY}{dt} = \frac{dA}{dt} \frac{1}{A(t)} + \frac{K(t)}{F(K,L)} \frac{dF(K,L)}{dK} \frac{1}{K(t)} \frac{dK}{dt}$$
$$+ \frac{L(t)}{F(K,L)} \frac{dF(K,L)}{dL} \frac{1}{L(t)} \frac{dL}{dt}$$

Then substituting growth rates g for the logarithmic derivatives $(1/X)(dX/dt)$ (see Appendix A: Mathematics and Statistics for an explanation of why this is allowed), we obtain

$$g_Y = g_A + \frac{K(t)}{F(K,L)} \frac{dF(K,L)}{dK} g_K + \frac{L(t)}{F(K,L)} \frac{dF(K,L)}{dL} g_L$$

As we indicated earlier, the quantities multiplying g_K and g_L are elasticities of output with respect to the two inputs, denoted by ε:

$$g_Y = g_A + \varepsilon_K g_K + \varepsilon_L g_L$$

For example, ε_K measures the percent increase in output when capital increases by 1%, holding labor input and technical change A constant (see Box 9.1). Therefore, output growth can be expressed as the (approximate) sum of productivity growth (technical change) and the growth of inputs, weighted by their elasticities in the production function.

Here is an example from Solow (1957). The data he used were the aggregate US time series for capital stock, the share of capital income in income, and private nonfarm Gross national product (GNP) per man-hour with an adjustment for capital and labor utilization.[2] He specialized the model to a Cobb-Douglas production function and assumed

---

[1] Note that this version of the model does not confine A to be efficiency of labor, but restores it to be a multiplier of the production function.

[2] During this time period, the difference between GNP and GDP, excluding overseas production and including domestic production by foreigners, was small and it was customary to use GNP as a measure of output, unlike the present day, when GDP is more commonly used. We use his term for labor input, although, of course, now we refer to this as person-hours rather than man-hours.

Box 9.1 Elasticity

The elasticity ε of Y with respect to X is defined by

$$\varepsilon_X = \frac{d\log Y}{d\log X} = \frac{X}{Y}\frac{dY}{dX} = \frac{dY/Y}{dX/X}$$

It is approximately equal to the percent increase in Y associated with a percent increase in X, holding all other variables constant.

---

the constant returns to scale. Recall that a Cobb-Douglas production function with constant returns has elasticities α and $1 - \alpha$ that are equal to the share of capital and labor in output, so we can write the growth in productivity or technical change as the following, where r and w are the prices of capital and labor measured relative to the price of output:

$$g_A = g_Y - \frac{rK}{Y}g_K - \frac{wL}{Y}g_L \tag{1}$$

A typical computation using data averaged over the 1909–1949 time period is shown below:

$$
\begin{aligned}
g_A &= g_Y - \frac{rK}{Y}g_K - \frac{wL}{Y}g_L \\
g_A &= 2.72\% - 0.34 \cdot 1.53\% - 0.66 \cdot 1.00\% \\
&= 2.72\% - 0.52\% - 0.66\% \\
&= 1.54\%
\end{aligned}
$$

The conclusion Solow reached and this computation shows is that more than half of output growth (= 2.72%) is not explained by growth in capital and labor inputs (= 1.18%). This quantity (g_A) is often called the *residual* or *total factor productivity growth*. A similar conclusion using somewhat different data and a longer time period was reached by Abramovitz (1956).

Figure 9.1 shows that the index A derived by Solow came close to doubling in the 40 years between 1909 and 1949. During this period, average productivity growth was 1.7% per annum. We will return to the question of where this growth came from later in the chapter.

9.3 Modern Growth theory

Beginning with Arrow (1962b), a long series of papers have suggested modifications to the Solow growth model that incorporate the idea that A is not an unknown exogenous productivity level, but is generated by changes in the knowledge and human capital in the economy. In parallel, a number of empirical researchers approached the problem by improving the measures of both labor and capital to reflect quality change and to incorporate conscious investments in technical change on the part of individual firms. We will discuss their efforts in Section 9.4 of this chapter.

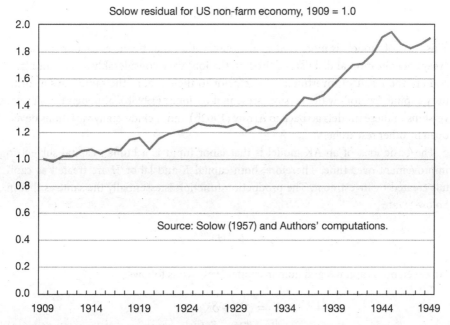

Figure 9.1 Solow's estimated A for the US nonfarm economy.

As we saw in the previous section, one of the implications of the simple Solow-Swan growth model that incorporates savings is that the capital-output ratio and labor productivity converge to a steady state that is a function of depreciation, savings, population growth, and exogenous productivity growth, the so-called balanced growth path, where capital, labor, and output grow in lockstep with each other. Many researchers pointed out that elements of this picture are contradicted by the evidence. For example, Mankiw, D. Romer, and Weil (1992) argue that when countries are compared, their data display too high a labor productivity response to savings and population growth, implying omission of a key variable, which they suggest is human capital, the knowledge and skills of the workers in the country.

In this section, we review the models that incorporate increases in the level of an economy's knowledge in an attempt to produce more realistic versions of economic growth. We focus first on the models that incorporate investments in human capital, sometimes called AK models, and then we present the full-blown endogenous growth models.

One note on our presentation: Most of these models are full GE models. They are closed by including an equation for the intertemporal utility of consumption that includes a rate of time preference and from which the savings/investment rate can be derived. That is, maximization of the utility of consumption tells the model how to trade off current production/consumption for future production/consumption and therefore investment to ensure that future. In our presentation here, we largely ignore this part of the model to keep things simple, but any welfare conclusions will rely partly on what the researchers have assumed about consumption preferences.

9.3.1 AK Models

This class of models is motivated by the observation that the levels of human capital (years of education and skills acquired on the job) vary considerably across countries and are the result of investments made prior to their use, in the same ways as ordinary capital. We follow the version presented by Jones (1995b), although the simpler versions of these models go back to Arrow (1962b) and include many variations developed by other researchers.

The basic idea of an AK model is that labor input is a human capital subject to improvement over time. Therefore, both capital K and labor H are treated as capitals created by investment. The production function is essentially the same as that in Solow-Swan:

$$Y_t = AK_t^\alpha H_t^{1-\alpha}$$

However, both capital K and human capital H evolve as follows:

$$\dot{K}_t = i_t^k Y_t - \delta K_t$$
$$\dot{H}_t = i_t^h Y_t - \delta H_t$$

where the i_t's are gross investment rates in capital and human capital; depreciation is assumed to be the same for both.

Jones closes this model with an equation for intertemporal consumption preferences and shows that capital and human capital will accumulate at the same rate in this simple model and that the equilibrium ratio of the two will take the following form:

$$\psi = \frac{H}{K} = \frac{(1-\alpha)}{\alpha}$$

Therefore, the production function can be written as a function of capital only, which is why this class of models is called AK:

$$Y_t = \tilde{A}K_t$$
$$\text{with } \tilde{A} = A\psi^{1-\alpha}$$

He then goes on to derive the steady-state growth rate of output, which turns out to be a simple linear (affine) function of the investment rate i^k for physical capital:[3]

$$g_Y = -\delta + \tilde{A}i^k$$

Because growth rates in most Organization for Economic Cooperation and Development (OECD) economies since 1950 fluctuate without a general increasing tendency, while investment rates in several countries grew at least until about 1990, Jones rejects the AK model as a poor representation of the growth process. This is perhaps not surprising

---

[3] He shows that H/K is always equal to $(1 - \alpha)/\alpha$ in the absence of adjustment costs so that the investment rate for human capital is determined by that for physical capital.

given the strong assumptions used to generate the growth equation. A second problem with this model is that unlike the Solow-Swan model, it predicts constant returns to capital accumulation rather than diminishing returns. As the next model shows (along with many others), diminishing returns to capital are more usually supported empirically.

9.3.2 The MRW Model

Mankiw, Romer, and Weil (1992) took a slightly different approach to incorporating human capital into the production function model, adding a separate human capital term to the version of the Solow-Swan model that we presented in Section 9.2.1 in addition to the AL term describing "effective" labor input. As in the AK model, they assumed capital and human capital evolved similarly as a function of investment, but with constant gross investment rates s_k and s_h rather than time-varying:

$$Y_t = K_t^\alpha H_t^\beta (A_t L_t)^{1-\alpha-\beta}$$
$$\dot{k}_t = s_k y_t - (n+g+\delta)k_t$$
$$\dot{h}_t = s_h y_t - (n+g+\delta)h_t$$

where once again, we have normalized the capitals and output by effective labor: $y = Y/AL$, $k = K/AL$, and $h = H/AL$. This model contains both exogenous evolution of productivity (via the growth g in A), as well as endogenous growth in knowledge and skills that is spread across the economy. It converges to a steady state in a similar way as the original Solow-Swan model and yields an empirical expression for labor productivity that can be taken to the data:

$$\log(Y_t / L_t) = \log A_0 + gt - \frac{\alpha+\beta}{1-\alpha-\beta}\log(n+g+\delta)$$
$$+\frac{\alpha}{1-\alpha-\beta}\log s_k + \frac{\beta}{1-\alpha-\beta}\log s_h$$

Note that unlike the Solow empirics described in Section 9.2.2, here the functions of α and β will be treated as unknown parameters to be estimated, rather than derived from factor shares.

In the empirical work, Mankiw et al. proxy the capital investment rate s_k by the investment-GDP ratio and the human capital investment rate s_h by the share of the population in secondary school. n is the rate of growth of the working age population, and $g + \delta$ is simply set to 0.05.[4] The resulting estimates show that the omission of human capital in the original model did bias coefficients upward, and that adding even their admittedly poorly measured proxy corrects this bias and yields reasonable results. The estimated capital and human capital shares (α and β) are both around 0.3, leaving 0.4 for labor. Constant returns in all three inputs are accepted, which implies diminishing returns to the two capitals.

---

[4] They report that estimates are not sensitive to this choice.

Note that in this model human capital is not proportional to the number of workers, but can be viewed as a general level of knowledge in the economy. There is nothing requiring it to be embodied in workers; it could instead be interpreted as the knowledge capital that is the output of R&D as in the endogenous growth models we consider next. In the empirical exercise, H is proxied by the level of secondary education in the economy, but the correlation of various education measures with R&D intensity across countries is typically above 0.5, so distinguishing the human capital measure from a measure based on R&D spending would be difficult.

9.3.3 Endogenous Growth Models

Dissatisfaction with the failure of existing models to fully incorporate the role of innovation and R&D in economic growth led a number of researchers to develop models of growth that included features intended to capture the idea that the conscious activities of firms generate growth via their investments in innovation. Hence, the name *endogenous*, or "generated within the system, having an internal cause," has been given to these models. The main endogenous growth models are those of P. Romer (1990), Aghion and Howitt (1992), and Grossman and Helpman (1991, 1994).

The key insight in these models, discussed at length in P. Romer (1990), is that knowledge relevant for innovation is both nonrival and partially excludable, as we discussed in Chapter 2 and elsewhere. That is, firms generating such knowledge will have an advantage over others because they can partially exclude or delay their use, but will not capture the full benefit to society of its creation. The impact of these insights is two-fold. First, when undertaking innovation, firms will need some rents or profits to pay the cost of innovation, leading to imperfect rather than perfect competition, a more realistic assumption. Second, at the aggregate level, the social returns to innovative activity by firms may exhibit increasing returns, even if each firm faces diminishing returns. This increasing returns characteristic is the central difference from the traditional growth models such as Solow-Swan.

Because of the addition of firms earning some monopoly profits, these models are more complex than the preceding, as they require an intermediate sector producing goods under imperfect competition and selling them to the final output sector that produces goods for consumption. Innovation is performed in different ways in the three models (Romer, Aghion-Howitt, Grossman-Helpman) but with generally the same impact on aggregate growth:

- *Romer.* Individuals produce new designs, sell to intermediate goods firms which produce using them, these firms sell above marginal cost, and their quasi-rents cover the cost of purchasing the designs. There is entry until profits are zero.
- *Aghion-Howitt.* There are a sequence of innovations, each of which improves on the previous (a quality ladder), and whose provision is determined by comparing the cost of raising the expected probability of an improvement to the wage. Each innovation will earn rents until it is displaced by an improved product, which is a way of incorporating creative destruction.
- *Grossman-Helpman.* At various times, these scholars have used versions of both of the above, calling them variety expansion and quality expansion, and showing that the results are similar, although the welfare implications are different.

In general, the mathematical development of these models is beyond the scope of this textbook, but we will present a very simple version due to Jones (1995a) here. As in most of these models, labor has two components L_Y and L_A with total labor $L = L_A + L_Y$. L_Y is labor used in production and L_A is labor used in knowledge production (usually considered more highly skilled than L_Y). In this simple version, total labor grows exogenously at a rate n. The key feature of the model is the equation for knowledge accumulation where the rate of increase depends on the current level of knowledge A and the number of skilled workers L_A generating new knowledge:

$$\dot{A} = \gamma A^{\phi} L_A^{\lambda} \quad \text{with } 0 < \lambda \leq 1$$

The parameter ϕ is interpreted as introducing research externalities or spillovers into the model. When it is less than zero, research productivity declines over time, sometimes referred to as *fishing out*. When ϕ is zero, the current level of knowledge has no impact on research productivity, and when ϕ is greater than zero, we have increasing returns in research. The parameter λ is less than 1 when there is duplicative R&D (racing behavior) in the economy or when some of the R&D workers are less productive or skilled than others.

Most of the endogenous growth models have assumed that ϕ and λ are both equal to 1. However, both Jones (1995a) and Solow (1997) have argued that assumptions of this kind lead to a solution of the model that is not very sensible, as it implies growth without bound when incorporated into the full model. That is, a central problem of the basic endogenous growth models is that they imply that an increase in the level of resources devoted to R&D should lead to a permanent increase in the *growth rate* of the economy, something that is strongly contradicted by the evidence.[5]

Jones shows that if we assume that $\phi < 1$, the model yields a balanced growth path where knowledge, output per worker, capital services per worker, and the capital-labor ratio all grow at rate g given by the following:

$$g = \frac{\lambda n}{1 - \phi}$$

which implies that growth is proportional to labor input (or population) growth with a proportionality constant given by the characteristics of the knowledge production function. If the knowledge accumulation function exhibits higher spillovers (higher ϕ), growth will be higher. If there are greater diminishing returns to R&D labor (lower λ), growth will be lower. Note that there is no balanced growth path for $\phi \geq 1$.

One of the interesting results that Jones generates from this simple model is that a decentralized economy with this structure will tend to underinvest in R&D relative to the social optimum, given the presence of potential externalities ($\phi > 0$).[6]

---

[5] For example, see Bloom et al. (2020) for evidence that research resources have grown while research productivity has fallen.

[6] Identification of ϕ with externalities is not obvious from our simple presentation. The full model has many individual firms each conducting R&D according to their own profit maximization and adding to the pool A. Hence, A implicitly incorporates knowledge that is freely available to all firms.

9.4 Explaining the Growth in
Total Factor Productivity

In this section, we consider the measurement of growth and its components. Solow's finding that most of the US output growth during the first half of the 20th century was not explained by growth in capital and labor led to a great deal of empirical work that tried to explain this result, first by improving the measures of capital and labor to incorporate quality change, and then by asking whether including measures of disembodied knowledge capital could increase explanatory power.

We first describe the empirical approach to measuring the sources of productivity growth that is based on data in the systems of national accounts, in Section 9.4.1. Then we discuss the problem of relating productivity to investments in R&D and innovation at the aggregate level.

9.4.1 Sources of Growth

The pioneers in the empirical and econometric sources of growth literature were Jorgenson, Griliches, and Denison. An influential paper by Jorgenson and Griliches (1967) laid out the measurement challenges using the framework and data from the US NIA. Their work built on Solow's finding that the growth in factor inputs explained less than half of the growth in output of the US economy during 1909–1949. They took a more careful look at how to measure both real output and real input using the data commonly available from NIAs.[7]

Jorgenson and Griliches considered the case of many outputs and many inputs and began with the accounting identity implicit in NIAs. Define Y_i as the quantity of the ith output and X_j as the quantity of the jth input. q_i and p_j are the corresponding prices. Then the following is the fundamental accounting identity:

$$q_1 Y_1 + q_2 Y_2 + q_3 Y_3 + ... = p_1 X_1 + p_2 X_2 + p_3 X_3 + ...$$

$$\text{or} \sum_{i=1}^{N} q_i Y_i = \sum_{j=1}^{M} p_j X_j$$

For example, Y_1 might be food products, Y_2 an index of apparel, Y_3 autos, and so forth. The X_i are various types of capital and labor input with different skills levels.

TFP growth is obtained by differentiating this identity with respect to time and dividing each side by the total values. For example, total output growth can be written as follows:

---

[7] Their work and subsequent work by Jorgenson and coauthors have had a considerable impact on how these accounts are constructed and measured in many countries. A full discussion of this topic is beyond the scope of this textbook. For the early history of NIAs, see Kendrick (1970). Present-day NIAs for many developed economies can be obtained at stats.oecd.org. For the US NIPA, see https://www.bea.gov/resources/methodologies.

$$\frac{d}{dt}\sum_{i=1}^{N}q_iY_i = \sum_{i=1}^{N}\left(\dot{q}_iY_i + q_i\dot{Y}_i\right) = \sum_{i=1}^{N}\left(\frac{\dot{q}_iY_i + q_i\dot{Y}_i}{\sum q_iY_i}\right)$$

$$= \sum_{i=1}^{N}\left(\frac{\dot{q}_iY_i}{\sum q_iY_i}\frac{q_iY_i}{q_iY_i} + \frac{q_i\dot{Y}_i}{\sum q_iY_i}\frac{q_iY_i}{q_iY_i}\right) = \sum_{i=1}^{N}w_i\frac{\dot{q}_i}{q_i} + \sum_{i=1}^{N}w_i\frac{\dot{Y}_i}{Y_i}$$

where the weight w_i is the relative share of the ith output in total output:

$$w_i = \frac{q_iY_i}{\sum q_iY_i}$$

Thus, total output growth is the sum of two indices: one for its quantity and the second for the price:

$$\frac{\dot{Y}}{Y} = \sum_{i=1}^{N}w_i\frac{\dot{Y}_i}{Y_i} \quad \text{and} \quad \frac{\dot{q}}{q} = \sum_{i=1}^{N}w_i\frac{\dot{q}_i}{q_i}$$

Similar computations can be done for the input factors X_i. Formulas of this type are sometimes referred to as *Divisia* or *Tornquist indices* after their creators (see Appendix A: Mathematics and Statistics).

With these equations in hand, we can define productivity as the ratio of real output to real input, suitably aggregated: $P = Y/X$. Therefore, productivity growth is defined by the usual time derivative of this quantity:

$$TFP = \frac{\dot{P}}{P} = \frac{\dot{Y}}{Y} - \frac{\dot{X}}{X}$$

Now let's simplify the problem so it looks like the growth accounting that Solow did, keeping in mind that the general framework tells us how to proceed if we wish to add additional factors or break down one of the factors into its constituent parts. But for now we identify Y (real output) with real private GDP from the NIAs.[8] Both the quantity and the price (the implicit deflator) have been constructed using formulas like those above from a wide range of outputs of the economy.

Thus, equation (1) becomes

$$TFP = \frac{\dot{Y}}{Y} - \frac{rK}{Y}\frac{\dot{K}}{K} - \frac{wL}{Y}\frac{\dot{L}}{L}$$

where K and L are both real quantity measures. One important complication that we have ignored until now is that the appropriate concept for capital in the production function is *capital services* that essentially is capital times its rental price for the period, with adjustments for depreciation and utilization.[9]

Suppose there are a number N of capital inputs K indexed by i. These inputs may be of different types, for example, computers, mobile phones, autos, and they may be of the

---

[8] This quantity excludes government output and output produced in the rest of the world by US entities.
[9] Solow's computations shown in Figure 1 did adjust capital for utilization, although he included the stock rather than a flow of capital services in his computations.

same type but with different vintages, which may be of different quality and therefore priced differently. One example might be new and used trucks of the same model, which clearly will have different prices depending on their age. Or think about comparing different vintages of computer or mobile telephones, all of which may be useful in production, but that clearly are of differing quality, depending on their age.

Each type of capital is created by investment I^i and depreciates at the rate δ_i.[10] Then the quantity K^i and price p^i of each capital are given by the following equations:

$$K^i_{t+1} = (1 - \delta_i)K^i_t + I^i_t$$
$$p^i_t = q^i_t \left(r + \delta_i - \frac{\dot{q}^i_t}{q^i_t} \right)$$

where r is the interest rate, the required net rate of return to capital. To create the capital aggregate, these individual capitals are aggregated using the Divisia index formula from above:

$$\frac{\dot{K}_t}{K_t} = \sum_{i=1}^{N} w_i \frac{\dot{K}^i_t}{K^i_t}$$

where the weights are once again the share of the implicit rental value for each capital, which is equal to $p^i K^i / pK$. For labor input, a similar procedure needs to be followed, but things are simpler because the prices are directly measured via wages for different types of labor.

A second issue in measuring the inputs to productivity is the proper measure of utilization of both capital and labor. Idle machines or reserve employees do not contribute directly to current output. They may still be productive in the sense that they reduce future adjustment or hiring costs. One possible solution is to use indices of power usage over time to proxy for utilization of capital. For labor, it is common to obtain actual person-hours instead of the number of employed persons.

Jorgenson and Griliches (1967, 1972) applied this methodology to US productivity measurement for the 1950–1962 period and showed that measuring labor, capital, and output more carefully reduced the unexplained residual TFP from 1.96 to 1.03%.[11] The most important changes were due to measuring utilization and the use of capital services rather than capital stock.

More recently, both Jorgenson et al. (2008) and Byrne et al. (2013) have used the sources of growth methodology to analyze the contribution of a major set of innovations to the US economy, namely, innovation in information and communication technology. The contribution of these innovations comes both through their impact on improvements in capital equipment and also via the contribution of the producing sectors to multifactor productivity (MFP).[12] Table 9.1, reproduced from Byrne et al.,

---

[10]   For capitals of different vintages, investment outside that vintage year will be zero, of course.

[11]   These numbers come from the 1972 version of Jorgenson and Griliches's computations, which was a response to Denison's (1972) critique of their methods.

[12]   MFP is productivity measured after taking account of multiple inputs, so it is essentially the same as TFP.

Table 9.1 Contributions to the Growth of Labor Productivity in the US Nonfarm Business Sector

	1974–1995	1995–2004	2004–2012
Growth of labor productivity*	1.56	3.06	1.56
Capital deepening	.74	1.22	.74
IT capital	.41	.78	.36
Computer hardware	.18	.38	.12
Software	.16	.27	.16
Communication equipment	.07	.13	.08
Other capital	.33	.44	.38
Labor composition	.26	.22	.34
MFP	.56	1.62	.48
Adjustment costs	.07	.07	−.02
Utilization adjustment	−.01	−.06	.16
MFP after adjustments	.50	1.61	.34
IT-producing sectors	.36	.72	.28
Semiconductors	.09	.37	.14
Computer hardware	.17	.17	.04
Software	.06	.10	.08
Communication equipment	.05	.07	.02
Other nonfarm business	.13	.90	.06
Total IT contribution = IT capital plus IT-producing sectors	.77	1.50	.64

Source: Byrne et al. (2013).
*Measured as 100 times the average annual log difference for the indicated years.

shows the contributions of various measurement and IT components to both labor productivity and MFP.

Labor productivity growth is the growth of output per hours worked (growth in Y/L). Labor composition is essentially the improvement in the human capital of labor H/L due to education and experience. The table is based on the following underlying equation, which is recognizable as a version of the TFP equation above, with constant returns imposed:

Labor productivity growth = capital deepening (growth in K/L) + labor composition improvement (growth in H/L) + MFP (the residual)

Capital deepening is a measure of the increase in capital that makes labor more productive, and labor composition reflects increased education of workers as well as labor's age and gender composition. The adjustment cost correction to MFP accounts for lost output when new capital is installed, and utilization is a measure correcting for idle capital and labor.

The key idea in this decomposition is to separate out the contribution of IT capital to capital deepening and the contribution of the IT sector to MFP. The table shows that until 2004, IT capital investment contributed more than half of the capital deepening, but that this declined in the post-2004 period, especially for hardware. In contrast, the IT-producing sectors accounted for two-thirds of MFP in the 1974–1995 period, then their share fell somewhat while MFP grew, but by 2004–2012, IT-producing sectors were essentially the only ones showing productivity growth.

The bottom line is that IT accounted for about half of labor productivity growth between 1974 and 2004, but that the IT share declined slightly to 40% of labor productivity growth thereafter. This slowdown has sometimes been attributed to the slowdown of Moore's law, which is the idea that quality-adjusted semiconductor manufacturing costs fall continuously at a constant rate. Flamm (2021) shows that this rate has fallen since about 2004 due to limits on miniaturization of semiconductors and the heat they generate in operation. The slowdown in the quality-adjusted computer hardware contribution to capital deepening in the final period supports this idea.

9.4.2   TFP and R&D Investment

Given the presence of an unexplained residual identified with technical change in the Solow growth model, it was natural to try to explain the residual using the R&D investment in the economy. This effort was undertaken by researchers even before the development of modern growth theory models that explicitly incorporated innovation. The basic method is to include a measure of the stock of R&D as an input to the production function:

$$Q = AF(K, L, R)$$

where R is a measure of the knowledge stock (usually constructed from past R&D investment) and A is now residual productivity change not captured by investments in R&D. In practice, when this relation is estimated empirically, A will be proxied by a time trend or a set of time dummies (in the case of estimation using panel data). Given the augmented production function, we have the following:

$$\frac{\partial F}{\partial R} = \text{marginal product of } R \text{ (gross rate of return)}$$

$$\frac{R}{Q}\frac{\partial F}{\partial R} = \varepsilon_R = \text{elasticity of output wrt R}$$

This leads to a revised growth accounting equation:

$$g_Q = g_A + \varepsilon_K g_K + \varepsilon_L g_L + \varepsilon_R g_R$$

At first, this model was mainly applied to data on individual firms and industries. For example, Griliches (1980) used US data from 1957 to 1965 to find an R&D elasticity of about 0.07, and private R&D growth of around 15% per year, which implies that the contribution to growth was 1 percent during that period ($0.07*0.15 = 0.0105$).

Subsequently, the productivity formulation has been used many times to estimate elasticity of output with respect to R&D or the returns to R&D, as we discussed in Chapter 6. There are also numerous surveys of the results in the literature (e.g., Hall et al. 2010; Ugur et al. 2016). The model has also been applied at the country level, raising a number of new problems of measurement that we discussed earlier or in the next section, such as the definition and scope of output, and the measurement of quality change, along with the simultaneity of the growth–R&D investment relationship.

One example of an investigation of the growth–innovation relationship is Hasan and Tucci (2010). They use data on 58 countries for 1980–2003, separating them into two groups: high- and upper-middle-income versus lower-middle- and low-income countries. They use a standard per capita growth equation with many controls and various econometric methods to show that both R&D and patents are associated with subsequent economic growth in both groups of countries, controlling for the literacy and technology level of the economy among other variables. In causality tests, they find that although causality runs in both directions between the innovation variables and growth, the direction from innovation to growth is much stronger, validating the fact that innovation can lead to per capita economic growth at the country level.

9.5 Measuring R&D Spillovers

One implication of the newer endogenous growth models is that disembodied unpriced knowledge creation plays an important role in generating output growth. As we have emphasized, knowledge is a non-rival and only partially excludable good. Because of imperfect patent protection, inability to keep innovations completely secret, and imitation via reverse engineering, some of the knowledge and benefits from R&D are not kept within the firm. We refer to these unpriced knowledge transfers to entities outside the one that generated the knowledge as spillovers.

The topic of knowledge spillovers is closely related to that of social returns to innovation, as they are the means by which we frequently find that social returns exceed private returns. Spillovers can come from other firms in the industry; firms in other industries; public research institutes and laboratories; and even from firms, research institutions, and governments in other countries.

Given the admitted benefits to society from these unpriced knowledge spillovers, researchers have explored whether this is visible in the data using a number of methods, including case studies as well as productivity studies at various levels of aggregation.

9.5.1 Case Studies of Spillovers

Examples of case studies include Griliches (1958) on hybrid corn, Mansfield et al. (1977) and Tewksbury et al. (1980) on various industrial innovations, and Bresnahan (1986) on mainframe computers.

Griliches (1958) used the previously discussed hybrid corn diffusion data to construct social returns to the research that produced hybrid corn and estimated a social rate of return to that research (both private and government) of 35–40%. Mansfield et al. (1977) and Tewksbury et al. (1980) took similar approaches to the problem of estimating social returns to a number of industrial innovations. In each case, they interacted with the innovating firms to collect detailed data that allowed them to perform the following steps to compute social and private returns:

- *Private returns*
  - Compute direct investment (R&D, capital, marketing, etc.) and profits gross of investment for the life of the investment.
  - Deduct profits from displaced products of the firm, if any.
  - Assign a share of uncommercialized R&D, if any, to the innovation.
  - Compute net profits per year, convert to constant dollars.
  - Compute the internal discounted cash flow rate of return.
- *Social returns (in addition to the previous steps)*
  - Add investment and profits of firms that imitate the innovation, if any.
  - Deduct profits from displaced products of firms competing with the innovator.
  - Assign a share of uncommercialized R&D of the imitating firms as a cost.
  - Add the savings to the consumers of the innovation (the difference between willingness to pay and the price charged).
  - Add or subtract other benefits and costs such as improved safety, environmental costs, and so forth.
  - Compute the internal discounted cash flow rate of return (again using constant dollars).

We give an example of such a computation drawn from Tewksbury et al. (1980) in Table 9.2. The innovation was a part of a widely used machine that improved safety considerably. For confidentiality reasons, neither the actual years nor the constant dollar figures could be shown, although the returns figures computed using constant dollar numbers were reported. The internal rate of return is the discount rate that makes the discounted cash flow from a project equal to zero (see Appendix A: Mathematics and Statistics for details). The internal rates of return were computed using the IRR function in Excel.

The interesting thing about this innovation was that it replaced an earlier innovation by the same firm that was commercially less successful and had a negative social rate of return. The present innovation reduced the cost of the product in question substantially. The firm reported that the learning in the first innovation was important for the second. It is unclear whether all these costs were included in the computations in Table 9.2. However, this example does illustrate the cumulative nature of innovation and the contribution that initially unproductive R&D can make to future innovations. The initial innovation looks like a failure until one sees its impact on the second successful innovation.

It is fairly clear from reading the steps in these computations that there will be considerable uncertainty about the precise answer, and that they will involve a number of assumptions. Nevertheless, both Tewksbury et al. and Mansfield et al. found plausible

Table 9.2 Sample Computation of the Private and Social Rates of Return to an Innovation

Year*	Private return = 31% (real 24%)					Social return = 130% (real 123%)				
	R&D	Capital expenditures	Direct profit	Indirect profit	Total	Imitator's return	Consumers' surplus	Displaced profits	Safety benefits	Total
1	-1				-1					-1
2	-1	-1			-2					-2
3	-1	-2	-2		-5	-1				-6
4		-2	-1		-3	-2	21			16
5	-2		1		-1	-2	30	-1	2	28
6		-17	5	0.5	-11.5	-17	33	-5.5	4	3
7			10	1	11		33	-11	10	43
8		-3	15	1	13		33	-13	23	56
9			20	1	21		33	-21	38	71
10		-5	25		20		33	-20	47	80
11		-10	19	2	11		33	-11	61	94
12		-2	13	6	17		33	-17	85	118

* Hidden for confidentiality reasons.

All numbers are in current millions of dollars for confidentiality reasons, so the return figures are shown gross of inflation with the real numbers in parentheses.

Source: Tewksbury et al. (1980), Table 3.

private and social returns that averaged 25–27% (private) and 56–99% (social) across the innovations they considered. Note that in the example above, the loss of competitors' profits roughly balances the increased profit of the innovator. The high social return is due to consumer surplus and the safety benefits of the innovation. Potential benefits from the increases in knowledge of how to make the product safe, how to reduce cost, and the like are not considered.

Bresnahan tackles the problem of inferring consumer benefit from improvements in the price-performance ratio in computers over the 1958–1972 period. The problem he confronts is that many of the downstream sectors that benefit from computer improvements, such as health, finance, education, and research, have output that is difficult to measure in real terms, making traditional growth accounting methods infeasible or at least misleading. His solution is to measure the benefits to the consumer of the improvements in computing using the willingness to pay for computers in the banking, financial, and insurance sectors. Using a method related to the growth accounting framework, he estimates that the spillover from the adoption of mainframe computers in these sectors was at least five times the expenditure needed to bring it about.

9.5.2 Econometric Spillover Studies

With case studies, there is always a tendency to examine winners, that is, innovations that succeed, for which there is a good track record of data. In addition, it is often difficult to track true knowledge spillovers that are not accompanied by some kind of transaction, as these examples demonstrate. Therefore, there is a role for the cross-industry or cross-country study of the topic that attempts to include all the elements involved by looking at aggregate performance.

The idea is that if one does a productivity-R&D analysis using firm-level data, the measured return to R&D will be only private returns. But Eberhardt et al. (2013) provide evidence that omitting others' R&D from the equation introduces upward bias in the estimates, given the correlation of R&D intensities across firms within industries. Doing the analysis at the industry level should generate a measure that incorporates the returns to all the firms in the industry to all the R&D done in the industry, which means that the estimate is partial social returns to R&D, those realized within the industry.

Ugur et al. (2016) survey these kinds of efforts and conclude that industry-level estimates are not that much higher than firm-level estimates, suggesting that social returns are not much greater than private returns. However, both types of estimates (firm and industry) suffer from a number of problems that makes comparing them difficult. Industry data on R&D are normally obtained via firm-level data and are therefore sometimes not attached to the correct industry, especially in the case of the mega firms that do most of the R&D. As Eberhardt et al. (2013) pointed out, estimated private returns may be biased upward by the presence of social returns via the effect described above, which implies that a comparison of industry-level to firm-level results will underestimate the difference between the two.

Estimating at the country level is intended to allow us to obtain the "true" social return to R&D, at least in a semi-closed economy. However, this, too, is problematic, partly because time-series estimation is confounded by high correlations with other variables that change over time and also by causality issues. That is, does economic growth cause R&D investment, or does R&D investment cause economic growth, or do they simply move in tandem? Guellec and van Pottelsberghe (2004) have useful estimates of this kind for 16 OECD economies, estimates that were obtained using careful econometrics. They find that both public R&D and foreign R&D have a greater impact on productivity than business R&D, and that the impact is higher when business R&D intensity is greater. This supports the idea that absorptive capacity is important when taking advantage of R&D done elsewhere (by government or in other countries).

The basic framework for econometric studies of knowledge spillovers is the production function or growth accounting framework we discussed earlier. The standard production model is modified by adding a term S that measures the contribution of external R&D or innovation to own productivity:

$$Q = AF(K, L, R, S)$$

The quantity S is constructed as a weighted average of R&D performance by those external to the firm (or industry or country), with weights proportional to some measure of the "closeness" of the external actor to the one being considered. Let i index the firm, industry, or country being analyzed, and j index other firms, industries, or countries that might spill knowledge to i. Then we can write S as follows:

$$S_{it} = \sum_{j \neq i} a_{ij} R_{jt}$$

where the a_{ij} are the weights that describe the closeness of j to i. This closeness has been measured by a whole range of factors:

- Closeness in technological space as measured by patent profiles (Jaffe 1986, Bloom et al. 2013, Arts et al. 2023)
- R&D intensity of intermediate input and capital purchases (Sveikauskas 1981)
- Attendance at workshops and trade fairs, collaborations
- Patent flows between industries (Scherer 1984)
- Imports (Mohnen 1992, Coe and Helpman 1995, van Pottelsberghe and Lichtenberg 2001)
- Worker mobility among firms (Stoyanov and Zubanov 2012)
- Various measures of technological and product market closeness (Bloom et al. 2013)

Some of these papers and many others have been summarized in Hall et al. (2010). With few exceptions, they generally find social returns that are greater than private returns, but with highly variable values, ranging from close to zero to almost 200%. As we discussed in Chapter 6, this variability is expected, given that economic forces do not generally discipline unpriced knowledge spillovers.

In an important paper already discussed in Chapter 8, Bloom et al. (2013) separate the impact of technical or knowledge spillovers from the effects of product market interactions at the firm level. The idea is that innovative firms interact with other firms in two ways: They exchange knowledge spillovers with firms that are close to them technologically and at the same time compete in the product market with the same and also different firms using their innovation investments. The former activity increases social welfare via spillovers, while the latter may lead to excessive and duplicative R&D, so measuring spillovers can be contaminated by the impact of product market competition on R&D.

Technological closeness is measured using patent classifications to construct the similarity of patenting profiles (as in Jaffe 1986). Market closeness is measured in a similar way using the sales share profiles of the firms across the standard industrial classifications. They give as an example of these relationships the firm IBM, which is close to Intel, Apple, and Motorola technologically using their measure, but only to Apple using the sales measure. Intel and Motorola specialized in semiconductor chips during the period they consider (1980–2001), while IBM was more oriented toward computers, as was Apple. They estimate equations for R&D, patenting, productivity, and market value using these variables and find that technology spillovers dominate and that the social returns to R&D are at least twice as high as the private returns. It is noteworthy that the estimation controls for the endogeneity of R&D investment using various tax variables that introduce variations in the cost of R&D.

An interesting question for many countries is the extent to which R&D external to the country can contribute to their own productivity and growth. That is, to what extent can they free-ride on others' R&D. Coe and Helpman (1995) attempted to answer this question using an external R&D stock constructed using weights proportional to the share of imports to the country being analyzed from the country performing the R&D. That is, if m_{ijt} are imports from country j to country i at time t and R_{jt} is the stock of R&D in country j at time t, the foreign R&D stock available to country i is defined as follows:

$$S_{it}^f = \sum_{j \neq i} \frac{m_{ijt}}{\sum_{j \neq i} m_{ijt}} R_{jt}$$

Building on the endogenous growth models, Coe and Helpman estimated a model that related the logarithm of TFP to the logarithms of domestic and foreign R&D stocks, finding that their elasticities were more or less comparable and equal to about 0.06 to 0.09.[13] If anything, the elasticity with respect to foreign capital was higher.

Although this evidence of international R&D spillovers is of considerable interest, there are a couple of problems with it. First, Keller (1998) showed that although foreign R&D is indeed associated with TFP, weighting it by random import shares rather than country-specific import shares produces the same result, suggesting that imports are not the source of spillovers. Second, the cointegration specification used by Coe and Helpman excluded time dummies, which effectively meant that the R&D stocks (which did grow during the period) were the only variables available to explain increasing productivity. This means any variables that could drive both R&D and productivity were omitted, possibly leading to spurious correlation or upward biased coefficients.

---

[13] Coe and Helpman used data for 22 highly developed economies during 1971–1990, including all the G7 countries. They also used time-series econometrics to show that the relationship was a cointegrating one, justifying estimation in log levels.

Fortunately, we have other evidence that is more direct and micro-oriented that suggests imports are indeed associated with innovation in the importing country. MacGarvie (2006) studied the international patent citation patterns that followed importing and exporting by French firms. She found that the inventions of importers were significantly more likely to be influenced by foreign technology than are the inventions of firms that do not import. In addition, importers' own citations increased relative to similar firms after they start importing. In contrast, French firms that began exporting to other countries did not cite those countries' patents more. However, Aghion et al. (2021) found that when French firms begin exporting to a new foreign market, citations to their technology *from* firms in that market increase, which is consistent with MacGarvie's findings.

9.5.3 Geographic Spillovers

Economists and others have long observed that there appear to be important concentrations of innovation at various times and places: Silicon Valley for digital hardware and software today; Detroit, Michigan, for automobiles in the first half of the 20th century; the fashion industry in Paris, and then London and Milan; and many others. This observation has also attracted the interest of many local policymakers, who would like to see their region become an innovation center of some kind. Informally, it is very clear that in such innovative regions there must be localized knowledge spillovers from chance encounters and employee mobility, reflecting the importance of tacit knowledge in furthering innovative activities. This must exist in addition to other factors that favor geographic concentration, of course, such as the location of specialized suppliers, relevant university training, and so forth.

In a highly cited paper, Jaffe et al. (1993) used patent data to show that citations from one patent to another were more probable if the patents were co-located. They chose a set of about 2,000 patents applied for in 1975 or 1980 and matched them to control patents by application year, US patent technology class (about 400 in number), and grant date. They then compared the inventor locations in the patents that cited these patents between the focal patents and the controls. They found that about 5% of the citations to the focal patent are localized at the standard metropolitan statistical area (SMSA) level, compared to 1% of the citations to the control patents, which is a highly significant difference. They argue that citations from one patent to another are a proxy for knowledge flow from the inventors on the cited patent to those on the citing patent, and that this result is evidence of localized knowledge spillovers.

Although the use of patent citations in this way can be and has been critiqued, Jaffe et al. (2000) report the results of an inventor survey that supports the idea that some (not all) of the citations represent knowledge flows. Thompson and Fox-Kean (2005) critiqued their work on the grounds that matching by technology class was too coarse, and they repeated the analysis using subclass matching. Unfortunately, this meant dropping a number of patents that could not be matched so the samples are not comparable. Nevertheless, Thompson and Fox-Kean did find that matching at this level eliminated the intranational localization but not the international localization differences. This result suggests that some of the localization findings were due to concentration on narrow technology areas within the SMSAs, which itself may be evidence of geographic localization of spillovers in the form of areas to be researched.

Balsmeier et al. (2023) sidestep the problem highlighted by Thompson and Fox-Kean by relying on inventor-level information. They show that when an inventor on a patent with multiple inventors dies before the patent issues, the patent is cited less often by others in close geographic proximity to the deceased inventor relative to those that are still alive. This suggests that some of the localized knowledge spillover is indeed coming from personal contact.

Feldman and Kogler (2010) summarize the stylized facts about the geography of innovation. First, innovation does tend to concentrate spatially. Second, the geographic location serves as a platform for innovation, generally both urban and diverse. Third, spillovers are subtle and pervasive, as well as difficult to measure (see the previous discussion). Fourth, local universities are necessary, but not sufficient, for innovation. Fifth, although much knowledge is transferred locally, connection to external sources around the globe is essential. Finally, innovative places evolve over time organically and are therefore difficult to manage or to bring into being using direct policy.

9.5.4 Social Returns

What do these models and estimates have to say about social returns to innovation? At the aggregate level, it is possible to show that balanced growth models like those in Section 9.3 can deliver a relatively simple expression for social returns, one that abstracts from the allocation of those returns among firms and individuals in the economy. Jones and Williams (1998) and Jones and Summers (2022) both make use of a variational argument to construct a simple equation for the social return to innovation.

The idea in Jones and Williams is to imagine that R&D is increased in one period so that consumption in the next period is higher, and then decreased in the next period to leave the level of knowledge A the same as it was before. The gain in consumption in the year following the increased R&D is the social rate of return. They show that the social rate of return for the period in which R&D is increased is the sum of a dividend term and a capital gains term. The dividend term is, in turn, the sum of increased output from the R&D and the increased R&D productivity in the future from an increase in A. The capital gains or loss term reflects any changes in the cost of producing new ideas between the two periods.

Jones and Williams go on to use a model like those in Section 9.3.3 to show that this rate of return does not depend on factors like market structure, taxes, and so forth. In addition, they are able to show that although the regression methods for estimating spillovers at the microeconomic level in the previous section omit some features of the R&D process, such as potential congestion and long-run (as opposed to immediate) impacts, the size of the biases are fairly small. Their computations using their simple model suggest that the optimum R&D investment rate in the US economy is two to four times the actual rate.

The model of Jones and Summers is even simpler, as they abstract from any functional forms for the productivity and knowledge accumulation functions, relying instead on a balanced growth assumption and a fairly strong assumption about the impact of R&D on growth. Assume that output per capita and R&D per capita are growing at rate g, as in a balanced growth model, so the R&D intensity in the economy is constant, an assumption that is not unrealistic for many developed countries in the recent past. Now imagine turning off the R&D at some time t and leaving it off forever.[14] Assume this causes output per capita to stop growing, that is, the only thing generating output per capita or labor productivity growth is R&D. They show that in this case the ratio of the social benefits B to social cost C of R&D is given by the following:

$$\frac{B}{C} = \frac{Y}{R}\frac{g}{r}$$

where r is the economywide discount rate. The social return to R&D is the rate r^* that makes benefits equal to costs ($B/C = 1$):

$$r^* = g\frac{Y}{R}$$

A back of the envelope computation using recent US data with R&D intensity R/Y equal to 2.7% and growth rate equal to 1.8% implies an average social rate of return to R&D of 67%. Although relying on some fairly strong assumptions, this is a very useful base case. It is also in the middle of the various micro estimates that have been made over the years.

Jones and Summers go on to consider why the returns might be higher or lower. First, returns might be lower because of lags in the productivity of R&D. For example, the US Bureau of Economic Analysis (BEA), which is responsible for the national income and product accounts (NIPAs), has explored using gestation lags of 1 or 2 years until the results of R&D projects are commercialized. Second, some of the benefits of R&D are received via their incorporation into new capital goods, which means that additional investment is required to make the R&D useful. Third and related to the previous, there may be other associated innovation costs such as training expenses that are not incorporated into the costs in the measures above.

On the other hand, the benefits to R&D could be higher if our output measure is downward-biased due to the difficulty of incorporating new goods and quality improvements. The Boskin Commission (Boskin et al. 1996) found that the US consumer price index (CPI) was upward-biased by 1.1% per year, over half of which was due to quality change. Gordon (1999) reevaluated their work using changes already incorporated by the government agencies, finding that the bias had reduced to 0.65% per year. Revaluation at a lower CPI would increase measured output. Innovations due to the rise of digital services, especially free services, have made measuring output even more challenging.[15]

Another reason our measure of benefits is too low is that much of the aggregate R&D (both public and private) is directed toward things that are omitted from output (or included, but only at cost rather than with their full benefit). The leading examples are R&D expenditures targeted to health and defense R&D. In the case of health expenditures, the difficulty is that the output is ultimately a better quality of life and

[14] They also show that if you use a discrete time model and turn off R&D for one period, the same result holds.

[15] See Corrado et al. (2021) for the current state of the art.

longevity, neither of which are really captured by expenditure and profit-based measures in the NIAs, except indirectly.[16]

The first problem is that measuring the health care sector in national accounts requires a measure of the sector's revenue and a health care price index. In many countries, the government provides at least some health care free of charges and so revenue is difficult to measure, leading to the use of cost as a revenue measure. But the big problem is the price index and its associated quality change. Besides the obvious problems associated with measuring health outcomes such as morbidity and mortality, there is the issue of moral hazard that arises from the fact that the agent making the purchase decision (a health care professional) is not the same as the consumer (patient) who will pay for it, which means that willingness to pay is incorrectly measured. Berndt et al. (2001) also stress the fact that technical change is rife in this sector, meaning that quality change is likely to be a bigger problem here. A final problem from the perspective of welfare is that much of the technical change is cost-increasing, with possibly limited benefits for patients.

A final omission in the measurement of social returns described in this section is the fact that measures based on an economy's growth and R&D intensity neglect the potential for spillover returns both to and from the R&D and innovation done in other countries.

9.6 R&D in the NIAs

Recently, fuller understanding of the investment nature of R&D and its increasing importance in investment spending has led to a move by government statisticians to include spending on R&D and other intangibles in NIPAs as investment. Previously, R&D was simply a current expense. The change to treating it as capital investment increases GDP and also the services from capital.

In the United States, an R&D satellite account was developed beginning in 1994 and R&D was incorporated into the main NIPA in 2013.[17] In the EU, ESA2010 specified that R&D should be included in a satellite account and moved to the core account as its measurement improved and was harmonized across member states. At the current time, it appears that both Ireland and the United Kingdom capitalize R&D in their main accounts. The US and EU changes followed the release in 2009 of a major revision to the international framework and guide for systems of national accounts (SNAs) by the United Nations in cooperation with the European Commission (EC), the International Monetary Fund (IMF), the OECD, and the World Bank (United Nations et al. 2009). Among many other changes, for the first time this publication recommended that R&D be capitalized in SNAs.

A complete and detailed description of the US NIAs is given in the NIPA handbook provided by the US Bureau of Economic Analysis.[18] The basic setup as of 2018 is shown in Table 9.3, with the key components highlighted. SNAs generally use a similar

---

[16] Aizcorbe et al. (2018) and Berndt et al. (2001) offer more complete discussions of these problems.

[17] For details on R&D in NIPA, see US Bureau of Economic Analysis (2013) and Moylan and Okubo (2020). For information on data sources behind the addition of R&D to NIPA, see https://www.nsf.gov/statistics/2015/nsf15315/overview.htm.

[18] https://www.bea.gov/resources/methodologies/nipa-handbook.

Table 9.3 National Income and Product Accounts for 2018

(billions of current dollars)			
Gross Domestic Income		**Gross Domestic Product**	
Compensation of employees, paid	10,941.40	Personal consumption expenditures	13,998.70
Wages and salaries	8,901.40	Goods	4,364.80
Domestic	8,881.80	Durable goods	1,475.60
Rest of the world	19.6	Nondurable goods	2,889.20
Supplements to wages and salariess	2,040.00	Services	9,633.90
Taxes on production and imports	1,441.80	Gross private domestic investment	3,628.30
Less: Subsidies	64.4	Fixed investment	3,573.60
Net operating surplus	4,959.20	Nonresidential	2,786.90
Private enterprises	4,965.70	Structures	633.2
Current surplus of government enterprises	−6.5	Equipment	1,222.60
Consumption of fixed capital	3,291.40	Intellectual property products	931.1
Gross domestic income	20,569.40	Residential	786.7
Statistical discrepancy (6–20)	10.8	Change in private inventories	54.7
		Net exports of goods and services	−638.2
		Exports	2,510.20
		Imports	3,148.50
		Government consumption expenditures and gross investment	3,591.50
		Federal	1,347.30
		National defense	793.6
		Nondefense	553.7
		State and local	2,244.20
= Gross domestic product	20,580.20	Gross domestic product	20,580.20

Source: https://apps.bea.gov/scb/2019/08-august/0819-nipa-update.htm#pfi.

double entry bookkeeping methodology to that of firms, where every dollar or other currency produced generates a corresponding amount in income. Thus, the table has two columns, with income on the left and production on the right. Because of the level of complexity in generating these numbers for the entire country, there is always a statistical discrepancy that the government statisticians try to make as small as possible. In this case, it equals 0.05% of GDP, which is not bad.

In Table 9.3, private investment in IP products including R&D investment was US$931billion, approximately 4.5% of GDP. IP products consist of software ($379billion); R&D ($462billion); and entertainment, literary, and artistic originals ($90billion). Table 9.4 gives a more detailed breakdown of these IP investments.

It is interesting to review the steps involved in adding R&D to investment, that is, to capitalizing R&D rather than treating it as an expense. A complete accounting of the history of the R&D satellite account and its incorporation into the NIPA is given in Moylan and Okubo (2020). Here, we give a brief overview.

Prior to the capitalization of R&D in the NIAs, R&D expenditures appeared as expenses for private firms, and as consumption for nonprofit institutions and government. For private firms, the change to treating R&D as a capital investment required adding it to investment and removing it from the expenses, increasing profits. The depreciation or obsolescence of the R&D is included in the consumption of fixed capital with depreciation rates drawn from Li and Hall (2020). These depreciation rates are somewhat higher than the 15% often used by researchers and vary by industry.

The R&D funded by government and nonprofits is now also recognized as investment, in contrast to its treatment in the initial R&D satellite account. Depreciation of government R&D is included in government consumption, and that for nonprofits in the consumption of fixed capital. All this has required estimation of a price deflator for R&D as well as some assumptions about the imputed rate of return to R&D as opposed to other investments. In the absence of a thick market for R&D assets, the deflator used has been an input cost deflator based on the R&D services sector and all other industries. However, note that the declining research productivity documented in Bloom et al. (2020) might imply that the price deflator be much higher and the measured research output lower.

Moylan and Okubo (2020) report the impact on measured GDP of treating R&D as capital investment for a number of years from 1959 through 2012. In 1959, including R&D investment increased measured GDP by 1.5%, whereas in 2012 the increase was 2.4%.

9.7 Summary

Simple growth models of output as a function of capital and labor weighted by their shares in compensation leave a large share of growth unexplained. Correcting capital and labor for increases in their quality over time reduces the unexplained growth but does not eliminate it. Economists have identified this unexplained growth or "residual" as being associated with innovation and technical change in production.

Table 9.4 Breakdown of NIPA Investment in Intellectual Property Products, 2018

Private fixed investment in intellectual property products	Shares
Software	**41.9%**
Prepackaged[1]	18.0%
Custom	17.0%
Own account	7.0%
R&D[2,3]	**48.7%**
Business	45.9%
Manufacturing	28.3%
Pharmaceutical and medicine manufacturing	8.4%
Chemical manufacturing, excluding pharmaceutical and medicine	1.1%
Semiconductor and other electronic component manufacturing	3.6%
Other computer and electronic product manufacturing	4.9%
Motor vehicles, bodies and trailers, and parts manufacturing	2.7%
Aerospace products and parts manufacturing	1.4%
Other manufacturing	6.1%
Nonmanufacturing	17.6%
Scientific R&D services	1.1%
All other nonmanufacturing	16.5%
Software publishers	3.8%
Financial and real estate services	0.9%
Computer systems' design and related services	1.7%
Other nonmanufacturing	10.1%
Nonprofit institutions serving households	2.8%
Universities and colleges[4]	0.6%
Other nonprofit institutions	2.2%
Entertainment, literary, and artistic originals	**9.4%**
Theatrical movies	1.9%
Long-lived television programs	5.3%
Books	1.0%
Music	0.8%
Other	0.4%

Notes:

1. Excludes software embedded, or bundled, in computers and other equipment.

2. R&D asset types are defined by the type of funder.

3. Includes R&D expenditures for software.

4. Includes R&D investment by private universities and colleges. R&D investment by public universities and colleges is included in state and local government investment.

Source: BEA NIPA, Table 5.6.5, "Private Fixed Investment in Intellectual Property Products by Type."

Putting a measure of R&D or knowledge capital into the growth accounting framework does help to explain this residual growth. However, R&D investment is composed of capital and labor, which are already accounted for, so the implication is that R&D is creating a knowledge capital above and beyond that which is monetized by the firm. This has led to considerable research on R&D and innovation spillovers, the unpriced products of R&D investment that benefit other firms, individuals, and countries. The broad conclusion is that they are substantial and at least high-income countries are underinvesting in R&D.

An interesting result has emerged from the research that has attempted to measure knowledge spillovers using various different approaches and data from a number of countries: macro modeling, empirical macro estimation, production function estimation, and microeconomic studies. Although imprecise, almost all these studies have found social rates of return to R&D that are consistent with the Jones and Williams (2000) estimates of two to four times the private rate of return.

Belief in the importance and value of the knowledge base to an economy has led countries to develop their systems of national accounts to include measures of R&D capital and other intangible assets, treating these as investments rather than expenditures, by analogy to ordinary fixed capital investment.

10

Innovation Policy

Learning Objectives

After reading this chapter, you will be able to understand and explain the following concepts:

- Market failure and other arguments as justifications for innovation policy
- The role that governments play in promoting innovation through policy
- How to determine the optimal government subsidy
- Different policies to address market failure
- The role of IP tax credits and subsidies in promoting private R&D spending
- The role of direct government support of R&D
- National innovation systems

10.1 Introduction

It should be obvious from what we have already learned in the previous chapters that there is a role for government policy directed toward the encouragement and support of innovative activities on the part of firms and individuals. In fact, there are almost no countries without some kind of innovation policy, irrespective of the country's political structure and even its development level. These policies include support for higher education, both to institutions and students, direct spending on R&D in some areas like defense and health, tax subsidies for innovative activity in private firms, the IP system, government standard setting, and regulatory standards that encourage innovation directed toward societal goals such as reducing pollution.

The justification for innovation policy is frequently the simple market failure argument that there are both unpriced spillovers and also financing constraints, the latter due to the fact that the inventor/entrepreneur is not the same as the potential financier of innovation (see Box 10.1). However, there are many other but related reasons for governments to have policy in this broad area that we discuss in the first section of this chapter, such as the necessity for R&D to support the creation of government-provided public goods (defense, health services, etc.).

A central question when designing policy is the question of which instrument is effective for which problem, and how much to spend on this instrument. We discuss ways to determine the optimal subsidy, but it is clear from the discussion that even determining the amount of the subsidy is a difficult question. We then review the various

The Economics of Innovation and Intellectual Property. Bronwyn H. Hall and Christian Helmers, Oxford University Press.
© Oxford University Press 2024. DOI: 10.1093/oso/9780197630914.003.0010

Box 10.1 Market Failure

A situation where the individual incentives for rational behavior do not lead to the optimal outcome for society. Literally, the market fails to deliver the amount of the good that would be optimal for society.

---

methods used to correct for the market failure implied by the spillover externalities and problems of innovation financing. We look also at some of the evidence on their effectiveness, although a full review of the many policy studies in this area is beyond the scope of this textbook.[1]

The final part of the chapter takes a more holistic view of the policies and how they interact to create what is sometimes called a *national innovation system*. The comparative national innovation system approach does not reach strong conclusions about the "best" system design. However, there are some useful insights and suggestions that are revealed by that literature.

10.2 Why Do Governments Have Innovation Policies?

The central reason that governments have innovation policies was discussed at length in the preceding chapters: a belief supported now by considerable evidence that the social return to R&D and innovation is greater than the private return, suggesting that the private sector will not provide enough innovation on its own. It is perhaps fairly obvious that the social–private return gap may vary considerably across the types and goals of R&D and innovative activity. There are a number of other related reasons that may provide a guide to which particular innovation areas might be targeted by government incentives. Therefore, it is worth unpacking the arguments for innovation policy in a bit more detail.

But first, we remind ourselves of the types of spillovers or sources of positive externalities:

- *Knowledge (nonpecuniary) spillovers.* Knowledge created by one agent can be used by another without compensation, or with investment that is less than the cost of the knowledge creation.
- *Market (pecuniary) spillovers.* Some of the benefits of the knowledge creation that leads to new products and processes flow to purchasers via the operation of market forces, reducing the price.
- *Network spillovers.* The value of a new technology is strongly dependent on the development of related technologies (e.g., the hardware/software case).

Knowledge and network spillovers, which are unpriced, generate what are called *market failures*, the failure of the market to generate the appropriate level of the activity

---

[1] A useful source for studies of government R&D subsidy policy and its performance is the Science, Technology, and Economic Policy Board of the US National Research Council. For their publications, see https://nap.nationalacademies.org/author/STEP/policy-and-global-affairs/board-on-science-technology-and-economic-policy.

that produces them. At an abstract level, the argument for all government policy toward innovation can be derived from some kind of market failure argument, but often it appears that other factors lie behind the funding decision.

The first argument for policy is that it is more difficult to evaluate and fund some types of research in the private sector. This can be because the risk and size of the effort are large relative to the size of the market, even though society might think such efforts are worth undertaking for fairness reasons. A good example of this is orphan drugs, those lifesaving pharmaceuticals for rare disease. Other examples are vaccines that prevent disease and therefore potentially reduce future pharmaceutical demand and treatments for diseases that are only prevalent in low-income countries, such as malaria and schistosomiasis (a parasitic illness).

For some innovations, the benefit is very diffuse, and it is difficult to identify those who benefit, making it difficult to collect payment from the users. Examples include improvements to air quality via pollution-reducing equipment innovations. Related to this are pure public goods such as some kinds of standards, for which government support may be needed. One important area that has elicited considerable government-funded R&D both now and in the historical past is defense and the military (Mowery 2010).

Related to the argument for defense spending is the *strategic industry* argument. The idea here is that some industries are very important for national security. They may be closely linked to other industries, and technical advance in them would facilitate progress in other industries. A leading contemporary example is the semiconductor industry. Recently, US government policy has been directed toward strengthening this industry domestically; the Creating Helpful Incentives to Produce Semiconductors (CHIPS) Act contains a number of incentives for R&D in addition to manufacturing subsidies (see Box 10.2).

Box 10.2 US CHIPS and Science Act

In the United States, the CHIPS and Science Act was signed into law in August 2022. The main goal of the CHIPS Act is to spur investments in domestic semiconductor fabrication facilities and to provide incentives for the development and commercialization of certain new technologies such as AI, quantum computing, and nanotechnology.

Semiconductors are the backbone of the modern economy and play a central role in the defense industry and the development of AI technology. The act was motivated by a significant decline in domestic manufacturing of advanced microchips. While US firms are leaders in chip design (e.g., Qualcomm, Nvidia), the US share in the worldwide manufacturing supply of microchips dropped from nearly 40% in 2000 to only 12% in 2021 (Hufbauer and Hogan, 2022). Instead, chip manufacturing is increasingly concentrated in Taiwan. This triggered concerns that global geopolitical tensions could undermine the reliable supply of semiconductors. Another motivating factor was a broader concern over China's recent technological advances in semiconductor manufacturing.

The act provides a total of US$76billion of funding for semiconductor manufacturing and R&D incentives in the form of grants of 5–15% of a company's capital expenditures for a project (not exceeding 35% of cost) and a tax credit reimbursing 25% of plant construction and equipment. The act also contains specific provisions that bar companies that receive funding from the CHIPS Act from investing in advanced semiconductor facilities in China during a 10-year period.

While it is clearly too early to assess the impact of the CHIPS Act, the construction of new semiconductor manufacturing plants is already booming across the United States. Taiwan's TSMC is investing $40billion to construct new manufacturing facilities in Arizona, Intel is investing a total of $40billion in two new factories in Ohio and another two factories in Arizona, and Samsung and Texas Instruments are investing $17 and $30billion, respectively, in new manufacturing facilities in Texas.

National security was also part of the argument for the controversial US flat panel display program, which ultimately failed in the sense that it was overtaken by the fact that commercial innovation in flat panels rendered it somewhat unnecessary and costly. Innovation in this area turned out to be driven by the huge consumer market, especially for small versions such as those we use every day, so there was less need for specialized defense industry flat panel innovation.

In some cases, the externalities are large but the relevant innovators are small, so it is difficult for them to finance the necessary research and the risk is too great for any individual agent. Cooperation at a larger scale to enable research to be undertaken would be difficult and precluded in some cases by antitrust considerations. An example of this kind of situation in many countries is agricultural innovation, which is often provided by cooperative research organizations, or agricultural extension offices at educational institutions. But the same could be said about many new industries with small startups. In some countries, VC fills this gap by pooling risk across similar companies, but VC financing is notoriously faddish and not suitable for all technologies (Lerner and Nanda 2020).

All of these (defense, health, environment, agriculture) are often referred to as *mission-oriented R&D*. That is, although one could argue that they reflect some form of market failure, the impetus that drives them is perhaps broader than the idea that industry will underfund research in these areas, although in some cases such as energy and environmental research, the market failure argument may also provide an impetus. In the case of environmental research in particular, another argument for government involvement is the double externality problem: Not only will the market perform less research than is socially optimal, but there are also unpriced negative spillovers from pollution and climate change that should be mitigated.

A final area where almost all governments subsidize the creation of intangible human capital directed toward research is higher education. The justification here is fairly clear. Imperfect capital markets together with moral hazard and adverse selection problems mean that the private sector will not supply finance for higher education except at high interest rates. This plus the need to forgo income for a period will lead individuals to underinvest in advanced training. In addition, one can argue that a highly trained workforce is essential to the economy and that many such individuals do not capture the full return to their human capital, implying positive spillovers to the rest of the economy.

Figure 10.1 shows the allocation of government spending on R&D for six major OECD economies. Clearly, there are major differences across countries. The United States spends by far the largest share on defense and health, and lowest share on higher education. The education share of spending reflects the fact that in the United States a larger share of higher education is either privately financed or financed by the states via public education institutions. Some additional federal spending on education-related R&D comes through support for advanced training via research funding. Germany, Japan, and Korea spend a larger share on industrial productivity and technology. In the case of Japan and Germany, the allocation partly reflects the fact that neither country was allowed to (at first) or wished to have a large defense establishment following World War II, although this has been changing recently. The main takeaway from Figure 10.1 is that the majority of the government R&D spending in all countries is on what is termed *mission-oriented R&D*. This type of R&D is less motivated by market failure arguments and more by perceived national needs.

The conclusion from the discussion in this section is that governments have innovation policies for a range of reasons, not all of which are "market failures," strictly speaking, although all exhibit the characteristic that from society's perspective, the market will fail to deliver the "right" amount of innovation in the area, left to its own devices.

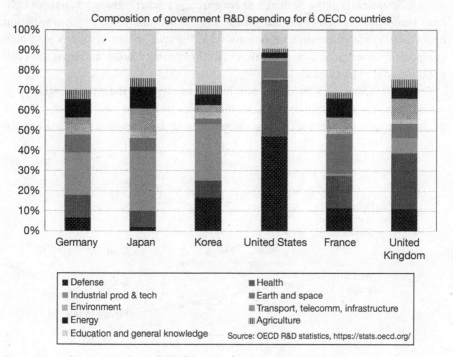

Figure 10.1 Government spending allocation for major OECD countries.

10.3 Determining the Optimal Subsidy

Much innovation policy, even the mission-oriented type, involves subsidies or tax incentives directed toward private firms. If one is going to subsidize or otherwise create incentives for innovation, the natural question is by how much. The simple graph below in Figure 10.2 presents a stylized version of the impact of a tax subsidy on R&D spending by the firm. The horizontal axis gives the level of R&D spending and the vertical axis its price in terms of cost of capital or rate of return. The firm's return to R&D is assumed to slope downward, as does the return to society as a whole, but society's return is higher because of spillovers. The cost of capital is assumed to increase with an increase in R&D, although this is not essential for the argument and it could be constant.

What we usually observe in the various econometric studies of R&D returns described in Chapter 6 is the gap between point A (the social returns to the firm's choice of R&D) and point C (the private returns to R&D at the firm, chosen to be equal to the expected cost of capital). In order to move the firm's R&D from the competitive level R_c to the socially optimal level R_s, the subsidy required is a reduction in cost from point S to point B, which is not necessarily of the same magnitude as A–C, unless the return lines are parallel.

The fact that the vertical distance A–C is not the same as S–B is only one of the things wrong with this simple graph. Another problem is that the magnitude of the spillover gap varies considerably, by country, by industry, and by technology type. For example, international spillovers to and from small open highly developed countries such as those in Scandinavia or the Netherlands are generally relatively greater than those from large semi-open economies like the United States and China. An example of variation by industry might be consumer electronics and "lifestyle" pharmaceuticals with high appropriability versus pharmaceuticals for life-threatening diseases and environmental pollution control (see Box 10.3).

One might also expect the nature of spillovers to vary with the different varieties of research. Pure science such as quantum mechanics and Einstein's theory of relativity might have very long and diffuse payoff periods. In contrast, goal-oriented applied

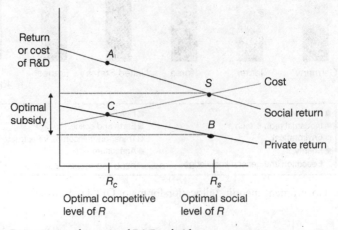

Figure 10.2 Determining the optimal R&D subsidy.

Box 10.3 "Lifestyle" Drugs

This is a class of pharmaceuticals for which a great share of use may exist for indications that are a matter of personal choice, such as drugs for erectile disfunction or obesity. These drugs might also be indicated for medical reasons for a subset of the patient population, but there are substantial incentives to market them more broadly (Gilbert et al. 2000).

---

research such as Edison's light bulb and phonograph or improved electric batteries is easier to fund and easier to find a market for. Research in *Pasteur's quadrant* as described in Chapter 2, such as bacteriology via research on wine or mathematics that is useful in encryption, will tend to have spillovers more like those of pure science, although its expected practical applications will make it somewhat easier to fund.

Finally and even more important, project ordering can differ according to whether you use social or private returns to rank projects. Think about cures for developing country diseases versus developed country diseases. The former has much higher social than private returns, whereas the latter may have social returns close to private returns. Another example is the social returns to "me too" drug innovation, which may be small, even if the private return is high to the innovator (Box 10.4).

Choosing policy design for innovation also involves a number of trade-offs. For example, it is not obvious who is better at choosing projects and approaches to a problem. Governments may be better at selecting high social return projects, given their goals—this is one reason why we have mission-oriented research. However, often innovating firms have a much better idea of the feasible projects, their technical solutions, and consumer tastes.

Related to this is the question of who will perform a given project better. Firms seem to be somewhat better at things like speed of action, with less bureaucratic delay. They may also be able to kill off unsuccessful projects sooner. As Cohen and Noll (1991) point out, large federal projects tend to create a constituency in the form of members of Congress and employees who make it difficult to stop a project even if it is clearly not useful. This phenomenon is part of the general problem of political capture of government programs.

Also keep in mind that the analysis above is a partial equilibrium analysis, appropriate for a situation where the tax subsidy is fairly small. In that case, the impact of increases in firm R&D will not necessarily lead to big changes in other firms' strategies or the prices of R&D inputs. But if the tax subsidy is of any size, or if it is a sudden change in the price of R&D, the short-run effect will partly be to increase the price of

---

Box 10.4 "Me Too" Drugs

These pharmaceuticals have the same or slightly improved function as a successful pharmaceutical produced by another firm. They may be highly profitable for the firm that produces them without improving clinical outcomes for patients by much.

R&D inputs, in particular to raise the wages of scientists and engineers, as this is the majority of R&D cost.

Goolsbee (1998) studied this possibility for the United States and found that a permanent 1 standard deviation increase in R&D spending raises wages 1% immediately and an additional 2% over the next 4 years. His model was admittedly quite simple and did not focus specifically on the R&D tax credit, but the results are suggestive. Results for the Netherlands find a modest long-run elasticity of 0.24 of wages with respect to the R&D tax credit (Lokshin and Mohnen 2013).

10.4 Policy Instruments for Market Failure

The standard policy tools for dealing with market failures are the following: (1) Internalize the externality, that is, bring the spillover within the innovating entity so that it has the correct incentives. This essentially hands the potential social return to the firm. (2) Subsidize the activity if the externality is positive; tax the externality if it is negative. (3) Direct government regulation, that is, mandates for a particular preferred behavior.

10.4.1 Internalizing the Externality

Internalizing the externality means granting ownership of the externality to the entity that is creating it. In the traditional example of downstream river pollution from a factory, it might mean granting the downstream entity the right to clean water and allow them to sell the rights to pollute to the upstream factory. If these are the only parties involved, this mechanism allows the downstream entity to choose the level of pollution it finds optimal and to be compensated for it. In this way, the downstream entity captures the (negative) social return to pollution.

Superficially, this is very appealing if it can be done, but usually it allows the entity maximizing social returns to create DWL, as in the case of a monopoly. For example, one way to reduce the cost that spillovers create for the firm that generates them when there are close competitors is to exempt R&D joint ventures and standards-setting organizations from antitrust regulation, as in the US National Cooperative Research Act (NCRA) of 1984 and the National Cooperative Research and Production Act (NCRPA) of 1993.[2] The EU has also encouraged joint ventures in innovation and R&D across member states for some time via the Framework programs.

A version of internalizing the externality is creating a property right in the output of the innovative activity (e.g., a patent, trademark, copyright). This allows the firm exclusive use of the innovation (monopoly), eliminating most of the spillover to a potential imitator, and may allow trading of ideas, facilitating cumulative and complex

---

[2] The NCRA (1984) allowed rule-of-reason evaluation of R&D joint ventures and limited the damages available from potential related violations of antitrust law (Scott 1989). The 1993 NCRPA Act essentially expanded the permissible activities to include production joint ventures.

innovation. We discuss the role of IP rights in encouraging or discouraging innovation at length in the rest of this textbook.

Neither of these solutions goes beyond simply limiting spillovers to competitors, either reducing them or moving them within the firm or joint venture. But the majority of beneficial nonpecuniary spillovers cannot be addressed using mechanisms of this kind.

10.4.2 Subsidize or Tax the Activity

The first option, which is very widely used, is direct government subsidy, where the social–private returns gap is large and the beneficiaries uncertain and diffuse. Examples of this are scientific and basic research; higher education; and the health, defense, and space sectors, as we saw in Section 10.2. One then confronts the problems of who chooses and performs the projects as described earlier. We discuss R&D subsidy programs further in Section 10.6.

The second subsidy option is to use tax policy. Here, we expect the spillover gap to be smaller and we use taxes to reduce the marginal cost of industrial R&D. This takes several forms: First, in most countries, R&D is expensed, which amounts to using a depreciation rate of 100%, even though the economic depreciation of R&D investment is likely to be much lower. Second, many countries and a few regions within countries offer an R&D tax credit or super-deduction, which lowers the cost even more. In addition, some countries offer reduced taxes on income generated by IP assets. We discuss these possibilities in Section 10.5.

A final tax subsidy is that the returns to foreign R&D can often be repatriated to the home country at a low tax rate, one of the features of international corporate taxation that favors investment in intangibles. A multinational corporation has the option to establish ownership of intangibles and the income they generate in a low-tax country, charging royalties to their subsidiaries in high-tax countries, which reduces profits there. Although this is an incentive for R&D because it reduces its cost, the practice has unintended negative consequences for the tax revenue available for other purposes in medium- and high-tax countries. Given the increased importance of intangibles in generating profits for multinational firms, avoiding corporate tax in this way has received increased attention from policymakers in high-income countries where such firms usually have their headquarters.[3]

10.4.3 Regulation

The final somewhat indirect policy option designed to encourage or change the direction of innovation is regulation. This often takes the form of a mandate for some kind of efficiency improvement in a product. The leading example is fuel efficiency standards for automobiles. These are widespread, especially in the major auto-producing countries: Brazil, Australia, China, South Korea, EU, Ukraine, Canada, United States (IEA

---

[3] See https://www.oecd.org/tax/beps/ for the current state of play of the Base Erosion and Profit Shifting (BEPS) tax reform project.

2017). Achieving these standards has led to substantial innovation in both traditional gasoline engines and in electric and hybrid automobiles.

Another example is environmental regulation of pollution caused by sulfur dioxide and nitrogen dioxide in coal-fired power plants. In many countries, this has led to considerable innovation in combustion techniques and post-combustion treatment of gases, as measured by patenting in these areas (Popp 2006).

10.5 R&D and IP Tax Credits

Encouraging private firms to perform R&D via the tax system is widespread, especially in high- and sometimes middle-income countries. Beginning with initiatives in Canada, France, and the United States during the 1970s and early 1980s, this policy has spread, with 34 of 38 OECD countries having some kind of tax incentive for R&D. It can be argued that economic evidence on the large social returns to R&D has helped to persuade policymakers that lowering the cost of R&D to firms would be good policy.

What are the advantages of using tax credits to subsidize R&D rather than directly funding the R&D? Normally, the firm benefiting from the tax credit chooses the areas in which to invest, rather than the government choosing them. The main exception is credits directed at firms paying for research conducted by universities, which are rare. This is an advantage if we believe that firms specializing in particular sectors have a better idea of what projects in those sectors are worthwhile. It also requires less time and management by the government and is less subject to lobbying pressure for specific projects. In addition, having firms in a specific area competing with varying approaches to a problem may produce better outcomes (Pavitt 2005).

The disadvantage is that project choice will be based on maximizing private returns rather than social. As we discussed earlier, using social rather than private returns to rank projects may lead to a very different ranking. For this reason, we do not expect the tax credit alone to close the gap between social and private returns, and most governments use targeted subsidies and also invest heavily themselves in some areas.

In addition to the widespread use of R&D tax credits, some countries have introduced what they call IP boxes, which provide for reduced tax rates on income generated by IP, or in some cases, just by patents. These are often a consequence of the international mobility of such income that arises from the fact that intangible assets are easily moved from one country to another. The reduced tax rates are an attempt to keep the income at home in the country.

We examine both R&D and IP tax subsidies in more detail in the discussion that follows.

10.5.1 Who Uses R&D Tax Credits?

R&D tax credits are used mostly by high-income countries as well as by large middle-income countries (Brazil, China, and Russia). This presumably reflects the importance of R&D investment in these countries. In the case of the many EU countries with a tax

Box 10.5 Tax Term Definitions

Super-deduction: in a corporate tax system, a deduction of expense that is larger than 100% of their level.

Tax credit: in a corporate tax system, an amount deducted directly from taxes. If there are no taxes payable, in some systems the amount may be carried forward or back to a situation where the firm did pay taxes.

credit, it also reflects their desire to increase R&D to the Lisbon agenda target of 3% of GDP.[4]

These credits take a variety of forms. The most common is a provision that allows a credit of some percent of R&D spending against corporate tax, anywhere from 15% to 50%. Some countries allow a super-deduction of R&D spending instead, generally 150–200% of expense (as opposed to the normal 100% expensing rule). Many countries cap the credit available for large firms, fearing the impact on the government budget. Some have a separate subsidy or accelerated depreciation for equipment used in research. See Box 10.5 for the relevant definitions.

The majority of R&D spending is usually the wages and salaries of scientists and engineers. For this reason, another way to reduce the cost of R&D using the tax system is to forgive or reduce the social charges (for social security, unemployment insurance, etc.) on these employees. This has the advantage that it is immediate and benefits companies that do not yet have profits on which to pay tax. If the idea is to provide tax subsidies for new startups as well as established firms, this form of the R&D tax subsidy may be preferred.

Figure 10.3 shows the use of R&D tax subsidies of various kinds around the world. Clearly, they are concentrated in high- and upper-middle-income countries, and there is substantial variation over the form that they take: credit, super-deduction, or payroll subsidy.

10.5.2 Why Incremental?

Many countries have experimented with some kind of incremental tax credit, which gives the firm a credit only for the amount of R&D spending they have done above and beyond their prior spending history. The argument is that the firm will do some level of R&D without the credit, and it would therefore be cheaper for the government if they only give the firm a credit on the amount of spending in excess of what they would have done anyway. Of course, the same is true for all types of investment tax credits, but it is especially salient in the case of R&D because such investment tends to be fairly smooth over time, unlike physical tangible investment.

Figure 10.4 illustrates this idea for a credit that achieves the same increase in R&D $(R_1 - R_0)$ whether it is ordinary or incremental. But if the credit is incremental, the tax

[4] https://portal.cor.europa.eu/europe2020/Profiles/Pages/TheLisbonStrategyinshort.aspx.

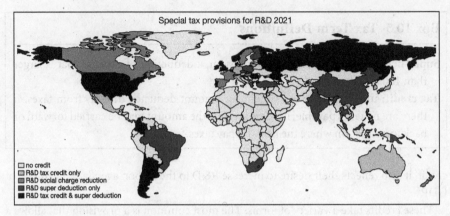

Figure 10.3 R&D tax provisions around the world.

revenue loss is only the dark shaded rectangle, whereas the ordinary credit costs the entire shaded rectangle (light and dark gray). The problem is that government policy would like to target only the marginal cost of additional R&D and an ordinary tax credit impacts the average cost as well as the marginal cost.

An incremental tax credit sounds like a good idea, but there is a difficulty: How should we determine the level of R&D precredit? When the first US R&D tax credit was introduced, an average of the past 3 years of R&D spending by the firm was used, but very quickly economists (Mansfield 1986b, Eisner et al. 1984) pointed out that this had the perverse incentive that past increases reduced the credit available in the future, rendering it much less effective than originally contemplated.

To see how this works, define the following symbols:

- θ = tax credit rate
- R = R&D
- b = current tax bill
- B = PDV of the tax bill
- β = discount rate

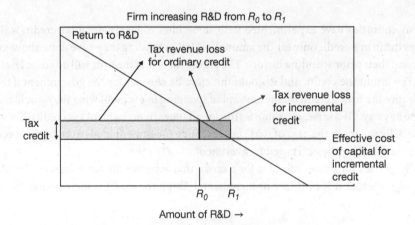

Figure 10.4 Incremental versus ordinary credit.

Then assume that the spending eligible for the credit is the amount above the average of the last 3 years' spending on R&D. If in year t the firm increases R_t by ΔR_t, the tax credit benefit to the firm is $\Delta b_t = -\theta \Delta R_t$. However, for the next 3 years, this increase is in the base R&D, so there is a cost each year given by $(\theta/3) \Delta R_t$. Therefore, the marginal tax benefit of a one-unit increase in R&D at year t is not θ, but the following:

$$\frac{\partial \Delta B_t}{\partial \Delta R_t} = -\theta \left[1 - \frac{(\beta + \beta^2 + \beta^3)}{3} \right]$$

If there is no discounting ($\beta = 1$), then the increase in the PDV of profits from the credit is zero. It is easy to see that for plausible values of the discount rate (e.g., 0.9 or 0.95), the effective tax credit is considerably less than the statutory value of θ. For example, when the discount rate is 0.9, the effective tax credit is $\theta(1 - (0.9 + 0.81 + 0.729)/3) = 0.187 \, \theta$. For this reason, many countries have moved away from an incremental credit toward a "volume" credit that is based on all of the firm's R&D spending.

The second problem with the incremental tax credit is that it is not suitable for startups that do not have a history of spending. For these firms, many countries use a simple volume credit, often with a credit rate that is somewhat higher than the credit rate for established firms.

10.5.3 Empirical Evidence on Tax Credit Effectiveness

Analysis of the effectiveness of R&D tax credits has focused on determining the firm-level R&D spending response to a reduction in the cost of R&D via the tax credit. The cost is either measured as the *tax price*, the effective after-tax price paid for R&D spending that costs $1 or other currency unit before tax, or as the user cost of capital, which is closely related. We show the computation of the user cost of R&D capital for a firm that may or may not have taxable income in the current year, and where the tax credit might be incremental.[5] We use the following definitions:

- θ = tax credit rate
- τ = corporate tax rate
- r = interest rate
- δ = depreciation rate for R&D
- k = no. of periods over which base R&D is computed
- N_t = no. of periods until firm exhausts loss carryforwards (usually equal to zero)
- D_t = indicator for taxable income in current year
- B_t = indicator for R&D above base value in current year

---

[5] This computation is based on the appendix in Hall and Van Reenen (2000), which is, in turn, based on R. E. Hall and Jorgenson (1967).

With these definitions, the user cost of R&D is given by the following:

$$c_t^R = (r+\delta)\frac{1-D_t(1+r)^{-N_t}\,\tau-\theta_t\left(B_t-\dfrac{1}{k}\displaystyle\sum_{i=1}^{k}(1+r)^i\,B_{t+i}\right)}{1-D_t(1+r)^{-N_t}\,\tau}$$

If the tax credit is not incremental (the base value is always zero and $k = 0$) and the firm has taxable income, this formula becomes much simpler:

$$c_t^R = (r+\delta)\frac{1-\tau-\theta_t}{1-\tau}=(r+\delta)\left(1-\frac{\theta_t}{1-\tau}\right)$$

Clearly, the cost of R&D capital is lower when the corporate tax rate or the R&D credit rate is higher. A typical tax credit evaluation regresses the log level of real R&D spending by a firm on the log cost of R&D capital as measured above to determine the elasticity of R&D with respect to its cost.

There is a reasonably long history of the R&D tax credit in many countries, and therefore, a number of studies that evaluate its impact already exist; the fact that the impact depends to some extent on the tax position of the firm and the details of the credit computation helps with identification because it yields variation in the cost of R&D faced by firms within country and time period. The general consensus from these studies is that tax credits have an impact on R&D spending and that the elasticity of spending with respect to the cost of R&D net of the credit is about 1 or, in some cases, higher. The implication is that for every currency unit of tax savings, R&D increases by at least one currency unit and possibly by more (Hall and Van Reenen 2000, Blandinières and Steinbrenner 2020).

A few studies have evaluated whether the estimates they obtain imply that the amount of increased R&D obtained is more or less than the tax revenue forgone. This is a rough benefit–cost computation, although it cannot tell us whether there are government expenditures with higher benefit–cost ratios that might be a better use of limited funds. In general, the conclusion is that the lost tax revenue is replaced in the short run by increased business R&D, and the expectation is that the long-run benefits may be even larger.

One concern that is often expressed by critics of policy instruments like the R&D tax credit is that it leads to wasteful tax competition among jurisdictions. There is some evidence that this may be a problem, given the ability of firms to respond to attractive tax regimes by moving some of their R&D efforts to such locations. This can admittedly be a costly strategy, especially internationally, entailing some loss of human capital as R&D employees are unwilling to move.

Two studies of major economies have found that R&D in one country not only responds positively to a reduction in R&D cost domestically but also negatively and with a similar magnitude in terms of elasticity to a reduction in foreign R&D cost, suggesting some substitution across countries (Bloom and Griffith 2001, Corrado et al. 2015). There are similar, but even larger, results for US states (Wilson 2009). The difference in results between these two studies is to be expected if the cost of shifting R&D between states is lower than the cost of shifting it across countries.

It is important to note that the equal and opposite elasticities found in these studies do not necessarily imply zero-sum changes in R&D. Under the assumption of constant elasticity (which has not been tested), the impact in large or high R&D countries will be bigger in absolute level than in small low-R&D countries, which argues that the R&D tax credits will be more effective globally if they are used by the larger countries.

10.5.4 IP Boxes

Some countries, mostly in Europe, but also Brazil, Canada, and India, have recently introduced some form of IP tax treatment, often called an *IP box*. The IP covered by this tax instrument varies across countries but usually includes patents, utility models, and software. In many cases, the motivating force is the fact that multinational firms are able to locate ownership of their intangible assets in low-tax jurisdictions, enabling them to pay lower taxes on any income they earn from those assets. This strategy was obviously not as easily available for tangible assets, but as the importance of intangibles has risen, the incentives to avoid taxes this way have risen also. Figure 10.5 shows the use of IP boxes around the world.

Given the fact that some of intangible income will migrate anyway, reducing the tax revenue in countries with higher tax rates, it seems like a good idea to reduce tax rates on such income in order to keep it at home. It has also been argued by those who favor the introduction of an IP box that this is a way to subsidize successful innovative activity. But is this better than using a direct tax subsidy to R&D? There are a number of reasons that it might not be. We review them here, focusing on the mostly widely used instrument, the patent box. This is also the part of the IP box that has been most thoroughly studied.

- R&D spending is directly under control of the firm so the incentive is more immediate (and therefore salient to the decision-makers in the firm). Patent-generated income may depend on some R&D investment, but it is influenced by many other factors, including luck.

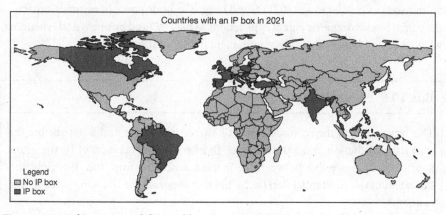

Figure 10.5 IP boxes around the world.

- Patent boxes target the most directly appropriable part of innovation. This part already receives an incentive from the patent grant, and it doesn't seem like the type of innovative activity that needs subsidizing.
- Patent boxes subsidize patent enforcement since all the income of a patent assertion entity (PAE) is arguably patent-related income.
- Patent boxes give firms another incentive to renew patents that might otherwise be abandoned, thus extending potential market power and raising inventor search costs.
- The design of a patent box is difficult as it involves the allocation of costs for the nonpatent assets that are used in generating the patent income. Correspondingly, government audit costs, which are already high for the R&D tax credits, are even higher for the patent box.

One feature of patent box legislation that is important is its applicability to patents that are transferred into the jurisdiction. Some countries require patented inventions whose income is taxed at a lower rate to have been developed in the country or at least that some further development has taken place domestically. This feature is one way to prevent simple tax shifting and ensure that the policy at least has some impact on local innovation. It is also a component of the previously mentioned OECD base erosion and profit shifting (BEPS) project. This project recommended in 2015 that there be a local development requirement for the patent to be eligible for reduced taxation (OECD 2015b, p. 23). BEPS refers to such a requirement as a "nexus" requirement, that is, a requirement for significant economic presence in the country (Box 10.6).

How do firms respond to patent boxes? A number of researchers have looked at various aspects of the impact, although the relatively small number of countries with IP boxes in the early days of their application and the variations in legislation across countries have made identification of specific effects difficult to determine. First, there is some evidence that the nexus requirement is important, in that patent transfers increase following the introduction of a patent box only when there is no requirement for local development. Transfers are also deterred if the tax rate on patent income in the current location is low, supporting the view that the purpose of the legislation is to keep patent income within the country.

As a spur to innovation, the patent box seems to be unsuccessful at the country level, at least so far. Gaessler et al. (2021) found insignificant or possibly negative impacts of the patent box on domestic patent applications to the EPO and business R&D spending, whether or not there was a nexus requirement in the legislation.

Box 10.6 Nexus Principle

This term refers to the requisite contact between a taxpayer and a state before the state has jurisdiction to tax the taxpayer. In international taxation of IP, the nexus approach requires a link between the income benefiting from the IP regime and the extent of the substantial R&D activities that generate the IP taking place in that country.

The conclusion from the evidence thus far is that IP boxes are probably not the best way to encourage innovative activity. More direct ways of discouraging the tax shifting of intangibles seemed to be called for. This is the goal of OECD's BEPS project and as of January 2024, over 135 countries have signed on to the global minimum corporate tax of 15% for large MNES proposed by OECD.[6]

10.6 Government Support for R&D

Figure 10.1 above showed the composition of direct government spending on R&D for a number of countries. That figure made it clear that government-funded R&D covers a wide range of technologies and also that its composition varies considerably across countries. Also varying across countries are the methods of delivery. These can include direct spending funded and performed by the government; spending at government-owned laboratories and research institutions; spending at private non-profit laboratories and research institutions; and competitive grants to industry, universities, and research institutions.

Figure 10.6 shows the composition of government-funded R&D spending in a number of economies, sorted by the total size of the government R&D budget. This figure makes it clear that countries vary in the ways they allocate government funding, with the slightly smaller of these economies allocating more to higher education and less to the other sectors. Russia is an outlier in the share it spends in industry; it turns

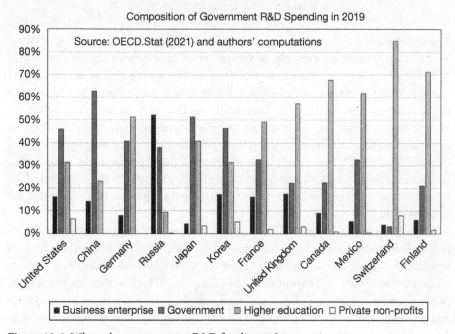

Figure 10.6 Where does government R&D funding go?

[6] https://www.oecd.org/tax/beps/summary-economic-impact-assessment-global-minimum-tax-january-2024.pdf

out that about 60% of business enterprise R&D in Russia is funded by the government, a much larger figure than in other countries, where it averages less than 10%.

What are the benefits of public R&D spending?[7] First, there are the directly valuable additions to the knowledge base. Some examples are the editing of genes using the CRISPR technique and the mathematics behind common encryption methods used on the internet. The internet itself is an outgrowth of ARPANET, funded by US defense R&D, and the work of Tim Berners-Lee at an intergovernmental research laboratory, CERN, funded by 23 European member states. Another important innovation with huge economic benefits around the world is the Global Positioning System (GPS), originally developed by US defense R&D during the 1950s–1970s and made open and free to the public in the mid-1990s (O'Connor et al. 2019).

Scientific knowledge created by public and university R&D also guides and informs applied R&D. For example, mapping the genome has created many opportunities for biotechnology firms seeking targets for new drugs that might alleviate or cure disease. The work of Einstein was important in understanding the photoelectric effect (light as both wave and particle), and this understanding underlies the present-day photocell and solar cell.

Important benefits from public R&D also include the human capital created by research training and graduate funding, which are not fully captured by the wages of those trained. For example, the postdoctoral circulation of researchers that embody and transfer tacit knowledge increases the knowledge base and leads to new discoveries.

10.6.1 The US Experience

The evolution of public support for R&D in the United States during and after World War II is an important example of the power of government-funded research in generating long-lasting spillovers and creating self-sustaining geographic technology clusters. World War II research by the US government was initiated by the creation of the National Research Defense Committee (NRDC) in June 1940, even before the United States entered the war after Pearl Harbor. It was expanded into the Office of Scientific Research and Development (OSRD) in June 1941, which was eligible for congressional budget appropriations (Gross and Sampat 2023). Both agencies were headed by Vannevar Bush, who authored *Science, the Endless Frontier* (1945) at the end of the war. This report set the agenda for further government support for R&D, including the creation of the NSF.

Research conducted by the OSRD during the war led to developments, many foundational, in radar, electronic communications, computing, sonar, rockets and jet propulsion, atomic fission, mass-produced penicillin, new vaccines, new malaria treatments, and many other areas. Gross and Sampat (2023) show that this shock to research funding was very unevenly distributed across the United States, as it tended to go places where there were universities and scientists equipped to undertake the research. They also show that the effects were persistent, leading to (semi-)permanent increases

---

[7] A useful if slightly dated summary of research on the benefits of publicly funded research can be found in Salter and Martin (2001).

in patenting activity in the areas and technologies targeted. Thus, the wartime increase in public funding had huge benefits for subsequent research, but it also led to further concentration of research and its spillovers.

Today in the United States, R&D spending has the following components:

- Fundamental and basic scientific research of all types (NSF, National Institutes of Health, energy, and space science)
- Research for military and space applications (National Aeronautics and Space Administration (NASA), Department of Defense)
- Research in applied technology areas perceived to be of national importance in health, energy, and agriculture (e.g., Environmental Protection Agency, Department of Agriculture)
- Commercialization and adoption programs/demonstration programs like the clean coal demonstration (Small Business Innovation Research (SBIR), Advanced Technology Program (ATP), Cooperative Research and Development Agreement (CRADA))
- Cost-sharing private R&D in commercial areas, for example, Sematech and the flat panel display project (ATP)

The United States also has the longest time series available for detailed data on the direction of government spending. Figure 10.7 shows the evolution of US federal nondefense R&D spending over the past 6 decades. It is very striking to see how priorities have changed. A huge amount was devoted to space research after Sputnik and prior to the moon landing of 1969. During the 1970s, there was a boom in spending on energy research in response to the oil price shocks of 1973–1974 and 1978–1979. At the

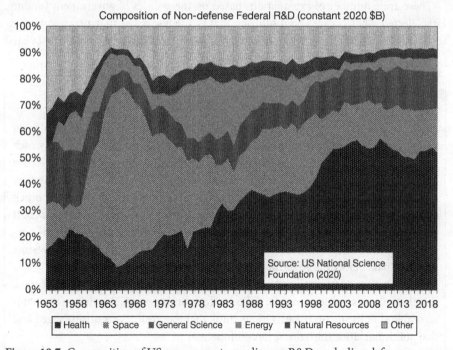

Figure 10.7 Composition of US government spending on R&D, excluding defense.

same time, the priority began to shift to health, with growth in health R&D to 50% of nondefense R&D in the last decade.

Cohen et al. (2002) used the 1994 Carnegie Mellon Survey of R&D laboratories in manufacturing to look at the influence of public (government) research in the United States on industrial R&D. They found that it affected R&D across most of the manufacturing sector via published research, conferences, informal exchanges, and consulting. Public research outputs were very important to industry research projects in high-technology industries such as pharmaceuticals, semiconductors, and other electronics, but were used by a third of projects across all industries. The most important fields of research were chemicals, computer science, and materials science, consistent with earlier work by Mansfield (1991, 1995) using data from 1975 to 1985.

10.6.2 Political Economy of Government R&D

In a democracy, the closer government R&D spending is to commercial activities, the more controversial it becomes. One reason is that it is easier to argue that the spillover benefits are small given the commercial possibilities. A second reason is that governments are ill-equipped to evaluate the potential of each project and are bad at "picking winners." Cohen and Noll argued in a 1991 book that spending on commercial innovation projects by government has historically been subject to underperformance and cost overruns. Some point to the failure of Solyndra as a recent example of poor government performance in funding R&D, in this case via loan guarantees of half a billion dollars (Box 10.7). Why might government management of precommercial R&D be prone to failure?

There are a number of explanations based on the politics of government funding. First, elected officials care about *saliency*, that is, the few issues that attract voters' interest. R&D spending is salient only when it is related to a national priority, associated

---

Box 10.7 Solyndra

Solyndra was a US-based company founded in Silicon Valley in 2004 to build solar panels using copper indium gallium selenide rather than polysilicon, which were more expensive to make but cheaper to install. The company received a US$535million loan guarantee from the Department of Energy in 2009. The firm went bankrupt in August 2011, partly because polysilicon had become much cheaper in 2008 and Chinese firms had begun to crowd out the American market. It was unclear in early 2010 whether Solyndra would survive as a business, but the government extended and increased the loan, also guaranteeing that private investors would be paid before the government.

The Solyndra story is somewhat controversial and undecided. Some would argue that this failure is only one in a portfolio of efforts and was arguably driven by an unfavorable shift in silicon prices. Others think that the project was mismanaged and that political relationships drove its continuation.

with a scandal, or has a local interest factor (often jobs). The increase in the US space research share of the government R&D budget after the USSR launched Sputnik in 1956 is an example of the power of a national priority. Saliency is also more likely if a few people care a lot, or are already organized, such as a labor union or an industry organization.

Elected parliaments tend to be impatient due to their relatively short terms and also risk-averse. Agencies that implement projects have more information than parliaments and tend to ally with industry, so the preferences of industry may be prioritized over the public good.

There is asymmetry in the political support for projects. It is cheap to start a project, so many may be started that appeal to some share of the electorate. Once a project has begun, it becomes hard to cancel if there is a large local job base associated, even if the project has been shown to be technically infeasible or worthless.

The implications of the forgoing are that governments are more likely to do programs oriented toward a concentrated industry given that such an industry is more able to focus its lobbying in particular directions. This is inconsistent with an optimal public goods policy, as these are the industries more likely to be able to undertake R&D with a particular focus on their own.

Short time horizon projects with no radical change in the technical base of the industry are more attractive to both parliaments and industries, which is inconsistent with the market failure arguments for policy, which imply that support is needed for riskier projects without existing financing. Another reason direct government performance is more suited to risky projects is that because government does not go out of business, it may be better able to capture the useful information when a project fails, although this is somewhat speculative.

The projected net benefits of a project are important early on in the decision to undertake it, but their importance declines as stakeholders are created by the project, implying that projects will be kept going even when they are not expected to yield much in the way of benefits.

Table 10.1 summarizes the findings of Cohen and Noll (1991) for the United States and adds a couple of additional more recent examples. These projects satisfied the market failure criterion for public R&D in principle (except possibly the SST, which might have been left to the private sector to determine whether it was a good idea). The cost–benefit rationales made two mistakes, both of which were due to "technological optimism." First, they assumed that the R&D would achieve objectives with certainty, instead of building in a benefit deduction for risk. Second, they compared the proposed program with a very narrow range of alternatives early on. For example, instead of using Western coal, which was more suitable, the synfuels project focused only on Eastern coal for political reasons. A final reason for failure was the failure to anticipate relative price movements that made the technology less useful, as in the case of synfuels and the copper indium gallium selenide used by Solyndra. This latter reason can afflict private technology projects also, but they may be easier to kill when prices move.

In some cases, the projects were successful in the sense that they laid the groundwork for further private R&D in the area, but this took a long time, well beyond the date of Cohen and Noll's study. All were subject to a boom–bust in spending for political reasons as they were based on fragile coalitions in Congress that changed every 2 years

Table 10.1 Federal R&D Projects from Cohen and Noll (1991), Updated

Project	Field	Technical Outcome	Political Outcome
SST (supersonic transport)	Aerospace	Too costly	Killed before a constituency developed.
Communication satellites	Electronics and aerospace	Success	Became less salient and was killed in 1974; groups that would benefit were not represented (new firms).
Space shuttle	Aerospace	Cost too much and flew too infrequently.	Challenger disaster a setback; missions became very costly and program discontinued in 2011.
Clinch River breeder reactor	Nuclear energy	Failed	Killed too late, absorbed a large part of nuclear technology budget, due to local jobs and interests, etc.
Photovoltaic commercialization	Energy	Success, but oil prices moved against it; eventually, climate change worries meant it became a long run success.	Scaled back for political reasons, benefits very decentralized and nonfocal at the time, although since then climate change has refocused attention.
Synfuels research	Energy	Probably too costly. One success, but generally misdirected (Eastern coal rather than cleaner Western coal); oil prices moved against it.	Ultimately scaled back due to technical and economic difficulties; much pursuit of uneconomic technologies; oil prices fell after many such programs were established.
Flat panel display	Electronics	Success, but manufacturing is all in East Asia.	Consumer demand drove the technology; US firms exited when funding ran out, but are still involved in R&D and co-development.
Solyndra	Energy	Failed; input prices fell, favoring alternative flat solar panel tech.	Firm financed by government loan, went bankrupt when prices moved against the technology.

with a new Congress. As we have learned, optimal R&D spending for most projects is smooth and grows over time.

10.6.3 Policy Evaluation and the Productivity of Government R&D

Looking across countries, the direct productivity of government spending on R&D is generally lower than that of private R&D. There are a number of reasons why this might be true. First, much of it is defense spending, which has little private product, and can sometimes lead to so-called gold-plating, that is, excessive investment in quality. Evidence from Guellec and Van Pottelsberghe (2003) shows that defense R&D tends to make the productivity impact of business R&D lower, in contrast to nondefense government R&D. Second, another large share is directed at unmeasured welfare improvements in health and the environment, which will not show up in aggregate productivity (Griliches 1994).

A third reason is that most productivity measures are short-term, while investments like basic science and higher education and research have long-term payoffs, sometimes decades. Lower short-term "productivity" is not a bad thing if the spillovers from this spending are large. Finally, some government R&D investments respond more to political forces, such as employment creation in particular regions, which means that the goal is not necessarily short- or long-term productivity enhancement. However, for the remainder of this section, we will assume that the policy is to be evaluated by whether it induces R&D & innovative effort and by its returns.

Most governments wish to evaluate the effectiveness of any policy they introduce, and a large literature has developed concerning the appropriate methodologies.[8] A simple econometric model due to Jaffe (2002) illuminates the problems. Assume Y_i is the output of interest for applicant i and X_i are the observed applicant characteristics, used as controls in the regression. Then a version of the following equation is generally used to evaluate the impact of receiving a government grant:

$$Y_{it} = \beta_i D_{it} + \lambda X_{it} + \alpha_i + \mu_t + \omega_{it} + \varepsilon_{it}$$

D_{it} is a dummy equal to 1 if the applicant i receives a grant at t or earlier, and β_i therefore measures the impact of the grant for that applicant on the output measure. Here, we have assumed that there is more than one period of observation for each applicant so that the individual β's are identified. Alternatively, if there is only one period, we would estimate a common β across applicants, possibly interacted with the characteristics X.

The disturbance term in this regression has four components. The first two are dummies for the applicant (α) and the time period (μ). The last two are the regression error, broken into two pieces. ε is the usual error assumed uncorrelated with the other variables in the regression. ω is the error that causes all the trouble--it is the period- and applicant-specific quality or productivity, which we do not see, but is observable to the granting agency. The presumption is that this observability induces correlation

---

[8] Good surveys that are specific to the innovation subsidy context are Jaffe (2002) and Klette et al. (2000). For a general treatment of the econometrics of policy evaluation, see Angrist and Pischke (2009).

Box 10.8 Difference-in-Difference Estimation

This kind of estimation compares an outcome variable between observations where one set received some treatment and one did not. One differences the outcomes for the two sets before and after the treatment and then differences these results to find the effect of the treatment. This is essentially equivalent to including both time dummies and unit of observation dummies in the outcome regression.

---

between the regression error and D, the grant success, because expected productivity predicts both receiving a grant and its outcome.

Jaffe reviews the various ways to deal with the bias introduced by the fact that grant success may be correlated with the unobserved qualities of the applicant and the project. These include using controls that might proxy for future productivity, matching on observables, difference-in-difference estimation (see Box 10.8), and instrumental variables. For the latter, one must find an instrument that predicts obtaining a grant but is unrelated to productivity once the grant is obtained.

A widely used approach to policy evaluation that solves some of the problems above is available if the proposals have been ranked in some ways before the decision is made. This method is known as regression discontinuity design (RDD). Given a score and a cutoff score, one can compare observations just above and below the cutoff, on the assumption that they are very similar except that some received a grant and the others did not. A recent example by Santoleri et al. (2020) studies R&D grants to small- and medium-sized enterprises in the EU. They use RDD to show that such grants increase investment (especially in intangibles) and cite-weighted patents; they also lead to faster growth in assets, employment, and revenues and a higher likelihood of receiving follow-on equity financing and lower failure chances. Importantly, they also find that these impacts are greater for smaller, younger, financially constrained firms, and for those in less developed European regions.

Interpretation of the results of R&D and innovation grant programs can be challenging in the presence of risk. For any portfolio of innovation projects, one must expect some failures; otherwise, it is probable that too little was invested. Here is a very simple model due to Rodrik (2014) that encapsulates the idea that project failure is to be expected. Consider a typical precommercial funding program, where there are funds available to be allocated to a number of applicants, each of whom has a probability distribution of success or failure that is known to the funding agency. Assume that there exists a continuum of applicants indexed by $z \in [0, 1]$ with probability distribution function $f(z)$. Given the distribution function for the applicants $f(z)$, the probability of success for applicant z is $P(z)$. When $z = 0$, the probability of success is zero, and when $z = 1$, success is certain. Assume each project costs the same and generates net return π if it is successful.[9]

---

[9] This is a simplifying assumption that makes the problem tractable. It would be possible, but much more complicated to consider a model where each project costs different amounts. The central conclusion of the model would remain true.

The funding agency faces an opportunity cost of funding equal to r (normally the interest rate). To achieve this expected return, it needs to figure out how many projects to fund by finding the level of z above which the probability of success will generate just enough returns to be equal to the opportunity cost. The number of such projects is defined by this equation, where k is the number of such projects chosen:

$$r = \int_{z=k}^{z=1} \pi f(z)dz = \pi\left[1 - P(k)\right]$$

Note that we have implicitly assumed that the net return from each project is greater than r. If that were not true, it would suggest discontinuing the program entirely. Nevertheless, even though $\pi > r$, some projects will fail even if the program is successful and earns an overall net return that satisfies this constraint.

Now consider the case when the rule for choosing the projects depends on the social return rather than the interest rate. In this case, the cutoff return is higher and the agency can afford to take on riskier projects:

$$r + \theta = \pi\left[1 - P(k^*)\right] > r = \pi\left[1 - P(k)\right]$$
$$\Rightarrow \theta = \pi\left[1 - P(k^*)\right] - \pi\left[1 - P(k)\right] > 0$$
$$\Rightarrow \pi(P(k) - P(k^*)) > 0$$
$$\Rightarrow P(k) > P(k^*)$$
$$\Rightarrow k < k^*$$

The implication is that when the social return $(r + \theta)$ is greater than the interest rate or opportunity cost, the agency will choose a larger piece of the probability distribution (a lower cutoff $z = k^*$) and there will therefore be more failures in the pool of projects. This point is worth emphasizing as it is often missed by evaluators looking for success in a program.

The main alternative to the econometric approach to evaluation is a detailed case study. For an excellent example of this method, see the 2001 report from the National Research Council on energy research at the US Department of Energy (DOE). This report looked at the results of DOE spending on energy efficiency and fossil energy programs during 1978–2000, spending amounting to $22.3billion. They analyzed 39 case studies using a common evaluation matrix that specified economic, environmental, and security benefits in three categories: realized benefits, options for the future, and knowledge benefits. Many of the projects had more than one kind of benefit, and some were considered failures. The largest benefits were from avoided energy costs in the building sectors due to improvements in energy efficiency and avoided environmental costs from nitrous oxide emissions. The buildings sector is very fragmented and a good example of a sector where the individual actors do not have the funds or ability to invest in the R&D themselves.

A study by Babina et al. (2023) highlights the difficulty of shifting the research strategies of university scientists via research funds targeted to specific areas. They looked at the impacts of large cuts to federal funding in specific narrow fields of research and found that the outcome typically was a shift to private funding, a loss of higher-quality publications, and an increase in patenting, mostly of lower quality. That is, the researchers generally look outside for funding in a research area that has lost government interest, rather than shift their research to a new field.

10.7 National Innovation Systems

The idea that a country's innovation policies operate together to form a national innovation system goes back to a German political economist in the 19th century, Friedrich List (1841), but has been revived and further developed by innovation economists influenced by List and Schumpeter such as Chris Freeman (1995), Bengt-Ake Lundvall (1992), and Richard Nelson (1993). The elements of the system are usually education, training, and public research institutions, user–producer interactive learning, financing of new ventures via VC or government finance, strategic industrial policy including competition policy, and policies targeting particular technologies. These elements work together to provide the environment and mechanisms that allow innovation to flourish. Although the term *system* is used to describe the collection of policies and structures, in most countries this is not a top-down conscious planned system but rather something that arises from the country's particular history and culture. The main contribution of this literature is to emphasize the complementarities of some policies, which can make the system as a whole either more or less than the sum of its parts.

Freeman (1995) uses these ideas to contrast the development of Japan versus the USSR during the 1970s, and East Asia versus Latin America in the 1980s. Japan and the USSR both had high R&D intensity and a well-educated population, along with high economic growth in the 1950s and 1960s, but the USSR R&D was heavily targeted to military and space endeavors, and there was considerably less industry spending. They also had relatively weak links between their research institutes that were separated by basic, different industrial sectors, and plant and technology design, as well as weak links between research and industry. Compared to Japan, incentives to innovate were also weak, both because of production quotas rather than profits as a goal and because of a lack of international competition. The outcome was catchup by Japan during the 1970s, and economic decline for the states in the USSR into the 1980s, contributing to its breakup.

From 15 country studies for countries as diverse as Brazil, Japan, and Canada, Nelson (1993) drew a few tentative conclusions as to which features were important in encouraging innovation and development. First was the general competence of the firms in the industries that were important to the country: effective management, links to upstream and downstream markets, product design and production, and so on. Second was education and training systems that provided firms with the requisite knowledge and skills needed by industry. This includes external training systems linked to firms or training by the firms themselves, as in Japan. Education and a skilled workforce were important for the fairly rapid development of East Asian countries such as Taiwan and Korea, but they are not enough, as evidenced by some of the Latin American countries. There also needs to be a link between the education and training and the firms' needs.

The studies found that exporting is important for innovation and development as it forces firms to compete in a world market. Few countries other than the United States and China have home markets big enough to create effective competition. In the same spirit, protection from import competition can be important early in development but will hold back firms eventually. Looking at publicly supported research, in successful countries the universities and public research organizations did research that was linked to their strong industrial sectors. As to military R&D spending, which varies widely across country, its value to the civilian economy depends on how much it spends on broad new generic technology, as opposed to sophisticated weapons systems that are only of use to the military. The United States seems to have benefited from spending on electronics R&D up until the 1960s, but few countries have been able to emulate that success, with the possible exception of Israel.

The study concludes with a non-conclusion about the role of infant industry protection and industrial policy in moving countries to the technology frontier. One can find plenty of evidence for either failure or success in projects intended to catch up with the leaders in any technological area, and it is difficult to sort out the exact predictors of the differences. That's why it is called a "system."

A series of studies by Keun Lee and his co-authors attempts to quantify the relationship between national and regional innovation systems and growth using measures of the knowledge environment based on patent and in some cases trademark data (Lee and Lee 2021, Lee et al. 2021, Kim and Lee 2022). They focus on middle-income countries and relate measures of local knowledge generation, technological diversification, technology cycle time, originality, and the concentration across firms of patenting activity. For both national and regional data, they find that catchup in terms of economic growth is related to shorter technology cycle times as well as increasing local knowledge generation. Technology cycle time is measured by the average citation lag for the US patents held by the country, measured relative to all US patents. Short cycle times are associated with ICT technologies, whereas long cycle times are more likely in pharmaceutical technologies.

10.7.1 Taxes versus Subsidies

As should be clear from the forgoing, one interesting question that is by no means fully understood is how to choose the optimal mix of innovation policies. Although it is fairly clear that some kinds of mission-oriented innovation need to be undertaken by a central government and that human capital building investments are essential, how should we balance the use of tax incentives with the use of direct government spending for supporting R&D that is not part of a government mission?

As discussed earlier, these two instruments tend to operate quite differently. Like IP rights, tax incentives leave the choice of R&D and innovation projects to the firm, whereas government spending is more clearly targeted, if only to particular broad areas. Government spending comes in many flavors, from specific projects paid for and undertaken by government agencies to loan guarantees for innovative commercial firms. Figures 10.8 and 10.9, taken from the most recent OECD R&D tax incentives database, give an idea of how much the support patterns vary across country, as a share of that country's GDP.[10]

---

[10] These figures ignore any subnational policies benefiting industry R&D, which affects at least Canada, Hungary, Switzerland, and the United States. Also note that both Finland and Germany introduced an R&D tax credit in the years immediately after the date of these data.

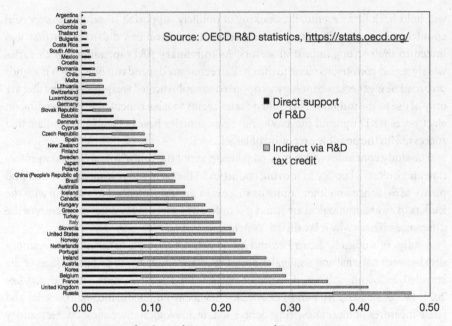

Figure 10.8 Government funding of R&D as percent of GDP in 2019.

Figure 10.8 shows that only Russia, the United Kingdom, and France have a level of government support for industry R&D above 0.3% of GDP, and even these three countries have a very different composition of support, with Russia relying much more on funding R&D directly. It should also be noted that the number for Germany may be an underestimate as it does not include funding supplied by the individual Länder.[11] With the exception of a few middle-income countries that have a share below 0.03%, there is no obvious pattern in the ranking of the mostly high-income countries in the figure.

Figure 10.9 ranks the countries by their share of indirect tax support in the total government subsidy to industry R&D. It, too, shows considerable variation, all the way from 10 countries with no R&D tax credit to 9 where the share from the credit is greater than 80%. Once again, there is no obvious pattern to the ranking. Compare Estonia to Lithuania or Italy and Portugal to Spain.

There is a limited literature that attempts to assess the relative importance and success of tax credits and subsidies in promoting R&D. For example, Busom et al. (2014) use data on Spanish firms to suggest that these instruments reach different types of firms, depending on their size and whether they face financing constraints. SMEs make more use of subsidies than tax credits when they are financially constrained. A meta-regression combining about 50 estimates of the impact of tax credits and subsidies on firm R&D spending finds their impact to be similar. Tax credits are more effective in large firms (Dimos et al. 2022). At least one study finds that subsidies and tax credits are substitutes in eliciting R&D spending (Guellec and Van Pottelsberghe 2003).

---

[11] State or Länder funding may amount to as much as half of all government funding of R&D in Germany. See https://www.research-in-germany.org/en/research-landscape/why-germany/research-funding-system/government-funding.html.

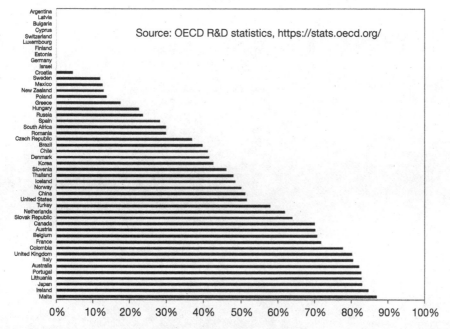

Figure 10.9 Tax credit share of industry R&D support in 2019.

10.8 Summary

Government policy toward R&D and innovation is widespread and takes many forms: higher education support, basic research spending, research targeted to national needs, IP policy, regulation, standard setting, and various tax policies to encourage innovation. Different countries place varying weights on each of these in their spending. In high-income countries, government spending on R&D tends to be somewhat less than that by industry, while the opposite is true in low- and middle-income countries.

Evaluation of government policy in this area tends to show effectiveness in most cases, in the sense that R&D policies tend to encourage R&D spending by firms. However, determining the optimal policy mix and level remains challenging. In addition, full evaluation of government programs needs a full accounting of benefits, which will include those that are not counted in GDP, such as health and environmental.

Innovation policy works together with other features of an economy's structure and linkages to create what we call a national innovation system. Unfortunately, some of the most beneficial features of such a system may come from past history and culture, or from institutions that are difficult to change, which implies that progress in improving the system can be slow.

II.
INTELLECTUAL PROPERTY RIGHTS AND THEIR USE

11

Patents, Utility Models, Design Rights, and Plant Breeder Rights

---

Learning Objectives

After reading this chapter, you will be able to understand and explain the following concepts:

- The basic structure and purpose of the patent system
- The process and legal requirements to obtain a patent
- The economics underlying the patent system
- The definition of patent quality and patent value, and different methods to estimate patent quality and patent value
- The characteristics and purpose of utility models, design patents, and plant patents

---

11.1 Introduction

A patent gives its owner the right to exclude everyone else from exploiting the patented invention. In practice, this means that the patent owner can sue for patent infringement in court if a third party makes, uses, sells, or imports the patented invention into the jurisdiction where the patent is in force. The ability to exclude others is often referred to as a *monopoly* over the patented invention. The patent monopoly is particularly powerful because infringement occurs even if the infringing party had no knowledge of the patented invention--for example, if they independently came up with the same invention without any awareness of the patented invention. In other words, a patent offers much broader recourse than other forms of legal protection such as copyright because it protects against *any* use of the patented invention.

The economic motivation underlying the granting of such broad legal rights is to encourage investment in innovation. We reviewed the broader list of arguments for the patent system in Chapter 4. The main policy question regarding the patent system is to what extent it achieves its objective. There is even a possibility that the patent system has the opposite effect, that is, it could discourage rather than encourage innovation. Ultimately, the question is whether a patent is necessary to incentivize innovation or would parties innovate without it?

In practice, the answer to the question about the effect of patent protection on innovation revolves more around the specifics of how the patent system is designed and

The Economics of Innovation and Intellectual Property. Bronwyn H. Hall and Christian Helmers, Oxford University Press.
© Oxford University Press 2024. DOI: 10.1093/oso/9780197630914.003.0011

implemented, rather than the broader question of whether patents are helpful altogether or not. In this chapter, we review the basic economic rationale for the patent system, and provide an overview of the legal requirements and procedures to obtain a patent. It is important to remember that this is not a legal textbook, so the discussion of the legal requirements and procedures is intentionally kept short and abstracts from many legal particulars. Nevertheless, the chapter introduces and defines language and terms specific to the patent system that you should know in order to understand the more in-depth discussion of the economics of the patent system in Part III of this book. The discussion in this chapter focuses largely on the US and European patent systems. However, it also discusses international aspects of patent protection, including international agreements, institutions, and harmonization efforts. Finally, the chapter also offers a brief overview of "other" patent rights, including utility models, design patents, and plant patents.

11.2 Background

The first (technological) *patent* was granted in 1421 by the city of Florence in Italy to Filippo Brunelleschi for new means to transport marble from the quarries at Carrara up the Arno River, which was an important transport route to Florence (Prager 1946). While Brunelleschi's patent had many things in common with a modern patent, we were still a long way from anything close to our modern patent system.

The first administrative patent system was created in the Republic of Venice in 1474. The Venetian Patent Statute granted exclusivity over an invention and established an enforcement mechanism. The law also mandated disclosure and the availability of some limited form of compulsory licensing of a patented invention. Importantly, the law required inventions to be novel and non-obvious and even required a practical demonstration of usefulness. As such, it was in many ways remarkably similar to the patent system as we know it today (Guellec and van Pottelsberghe 2007, Chapter 7).

Nevertheless, the patent system has evolved enormously since those early days. It has become a lot more complex, and it has been adopted by virtually all countries around the world. Figure 11.1 shows annual patent filings in the world's most important countries in terms of patent filings between 1985 and 2020.[1] We see enormous growth in patent filings across countries over time with the exception of Japan. In the United States, the number of filings increased from slightly more than 100,000 annual filings in the mid-1980s to over 600,000 in 2019. Even more impressive is the growth in patent filings in China. The Chinese patent office received fewer than 10,000 annual filings toward the end of the 1980s. In 2020, it received almost 1.5 million filings. China is now by far the country with the largest number of patent filings in the world.

The use of patents differs substantially across economic activity. There are several reasons. For one, patents protect technological inventions. This makes patent protection more applicable in manufacturing industries. But even within

[1] To be precise, these are the filings at patent offices in these countries and at the EPO. The filings may come from inventors in the country itself, or from inventors in any other country.

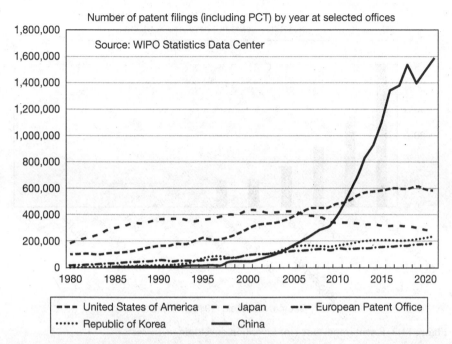

Figure 11.1 Patent filings at the five major offices.

manufacturing industries, there are large differences in the use of patents. This is mainly explained by differences in the effectiveness of patents in helping firms appropriate returns to innovation. Indeed, Figure 11.2 shows the results from a survey where manufacturing firms were asked directly whether patent protection was critical for their decision to develop or commercially introduce an invention (Mansfield 1986b).[2] We see that firms in pharmaceuticals and chemicals consider patent protection much more effective than all other industries. In fact, in some industries, such as textiles, patent protection does not appear to play any role, at least at the time the survey was conducted. What accounts for these significant differences in the effectiveness of the patent system across industries? We will review some of the reasons below, and Chapter 14 provides a more comprehensive answer to this question.

11.3 Patent Procedures

In this section, we provide some information on patent eligibility, application process, and other legal requirements that are useful to know if you want to understand the economics literature on the patent system (or if you are planning to do research on the patent system).

---

[2] While the survey is admittedly somewhat dated, Mezzanotti and Simcoe (2023) report similar findings for more recent data collected by the US Census for the 2008–2015 period.

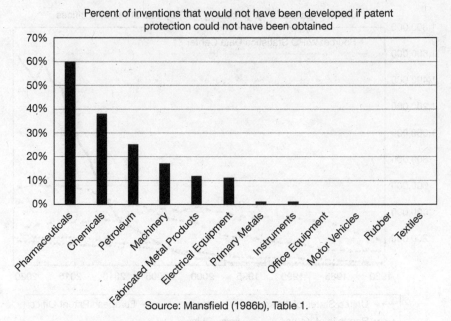

Source: Mansfield (1986b), Table 1.

Figure 11.2 Patent importance for invention development by sector.

11.3.1 Patentability

Patents are government-granted, registered IP rights. In order to obtain patent protection, an applicant has to apply for a patent with the relevant patent office. For the patent office to grant patent protection, the patent application has to meet certain criteria, referred to as *patentability requirements*. This application process distinguishes patents from other IP rights, such as copyright, because the creation of an invention does not automatically lead to patent protection. Instead, an inventor has to make the decision to apply for patent protection at a relevant patent office and successfully undergo patent examination before legal protection is granted. During patent examination, a patent examiner verifies that a patent satisfies the following patentability requirements (this is referred to as *substantive examination*):

1. **Novelty.** Novelty requires that a given invention be new, that is, not already (at least nominally) disclosed to the public through a prior publication, product offered for sale, or public use. This avoids situations in which an invention that is already known to the public and potentially in use is granted exclusivity. A patent examiner will evaluate the so-called state of the art in order to establish novelty. The term *state of the art* describes everything that was available to the public in any form anywhere in the world before the patent's first application date (also referred to as the priority date––more on this further below).[3] Note that *publicly available* does not mean that the patentee had to have access to the information. It merely means that the

---

[3] This statement is not entirely correct. Some countries recognize so-called grace periods that provide exceptions to prior art provisions.

information was publicly available and the patentee, in principle, could have accessed it. It also does not matter who made the information public, a competitor, researcher, and the like. In practice, to establish novelty, a patent examiner will look for a single "prior art reference" in which the invention described by the patent application is disclosed. For example, the examiner could find an existing patent or a published academic journal article that contains all the relevant features of the invention described by the patent application.

2. Non-obviousness (inventive step). Provided an invention is novel, this requirement asks whether the invention represents more than an obvious--to a person having ordinary skill in the art (PHOSITA)--extension of something that already existed before the patent's priority date. This requires a showing that the claimed invention provides a nontrivial advantage over the prior art. Hence, it is possible for an invention to be novel, while still being obvious. While the novelty test asked whether the claimed invention existed and had been disclosed already "as a whole," the non-obviousness test allows for a combination of different pieces of prior art. So, in practice, to assess non-obviousness, the patent examiner can combine elements from different patents as long as the examiner can argue that a PHOSITA would have been motivated to do so to arrive at the claimed invention. The latter requirement, that a PHOSITA would have indeed combined the different elements, is a critical yet difficult question to answer in practice. The non-obvious requirement is referred to as "inventive step" in Europe.

3. Utility (industrial application). The third requirement asks whether the patent applicant has articulated a specific and substantial use for the invention. This does not require any actual prior use or construction of the invention; the requirement only asks whether an invention is capable of industrial application. This also implies there is no need to demonstrate that the claimed invention actually works in practice. It is sufficient to claim that theoretically a PHOSITA would understand that the claimed invention has a particular industrial application. As a result, this requirement generally does not represent much of a hurdle for applicants.[4]

These patentability requirements are designed to ensure that only sufficiently new, previously unknown, and useful inventions receive patent protection.

While, in principle, all countries apply these same criteria,[5] their application by patent offices and courts differs substantially across countries (see Section 11.8 below).

Apart from the three patentability requirements presented above, there is an additional important hurdle: The invention has to be patentable subject matter. The term *patentable subject matter* describes types of inventions that are eligible for patent protection provided they satisfy the patentability requirements. In the United States, patentable subject matter is broadly defined to include "a process, machine, article of

---

[4] A curious exception is a patent application for a perpetual motion machine. Since the laws of physics make the creation of a perpetual motion machine impossible, there cannot be any use for such an invention.
[5] See Article 27(1) of TRIPS.

manufacture, and composition of matter." However, some inventions are excluded from patentability either because they are not considered inventions for the purposes of patent law or because of overriding policy concerns. For example, patent protection is not available for newly discovered laws of nature and natural phenomena. Aesthetic creations, such as literary, dramatic, musical, and artistic works, are also not patentable (they are covered by copyright as explained in Chapter 13).

While these restrictions to patentable subject matter apply across countries, Article 27 of TRIPS still gives countries considerable flexibility to define patentability.[6] For example, the EPO excludes business methods and software from patentability,[7] while the USPTO, in principle, grants patents on both business methods and software (see Chapter 17 for a discussion of the changing environment in this area as a result of various court decisions).

11.3.2 Procedures

In this section, we describe the procedures to obtain a patent. While some of these procedures may appear overly legalistic, a basic understanding is helpful as these procedures have important consequences for the use and functioning of the patent system.

To give you a better understanding of what a patent actually looks like, Figure 11.3 shows you one of the patents that protect the Nintendo Switch, a popular video game console.[8] The title of the patent is "Game controller" and its patent number, which acts as a unique identifier, is US 9,751,008. We will refer to this figure as we explain different aspects of the patent application procedure and patent document. You can look up the complete patent text online using the patent number on Google patents or the USPTO search facility.

11.3.2.1 Application
A patent can be filed by a legal or natural person; the applicant does not need to be the inventor.[9] Patent offices rely on a so-called first-to-file approach. Under a first-to-file approach, priority is established by being first to file a complete patent application with a patent office. In contrast, under a first-to-invent approach, priority is established at the time the invention was made. The former approach is much easier to administer since it is easy to establish who filed first for a patent on a given invention. The first-to-invent approach is more complicated because the entity that filed for a patent first might not be the one that came up with the invention first. In such a case, the entity that first conceived the invention would have to prove so in order to establish priority over

---

[6] While TRIPS mandates that patent protection be available in all fields of technology, this requirement does not apply if an invention is not patent-eligible. The reason is that it is not considered an invention from the perspective of patent law and hence does not fall within the scope of the TRIPS obligation.

[7] Specifically, "schemes, rules and methods for performing mental acts, playing games or doing business, and programs for computers" are excluded from patentability [Article 52(2c) of the EPC].

[8] https://www.nintendo.com/us/patents.

[9] In the United States before the changes introduced by the AIA in 2011, only inventor(s) could apply for a patent. Now the applicant (usually the employer) can apply on their behalf.

(12) **United States Patent**
Fujita et al.

(10) **Patent No.:**   **US 9,751,008 B2**
(45) **Date of Patent:**   **Sep. 5, 2017**

(54) **GAME CONTROLLER**

(71) Applicant: **NINTENDO CO., LTD.,** Kyoto (JP)

(72) Inventors: **Kumpei Fujita,** Kyoto (JP); **Shinji Hirose,** Kyoto (JP)

(73) Assignee: **NINTENDO CO., LTD.,** Kyoto (JP)

(*) Notice: Subject to any disclaimer, the term of this patent is extended or adjusted under 35 U.S.C. 154(b) by 0 days.

(21) Appl. No.: **15/179,011**

(22) Filed: **Jun. 10, 2016**

(65) **Prior Publication Data**

US 2016/0361633 A1   Dec. 15, 2016

(30) **Foreign Application Priority Data**

Jun. 12, 2015	(JP)	....	2015-119707
Jun. 8, 2016	(JP)	....	2016-114668
Jun. 8, 2016	(JP)	....	2016-114669
Jun. 8, 2016	(JP)	....	2016-114670
Jun. 8, 2016	(JP)	....	2016-114671

(51) **Int. Cl.**
A63F 13/23   (2014.01)
A63F 13/21   (2014.01)
(Continued)

(52) **U.S. Cl.**
CPC *A63F 13/23* (2014.09); *A63F 13/21* (2014.09); *A63F 13/24* (2014.09); *A63F 13/92* (2014.09); *A63F 13/98* (2014.09)

(58) **Field of Classification Search**
None
See application file for complete search history.

(56) **References Cited**

U.S. PATENT DOCUMENTS

5,627,974 A   5/1997   Watts, Jr. et al.
5,657,459 A   8/1997   Yanagisawa et al.
(Continued)

FOREIGN PATENT DOCUMENTS

CN   104 436 646 A   3/2015
EP   1 759 745 A1   3/2007
(Continued)

OTHER PUBLICATIONS

Koizumi et al., U.S. Appl. No. 15/179,022, filed Jun. 10, 2016 (210 pages).
(Continued)

Primary Examiner — Tramar Harper
(74) *Attorney, Agent, or Firm* — Nixon & Vanderhye P.C.

(57)   **ABSTRACT**

An example game controller is removably attachable to a main unit. The game controller includes an operation section and a controller-side slide member. The controller-side slide member protrudes from a first surface of the game controller and is configured to slidably engage with the main unit-side slide member in a slide direction. The controller-side slide member has a first end and a second end in the slide direction, and the game controller is configured to be attached to the main unit by inserting the controller-side slide member into the main unit-side slide member at least from the first end. The game controller includes a stop member. The stop member is configured to protrude from the first surface of the game controller or from a side surface of the controller-side slide member, which side surface is substantially perpendicular to the first surface.

25 Claims, 63 Drawing Sheets

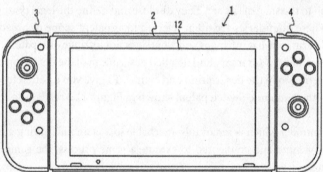

Figure 11.3 US patent 9,751,008.

the entity that filed first. In practice, this might be a complicated endeavor. The United States relied on the first-to-invent approach until 2013 when it replaced it with a first-inventor-to-file system.

11.3.2.2 Priority and Application Dates
The filing date of a patent is the date when a patent application is filed with a patent office. The priority date is the first filing date of a patent. It is necessary to distinguish

between the first filing date of a patent (priority date) and other filing dates because patents can be filed in different jurisdictions within 12 months of the first filing date.[10] All other patent offices where the patent is filed afterward will have a later filing date but rely on the same priority date (first filing date) for examination. This is important because the priority date determines the cutoff date for the assessment of patentability.[11] For example, the patent shown in Figure 11.3 was first filed in Japan on June 12, 2015. It was then filed at the USPTO on June 10, 2016. The patent's priority date is June 12, 2015. This means that although its filing date at the USPTO is June 10, 2016, the USPTO examined the patent based on its earlier June 12, 2015, priority date, so material that emerges between June 12, 2015, and June 10, 2016, cannot be considered prior art.

11.3.2.3 Publication Date

Patents are published after 18 months counting from the priority date. This is an important aspect of the patent system. It grants exclusivity but, in return, requires disclosure of the invention. Disclosure has a number of functions. First, it provides information to the public about an invention and hence allows third parties to learn about the invention. In fact, disclosure by a patent has to be sufficient to allow "someone skilled in the art" to make or use the patented invention; otherwise, the patent is considered invalid (for lack of enablement or insufficiency). Disclosure is also important because it provides notice to the public about the property right. It informs the public about patent protection and therefore (at least in theory) allows third parties to avoid trespassing or negotiate access to the patented invention.[12]

11.3.2.4 Patent Document

A patent consists of different elements; the most important from a legal perspective are the claims. They are the core of a patent as they describe the technical contribution of the invention to the state of the art. They disclose and define the legal boundaries of the invention. These boundaries are often referred to as patent scope or breadth. As such, the claims determine what infringes and what does not infringe on a patent. In addition, a patent also contains a summary and detailed description of the invention and optional drawings referred to in the description and claims. To give you a concrete example, the first claim of the Nintendo Switch patent shown in Figure 11.3 reads as follows:

> A game controller which is removably attachable to a main unit having a main unit-side slide member and configured to execute a game process, the game controller comprising:
>   an operation section; and

---

[10] Priority dates also matter because in some jurisdictions, applicants can file subsequent applications based on earlier filings. For example, in the United States, applicants file so-called continuations and continuations-in-part based on an earlier filing. At the EPO, applicants can file so-called divisional applications. The subsequent filings all retain the priority date of the first filing from which they originated.

[11] Some countries recognize grace periods that excuse prefiling disclosures under certain conditions.

[12] The publication date is also important because, for example in the United States, patent owners can sue for patent infringement after a patent has been granted for any infringing act that has occurred after the patent publication date even before a patent was granted, provided the infringer had actual notice of the published patent application.

a controller-side slide member protruding from a first surface of the game controller and configured to slidably engage with the main unit-side slide member in a
slide direction, wherein:

the controller-side slide member has a first end and a second end in
the slide direction;

the game controller is configured to be attached to the main unit by
inserting the controller-side slide member into the main unit-side slide member
from the first end;

the game controller includes a stop member configured to resist a
slide movement, in an opposite direction, of the controller-side slide member
against the main unit-side slide member, the opposite direction being a direction opposite to a direction in which the controller-side slide member is inserted into main
unit-side slide member; and

the stop member is configured to protrude from the first surface of the
game controller or from a side surface of the controller-side slide member, which
side surface is substantially perpendicular to the first surface, and the stop member
is on the second end side of a center of the controller-side slide member in the slide
direction.

In practice, defining patent scope presents a significant challenge. The broader the
claims, the broader is the protection afforded by a patent. This makes it more difficult for third parties to invent around a patent and hence results in fewer competing
inventions in the marketplace. Thus, broader claims tend to translate into fewer available substitutes and more market power for the patentee. However, broader claims also
make it more likely that the claimed invention has already been disclosed in the existing
prior art and therefore fails to satisfy the novelty and non-obviousness requirements.

Most patents have more than one claim. For example, the Nintendo Switch patent
shown in Figure 11.3 has 25 claims. If there are several claims, a distinction is made between independent and dependent claims. An independent claim defines the broadest
boundaries of the invention. The broad boundaries are then narrowed down by dependent claims. It is important to note that the presence of several claims does not
imply that a patent contains more than one invention. In fact, a patent must not disclose
more than a single invention.

We said above that claims define the boundaries of an invention. In practice, moving
from the claim language to the definition of patent scope can be challenging. This is
because claims are subject to interpretation. This is where the patent description and
drawings come in handy. They are used in combination with the claims to define the
boundaries. The interpretation of claims differs across countries. Many countries offer
some flexibility under the so-called doctrine of equivalents by not requiring a literal
claim interpretation.

Finally, it is helpful for economic analysis to distinguish between different claim
types. We can make a basic distinction between product and process claims. A product
claim generally refers to a device, embodiment, or chemical compound or substance.
Patent protection guarantees that no third party can make the same product regardless of how it is made. That is, if a certain active ingredient is patented, it is irrelevant
if another company manages to produce the same active ingredient using a different

production method. This is different for process claims. Here, what is protected is a specific method of making or using a product. Now if a third party manages to make or use the same product employing a different method, the product does not infringe the process patent. There are many other types of claims, but a more in-depth discussion goes beyond the scope of this chapter.

11.3.2.5 Expiration and Renewal

Patents are normally valid for a maximum of 20 years counting from the date of filing. However, depending on the jurisdiction, limited extensions beyond 20 years may be available.[13] In order to keep a patent in force during its statutory lifetime, a patent owner has to pay maintenance (also called renewal) fees.[14]

A patent expires either because it reaches its limit of the statutory patent term or because it lapses due to nonpayment of renewal fees. Once a patent expires, it can no longer be infringed (although it is possible to sue for infringement after a patent has expired if the alleged infringing act occurred prior to the expiration of the patent). At this point, the patented invention, which is disclosed in the patent document, enters the public domain.

11.3.3 Patent Classification

To facilitate the search process for prior art during patent examination, patents are categorized into hierarchical patent classifications according to the technologies that they cover. There are several such patent classifications. The International Patent Classification (IPC) system was established in 1971 to provide a harmonized hierarchical system to classify technology contained in patents. The United States relies instead on the US Patent Classification (USPC) system. In 2010, the EPO and USPTO created a joint harmonized classification system, the Cooperative Patent Classification (CPC) system, which is very similar to the IPC in structure. The CPC replaced the EPO's European Classification (ECLA) system, while the USPTO continues to use both USPC and CPC. These patent classifications are regularly revised to take into account technological changes and new developments.

To understand the structure of patent classifications, let's look at the example of Apple's patent US 8,289,400, "Image capturing device having continuous image capture." The patent covers a technology that is designed to improve the quality of photos taken with the iPhone. The patent office assigned the patent a total of 13 IPCs, all with a main class H04N.[15] It is common for patents to have more than one IPC since different features contained by a patent may relate to different technologies. Take, for

---

[13] For example, in Europe, the EPO grants supplementary protection certificates (SPCs) for pharmaceutical and agrochemical inventions that offer an additional 5 years of protection.

[14] Fees are payable during fixed intervals that vary across jurisdictions. However, fees usually increase over time to ensure that only valuable inventions are kept on the patent register for the full 20-year patent term.

[15] In fact, the USPTO assigned CPC classes rather than IPC, but in this case the two classifications are the same so we refer to them as IPC for simplicity. The broader H04N class does have some differences between IPC and CPC, however. For details, you can consult https://www.uspto.gov/web/patents/classification/cpc/html/cpc.html.

example, IPC symbol H04N 5/144. The letter "H" denotes the section "Electricity," a broad technological area. Currently, the IPC has eight such broad sections. H04 is the patent class. It describes a narrower technological area, to which the IPC and CPC have assigned the title "Electric Communication Technique." Next, H04N is the patent subclass "Pictorial Communication." There are currently 129 classes and 638 subclasses. H04N 5 denotes the main group and H04N 5/144 denotes the subgroup ("Movement Estimation") of which the IPC contains over 70,000. The subgroup title "Movement Estimation" is supposed to provide a precise description of the patented technology. As an exercise, you should find the patent classifications listed on the Nintendo Switch patent illustrated in Figure 11.3 and see if you can identify the corresponding technologies.

Patent classifications make it easier to find technologically similar prior patents both for applicants and patent examiners.[16] The focus on aiding prior art search means that patent classes do not map directly into technology areas that correspond more closely to areas of economic activity. There have been several attempts at creating such correspondences, the most widely used one of which is the concordance proposed by Schmoch (2008). The concordance maps IPC classes into 35 broad areas of technology. For example, Apple's patent discussed above, according to Schmoch's correspondence, IPC H04N 5/144 maps into "Audio-visual technology" within the broad technology area "Electrical Engineering." Mapping IPC classes more directly to economic activity is even more challenging because technologies often can be used in a wide range of economic activities. One solution is to match patents to firms and then rely on the economic activity of the firm to assign the same economic activity to the patents held by the firm. Lybbert and Zolas (2014) propose an alternative approach. They map IPC classes directly to different classifications of economic activity, including the Standard International Trade Classification (SITC) and the International Standard Industrial Classification (ISIC). Lybbert and Zolas rely on keyword matching between patent abstracts and titles and the description of the industry classifications. Returning to our example of US 8,289,400, the algorithm assigned H04N to several industry classes including "Photographic apparatus and equipment."

11.3.4 Inventor and Ownership

11.3.4.1 Inventor

An inventor is anyone who contributed to any of the essential elements of the invention claimed by a patent. In practice, there are often several individuals listed as inventors, who are also referred to as co-inventors. By default, co-inventors are assumed to have equally contributed to the patented invention and hence are entitled to an equal share of the property right. There are, in fact, two inventors listed on the Nintendo Switch patent shown in Figure 11.3: Kumpei Fujita and Shinji Hirose.

---

[16] It also helps patent offices in assigning incoming patent applications to examiners with the relevant subject matter expertise. Larger patent offices divide examiners up by technology (e.g., at the USPTO, examiners are assigned to Technology Centers (TC) and within TCs, into Art Units).

11.3.4.2 Assignee

The patent system separates inventorship from ownership. That is, the owner of a patent is not necessarily the inventor. Ownership of a patent can be transferred at any point during the lifetime of a patent; such a transfer is referred to as reassignment. You can see in Figure 11.3 that the Nintendo Switch patent is assigned to Nintendo.

A patent can also be assigned to more than one party. In such a situation, the patent is co-owned. The rules regarding co-ownership vary across jurisdictions (see Chapter 20). In all jurisdictions, co-owners have the right to exploit the patented invention themselves free from interference by any of the other co-owners. However, in some jurisdictions, such as Germany or the United Kingdom, co-owners require consent from other co-owners if they want to license or reassign the patent. In other jurisdictions, such as the United States, no consent is required.

11.3.5 International Dimension

It may come as a surprise, but there is no such thing as an international patent. Patents are national rights. If an applicant seeks patent protection in several countries, they have to file and prosecute separate patent applications in each jurisdiction in which they wish to obtain patent protection.

The 1883 Paris Convention established the national treatment of foreigners, which means patents must be available to foreign nationals, and they receive the same rights as nationals. The Paris Convention also facilitated the filing of patent applications in multiple jurisdictions by allowing the use of the first filing date of a patent application in any member state of the convention within 12 months of that first filing date (this is what happened in the case of the Nintendo Switch patent). As explained above, without the 12-months period, an applicant would have to file their patent on the same day in all jurisdictions where they seek patent protection. Otherwise, any later filing would be rejected on the basis of a prior filing of the same patent in another jurisdiction. Patents that protect the same invention in different countries belong to the same "patent family." Note that the Paris Convention is not an international patent system; it merely provides the possibility to file the same application in multiple jurisdictions within a 12-month period (instead of having to file them all simultaneously).

A direct consequence of the national character of patents is that they are only enforceable in countries where they have been granted. For example, Amazon's patent US 6,317,722 titled "Use of electronic shopping carts to generate personal recommendations" has been granted by the USPTO. However, there is no patent at the EPO that protects the same invention, presumably because the EPO does not consider the invention patentable subject matter. As a result, the invention does not benefit from patent protection in any of the EPC member states. Instead, Amazon's invention benefits from patent protection only in the United States. This, in turn, means that patent protection only applies to any infringing acts within the borders of the United States. Indeed, in 2009, Amazon sued Discovery Communications (the company that runs the Discovery Channel among others) for infringement because it allegedly relied on the patented technology in its online store.[17] Amazon did not have the same recourse outside of the US It could not have sued Discovery Communications for infringement anywhere else in the world even if the online shop was also available to customers elsewhere.

While there are no international patents, WIPO's PCT of 1970 simplifies the application procedure of obtaining patent protection in multiple countries. The PCT system currently has 157 contracting states and therefore covers almost the entire world. It facilitates obtaining international patent protection by allowing applicants to file a single international application instead of separate applications in each jurisdiction where patent protection is sought. The PCT system also partly addresses concerns over duplication of patent examination because it centrally produces a single search report that is then made available to national offices. Box 11.1 describes the PCT process in more detail; it is quite different from the regular application process.

Although there is no international patent, governments have undertaken major progress toward the international harmonization of the patent system with the 1994 TRIPS agreement. The TRIPS agreement was part of a major WTO agreement on trade, the so-called Uruguay Round, and therefore signed by all WTO member states. An important feature of TRIPS as a WTO agreement is that disputes over compliance can be brought before the WTO, which has the authority to impose trade sanctions. This ensured swift compliance with the agreement. TRIPS specified certain minimum standards of IP protection that each signatory must provide. Before the agreement, there were substantial differences across countries in terms of the level of patent protection provided. For example, some countries, such as India, did not grant product patents on pharmaceuticals. Also, in some countries the statutory patent term was significantly shorter than 20 years, just 7 years in the case of India. Developing countries were accorded transition periods depending on their level of development to implement the agreement. While the overall impact of TRIPS is contested (see Chapter 15), there is widespread agreement that TRIPS led to a substantial strengthening of patent protection in most developing countries.

Despite the harmonization of national patent systems around the world achieved by TRIPS, there is still no global patent system. However, a number of regional patent systems exist. Currently, there are four regional patent systems: the ARIPO, the OAPI, the Eurasian Patent Convention, and the European Patent Convention (EPC). By far the most important of these four is the EPC. Signed in 1973, it currently has 38 member and 2 extension states.[18] The EPC is not part of the EU, although all EU countries are member states of the EPC. That said, there are many EPC member states that are not part of the EU, including the United Kingdom and Turkey. The EPC provides a single route to obtaining a patent grant in all member and extension states. The EPC created the EPO, which centrally accepts patent applications, examines them, and grants the

---

[17] *Amazon.com Inc. v. Discovery Communications Inc.*, No. 09-cv-00681, 2011 WL 13228465 at *1 (W.D. Washington, January 11, 2011).

[18] Extension agreements are usually signed before accession to the EPC. Patents granted by the EPO can be validated in extension states.

Box 11.1 PCT Application Process

The PCT filing process proceeds as follows:

- **Filing of international application:** The applicant files a single patent application with their national or regional office or directly at WIPO (these patent offices are referred to as Receiving Offices or RO). Filing fees are much more substantial for a PCT filing than regular national or regional filings (around US$1,300). In order to file a PCT application, at least one applicant has to be a national or resident of a PCT contracting state.
- **International search:** An International Search Authority (ISA), which are a select set of patent offices including WIPO, conducts prior art search and issues an international search report as well as a written opinion about the patentability of the invention. The search fee varies substantially by ISA between US$150 and US$2,000. The competent ISA that carries out the search is determined by the RO. Some ROs allow applicants to choose among multiple ISAs, although in most cases there is only one competent ISA for a given RO.
- **International publication:** Eighteen months after the first filing date of the application, the application and the international search report are published and hence disclosed to the public.
- **Optional supplementary international search/preliminary examination:** If requested, another ISA can conduct another international prior art search. Also, if requested, an ISA carries out additional investigation regarding the patentability of the filed invention.

National phase: After the above steps are concluded, commonly after around 30 months counting from the earliest filing date, the international application together with the international search report is forwarded to the national and regional offices in which the applicant seeks patent protection for examination. National and regional offices also require payment of national or regional filing fees. National and regional offices then conduct their own regular examination and decide on granting the patent. Once granted by a national or regional office, the patent has to be maintained in force in each national or regional office where the patentee wants protection.

European patent. Importantly, although the EPO grants a patent, the granted patent does not have unitary effect in all EPC signatory states. Instead, the granted patent has to be validated in each member state in which protection is wanted, and the patent is then subject to national law. The validation process is complex since validation requirements differ across countries. Apart from validation fees, there are also translation requirements that will increase the cost of validating a European patent. Also note that the EPC coexists with national patent systems, which means applicants have a choice to obtain patent protection either directly via the national patent system or via the EPO.

The participating states are: Austria, Belgium, Bulgaria, Denmark,
Estonia, Finland, France, Germany, Italy, Latvia, Lithuania, Luxembourg,
Malta, the Netherlands, Portugal, Romania, Slovenia, Sweden.

Figure 11.4 Unitary Patent states.

The advantage of the European patent is central examination. Instead of having to
file separate patent applications with national offices, an applicant can file a single application at the EPO. However, once granted by the EPO and validated in a member
state, the patent needs to be enforced separately in each member state. Mejer and van
Pottelsberghe (2012) document the potential inconsistencies that can result from such
fragmented national enforcement. In the 1980s, Epilady patented its then popular hair
removal device for women. Not too long after receiving its patent (EP0101656), Epilady
sued competitor Remington for infringement in Austria, Belgium, Germany, France,
Italy, the Netherlands, and the United Kingdom. The courts in Belgium, Germany, Italy,
and the Netherlands found Epilady's patent infringed. In contrast, the courts in Austria,
France, and the United Kingdom found no infringement.

To address these shortcomings, the European patent with unitary effect, or short the
Unitary Patent system, was created in 2012. As shown in Figure 11.4, there are currently 18 states that participate in the Unitary Patent system, which became operational
in June 2023. Unlike the "classic" European patent, the Unitary Patent has unitary effect and therefore does not require validation in those 18 individual member states.
The Unitary Patent makes it cheaper to obtain and maintain broad patent coverage
since no fees are payable to individual member states. Importantly, enforcement occurs
at the newly formed UPC.[19] Given the patent's unitary effect, the court's decisions

---

[19] Note that following Brexit, the United Kingdom is no longer part of the Unitary Patent system since the
UPC would have been bound by EU law and Court of Justice of the European Union (CJEU) decisions. The
United Kingdom nevertheless remains part of the EPC since it is decoupled from the EU.

automatically affect all 18 jurisdictions that are part of the Unitary Patent system. As such, the Unitary Patent system is designed to avoid the inconsistencies associated with the "classic" European patent illustrated by the Epilady example above.

11.4 The Economics of Patents

Patents are generally considered the strongest of IP rights. Patent applications undergo examination at national or regional patent offices, which verify that they satisfy the statutory requirements for patentability. Once granted, patents provide a range of rights to their owners. Most importantly, a patent grants its owner the right to exclude everyone else from the exploitation of the patented invention. This ability results in exclusivity, which motivates the view of a patent as a monopoly. Moreover, since a patent is a property right, it can be sold, licensed, or even used as a security in financial transactions.

On the flipside, patents are usually vulnerable to invalidation throughout their life. The fact that a granted patent could be invalidated at any point during its lifetime reflects the difficulties inherent in patent examination.[20] For many of the same reasons, the scope of protection of a given patent also can sometimes be difficult to ascertain without recourse to litigation.[21]

In short, patents are property rights that grant their owners broad legal protection. At the same time, there is considerable uncertainty associated with both the validity and scope of the property right. As we will see below and throughout Part III of this textbook, the combination of a strong legal right and uncertainty has important implications for the use and impact of patents on innovation and competition.

How do economists think about patents? Take a look at Figure 11.5. It describes a company that initially finds itself in perfect competition. The firm has marginal cost MC_1, the market price is P_1, and the firm's profit is zero. Next the firm comes up with a drastic process innovation. The innovation allows the firm to lower its marginal cost from MC_1 to MC_2. If the innovation is not patented, we assume that it becomes immediately available to all other firms in the market as well, for example, through reverse engineering. If all other firms can also lower their marginal costs, the innovator finds itself producing at MC_2 with a market price of P_2. Again, the innovator makes zero profits despite having produced the cost-reducing innovation. Note, however, that consumers are much better off since the consumer surplus triangle has increased from area ABC to AFH.

If the firm can protect its innovation with a patent instead, we assume that no other firm can access the innovation. This means the innovator can produce at a marginal cost lower than any of the other firms and hence will become a monopolist in the market. As a monopolist, it maximizes profits by setting marginal revenue (MR) equal to marginal costs: $MR = MC_2$. The price the innovator charges

---

[20] There are a range of reasons why a patent may have been erroneously granted. For example, it later becomes apparent that a patented invention was, in fact, not novel. Given the limited time and resources available to patent examiners, an examiner could simply fail to discover the relevant prior art during the examination process (Frakes and Wasserman 2017). It is also possible that the patent did not disclose the invention sufficiently to allow a PHOSITA to perform the invention.

[21] Chapter 17 discusses this in more detail in the context of software patents.

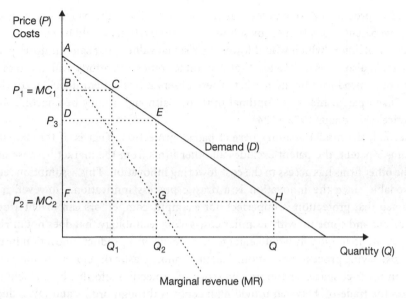

Figure 11.5 Drastic process innovation.

is therefore P_3. The effect of patent protection is that market structure changes from perfect competition to monopoly and, as a result, the innovator moves from zero profit to positive profit described by area *DEGF*. Consumers are worse off because of the patent; their surplus shrinks from *AFH* to *ADE*. That said, they are still better off with the innovation despite the monopoly since without the innovation their surplus is only *ABC* with *ADE* > *ABC*. At the same time, patent protection and resulting monopoly pricing lead to DWL, area *EGH*. Hence, the impact of patent protection is on the one hand a positive profit *DEGF* for the innovator and on the other DWL *EGH*.

While Figure 11.5 is static, it still allows us to understand the fundamental trade-off involved in granting patent protection. On one side of this trade-off, there is the innovator. If the innovator obtains patent protection, the innovator receives the monopoly profit described by area *DEGF*. The prospect of profit *DEGF* is the incentive provided by the patent system as it allows the innovator to recoup their investment in R&D to generate the cost-saving invention. On the other side, if the innovator sets a monopoly price thanks to patent protection, there will be DWL described by area *EHG*. It is important to bear in mind that patent life is limited, which means once a patent expires, the DWL disappears and both areas *DEGF* and *EHG* turn into consumer surplus.

A number of questions about the design of the patent system arise from these simple observations. First, what is the optimal duration of patent protection? In other words, how much profit is necessary to induce the innovator to incur the necessary R&D expenses to produce the innovation? This is a long-standing question first posed by Nordhaus in 1967. An increase in patent protection will increase profits and thereby the marginal incentive to invest in R&D. However, increased incentives are not always necessary or even desirable. For example, some inventions would be produced also with less patent protection. Since the patent system grants uniform patent protection set by statute, those innovations would benefit from "too much" protection, which would lower their social value. That said, uniform patent protection also leads to "too little" protection for other inventions, which will therefore not be produced by the market. These observations led Nordhaus to conclude that "fixed patent life is not optimal in theory, although it may be unavoidable in practice" (Nordhaus 1972, p. 34).

Second, the model assumes perfect patent protection. That is, if the innovator obtains a patent, the patent excludes all other firms from the market because none of the other firms has access to the cost-lowering innovation. This assumption seems reasonable since the innovation is a drastic process innovation. However, if we assumed that protection is imperfect, for example, competitors can invent around the patent and come up with a similar cost-saving technology that does not infringe the patent, no monopoly would emerge. If we focus on a product innovation instead of a cost-saving process innovation, demand is more elastic the closer products compete in product space. Therefore, the scope of protection afforded by a patent also affects the trade-off between providing incentives through profits and DWL due to market power.

Finally, there is also the possibility of duplication of R&D expenses if firms engage in so-called patent races, where they try to be first to obtain exclusivity over an innovation in the form of a patent. While not shown in Figure 11.5, the figure still conveys the intuition. If only one party can obtain a patent over a given innovation, assuming perfect protection, the party that obtains the patent will obtain all the profits associated with that innovation. Hence, if there are initially two companies investing in R&D to produce an innovation, only the company that succeeds first will be awarded the patent. The other company will have wasted its R&D since it won't be able to use the innovation because the other party holds the relevant patent. This type of situation leads to duplication of R&D, which is wasteful from a social perspective. The extent to which this problem arises depends on patent scope (still assuming perfect protection). To see this, imagine that the patent obtained by the first successful inventor provides only narrow protection. In this situation, the second company might still be able to use its own innovation if it is sufficiently different from the first company's innovation, as claimed in its patent.[22]

11.5 Patent Quality and Patent Value

The economics literature on the patent system is replete with references to *patent quality*. This term is also often invoked in policy debates on the functioning of the patent system. However, patent quality is not a legal concept and has proved an elusive concept to define. Despite its prominence in the literature and policy debates, a fair amount of ambiguity persists about its precise meaning. One source of confusion is the fact that quality can refer to the quality of the patent right, that is,

---

[22] Note that the model's predictions also depend, among other factors, on our assumptions about any uncertainty involved in the research process.

the likelihood that a patent would be upheld if challenged, or to the underlying invention. Of course, the two qualities will be related, but they are different in conception.

A second concept that is often used in reference to patents is *patent value*. Again, this can refer to the value of owning the patent, or to the value of the underlying invention. In addition, the value of a patented invention may be private, that is, the value it creates for its owner via profits, or social, that is, the value it has for society including the private value for the owner.

Higham et al. (2021) use a variety of patent indicators known at the time of the patent grant to demonstrate that their association with *ex post* outcomes in the form of market valuation, renewal status, and the number of times they are cited is highly variable across the outcomes. Their results are evidence that what they term "patent quality" (but which includes some concept of value) has multiple dimensions. For example, it is plausible that market valuation measures relate to private value, whereas future citation may be more closely related to the social value of the invention.

Below we discuss further what we know about how to measure the quality and value of the patent right and the invention it covers.

11.5.1 Quality and Value of the Patent Right

Hall and Harhoff (2004, p. 991) propose several criteria for a patent to qualify as *high-quality*. According to their definition, high-quality patents:

1. describe inventions that are truly new, rather than inventions that are already in widespread use but not yet patented.
2. enable those "skilled in the art" to comprehend the invention well enough to use the patent document to implement the described invention.
3. have little uncertainty over [their] validity and the breadth of [their] claims.

According to this definition, patent quality is determined by the actual implementation of statutory patentability requirements by patent offices during examination. Patent examiners assess patentability and "negotiate" with applicants over amendments to the patent application. The outcome of this process determines patent quality. Hence, patent quality could be understood as the degree to which a patent office implements the legal standards for granting patents. This discussion also implies that patent quality is distinct from what the literature refers to as *patent strength*. Patent strength is the degree of protection afforded by a patent system. For example, longer statutory patent life results in stronger patents but does not affect patent quality directly, although it does affect the value of the patent right.

De Saint-Georges and van Pottelsberghe (2013) attempt to measure the quality of patents granted by the 32 different patent systems around the world by creating an index combining the rules and regulations of the office with the workload and incentives faced by the patent examiners. They found that the demand for patents was lower in systems with higher quality, controlling for research efforts, patent fees, and the strength of patent enforcement in the country. By their measure, the EPO, UK IPO,

Table 11.1 Schankerman-Pakes and Bessen Estimates of the Value of a Patent Right

Country	Median Value (2022 US$)	Top 1% Value (2022 US$)
United Kingdom	$1,861 ($6,681)	$82,475 ($296,085)
France	$897 ($3,220)	$101,473 ($364,288)
Germany	$5,710 ($20,499)	$208,061 ($746,939)
United States (all patents)	$7,000 ($14,770)	N/A
United States (public manufacturing firms)	$18,000 ($37,980)	N/A

Source: Schankerman and Pakes (1986) and Bessen (2008).

and Scandinavian patent systems had the highest quality and the United States ranked rather low, even after the various reform efforts of the 2000s.[23]

The value of a patent right will be related to the quality of the system, the size of the market covered, and the ability to enforce the patent. The value of the patent right is the value of excluding others from practicing the invention; a patent owner who lets the patent lapse can still practice the invention. Measuring this value is challenging given its correlation with the underlying value of the invention. However, the value of a patent can diverge from the value of the underlying invention, for example, if patents are used for strategic reasons (see Chapter 18).

One approach to the measurement of the value of the patent right itself, as opposed to the value of the invention, relies on the fact that patent owners let the overwhelming majority of patents lapse before the end of the 20-year statutory patent term to avoid the cost of renewal. The renewal value of a patent captures the incremental value of legal protection provided by the patent because if a patent is not renewed, the invention can still be used by the owner of the lapsed patent. If the patent is sold, however, the new owner can block the use of the invention by the original owner. As such, the "renewal value" of a patent right differs from its "asset value" (Harhoff et al. 2003).

The renewal approach was first proposed by Pakes and Schankerman (1984) and Schankerman and Pakes (1986). Schankerman and Pakes (1986) use data on patent renewals for the United Kingdom, France, and Germany for patents applied for between 1950 and 1979. The estimates of patent value produced by this approach are low. We show these estimates for the median and the top 1% of patents in Table 11.1. The table shows their estimates and the value converted to US dollars in 2022. All of these values are smaller than the estimates obtained from the PatVal survey or market value estimates discussed below.

The United States did not require the payment of renewal fees for patents until 1980, so Schankerman and Pakes were not able to use US data. Bessen (2008) used data from 1985 to 1991 and a similar model to estimate the value of patent rights in the United

---

[23] The low ranking of the United States was due to the existence of the grace period, the possibility to avoid publication of the application, the lack of a search report, and the availability of continuations.

States. The final two rows of Table 11.1 show his estimates, which are similar to the Schankerman-Pakes estimates but somewhat higher.

One problem with the renewal approach to estimating the value of a patent right is that patent values tend to be very skewed, so the average value is driven by the right tail of the distribution (see Figure 11.6). Because of the paucity of observations in the right tail and the relatively low values of renewal fees, the renewal approach is unable to measure the value distribution well without a parametric assumption about the value distribution that allows extrapolation to the most valuable part of the distribution. For example, Schankerman and Pakes use the lognormal distribution to estimate the potential returns to a patent right and hence its value. Because the renewal fees are very low relative to the value of the most valuable patents, the use of a different distribution to extrapolate could produce different results.

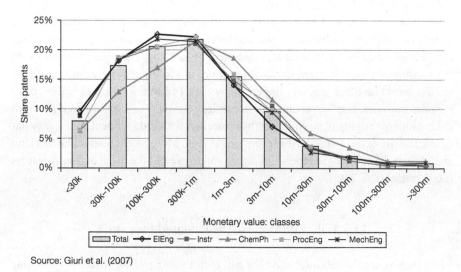

Source: Giuri et al. (2007)

Figure 11.6 The value distribution of European patents.

11.5.2 Quality of the Patented Invention

The distinction between the quality and value of a patented invention is somewhat less clear. By quality, we generally mean the intrinsic value of the invention as an inventive step, or contribution to knowledge. This implies that for society, value and quality of an invention are essentially the same: A high-quality invention is one that creates value for society. But for the owner, a patented invention may create considerable value without being of high quality. This can happen if the invention is only a modest improvement over a competitor's invention but displaces it in the market.

By far the most common approach to measuring the quality of a patented invention is to proxy it through observable patent characteristics. Motivated by the idea that patent quality is related to observable patent characteristics, Lanjouw and Schankerman (2004) proposed an approach that treats quality as a common factor. The intuition underlying this approach is that patented invention quality is a latent variable that is correlated with a patent's observable characteristics. As Lanjouw and Schankerman (2004, p. 448) explain, "We call the common factor "quality" because we find it difficult to think of any other characteristic that would be common to all" patent characteristics included in the model. Lanjouw and Schankerman (2004) rely on four patent characteristics in their model: the number of claims, backward citations, forward citations, and family size. They specify the following linear common factor model:

$$y_{ki} = \theta_k + \lambda_k q_i + e_{ki} \tag{1}$$

where y_{ki} denotes characteristic k (with $k = 1, \dots, K$) of patent i; λ_k are factor loadings; and ε_{ki} is a random normally distributed error term. q_i is the latent patent quality that will be estimated by equation (1). Note that this approach does not explicitly produce a measure of quality; it merely finds a single common indicator that combines measures that are believed to be related to quality.

The measure obtained by Lanjouw and Schankerman is a broad measure of the quality and impact on subsequent patented inventions of the patented invention, which can be interpreted as its social value. Subsequent research has highlighted some flaws in the measures they chose. Many backward citations in a patent may be indicative of a derivative invention that is not very important by itself. In addition, the measure of claims includes both independent claims and dependent claims. The latter are likely to limit the breadth of the patent, so counting them together with independent claims may not be informative of the quality of the invention covered. More recent research of this kind tends to use the count of independent claims and to expand the list of quality measures (Squicciarini et al. 2013).

11.5.3 Private Value of the Patented Invention

There is also considerable interest on the part of firms and investors in the private value of patented inventions. The private value is generally not the same as the social value or quality because it ignores DWL and spillovers. Understanding and empirically gauging the private value of patented inventions are important for policy (to determine the gap between private and social value) and private companies in making their business decisions.

It is not terribly meaningful to speak of the private value of a patented invention as distinct from the private value of a patent because the two are intrinsically connected. Only the renewal analysis described earlier is able to tease out the portion of value that is due to the patent right itself, rather than the combination of the patent and the invention it covers. When we observe the profits or market value associated with a patent, we observe the combined value of the patent right and the underlying invention. This value varies across technologies and institutional settings across jurisdictions, and also will depend on the patenting decisions by other firms and individuals. Moreover, most firms file more than a single patent, which means the value of a patent may depend on the firm's portfolio as well. If patents are complements, a portfolio may be more valuable than individual patents on their own.

Harhoff et al. (2003) use data from a small survey conducted in Germany in 1996 to elicit firms' valuations of their patents. Importantly, the survey only includes patents that were renewed for their entire statutory patent term, which is likely to bias patent value upward. The survey was conducted among patent holders, which included firms and individuals. They were asked, "If in 1980 you had known how its contribution to the future profitability of your enterprise would unfold, what is the minimum price for which you would have sold the patent, assuming that you had a good-faith offer to purchase?" Nearly three-quarters of respondents indicated a value of less than 1 million Deutschmarks (equivalent to about 500,000 euros). Only 1% of respondents reported a value of more than 40 million Deutschmarks (20 million euros).

Giuri et al. (2007) relied on a similar approach. They obtained information on patent value directly from inventors of granted European patents through the PatVal survey. Inventors were asked for the hypothetical minimum price for which their patent would have been sold on the day it was granted.[24] The results show again a highly skewed distribution (see Figure 11.6); only 7.2% of patents had a self-reported value of more than 10 million euros. In contrast, more than two-thirds of patents had a value of less than 1 million euros. Comparing the data across technologies, Figure 11.6 shows that there are more valuable chemical and pharmaceutical patents, while the opposite is the case for patents in electrical engineering, instruments, process engineering, and mechanical engineering. Further analysis of the data by Gambardella et al. (2008) suggests that the mean patent value is around 3 million euros, while the median is only 400,000 euros.[25]

Yet another approach to estimating patent value links a firm's stock market value and the firm's patent holdings, as we described in Chapter 6. The approach, first proposed by Griliches (1981), relates the financial market valuation of a firm to its tangible and intangible assets. This method provides estimates of patent value by obtaining an estimate of the marginal effect of an additional patent on a firm's market value. That is, the incremental effect of an additional patent is an estimate of the private value of the patent to the firm.

The approach also allows separating the value of a patent from the invention inputs by including not only a patent count measure but also R&D input in K. In his original application of this approach, Griliches (1981) used a small sample of 157 US publicly traded firms for the period 1968–1974 to obtain an average patent value of US$200,000 (about $718,000 in 2022).

To obtain a value estimate, we focus on results in Hall et al. (2005) for the simple regression of Tobin's q on the patent-stock ratio (equation 3 in their paper):

$$\log Q_{it} = \log\left(\frac{V_{it}}{A_{it}}\right) = \log q_t + \log\left(1 + \gamma\frac{K_{it}}{A_{it}}\right) + \varepsilon_{it}$$

---

[24] The inventors were provided with 10 intervals to choose from: less than Euro 30,000; 30–100,000; 100–300,000; 300,000–1 million; 1–3 million; 3–10 million; 10–30 million; 30–100 million; 100–300 million; more than 300 million.

[25] Their results also suggest that forward citations correlate with value, which provides some direct support for the widespread use of forward citations as a proxy for patent value in the literature.

where K is proxied by firm i's stock of patents suitably depreciated. This regression equation implies the following expression for the change in value from a one-unit increase in patent stock:[26]

$$\Delta V_{it} = \gamma q_t$$

Hall et al. (2005) obtain a patent coefficient of 0.6–0.7 depending on the time period. The firms in their sample have a mean Tobin's q of 1.73 and a median of 1.09, which implies that the value of an additional patent to US firms during the 1976–1992 period was approximately 0.6 to 1.2 million 1987 dollars.[27] This value was somewhat lower than the Kogan et al. (2017) estimate of 5.4 million 1982 dollars for the 1976–2006 period. But it is important to recognize that these estimated values will be highly variable across firms so that computations at the median or mean are only guidelines, and we do not expect different samples to give the same answer.

Hall et al. (2005) also extend the model to include patent forward citations. Their results indicate that citations per patent increase market value more than the patent itself and that valuation varies considerably across industry. However, the results also suggest a nonlinear relationship as only citations above the median citations per patent affect market value.

11.6 Utility Models

Utility model protection originated in the United Kingdom in 1843 with the Utility Designs Act in the form of *utility designs*. The law created protection for designs with functional features. However, utility designs in the United Kingdom were rather short-lived as they were abolished in 1919 by the Patents and Designs Act. Germany also created utility model protection in 1891, with the intention of offering protection for inventions that were excluded from patentability. Notably, the German patent system required a showing of a "technical advance," which effectively excluded many inventions from patentability. The utility model therefore offered protection to such inventions. Nonetheless, process inventions were excluded from utility model protection.

In Germany, the utility model (*Gebrauchsmuster*) still exists. It requires registration although it is not subject to substantive examination. Hence, utility models are presumed valid until a third party challenges validity. A utility model is valid for only 10 years counting from the application date. The structure of the utility model is the same as that of a patent: It consists of a description, claims, and possible drawings where the invention is disclosed in the claims. Utility models are granted much faster than patents and their prosecution is significantly cheaper. An important difference to the patent system is that novelty only focuses on written prior disclosure anywhere in the world and use in Germany. In contrast, prior oral disclosure or prior disclosure

[26] The easiest way to derive this result is to drop the disturbance ε and transform the equation to one for V_{it} instead of $\log Q_{it}$.

[27] Doing this computation requires us to recognize that A is measured in millions of dollars, so the units of K/A are patents per million dollars, and the units of γ are therefore a million dollars per patent. Q is the ratio of two quantities measured in the same currency units and therefore unitless.

through use outside of Germany is not considered novelty-destroying. Moreover, the German utility model system offers a 6-month grace period. That means utility model protection is available up to 6 months after disclosure of an invention. The German patent system does not offer such a grace period (unlike, e.g., the US patent system).

It is also possible to convert a patent into a utility model while the patent is still pending (so-called branching off) and even to obtain both a patent and utility model on the same invention. As such, the utility model offers a number of advantages relative to a patent: It is granted quickly, which enables swift enforcement; the novelty requirement is lower; it is cheaper to obtain; and it can be used in addition to a national or European patent. In light of these characteristics, it is not surprising that utility models are predominantly used to protect technical inventions that have a relatively short commercial life or as complements to regular patent protection. Empirical evidence for Germany suggests that products with a short life cycle are indeed more likely to rely on utility model protection because of the short grant lag compared to patents (Heikila and Lorenz 2018). This suggests that utility models might be useful in settings where quick protection is useful and the long lag times involved in the granting process make patents relatively less useful. That said, the evidence also suggests that firms regard patents and utility models as complements rather than substitutes (Heikila and Lorenz 2018).

Protection in the form of utility models, also referred to as *petty patents* or *small patents*, is not available in all jurisdictions around the world. While, for example, China, Japan, and Germany grant utility models, the United States and the United Kingdom do not.[28] It is also perhaps worth pointing out that in contrast to the availability of Europe-wide coverage of patents and design rights, there is no European utility model.

Even among those countries that grant utility model protection, there are significant differences in the legal requirements and type of protection afforded. The lack of harmonization across countries is explained by the fact that TRIPS does not mandate the granting of utility models. Still, the Paris Convention establishes the priority right for utility models and stipulates that priority can be established for utility models through the filing of a patent and vice versa. Moreover, the PCT also extends to utility models.

Figure 11.7 shows the number of utility (model) patent filings in China and Germany between 1985 and 2020. Note the difference in scale––the right-hand scale (China) is more than 10 times that for Germany. While utility model filings decrease slightly over time in Germany, there is a dramatic increase in utility patent filings in China. As in the case of patents, China has seen exponential growth in utility model filings and is now leading the world in terms of filings.

11.7 Design Rights

In 2019, car manufacturer Volkswagen alleged that Verotec Wheels Inc. and its owner Andy Varona infringed Volkswagen's design patent D721,028 titled "Vehicle wheel rim" (the patent is owned by Volkswagen's subsidiary Audi), which protects the ornamental

---

[28] To avoid confusion, we should remind ourselves that utility patents in the United States are not utility models. Instead, utility patent is just another name for invention patent.

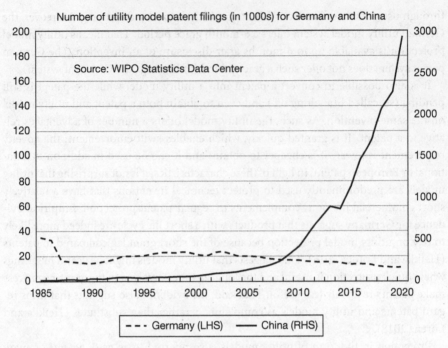

Number of utility model patent filings (in 1000s) for Germany and China

Source: WIPO Statistics Data Center

--- Germany (LHS)   —— China (RHS)

Figure 11.7 Number of utility model patent filings in selected countries.

appearance of its wheel rim. Volkswagen claimed that the design of the wheel rim on the right-hand side in Figure 11.8, sold by the defendant, is the "same or substantially the same" as the design protected by Volkswagen's design patent, shown on the left-hand side of Figure 11.8. Volkswagen claimed that "[t]he designs are so similar as to be nearly identical such that an ordinary observer, giving such attention as a purchaser usually gives, would be so deceived by the substantial similarity between the designs so as to be induced to purchase Defendants' products believing them to be substantially the same as the design protected by the '028 patent." The court granted summary judgment

US Design Patent D721,028	Infringing and Counterfeit Product
Fig. 1	

Source: Volkswagen Group of America inc. vs. Andy Varona and Verotec Wheels Inc., No. 19-cv-24838, 2021 WL 1997573, at *1 (S.D. Fla May 18, 2023).

Figure 11.8 Comparison of Volkswagen's design and the infringing design.

in Volkswagen's favor, finding willful infringement of its design patent, and awarded Volkswagen damages. If you have a hard time relating to the design of a wheel rim, take a look at Box 11.2, which discusses design protection of a product with which you are probably more familiar.

In the United States, design protection is available in the form of design patents. However, protection for designs varies substantially across jurisdictions; there is little international harmonization. TRIPS only loosely mandates design protection, and the agreement leaves considerable room for interpretation by individual member states on how to protect designs.[29] Apart from protection in the form of design patents, industrial designs are also protected by registered and unregistered design rights. Similar to patents and trademarks, there is an international agreement, the Hague Agreement Concerning the International Registration of Industrial Designs, that facilitates the international filing of design rights in different countries signatory to the agreement through a single filing with WIPO.

The economic purpose of design rights is to promote investment in the development of aesthetic aspects of products, which can result in higher prices. There is empirical evidence from Europe that in the market for visible automotive spare parts,

---

Box 11.2 *Apple v. Samsung* Design Patent Litigation

Apple sued Samsung in the Northern District of California in 2011 for the infringement of three of its design patents that protect the look of its iPhone (among other legal issues in the suit). Apple alleged that "Samsung has misappropriated Apple's patented mobile phone design in the accused products, including the Samsung Galaxy mobile phone." The figure below shows the direct comparison provided by Apple in its complaint filed with the court for one of its design patents (D618,677) with Samsung's Galaxy phone.

Apple's US Design Patent D618,677   *Samsung Galaxy Smartphone*

Source: *Apple Inc. v. Samsung Electronics Co. Ltd.*, 920 F. Supp. 2d 1079 (N.D. California, January 29, 2013).

In 2012, a jury in the case found in Apple's favor and imposed a total damages award of over US$1billion. The figure below shows the table from the jury verdict regarding infringement of Apple's design patent D618,677:

---

[29] See Article 25(1) of TRIPS. TRIPS does, however, require a minimum term of protection of 10 years [Article 26(3) of TRIPS].

For each of the following products, has Apple proven by a preponderance of the evidence that Samsung Electronics Co. (SEC) and/or Samsung Telecommunications America (STA) has infringed the D'677 Patent?

(Please answer in each cell with a "Y" for "yes" (for Apple), or with an "N" for "no" (for Samsung). Do not provide an answer for any cell that is blacked out.)

Accused Samsung Product	Samsung Electronics Co., Ltd.	Samsung Telecommunications America, LLC
Fascinate (JX 1013)	Y	Y
Galaxy Ace (JX 1030)	N	
Galaxy S (i9000) (JX 1007)	Y	
Galaxy S 4G (JX 1019)	Y	Y
Galaxy S II (AT&T) (JX 1031)	Y	Y
Galaxy S II (i9100) (JX 1032)	Y	
Galaxy S II (T-Mobile) (JX 1033)	Y	Y
Galaxy S II (Epic 4G Touch) (JX 1034)	Y	Y
Galaxy S II (Skyrocket) (JX 1035)	Y	Y
Galaxy S Showcase (i500) (JX 1017)	Y	Y
Infuse 4G (JX 1027)	Y	Y
Mesmerize (JX 1015)	Y	Y
Vibrant (JX 1010)	Y	Y

On appeal, the Court of Appeals of the Federal Circuit (CAFC) affirmed the design patent infringement but substantially reduced the damages award to Apple. However, Samsung appealed further to the US Supreme Court. In 2016, the Supreme Court questioned the way damages were calculated by the lower courts and referred the case back to the district court to reassess the damages. Ultimately, in a second trial, the design patents were found infringed and damages totaling more than US$500million were imposed, as shown in the figure below. The case is certainly unusual in its complexity, but it did create a widespread perception that design patents are valuable assets in a firm's patent portfolio.

1. What is the total dollar amount that Apple is entitled to receive for Samsung's infringement of the D'677, D'087, and D'305 patents?

$ __533,316,606__ .

the availability of design protection results in around 6% higher prices (Herz and Mejer 2021). Design rights also offer protection for low-tech products, which otherwise could not benefit from patent or utility model protection. Indeed, empirical evidence from Europe indicates that industries that rely more on design protection are relatively low-R&D-intensive, consumer goods industries, such as furnishing, and clothing (Filitz et al. 2015). Design rights can also help specialization as they allow upstream design firms to license their designs downstream to manufacturers. Moreover, they may enable product differentiation. These effects may benefit in particular smaller firms. Evidence from design patent litigation in the United States indicates that around half of court cases involve small- and medium-sized firms as both plaintiffs

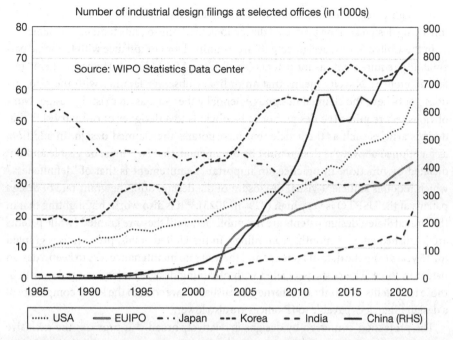

Number of industrial design filings at selected offices (in 1000s)

Source: WIPO Statistics Data Center

| ...... USA | ——— EUIPO | – · · Japan | – – – Korea | – – India | ——— China (RHS) |

Figure 11.9 Number of industrial design filings at 6 major offices.

and defendants, which is a much higher share than in patent litigation (Schwartz and Giroud 2020).

Figure 11.9 shows design filings for a selected number of jurisdictions, again with China on a separate right-hand scale. The most striking feature of Figure 11.9 is the dramatic increase in design patent filings in China, from around 2,000 in the late 1980s to over 800,000 in 2021. Among the other jurisdictions, we also see a steep increase in design filings over time in the United States, Korea, India, and Europe--the EUIPO started granting registered design rights in 2003. The data for India show that design rights are important in developing countries for appropriating returns to innovation. The data shown in Figure 11.9 also reveal an interesting downward trend in design filings in Japan, similar to what we already observed in Figure 11.1 for invention patents.

Protection in the form of design patents or rights is only available for the visual appearance of a product,[30] that is, protection is only available for a design that is ornamental. In contrast, a design that is dictated by the function or purpose of a product is not protected. This requirement is the core distinction between design protection and patents.

Design patents are much simpler than patents. The design patent specification consists only of the patent title, description, and a single claim. The drawings are what matters; they disclose the patented invention and define the scope of protection. That is, the scope of design patents is not construed based on a verbal description of the design but instead based solely on the graphical depiction of the design. Infringement

---

[30] More precisely, an *article of manufacture* is a term of art that includes a wide range of products, including shapes, molded objects, and even graphical user interfaces (GUIs).

of a design patent is established through a visual test of similarity: Do the allegedly infringing design and the protected design look the "same or substantially the same"?[31]

In the United States, design patents are examined for compliance with the same patentability requirements as for patents (see Section 11.4.1 above). However, there are a few differences. Novelty means that an ordinary observer familiar with the prior art does not believe the claimed design is essentially the same as an existing design. Non-obviousness requires the design not to be obvious to a designer of ordinary skill that designs articles such as the article that incorporates the claimed design. In addition, as mentioned above, the design must be ornamental, that is, it must be visible and not dictated by function. In practice, an important requirement is that of "definiteness," which requires sufficient visual disclosure of the design. Still, the grant rate of design patents at the USPTO is very high (82% in 2023).[32] It is also worth highlighting that in the United States, design patents are not published until they are granted (while patents are published after 18 months from filing). In the United States, protection is granted for 15 years from the date of issuance and there are no maintenance fees to keep a design patent in force. The costs associated with obtaining design protection are lower than those for patents. Not only are attorney fees usually lower due to the lower complexity of a design filing, fees payable to IP offices are also lower.[33]

The protection conferred by designs is relatively broad.[34] It provides the exclusive right to use the design, and it even goes beyond the exact registered design. It also protects any design "which does not produce on the informed user a different overall impression." As in patent law, infringement does not require willfulness; infringement also occurs if the infringer had no knowledge of the registered design. This is different from copyright, where only copying constitutes infringement (for copying to occur, the copier must have been aware of the copyrighted work). It also distinguishes registered from unregistered designs; unregistered designs only protect against copying (because they are not registered and hence it requires finding the existing unregistered design in the marketplace).

In Europe, there is registered and unregistered design protection at the national level and since 2003 also at the EU level. The EU-level rights have a unitary character, which means they automatically extend to all EU member states. There are some important differences in protection available to registered and unregistered designs. The requirements for unregistered designs are generally lower, but the scope of protection afforded is weaker and the statutory term of protection shorter.[35] In Europe, there is no examination of registered design rights. In contrast to patent law, prior art may not be necessarily novelty-destroying. Earlier disclosed designs are to be ignored if they "could not reasonably have become known in the normal course of business to the circles specializing in the sector concerned" within the EU. Hence, earlier disclosed designs

---

[31] Note this is distinct from the test applied under trademark law that focuses on potential consumer confusion.

[32] https://www.uspto.gov/dashboard/patents/design.html.

[33] For example, at the USPTO, the filing fee for a utility patent is US$300, while that for a design patent is US$200 (see the USPTO Fee Schedule as of August 2022).

[34] The relief available includes preventing outright copying and counterfeiting, royalties, stopping imports, disgorging profits (a remedy not available to utility patents), and an injunction to stop sale.

[35] The unregistered design automatically provides protection for 3 years counting from the disclosure of the design in the EU.

outside of the EU could be irrelevant. There is also a 12-month grace period, that is, an applicant has 12 months to register their design after disclosing it (e.g., to do market testing).

There is little overlap between design protection and patents because patents protect the technical aspects of an invention, while a design protects only its ornamental aspects. That said, there is potential for overlap with copyright and trademark protection. In the United States, the overlap with trademark protection arises mostly because of so-called trade dress protection available under trademark law. A trademark may also protect the design of a product as long as the design satisfies the legal requirements for trademarkability (see Chapter 12). Indeed, in the case described in Box 11.2, Apple also enforced alleged trade dress rights against Samsung alongside its design patents. Because copyright protects the creative expression of an idea, a design usually also qualifies for copyright protection (see Chapter 13).

11.8 Plant Patents

In the United States, the 1930 Plant Patent Act (PPA) created a new IP right, the plant patent, to protect new, asexually reproduced plant varieties. The PPA was motivated by the demand by plant breeders for legal protection. As shown in Figure 11.10, prior to the PPA, some plant breeders went to extreme measures to prevent copying. The Stark Brothers nursery built a cage secured with an alarm around their first Golden Delicious apple tree to prevent competitors from stealing cuttings from the tree (Moser and Rhode 2012).[36] The need for IP protection was motivated by the characteristics of the plant-breeding industry. It takes a relatively long time to develop new plant varieties, and the process is associated with high development costs. At the same time, imitation is relatively easy and fast. Some plant varieties are self-reproducing, which means that no reverse engineering is necessary; just access to such varieties is sufficient for reproduction. The problem is compounded by commercial uncertainty; only very few plant varieties achieve commercial success. Therefore, the intention behind the PPA was to grant protection to plant breeders to incentivize private investment in R&D in order to help the domestic plant-breeding industry develop. The creation of a new form of legal protection was also considered necessary, because at the time, there was considerable uncertainty regarding whether the existing patent system would provide protection for modified organisms.

Plant patents have narrower scope than patents. They only cover the asexual reproduction of a specific plant grown in cultivation, not the seeds, or similar plants. The patentability requirements also differ. For a plant to be patentable, it has to be new, distinct, and not found in the wild. Plant patents provide protection for 20 years counting from the filing date.

Protection in the form of patentlike PVP certificates was extended to sexually propagated plants, that is, reproduction through seeds, by the Plant Variety Protection Act (PVPA) in 1970. In 1980, in its *Diamond v. Chakrabarty* decision, the US Supreme

---

[36] Note that plant breeders propagate the Golden Delicious apple tree asexually by grafting or budding. Sexual propagation through pollination is also possible but uncommon.

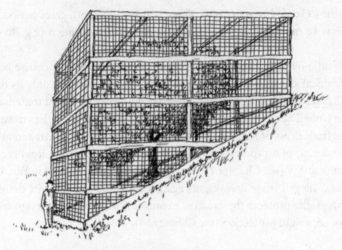

Source: Moser and Rhode (2012)

Figure 11.10 Cage to protect Golden Delicious apple tree.

Court extended utility patent protection to living organisms and therefore opened the door to the patenting of biological organisms.[37] Again the Supreme Court, in its 2001 decision in *J.E.M. Ag Supply Inc. v. Pioneer Hi-Bred*, extended utility patent protection to plant seeds and plants themselves.[38]

Apart from the United States, Japan and Korea also grant plant patents, although in some jurisdictions, conventional patent protection may also be available to plant breeders, for example, in Australia. However, not all countries grant plant patents or allow plants to be protected by patents (the EPO, e.g.). Instead of (also in addition to) patents, countries grant *sui generis* protection in the form of plant breeders' rights (PBRs). PBRs were created in 1961 at the International Convention for the Protection of New Varieties of Plants organized by the Union pour la Protection des Obtentions Végétales (UPOV), which had been set up by a number of European countries in an attempt to harmonize plant protection internationally. TRIPS mandates protection for plant varieties either in the form of patents or *sui generis* protection such as PBRs. Like patents, PBRs also provide temporary (20 years) exclusivity over plant varieties. PBRs require a plant variety to be novel (only with respect to commercialization), distinct from existing varieties, and uniform and stable, that is, plant characteristics should be the same and not change over generations. PBRs may be subject to breeders' exception and farmers' privileges. The farmers' privilege gives farmers the right to use their harvest to reproduce previously purchased protected plant varieties. The breeders' exception grants breeders access to protected plant varieties for research and experimental purposes.

The economic importance of plant patents is unclear. Moser and Rhode (2012) suggest that plant patents were not the main driving force behind the emergence of the US rose industry following the PPA. Alson and Venner (2002) arrive at a similar

---

[37] *Diamond v. Chakrabarty*, 447 US 303 (1980).
[38] *J.E.M. Ag Supply Inc. v. Pioneer Hi-Bred International, Inc.*, 534 US 124 (2001).

conclusion in their analysis of the impact of the 1970 PVPA on wheat varieties. They find no evidence for any positive impact on private investment in wheat breeding, or any evidence of increases in experimental or commercial yields of wheat. Thomson (2015) reaches a more negative conclusion regarding the impact of the introduction of PVP in Australia on wheat breeding. The results suggest that plant protection led to a decrease in new wheat variety output. One potential explanation advanced by Thomson (2015) is that PVP reduced spillovers in the form of exchange of germplasm between breeders.

11.9 Summary

This chapter provides an introduction to the economics of patent protection. The basic economic argument for granting the "patent monopoly" is that temporary exclusivity encourages investment in innovation. The chapter also offered an overview of the legal requirements and procedures to obtain patent protection. Although we only scratched the surface, it is clear from the discussion that the patent system is fairly complex and its specific design differs significantly across jurisdictions.

We also discussed the concepts of patent quality and value, and their empirical measurement. Although patent quality is a concept that is widely used in the economic literature and policy discussions, its definition and measurement are challenging. Conceptually, it is helpful to distinguish between the quality of the legal right that a patent confers on its owner and the quality of the underlying invention. The same is true for patent value, although here we have to deal with the additional complexity that there is yet another distinction, that between the private and social value of the patented invention.

Finally, in addition to patents, the chapter provides brief overviews of utility models, design patents and rights, as well as plant patents and PBRs. We explained the differences between these rights and invention (utility) patents, and the economic arguments for why some jurisdictions grant them.

12

Trademarks and Brands

Learning Objectives

After reading this chapter, you will be able to understand and explain the following concepts:

- The basic structure and purpose of the trademark system
- The process and legal requirements to obtain a trademark
- The characteristics and purpose of collective marks, certification marks, and geographical indications
- The economics underlying the trademark system
- The connection between trademarks, innovation, marketing, and economic performance
- The use of trademarks in combination with other IP rights
- The link between trademarks and product market competition
- Trademark squatting
- The trade-off involved in disclosure of information due to a trademark and trademark protection
- Trademark non-use, cluttering, depletion, and congestion
- The link between trademarks and e-commerce, including the link between trademarks and domain names and trademarks and online search

---

12.1 Introduction

Trademarks are everywhere in the modern economy. Literally billions of people recognize brand names such as Coca Cola, McDonald's, Google, or Facebook. These companies own and carefully maintain very large portfolios of brand names protected by trademarks. But not just multibillion dollar companies rely on trademarks to protect their brands. Trademarks also play an important role for smaller companies in building and protecting brand recognition.

Therefore, it is not surprising that trademarks are widely used throughout the world. There were more than 10.8 million trademark filings worldwide in 2018, as opposed to fewer than 3.3 million patent filings.[1] Growth in trademark filings has even

---

[1] The number of trademark filings refers to class counts, that is, applications are counted once for each class they cover; for more explanation on trademark classes, see Section 12.3 below (*Source:* WIPO Statistics).

The Economics of Innovation and Intellectual Property. Bronwyn H. Hall and Christian Helmers, Oxford University Press.
© Oxford University Press 2024. DOI: 10.1093/oso/9780197630914.003.0012

Table 12.1 Top Corporate Trademarkers in the United States in 2019

Company	Sector	US Trademarks Registered in 2019
Novartis AG	Pharmaceuticals	226
Samsung Electronics Co., Ltd.	Technology	204
Aristocrat Technologies Australia Pty Ltd.	Games	190
Daimler AG	Automobiles	139
Warner Bros. Entertainment Inc.	Entertainment	124
Amazon Technologies, Inc.	Technology	99
AGS LLC	Games	98
LG Electronics Inc.	Technology	94
King Show Games Inc.	Games	91
Johnson & Johnson	Pharmaceuticals	89

Source: USPTO's 2019 Performance and Accountability Report.

outpaced the accelerated growth in patent filings over the last decade.[2] Noteworthy is also the large number of trademark filings made in developing countries by developing country residents, which stands in stark contrast to their use of the patent system.[3] Since trademarks can, in principle, cover any type of product or service, they are also much more widely used across the entire economy than other IP rights, notably patents. Table 12.1 shows the top trademarking for-profit companies in the United States in 2019. The table shows a diverse mix of companies, including companies in pharmaceuticals, technology, automobiles, and (online) gaming. The widespread use of trademarks is to be expected given the close relationship between trademarks, brands, and marketing. In contrast, the link between trademarks and innovation is more complex.

This chapter provides an overview of the design and functioning of the trademark system; it discusses the economics of trademarks, and a range of topics related to the use of trademarks in the marketplace. The discussion also includes certification marks, collective marks, and geographical indications, which are available in a number of jurisdictions in addition to trademarks.

12.2 The Trademark System

According to the definition provided by the TRIPS agreement, a trademark is any sign, or any combination of signs, capable of distinguishing the goods or services of one undertaking from those of other undertakings." The definition provided by the US Lanham Act of 1946 (Trademark Act) is somewhat more comprehensive: A trademark

---

[2] Between 2000 and 2018, growth in worldwide trademarks averaged 8.5% per year, while patent filings increased, on average, by only 5% per year (*Source:* WIPO Statistics).

[3] For example, see Abud et al. (2013) for evidence on Chile and WIPO (2013). See also Chapter 15.

is "any word, name, symbol, or device, or any combination thereof . . . used by a person . . . to identify and distinguish his or her goods . . . from those manufactured or sold by others and to indicate the source of the goods." These definitions suggest that the purpose of a trademark is to distinguish one product from another and to identify the source of the product.[4]

For a sign to achieve these objectives as a trademark, it has to be distinctive. Conceptually, it is helpful to distinguish between "source distinctiveness" and "differential distinctiveness" (Beebe 2005). *Source distinctiveness* means that a trademark must allow consumers to identify the source or origin of the trademarked product. This requirement defines trademarkable subject matter and distinguishes a trademark from a purely decorative or functional product feature and sets it apart from other IP rights, notably registered design rights.[5] It also implies that generic words, simple colors, and conventional shapes that are purely functional cannot be trademarked. Since source distinctiveness defines trademarkable subject matter, it is a binary concept: A trademark either identifies a source or it does not.

Differential distinctiveness, in contrast, is a continuous concept; it describes the "uniqueness" of the trademark and is often also referred to as *trademark strength*. Although some marks are inherently more distinctive in this sense than others, differential distinctiveness generally is acquired over time with use of a trademark in commerce and investment in building the reputation and goodwill that the public associates with a mark. There is an obvious correlation between the two concepts of distinctiveness. In particular, descriptive trademarks that do not inherently identify a source can still qualify for trademark protection by acquiring source distinctiveness through so-called secondary meaning over time. This occurs when the mark achieves differential distinctiveness despite its descriptive nature. In practice, establishing acquired distinctiveness is often challenging, and it is generally unclear whether a high degree of differential distinctiveness implies a high degree of source distinctiveness or vice versa.

Provided a trademark is distinctive, it serves several purposes:

- Trademark owners are entitled to advertise a sign as a (un)registered trademark and signal to others that the mark is legally protected, that is, that they have the exclusive right to use the trademark for protected products in commerce.
- The legal property right protection afforded by trademarks allows trademark owners to prevent other firms from imitating the trademarked words and signs, and hence from free riding on the reputation and goodwill embodied by the brand that the trademark protects.
- Trademarks can also be licensed for use by third parties or sold, although usually it is required that both the mark as well as the protected products be licensed or sold. That is, a trademark as such usually cannot be licensed or sold in isolation. Still, trademarks offer the possibility to license or sell an intangible asset in the form of goodwill or reputation to third parties.

[4] Note that trademarks protect both products and services—however, for brevity, unless necessary, we will refer only to products throughout the chapter.

[5] Note that trademarkable subject matter is a malleable concept that can change over time. For example, in the United States before the 1946 Trademark Act, slogans, trade names, and trade dress could not be protected by a trademark (Lunney 1999).

The first purpose of the trademark system shows that there is a close link between trademarks and brands. Both terms are often used interchangeably, but trademarks are the legal instrument in the form of an IP right that protects the reputational value embodied by a brand. The link between trademarks and brands is discussed in more detail below.

Trademarks are also often associated with innovation.[6] However, from a legal point of view, there is no requirement that a product be innovative or new to benefit from trademark protection. From an economic perspective, unlike the patent system, the trademark system does not have the purpose of promoting innovation. That said, new trademark registrations are usually triggered by the introduction of new products or changes to existing products, which often reflect the outcome of some innovative activity. It is also true that the ability to protect brand names of new products helps innovators appropriate returns to their innovation.

12.3 Trademark System and Procedures

This section provides an overview of the structure of the trademark system and its procedures. There are significant differences between jurisdictions around the world. Nevertheless, there are some important characteristics shared by all trademark systems.

12.3.1 Trademarks

12.3.1.1 Trademark-Eligible Subject Matter
According to Article 15 of the TRIPS agreement, trademark-eligible subject matter is broadly defined. In principle, any product or service can be protected by a trademark. Trademark protection is available for "any combination of signs, capable of distinguishing the goods or services of one undertaking from those of other undertakings." Subject matter is mainly excluded because of an inherent lack of distinctiveness. For example, a word that is generic and merely describes a good, such as "coffee," cannot be trademarked as it inherently lacks distinctiveness. As such, also purely decorative or essential functional features of a product cannot be trademarked. While such marks are considered to inherently lack distinctiveness, they may nevertheless acquire distinctiveness over time through use and therefore become trademark-eligible as long as they are not generic.

12.3.1.2 Geographical Scope
Trademark applications are submitted to and granted by national IP offices as trademarks are territorial rights. They can only be enforced within the jurisdiction in which they were granted. The geographical scope of a trademark also determines an applicant's ability to register the trademark. Unlike the case of patents, the examination of a trademark filing only verifies whether there exist any confusingly similar marks in the geographic area for which trademark protection is sought (this is also referred to as

---

[6] For an overview of the literature, see Schautschick and Greenhalgh (2016. Section 3.1).

relative grounds examination).[7] This means that identical trademarks covering the same goods and services can be registered by different companies in different jurisdictions.

Similar to the patent system, under the Paris Convention there is an international priority right that allows trademark applicants to claim priority from a filing at another trademark office within 6 months of the first filing. There are also regional trademark systems, such as the EUIPO, that grant trademark protection in all EU member states or the ARIPO, which offers trademark protection in 10 African member states through a single trademark registration.

WIPO administers the so-called Madrid system, established under the Madrid Agreement Concerning the International Registration of Marks and the Protocol Relating to the Madrid Agreement, which offers a streamlined system for obtaining trademark protection in countries that are part of the system through a single application in a single language. The Madrid system also simplifies fee payments and trademark renewals since there is a single procedure within the system. That said, applications filed through the Madrid system still have to be approved and registered by the national offices designated by the applicant and, once registered, trademarks are subject to national law. This implies, for example, that if a trademark is cancelled in one jurisdiction, the cancellation does not affect the legal status of any registered trademarks in other jurisdictions.[8]

There are also a number of international agreements that facilitate obtaining international trademark protection; their role is mostly to simplify and harmonize administrative procedures. For example, the Trademark Law Treaty TLT and the Singapore Treaty on the Law of Trademarks regulate the information applicants have to provide in all signatory states, how goods and service classes should be specified, and so on.

12.3.1.3 Scope of Protection

Trademarks are classified into 45 classes according to the Nice classification system. It distinguishes broadly between 34 product and 11 service classes. Trademark classes assume an important role in affording legal protection––however, the precise role of the classification system in granting protection differs across jurisdictions. Some offices require applicants to specify only entire high-level Nice classes; others require applicants to specify product or service class headers; again, others require applicants to choose specific product and services groups from lists within each class. These differences have important implications for legal protection as generally only products and services specified in any of these more or less restrictive ways benefit from legal protection. The legal importance of the Nice classification in the trademark system also means that, in principle, different parties may be able to register the same or similar marks in different classes or product/service categories.

---

[7] So called well-known marks benefit from special protection. See https://www.wipo.int/edocs/pubdocs/en/marks/833/pub833.pdf.

[8] The exception is the trademark registered in the applicant's country of origin. If that trademark is for any reason removed from the register within 5 years from the date of the international registration, the international registration is no longer protected (although the international registration may be transformed into national applications). After the 5-year period, the legal status of the international registration is independent of that of the registration in the applicant's country of origin.

Note also that depending on the national trademark system, applicants can request protection only in a single or multiple classes (so-called single- vs. multiclass systems). In multiclass systems, trademark holders may abandon a subset of classes (or they may be cancelled in administrative or court proceedings) while still maintaining the remaining trademark in force. Normally registered trademarks cannot be extended to cover product/service categories or classes not covered by the original registration. Hence, if a company wants to expand into new product categories, it has to file new trademarks on the same mark. This gives rise to filing patterns on the same mark where new filings in different classes are added over time.

12.3.1.4 Length of Protection

Unlike other IP rights, trademarks once registered can be maintained in force indefinitely. The requirements to do so differ across trademark systems, but generally the payment of renewal fees is required in regular intervals and in some jurisdictions also some proof that the good or service protected by the trademark is still used in commerce by the trademark owner (see Section 12.3.1.6 below). In the United States, for example, trademarks are initially granted for a period of 10 years and then have to be renewed every 10 years. At the EUIPO and ARIPO, renewals are also due every 10 years.

12.3.1.5 Registration

Although trademarks are registered IP rights, trademark protection is also available for unregistered marks. Protection for unregistered trademarks is granted when firms have established distinctiveness for a given mark by actively using it in commerce.[9] Although both registered and unregistered trademarks may benefit from legal protection, trademark systems around the world differ in the role that registration plays. In some systems, only registration provides legal protection, whereas in others, such as the United States, use results in legal protection, not registration. Hence, in the US system, registration is not sufficient for protection if the trademark is not used or there is no intent of use within a defined period of time. That said, there are still advantages to registering a trademark over relying on an unregistered right in the United States.[10]

12.3.1.6 Use Requirements

To gain legal trademark protection, the corresponding trademarks have to be used in commerce. The purpose of this requirement is to discourage rent seeking by simply registering trademarks on products sold by other companies or strategically occupying trademarks for potential future use while keeping competitors from using them. Such use requirements are enforced in different ways across jurisdictions. The EUIPO, for

---

[9] In practice, this is assessed by evaluating the product's market share, duration of use in commerce, geographic scope, and the investment by its owner in building goodwill in the brand. Note that in most systems the bar for legal protection is substantially lower for trade designations (e.g., company names); they usually acquire protection through simple use as long as they identify the source of a product.

[10] Arguably, the most important advantage is the nationwide priority right granted by registration. It also grants a nationwide exclusive ownership right regardless of the actual geographical scope of use within the United States. Moreover, after the fifth year counting from the registration date, a declaration of incontestability can be obtained that limits the grounds on which the trademark may be invalidated for the rest of its (in principle, infinite) lifetime. Finally, registration also creates a strong presumption of validity in any cancellation proceedings.

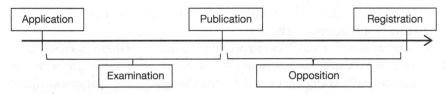

Figure 12.1 Trademark registration process timeline.

example, does not require any proof of use at any stage of the registration process or any time post-registration. Proof of use is only necessary if the trademark is subject to cancellation proceedings or enforced in litigation. In the US system, in contrast, applicants have to provide proof of use upon registration or, since 1989, make a *bona fide* declaration that the trademark will be used in commerce within 6 months (plus a 30-month extension). Nevertheless, registration and remedies for infringement are still contingent on actual use and proof of use. The US trademark office also requires proof of use 6 years following registration and every 10 years when the trademark is renewed.

12.3.1.7 Application and Grant Procedure

Upon filing of the application form, trademarks are examined (see Figure 12.1). Depending on the system, trademarks are either only formally examined or are examined both on formal and substantive grounds. Formal examination only assesses whether the filing concerns trademarkable subject matter and satisfies the formal requirements of a trademark application. The substantive examination (also called relative grounds examination), in contrast, assesses the distinctiveness of a mark and verifies that no likelihood of confusion exists with existing registered or unregistered marks (provided they are "renowned" in the sense of Article 6*bis* of the Paris Convention). The examiner assesses both inherent and acquired distinctiveness (i.e., secondary meaning) to ensure that the trademark identifies the source of the protected product and it is not confusingly similar to an existing trademark.

Following examination, a trademark is published in the gazette or trademark journal. Depending on the jurisdiction, the publication may coincide with the grant of the trademark. However, some systems allow for pregrant opposition, that is, following publication, third parties have the possibility to oppose the grant within a predetermined window of time (e.g., 30 days). Once that window is closed without a successful challenge, the trademark is automatically registered and the registered trademark published. Depending on the system, legal relief available to the trademark holder may only become available with registration, which makes this an important date in the lifetime of a trademark.

12.3.1.8 Trademark Types

There are different types of subject matter for which trademark protection is available:

- *Word mark*, which is a single word or combination of words, letters, and numbers, which are registered in standard black font on a white background.
- *Figurative mark*, which is a figure, such as a logo, without text.

- *Mixed mark*, which is a combination of a word and figurative mark where the word can have special fonts and be colored.
- *"Nontraditional" marks*: They comprise three-dimensional shapes, taste, sound, and scent marks. Three-dimensional shapes, taste, sound, and scent have to be nonfunctional to qualify as a trademark, and they must be capable of being represented graphically. Other nontraditional marks include holograms or moving image marks.[11]

12.3.1.9 Inherent Distinctiveness

Distinctiveness of trademarks is achieved in different ways. There are broadly conceived two types of trademarks that differ in their distinctiveness:

Inherently distinctive marks

- *Fanciful mark.* The so-called fanciful mark is an entirely new word that has no obvious connection with existing words (e.g., Kodak, Exxon). As such, fanciful marks are considered inherently distinctive as any association with a product is the result of investments and efforts made by its owner.
- *Arbitrary mark.* Arbitrary marks are existing words, symbols, and the like that have no obvious relation to the product that they protect (e.g., Apple, Adobe). This also implies that any association with a product is the outcome of investments and efforts made by the trademark owner.

Inherently nondistinctive marks

- *Descriptive mark.* Descriptive marks describe the product that they protect (e.g., Holiday Inn, Kentucky Fried Chicken) and hence have naturally a closer link with the product. They can, however, acquire distinctiveness by acquiring secondary meaning. That is, the public perceives the descriptive mark to primarily describe the protected products or services.
- *Suggestive mark.* A suggestive mark implies characteristics of the goods that it is used to name, but does not describe it (e.g., Financial Times, WhatsApp). This trademark type is somewhere between a fanciful and descriptive mark, although it is more narrow than descriptive marks but still inherently has a close, "suggestive" connection with the product that it protects.

12.3.1.10 Opposition and Cancellation

Oppositions are adversarial administrative proceedings that take place within a certain time window, either before or after registration of a trademark. If they take place before registration, they will occur following publication (see Figure 12.1). Trademark offices that offer opposition procedures differ in terms of grounds for opposition allowed. The basic distinction is between absolute (e.g., descriptive mark) and relative (e.g., likelihood of confusion) grounds. Opposition procedures also differ in the length of the time window during which third parties can oppose the registration of a trademark, which

---

[11] In the United States, trade dress protection is also available for visual aspects of a product or product packaging.

typically ranges between 30 and 90 days (e.g., in the United States third parties have 30 days following publication to oppose). The length of the time window trades off the likelihood of an opposition and the uncertainty for the applicant while the opposition window is open.

Some trademark offices also offer administrative postregistration cancellation proceedings. Again, there are differences across jurisdictions, for example, at the EUIPO trademarks can either be invalidated counting from the date the cancellation proceedings were initiated or alternatively *ex tunc*[12] retroactively, whereas in the United States no retroactive cancellation is possible. Also, in multiclass systems, individual classes can be cancelled, for example, if they are not maintained or no use is proven, while the remaining classes can still be maintained in force. In some jurisdictions, the ability of third parties to invalidate a trademark can be substantially curtailed, for example, in the US system after 5 years, certain grounds are no longer admissible for cancellation.

12.3.1.11 Fees
Trademark offices charge a range of fees that differ both in terms of level and structure. Trademark offices usually charge filing, publication, examination, and registration fees. There are also renewal fees postregistration. Offices may also charge a range of additional fees, for example, for changing the address of the applicant, re-assignments, and the like. The way these fees are structured varies across trademark offices. For example, some charge fees per class in which a trademark is registered; others may charge a fixed fee for a given number of classes. Some offices also award fee discounts to specific applicant groups, such as individuals or small- and medium-sized enterprises (SMEs), and WIPO grants a significant fee reduction for filings under the Madrid system to applicants in least developed countries. The level and structure of fees can have important implications for trademark filing behavior as discussed in more detail further below.[13]

12.3.1.12 Infringement
Another interesting aspect of the trademark system is that infringement is contingent on the likely confusion of consumers, and no actual confusion is required. In practice, proving confusion hinges on a range of different factors and can involve a certain degree of subjectivity,[14] although again there are substantial differences across jurisdictions.

---

[12] A legal term meaning "from the outset."

[13] De Rassenfosse (2020) and Herz and Mejer (2016) suggest that trademark filings react rather strongly to changes in filing fees. De Rassenfosse (2020) finds that a 10% increase in fees for filing a Madrid application leads to a decrease in filings by 3–4%. Herz and Mejer (2016) find even larger estimates of 5–10% for fees at 20 national offices in Europe.

[14] In the United States, for example, the so-called multifactor test is applied, which involves different factors such as the distinctiveness of the trademark and actual consumer confusion. The test varies across courts and affords substantial discretion to the court in its application. In establishing whether infringement has occurred, courts recognize different forms of confusion: (1) source confusion that arises when consumers are likely to mistake a product as the one protected by the trademark, (2) sponsorship confusion that describes a situation where a consumer may mistakenly think that a product is approved or promoted by the trademark owner, (3) initial interest confusion that arises before a product is purchased but disappears before the product is bought, and (4) postsale confusion that occurs when individuals other than the purchaser of a product believe the product originates from the trademark owner.

12.3.1.13 Reassignment and Licensing

Generally, trademarks are attached to the products and services that they protect. In that sense, trademarks cannot be traded without the product or service that is covered by the trademark.[15] In the United States, for example, it is not possible to sell or license a trademark unless the transaction is accompanied by the sale or licensing of the right to produce the protected good or service.[16] This is an important distinction to, for example, the patent system, where patents can be easily reassigned as there is no requirement for patented inventions to be practiced. The argument for this restriction on licensing and assignment in gross reflects the basic function of the trademark system (see Section 12.4), allowing trademarks to be detached from the products they protect could increase rather than decrease consumer confusion and search costs.

This argument is less important with regard to licensing (as opposed to sale) because if the licensee offers a product of inferior quality under the trademark, they will undermine the trademark and lower the value of the license. This creates incentives for the licensor, the trademark owner, to ensure that the licensee maintains the same quality as the public expects from the trademarked product. There is another, related issue that distinguishes trademarks from patents: If a company goes out of business, its trademarks cannot be transferred to a creditor unless the creditor continues to use them in commerce. Instead, the trademarks are considered abandoned. This limits the ability of trademark owners to use them to collateralize debt (in contrast, patents can be used for that purpose). More generally, any security interest in a trademark has to include an interest in the associated goodwill and ideally also any assets required for the use of the trademark (Bramson 1981).

12.3.2 Collective Marks, Certification Marks, and Geographical Indications

Collective marks are registered by collective groups or organizations that award them to their members. The purpose of the collective mark is to associate certain characteristics with a product, such as geographical origin or method of manufacturing that are characteristic of a group or organization. As such, a collective mark identifies products that belong to a group and sets them apart from products that do not belong to the group. Collective membership marks are used to indicate membership of a group (e.g., "CPA" that identifies members of the Society of Certified Public Accountants). The main distinction between collective and regular trademarks is that collective marks are used by multiple members of a group that are part of the collective organization that owns the mark. The application and registration process is similar to the one for trademarks described above, although there are important differences across jurisdictions, with some not recognizing collective marks.

Certification marks certify that a product satisfies a certain standard. For example, it can certify that a good was produced with a certain method of manufacture or that the product consists of certain material (e.g., Woolmark that identifies goods that consist

---

[15] Note that collective and certification marks are not transferable.
[16] Exceptions apply to promotional goods and service marks.

of 100% wool). To register a certification mark, the entity that awards the certification has to establish rules that define the standard that warrants certification. The entity itself cannot engage in the production of goods that obtain certification and instead awards the certification to any third parties that meet the requirements. The entity is also tasked with ensuring that only products that meet the requirements use the certification mark. The purpose of certification marks is therefore to allow producers to identify their products as meeting certain standards or have certain characteristics that warrant obtaining the certification mark. As for collective marks, the application and registration process is similar to that of trademarks, with the additional requirement that the certifying organization has to submit the rules and regulations for obtaining the certification. In some jurisdictions, collective marks also include certification marks, while in other jurisdictions, collective marks are not recognized.

The main difference between certification and collective marks is that collective marks are reserved for members of the association that owns the mark, whereas certification marks are available to anyone who satisfies the established requirements.

Another IP right that serves as a product identifier are GIs.[17] GIs are granted for products (and in some jurisdictions also for services) if their specific geographical origin accounts for their characteristic attributes or reputation (e.g., Champagne, Roquefort, or Parmigiano Reggiano). GIs serve similar functions as trademarks; notably, they identify the source of a product that is associated with certain characteristics, and in some jurisdictions are therefore considered part of the trademark system (e.g., the United States). In these systems, GIs are protected through collective or certification marks (and to some limited extent also through regular marks). In other jurisdictions, *sui generis* protection for GIs is granted in the form of a separate IP right (e.g., EU). Depending on how GIs are protected, there are differences in the requirements for protection and scope of protection. Geographical indications can be particularly useful in settings where production is highly fragmented and individual producers are too small to convey individually the quality of their products (Moschini et al. 2008).

12.4 The Economics of Trademarks

The economics of trademarks are based on the insight that markets are generally characterized by asymmetric information (Akerlof 1970). Sellers and buyers have different information about the product they intend to sell or buy. In nearly all markets, quality is to some degree unobservable to consumers before purchasing and consuming a product or service. An extreme case in point is an experience good where quality can only be assessed after consumption (e.g., a meal at a restaurant).

In such a setting, trademarks can help reduce asymmetric information by allowing sellers to identify themselves and to signal that their products are of a certain, consistent

---

[17] GIs are defined in Article 22(1) of TRIPS as "indications which identify a good as originating in the territory of a Member, or a region or locality in that territory, where a given quality, reputation or other characteristic of the good is essentially attributable to its geographical origin." In some jurisdictions, they are also referred to as appellations of origin or designations of origin. Article 23 provides enhanced protection for wines and spirits.

quality. In other words, asymmetric information provides a role for reputation that can be gained and protected by trademarks. Trademarks achieve this objective by providing their owners with an exclusive right to deny others the use of that mark to sell their products. In fact, trademark owners can often keep others from selling their products under different trademarks provided they are considered so similar that they are likely to confuse consumers about the source of the product. The economic argument is straightforward: If consumers think that two distinct products that are of different quality are the same, a trademark would no longer reduce asymmetric information (Landes and Posner 1987).

Even in the absence of asymmetric information, trademarks can also play a role if products contain noncontractible elements, that is, if certain characteristics and features of a product cannot be fully described in a contract and would therefore be difficult to enforce in court. In that case, trademarks can serve a purpose similar to that of a private contract since they provide some form of guarantee regarding the noncontractible elements of a product (DeAlessie and Staaf 1994). In case a company does not provide the expected noncontractible features, the company's trademark will suffer a loss of goodwill.[18] This role of trademarks may help explain why firms in markets with little asymmetric information still obtain and invest in trademarks.[19]

If trademarks reduce asymmetric information, consumers are willing to pay a higher price because they incur lower search costs. Landes and Posner (1987) formalize this idea in a simple model.

Assume the full price faced by consumers for product x manufactured by a company is p. It consists of the "money price" m paid by consumers to the company and their search costs $s(t, z)$:

$$p = m + s(t,z) \tag{1}$$

Search costs are costs incurred by consumers in obtaining information on product x. They depend on trademark t as well as a range of other factors z, such as advertisement. We assume that s decreases in t $\left(\dfrac{\partial s}{\partial t}<0 \text{ and } \dfrac{\partial^2 s}{\partial t^2}>0\right)$, that is, the "stronger" a trademark is, the lower the corresponding search costs. The firm's profit function then is

$$\pi = mx - cx - rt \tag{2}$$

where π denotes firm profits, c are marginal costs of producing x, and r is the marginal cost of "producing" trademark recognition/protection t. Now substitute equation (1) into (2) to obtain

---

[18] If such reputational loss occurs, the consumer who was disappointed by the product usually does not derive any direct benefit from that loss. This means that the consumer has no incentive to behave in an opportunistic way.

[19] Landes and Posner (2003) suggest that trademarks serve yet another purpose: They enrich the language by incentivizing the creation of new words and of distinctive design features (e.g., a Perrier bottle). Some of these new words may then even become generic identifiers for entire product groups, such as Aspirin, Xerox, Kleenex, or cellophane.

$$\pi = \big[p - s(t,z) \big] x - cx - rt \tag{3}$$

In this simple model, firms are assumed to be in perfect competition. The first-order conditions (FOCs) of equation (3) with respect to the firm's two choice variables x and t are, respectively,

$$p - s(t,z) - c = m - c = 0$$
$$-\frac{ds}{dt} x - r = 0 \tag{4}$$

The first FOC says that money price is equal to marginal costs. In other words, firms are in a perfectly competitive market and make zero profits. The second FOC implies that the firm invests in t up to the point where it equates the marginal cost of a little more trademark protection r to the marginal return in the form of lowering search costs a little further ($-ds/dt$), which applies to all units of x sold in the market.

The model helps illustrate two features of trademark protection: (1) Firms invest optimally in trademark protection to the point where marginal benefits equal marginal costs; (2) even in a perfectly competitive market, trademark protection allows companies to charge a higher price m since for a given p, the lower is s, the larger is m.

Trademarks only achieve their objective of reducing asymmetric information and allowing enforceability of noncontractible product characteristics if companies maintain a consistent quality that consumers associate with the trademarked products. Obviously, firms could attempt to use their reputation to make short-run gains, for example, selling a lower-quality product at the price of a high-quality product under their high-quality brand name. But that would generate reputational loss that might be more costly than the short-run gains. This generates a self-enforcing mechanism. Hence, the ability to build and protect reputation that will allow a firm to credibly signal its quality to consumers will also provide incentives to companies to invest in quality even when it is not directly observable to customers.

The arguments above provide a relatively straightforward efficiency argument for the existence of the trademark system. This has also meant that the role of the trademark system has been relatively uncontroversial among legal scholars and economists (Boldrin and Levine 2005).

Instead of questioning the purpose of the trademark system, the policy debate focuses on the degree to which trademark protection should provide exclusivity and the conditions under which such exclusivity is granted.

12.5 Link between Trademarks, Innovation, Marketing, and Economic Performance

12.5.1 Trademarks and Innovation

From a legal perspective, there is no requirement that a trademark protect something new (an innovation). The only requirement is that the mark be distinctive and that it is not likely to lead to consumer confusion due to conflicts with existing trademarks. As such, the trademark system *per se* is not tasked with promoting innovation and there is no reason to assume that a trademark reflects innovative activity.

That said, the ability to legally distinguish a product from other, often similar products may nevertheless create incentives for firms to invest in the development and introduction of new products. Hence, one might expect new products to trigger new trademark registrations. As such, trademarks reflect innovative activity insofar as these new products reflect innovative activity. Moreover, given the cost of registering and policing a trademark, it is reasonable to assume that companies trademark more valuable and hence potentially innovative products. Also, firms in industries, especially services, that produce few patentable inventions may rely on trademarks relatively more to appropriate the returns to their innovative activity (Schmoch 2003).

Empirically, it is true that firms tend to trademark in particular new products and services, which creates a link between trademark registrations and innovation or new product introductions (Mendonca et al. 2004). However, new product introductions do not necessarily reflect innovative activity as they may be variations of existing products that embody little innovation. Trademark registrations offer little information that would allow inferring anything on the degree to which the underlying product is indeed novel.

One way to investigate this concern is to link product innovation directly to trademarking activity. Table 12.2 shows data from the UK Community Innovation Survey where firms are asked to what extent they rely on different forms of IP protection. The table distinguishes between firms according to their self-reported innovative activity. For comparison, the table shows data for trademarks and patents. It suggests that firms rely substantially more on trademark than patent protection. The data also

Table 12.2 Use of Trademarks and Patents

Share (%) of Firms Reporting That the IP Was...	Not Used	Low Use	Medium Use	High Use	Total
Trademark					
Product innovation	59.8	10.9	13.8	15.5	100
Process innovation	76.2	8.4	8.1	7.3	100
Product and process innovation	53.2	13.7	15.2	17.9	100
No innovation	85.3	5.2	4.9	4.7	100
Patent					
Product innovation	69.6	10.1	8.1	12.2	100
Process innovation	81.6	6.8	5.2	6.4	100
Product and process innovation	62.0	12.2	9.8	16.0	100
No innovation	90.2	4.0	2.8	3.0	100

Note: Data from the UK Community Innovation Survey (see Hall et al. 2011).

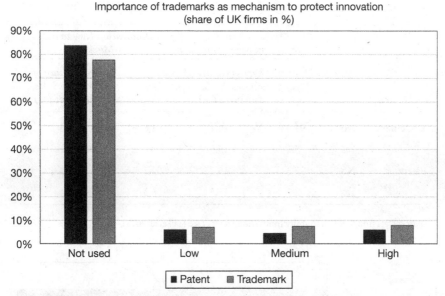

Source: Data from UK Community Innovation Survey (See Hall et al., 2011, Table 9).

Figure 12.2 Importance of trademarks as mechanism to protect innovation.

suggest that firms with product innovations tend to rely most on trademark protection. Similar patterns have been found for various other countries.[20]

Figure 12.2 suggests that one of the reasons for the relatively higher use of trademarks to protect innovations by firms is that they believe trademarks are more important/effective in protecting their innovation than, for example, patents.

Another way to investigate further the link between trademarking and innovative activity is to correlate measures of innovative input and output with trademarking activity. The use of trademarks has been found to correlate positively with the share of new products and services in a company's sales (Gotsch and Hipp 2012), and firms' R&D expenditure more broadly (Jensen and Webster 2009). Table 12.3 again displays data from the UK Community Innovation Survey. The table distinguishes between so-called innovations "new to the firm" and those "new to the market." The latter are considered genuine innovations, whereas the former are often simple modifications of existing products or some form of imitation/replication. The table shows that trademarking firms have a significantly larger share of innovative products in total turnover than nontrademarking firms for innovations that are new to the market. The difference in the share between trademarking and nontrademarking firms is much smaller when innovations are considered that are merely new to the firm. This suggests that trademarking firms tend to be innovative, and hence their trademarking activity indeed reflects their innovation output.

It is also empirically the case that innovative firms tend to use multiple IP rights. The available empirical evidence suggests that patenting firms often also file for trademarks (Abud et al. 2013, Helmers and Schautschick 2013). Figure 12.3 offers data on all

---

[20] See Jensen and Webster (2009) and Gotsch and Hipp (2012).

Table 12.3 Use of Trademarks and Patents by Share of Turnover due to Innovation

		Innovation New to the Firm		Innovation New to the Market	
		% of Firms	Average Share of Innovative Sales in Turnover (%)	% of Firms	Average Share of Innovative Sales in Turnover (%)
Trademark	No	94.9	16.1	91.6	10.8
	Yes	5.1	15.9	8.4	14.1
Patent	No	97.3	16.2	93.7	10.7
	Yes	2.7	13.3	6.3	18.1

Source: Data from UK Community Innovation Survey (see Hall et al. 2011).

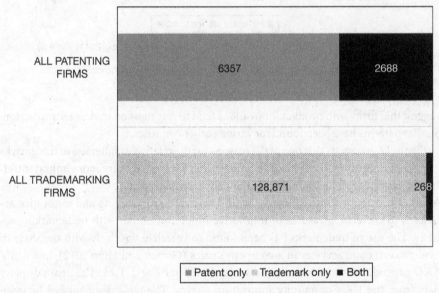

Source: Data on patents and trademarks from the Chilean Intellectual Property Office (INAPI). See Abud et al. (2013).

Figure 12.3 Use of trademarks and patents in Chile.

patenting and trademarking entities with the Chilean Intellectual Property Office. The figure shows that among patenting entities, around a third also file for trademarks. If patenting reflects innovative activity, Figure 12.3 suggests that despite the absence of a legal requirement that trademarks cover only innovative new products and services, there is nevertheless a strong correlation between innovative output and trademarking activity.[21]

---

[21] Note however that while there is some empirical evidence on the use of trademarks by innovative companies, no empirical evidence exists that shows trademarks contribute to the creation of (product) innovation, that is, that in the absence of trademarks firms would not have introduced their product innovations.

12.5.2 Trademarks and Marketing/Branding

A brand represents the result of all activities undertaken by companies to shape its public image and reputation. It embodies the perception by the public of a company's characteristics, attributes, and often also its values. Companies often invest heavily in the creation and maintenance of brands as a way of securing a competitive advantage in the marketplace. The main tool to influence consumer perception of a brand is marketing. But a brand depends on many other factors, too, such as consumer experience, perceptions of reliability, and so forth. In short, a brand is built on reputation. Trademarks protect the reputation embodied by a brand, which explains why the terms trademark and brand are often used interchangeably. Empirically, there is indeed a close link between trademarks and brands. A quick look into the trademark register reveals that all of the world's most valuable brands rely heavily on trademark protection.

It is not surprising that the purpose of a brand overlaps heavily with that of a trademark. Firms create brands to reduce asymmetric information and hence consumer search costs. Brands also act as an implicit contract over noncontractible product characteristics as consumers can punish firms (often very severely) by causing reputational damage in case firms do not perform on their noncontractible promises. But branding achieves a number of additional objectives. For example, a strong brand image can make it easier for firms to differentiate their offerings as new products can benefit from the existing goodwill associated with the brand. The same is true if companies expand into new geographic markets. Brands also make it easier to achieve consumer loyalty. Firms are also able to charge higher prices if consumers are willing to pay for intangible product attributes, most notably brand recognition as in the case of luxury products.

Because of the close link between trademarking and branding, trademark filings are often considered a proxy for a firm's investment in building and guarding its public image and reputation.[22] The link is perhaps a lot closer than between trademarks and innovation.[23]

There is also a large literature on brand valuation. Despite the close link between brand value and trademarks, insights from valuing brands do not translate directly to the question of how to measure the value of trademarks. This literature therefore only offers limited guidance with regard to estimating the value of trademarks. The fact that a trademark is the legal right that protects brand recognition also means that a trademark per se does not have value. Its only value lies in the reputation enjoyed by the product that it covers. In other words, goodwill is the necessary condition for a trademark to have economic value and hence enjoy legal protection. However, the goodwill achieved by a brand also depends on a trademark, which creates interdependency between the value of a brand and that of a trademark. This makes isolating and measuring the value of a trademark challenging.

In practice, the value of a trademark depends mainly on so-called trademark strength, which can be regarded as a measure of inherent distinctiveness or uniqueness of a trademark. This is what was previously described as differential distinctiveness. Economides (1998. p. 528) suggests three factors that determine trademark

---

[22] See, for example, Krasnikov et al. (2009).
[23] For further discussion, see WIPO (2013).

strength: (1) a consumer's ability to recall the mark and its associated features, (2) the ability of others to use a confusingly similar mark, and (3) the reluctance of the trademark owner to change the variety and quality features of the trademarked product over time. These factors, in turn, depend on a number of trademark and brand characteristics. For example, our discussion above suggests that descriptive and suggestive marks are broader and potentially more effective in excluding competitors. They also provide information to consumers that partly substitutes for advertising. These considerations would suggest that these trademark types are, on average, more valuable. However, they are more likely to become generic and hence to lose trademark protection. Moreover, it often takes time to acquire secondary meaning as goodwill can only be built over time. Trademark strength also depends on brand awareness. Brand awareness is usually seen as a combination of name awareness, loyalty toward the brand, perceived quality, and any other associations that consumers have with the brand name. All of these factors are inherently intangible and therefore hard to measure.

It is obviously difficult to operationalize and measure the concept of trademark strength in practice. Instead, firms rely mostly on a few standard valuation methods to compute the value of a trademark:

- *Cost valuation.* This method evaluates the total cost of obtaining a trademark, which includes registration and legal fees, marketing and advertising costs, and the like. This accounting method is relatively easy to implement, but it is likely to undervalue the trademark as it essentially equates trademark strength with marketing and advertising costs that usually account for the bulk of expenses associated with a trademark.
- *Expected income.* This method computes the present value of all expected earnings made with the trademark. Therefore, this method attempts to project the future returns associated with a trademark, which is naturally associated with a lot of uncertainty and requires a number of strong assumptions. These assumptions are necessary to isolate earnings due to the trademark from earnings due to the many other factors that affect income. If data are available, trademark holders can also compute hypothetical royalty rates, how much they would have to pay in royalties if they had to license their trademark from a third party. But licensing markets for trademarks are relatively thin, and such data are relatively difficult to come by, which means that it may be difficult to find truly comparable trademarks and royalty rates.
- *Market value.* The method relies on the so-called fair market value, which simply measures how much third parties would pay for a trademark if it were sold or licensed. The standard way to measure this is to rely on historic sales or licensing price data of comparable trademarks. Similar to the hypothetical royalty rate measure, this approach is challenging in the context of trademarks because the market is relatively thin and hence there are few transactions that can serve as reference points.

12.5.3 Trademarks and Economic Performance

Given the importance of trademarks for branding and their close link with innovation, it is not surprising to find an association between trademarks and economic performance. Trademarks can help companies sustain a brand premium in the marketplace, which can translate into positive mark-ups. Less competition can also help companies grow faster. This, in turn, can further incentivize companies to invest in branding and advertisement, and even encourage innovation. While trademark use is associated with positive private returns, their impact on branding, innovation, and ultimately company performance could also have adverse social effects due to less competition and increased market concentration.

The existing empirical evidence suggests that trademarking is positively associated at the firm level with market value, employment, and revenue growth as well as productivity. This positive effect of trademarks on firm performance holds in both industrialized and developing economies.[24] At the macro-level, Dinlersoz et al. (2023) provide evidence that the trademark system increases welfare because it encourages the allocation of production inputs and consumption to higher-quality firms in the economy. Unfortunately, there is no comprehensive evidence on the potential social costs of the trademark system due to its dynamic effect on product market competition.

12.6 Topics Related to the Trademark Protection and Use of the Trademark System

This section discusses a range of issues related to the way companies use the trademark system that are relevant for trademark, innovation, and competition policy.

12.6.1 Trademark Use in Combination with Other IP Rights

As discussed above, trademarks protect source and differential distinctiveness by allowing companies to prevent consumer confusion by enjoining other companies from using similar or identical marks to market their products or services. Trademarks do not protect directly the innovation, technology, or design of a new product.[25] This provides a role for other IP rights, notably design rights, patents, and copyright to be used in combination with trademarks to protect an innovation.

As shown in Figure 12.3, about a third of patent applicants also file for trademarks. The combination of patents and trademarks may be explained at least partly by the fact that it is easier for companies to build reputation if their product (or rather the underlying innovation) enjoys exclusivity from patent protection. Consider Xerox as an example: The company was so successful in building consumer recognition for its patented photocopier that its trademarked name has arguably become generic (Parchomovsky and Siegelman 2002). Conversely, trademarks also offer an opportunity

---

[24] See Dinlersoz et al. (2018) for evidence for the United States, Greenhalgh and Rogers (2006) for the United Kingdom, and Fink et al. (2021) for evidence for Chile. Thoma (2019, 2020, 2021) developed a composite indicator of trademark value to show that it is a predictor of the market value of US publicly traded high-tech firms, controlling for patents, R&D, and advertising.

[25] Although in the United States, trade dress protection is available for visual aspects of products.

to capitalize on the temporary exclusivity afforded by patent protection, a phenomenon best illustrated by Bayer's Aspirin.

Companies can also strengthen legal protection by combining trademarks with other IP rights (Helmers and Schautschick 2013). A British nursing bottle maker alleged infringement in court of its nursing bottle "Dr Brown's Natural Flow," which has a specific design that avoids the forming of a vacuum when the bottle is inverted to feed an infant and hence prevents the infant from swallowing air. The manufacturer sued at the High Court of England and Wales for patent, trademark, and copyright infringement against a former distributor that had created a rival bottle. The court invalidated the patent but found for trademark and copyright infringement. This shows that exclusivity (and hence commercial success) hinges on multiple product characteristics, which are protected by different types of IP rights. This also helps explain the observation from innovation surveys that the use of different IP rights by firms is positively correlated, that is, if a firm uses one type of IP right, it is more likely to use another one, too.

Figure 12.4 illustrates another case of trademark use in combination with other IP rights. Italian espresso and coffee machine maker Ariete filed a patent on a new technology to expel prepackaged capsules for espresso machines. Shortly thereafter, the company filed for a EU trademark for a product line called "Capricci," espresso capsules for use in machines that have the patented technology. Finally, the company filed for a design right that protects the design of the espresso machine that would shortly thereafter be sold in the market. It turns out that similar examples could easily be constructed for other espresso machine makers, such as Nespresso, where patents usually protect aspects of the capsule technology, design rights the look of the machines and capsules, and trademarks the names of the machines and capsules.

Another example are GUIs, display screens, and icons for digital devices, notably smartphones, tablets, and other smart devices. Here, for example, the same display icon may be protected by copyright, design rights, and trademarks. A famous example is Apple's trademark for the design of the display of its first iPhone that was protected by a trademark (No. 3,470,983) and design patent (USD 604,305), which Apple asserted in its protracted landmark litigation against competitor Samsung.

In some cases, encouraging the use of copyright and design rights in combination with trademarks helps companies avoid seeking trademarks with overly broad boundaries. For example, products often have attributes that have aesthetic features;

Source: Helmers and Schautschick (2013).

Figure 12.4 Trademark use in combination with other IP rights.

perhaps the simplest case is a specific color. The color has no function, but if the color is inherently associated with a product, it could effectively exclude other companies from using that aesthetic feature in their products (see Box 12.1).

There is also a concern that the boundaries between the different rights intersect. Take, for example, the famous cartoon character Mickey Mouse. Mickey Mouse is a visual character and, as such, can be protected by both a trademark and copyright (Ginsburg and Calboli 2020). Kaiser et al. (2023) show that trademark protection of cartoon characters applies much more widely than just Mickey Mouse. Because copyright expires while trademark protection does not (provided a trademark is renewed), the combined use of a trademark and copyright can provide substantial additional protection. Similar overlap exists between trademark and design protection because product shapes can be protected by both trademarks and design rights. Since trademarks do not require novelty and non-obviousness, but design rights do, it is possible that applicants

---

Box 12.1 *Louboutin v. YSL*

Christian Louboutin is a well-known brand in the market of luxury shoes. Its shoes typically feature a lacquer red outsole (see Figure 2). In the United States, Louboutin successfully registered the red sole as a trademark in 2008 (registration number 3,361,597; see Figure 1).

Figure 1 US trademark registration number 3,361,597.

Figure 2 Louboutin shoe with red outsole.

Figure 3 YSL monochrome red shoe.

Louboutin filed a lawsuit in 2011 alleging trademark infringement against fashion company Yves Saint Laurent (YSL) after YSL had launched an all-red shoe (see Figure 3). Louboutin sought a preliminary injunction to stop YSL from selling its all-red shoe. The district court denied the request for a preliminary injunction on the basis that the single-color trademark was likely invalid since the color was inherently functional. On appeal, the Circuit Court found that Louboutin's trademark was, in fact, valid as it had acquired secondary meaning.* However, the court limited the trademark to shoes where the red sole contrasts with the upper part of the shoe. As a result, it does not apply to all red shoes. The Circuit Court therefore denied the injunction.

Source: Christian Louboutin S.A. v. Yves Saint Laurent Am. Holding, Inc., 696 F.3d 206 (2d Cir. 2012).

* Secondary meaning signifies here that consumers identify a red outsole as a Louboutin shoe.

obtain first a design right and then extend protection through a trademark. That said, obtaining a trademark on a shape or form requires secondary meaning as generally a shape or form does not possess inherent distinctiveness. This may limit the ability to substitute one right with another.

12.6.2 Trademarks and Competition

Trademarks grant a monopoly to their owners. However, unlike patents, where owners obtain a right to an innovative idea, which prevents copying of the invention, it is possible under trademark protection to imitate a product except for its trademarked characteristics. This limits the monopoly power as trademarks, in fact, allow for the existence of almost arbitrarily close substitutes in terms of product characteristics. Moreover, by limiting the scope of trademarks by excluding generic terms and decorative or functional features, the monopoly power is further constrained.

The economic argument for granting a property right with limited monopoly power is that trademarks should only protect products that have acquired goodwill. Only if a trademark is recognized by the relevant part of the public, consumer confusion can arise if a competitor were to offer a product under the same or a similar name.

By the same token, most trademark systems grant some exclusivity before goodwill has been established (no use, lagged use, or intent to use requirements) and protection might be granted in areas other than where the product has acquired goodwill. In particular. the latter aspect can undermine competition as it may result in relatively broad exclusivity despite the statutory limitations on trademark protection. Descriptive marks can also harm competition when they afford their owners control over parts of the name space that are particularly powerful in associating brand names with product characteristics. Think of brand name "ActivTrak" for a fitness tracker, which might make it difficult for competing fitness products to use the words "active" and "tracker" (Buccafusco et al. 2023). Hence, despite the constrained exclusivity conferred by trademarks, they still have the potential to be used anti-competitively, in particular to prevent entry of new competing products.

In practice, trademark protection has to strike a balance between providing effective exclusivity to the rights holder while not unduly restricting competition by granting overly broad exclusivity (Economides 1998). The main practical challenge consists of determining whether the exclusion of competing products or services represents a legitimate use of the negative right conferred by a trademark or anti-competitive behavior.

In court, if a trademark owner wants to prove trademark infringement, the owner has to show that there is likelihood of confusion, that is, consumers must likely believe that the infringing product or service belongs to the trademark owner. A related concept is dilution, where a trademark owner can prevent a third party from using the trademarked word, shape, and so forth even if there is no risk of confusion. Instead, the trademark owner has to prove that the act tarnishes the reputation or blurs distinctiveness of the brand. This issue arises usually when a firm wants to use the same trademark or a variation for a product entirely unrelated to the existing trademark. It is important to emphasize that dilution and confusion are different concepts. Confusion is directed at competing products, whereas dilution is not. Nevertheless, dilution can affect product market outcomes by preventing entities from using a mark in areas unrelated to the existing mark.

There is no direct empirical evidence on the anti-competitive effect of trademarks. However, that does not mean anti-competitive use of trademarks is merely a theoretical construct. Anecdotal evidence, for example, suggests that trademark protection of pharmaceuticals creates inertia and delays consumer switching once market exclusivity due to patent protection expires. Since this means that producers are able to charge higher prices despite the existence of cheaper therapeutically equivalent drugs, this may result in DWL. The concern is that a firm may invest resources to create a perception of high quality among consumers by, for example, generating a public image through extensive marketing campaigns. This may lead consumers to forgo purchasing cheaper equivalent products or superior alternatives at the same price (Landes and Posner 2003).[26]

12.6.3 Trademark Squatting

One of the motivations behind imposing an (intent to) use requirement is to prevent rent seeking in the form of trademark squatting. Squatting describes a situation in which someone who has not created the trademark and invested in building the associated goodwill registers the mark with the trademark office. In most cases, the intention of squatters is to extract rents from the actual brand owners. There have been many examples of squatting behavior; when entering the Russian market, Starbucks was confronted with a squatter who had registered the Starbucks trademark and demanded $600,000 for reassignment to Starbucks. Tesla faced a similar situation when entering the Chinese market. However, in China trademark registration poses particular problems due to the frequent coexistence of several names for the same brand, the original foreign name, a pinyin transcription into Chinese, and a potentially entirely distinct transliteration under which a brand becomes known to the public in China.[27] Apart from the anecdotal evidence, there is little systematic evidence on the extent to which trademark squatting occurs and what its impact is on brand owners or the trademark system more generally. The available evidence for Chile suggests that trademark squatting is a relatively rare, albeit systematic occurrence (Fink et al. 2018). Squatters, which are both individuals and companies, target the most valuable, mostly foreign brands, overwhelmingly related to the fashion industry. There is also some evidence that brand owners react to squatting by filing

---

[26] One can make the argument that in the case of pharmaceutical and chemical products, where two products may have the same chemical formula, consumers may be willing to pay a higher price for the trademarked product because they can rely more on the promise that the product is produced according to certain quality standards. However, at least with regard to pharmaceuticals, this is a rather weak argument as health regulation assumes this role and ensures products contain the chemical compounds that they claim to contain and that they have the intended effect.

[27] A case in point is Pfizer's battle over control of the Chinese transliteration of its Viagra trademark in China. While Pfizer had registered its trademark in English, it had failed to trademark the Chinese transliteration under which Viagra became known to the Chinese public. Instead, the name was registered first by a Chinese competitor, Viamen. Under China's first-to-file system, Pfizer struggled to challenge the trademark's validity and eventually lost the legal challenge (Chow 2012).

trademarks preemptively, including in classes not directly related to the product marketed by the companies.

Despite the risk of having one's trademark squatted, it may indeed be rational for firms to forgo trademark protection and hence allow for squatters to register the firm's trademark. The most likely scenario in which firms decide to forgo trademark protection concerns protection in new markets. That is, when companies, for example, launch a new product, they will routinely obtain trademark protection for that product in their home and other core markets. Often firms eventually sell the product also in other countries. Because that is hard to predict at the time the product was launched, companies may not obtain early trademark protection in all of the countries in which they eventually sell their products. If a country is part of the Madrid system, filing a trademark application internationally is easier and cheaper, which means that brand owners may be more likely to obtain trademark protection preemptively in countries that are part of the Madrid system. Conversely, there may be more opportunities for trademark squatters in countries that are not part of the Madrid system.

The ability to successfully squat a trademark also depends on a number of institutional factors. As mentioned above, under a first-to-file rule, the first entity to register a trademark is entitled to protection, whereas under a first-to-use system, the entity that can prove it used the mark first is entitled to protection. Also, a use requirement makes it obviously more difficult to squat a mark as squatting usually means the trademark is not used in commerce. Different forms of a use requirement can have different effects, for example, at the EUIPO, no use has to be demonstrated although enforcement does require proof of use. In the United States, an intent-to-use statement makes it, in principle, possible to squat a trademark, but registration is contingent on proving use. In China, trademarks can be registered without proof of use but will be invalidated if no use can be demonstrated within 3 years of registration. Another important factor is the type of examination applied by trademark offices. If an office only conducts formal examination, a squatter has better chances of registering another company's brand than if the office conducts a relative grounds examination.

WTO members recognize under Article 16 of the TRIPS agreements the so-called well-known mark provision within the meaning of Article 6*bis* of the Paris Convention. The provision overcomes national and regional aspects of trademark protection by granting owners of a famous mark protection without prior registration in a foreign country. Hence, the provision provides a way for brand owners to remove conflicting trademarks from the register. Famous marks therefore enjoy special treatment under national trademark laws. As a result, if a company is able to show that its brand was famous in a given country before a squatter registered the trademark, the squatted trademark will be removed from the register through opposition or cancellation proceedings even if it was filed first under a first-to-file system.[28]

---

[28] The main practical challenge in this context is to establish criteria for determining what qualifies as a well-known mark. The 1999 WIPO Joint Recommendation Concerning Provisions on the Protection of Well-Known Marks did not provide a definition and instead offers various factors that national offices can take into account, such as determination of the relevant sector of the public, consideration of bad faith, consideration of dilution protection, conflicting business identifiers, and the like.

12.6.4 Combining Trademark Protection and Secrecy

A trade-off common to all registered IP rights is between obtaining legal protection and required disclosure of information. Trademarks are no exception. The trademark owner has to disclose the trademark, often a brand name, as well as the classes in which protection is sought (in the United States more detailed information on specific goods and services is required). Disclosure occurs in most jurisdictions almost immediately upon filing of a trademark because the trademark will be made visible in an online register (which is distinct from publication for opposition purposes, which occurs later). This can be valuable information for competitors.

Trademark-based market intelligence helps competitors adjust their own product development and product positioning. For example, it can allow competitors to learn about new product announcements since companies usually secure legal protection by filing a trademark before launching the corresponding product in the marketplace. New brand names may convey additional information, such as entry into new product markets (e.g., Apple Watch). Even when the brand name is already known, new trademark filings in additional classes may indicate brand extensions and entry into new product categories. This information is not only potentially useful for competitors, it can also be exploited by trademark squatters.

This creates a challenge for companies' trademark filing strategies. They can delay the filing of a trademark until the official announcement or even launch of a new product to avoid early disclosure of information. However, that creates legal risk since a third party might file the same trademark or a potentially confusingly similar one in the meantime. This could create challenges when the company files its trademark, especially if the product has already been announced or launched.

A number of companies in the United States have found a way to evade this trade-off by relying on a creative filing strategy coined *submarine trademarks* by Fink et al. (2022). They file their trademark first in a remote jurisdiction that does not have an online trademark register, or if there is an online register, the trademark office significantly delays publication of incoming trademarks and generally makes searching the register for specific trademarks difficult. Such jurisdictions include countries like Trinidad and Tobago, Tonga, or Saint Lucia. Under the Paris Convention, applicants have 6 months to file the same trademark in the United States, where they get to claim the original filing date in the foreign jurisdiction as the US filing date. Since the trademark is not published in the foreign jurisdiction during that 6-month period, the applicant keeps the trademark filing secret while still securing legal trademark protection in the United States. Examples of brands for which this filing strategy has been used include iPhone, iPad, Kindle Fire, Amazon Echo, and Google Chrome. Figure 12.5 shows the example of the trademark for the first version of the iPhone.

Companies also use yet another, alternative filing strategy to sidestep the secrecy-legal protection trade-off. Instead of filing in their own name, they set up shell companies whose only purpose is to file a trademark. This can also afford secrecy in combination with legal protection if competitors are unable to connect the filing by the shell company to the brand owner. Eventually, the trademark is reassigned to the brand owner. Figure 12.5 shows that the iPhone trademark was filed by a shell company called

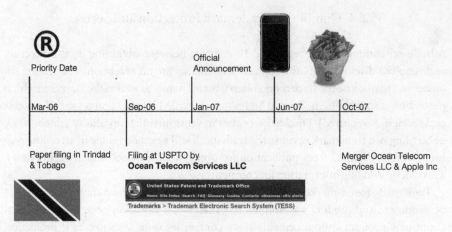

Figure 12.5 Combining trademark protection and secrecy.

Ocean Telecom Services LLC instead of Apple, and about 18 months after filing, Ocean Telecom Services was absorbed by Apple.

This phenomenon also raises a broader issue. While companies value secrecy, even temporary secrecy undermines the transparency of the trademark register. The private benefits that firms obtain from secrecy likely translate at least to some extent into social benefits. Less transparency in the trademark register, in contrast, creates a social cost. This creates the challenge for the trademark system to balance these benefits and costs. Currently, the trademark system in most jurisdictions favors transparency over secrecy by almost immediately publishing trademark applications online after filing.

12.6.5 Trademark Non-Use, Cluttering, Depletion, and Congestion

Trademark *cluttering* is defined as the existence of trademarks on the register that are not used by their owners. Closely related is the issue of overly broad trademarks, that is, marks that cover classes or goods and services that are currently not used by the trademark owner and where even future use is unlikely. The latter is mostly a concern in jurisdictions that do not require proof of use.

The concern over the fact that the owner does not use the registered trademark is different from the rent-seeking concern in the case of squatting. Here, the concern is that of *negative use*, that is, an entity holds the trademark mainly to keep others from using it. Apart from keeping other firms from using a mark in commerce, clutter on the register may also make it harder for companies to come up with new trademarks if one accepts the notion that the "name space" from which new trademarks can be drawn is finite. The main concern with trademark clutter is that the large volume of trademarks increases costs for firms to search the trademark register and successfully register new and sufficiently distinctive trademarks. However, even in the absence of negative use, there can be trademark *depletion*. This is a situation where the supply of "competitively effective" trademarks is, in fact, limited and the number of unclaimed trademarks is shrinking.

There is indeed evidence for both depletion (Beebe and Fromer 2018) and for firms incurring large costs in searching trademark registers and in ensuring there are no potentially conflicting existing marks (von Graevenitz 2013, von Graevenitz et al. 2015).[29] The latter is at least partly a result of *congestion*, which can also occur in the absence of cluttering.

Congestion arises when a trademark that has been registered is increasingly also claimed by others to cover other goods and services. Beebe and Fromer (2018) offer the example of word mark "ACE." The trademark was first registered in the United States to cover adhesive bandages. Later it was registered for hardware goods and hardware store services. Beebe and Fromer (2018) counted a total of 130 different registered trademarks for ACE across different classes and owned by 95 different trademark owners.

However, the view that the trademark space is limited is not uncontroversial as one could argue that the name space is infinite and hence no increased transaction costs should result from depletion and congestion (Landes and Posner 1987, 2003). In principle, the supply of fanciful trademarks is indeed infinite. The same is not true for suggestive and especially descriptive marks. They are commonly considered to be broader and to substitute to some degree for advertising since they describe the product more directly. However, key to understanding the depletion and congestion arguments is that not all potential trademarks are equally effective from a company's perspective. Beebe and Fromer (2018) argue that certain types of marks, common standard English words, one-syllable words, short and pronounceable neologisms, as well as common US surnames make for more competitively effective marks on the US market, and their supply is indeed limited.

12.6.6 Trademarks and e-Commerce

The internet and the explosion of e-commerce have created a number of new challenges for the trademark system. We focus here on two issues: (1) the link between trademarks and domain names and (2) trademarks and online search.

12.6.6.1 Trademarks and Domain Names
Domain names are "web addresses" that link to websites. For example, in www.google.com, google is the domain name, while .com is the top-level domain. Companies usually trademark their trading names. This means that the domain name and trademark of a company are usually the same since the company wants to be easily found online by consumers simply inputting the company name in the browser URL bar. The domain name system is administered by the Internet Corporation for Assigned Names and Numbers (ICANN). The domain names themselves can be purchased from domain name registrars, such as GoDaddy. It is possible for anyone to purchase domain names even if the domain name is a registered trademark owned by a third party. The system functions on a first come, first served basis.

---

[29] There is also anecdotal evidence from the beer brewer industry, see https://www.npr.org/sections/thesalt/2015/01/05/369445171.

ICANN offers an arbitration system, the Uniform Dispute Resolution Policy (UDRP), that deals with domain name disputes. Such disputes include domain name squatting, also referred to as cybersquatting. A third party registers a domain name in bad faith with the intention of benefiting from the domain name by either reselling it to the company the domain name corresponds to or by benefiting in some other form from the goodwill of the company name. ICANN has also created the Uniform Rapid Suspension (URS) mechanism and a trademark clearinghouse to help avoid trademark conflict as a result of the top-level domain expansion (which created domains such as .google or .hotels). The URS offers a streamlined and faster UDRP procedure that leads to the suspension of domains. The trademark clearinghouse offers trademark owners the possibility to register their trademarks with ICANN. They are then notified when new domain name registries become available or a domain that corresponds to a registered trademark is registered.[30]

In 1998, in *Brookfield Communications v. West Coast Entertainment*, the US Ninth Circuit Court rendered an important decision on the link between trademark infringement and domain names.[31] The domain name www.moviebuff.com had been registered by a company called West Coast Entertainment. Another company, Brookfield Communications, offered an online database called MovieBuff and registered the name as a trademark. When West Coast Entertainment launched a similar database on its www.moviebuff.com website, Brookfield Communications sued for trademark infringement. The appeals court found that there was likelihood of confusion and West Coast Entertainment had infringed Brookfield's MovieBuff trademark. The court also found trademark infringement due to West Coast Entertainment's use of so-called metatags, where it included MovieBuff in its html code to direct search engines to its website if anyone searched the Web for the term "MovieBuff."

Despite the importance of this topic for e-commerce, so far there has been little economic research on the topic.

12.6.6.2 Trademarks and Online Search

Search engines such as Google allow companies to bid for search terms so their ads are displayed in addition to the search results. That is, Google sells to advertisers the ability to display their ads to consumers that search for specific keywords. Such keyword-based advertisement includes registered trademarks. For example, a consumer might search for the term "lenovo thinkpad" (a laptop), where both "lenovo" and "thinkpad" are registered trademarks owned by Chinese computer manufacturer Lenovo. The consumer will then see an ad in the form of a search result displayed on top of the regular search results. This ad belongs to the advertiser that placed the highest bid on the specific keywords, in this case, "lenovo thinkpad." In addition to these text-based ads, Google also displays product placement ads (PLAs). For example, a Google search for "xiaomi mi" (a smartphone), where both "xiaomi" and "mi" are registered trademarks owned by Chinese smartphone maker Xiaomi Communications, returns the results shown in Figure 12.6. The figure shows that the PLAs might contain other brands, such as the Apple iPhone. Both text-based ads and PLAs are clearly marked as advertisements and

---

[30] For a review of these mechanisms, see Karanicolas (2020).
[31] *Brookfield Communications Inc. v. West Coast Entertainment Corp.*, 174 F.3d 1036 (9th Cir. 1999).

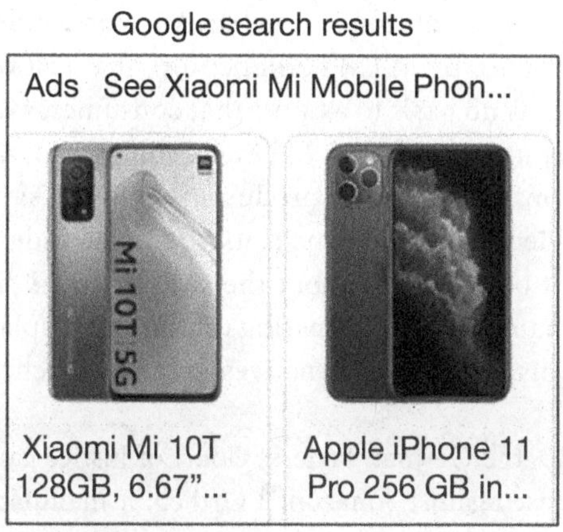

Google search results

Figure 12.6 Google search results.

placed either on top or on the side of the search results to also set them apart visually. PLAs provide more information on products including images and prices than text-based ads. PLAs are chosen by Google's algorithm that matches information provided by the advertiser with search queries. In contrast, text-based ads are displayed as a result of the advertiser's bidding for specific keywords.

Trademark owners have argued that both the advertiser and the search engine are liable for trademark infringement. The core argument is that the display of products other than the product protected by the trademark that a consumer searched for would result in likely consumer confusion.

The economic question is whether a search engine's display of the competing product in addition to the trademarked product the consumer searched for increases competition or only causes consumer confusion. If the latter is the case, this practice would undermine the functioning of the trademark system. However, if it provided consumers with more information, choice, and hence increased competition, those pro-competitive effects might outweigh any negative effects on trademark owners. Bechthold and Tucker (2014) offer empirical evidence based on internet user-browsing behavior that suggests both effects are at play. Consumers who look specifically for the trademarked product when using the trademark in their keyword-based search are less likely to go to the trademark owner's website. However, consumers who use the trademarked keyword for a more general search are more likely to visit the trademark owner's website.

The problem is even more acute on online marketplaces such as Amazon since their own search engines have the goal of selling products to consumers. Amazon relies on its own proprietary search engine that allows consumers to search for items on its site. In the United States in 2013, Multi Time Machine (MTM), the manufacturer of high-end rugged watches, sued Amazon for trademark infringement.[32] MTM does not sell its watches on Amazon, nor does it allow authorized retailers to sell them on Amazon. However, when a consumer entered MTM's trademark

---

[32] See Hall (2016) for a discussion of the case.

"MTM special ops" into the Amazon search bar, Amazon would offer a list of search results, displaying watches by MTM's competitors that sell on Amazon. Amazon countered that there was no basis to assume that consumers who search for MTM's trademark wanted to purchase only an MTM watch. Instead, Amazon offered these consumers new information on other products within the same product category. The district court sided with Amazon in its summary judgment. It argued that consumers would not be confused about the search results since Amazon clearly identified the brand names of the competing products it displayed. Confusion over why Amazon should display these alternatives to MTM watches was not covered by the Trademark Act.[33]

In Germany in 2019, the German Federal Court of Justice came to a different conclusion in a similar case against Amazon.[34] Ortlieb, a manufacturer of sports bags, sued Amazon because Google displayed Amazon ads when users searched for "ortlieb fahrradtasche" ("ortlieb bicycle bag"). The Amazon ads that were displayed by Google as a result of keyword advertisement linked directly to the Amazon website where users would be confronted with a list of products that contained Ortlieb as well as competing products. The court found that Amazon misled consumers because the ads that appeared on Google suggested the search would only lead to a display of Ortlieb products. The case differs in this important aspect from the *MTM v. Amazon* case in the United States. In an earlier decision, the German court did not object to the display of competing products on the Amazon site when Ortlieb keywords were used as a query in the Amazon search bar. What the court ultimately objected to was the misleading character of the Amazon ads displayed on Google.

12.7 Summary

Trademarks are by far the most widely used IP right. There is a close link between trademarks, brands, and marketing. Trademarks are a critical tool used by companies to create and protect brand recognition and appropriate returns to marketing. The link between trademarks and innovation is more complex. New products and services are often protected by trademarks and therefore trigger new trademark filings. As such, trademarks can help companies obtain returns on innovation. That said, there is no legal requirement that trademarks protect anything new; existing brand names can still be trademarked. In fact, the purpose of the trademark system is not to encourage innovation but to reduce asymmetric information in the marketplace by allowing companies to distinguish their products from other products and to allow consumers to identify the source of the product. A trademark gives its owner the right to stop third parties from imitating the trademarked words and signs. This prevents free riding on the goodwill created by the trademark owner.

[33] On appeal, the Ninth Circuit Court first overturned the district court decision to shortly thereafter reverse its own opinion. The Circuit Court affirmed the district court decision, finding no likely consumer confusion with respect to the origin of the products displayed by Amazon.

[34] Ortlieb II (Federal Court of Justice, judgement of 25.07.2019, I ZR 29/18).

This chapter also reviewed the link between trademark protection and competition, and various related topics, including squatting, secrecy, cluttering, depletion, and congestion. Finally, the chapter also highlighted new challenges for the trademark system in the online context, especially the link between trademarks and online search. The role of the trademark system in e-commerce is so far an underexplored topic that deserves more attention.

13
Copyright

Learning Objectives

After reading this chapter, you will be able to understand and explain the following concepts:

- The basic structure and purpose of the copyright system
- The process and legal requirements to obtain copyright protection
- The economics underlying the copyright system
- The link between copyright, software, and artificial intelligence
- The link between copyright and digitization

13.1 Introduction

When a number of states in the United States entered their first COVID lockdown in March 2020, public libraries shut their doors as well. At least initially, that meant the lending of physical books ground to a sudden halt. In response, the Internet Archive, a nonprofit organization that also maintains the Wayback Machine, created the "National Emergency Library." The Internet Archive had been operating a library prior to COVID, the "Open Library." It offered scanned books for users to borrow online. Importantly, the Internet Archive only allowed one user at a time to digitally check out a book. In this way, the Internet Archive mimicked the traditional offline lending of physical books, which is permissible under copyright law (owing to the first-sale doctrine, which we will explain later in this chapter). However, because of the COVID lockdown and resulting closure of brick and mortar libraries, the Internet Archive lifted the "one at a time" restriction and allowed different users to check out the same book at the same time. The library was set to revert back to its regular lending restrictions on June 30, 2020.

However, on June 1, 2020, a group of publishers, including Hachette Book Group, HarperCollins, Penguin Random House, and John Wiley & Sons sued the Internet Archive for copyright infringement of 127 of their books that were available on the National Emergency Library. To preempt the lawsuit and a possible injunction, the Internet Archive terminated the emergency library early on June 16, 2020.

The case may remind you of an earlier case that received a lot of public attention, *Authors Guild v. Google*,[1] a class action suit filed in 2005. The Authors Guild, which is America's largest professional organization representing authors, alleged that Google

[1] *The Authors Guild Inc., et al. v. Google, Inc.* 721 F.3d 132 (2d. Cir. 2015).

The Economics of Innovation and Intellectual Property. Bronwyn H. Hall and Christian Helmers, Oxford University Press.
© Oxford University Press 2024. DOI: 10.1093/oso/9780197630914.003.0013

Books infringed the copyright of the books it made available online. Google Books, which was initiated in 2002, scanned books to create digital versions that are made available and searchable online. Books that are in the public domain were made available in their entirety, while for copyrighted work, only excerpts would be available to users. The case dragged on for over a decade, but ultimately the court sided with Google. The main argument was that because Google only made excerpts of books publicly available online, the "fair use" copyright exception applied and Google was not liable for copyright infringement (we will explain fair use later in this chapter). In particular, the court found that Google made it easier for users to discover books and enabled users to locate and purchase legal copies of a book.

Of course, in the current case against the Internet Archive, the facts are different because the whole purpose of the emergency library was to make an entire book available to users even when it was still protected by copyright. It is also unlikely that the National Emergency Library promoted sales of legal copies because the purpose of borrowing a book from a library is to avoid having to purchase the book in order to read it.

But there is more at stake than the ostensible dispute between a group of big publishing houses and the Internet Archive. In an attempt to facilitate digital lending, libraries across the United States had started so-called *controlled digital lending* (CDL). A library scans a book that the library already owns and lends out in physical form. It then makes the scanned version available online for check-out. However, only a single user is allowed to check out the scanned version at a time, and while the digital copy is on loan, the physical copy is unavailable to readers. This lending model is much more economical for libraries than the lending of e-books. They only incur the fixed costs of acquiring a physical copy of a book and of scanning it, but marginal costs of lending are low. In contrast, libraries pay for each time an e-book is borrowed, which means much higher marginal cost.

The Internet Archive lost the lawsuit in the first instance.[2] The district court ruled that CDL and hence the emergency library infringe the publishers' copyright. The court stated plainly that the Internet Archive's "fair use defense rests on the notion that lawfully acquiring a copyrighted print book entitles the recipient to make an unauthorized copy and distribute it in place of the print book, so long as it does not simultaneously lend the print book. But no case or legal principle supports that notion."

The case illustrates the tensions that exist around copyright protection. On the one hand, the Internet Archive made books available to readers, which allows users to access work at close to zero cost, which corresponds to the marginal cost of reproduction of an electronic book. In the example of CDL, you can also clearly see that copyright protection artificially creates rivalry. In principle, the benefit that Reader *A* gets from reading a scanned copy of a book is unaffected by whether Reader *B* also gets to read the same scanned copy at the same time. You may recall from Chapter 2 that non-rivalry is one of the core characteristics that sets intangible goods apart from tangible ones. However, because of copyright, if Reader *A* has borrowed the online version of the book, Reader *B* is not allowed to access it. On the other hand, publishers argue that unrestricted digital lending erodes their profits since they only get to sell one copy of a book to a library

---

[2] *Hachette Book Group, Inc. v. Internet Archive*, No. 20-cv-04160, 2023 WL 2623787, at *1 (S.D.N.Y. March 24, 2023).

while many more people read it. This illustrates the trade-off inherent in copyright protection. The creation of creative works requires investment. At the same time, reproduction of, for example, a book once it has been written is cheap; in digital format, marginal costs are, in fact, very close to zero. If an author or publisher sets price equal to marginal cost, we get the socially optimal amount of consumption. However, the author or publisher cannot recover their fixed investment in the creation of the book. Because the author understands this, they would never have written the book in the first place. Copyright law faces the daunting challenge of having to balance the interests of creators in requiring some positive profits and those of the public in obtaining access to creative works.

The example of the National Emergency Library and CDL more generally also illustrates that at the heart of copyright is the act of copying. In the case of an online library, the scanning of a physical copy of a book creates a digital copy, which is identical in content and format to the offline version. Because the digital copy can be made available to many users at the same time, it is effectively equivalent to the production of as many copies as people who want to read it. The group of book publishers that sued the Internet Archive argued (and the district court agreed) that this is contrary to copyright protection since it erodes a copyright owner's right to control the reproduction of their work and hence their market power. However, unauthorized copying clearly enables access at a lower or zero price and at a minimum has the benefit–from a social perspective––of maximizing diffusion.

The case against the Internet Archive has garnered a lot of public attention. One reason is that it concerns something that is near and dear to our hearts, access to books. This reflects another important fact about copyright: It is an IP right that concerns different forms of cultural and social engagement and communication, such as music, books, movies, performances and so forth. Not surprisingly, as a result, the debate on copyright has been quite ideological and often elicits strong moral views by different stakeholders. This chapter will focus less on this aspect of copyright and more on the underlying economics. That is not to say that the normative debate on copyright is less important.

Copyright is also closely associated with innovation and technological change. For one, copyright can protect scientific output, for example, in the form of a database, and it also protects computer software. But perhaps more importantly, copyright interacts with the creation of new technologies as they often change the way copyrighted works can be created, copied, and distributed. Copyright itself emerged in response to innovation, the advent of the printing press in the mid-15th century. Prior to its invention, the copying of books was very expensive because it had to be done manually in a very time-consuming and laborious process (Can you imagine copying this entire book by hand?). After the invention of the printing press, copying was much faster and cheaper, which allowed much more widespread distribution. Governments and the church sought control over the copying process in order to ensure that only texts in accordance with religious and state views would we copied and circulated. To regain control, governments issued licenses to printers that gave them typically the exclusive right to print a given work for a fixed number of years. This gave the printer the ability to prevent others from printing the same work, and although the exclusive right to print was limited to a given territory, they could also prevent importation of copies from abroad.

Technological change and copyright continued to co-evolve over time. Think, for example, of the launch of the Xerox photocopier in 1959, the audio compact cassette in 1963, and the spread of videocassette recorders (VCR) for home use in the late 1970s and early 1980s. All of these technologies had a major impact on consumers' ability to access and copy copyrighted works. In response to such technological change, copyright law had to adapt over time. For example in the United States, the Audio Home Recording Act of 1992 amended the US Copyright Act to allow the release of recordable digital audio tapes, while at the same time mandating for the first time copy-protection and anti-circumvention measures.

However, more recently, the rapid development of the internet and digital technologies has created unprecedented challenges for the copyright system. Digitization has dramatically reduced the cost of copying, transforming, storing, and distributing copyrighted works. It not only affected new works, but also existing works that could be transformed into digital format. The internet also changed how people consume copyrighted works, for example, the ability to stream music significantly increased music consumption and allowed listeners to consume more new and diverse music (Datta et al. 2018). Digital technologies also affected the creation of copyrighted works as the lines between creators and consumers blur. For example, it has become incredibly easy to record and edit a high-quality short video on a smartphone and upload it on social media platforms such as SoundCloud or TikTok. Digitization has also led to the creation of many new business models that are directly or indirectly based on some form of copying of copyrighted works. Examples include the various music- and video-streaming services, such as Spotify or Netflix; platforms that offer access to digital content, such as YouTube; and e-books, such as Amazon's Kindle Books. Another effect of these developments is that the transaction costs due to copyright, especially across jurisdictions, have become relatively more important and enforcement more difficult. The advent of powerful AI tools that facilitate and even automate potentially the entire production process of creative output poses new challenges for the copyright system. In particular, the question of authorship of creative output generated by AI could potentially have wide-ranging consequences for the creative industries and individual creators.

While digital technologies created many challenges for the copyright system, the copyright system is also sure to affect technological development. In fact, the courts, many times in the past, have had to weigh this issue, to determine to what extent certain new technologies were compatible with copyright protection. This underscores the role that copyright protection plays in shaping technological development, not only of consumer facing technologies such as social media platforms, but also hardware such as e-readers or three-dimensional printing. Copyright is likely to also play an important role in shaping the future of AI. Not only because of its impact on creative output, but also because of the importance of access to copyrighted material as input in the training process of AI algorithms.

This chapter reviews the legal and economic aspects of copyright protection. It notably examines the question of whether copyright achieves its economic objectives of incentivizing the creation of and providing access to original works. An important aspect in this discussion is the role that unauthorized reproduction, also known as copying, plays for both the incentives to produce creative works and their diffusion.

The chapter also reviews the more recent debate on copyright and digital technologies including AI.

13.2 Legal Aspects of Copyright

The Copyright Act of 1709, the Statute of Anne, established the first statutory copyright in Great Britain. It was limited to book authors and granted them the right to control the copying of their books for 14 years (it was renewable for another 14 years). A few decades later, in 1790, the US Congress passed the US Copyright Act. Copyright protection in the United States was modeled closely after the British Copyright Act and granted copyright only to books. In 1909, copyright protection was extended to all works of authorship, which included music.

Currently, in the United States, copyright protects "original works of authorship fixed in a tangible medium of expression," which encompasses literary, dramatic, artistic, musical, and other works including software. Works must be original to acquire copyright. However, in the context of copyright, original must not be confounded with the concept of novelty in patent law. In order to gain copyright protection, work does not need to be an expression of a novel or inventive idea. The specific requirements for originality differ across jurisdictions. For example in the United Kingdom, the requirement is that work originates from an author; it is not just a copy of preceding work; and its creation required skill, labor, and judgment by the author. The EU applies a different definition. Originality merely means that work is an author's own intellectual creation. In this context, it is also worth highlighting that copyright does not depend on the quality or merit of work. As such, the bar to obtaining copyright is low compared to other IP rights.

Copyright comes into existence simply through the creation of copyrightable subject matter (certain types of work that contain no original authorship such as a standard calendar cannot acquire copyright protection). No registration or examination is required to obtain copyright. Nor is publication a requirement for copyright protection since copyright protects both published and unpublished work. Instead, copyright is automatically acquired through the creation of the work and "fixing it" in a tangible medium. Nevertheless, in some jurisdictions such as the United States, registration with the Copyright Office is encouraged and confers certain advantages, for example, to establish ownership or for purposes of enforcement.

Copyright is an IP right because it grants an exclusive right to its owner. The right afforded by copyright includes a bundle of rights that cover different ways in which protected work can be exploited. It contains the exclusive right to control reproduction (including that of derivative work), distribution, performance, and display.

The scope of copyright protection is relatively easily defined, in particular compared to patents. Copyright only protects the literal expression of an idea, not the idea itself.[3] To see what this means, let's look at the example of Charles Selden.[4] In 1859, he wrote a short book titled *Selden's Condensed Ledger, or Bookkeeping Simplified* that contained

---

[3] See, for example, Section 102(b) of the 1979 US Copyright Act.
[4] For a more detailed account, see Samuelson (2005).

Notes: The picture on the left is the original photograph taken by Art Rogers. The picture on the right shows the sculpture made by Jeff Koons.

Figure 13.1 Illustration of *Rogers v. Koons* [960 F.2d 301 (1992)].

a simplified bookkeeping system. The book consisted "of an introductory essay explaining the system of book-keeping referred to, to which are annexed certain forms or banks, consisting of ruled lines, and headings, illustrating the system and showing how it is to be used and carried out in practice." In 1867, W. C. M. Baker produced a book that contained a similar bookkeeping system. Selden's wife (Selden himself had died in 1871) sued Baker for copyright infringement. While the lower courts all found copyright infringement, the US Supreme Court held in 1879 that "the mere copyright of Selden's book did not confer upon him the exclusive right to make and use account books, ruled and arranged as designated by him and described and illustrated in said book."[5] In other words, the specific way in which Selden's bookkeeping system was described in his book was protected by copyright. However, the bookkeeping system itself was not.[6]

While copyright protection is narrow in the sense that it protects against copying, copying does not necessarily mean exact replicas. For example, an artist of a two-dimensional artwork can prevent another artist from making a three-dimensional sculpture of the two-dimensional work (see Figure 13.1). Similarly, the author of a novel may prevent someone else from turning the book into a movie without their permission. This is an important point precisely because copyright does not protect the idea of the work; it only protects its expression. Still, that expression can take different forms and copyright can protect different expressions of the same idea. That said, no copyright infringement usually occurs if copying only concerns an insubstantial part of copyrighted works, although it is not easy to determine what that means in practice (for an example, see Box 13.3).

In addition to direct infringement, there is also the concept of indirect liability, which in some jurisdictions is referred to as secondary infringement. It arises when someone is not directly infringing copyrighted works but instead offers, for example, a peer-to-peer

---

[5] *Baker v. Selden*, 101 US 99 (1879).

[6] The US Supreme Court explained, "To give to the author of the book an exclusive property in the art described therein when no examination of its novelty has ever been officially made would be a surprise and a fraud upon the public.... The claim to an invention or discovery of an art or manufacture must be subjected to the examination of the Patent Office before an exclusive right therein can be obtained, and it can only be secured by a patent from the government."

Box 13.3 "Metall auf Metall": *Kraftwerk v. Pelham*

German electronic music pioneer Kraftwerk sued German music producer Moses Pelham in 1999 for the use of a 2-second sample of Kraftwerk's song "Metall auf Metall" from 1977 for a new song produced by Pelham (the song is called "Nur mir" and was recorded by hip-hop artist Sabrina Setlur in 1997). Kraftwerk alleged that by using a 2-second sample of their song without authorization, Pelham infringed their copyright (more precisely in Germany, phonograms are protected by so-called related rights). Pelham countered that the German copyright act (Section 24 UrhG) allowed the free use of a sample for the creation of new and independent work.

The German Federal Court of Justice (BGH) ruled in 2012 against Pelham and found that even a 2-second sample infringed on Kraftwerk's phonogram.

In response, Pelham filed a constitutional complaint because the decision would have effectively ruled out the unauthorized use of a sample, which would have affected in particular hip-hop as an entire music genre. The German constitutional court referred the case back to the BGH. The BGH itself referred the question of whether sampling required authorization from the rightsholder to the CJEU.

In 2019, the CJEU ruled that following the 2002 EU InfoSoc Directive, samples amounted to unauthorized reproduction under EU law. Nevertheless, the CJEU ruled that sampling, that is, unauthorized reproduction, is allowed provided the sample is unrecognizable to the ear of the average listener once it has been incorporated in the new work. This carve-out was necessary because sampling as a form of artistic expression is a fundamental right protected by the European Convention of Human Rights. The decision illustrates the delicate balance copyright law attempts to strike between protecting original works and not obstructing the creation of new works. In this particular setting, the scope of protection might make it difficult for artists to rely on the unauthorized use of snippets of existing music in their production of new music.

However, as it turns out, the case did not end with the CJEU ruling. After subsequent court rulings that could have ended the dispute, the case is currently back at the BGH, which has referred yet another question to the CJEU for clarification. As a result, the case is still ongoing after more than 20 years of intense litigation with potentially far-reaching implications for artistic creation and copyright protection in Germany.

---

file sharing service specifically designed to enable the exchange of copyrighted music and movies. In the United States, indirect liability rests on the common law doctrines of contributory infringement and vicarious liability. Contributory infringement means a party knowingly induces infringement by another party. Vicarious liability means that one party has control over the actions of another party and obtains some financial benefit from that party's actions. Indirect liability is important because it helps prevent the diffusion of infringing copies, especially in situations where it is difficult to take action against individual unauthorized copiers.

Indirect liability also affects the development of new technology. When VCR for home use emerged in the late 1970s and early 1980s, TV program producers and movie studios argued that VCR manufacturers should be liable for copyright infringement. The argument was that the devices enabled consumers to engage in illegal copying of TV shows and movies. People would record entire shows or movies on their VCR to watch them at a time convenient to them, rather than at the time they were broadcasted. There was an additional benefit to viewers and nuisance to broadcasters: Once recorded, viewers could skip commercials by simply winding the tape forward. The argument was that manufacturers were in a much better position to prevent copyright infringement than if copyright owners had to monitor and pursue individual consumers. The US Supreme Court weighed into the debate with its decision in *Sony v. Universal*.[7] The court rejected both contributory infringement and vicarious liability. It found no vicarious liability because the manufacturer cannot control what users do at home with their device. Contributory infringement was rejected because the technology had substantial non-infringing uses. The decision was important for the development of the VCR market, a market that ultimately proved extremely profitable to those film studios that had strongly opposed it.

13.2.1 Copyright and Criminal Law

In response to the sweeping technological changes brought about by the internet, there have been various efforts over the last two decades to strengthen copyright protection and enforcement, especially online. In the United States, several draft bills, including the Stop Online Piracy Act (SOPA) and the PROTECT IP Act (PIPA), contained provisions that would have imposed significant criminal penalties for copyright infringement. Criminal penalties already exist for copyright infringement and infringement of other IP rights, notably designs and trademarks. However, copyright stands out in the severity and frequency with which criminal penalties have been applied to infringers. What are the economic arguments in favor of criminal penalties for copyright infringement? This is an important question because potential overenforcement in the form of criminal sanctions can stifle technology development and adoption.

To answer this question, we have to first learn a bit more about the distinction between property rules and liability rules. A property right confers to its owner the exclusive right to dispose of the right. For example, the owner can refuse access to a third party. Instead, under a liability rule, the owner could not refuse access because the third party could simply compensate the owner for their unauthorized use. The latter seems economically efficient since a third party would only want to engage in unauthorized use if they value access sufficiently to pay compensatory damages to the right holder. The problem with this is, however, that it allows third parties to violate property rules. However, property rules exist because they enable market transactions that result in bargaining surplus, for example, the owner of a property right selling the right to a third party. This is where criminal sanctions come in. They serve as an additional (in addition to compensatory damages) penalty to deter such behavior. That is, criminal

---

[7] *Sony v. Universal City Studios*, 464 US 417 (1984).

sanctions help deter parties converting property into liability rules when it is not economically efficient to do so.

There are, however, also good arguments against criminal sanctions for IP infringement. First, the argument in favor of enforcing property rules hinges on low transaction costs as bargaining will only be possible to achieve efficient outcomes if transaction costs are sufficiently low (Calabresi and Melamed 1972). If transactions costs are high, property rules may be inefficient. Second, criminal penalties impose considerable costs on the public, including the cost of detection, prosecution, incarceration, probation, and the like. These costs are important because efficiency requires that an act should only be prevented if the net harm (net harm means damage caused minus gain to criminal) caused exceeds the cost of preventing it. Another argument that applies especially in the context of IP is the extent of the harm caused. We discuss in this chapter several economic arguments that question whether the net impact on the rightsholder of unauthorized access or copying is, in fact, always necessarily negative.

13.2.2 Economic and Moral Rights

Copyright law distinguishes between so-called economic and moral rights. Economic rights focus on the role of copyright in incentivizing the creation of original works. They are transferable rights that concern the commercial exploitation of copyrighted works such as reproduction or distribution rights. Moral rights, which originate from the French *droit d'auteur*, in contrast, focus on the personal rights of the individual creator and therefore are not transferrable. They ensure an author's moral right of attribution, that is, to be identified as the creator of original work, the right to have the integrity of their work preserved, as well as the right to withdraw their work from the public. In some countries, there is even a right for the author to be compensated on resale of the work (see Box 13.1).

Common law jurisdictions such as the United States do not usually recognize moral rights (although the 1990 Visual Arts Rights Act introduced moral rights for some visual artists in limited circumstances). Moral rights are more common in civil law jurisdictions. As we will discuss in more detail in Section 13.4 below, economic rights matter for an artist's incentives to create new work. However, moral rights may also achieve the same objective by granting status and recognition to the artist.

13.2.3 Term of Protection

Copyright protection lasts for a specific amount of time. Currently the Berne convention (see Chapter 4) specifies that it should extend at least 50 years after the author's lifetime. In the US, the EU, and elsewhere, the statutory copyright term has expanded considerably over time. The US Copyright Act of 1790 set the term at 14 years from the first publication. The term was extended to 28 years in 1831, and the option to renew copyright protection for another 28 years was added in 1909. In 1976, the term was extended substantially to the life of the author plus another 50 years after the author's death (or 75 years for work for hire). The 1998 Sonny Bono Copyright Term Extension

---

Box 13.1 *Droit de suite,* Blockchain, and NFTs

The *droit de suite* is a right that was created in France in 1920 and exists in the EU and a number of other countries around the world. It establishes a resale right for the artist. It is an *ad valorem* levy that is payable to the original artist for the re-sale of a painting above a certain price in public sale on the secondary market. In Europe, it is a non-transferable right that is designed to allow artists to benefit from any increased value of their work in the future. This can make a big difference to an artist's income because paintings often increase substantially in value over time and achieve much higher prices in the secondary market than when they are first sold by the artist. Contemporary artist Robert Rauschenberg's painting *Thaw* is often cited as an example. The artist created the painting in 1958 and sold it to an art collector for $900. It was resold at a Sotheby's art auction in the United States 15 years later in 1973 for $85,000. Because the United States does not recognize the *droit de suite*, Rauschenberg did not receive any money from the dramatically increased value of his painting.

Today, blockchain technology offers an alternative. The blockchain functions as a sort of public ledger that keeps track of all transactions over time in a decentralized way. A NFT is a numerical certificate that uniquely identifies a given work and can therefore be used to authenticate original work. It allows anyone to verify the date of creation and track its ownership. In principle, anything including nondigital, tangible works can be tokenized and transformed into an NFT. Transfers of an NFT are recorded on the blockchain. Each subsequent transfer then triggers a payment to the artist who created the work through a smart contract, which is a program that is built into the blockchain. In this way, the original artist automatically participates in the sale of their work according to the criteria set forth in the smart contract. As a result, the new technology does away with the need for a statutory right and replaces it with a decentralized solution that requires no enforcement or third-party intermediary (in fact, the *droit de suite* is limited to physical works of art and does not apply to NFTs).

Act extended this further to the life of the author plus 70 years (for work for hire, 95 years from the date of publication or 120 years from the date of creation).

The economic benefits of these various extensions are contested. On the one hand, a longer copyright term allows creators or their successors to make more money, including from new opportunities that may arise due to changing technology and new markets. This should encourage investment in the creation of works. However, the magnitude of the marginal impact on incentives is disputed. If the goal of an extension of statutory copyright terms is to incentivize the creation of original works, the question is to what extent these additional years after an author's death affect the present value of copyright (it is the present value that matters for an author's decision to create new work). Akerlof et al. (2002) suggest that the additional 20 years added by the Sonny Bono Copyright Term Extension Act had minimal impact on the present value of work. They estimated that the additional 20 years make up only 0.33% of the present value of the first 80 years of copyright protection. Instead, a retroactive extension almost exclusively benefits owners of copyrighted works that are about to expire. In the case of the Sonny Bono Copyright Term Extension Act, the Walt Disney Company had lobbied for the copyright extension to prevent its iconic Mickey Mouse character, which appeared for the first time in the *Steamboat Willie* short film in 1928, to enter the public domain (which it eventually did in 2024).

13.2.4 Ownership

Initial ownership of copyright pertains to the creator. Because copyright is a property right, it can be transferred, including beyond the creator's life. If work is created in the course of an author's employment (so-called work made for hire), the copyright is owned by the employer.[8] There is also the possibility of joint authorship, which results in common ownership. In case of joint authorship, all authors own the copyright, that is, each owns the same share. Depending on the jurisdiction, in case of common ownership, consent by all co-owners may be needed to grant a license. Note that there is a distinction between joint authorship and coauthorship. Under coauthorship, the contributions of different authors are separate from each other. For example in the case of a song, one person might write the lyrics, another the music. In the case of coauthorship, each author gains a separate copyright for their part of the work.

13.2.5 International Dimension

Copyright is a territorial right. That is, copyright is subject to national laws and therefore only enforceable in a given jurisdiction. However, a number of aspects of copyright protection were harmonized early on by the Berne Convention in 1886. The Berne Convention is an international treaty that sets minimum standards for copyright protection. It requires signatory states to grant protection for literary, scientific, and artistic works. It also requires national treatment for foreigners, that protection is available without a registration requirement, and that the minimum copyright term is the author's life plus 50 years. The convention also makes a distinction between moral and economic rights, and allows for certain copyright exceptions that permit reproduction without permission from the author.

It is noteworthy that the United States did not join the Berne Convention until 1989. In fact, the US copyright system did not recognize national treatment until 1891. Even after 1891, the United States granted copyright protection to foreigners only if their work was typeset in the United States (this provision was only abandoned in the Copyright Act of 1976). Until 1891, the US copyright system discriminated against foreign authors who did not enjoy copyright protection. As a result, foreign books, in particular by English authors, were usually copied immediately and were much cheaper in the United States. The famous English novelist Charles Dickens was especially affected

---

[8] Employment is different from commissioned works. For commissioned works, the creator is the owner of the copyright unless the parties establish an agreement to the contrary.

by lost royalties on his American editions and fought for an international copyright agreement throughout his life (Hudon 1964).

The 1994 TRIPS agreement also contains several provisions related to copyright.[9] Among others, it required the signing of the Berne Convention and required signatories to offer copyright protection for computer programs and databases. There are also a number of other important international agreements including the Rome Convention of 1961 on the Protection of Performers, Producers of Phonograms and Broadcasting Organizations, which created performer's rights, and the WIPO Copyright Treaty in 1996, which *inter alia* mandated the prohibition of circumvention of copyright protection and DRM.

Despite far-reaching international harmonization, there are still substantial differences in copyright protection across jurisdictions, such as differences in copyrightable subject matter, different requirements for originality, and differences in available exceptions and limitations.

13.2.6 Copyright Limitations and Exceptions

Copyright law recognizes certain limitations on copyright protection to account for situations in which the public's interest in obtaining access to copyrighted works outweighs the copyright owner's interest. These limitations include a closed list of exceptions from copyright liability. In the United States, these limitations include exceptions such as fair use and compulsory licensing. Compulsory licensing means that the use of copyrighted works is permitted under certain conditions and in exchange for specified royalties. Hence, permission from the rightsholder is not needed but compensation must be paid.

In practice, the most important exception is the fair use doctrine. Section 107 of the US Copyright Act lists a number of uses of copyrighted material that are covered by fair use, including "criticism, comment, news reporting, teaching, scholarship, or research." A similar exception exists also in other countries, for example in the United Kingdom, it is referred to as *fair dealing*. In the United States, courts apply a four-factor test to assess whether fair use applies based on Section 107 of the Copyright Act. The factors are: (1) the purpose and character of the use, including whether such use is of a commercial nature or is for nonprofit educational purposes; (2) the nature of the copyrighted work; (3) the amount and substantiality of the portion used in relation to the copyrighted work as a whole; and (4) the effect of the use on the potential market for or value of the copyrighted work.

Another important limitation of copyright is exhaustion. Exhaustion, also referred to as first-sale doctrine, means that once copyrighted work has been legally purchased, the copyright owner can no longer control the distribution of the work. This means that if you purchase a physical copy of a book from your campus bookstore for a course you are currently taking, you can legally resell the book after you are done with your course without infringing the book's copyright. Box 13.2 discusses a similar situation that tested the geographical boundaries of the first-sale doctrine.

---

[9] https://www.wto.org/english/docs_e/legal_e/27-trips_04_e.htm.

Box 13.2 Copyright and Exhaustion: *Kirtsaeng v. John Wiley & Sons, Inc.*, 568 US 519 (2013)

Supap Kirtsaeng, a Thai national, imported to the United States foreign-edition academic textbooks from Thailand, where the books had been purchased legally. Supap effectively took advantage of international price discrimination practiced by academic book publishers. They usually price textbooks much higher in the United States, especially when compared to developing countries with lower purchasing power. Publisher John Wiley & Sons sued Supap for copyright infringement arguing that the importation of copyrighted works without the authorization of the US copyright owner was prohibited; in other words, copyright exhaustion applied only nationally. The US Supreme Court, however, held that the sale of copies lawfully made abroad was covered by the first-sale doctrine, that is, copyright exhaustion applies internationally. This meant that books legally purchased abroad could be imported to the United States without the permission of the US copyright owner.

13.3 Copyright on Software and AI

Copyright protection for software is still relatively new. In the United States, software obtained statutory copyright protection as "literary works" through the 1980 amendment of the 1976 Copyright Act and subsequent case law. Similarly, in other jurisdictions, such as the United Kingdom, software is copyrightable subject matter as it qualifies as literary works. One particular challenge for copyright in the software context is the distinction between the software's underlying idea and function, and its expression in the form of code. This is important for determining the scope of protection. If only the literal expression in the form of a specific code was protected, it would be easy for others to copy the essence of the code without infringing its copyright by, for example. rewriting the code while preserving its function and structure. However, if copyright protects also against nonliteral copying of software, it would offer broader protection but risks protecting the underlying idea, rather than just its expression. This would result in protection similar to patents, albeit without examination and with a much longer statutory term of protection. This tension in the copyright protection of software became apparent in a copyright infringement lawsuit litigated in the early 1990s by software developer Lotus against competitor Borland. Lotus 1-2-3 was a popular spreadsheet program created by Lotus in the early 1980s. Borland released competing software, the Quattro Pro, in the late 1980s. In the first instance, the district court found copyright infringement because Borland had copied the Lotus 1-2-3 menu commands and structure,[10] even though Borland "did not copy any of Lotus's underlying computer code."[11] However, on appeal, the US Court of Appeals for the First Circuit reversed the district court's decision.[12] It found that the Lotus 1-2-3

---

[10] *Lotus Development Corporation v. Borland International, Inc.*, 831 F. Supp. 202 (D. Massachusetts, June 30, 1993).

[11] *Lotus Development Corporation v. Borland International, Inc.*, 49 F.3d 807 (1st Cir. 1995).

[12] *Id.* The decision was affirmed by the US Supreme Court [*Lotus Development Corporation v. Borland International, Inc.*, 116 S. Ct. 804 (1996)].

menu structure, which Borland had copied, was a method of operation and, as such, not protected by copyright.

Apart from the question of whether software is protected by copyright, there is also the question of whether software, or rather AI, on its own can create work that benefits from copyright protection (for a discussion of AI and patent protection, see Chapter 17). Due to recent technological advances, generative AI is now easily capable of producing new works without direct human intervention that, in principle, could benefit from copyright protection, such as images (e.g., Midjourney or OpenAI's DALL-E 3) or music (e.g., Amper Music or AIVA). The question is whether works generated by AI can acquire copyright protection and, if so, who should be the author. While the legal standard for originality differs across jurisdictions, the basic question is the same: Does AI satisfy the originality requirement? In the United States, for example, this requirement mandates some level of creativity and that the work be an independent creation by its author. Provided AI-generated work qualifies for copyright protection, who should be able to claim authorship? The person who wrote the source code or the person who used the AI to generate the work?

A recent court case clarified that in the United States, creative works autonomously generated by AI are not eligible for copyright protection.[13] Stephen Thaler tried to register a copyright for a piece of visual art called *A Recent Entrance to Paradise* that was, according to Thaler, autonomously generated by an AI system called the "Creativity Machine." While he claimed ownership of the copyright, the Creativity Machine was listed as the author. The US Copyright Office refused registration on the basis that the work lacked human authorship. Thaler challenged the decision in federal court. The court, however, affirmed the copyright office's decision and clarified that the question of who owns the copyright to *A Recent Entrance to Paradise* does not even arise because "the work at issue was never subject to copyright protection" due to its lack of human authorship. To be clear, the court's decision still allows for copyright protection of creative works involving AI provided there is human input. However, the court also acknowledged that "[t]he increased attenuation of human creativity from the actual generation of the final work will prompt challenging questions regarding how much human input is necessary to qualify the user of an AI system as an 'author' of a generated work. . . ." Although this is not a new debate--the issue was, in fact, discussed already in the early 1980s (see, e.g., Butler 1982)--it will become more urgent given the speed at which AI advances. The outcome of the debate has potential economic implications as the availability of copyright protection for AI-generated works will shape incentives for the development and application of AI technology.

Copyrighted works also play an important role in the training of AI algorithms. The question here is whether that use is covered by existing copyright exceptions, such as fair use in the United States. Several lawsuits have been filed recently in the United States and Europe against AI companies alleging copyright infringement. For example, Getty Images sued Stability AI both in the United States and United Kingdom claiming that Stability AI had copied millions of images from Getty's database without authorization. The Authors Guild and 17 prominent writers, including John Grisham and George R. R. Martin, filed a class action suit in the United States against Open

---

[13] *Thaler v. Perlmutter*, 22-cv-1564, 2023 WL 5333236, at *1 (D.D.C., August 18, 2023).

AI alleging infringement of copyrighted works of fiction used as input for training ChatGPT. The outcome of these legal disputes is uncertain, but it is likely to have potentially far-reaching economic implications since copyrighted material is a key input for generative AI systems.

13.4 The Economics of Copyright

In principle, the economics of copyright are straightforward. The fixed costs of creating new works are high (think of how many hours it takes to write a novel or compose and record a music album), especially when compared to the low marginal cost of reproduction. We would like an author to price at marginal cost to allow everyone to enjoy the work who can afford to pay the marginal cost. However, at that price, the author would not be able to cover the fixed costs incurred in their creation of the work (this would lead to what is sometimes referred to as *underproduction*). Copyright allows the author to price above marginal cost. As a result, the author makes a positive profit, which covers their fixed costs. However, this comes at the expense of consumers since due to higher prices, fewer consumers are able to afford the work (this is sometimes referred to as *underutilization*). The result is a trade-off between avoiding underutilization and underproduction. We have already encountered this trade-off in our discussion of the patent system in Chapter 11. However, the economics of copyright differ somewhat for two reasons: (1) Unauthorized copying is very common and (2) new works often rely in some form or fashion on existing works.[14]

Let's discuss the second point in more detail first. It says that existing works often serve as input for the creation of new works. If copyright protection is strong, the cost of creating new works increases because creators infringe the copyright on some of the elements they relied on when creating their new works.

To make our discussion more concrete, take a look at Figure 13.1. The figure shows a black-and-white photograph (left-hand side) and a sculpture in color (right-hand side). The photo, titled "Puppies," was taken by professional photographer Art Rogers and sold as a postcard. Famous contemporary artist Jeff Koons created the sculpture. Koons freely admitted that the sculpture was based on the photo printed on a postcard that Koons had purchased at an airport gift shop.[15] Koons showed the sculpture at an exhibition and sold three copies for a total of US$367,000 in 1988 (about US$925,000 in 2022). Rogers sued Koons in 1989 for copyright infringement.[16] It is obvious that a sculpture is not a photo. However, it was also clear that Koons relied on the photo, which was protected by copyright, as input for his sculpture. The question for the court to decide, therefore, was whether by making his sculpture, Koons had actually copied Rogers's work. Koons argued that the fair use parody exemption should apply because his work should be seen as a commentary on contemporary culture, and he had transformed the original black-and-white two-dimensional work into a colorful

[14] To be clear, both issues also apply to patent protection. However, they are more pronounced in the context of copyright protection, especially (1).
[15] https://www.nytimes.com/1991/09/19/nyregion/a-picture-a-sculpture-and-a-lawsuit.html.
[16] *Rogers v. Koons*, 960 F.2d 301 (2d Cir. 1992).

Notes: The picture on the left is the original photograph taken by Andrea Blanch.
The picture on the right shows the collage created by Jeff Koons.

Figure 13.2 Illustration of *Blanch v. Koons* [467 F.3d 244 (2006)].

three-dimensional sculpture. The court rejected Koons's defense and found that Koons had infringed Rogers's copyright.

The *Rogers v. Koons* case illustrates how prior works serve as input for the creation of new works. It also shows that it is often not so easy to determine whether existing works serve only as input or whether subsequent works are effectively a slightly altered copy of the prior original works and hence infringe on the original works' copyright. How difficult it actually is in practice can be seen in another case involving again contemporary art made by Jeff Koons based on a photo. In this case, *Blanch v. Koons*,[17] photographer Andrea Blanch sued Koons for copyright infringement of a photo called "Silk Sandals by Gucci" that had appeared in a fashion magazine (see Figure 13.2). Koons took the photo and placed it in a collage painting that contained several other elements. Again, there was no dispute about the fact that the photo enjoyed copyright protection and that Koons had copied the photo without authorization and incorporated it directly into his art piece. Therefore, again the question was whether Koons's work was an unauthorized reproduction or the use of the photo was permitted as a component of an original, new art work. In this case, the court found in Koons's favor. The court determined that the fair use exception applied. Because "Koons used Blanch's work in a transformative manner," it had no negative economic effect on Blanch's work, and "the amount and substantiality of Koons's copying was reasonable in relation to the purpose of the copying." To sum up, we see that in both cases Koons relied on the unauthorized use of copyrighted material to create new art. In one case, his use infringed copyright; in the other, it did not. Where the law draws the line between unauthorized reproduction and non-infringing use has a direct impact on the creation of new works.

We can use a simple model to formalize the trade-off that emerges between providing incentives for the creation of new works by granting copyright protection and the cost that copyright protection generates for the use of existing works in the production of new works. In the model, proposed by Landes and Posner (1989), there is an artist who produces original art. There is also a copycat who makes unauthorized, identical copies of the original artist's work. Think, for example, of contemporary artist Andy Warhol as

---

[17] *Blanch v. Koons*, 396 F. Supp. 2d 476 (S.D.N.Y., November 1, 2005).

the original artist. Warhol was known for the mass production of art in his studio known as "The Factory." That is, while every copy of his art is considered an original Warhol, he still manufactured many identical copies of his art. The total quantity supplied by the artist is denoted as x. The total quantity supplied by the copycat is denoted as $y(p, z)$, where $z \geq 0$ denotes the overall level of copyright protection ($z = 0$ means that there is no copyright protection).

The total quantity of artworks supplied in the market is $q = x + y$. If we assume that consumers cannot distinguish between the original and unauthorized copies, the price of a copy--regardless of whether it is made by the artist or the copycat--is denoted by p. The artist incurs constant marginal cost c to make a copy of their work. The original artist also incurs costs $e(z)$ to create their new artwork. You can think of $e(z)$ as the cost of coming up with an idea and expressing the idea in some tangible form. Apart from the time and material cost of creating new art, you can also include costs such as the royalty payments of copyrighted material that is used as an input, or the transaction cost involved in locating the owner of the copyright and negotiating access.

Next, we assume that the supply of copies by the copycat increases in the price of the work $\dfrac{\partial y(p,z)}{\partial p} > 0$ and decreases in copyright protection $\dfrac{\partial y(p,z)}{\partial z} < 0$. The latter assumption could be justified, for example, by potential damages payable by the copycat if the illegal copying is detected. We also assume that the cost of creating new original work e increases in the overall level of copyright protection z, that is, $\dfrac{\partial e(z)}{\partial z} > 0$.

We can then write the artist's profits π as

$$\pi = (p-c)x - e(z) \tag{1}$$

If we replace the quantity x supplied by the artist using the fact that $x = q - y$, we obtain the following expression for π:

$$\pi = (p-c)\left[q - y(p,z)\right] - e(z) \tag{2}$$

If we take the first derivative of the artist's profits with respect to copyright protection z, we can examine the impact of a change in copyright protection on the artist's profits:

$$\frac{\partial \pi}{\partial z} = \underbrace{-[(p - c)\frac{\partial y(p,z)}{\partial z}]}_{\substack{Revenue\ effect \\ +}}\ \ \underbrace{- \frac{\partial e(z)}{\partial z}}_{Cost\ effect\ -} \tag{3}$$

Equation (3) shows that a strengthening of copyright protection has two opposing effects on the artist's profits. The first part on the right-hand side of equation (3) captures the positive effect of a strengthening of copyright on the artist's profits due to its negative effect on the supply of art by the copycat. If copyright protection increases, less is supplied by the copycat and more by the artist. We call this the revenue effect. The second part of equation (3) captures the negative effect of a strengthening of copyright protection on the artist's profits. The negative effect is a direct consequence of our assumption that the artist's cost $e(z)$ increases in z. In other words, stronger copyright protection makes it more expensive for the artist to create new works, for example, because as in the court cases involving Jeff Koons described above, the artist has to pay royalties on existing work that they rely on as input for their work. Box 13.3 provides another example from the music industry that illustrates this point in practice. In certain genres, music producers routinely rely on samples of existing music for the creation of new songs. Copyright protection has a direct impact on their ability to do so, as the case discussed in Box 13.3 illustrates.

An important empirical question is how responsive creators are to the revenue effect. Some might argue that artists have a fairly inelastic supply with respect to financial compensation. Moreover, in practice, the royalty income distribution is highly skewed. Very few superstar artists earn a lot, while everyone else makes hardly any money (Corrigan and Rogers 2005).[18] However, empirical evidence on the impact of copyright does suggest large effects on prices (Li et al. 2018, Reimers 2019). Giorcelli and Moser (2020) show that copyright also affects the supply and quality of creative work. Specifically, they show that the introduction of copyright in Italy in the early 19th century significantly increased the creation and quality of new operas. Composers benefited from copyright because it gave them the right to obtain royalties from repeat performances (without copyright, they only got paid for the original composition of the opera).

Now let's return to the first point we mentioned above: Unauthorized copying is common. Think, for example, of illegal streaming or downloading of music or movies on now defunct platforms such as The Pirate Bay or Megaupload. Popular songs and movies were available online on those platforms for free as unauthorized copies (we discuss online piracy in more detail in the next section). The existence of relatively easily accessible pirated copies of original works is a common occurrence in markets for copyrighted works. There are several reasons for this. First, copying and distribution are often cheap, especially of digital works. Second, copyright enforcement is costly and time-consuming, while the economic damage caused by an individual copy may be low. This means that enforcement may be difficult, especially if those that produce and distribute unauthorized copies are out of a copyright owner's legal reach. This happens because copyright regimes and enforcement differ substantially in practice across countries.

In terms of the economics of copyright, the presence of copies creates de facto competition for the artist. Even if we assume that unauthorized copies are not perfect substitutes of original works (e.g., they could be of inferior quality), the resulting market structure looks more like monopolistic competition. Hence, despite exclusivity granted by copyright, in practice copyright owners have limited market power. This limits their revenue and in particular their ability to price-discriminate. At the same time, competitive pressure from copying may, in fact, have an *escape competition effect*

---

[18] *The Economist* reported in 2017 that the 13 most popular Christmas songs on Spotify alone accumulated 1 billion plays. The most popular among them, Mariah Carey's "All I Want for Christmas," accounted for over 200 million plays and earned over US$60million since it was released in 1994.

(Aghion et al. 2005; see also Chapter 5). Indeed, Bradley and Kolev (2023) show, for a sample of publicly traded software firms, that increased piracy lead to an increase in R&D spending (although the effect is relatively small) due to a perceived increase in product market competition.

In fact, the economics literature suggests that the existence of routine copying may not be such a bad thing even for copyright owners. Allowing some degree of copying can be profitable for an artist in the presence of network externalities (Conner and Rumelt 1991, Takeyama 1994), that is, when the utility of a consumer increases in the number of consumers of the same product. Think, for example, about software where the use of the software depends directly on the total number of users (your benefits from using a software increase in the number of other people using the same software); or think of platforms where users exchange information about the software--the more users there are, the more active such a platform will be. This will benefit users who acquired the software legally even if many of the other users who exchange information obtained a pirated copy. In such a situation, copying can effectively act as a way to price-discriminate among consumers. The copiers are charged a price of zero, while others pay a price that incorporates the network effect generated by copiers. If copying were prevented, the same network size could only be obtained by charging a lower uniform price for everyone. As a result, it may be optimal to allow some degree of copying and thereby engage in price discrimination.

There is another way in which a copyright owner can rely on price discrimination in the presence of unauthorized copying. The idea, referred to as indirect appropriation (Liebowitz 1985), works as follows: If the artist knows who will use their legally purchased version for unauthorized copying, the artist can charge that user more. The idea is that the artist price-discriminates among buyers as a function of the number of copies that will be made with each original work. Indirect appropriation can also occur through complementary products. For example, artists can increase profits through live concerts. If copying of an album increases demand for concert tickets, the resulting increase in prices of concert tickets can mitigate decreased revenue due to copying. Now you can also see why this is called indirect appropriation: The owner of copyrighted works appropriates their returns indirectly from copiers.

The data for concert prices in the United States did indeed show a steep increase starting in the late 1990s when Napster appeared. However, this pattern could have also been explained by artists setting higher prices because concerts had less impact on record sales due to piracy instead of piracy driving up demand (Krueger 2005). That said, Mortimer et al. (2012) offer evidence to suggest that in particular lesser known bands saw their revenue from live concerts increase in the post-Napster period. This effect is consistent with file sharing allowing consumers to listen and discover a more diverse set of music, hence driving demand for concert tickets of lesser known bands and resulting in indirect appropriation. However, evidence from songs that entered the public domain in the United Kingdom after their recording copyright expired suggests that the relationship between concerts and copyright is more complex. Watson et al. (2022) show that the number of reissues increased, although the songs were performed less frequently live in concert. The latter is explained by artists preferring to promote their copyrighted works.

Apart from incentivizing the creation of original works, statutory copyright protection also has the objective of avoiding overinvestment in private copy protection. Private copy protection describes measures, such as DRM, that creators can take to impede unauthorized copying and access of copyrighted material. Copy protection serves as a substitute to legal copyright protection. Typical examples of DRM include encryption, digital watermarks, or authentication protocols. Box 13.4 discusses so-called geo-blocking as a way of controlling access to copyrighted works.

Box 13.4 Geo-Blocking and Price Discrimination

Geo-blocking is a technology that allows content providers to block access to digital content, such as movies, music, or e-books, based on a user's geographical location. To apply geo-blocking, a content provider has to access a user's physical location using, for example, the user's IP address or GPS coordinates. The technology also allows content providers to tailor content to users depending on their location. As a result, the technology can also be used to price-discriminate against users across locations. Below, you can see the screenshot from YouTube that visualizes geo-blocking. You are shown this message if you try to access content that is not available in your location. In contrast to YouTube, geo-blocking applied to price-discriminate is usually not visible to customers. They are simply automatically displayed different prices or rerouted based on their location.

Geo-blocking allows content providers to avoid copyright infringement and instead benefit from geographically differentiated licensing. For example, Netflix can stream a given TV show in only a subset of countries where its streaming service is available to avoid paying for a global license. Geo-blocking can also be used to prevent access for users in a certain country for other legal reasons, such as laws prohibiting online gambling. However, geo-blocking is relatively easily circumvented through the use of virtual private networks (VPNs) or anonymous proxy servers. This is an example of a circumvention technology that can be used for unauthorized access to copyrighted material, but that also has a wide range of legal applications including ensuring privacy.

There are a number of potential drawbacks to the use of copy protection. First, it requires private investment in access and copy control. This increases the cost of producing and distributing original works. It also provides copyright owners with the ability to limit non-infringing uses, such as those covered under fair use in the United States. This can therefore reduce access to copyrighted works above and beyond what copyright protection is supposed to provide. There is even the potential for private copy protection to be used anti-competitively. This happens if copy protection can be used as a way of excluding competitors.

An example is the case brought by video console and game maker Nintendo against PC Box in Italy. PC Box sold a device, a mod chip, that allowed users to circumvent restrictions Nintendo built into its game consoles, such as the Wii, to prevent third-party content from being played. Nintendo claimed that the restriction was necessary to prevent copyright infringement of its video games since unauthorized copies must not be played on its hardware. However, the restriction also meant that Nintendo was able to prevent any third-party content from being played on its consoles, which allowed it to act as a monopoly in the market for compatible video games. PC Box argued that its circumvention device enabled additional legal uses of Nintendo's console for purposes such as playing MP3 files or movies. The CJEU ruled on the one hand with respect to technological protection measures such as those used by Nintendo that national courts have to weigh their impact on "preventing or restricting not only acts which require the rightholder's authorisation . . . but also acts which do not require such authorization." On the other hand, with respect to circumvention devices such as PC Box's mod chip, the court ruled that national courts must take into consideration the extent to which these devices "can be used for legitimate purposes other than allowing acts which require the rightholder's authorisation".[19]

13.5 Copyright and Digitization

All IP rights have been fundamentally affected by digitization. However, copyright has played a central role in shaping the development of new digital technologies and online marketplaces. Copyright law has also been challenged by these developments and had to adapt quickly to accommodate dramatic changes in which copyrightable works are created, distributed, and consumed.

In particular, digitization has had a pronounced impact on the media industries that heavily rely on copyright, including music, film, and books. When media only existed in physical format, say, as a printed book or a music compact disc, copying was more laborious and time-consuming. Once digitized, copying is much faster and easier, and ultimately cheaper. Marginal costs of copying and distribution have essentially fallen to zero.

Resulting widespread piracy eroded the music industry's profits starting in 1999 (although the exact magnitude of the effect of piracy on sales is contested).[20] Some of you might be old enough to remember the file-sharing site Napster. It was created in 1999

---

[19] Case C-355/12, *Nintendo Co. Ltd. v. PC Box Srl* (January 23, 2014).
[20] For different estimates, see, for example, Liebowitz (2006) and Oberholzer-Gee and Strumpf (2007).

and allowed peer-to-peer file sharing of copyrighted works. Napster was shut down in early 2001 after a US court found contributory and vicarious copyright infringement. However, the shutdown did little to stop peer-to-peer file sharing since several other peer-to-peer sites popped up that were much harder to reach because they did not rely on a central server in a single location. This allowed users around the world to up- and download music and movies without much regard for copyright protection.

While it seems intuitive to assume that piracy was the sole culprit of reduced demand for copyrighted works, caution is in order. There is the possibility that free access to copyrighted works allowed consumers to sample and thereby increase demand (Peitz and Waelbroeck 2006). Working out the net effect is difficult, however. Think of popular music, for example a song by pop star Taylor Swift. There is clearly a positive correlation between the legal sales of that song and how often it is shared illegally on file-sharing websites. But that does not mean the illegal sharing causally drives up demand, nor does it mean that everyone who obtained an illicit copy would have otherwise legally purchased a copy (although the record industry often made that latter claim to inflate its estimates of the damages suffered).

Survey-based evidence suggests that piracy and legal sales are indeed substitutes. Using data from a European consumer mail survey in 2001, Zentner (2006), for example, found that regular users of file-sharing sites and those downloading MP3 files from the internet were 32% less likely to legally purchase music. There is also evidence that suggests a strengthening of copyright enforcement online leads to less internet traffic, which is an indicator of reduced peer-to-peer file sharing activity, and an increase in legal music sales (Adermon and Liang 2014). Both effects indicate that piracy and legal sales are indeed substitutes, albeit certainly not perfect ones. However, this finding does not necessarily carry over to other types of creative works. Nagaraj and Reimers (2023) show that the free availability of books in digital format on Google Books increased sales of their physical counterparts because it facilitated consumer search and discovery. This effect is likely to dominate substitution of paid-for physical books for free online versions because consumers do not consider them perfect substitutes and their improved ability to search online expands demand sufficiently.

Another important consequence of digitization is that the costs associated with production, distribution, and promotion have also fallen dramatically. In addition, the industry was disrupted by the entry of new global platforms that facilitated distribution and access to creative content. Apple's iTunes Store was created in the early 2000s and profoundly changed the market structure in the music industry. One of the major innovations introduced by iTunes was the unbundling of music. Previously, consumers had to purchase a compact disc that typically contained an entire album, rather than only the one or two songs a listener was interested in. iTunes offered consumers the ability to purchase only individual songs for a much lower price than the entire album.

Soon thereafter, in 2005, YouTube was launched, which allowed users to upload and watch videos. Netflix also emerged, initially as a DVD rent-by-mail company, which then started to stream in 2007. The development of complementary technology such as Apple TV made it soon easy to stream content on TVs rather than the computer. It also helped that TV hardware improved fast during that time period, which made plasma TVs quickly bigger and much more affordable. The book market was also disrupted by the advent of Amazon's Kindle reader and the launch of e-books on Amazon's on-line store.

These technological developments also gave content creators direct access to consumers, which facilitated entry into the market. That is, it has not only become cheaper to make new content but it has also become cheaper to store and offer content to consumers. In fact, it has also become a lot cheaper to rely on content as input be-cause the storage of content has become drastically cheaper and a number of platforms have emerged that allow creators to shop for input. Online marketplaces like Beatstars, for example, allow users to license beats from other users that they can use as input for their own music production. Anyone can record themselves with their smartphone, perform a song, and upload the video to YouTube or make it available for sale on iTunes or for streaming on Spotify. Similarly, anyone can now self-publish a book and sell it on Amazon via Amazon's Kindle Direct Publishing platform or as a physical print-to-order book via self-publisher services such as Lulu. Professional and amateur photographers alike can monetize their works through stock photo licensing platforms such as iStock or Shutterstock. New AI-based tools are poised to boost this development and further blur the lines between consumers and creators.

Owners of copyrighted works deal with the challenges posed by digitization in var-ious ways (Varian 2005). They can lower prices to discourage the use of unauthorized copies of lower quality; they can also engage in bundling through subscriptions (e.g., Amazon Prime) and sell personalized access (e.g., playlists on Spotify); they can make it harder to copy or gain unauthorized access by using DRM; they can also sell phys-ical or service complements (e.g., software companies can provide customer service or regular free updates).

13.6 Summary

This chapter reviewed the legal and economic foundations of copyright protection. Copyright protects the expression of an idea, not the idea itself. It is acquired by the creation of original works that fall within the definition of copyrightable subject matter. There is no examination or requirement of registration to benefit from copyright pro-tection. Although copyright protection has been substantially harmonized internation-ally, important differences remain across jurisdictions.

The economics of copyright center on the trade-off between granting exclusivity to allow authors to recoup their fixed investment in the creation of original works and ensuring the widest possible access to the works. This trade-off is complicated by the fact that unauthorized copying is common and that the creation of original works almost invariably relies on existing copyrighted works as input. The chapter also discussed the role that statutory copyright plays in shaping a creator's incentives to engage in pri-vate copy protection. Finally, the chapter also discussed the unique challenges posed by digitization and AI for the copyright system.

14

Alternatives to Intellectual Property

Learning Objectives

After reading this chapter, you will be able to understand and explain the following concepts:

- Different informal appropriation mechanisms including secrecy, lead time, and first-mover advantages
- The use of formal and informal mechanisms in practice
- Factors that determine the choice between formal and informal mechanisms, in particular patents and secrecy
- Collective invention and the "open sharing" knowledge production system
- The role of prizes and awards as incentive mechanism for innovation

---

14.1 Introduction

The economics literature has traditionally focused on IP in the form of patents. However, as we discussed in Chapters 11–13, there are a number of other IP rights available, including trademarks, design rights, utility models, and copyright. All these IP rights are also referred to as *formal* appropriation mechanisms to distinguish them from *informal* appropriation mechanisms. Informal or "alternative" mechanisms include secrecy, confidentiality agreements, lead time, complexity, complementary sales or assets, and so forth. The literature refers to them as *alternative appropriation mechanisms* because they allow firms to obtain returns on their innovations and they are different from IP––hence the label "alternative."

What all informal mechanisms have in common is that they do not require any form of official registration or examination (although as you already know, certain IP rights do not necessarily require registration or examination either). In fact, the legal protection afforded by these mechanisms is limited; they do not benefit from legal protection that grants (temporary) exclusivity, although confidentiality agreements and trade secrecy are legally enforceable, normally in civil courts. Limited legal protection does not imply that these alternative appropriation mechanisms are necessarily any less effective in enabling innovators to appropriate returns to their innovations. Indeed, their effectiveness combined with the fact that they do not require any registration or examination makes them popular among innovators.

The Economics of Innovation and Intellectual Property. Bronwyn H. Hall and Christian Helmers, Oxford University Press.
© Oxford University Press 2024. DOI: 10.1093/oso/9780197630914.003.0014

Still, it might be tempting to assume that informal appropriation mechanisms are less important because anything of value will be protected by IP, in particular patents. Would it surprise you to learn that the magnetic stripe, which is found on virtually every credit and debit card, has never been patented? In 1960, IBM engineer Forrest Parry came up with the idea to attach a magnetic strip to a plastic card to store data directly on the card. At the time, IBM made the decision not to patent the technology and instead drive diffusion as widely as possible by making the technology freely available to everyone. How then did IBM appropriate the returns to its invention? After all, IBM had spent millions of dollars on the development of the technology. Jerome Svigals, IBM's magnetic stripe project manager at the time, provides the answer: "For every buck we spent on developing the mag stripe, we got [US]\$1500 back in computer sales. . . . Our motive was to drive computer sales, and we did".[1] The magnetic stripe is an example of an invention that was not patented; instead, it was disclosed and freely made available to the public. Appropriation occurred via the sale of a complementary proprietary technology, computers, IBM's main line of business.

Another example of a commercially and highly successful invention that was clearly patentable but still never patented is WD-40, a multi-use product that "protects metal from rust and corrosion, penetrates stuck parts, displaces moisture and lubricates almost anything."[2] The product was launched in 1958 and has since become a staple of the American household generating hundreds of million US dollars in annual sales worldwide. Although the chemical formula of WD-40 could have been protected by a patent, the WD-40 company opted for secrecy instead. While this allowed competitors to bring very similar products to market, the company has avoided disclosure of the chemical formula until this day. A patent would have expired probably at some point in the late 1970s, and competitors would have been able to produce an exact copy of WD-40.

These examples show that innovators may choose to forgo patent protection and instead appropriate returns to their inventions in other ways. There are, in fact, many historical examples of new technologies that were developed without patent protection (we discuss these examples in more detail in Section 14.5.2 below), including textile looms (Foray and Hilaire-Perez 2006), the Cleveland (UK) iron industry (Allen 1983), and Cornish pumping equipment (Nuvolari 2004). Using data on thousands of innovations exhibited at the Crystal Palace World's Fair in London in 1851 and the Centennial Exhibition in Philadelphia in 1876, Moser (2005) shows that countries without patent systems still produced plenty of innovation despite the absence of patent protection. However, the absence of patent protection strongly affected the type of innovative activity. Countries that did not have patent protection at the time, such as Switzerland, specialized in industries where secrecy was more effective at the time, including textiles, food processing, scientific instruments, and watch making. In contrast, countries with patent protection, such as the United States, focused on machinery for which patent protection is more effective.

There are also many more recent examples of inventions that emerged in the absence of patent protection. As we discuss in Chapter 18, in the early days of the modern US software industry, software was, in fact, not even patentable. Regardless, the industry innovated at breakneck speed, paying little attention to the patent system, at least

---

[1] https://www.ibm.com/history/magnetic-stripe.
[2] https://www.wd40.com.

initially. Boldrin and Levin (2013) argue more generally that major innovations that often drive the creation of entire new industries typically do not rely on patent protection at an early stage. Instead, they argue that patents become more important only as the industry matures and incumbents turn toward patent protection to secure rents and prevent entry.

In this chapter, we review the most widely used alternative appropriation mechanisms. This includes not only informal appropriation mechanisms and the "open sharing" model, but also prizes and awards. We discuss the choice that innovators face between these different appropriation mechanisms. The choice between different appropriation mechanisms is important for the design of the optimal incentives to innovate. The formal IP system was created with the express goal of incentivizing innovation and creative works. However, if innovators rely on alternative mechanisms instead, we need to understand why as this informs us about the functioning of the IP system. We will see that, in practice, the choice is not so stark and innovators often combine different mechanisms––especially over time as different mechanisms may be more useful during different stages of the R&D and commercialization process.

14.2 Informal Appropriation Mechanisms

In this section, we review a number of informal appropriation mechanisms. We focus on those mechanisms that have received the most attention in the literature, although there are may be others that are also important to innovators in practice.

14.2.1 Secrecy

Secrecy is one of the most popular methods of appropriating returns to innovation, as we will see later in this chapter. In principle, anything can be kept secret, at least to some extent and for a certain period of time. However, that does not make the information automatically a secret that is protected by trade secrecy. When we talk about secrecy as an appropriation mechanism, what we usually mean is trade secrecy. What is the difference between a secret and a trade secret? And why does it matter when it comes to appropriating returns to innovation?

The difference between a secret and trade secret is legal protection. Trade secret law generally grants owners of a secret that qualifies as a trade secret certain legal recourse in case the secret is misappropriated, where misappropriated means "acquired by improper means," for example, theft or breach of duty of confidentiality. Because it is protected by legislation and enforceable via litigation, trade secret protection is actually something of a hybrid between formal and informal protection methods. In some jurisdictions, the protection of trade secrets is explicitly regulated, whereas in others, such protection is part of unfair competition legislation.[3] In order to benefit from legal trade secrecy protection, the information that is kept secret has to satisfy two conditions:

---

[3] https://www.wipo.int/tradesecrets/en.

1. The information has independent commercial value based on the fact that it is not readily available to others.
2. The holder of the secret has to take reasonable precautions to prevent its disclosure.

The first condition is relatively weak as one would expect that competing companies are only interested in information that translates into some commercial advantage. Take the example of a company's customer list. Such a list has clear commercial value and, if disclosed, would benefit competitors. The second condition is more stringent. It imposes a duty on the owner of the information to take active measures to prevent inadvertent disclosure of the information. While "reasonable" can mean many things, in the United States, the UTSA[4] defines reasonable efforts to include (1) advising employees of the existence of a trade secret, (2) limiting access to the secret on a need to know basis, and (3) controlling plant access (i.e., the physical location where the secret is held). As opposed to, for example, patents, firms do not need to register their trade secrets. There is also no term limit on trade secrets; in principle, they can be kept secret indefinitely, as long as they are not inadvertently disclosed or misappropriated. A famous example of a long-standing trade secret is the original recipe for Coca Cola.

It is worth pointing out that a trade secret is not a property right since its holder does not acquire an exclusive right to the secret. If the secret leaks or another company discovers the same invention independently by legal means, the holder of the trade secret has no legal recourse. In practice, leakage occurs more frequently than you might imagine. Usually, some mishap is at the origin of the leakage. Take the example of a trove of confidential documents that were inadvertently made publicly available on a court's online cloud storage folder during the discovery stage of a recent court case of Fortnite game developer Epic Games against Apple.[5] The secrets related to a vast range of internal business information involving the litigants, Epic Games and Apple, but also related to business dealings with third parties, such as Netflix and Microsoft. While the documents were quickly removed from the cloud storage, the horses had already left the barn and the information had already widely spread and was soon publicized by various news outlets.[6] It was also a simple mishap that led to the public revelation of Apple's iPhone 4 well ahead of its official announcement date in 2010.[7] An Apple engineer had accidentally left the prototype in a bar. Because trade secrecy only provides legal recourse in case of misappropriation, not in situations like the ones described, where an oversight leads to inadvertent disclosure, it does not grant a legal right to exclusive use. Exclusive use is only obtained by ensuring that the secret remains secret.

While in practice misappropriation may be difficult to prove, nowadays it often takes the form of obtaining access to digital information. Take the example of a former Apple hardware engineer that was accused of trade secret theft because he downloaded

---

[4] The UTSA aims to harmonize state-level legal protection of trade secrets.
[5] *Epic Games, Inc. v. Apple Inc.*, 559 F.Supp. 3d 898 (N.D. California, September 10, 2021).
[6] https://www.theverge.com/c/22611236/epic-v-apple-emails-project-liberty-app-store-schiller-swee ney-cook-jobs.
[7] https://gizmodo.com/this-is-apples-next-iphone-5520164.

several Apple internal files that contained information on Apple's driverless technology shortly before giving notice and announcing his move to China to take up employment with Guangzhou-based start-up Xiaopeng Motors, which worked on similar technology.[8] Note that depending on the jurisdiction, trade secrecy misappropriation can be a crime. In the United States, for example, under the Economic Espionage Act, theft of a trade secret used in interstate or foreign commerce can result in imprisonment, as it did in the case of the former Apple engineer.

An interesting aspect of trade secrecy theft is that it could have a positive effect on innovation because it makes the information available to a competitor, which could induce competition and lower prices. Obviously, the downside of misappropriation is reduced incentives to innovate if there is no legal recourse against misappropriation and it would incentivize investing resources in theft as the means to acquiring information. However, since the law penalizes only misappropriation but not reverse engineering, the law incentivizes investment in reverse engineering but not misappropriation. This makes sense from a legal and economic perspective since it might be difficult to prove reverse engineering in practice and reverse engineering can lead to learning and incremental innovation. This argument also teaches us something more generally about the economics of secrecy. The main economic argument for the legal protection of trade secrets is simple: Protection against the misappropriation of new ideas encourages investment in R&D, and it discourages investment in misappropriation.

The legal framework of trade secrecy protection differs substantially across countries. Trade secrets are protected by statutory provisions specific to secrecy, as well as provisions across a wide range of areas, including unfair competition law, employment law, contract law, criminal law, and common law. In practice, companies bolster trade secrecy protection by relying on private contracts with employees and business partners such as non-disclosure, confidentiality, or non-compete agreements. These private contracts make it more difficult for information to travel via employee mobility or information exchange with other companies as part of a (prospective) business transaction.

In their seminal discussion of the economics of trade secrets, Friedman et al. (1991, p. 61) said that "the law of trade secrets is a neglected orphan in economic analysis." Although this statement was made more than 30 years ago, and the literature has made some progress, we know surprisingly little about the economics of trade secrets, especially in comparison to the vast literature on the economics of patenting. But perhaps it is not that surprising after all because due to the very nature of the subject, secrecy, it is particularly hard to study. One way to obtain some insight into the importance of secrecy and its use is to ask firms directly in surveys. A large number of surveys, which we discuss in the next section, have produced remarkably consistent results. Secrecy is considered by far the most effective way of appropriating returns to innovation. This may be surprising since secrecy requires firms to somehow maintain the veil of secrecy while still commercializing products or services that rely on the innovations that are being kept secret. Nevertheless, secrecy is, in fact, the most widely used form of protection. This is true regardless of whether the underlying invention is a product or process. However, there are differences between discrete (e.g., pharmaceuticals and chemicals)

---

[8] https://www.justice.gov/usao-ndca/pr/former-apple-employee-indicted-theft-trade-secrets.

and complex (e.g., computers and communication equipment) technologies, with secrecy being more important in complex technologies.[9]

As we already pointed out above, the main economic argument for the legal protection of trade secrets is to encourage investment in R&D. However, there are other
benefits to trade secrecy protection. First, it allows firms to disclose inventions to
those who have signed a non-disclosure agreement and thereby can enable trade and
collaboration between firms. Second, it avoids overinvestment in keeping secrets secret. Fromer (2011) illustrates this benefit by pointing to Roald Dahl's famous story of
Charlie and the Chocolate Factory. As some of you probably remember, Willy Wonka,
the main character in the story, ran a highly innovative and successful candy company. Wonka relied mainly on secrecy to protect his astonishingly innovative recipes
and production methods. Desperate to catch up, his competitors infiltrated spies into
Wonka's workforce tasked with stealing Wonka's trade secrets in order to copy his candy
creations. Frustrated by the blatant theft of his creations by his competitors and the financial implications-- Wonka had to invest heavily in the creation and production of
new candy while his competitors would copy them at no cost--Wonka took the drastic
step of shutting down his factory.

Eventually, Wonka found an unconventional solution to his predicament. He discovered the tribe of Oompa-Loompas who lived in a remote place called Loompaland. The
Oompa-Loompas found themselves in a predicament of their own. They revered the
cacao bean, but it was extremely hard to come by in Loompaland. Therefore, it was not
difficult for Wonka to convince them to live and work in his factory in exchange for un-
limited access to cacao beans and chocolate. Wonka's new Oompa-Loompa workforce
solved his problem because the Oompa-Loompas would never leave his factory, had no
contact with the outside world, and due to their distinctive appearance, competitors
could no longer infiltrate any of their spies disguised as Wonka's workers.

While of course fictional, the story and in particular the extreme measures Wonka
was forced to take are a good example of private overinvestment in secrecy. Such
overinvestment could have been avoided, if Wonka had had legal recourse against the
outright theft of his trade secrets by his employees. You can see that this is where legal
trade secrecy protection comes in. By offering legal protection against misappropriation
in exchange for only requiring reasonable measures to maintain secrecy, legal trade secrecy protection helps avoid private overinvestment in measures to keep secrets secret.

However, there are also downsides to the use of secrecy to appropriate returns
to innovation. First, if companies maintain information on their innovations as secret, there is increased potential for duplication of R&D. Second, and more importantly, companies' efforts to maintain secrecy reduce knowledge spillovers. Png
(2017) provides empirical evidence regarding this argument. His results suggest
that a strengthening of legal protection of trade secrets in the form of the UTSA in
the United States lead to an increase in R&D expenditure by larger manufacturing
companies and companies in high-tech industries. Importantly, the results cannot distinguish between two competing explanations for the observed effect. It is possible

---

[9] Cohen et al. (2000, p. 19) explain the distinction as follows: "The key difference between a complex and
a discrete technology is whether a new, commercializable product or process is comprised of numerous separately patentable elements versus relatively few."

that the results are driven by the fact that for these firms spillovers and own R&D are substitutes. Alternatively, the results could also be explained by the appropriation effect dominating the negative effect from reduced spillovers, assuming own R&D and spillovers are complements.

In practice, employees are one of the main vehicles for trade secrecy misappropriation (Almeling et al. 2010). This can happen either through outright espionage (as in Willy Wonka's case) or worker mobility. When employees move on to a new job, they may take codified information, for example, documents that contain secret information, with them. One highly publicized episode of this type was Anthony Levandowski's move from Google's Waymo to Uber in 2016 and the subsequent litigation between the two firms as well as Levandowski over trade secret theft.[10] The first case was settled between Uber and Waymo in 2018 for US$245million. The case of Waymo against Levandowski continued, and he was sentenced to 18 months in jail and owed Waymo US$179million.[11]

Misappropriation can also occur without outright stealing documents because R&D often contains substantial tacit elements and employees can simply relay those trade secrets to their new employer. Companies therefore attempt to restrict worker mobility in various ways, most importantly through contractual agreements such as non-disclosure and non-compete agreements. Conti (2014) offers empirical evidence from US companies over the period 1990–2000, which suggests that firms in states with stricter enforcement of non-competes engage in riskier R&D. The intuition for this result is simple: If employees of successful projects are more likely to be poached by competitors, non-competes help retain such employees and hence increase a firm's ability to appropriate the returns to such high-risk, high-return R&D.

Contagiani et al. (2018), on the other hand, suggest that stronger secrecy protection in the form of restrictions on employee mobility has negative effects on patenting, especially citation-weighted patent counts. The explanation is not so much that firms substitute patents with secrecy, but rather reduced incentives for inventors because of reduced mobility. More generally, as discussed in Chapter 6, worker mobility is an important channel through which knowledge spillovers occur in practice. Since there is empirical evidence that suggests non-compete agreements restrict inventor mobility (Marx et al. 2009), they are likely to limit knowledge spillovers, which could negatively affect overall innovative activity.

14.2.2 Lead Time and First-Mover Advantage

There are a number of other informal mechanisms than secrecy that firms rely on to appropriate returns to innovation. According to the firm-level surveys that we discuss in more detail in the next section, lead time is even more popular among firms than secrecy when it comes to protecting product innovations. The survey evidence

[10] https://news.bloomberglaw.com/ip-law/uber-settles-waymo-litigation-in-saga-that-drew-in-thiel-trump.

[11] Levandowski was pardoned by President Trump in 2021, and in 2022 Uber and Waymo agreed to settle his case.

also suggests that lead time is particularly useful for smaller companies (Leiponen and Byma 2009, Thomä and Bizer 2013). But what exactly is lead time?

Lead time describes the time a firm takes to bring an innovation from its inception to market (Clark et al. 1987). Another way to think about lead time is that it reflects how much faster a company can bring a new product or service to market than its competitors. The Yale survey by Levin et al. (1987) discussed in the next section defined lead time as "being first with a new process or product." This shows that lead time is closely related to another informal mechanism: first-mover advantage. First-mover advantage describes the edge that a firm gains from introducing an innovation first to a new industry or product category. Firms are first for different reasons. Usually, they have some technological edge that then translates into being first thanks to specific capabilities, foresight, or just luck (Lieberman and Montgomery 1988). Being first is useful for a number of reasons. Companies that are first have more time to build expertise, prevent access by competitors to scarce resources, and they benefit from temporary exclusivity simply by being the only one on the market. However, temporary exclusivity can translate into lasting market power by creating customer loyalty (Schmalensee 1982). In network industries, the first mover may be able to build a market share advantage that helps it become the dominant producer.

The effectiveness of lead time varies depending on the pace at which technology is evolving and the market expanding. Suarez and Lanzolla (2005) point to the example of William Henry Hoover's vacuum cleaner launched in 1908. Hoover was the first to sell an upright bag-on-stick vacuum cleaner. However, uptake was relatively slow and so was the technological development. According to Suarez and Lanzolla (2005), the combination of slowly expanding demand and slow technological progress meant that Hoover was able to cement his first-mover advantage to the extent that his name became synonymous with an entire product category.

Suarez and Lanzolla (2005) contrast the Hoover vacuum cleaner with the internet browser Netscape. The company released its Web browser Mosaic Netscape 9.0 in 1994 (later renamed Netscape Navigator). In the mid-1990s, it dominated the emerging and fast-growing browser market. However, Netscape quickly lost its dominant position to Microsoft and the company eventually disbanded and the browser was discontinued. Here, first-mover advantage did not result in lasting competitive advantage as the market was expanding extremely fast and technology was evolving rapidly (and Microsoft (ab) used its market power in operating systems to promote its own browser).[12]

14.3 The Use of Formal and Informal Mechanisms

You may still be under the impression that innovation and patenting are inextricably connected (Chapter 11 has certainly reinforced that view). However, there is plenty of empirical evidence to suggest the contrary. Hall et al. (2013) report that even among innovative companies in the United Kingdom, those that conduct R&D and report having had an innovation, only 4% applied for a patent. This figure is much lower than what we would expect to see if all innovative companies protected their inventions by

---

[12] *United States of America v. Microsoft Corporation*, 253 F.3d 34 (D.C. Cir. 2001).

Table 14.1 Importance of different IP mechanisms to US firms in 2008 (%)

	All firms	*R&D-doing firms*
Patent	5	41
Design patent	6	33
Trademark	15	60
Copyright	12	50
Trade secret	14	67

Population-weighted share of firms that rate the IP mechanism as somewhat or very important to their firm. Source: Hall et al. (2014).

patenting. Table 14.1 shows similar data for the United States. The data come from the US National Science Foundation's new Business R&D and Innovation Survey (BRDIS). Table 14.1 provides a breakdown by formal IP right. It shows that there are substantial differences across IP rights, with trademarks being considered important by the largest share of firms. Utility patents, in contrast, are considered far less important regardless of whether we look at all firms or restrict our attention to R&D-conducting firms. However, secrecy, the only informal mechanism in Table 14.1, is still considered much more important by R&D-doing firms than any type of formal IP.

Table 14.2 reports results from the so-called Yale I survey by Levin et al. (1987). The survey asked firms to report the effectiveness of different appropriation mechanisms in their industry. We see in Table 14.2 that patents are not considered the most effective means to appropriating returns to either product or process innovation. Instead, informal mechanisms are considered much more important. The Yale survey also offered some qualitative insights into why companies shunned patenting. Most importantly, the view was that patents required too much disclosure of information, while at the same time being relatively easy to invent around.

Figure 14.1 shows the Yale survey results on the effectiveness of patent protection across industries. There is substantial heterogeneity across industries. The effectiveness of patents for product innovation varies between 3.3 (pulp, paper, and

Table 14.2 Yale survey results by appropriation method (1983)

Method of appropriating the benefits from innovation	*New and improved product*	*New and improved process*
Patents to prevent duplication	4.33	3.52
Patents to secure royalty income	3.75	3.31
Secrecy	3.57	4.31
Being first with an innovation	5.41	5.11
Moving quickly down the learning curve	5.09	5.02
Superior sales or service efforts	5.59	4.55

From 1 (least effective to 7 (most effective). Source: Levin et al. (1987)

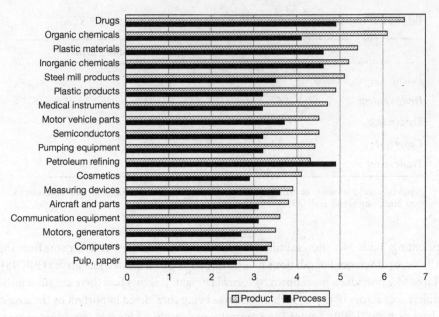

From 1 (least effective to 7 (most effective), for process and product inventions separately.
Source: Levin et al. (1987)

Figure 14.1 Yale survey results: Effectiveness of patents by industry (1983).

paperboard) and 6.5 for the pharmaceutical industry. Complex product industries, such as computers and communication equipment, also rate the effectiveness of patent protection low. In contrast, discrete product industries, such as pharmaceuticals and chemicals, all consider patents much more effective in helping firms appropriate returns to their innovations. This is a result of patents successfully excluding imitation in chemical sectors, where new inventions can be relatively precisely described by a chemical formula. This fact, which is not characteristic of other technologies, makes the boundaries of the idea the patent covers clearer and therefore easier to defend.

More recent evidence is given in Table 14.3, which shows results from the Carnegie Mellon survey by Cohen et al. (2000). The data come from a survey of R&D managers conducted in 1994 and cover the US manufacturing sector. Table 14.3 shows the percentages of innovations that respondents reported to be effectively protected by a given appropriation mechanism. The table distinguishes between product and process innovations. It is clear from Table 14.3 that patents are considered the least effective mechanism, with only around 35% of respondents considering patents effective for product innovation and 23% for process innovation. Secrecy, in contrast, is equally popular for product and process innovation, with a percentage of slightly above 50% for each. Lead time is considered the most effective mechanism for product innovations, even more so than secrecy. However, it is considered less effective for process innovation, with 38%. That said, it is still much more effective than patents. Complementary sales and manufacturing are also considered more effective than patents, but less so than secrecy or lead time.

In light of the relatively low effectiveness of patents, Cohen et al. (2000) are careful to highlight that respondents to the survey interpreted effectiveness to refer to the returns

Table 14.3 Carnegie Mellon survey results (1994)

Method of appropriating the benefits from innovation	Average share of innovations for which mechanism effective (%)	
	Product innovation	Process innovation
Patents	34.8	23.3
Secrecy	51.0	50.6
Lead time	52.8	38.4
Complementary sales or service efforts	42.7	30.7
Complementary manufacturing	45.6	43.0

Source: Cohen et al. (2000)

due to commercialization or licensing of the patented inventions. This is a relatively narrow definition as patents can serve myriad other purposes, which we discuss in more detail in Chapter 18.

Surveys similar to the Yale and Carnegie Mellon surveys have been conducted also outside of the United States, notably in Europe in the form of the Community Innovation Survey (CIS).[13] The results across surveys are remarkably consistent. Informal mechanisms, especially lead time and secrecy, are considered more important mechanisms than patents. Secrecy is more important to smaller firms. However, patents are important in pharmaceuticals and chemicals.

One potential shortcoming of these surveys is that information is self-reported. Figure 14.2 shows results for the United Kingdom from the combination of self-reported data (CIS for 1998–2006) and firms' actual patent filings (Hall et al. 2013). Figure 14.2 reports the share of innovating firms that rate a given appropriation mechanism as important, distinguishing between firms that have filed for a patent and those that have not. We see that a much larger share among patenting firms regards formal IP protection as important. In contrast, there is a much smaller difference between patenting and nonpatenting firms with respect to the importance of informal mechanisms (the three mechanisms on the right of the figure). That said, the fact that patenting firms still rate the effectiveness of informal mechanisms highly suggests that innovative firms may treat informal and formal IP as complements, rather than substitutes.

14.4 The Choice between Formal and Informal Mechanisms: Patenting versus Secrecy

The empirical evidence strongly suggests that firms consider informal mechanisms as, on average, more important and effective in appropriating returns to their

[13] Examples include surveys in Switzerland (Harabi 1995); the Netherlands (Brouwer and Kleinknecht 1999); Germany; Luxembourg; the Netherlands; Belgium; Denmark; Ireland; and Norway (Arundel 2003). More recently, a similar survey was conducted among third-party app developers on the Apple App Store (Miric et al. 2019).

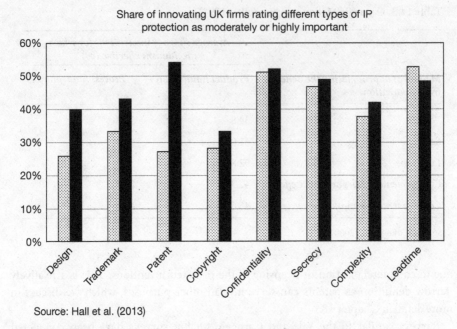

Source: Hall et al. (2013)

Figure 14.2 How innovating firms rate different types of IP protection.

innovative activity. However, the evidence also suggests that the importance of formal mechanisms, in particular patents, relative to informal mechanisms, notably secrecy, differs substantially between product and process innovations as well as more broadly across industries.

In this section, we review what we know about why firms choose informal or formal IP protection. To keep things simple, we focus on the choice between patenting and secrecy. This is also a useful starting point to think about an innovator's choice because, in principle, secrecy and patenting are mutually exclusive. Patenting requires disclosure, while secrecy by definition rests on non-disclosure of an inventive idea.[14] This trade-off is less pronounced for the combination of other formal and informal mechanisms, such as copyright and secrecy. A computer program is protected by copyright, and to at least a certain extent it can also be kept secret. Similarly, other informal mechanisms such as lead time or complexity could be combined with formal protection including patenting. That said, many of the factors that influence an innovator's choice between patenting and secrecy also apply to other formal and informal appropriation mechanisms.

Table 14.4 summarizes the choices available to an innovator under the stylized assumption that the only mechanisms available to an innovator are patenting and secrecy. The table shows that the innovator has four choices. Apart from either choosing

[14] One might question the extent to which patents actually disclose information in practice. There is a substantial amount of evidence that suggests patents are not an important source of information for inventions. Gambardella et al. (2011) asked inventors to quantify time saved in the invention process compared to a situation in which information from patents had not been available. The responses yield time savings of, on average, 11.5 hours (the median was slightly less than 6 hours). There was also considerable heterogeneity across technologies, with median values ranging between 1 hour (digital communication technology) and 36 hours (organic chemicals).

Table 14.4 The choice between secrecy and patent protection

	Patent	*Don't patent*
Secrecy	Patent-secrecy combination	Secrecy only
Non-secrecy	Patent only	Disclosure-publishing

Source: Graham et al. (2004).

to patent or maintain secrecy, the innovator can also choose to combine patenting and secrecy (upper-left quadrant) or eschew both in favor of disclosure without protection (lower-right quadrant).

14.4.1 Patent Only versus Secrecy Only

Let's first focus on the mutually exclusive choices of patenting only and secrecy only. Table 14.5 provides an overview of the different factors that determine the choice between patenting and secrecy.

A crucial factor in determining the choice to patent is whether the invention represents patentable subject matter and whether it satisfies the legal patentability requirements (see Chapter 11). As such, secrecy is applicable to a much wider range of inventions than patents. It is also true that even among patentable inventions, patents are more useful for some inventions than others. This was reflected in the survey results discussed above, where we saw that patents were considered more effective for product

Table 14.5 Factors affecting the patent-secrecy choice

Factor	*Patent*	*Secrecy*
Disclosure (codifiable knowledge)	Yes	No
Disclosure (tacit knowledge)	No	No
Ease of delimiting invention	Yes	Not clear
Reverse engineering allowed	No	Yes
Subject matter	Statutory	Broader
Timing	After invention	Work-in-progress
Process vs product	Both	Easier for process
Length	20 years	Longer (potentially)
Cost to obtain	Higher	Nonzero
Enforcement cost	Expensive	Expensive
Management requirements	IP management	Knowledge management
Geographical scope	National	Global

Source: Hall et al. (2014)

innovations and pharmaceutical companies consistently considered patents as more effective. A patent prevents others from using the invention even if they came up with it independently without any knowledge of the patented invention.

Another difference is that patent protection expires after a maximum of 20 years, while secrecy could be maintained indefinitely as our example of WD-40 illustrated. Moreover, patenting is costly since it has to undergo a registration process and then requires payment of various fees throughout its lifetime in order to remain enforceable. While maintaining secrecy may also be costly due to the reasonable efforts that have to be undertaken to prevent inadvertent disclosure, the associated costs are likely lower. In contrast, secrecy does not protect against other firms coming up with the same invention as long as they do so by legal means. Finally, enforcement of both patents and secrecy is costly. Enforcement of secrecy may be particularly difficult also because it may risk disclosing the secret and involves an admission that the company was unable to keep its valuable intangible assets secure.

As mentioned above, another important difference is the disclosure of a patented invention. Secrecy avoids such disclosure. How do innovators decide whether to disclose their invention or keep it hidden? Anton and Yao (2004) propose a model to analyze the role of information disclosure required by a patent on a firm's choice between patenting and secrecy. In their model, disclosure has two effects: (1) It provides information that competitors can use to innovate and (2) it can signal a competitive edge to competitors. This generates a trade-off between the exclusionary effect of a patent and the disclosure required by a patent, which promotes competition. Anton and Yao's main (and somewhat counterintuitive) result is that large inventions are kept secret and only small inventions are patented.

The model is a three-stage signaling game with two risk-neutral firms, innovator i and competitor j. In the first stage, the innovator invests in R&D in order to produce a process innovation that lowers marginal costs c. The outcome of the R&D stage is uncertain. If the innovator fails to innovate, they will continue producing with their old technology that has marginal cost $\bar{c} > c$. There is asymmetric information because the outcome of the R&D stage is observable only to the innovator but not the competitor. Given the outcome of the R&D stage, the innovator chooses whether to rely on patent protection P or secrecy S. Regardless of the innovator's choice, the model assumes that some information on the process innovation becomes available to the competitor, which allows the competitor to produce at marginal cost s with $s \geq c$ (despite not investing in R&D themselves). In the second stage of the model, given the innovator's choice between P and S, the competitor has to decide whether to imitate i's technology and risk infringement if i has chosen P or rely on their existing technology (which also has cost $\bar{c}$). In the third stage, the innovator and competitor compete as Cournot.

To solve the model, let's start with the competition stage.

Competition stage. There are three possible outcomes depending on the previous two stages. If the innovator relied on S, the competitor can imitate without risking infringement and produce at marginal cost s. In this case, i and j simply compete as Cournot. If the innovator has chosen P, the competitor can imitate and risk infringement or stick to their old technology $\bar{c}$. In the latter case, firms again compete as Cournot but j now produces at $\bar{c} > s$. If the competitor chooses imitation instead, they can produce at marginal cost s, but they also risk infringement with probability γ. If the competitor is found to infringe, they have to pay damages in the form of royalties on their revenue $\tau p q_j$, where τ the royalty rate, p is price, and q is quantity. We can write the rate of expected infringement damages g as $\tau \gamma \equiv g$. In this case, the profits for the competitor j are net revenue minus expected damages for infringement:

$$\pi_j = (p - s)q_j - gpq_j \qquad (1)$$

The profits for the innovator are simply net revenue plus expected damages for infringement:

$$\pi_i = (p - c)q_i + gpq_j \qquad (2)$$

For simplicity, Anton and Yao assume a downward-sloping linear demand function $p = F(Q) = F(q_i + q_j) = \alpha - \beta Q$. Using this demand function, we can compute the best response functions for the innovator and competitor and solve for the equilibrium output choices:

$$q_j^* = \frac{1}{2\beta}\left[\alpha - \beta q_i - \frac{s}{1-g}\right] \qquad (3)$$

$$q_i^* = \frac{1}{2\beta}\left[\alpha - c - (1+g)\beta q_j\right] \qquad (4)$$

Equations (3) and (4) can be solved for the equilibrium quantities to obtain the following:

$$q_j^* = \frac{1}{\beta(3-g)}\left[\alpha - \frac{2}{1-g}s + c\right]$$
$$q_i^* = \frac{1}{\beta(3-g)}\left[\alpha(1-g) - 2c + \frac{1+g}{1-g}s\right] \qquad (5)$$

For the imitator to produce at all ($q_j^* > 0$), we must have $s < (1-g)(\alpha+c)/2$. Equations (5) show that q_i^* increases in s and q_j^* declines. That is, the higher j's price is (holding c constant), the less disclosure took place and therefore the innovator produces more of the output. In addition, one can show that weaker property rights (lower g) lead the imitator to produce more and the innovator to produce less.[15]

The *equilibrium* profits are

$$\pi_j = \frac{1-g}{\beta(3-g)^2}\left[\alpha + c - \frac{2}{1-g}s\right]^2$$
$$\pi_i = \frac{1}{\beta(3-g)^2}\left[\alpha - (2-g)c + s\right]^2 + \frac{gc}{\beta(3-g)}\left[\alpha + c - \frac{2}{1-g}s\right] \qquad (6)$$

---

[15] To show this, s has to be small enough for the imitator to be willing to produce more than zero output.

It is easy to see from these equations that higher s (less disclosure) means lower profit for the imitator, other things equal. The innovator faces a trade-off in choosing optimal disclosure, however. On the one hand, disclosure of information leads to lower s and hence lower profits. On the other, disclosure can also lead the competitor to infer that the innovator has low cost c.

Infringement-risking imitation stage. In this stage, the competitor chooses whether to imitate the technology and risk infringement. The competitor observes whether the technology was patented and how much information was disclosed. However, the competitor cannot see the innovator's marginal cost and therefore does not know the gap in marginal costs between themself and the innovator. If the innovator did not patent the technology, the competitor can imitate and produce at marginal cost s. If the innovator obtained a patent, the competitor can either imitate and risk infringement or rely on their existing technology.

Assume the innovator chose to patent and the competitor observes marginal cost s, which allows them to infer the innovator's cost c. If the competitor does not imitate, they will produce at $\bar{c}$ with $\bar{c} > c$. The corresponding imitator profits are $\frac{1}{3\beta}(\alpha - 2\bar{c} + c)$.

If the competitor imitates, however, they produce at lower marginal cost s. Yet, they run the risk of having to pay damages to the innovator. This yields the profit in equation (6). If we set both pay-offs equal, we can obtain an equal pay-off line in the marginal cost space along which the competitor is indifferent between imitating and relying on the old technology instead. Above the line where s is larger, the competitor chooses to not imitate, while below the line the competitor imitates. The intersection of the equal pay-off line and the 45° line defined by $s = c$ gives the cut-off level of inferred costs, above which the competitor has no incentive to imitate.

Anton and Yao show that this point is given by the following equation:

$$c^*(g, \alpha, \bar{c}) = \frac{2\bar{c} + \alpha[(1-g)h(g) - 1]}{1 + (1+g)h(g)}$$

$$\text{where } h(g) = \frac{3}{(3-g)\sqrt{1-g}} \tag{7}$$

Equation (7) means that the competitor imitates when--taking into account expected damages--the cost disadvantage of using the new technology over the inferred cost of the innovator is smaller than the cost disadvantage of using the existing technology compared to the inferred cost of the innovator.

Protection and disclosure stage. At this stage, the innovator decides whether to obtain a patent or to choose secrecy and how much information they want to disclose. In equilibrium, there are three outcomes. First, an innovator with high marginal costs and a small invention (small means $c > c^*$) prefers to patent and fully disclose the technology. Second, an innovator with a medium-size invention prefers to patent and only partially disclose the invention. Third, an innovator with a large invention chooses secrecy and partially discloses the invention.

If the innovator has a small invention $c > c^*$, the cost reduction for the competitor from imitating is small. Hence, it does not justify the risk of infringement. Therefore, the competitor does not imitate. In this case, the innovator has a strong incentive to patent and to disclose that information to the competitor.

If the innovator has a medium-sized invention $c > c^*$, the competitor has incentives to imitate. Now the innovator has no incentive to disclose fully. The innovator faces a trade-off between wanting to disclose low costs and not transferring knowledge to the competitor. Therefore, the innovator will only disclose partially.

If the innovator has a large invention, the trade-off becomes less attractive, and the innovator wants to rely more on the cost advantage and less on damages. Therefore, the innovator prefers to forgo patenting and limit disclosure of information to the competitor.

This leads to the counterintuitive result that large inventions are protected by secrecy rather than patenting. Anton and Yao provide the example of the Ford Motor Company in support of their finding. In 1913, the company introduced the moving assembly line process. Despite not having patented it, the company openly disclosed the process to the public. However, the disclosure was not sufficient for replication. Hence, the intention was to use disclosure to signal that Ford had low production costs to discourage competitors.

The Anton and Yao model only looked at the interaction between a single innovator and a potential imitator. However, in practice in many situations, there is more than one innovator who competes to innovate first. In settings where we have a race to innovate before others do, a situation often characterized by simultaneous discovery, innovators have to factor in that if they fail to patent first, a competitor will and effectively exclude them from the market. In such situations, "the patent isn't a carrot so much as a stick with which to threaten the slow" (Lemley 2012, p. 755). Hence, patenting assumes a more defensive role. This can overturn the disclosure results by Anton and Yao. That is, patenting dominates secrecy even in situations where secrecy offers stronger protection because the choice is now between patenting and letting a competitor patent.

We can illustrate the argument in a simple model by Kultti et al. (2006). Assume there are two firms that invest in R&D. With probability q, the R&D results in an innovation and with $1 - q$ it fails. Assume that the innovation can only be protected by secrecy, with secrecy being effective with probability α. If only one firm innovates successfully, it earns monopoly profits π^M. If both succeed, they earn duopoly profits $\pi^D < \frac{\pi^M}{2}$. The firms determine their success probability by choosing q_i where $i = 1, 2$, incurring $c(q_i) = Rq_i^2 / 2$, the quadratic cost function for innovation, with $c' = Rq_i$, where R is a scale parameter. We can write profits for Firm 1 as

$$\pi_1 = q_1(1 - q_2)\alpha\pi^M + q_1 q_2 \alpha\pi^D - Rq_1^2 / 2 \qquad (8)$$

If we allow the firms to opt for patent protection instead of secrecy, the firm has to decide whether to patent before it knows whether the other firm has successfully innovated. Further, assume that if both firms successfully innovate and apply for a patent, each obtains the patent with probability 0.5. If we denote the strength of patent protection by α_p, it is possible to show using equation (8) that patenting dominates secrecy even if $\alpha_p < \alpha$.

Apart from allowing for competition between innovators, we can also imagine a situation where there is strategic interaction among imitators and where that interaction influences an innovator's incentives to patent. For example, an innovator can strategically delay entry by imitators through a combination of secrecy and product complexity that increases imitation costs (Henry and Ruiz-Aliseda 2016). Alternatively, the innovator can use licensing of the knowledge necessary to use an otherwise unprotected invention to potential imitators in order to delay entry (Henry and Ponce 2011). Either of these strategies provides the innovator with sufficient lead time to appropriate returns despite the absence of a patent. These arguments also illustrate the role that other forms of informal appropriation mechanisms, such as complexity and lead time, can play in an innovator's choice between formal and informal mechanisms.

The choice between patenting and secrecy becomes even more complex if we acknowledge the cumulative and often sequential nature of the innovation process. An innovation process with a series of innovations that build on each other affects an innovator's incentives to patent because the associated disclosure makes it harder for rivals to patent subsequently but it also helps them to make innovations that build on the patented invention (Ponce 2011).

14.4.2 Patent–Secrecy Combination

Patents and secrecy do not have to be mutually exclusive. Different aspects of an invention can be protected by patents or secrecy, which means that a combination of both mechanisms can be better than choosing one or the other. This is the choice described by the upper-left quadrant in Table 14.4. For example, in pharmaceuticals, chemicals are easily codifiable and hence protected by patents. However, they also contain tacit elements, such as the specific combination of different ingredients, which may be more effectively protected by secrecy (Arora 1997). This is consistent with the survey data reviewed in Section 14.3, where pharmaceutical firms report relying heavily on both patents and secrecy (Cohen et al. 2000, Tables 1 and 2).

Firms may also use the patent system in ways that allow them to de facto combine patenting with secrecy. Graham (2004) documented the combination of patenting and secrecy through the use of so-called continuations in the US patent system. Prior to the American Inventors Protection Act (AIPA) in 1999, in the United States, patents were published only when they were issued. This allowed applicants to strategically delay publication while still maintaining their original priority date of the patent. Even after the adoption of mandatory publication after 18 months counting from filing as a result of AIPA, applicants that only sought patent protection in the United States were allowed to defer publication until grant. Still, Graham and Hegde (2015) show that inventors presented with the choice to delay publication overwhelmingly opt for pregrant disclosure (85%). This is true across industries and for both small and large entities. Yet, inventors in complex technologies, such as computers and communication, are twice as likely to opt for secrecy as inventors in discrete technologies, such as chemicals. These results suggest that if innovators choose to patent, secrecy may be less important than the benefits that come from a patent publication, such as credibly signaling to competitors or investors the existence of a patentable invention.

14.4.3 No Patent, No Secrecy: Disclosure and Publishing

This choice may seem counterintuitive at first. However, in the introduction, we already discussed the case of the magnetic stripe that was a patentable invention. Still, IBM decided to forgo both patenting and secrecy in order to promote widespread diffusion. The idea that appropriation through complementary assets can be more effective underlies the so-called open innovation business model. Innovators eschew patent protection, while not only disclosing their inventions, but also making them explicitly available to third parties. We discuss this choice in more detail in the next section below as well as in the context of the OSS business model in Chapter 17.

There are other reasons as well why firms may go without patent protection or secrecy. IBM used to have a publication, the *IBM Technical Disclosure Bulletin*, whose entire goal was to make IBM inventions public without them being patent-protected. Similarly, Google maintains a website, the Technical Disclosure Commons, that allows companies and individuals to disclose unpatented inventions.[16] The inventions published in the bulletin or on the website are referred to as a defensive publication. The goal of a defensive publication is primarily to ensure freedom to operate for the innovator, that is, to prevent others from patenting the same or similar inventions and thereby blocking the innovator. Defensive publications can also be used strategically to influence the state of the art and obstruct a competitor's patent strategy (Baker and Mezzetti 2005, Bar 2006). Apart from raising the prior art bar, defensive publications can also be used to signal a lead to competitors in a specific technology. For example, in a patent race, a leader may opt to disclose information on a research project even before successfully concluding it in order to convince a competitor to drop out of the patent race.

The next section gives some examples where innovators found the no patent, no secrecy choice preferable given the state of their technology.

14.5 Innovation without IP

As we mentioned earlier in the introduction, there are also cases where substantial innovation has taken place among communities that share information, rather than keeping it secret or protecting it with IP rights. This phenomenon is especially characteristic of the very early phases of a new technology and the industry it creates. But it is also familiar to those in the scientific research community. Scholars such as Polanyi (1962), Merton (1968, 1973), David (1998), and Dasgupta and David (1994) have developed a model of the organization of scientific inquiry that emphasizes the rewards of priority and the norms of the discipline in ensuring the performance of the system without an explicit market for the knowledge it produces. In the next two sections, we

---

[16] https://www.tdcommons.org/.

describe the two worlds of scientific research and collective invention. Then we present a model of the coexistence of the "open sharing" knowledge production system and the commercial privatized world of knowledge generation that relies on IP ownership as an incentive. This model illustrates the tensions between the two systems and the instability of the open sharing system.

14.5.1 Open Science

What motivates scientists? As Stephan (2012) suggests, puzzles and priority. That is, most scientists are driven to solve puzzles that arise in the course of their work. As the well-known physicist Richard Feynman said, "Once I get on a puzzle, I can't get off" (Feynman 1985, p. 21). Their rewards come in the form of intrinsic satisfaction and priority, that is, being the first to solve a puzzle, although priority, of course, translates into higher salaries, research grants, and promotion in most present-day cases. Centuries ago, they might have hoped for noble patronage to finance their activities (David 2008), but today they rely on universities, governments, and nonprofit research organizations.

The advantage of the priority system accompanied by (uncertain) rewards is that it ensures early publication of scientific results that everyone can access in principle. In contrast to the usual proprietary approach to securing returns to research via patents and other IP instruments, the open science system enables basic and sometimes applied scientific research to progress because it makes the "spillovers" from such research almost costless to access and ensures that they are spread as wide as possible. A second advantage of open science has been identified by Murray et al. (2016): In addition to increasing follow-on research, openness leads to the exploration of more diverse research paths because it enables a wider range of researchers to build on discoveries.

Merton (1973) described the open science system at various times as having five properties or norms:

- *Communism.* There is common ownership of scientific discoveries; scientists give up their IP in exchange for recognition and esteem.
- *Universalism* Claims to truth are evaluated in terms of universal or impersonal criteria, and not on the basis of race, class, gender, religion, or nationality.
- *Disinterestedness.* Scientists are rewarded for acting in ways that outwardly appear to be selfless.
- *Originality.* Novelty in research contributions.
- *Skepticism.* All ideas should be subject to rigorous, structured community scrutiny.

Naturally, the research systems in universities and government laboratories do not always fulfill these requirements completely, but they are general characteristics to which most participants in the "Republic of Science" adhere, to use Polanyi's (1962) term for the community.

Nevertheless, in today's world, there are numerous examples of breakdown in the system at the edges, in the form of scientists starting firms to exploit their discoveries accompanied by some kind of patenting strategy, or the operation of university TTOs, some of which pursue the licensing of technology for profit rather than maximal dissemination. All TTOs use IP to some extent to profit from university research, but some are more likely to grant non-exclusive licenses than exclusive licenses,[17] which increases diffusion and reduces the market power of the licensee. For example, Stanford University licensed the Cohen-Boyer patents, which cover inventions for splicing genes to make recombinant proteins that are foundational to the biotechnology industry, non-exclusively.

14.5.2 Collective Invention

Collective invention refers to a setting where there are a number of firms and inventors developing a technology in a specific area who choose not to protect their inventions but instead to share them with each other. This is often a feature of the very early stages of a new technology or industry when no single design or paradigm dominates, as in Klepper's work that we studied in Chapter 5. Allen (1983) posits three features of collective invention settings that he views as essential:

1. The overall rate of change is dominated by incremental innovations.
2. Firms make technical information about performance and operation of their inventions public.
3. Firms employ the common pool of knowledge thus generated to make further improvements.

Allen (1983) used the development of steel furnaces in Cleveland, United Kingdom, during the 1850–1875 period as an example. Firms in this area increased the height and feasible temperature of these furnaces in a series of small increments, using informal disclosure and publication in the engineering literature to diffuse their knowledge. They did not view their inventions as patentable. However, Allen points out that the failure of Britain to develop the open-hearth steel furnace for pig iron was because the development cost was too high under collective invention. This is an illustration of the weakness of the collective system when large expenditures are needed for a radical new innovation.

Nuvolari (2004) offers the Cornish pumping engine, a steam engine for pumping water out of the Cornish mineshafts, as an example. In 1769, James Watt had obtained a patent on his steam engine, which was extended by an Act of Parliament to 1800. In Cornwall, innovation in pumping engines did not take off until the expiration of Watt's patent; the miners there had resented having to take a license and pay royalties to Boulton (who was Watt's business partner) and were fairly anti-patent as a result. After 1800, they developed their own engines and in 1811 started a monthly journal to report technical characteristics, operating procedures, and the performance of each engine. This created some competition among engineers, who typically moved from firm to firm and could therefore improve their employment chances using publication as a quality signal.

---

[17] An exclusive license restricts the licensor from licensing to any other party, while a non-exclusive license allows the licensor to freely license to other parties as well. For further discussion, see Chapter 20.

Another peculiar feature of the Cornish setting was that typically investors held shares in multiple mines, which internalized the benefits of engine improvements that were shared across firms, reinforcing the knowledge-sharing model.

Another example, which illustrates the guild structure from which collective invention sometimes emerged, is given by Foray and Hilaire-Perez (2006), who studied the Lyons (a city in France) silk-weaving industry during the 18th and early 19th centuries. The Lyons government had set up a system of awards for inventions, requiring that they be shared with other local weavers and that the new inventions be taught, that is, diffused within the city. The size of the award was supposed to be proportional to the importance of the invention. This promoted innovation in the local silk-weaving industry (at the time roughly 25% of the Lyons economy) and the main competitor, which was the London-based industry, ultimately declined, partly due to lack of innovation. However, the most famous Lyonnaise inventor, Joseph-Marie Jacquard, was ultimately not happy with his award and fled to Paris to attempt to patent his invention.[18]

A more recent example of free knowledge sharing enforced by norms in a community is the example of haute cuisine French chefs described by Fauchart and von Hippel (2008). They interviewed some of these chefs and also surveyed a larger number. The chefs did not view their recipes as protectable via IP, but had strong norms on what type of imitation and borrowing was appropriate. In particular, they expect acknowledgment if another chef uses their recipe, and they do not share information with chefs who violate the various norms of the profession.

Professional norms and their community enforcement are also used among live, on-stage performers, including magicians and comedians, because of limited available IP protection.[19] A comedian interviewed by Oliar and Sprigman (2008, p. 1813) explains how the norm-based enforcement system works: "They police each other.... If you get a rep as a thief or a hack (as they call it), it can hurt your career. You're not going to work. They just cast you out." Fashion design is another industry where IP protection is limited. However, unlike in the case of haute cuisine chefs, magicians, or comedians, widespread copying of fashion designs is accepted if not encouraged within the industry as it hastens fashion cycles that drive demand (Raustiala and Sprigman 2006).

Other areas of recent collective invention are the early software sector, discussed by von Hippel (2006), and various types of sports equipment such as surfboards (Shah 2000) and other sporting equipment (Franke and Shah 2003). These are also cases where the typical developer/innovator is a user of the technology.

14.5.3 Proprietary versus Public Domain Regimes

The preceding two sections highlight the various settings when a free knowledge-sharing equilibrium has emerged: scientific research and certain industries at certain times. However, we usually observe that as time passes, innovation in these settings

---

[18] Jacquard's invention was the most important and famous from this period and had long-lasting impact. He designed a method for weaving patterns into fabric using punched cards to control the loom automatically (from which we got the punched card used in the early days of computing). Today, fabric of this type is termed *jacquard*.

[19] For a review of IP protection of magic tricks and illusions, see Markley (2020).

becomes privatized via IP, as in the example of Jacquard. The exception is basic scientific research, which is supported by a set of institutions (universities, government laboratories, nonprofit research organizations) that tend to ensure knowledge remains public. Even here, occasional deviations are observed and there is pressure to privatize the most valuable pieces of knowledge via the TTO.

Gambardella and Hall (2006), building on the insights of Olson (1971) and David (2003), constructed a model of the choice by a researcher to participate in public domain (PD) or proprietary (PR) research. They use the model to show that an equilibrium exists where some researchers work in the public domain and some privatize their research, but this equilibrium is not robust to changes in the profit environment. Thus, the PD part generally must be sustained by norms or other means. A researcher working in PD who discovers their profits are high has incentives to break the equilibrium and switch to the PR domain. This result corresponds to Olson's argument that without coordination, collective action is hard to sustain.

We outline the model here. There are N researchers, each of whom faces a utility function U that is a function of their choice of PD versus PR and the number of researchers working in PD. The utility of the nth researcher is given by the following:

$$U = z + \theta X(n-1)$$

$X(n-1)$ is the stock of knowledge generated in PD by the previous $n-1$ researchers, and $\theta \geq 0$ measures the extent to which their utility depends on the previous knowledge stock.[20] Such might be the case because their research builds on this or simply because they have a taste for research. z is the utility they obtain from their own research. If they work in PD, $z = x(n)$, their contribution to the knowledge stock. The function $x(n)$ can exhibit increasing or decreasing returns; that is, more researchers could make the next one less productive, or vice versa. On the other hand, if they choose to work in PR, $z = \pi$, the profits from the knowledge they create. All researchers with $x(n) \geq \pi$ will work in PD.

We assume that researchers are heterogeneous, so $[\pi - x(n)]$ has a distribution $F(.|n)$. That is, researchers vary in the difference between their potential PR profits and the benefits they receive from their contribution to the knowledge stock. A stable equilibrium is achieved when the following holds:

$$F(0\,|\,n^e) = n^e\,/\,N$$

where n^e is the share of researchers working under PD. In equilibrium, this share is equal to the share of researchers whose utility from π is not larger than the utility of their contribution $x(n^e)$ to PD knowledge. The equilibrium is stable if the slope of the distribution function F at that point is less than $1/N$. We show two possibilities in Figure 14.3. Note that there can be multiple equilibria. You can see the stability by assuming that a researcher switches from PR to PD, which increases n^e/N by $1/N$ but increases the

---

[20] We have assumed that the researcher receives utility from others' PD research whether or not they work in PD themselves. This seems plausible, although it is not essential to the conclusions.

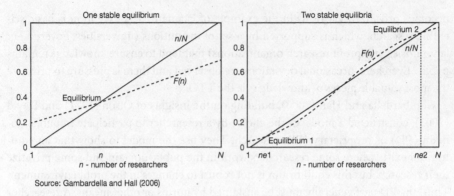

Source: Gambardella and Hall (2006)

Figure 14.3 Knowledge-sharing equilibria.

share of researchers with $\pi - x(n) \leq 0$ by less than $1/N$, so the move was not profitable. The argument for switches from PD to PR is similar.

Gambardella and Hall go on to show that it is possible a group of researchers able to coordinate would choose to join PD because it was jointly profitable, even if at least one of them had profits greater than the benefits they receive from PD research in which they participate. However, this equilibrium is unstable unless there is some form of co-ordination, as the researcher with large potential profits has an incentive to defect. In open science, coordination has generally been achieved via a number of social norms, as documented by Polanyi and Merton, although defection has been observed on occasion.

In the case of industry, there have also been norms and other mechanisms in the past, as documented in the Cornish mining industry and the French chef examples, but they are weaker, and the benefits of reciprocal knowledge sharing may also be lower after a technology has been standardized to some extent or a dominant firm has emerged in the sector. In the case of OSS, for example, the General Public License (GPL) mechanism, which requires that users of OSS release software that incorporates OSS under the GPL, is a mechanism that ensures coordination of PD software developers (see Chapter 17).

14.6 Prizes and Awards

The award system put in place by the Lyons silk-weaving industry to reward innovation and promote its diffusion is an example of yet another, non-IP incentive mechanism. Such prizes and awards are distinct from both the informal appropriation mechanisms and the open-sharing paradigm described above.

The idea underlying prizes is simple: Instead of awarding exclusivity through a patent to address the appropriability problem associated with knowledge, innovators are compensated directly through monetary awards in the form of prizes. If the prize-winning innovation enters the public domain, prizes have the advantage that there is no DWL due to exclusivity as opposed to patent protection. However, for this to work, we need to assume that innovators and prize sponsors have full information about the value of the invention before innovators successfully produce the innovation (Wright 1983). In practice, a more realistic assumption is that innovators have some private information regarding the value of an invention, which challenges the efficiency of prizes as an incentive mechanism.

Nevertheless, historical examples of prizes and awards abound. In 1773, Antoine-Augustin Parmentier won the Académie de Besançon Prize for Substitute Foods for proposing the use of the potato as a food source. Although the potato had already been discovered in South America, at the time it was still an unknown food staple in Europe. Another well-known award is the Orteig Prize, which was awarded to Charles Lindbergh in 1927 for accomplishing the first nonstop flight from New York to Paris. The prize purse was US$25,000 (around US$420,000 in 2023) and helped spur intense competition among aviators to accomplish the goal set by the prize challenge. Other canonical examples of historical prizes include the various prizes for the discovery of a method to determine longitude at sea. This had been a persistent, thorny problem in nautical navigation for centuries, and several countries established prizes to encourage efforts to find a solution (Spanish Longitude Prize of 1567, Dutch Longitude Prize of 1627, and British Longitude Prize of 1714).

There are also plenty of modern examples of prizes that reward innovation. For example, in 1996, IBM's Deep Blue creators won the Fredkin Prize for building the first computer chess program to beat the reigning chess world champion Gary Kasparov. The prize, which came with a reward of US$100,000, had been established in 1980 by academic computer scientist Edward Fredkin. Another highly publicized prize competition was the US$1million prize Netflix established for the best improvement of its algorithm that provides recommendations to Netflix subscribers. Even more prominently, the XPRIZE Foundation, a nonprofit founded in 1994, regularly creates prize competitions to encourage specific innovations across technology fields. The first XPRIZE competition was the Ansari XPRIZE in 1996, which awarded US$10million to the first reusable spacecraft that would fly 100 kilometers into space within 2 weeks. The Ansari XPRIZE is credited with having sparked private-sector interest in the development of a private space travel market. There even exist online platforms, such as Wazoku's innocentive[21] or topcoder,[22] where anyone can make prize challenges available to anyone interested in taking on the challenge.

Prizes have also been used by governments to procure innovation. For example, the Defense Advanced Research Projects Agency (DARPA) has launched a series of prize competitions since 2004, such as the subterranean challenge in 2017 which "seeks novel approaches to rapidly map, navigate, and search underground environments during time-sensitive combat operations or disaster response scenarios." There are also collaborations between public and private entities, such as the Lunar Lander Challenge that was jointly organized by NASA, private aerospace company Northrop Grumman, and the XPRIZE Foundation. Former US president Barack Obama's Strategy for American Innovation explicitly encouraged the use of prizes to incentivize innovation more broadly, and the America Competes Reauthorization Act of 2011 allowed federal

---

[21] https://www.innocentive.com.
[22] https://www.topcoder.com.

agencies to offer innovation prizes. In fact, the US government maintains a website of all prize challenges sponsored by government agencies.[23]

Prizes are also seen as a possible mechanism to address big social challenges, so-called grand missions, such as climate change or global public health. These challenges are not likely to be completely funded by the market, given the diffuse nature of the potential benefits and the fact that these problems have substantial externalities. Therefore, non-market-based mechanisms are seen as more promising than market-based mechanisms such as patents (Murray et al. 2012). As these examples suggest, there are many different types of prizes that differ along several dimensions. In fact, prizes can even be used to honor "negative" invention, such as the Ig Nobel Prize[24] or the Plagiarius Trophy described in Box 14.1.

Box 14.1 Negative Prizes

The prizes discussed in Section 14.6 all aim to directly incentivize innovation. However, prizes can potentially also achieve the same objective by dis-incentivizing behavior that is considered detrimental to innovation. The Plagiarius Trophy, created by German industrial designer Rido Busse, is awarded annually to copiers and imitators of the design of original consumer and industrial products.[25] The goal of the prize is to "name and shame" counterfeiters and to draw public attention to the problem. The figure shows two recent prize winners.

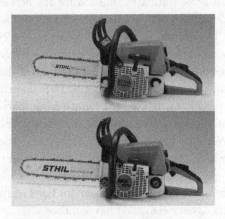

Figure 1 Plagiarius Trophy winners.

(a) Plagiarius Trophy winner 2021
 Chainsaw "STIHL MS 250"

(b) Plagiarius Trophy winner 2022
 Cutlery Set "KLIKK"

In both pictures, the picture on top shows the original; the picture at the bottom shows the imitation.

---

[23] https://www.challenge.gov.
[24] https://improbable.com/ig/about-the-ig-nobel-prizes.
[25] https://www.plagiarius.com.

14.6.1 Design of Prizes

First, we can draw a distinction based on the timing of the invention and the corresponding prize:

1. *Ex ante* **prizes:** sometimes also referred to as inducement prizes, are prizes where the requirements and criteria for winning a prize are specified before the innovation is produced. These are prizes targeted at the production of solutions to specific known problems for which the prize sponsor is seeking a solution. The prize challenges organized by the XPRIZE Foundation all fall into this category.
2. *Ex post* **prizes:** prizes awarded for an existing innovation. Take, for example, the Nobel Prize or the much more recently created Breakthrough Prize (which comes with an even bigger financial award than the Nobel Prize). These prizes reward new ideas often many years, if not decades, after they have been conceived. *Ex post* prizes reward new ideas that often solve problems that the prize sponsor did not even know existed, or for which no path to a solution was known. As such, *ex post* prizes tend to reward and hence encourage blue sky research, while *ex ante* prizes are more likely to generate solutions to specific well-defined problems, often of direct interest to the prize sponsor.

Second, we can also distinguish prizes depending on whether they come with a monetary reward or not. It might seem counterintuitive that nonmonetary prizes could be used to reward costly efforts to generate innovation. However, we are all familiar with the concept of nonmonetary prizes to induce effort as they are the most common reward in amateur sports competitions. In the context of innovation, take the example of the National Medal of Technology and Innovation awarded annually by the president of the United States for outstanding technological achievement. The list of recipients of this *ex post* prize contains many well-known inventors, including Steve Jobs, Robert Noyce, and Bill Gates. The main benefit of nonmonetary prizes is public recognition, expert validation, and reputation, which can be transformed into monetary gain.

Third, prize competitions may allow winners to retain the right to patent their invention or force winners to forgo patent protection. Prizes that force inventors to forgo patent protection amount to a patent buy-out.[26] For example, the Royal Society of Arts in the United Kingdom in the 18th century did not allow prize winners to patent their prize-winning inventions (Khan 2015). If no restrictions are imposed on a winner's ability to patent, then the winner can obtain compensation from patent protection in addition to the award.

14.6.2 Empirical Evidence on Prizes

The empirical evidence on prizes suggests that prizes can be successful in spurring innovation. Brunt et al. (2012) analyze a century of prizes awarded by the Royal Agricultural

---

[26] A patent buy-out means that the government purchases a patent from its owner at a price determined through a public auction and then puts the invention into the public domain (Kremer 1998).

Society of England from 1839 to 1939. The Royal Agricultural Society awarded both *ex ante* and *ex post* prizes. *Ex ante* prizes were monetary awards, while *ex post* prizes were awarded as medals. Brunt et al. found that an award had a positive impact on subsequent patent filings on the award-winning inventions, where the effect was more pronounced for medals than monetary prizes. Moser and Nicholas (2013) also rely on historical data to arrive at a similar conclusion. They analyze *ex post* prizes (without monetary award) awarded for innovations exhibited at the Crystal Palace Exhibition in 1851 to find large increases in patenting among prize-winning innovations compared to nonwinning innovations. Moser and Nicholas suggest that the main mechanism for the positive impact on patenting is increased publicity thanks to the award.

Given the positive impact of prizes on patenting, the empirical evidence raises the question about the relation between prizes and patents more generally. In theory, they are seen as substitutes; in particular, prizes are seen as a way to avoid the DWL associated with patent protection. However, in practice, prizes and patents are rather seen as complements (Murray et al. 2012). Khan (2015) discusses several historical examples to demonstrate the link between prizes and patents. For example, Michael Phelan and High Collender, who owned a billiards company, created a US$10,000 prize in 1863 to find a material to replace ivory in billiard balls. Attracted by the prize money, John Wesley Hyatt engaged in extensive experimentation that eventually led him to invent celluloid (i.e., plastic). While the invention initially did not satisfy the requirement for the prize money (the celluloid billiard balls would easily crack), he patented his invention and quickly discovered its wide applicability.

Hence, similar to our discussion of informal appropriation mechanisms and patenting, prizes and patents are better seen as complements than substitutes. This does not necessarily result in excessive rewards for innovators because in the presence of significant externalities and risk associated with the research, additional reward beyond patent protection may be warranted. Galasso et al. (2018), in fact, show that the combination of prizes and patents can improve welfare relative to the use of only patents or prizes in the presence of noncontractible aspects of innovation.

14.7 Summary

The available survey evidence suggests that firms consider patents relatively ineffective means to appropriating returns on their innovative activities. Informal mechanisms, such as lead time and secrecy, are considered more effective. However, the data also reveal substantial heterogeneity in the use of patents across type of innovation and economic activity. Moreover, the evidence also indicates that firms tend to regard different appropriation mechanisms as complements, rather than substitutes, even for the same innovation. In practice, firms often rely on bundles of mechanisms to appropriate returns to their innovations, adapting the combinations of formal and informal mechanisms flexibly depending on the specific characteristics of innovations and markets.

The chapter also reviewed the factors that determine an innovator's choice between patents and secrecy. It turns out the choice is fairly complex; many different factors play a role and their importance depends on the nature of competition in the marketplace.

The chapter also documents situations where researchers or innovators choose to freely reveal their information to others in exchange for free access to their knowledge. This is widespread in the academic science community, but also characterizes many infant industries and technologies.

The final section of the chapter reviewed prizes and awards as an incentive mechanism to induce innovation. There are many historical and modern examples of prize challenges, and historical evidence suggests that prizes can be successful in incentivizing innovative activity. However in practice, the optimal design of prize competitions is challenging due to lack of information on the cost and value of the invention that should result from the prize competition.

III.

THE PATENT SYSTEM

15

Intellectual Property Rights and Economic Development

Learning Objectives

After reading this chapter, you will be able to understand and explain the following concepts:

- Stylized facts about the use of IP by residents of developing countries
- The optimal IP policy as a function of a country's level of economic development
- The effect of patent protection on technology transfer to developing countries
- The effect of patent protection on domestic innovation in developing countries
- The effect of patent protection on economic growth
- The role of patents in the production and distribution of pharmaceuticals in developing countries

15.1 Introduction

The question of the proper role of intellectual property rights in developing economies is an important one, and one that has increased in importance as the role of knowledge in the economy has increased.[1] It is also a heavily debated topic, as the interests of those with large economies or more highly developed economies may conflict with those of smaller or less developed economies.

We begin by highlighting some facts about IP use in less developed countries. The data show that residents of the least developed countries make almost no use of IP protection, and that, with the exception of China, even those in middle-income countries hardly use patents, although they do employ utility models, trademarks, and industrial designs to some extent.

We then review the arguments for stronger or weaker IP rights as a support for development. We present some simple theoretical models that illuminate the trade-offs and suggest that this is ultimately an empirical question. Therefore, the majority of the chapter is devoted to empirical evidence on how IP rights affect both the countries in question and those who invest in the country.

The majority of the models and evidence we discuss in this chapter will turn out to be about one specific IP right, namely patents, partly for data availability reasons but also because of

---

[1] Some material in this chapter is excerpted from Hall (2022).

The Economics of Innovation and Intellectual Property. Bronwyn H. Hall and Christian Helmers, Oxford University Press.
© Oxford University Press 2024. DOI: 10.1093/oso/9780197630914.003.0015

their economic importance. Much of the discussion will, of course, apply to other IP rights such as copyright, design rights, and the like. However, there are some differences with respect to trademarks and geographic indications, and we will spend some time on these in particular.

15.2 Some Facts

Here, we present some background information on the use of IP by residents of low- and middle-income countries, using the World Bank classification that is also used by the WIPO statistical database. We look at trends in patents, trademarks, industrial designs, and utility models by four groups of countries, as classified by the World Bank at the present time: low, lower middle, upper middle, and high income.[2] The countries in each class are listed in Table 15.1.

Table 15.1 World Bank Countries Grouped by Per Capita Income

Low-income $1,045 or less	Lower-middle-income $1,046 to $4,095	Upper-middle-income $4,096 to $12,695	High-income $12,696 or more	
Afghanistan	Angola	Albania	Andorra	Nauru
Burkina Faso	Algeria	American Samoa	Antigua and Barbuda	Netherlands
Burundi	Bangladesh	Argentina	Aruba	New Caledonia
Central African Republic	Belize	Armenia	Australia	New Zealand
Chad	Benin	Azerbaijan	Austria	Northern Mariana Islands
Congo, Democratic Republic	Bhutan	Belarus	Bahamas, The	Norway
Eritrea	Bolivia	Bosnia and Herzegovina	Bahrain	Oman
Ethiopia	Cabo Verde	Botswana	Barbados	Palau
Gambia, The	Cambodia	Brazil	Belgium	Poland
Guinea	Cameroon	Bulgaria	Bermuda	Portugal
Guinea-Bissau	Comoros	China	British Virgin Islands	Puerto Rico
Korea, Democratic People's Republic	Congo, Republic	Colombia	Brunei Darussalam	Qatar

[2] Some of the countries will have changed rank, mostly for the better, during the long time periods we examine. The most notable example of this is China, which is now an upper-middle-income country, but was a low-income country in 1990.

Table 15.1 Continued

Low-income $1,045 or less	Lower-middle-income $1,046 to $4,095	Upper-middle-income $4,096 to $12,695	High-income $12,696 or more	
Liberia	Côte d'Ivoire	Costa Rica	Canada	San Marino
Madagascar	Djibouti	Cuba	Cayman Islands	Saudi Arabia
Malawi	Egypt, Arab Republic	Dominica	Channel Islands	Seychelles
Mali	El Salvador	Dominican Republic	Chile	Singapore
Mozambique	Eswatini	Equatorial Guinea	Croatia	Sint Maarten (Dutch part)
Niger	Ghana	Ecuador	Curaçao	Slovak Republic
Rwanda	Haiti	Fiji	Cyprus	Slovenia
Sierra Leone	Honduras	Gabon	Czech Republic	Spain
Somalia	India	Georgia	Denmark	St. Kitts and Nevis
South Sudan	Indonesia	Grenada	Estonia	St. Martin (French part)
Sudan	Iran, Islamic Republic	Guatemala	Faroe Islands	Sweden
Syrian Arab Republic	Kenya	Guyana	Finland	Switzerland
Togo	Kiribati	Iraq	France	Taiwan, China
Uganda	Kyrgyz Republic	Jamaica	French Polynesia	Trinidad and Tobago
Yemen, Republic	Lao PDR	Jordan	Germany	Turks and Caicos Islands
	Lesotho	Kazakhstan	Gibraltar	
	United Arab Emirates Mauritania	Kosovo	Greece	United Kingdom
	Micronesia, Federated States	Lebanon	Greenland	United States
	Mongolia	Libya	Guam	Uruguay
	Morocco	Malaysia	Hong Kong SAR, China	Virgin Islands (US)
	Myanmar	Maldives	Hungary	
	Nepal	Marshall Islands	Iceland	
	Nicaragua	Mauritius	Ireland	
	Nigeria	Mexico	Isle of Man	

(continued)

Table 15.1 Continued

Low-income $1,045 or less	Lower-middle-income $1,046 to $4,095	Upper-middle-income $4,096 to $12,695	High-income $12,696 or more
	Pakistan	Moldova	Israel
	Papua New Guinea	Montenegro	Italy
	Philippines	Namibia	Japan
	Samoa	North Macedonia	Korea, Republic
	São Tomé and Principe	Panama	Kuwait
	Senegal	Paraguay	Latvia
	Solomon Islands	Peru	Liechtenstein
	Sri Lanka	Romania	Lithuania
	Tanzania	Russian Federation	Luxembourg
	Tajikistan	Serbia	Macao SAR, China
	Timor-Leste	South Africa	Malta
	Tunisia	St. Lucia	Monaco
	Ukraine	St. Vincent and the Grenadines	
	Uzbekistan	Suriname	
	Vanuatu	Thailand	
	Vietnam	Tonga	
	West Bank and Gaza	Turkey	
	Zambia	Turkmenistan	
	Zimbabwe	Tuvalu	

Figure 15.1 shows the trend of total patent applications filed in the countries in each group. There are two things to note. First, China is ranked as an upper-middle-income country, but its patenting and other IP activity are now the highest in the world, so it dominates the data for upper-middle-income countries. For this reason, here and in all the subsequent figures, we show the data separately for China and upper-middle-income countries without China. Second, with the exception of China, almost all patenting worldwide takes place in high-income countries. Because patents only protect inventions in the jurisdictions where they are taken out, this means that there is little patent protection in most of the countries in the world.

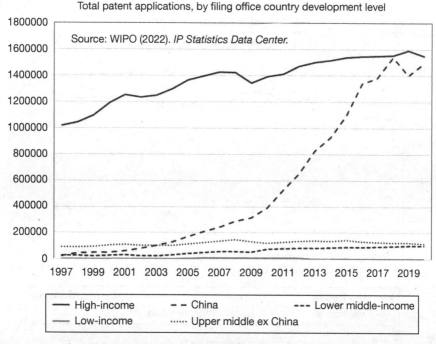

Total patent applications, by filing office country development level

Source: WIPO (2022). *IP Statistics Data Center.*

Legend: High-income — China — Lower middle-income / Low-income — Upper middle ex China

Figure 15.1 Total patenting by level of development.

Figure 15.2 shows the patent applications per capita made by residents in a country by development level.[3] In the aggregate, high-income countries average about 800 applications per million capita per year, and this has not changed much in the past 20 years. In contrast, China's per capita application rate has increased from almost nothing to over 900 applications per million capita, higher than the high-income country rate. The rate for the middle-income countries has increased very slightly since the late 1990s, and residents of low-income countries continue to file at a rate of less than one application per million capita.

However, as the well-publicized debates over access to medicines and vaccines have revealed, there is one technology where patenting is fairly active in the lower-income countries.[4] In Figure 15.3, we show the broad technology profiles for patenting in countries with different income levels. High-income countries have the largest share of their patenting in electrical (including information technology and communications) and mechanical (including transportation equipment) technologies. In contrast, as we move to lower incomes, patenting in the chemical sector including pharmaceuticals dominates. Recall from Figure 15.1 that this does not mean these countries patent more

[3] We limit the applications to those from residents in this figure because we are normalizing by the population from which they come. In fact, the figure looks roughly the same if one uses total applications instead of restricting it to those by residents, although, of course, the numbers are higher.

[4] For a review of the issues, see Lanjouw (2003). An example of the controversies is the well-publicized debate over access to HIV/AIDS treatments in Brazil, among other countries (Nunn et al. 2009). See also Chapter 16.

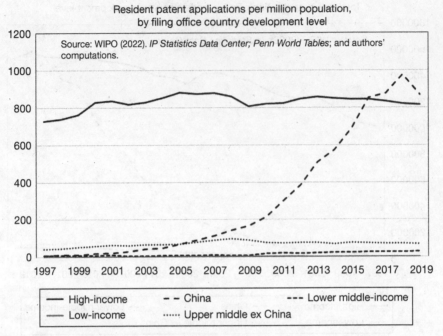

Figure 15.2 Resident patenting by level of development.

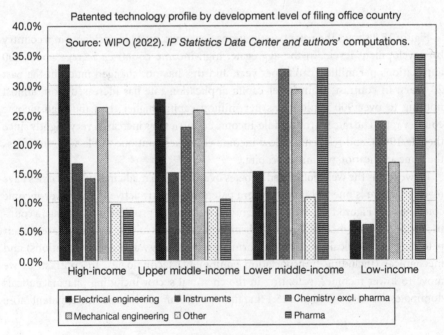

Figure 15.3 Patented technology profile by development level.

in this technology; it simply means that the limited number of patents that are taken out in these countries are more likely to be in chemicals. In fact, a great number of these patents are in the pharmaceutical and biotechnology subsector of the chemical area, as shown in the figure.

Why is this the case? Earlier, we discussed the fact that the boundaries of chemical technologies are easier to delineate, making the patents more enforceable and better suited for protection from imitation than those in other technologies. For example, motives for patenting by computing and information technology tend to be related to defensive concerns about competitors' patenting, rather than a desire to exclude imitators, as we describe in Chapter 18. In most developing countries, these concerns are much less important. In addition, the defensive motive coupled with the fuzziness of the patent boundaries in ICT and elsewhere leads to a strategy whereby firms take out hundreds if not thousands of patents, and the cost of doing this in a large number of less developed countries is simply not worth the possible benefits.

The pharmaceutical sector is completely different: Here, one or a few patents can serve to exclude imitators so the cost of protection is relatively lower, while the value can be quite high. We know that as a general rule, the economic value of a single patent on an invention tends to be much greater in this technology (Hall et al. 2005). So when we restrict the chemical technologies to the subset of biotechnology, organic fine chemistry, and pharmaceuticals, we find that the shares of patents for these technologies in low-, lower-middle-, upper-middle-, and high-income economies are 35, 33, 10, and 9%, respectively.

We illustrate this point with Figures 15.4 and 15.5 These figures show the differential patent coverage for Apple's gesture unlocking patent and an important pharmaceutical that treats hepatitis C.[5] Apple protects its IP only in countries that are likely to compete in mobile phones: the United States, Europe, China, Japan, South Korea, and Australia. In contrast, Gilead protects Sovaldi in over 40 countries, including a number of middle-income economies such as Brazil and South Africa.

Turning to trademarks, the picture is somewhat different. Here, middle-income countries show increasing and nontrivial use of this instrument for IP protection. By 2020, the total number of applications in the upper- and lower-middle-income countries excluding China is about the same as in the high-income countries. Compare this

Figure 15.4 Countries where Apple has a patent on unlocking a device by performing gestures on an unlock image.

---

[5] Patent protection for Solvaldi is based on the worldwide patent families of the US patents listed in the FDA Orange Book. This may not reflect all of the patents that protect Sovaldi outside of the United States.

Figure 15.5 Countries where Gilead has a patent on Sovaldi (to treat hepatitis C).

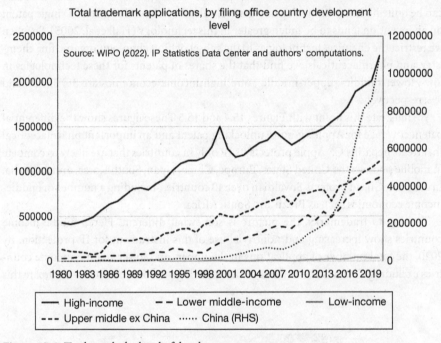

Figure 15.6 Trademarks by level of development.

to the ratio for high-income to middle-income patents of about 13. However, China is again an outlier, with 11 million trademark applications in 2020, a number so big that we show trademark applications in China using a different scale on the right-hand side of Figure 15.6.

Figure 15.7 shows the trends in applications for industrial designs. Once again, we use a separate scale for China, given the large number of applications at that country's office, most of which come from residents.

Finally, we show the trends in utility model applications in Figure 15.8. China is an extreme outlier in this figure, again shown on a separate scale. By 2020, there are nearly 3 million utility model applications in China versus 100,000 in the rest of the world. Utility models are often viewed as a path to development, which become less important as a country develops, and this is visible in the declining use of utility models by

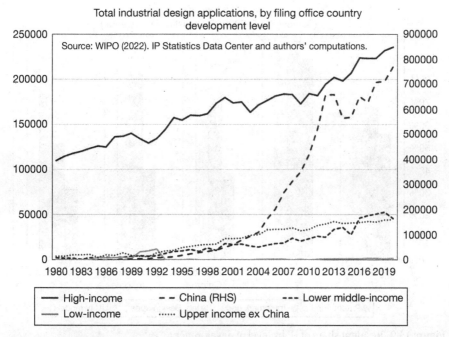

Figure 15.7 Industrial designs by level of development.

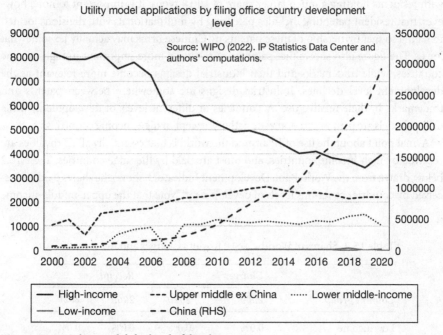

Figure 15.8 Utility models by level of development.

high-income countries. It is worth noting that only about 40% of countries with patent offices also have provision for utility models.

Figure 15.9 shows a summary for the four types of IP as of 2020, showing how the resident and nonresident shares differ across IP types. It clearly shows that China is an outlier,

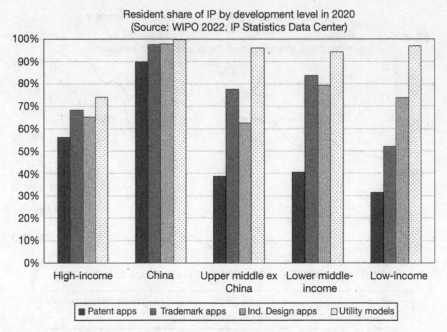

Figure 15.9 Resident share of IP by level of development.

with residents holding a much larger share of all IP types. It is important to note, however, that resident patenting includes patenting by multinationals with divisions located in China so that ownership of these patents by Chinese firms may actually be somewhat lower. The figure also shows that patents are relatively more important in high-income countries, while trademarks and then industrial designs become more relevant as the development level declines. Industrial designs are somewhere between patents and trademarks in their relative use by countries at different levels of development, while utility models are primarily a domestic activity, except in high-income countries.

A final point about the use of IP around the world is that essentially all IP royalties are received by high-income countries, and most are paid by the same countries. Table 15.2 below, drawn from the World Bank Development Indicators, shows the shares paid and received by countries at various levels of development. Note that the upper-middle-income

Table 15.2 Shares of Worldwide IP Royalty Charges and Receipts

	Charges		Receipts	
Country group	*2000*	*2020*	*2000*	*2020*
Low income	0.0%	0.0%	0.0%	0.0%
Lower middle income	2.4%	3.3%	0.3%	0.4%
Upper middle income	8.0%	18.8%	0.6%	3.2%
High income	89.6%	77.8%	99.1%	96.4%

Source: World Bank Development Indicators, balance of payments statistics

share of payments has increased from 8% to the 19% shown since 2000, due both to their increasing share of worldwide income and the increasing use of multinational patents to secure revenue in those countries. Low-income countries have essentially no IP trade.

From this overview of the facts about formal IP use around the world, we draw a number of conclusions:

- Formal IP is not very important in the least developed countries and only marginally important in the next tier.
- Trademarks and utility models seem to be more important in developing countries than patents.
- In the less developed countries, patenting is primarily in chemicals, especially pharmaceuticals, and these patents are usually held by nonresidents of the country.
- High-income countries capture all of the value in IP trade, mostly from each other, but with increasing shares from middle-income countries.

15.2.1 China

The preceding left us with a puzzle: the enormous increase in the use of IP by China, which was once a low-income country but has rapidly grown, becoming a lower-middle-income country in 2005 and an upper-middle-income country in 2015. Thus, the explanation for some of the growth in IP use lies in the relatively rapid growth of real GDP per capita in China, roughly 5.5% per annum between 1985 and 2020. But that is not enough to explain the 8–9% per annum growth of patenting and utility model sustained for 30 years, almost all of which is by residents.

A number of factors have contributed to this growth besides the obvious industrialization. China introduced its current patent system 7 years after Deng Xiaoping adopted the Open Door Policy in 1978. It was then amended several times during the next 2 decades and revised comprehensively as part of the National Intellectual Property Strategy in 2008.[6] This revision recognized the fact that imitation was no longer a viable strategy as China moved to the frontier in some technology areas.

This policy shift was accompanied by incentive programs to increase the patenting activity of domestic firms. Li (2012) documents how differences in these programs across regional jurisdictions affected patenting propensities. He argues that although patenting has increased due to increased R&D and new technologies as well as ownership reform that clarified the assignment of property rights as documented by Hu and Jefferson (2009), the post-2001 surge cannot be completely explained by those factors and is partly due to local incentive programs for patenting.

15.3 Optimal IP Policy for a Global Economy

A number of economic theorists have addressed themselves to the question of the choice of IP policy in an interconnected world (Grossman and Lai 2004, Angeles 2005,

---

[6] http://www.wipo.int/wipo_magazine/en/2010/06/article_0010.html.

Scotchmer 2004). Much of this research was driven by the negotiation of the Trade-Related Aspects of International Property Rights (TRIPS) agreement, which effectively imposed uniform standards (with some delay and exceptions) on all participant countries. Many scholars thought that this agreement was not optimal from a welfare perspective, arguing that benefits to less developed countries might not justify the costs imposed. Similar reservations about a one-size-fits-all IP system had been expressed earlier by Penrose (1951, 1973).

In order to more fully understand the issues, we describe the model of IP system choice and its welfare properties due to Grossman and Lai (2004). This model is written in continuous time so that expenses, profits, and the like are flows over time, which makes the mathematics somewhat easier to work with, but is highly stylized relative to reality. They begin by examining the optimal choice of IP strength in a closed economy and then look at what happens when there are two economies at different levels of development that trade with each other.

Beginning with the single economy model, they assume that every period a number of differentiated goods are invented and put on the market, whose prices are monopoly prices if covered by a patent and perfectly competitive prices if not. Patent holders (monopolists) earn a stream of profits π per consumer and good, and those without patents earn a profit of zero. All goods have a fixed lifetime equal to τ^*, and the PDV of \$1 or other currency unit from time zero until τ^* is denoted by $T^* = (1 - \exp(-\rho\tau^*))/\rho$, where ρ is the interest rate used for discounting (see Appendix A: Mathematics and Statistics for details on the computation of PDV over finite periods). The market size is given by M, which roughly corresponds to GDP rather than population. This captures the idea that an economy with higher income will be able to purchase more goods than one with the same population but lower income.

Patent strength is introduced in this model in two ways: (1) length of life of a patent τ, assumed to be less than or equal to τ^*, and (2) enforcement strength ω. They show that in their model strength can be collapsed into a single index Ω:

$$\Omega = \frac{\omega(1 - e^{-\rho\tau})}{\rho}$$

This index is the product of enforcement probability ω, with the PDV of \$1 over the life of the patent τ. Table 15.3 gives some values for Ω under the assumption that ω is 1, that is, the patent is perfectly enforceable over its lifetime. The values shown are the PDV of a patent generating an annual revenue of \$1 (or euro or other currency unit). Higher discount rates mean that future income matters less, so the PDV is lower. A longer patent life means that revenue is earned for a longer time, so the PDV is higher, but if there is high discounting, the longer revenue stream is much less important.

The invention of new goods is a flow over time $\phi(t)$ given by a constant elasticity of substitution (CES) function of human capital and labor devoted to research.[7] The remaining labor is used for production; all labor earns the same wage w and labor enters

---

[7] The CES production function is discussed in Appendix A: Mathematics and Statistics.

Table 15.3 Computing Ω

Patent life τ	Discount rate ρ			
	0.03	0.05	0.10	0.15
10 years	8.6	7.9	6.3	5.2
15 years	12.1	10.6	7.8	6.0
20 years	15.0	12.6	8.6	6.3

research until its relative marginal product falls to w.[8] Given all these assumptions, one can show that the value of a new patent is the following:

$$v = \frac{\omega M \pi}{\rho}(1 - e^{-\rho\tau}) = M\pi\Omega$$

That is, the value of each new patented invention is the market size times the stream of profits it generates times the strength of the patent protection.

With these ingredients, they are able to derive an expression for welfare at time zero $W(0)$ when a new patent system will be introduced. Welfare has three components: wages to production labor L_y, consumer surplus and profits $(C_m + \pi)\Omega$ while the products are sold by monopolists, and the consumer surplus after they become sold by competitive firms $C_c(T^* - \Omega)$. Recall that T^* is the value of a revenue stream of one currency unit over the entire lifetime of the product, as opposed to its patent lifetime. That is, each product is in the market during the period 0 to T^*, and during that time it earns monopoly profits until the patent expires or fails to be enforced; after that, the consumers receive C_c and the producer receives zero. Note that $C_c > C_m$ by the assumption of monopoly versus competition. Putting this together, we have the following equation for welfare W at time zero in the patent life:

$$W(0) = \frac{w(L_Y)}{\rho} + M\phi(C_m + \pi)\Omega + M\phi C_c(T^* - \Omega)$$

Using the above expression for welfare and maximizing with respect to patent strength Ω, they are able to derive an implicit equation for the optimal patent strength. This is a complex exercise because the invention stream ϕ is a function of the amount of labor devoted to research, which, of course, depends on the patent system. The resulting equation, which defines optimal patent strength under the assumptions of their model, is the following:

$$C_c - C_m - \pi = \gamma\left[C_m + C_c\left(\frac{T^* - \Omega}{\Omega}\right)\right] \tag{1}$$

---

[8] This is a fairly innocuous simplifying assumption here.

where γ is the responsiveness of innovation to the protection offered by the patent system. This equation shows that optimal patent protection is stronger (higher Ω) under three conditions: (1) longer useful product life τ^*; (2) more patient consumers (lower ρ and hence higher T^*); and (3) higher response of innovation to patenting (γ). One interesting result is that the impact of market size depends on the research production function. If the responsiveness of innovation to the patent system increases when R&D labor increases, optimal patent protection is an increasing function of market size, but when the responsiveness decreases with increased R&D labor, optimal patent protection is a decreasing function of market size. That is, decreasing returns in research mean that in larger markets, weaker patent protection is needed to induce "enough" R&D. If the research production function is Cobb-Douglas in form (a special case of CES), the optimal policy is invariant with respect to market size.

Grossman and Lai then use this understanding of single-country behavior to construct a noncooperative model of optimal patent system choice in two countries with different levels of development that trade with each other. As is common in the literature, they label these countries North and South (N and S). These countries are assumed to differ in wage rates w, level of human capital H, and market size M, with those variables all being higher in the North than the South.

The setup for each country is the same as before. New goods are produced from R&D labor and existing human capital, have a lifetime τ, and are patent-protected, with possibly different patent lives and strengths in the two countries, implying that the optimal policies differ, denoted Ω_N and Ω_S. They assume national treatment, as prescribed by TRIPS and also by the Paris Convention of 1883. This means that an inventor in the South who takes out a patent in the North receives the same protection as if they were an inventor in the North. They also exclude the possibility of parallel imports. This exclusion allows patent holders to price-discriminate across markets.

Invention and production of new goods take place in both countries and consumers are free to buy in both countries, so trade is free. However, each country benefits from markups on its own production due to its patent system, while consumers in both countries bear the cost in the form of monopoly pricing. Given greater productivity, human capital, and market size in the North, the resulting equilibrium will be asymmetric. The authors show that optimal patent policy in each country is determined by an equation similar to equation (1) above:

$$C_c - C_m - \mu_i \pi = \gamma \left[\frac{M_i \Omega_i}{M_S \Omega_S + M_N \Omega_N} \right] \times \left[C_m + C_c \left(\frac{T^* - \Omega_i}{\Omega_i} \right) \right] \quad \text{for } i = S, N \quad (2)$$

where $\mu_i = \phi_i / (\phi_S + \phi_N)$ is the share of worldwide innovation that takes place in country i. They also show that although human capital and labor productivity differ across the two countries, the supply elasticity of innovation γ is the same for both, thanks to their assumption of a CES innovation production function.

When we compare equation (2) to equation (1), the left-hand side shows that an open economy cares only about the share of profits earned within the country, while the right-hand side shows that in an open economy innovation is more weakly stimulated by the patent system because some of the innovator's profits are earned outside the country. Under the assumption that the elasticity of substitution between research labor and human capital is less than zero, Grossman and Lai use this to show that there is a unique Nash equilibrium and the optimal patent policies are weaker for open economies than closed economies.

They also show that, under the noncooperative equilibrium, if the North has a larger market size and higher human capital, the optimal policy in the North is stronger than in the South. The intuition is both that the North captures a larger share of innovators' profits and also has a greater capacity to conduct R&D. They also show that what matters for efficient global R&D effort is the market size weighted sum of the two patent policies and that achieving efficiency relative to the noncooperative Nash equilibrium would involve increased patent protection in at least one country. If the ratio of human capital to market size is greater in the North than in the South, the harmonized version of an efficient policy produces gains for the North if research production is Cobb-Douglas. Harmonization may produce gain or loss for the South. So for the all-important question of whether optimal harmonized patent policies benefit less developed countries, there is a somewhat ambiguous answer, even though the noncooperative outcome will yield weaker patent protection in the South.

Scotchmer (2004) uses a model that includes the possibility of public funding of R&D in place of patent protection and shows that the more innovative country prefers higher harmonized protection. In addition, national treatment generally increases incentives to innovate, but can lead to asymmetry where one country protects all innovation in a particular subject matter and consumers in other countries free-ride.

Clearly, these models are very stylized, and it is reasonable to ask what happens if we relax some assumptions, although for the most part this will be very difficult. For example, the stream of profits and consumer surplus from the invention is assumed to be constant until the patent ends (in the case of C_M and profits) or the product becomes obsolete (C_C). We might imagine that these grow and then decline, which is unlikely to affect the conclusions. However, they also ignore the stochastic arrival of products that displace the current one so that statutory patent life becomes unimportant. A second set of assumptions allows them to write a reasonably simple equation involving the patent policies for the two economies: that is, they assume that both the level of consumer surplus and profits for a product and the production function for innovations are the same in both countries. Therefore, any differences in consumer surplus and profits across countries have to come from different levels of the innovation stream $\phi(t)$, which, in turn, depends on higher levels of research labor and human capital.

The conclusions from the theoretical literature on the choice of IP system are fairly clear: In the absence of any kind of coordinated action, more developed countries will have stronger IP protection than less developed countries (Grossman and Lai 2004, Angeles 2005). In addition, harmonization generally leads to levels of IP protection that are higher than the social optimum, at least in the less developed countries (Scotchmer 2004). As these models predict, the tendency is for IP protection strength to harmonize upward rather than downward. However, the theory is less clear about the consequences of different levels of IP protection for development. As Fink and Maskus stress in the introduction to their edited volume on the topic, "[M]any effects of stronger IPR standards are theoretically ambiguous and thus need to be subjected to empirical analysis" (Fink and Maskus 2005, p. 2).

15.4 Patents, Innovation, and Development

Historically, patent systems have developed in response to a perceived need by governments and inventors to protect their creative and inventive endeavors. But that was not always true. In the early days, they were often a method of patronage that cost the ruler little but benefited those they wished to reward. In other cases, they were designed to attract craftsmen to a particular city or region. David (1994) cites some 14th-century examples of grants employed to encourage the introduction of foreign technologies through the immigration of skilled artisans from abroad: letters patent (an earlier term for the grant of exclusive use of a technology) given to the Flemish weaver John Kempe by Edward II in 1331; the protection granted to two Brabant weavers to settle at York in 1336; a similar grant conferred in 1368 upon three clock-makers from Delft, the Netherlands. Machlup and Penrose (1950) report that the granting of such monopoly privileges was widespread in Europe during the 16th and 17th centuries. After the French and American revolutions, patent systems democratized––no longer the prerogative of a king or ruler, now anyone with an invention could apply to have the right to exclude others from practicing it.

The US and French experience notwithstanding, the timing of patent system intro-duction and/or strengthening does seem to have been coincident or even after indus-trial development rather than preceding it. For example, in the 18th- and 19th-century United Kingdom, Mokyr (2009) expresses skepticism that patents were essential during the Industrial Revolution given the costly features of the system and the fact that a number of successful inventors made no use of it.[9] US industrial development during the 19th century does seem to have benefited from patents, although this development took place prior to the international patent harmonization of the Paris Convention and US inventors probably found the route to a patent easier than foreign inventors.

Among others, K. Lee (2013) and Kumar (2003) argue that Japan, Korea, and Taiwan followed a development strategy that emphasized a relatively weak patent system with narrow claim coverage and reliance on utility patents while catching up. Lee also suggests that this strategy went along with a technology strategy directed to-ward innovations with short cycle times. A modern-day example is China, as described above. However, thanks to TRIPS, the sequencing of development via first imitating and then instituting stronger patent systems is no longer possible, raising again the question of whether the one-size-fits-all approach is ideal for development and innova-tion in developing countries.

How do developing countries catch up? That is, what are the ways they can learn in order to close the knowledge gap? One channel is clearly the mobility of research and other skilled workers, as well as public resources such as scientific journals, the in-ternet, and international patents. None of this is greatly affected by the presence of a do-mestic patent system. A second channel is the purchase of investment goods embodying

---

[9] In the United Kingdom, filing fees prior to 1852 were estimated to be 100 pounds for an English patent, 300 pounds if the patent was also taken out in Scotland and Ireland, at a time when a skilled worker earned an annual income of 50–100 pounds (MacLeod et al. 2003). In today's money, 100 pounds is approximately equal to 12,700 pounds, or US$15,000. Hindmarch (1851) reports that the full cost of a patent in the United Kingdom including agent fees and the preparation of drawings, and so forth, was about 400 pounds. In addi-tion, obtaining a patent was a long, drawn out process involving many administrative offices.

new innovations, imitation and reverse engineering, licensing of patented technologies and technology information from foreign innovators, direct technology transfer by multinational corporations to their subsidiaries, and potential spillovers from those subsidiaries to domestic firms. This latter channel will be sensitive to the presence of a functioning domestic patent system.

Willingness to transfer technology in the form of investment goods, licensing, and know-how to both domestic firms and multinational subsidiaries is likely to be affected by the protection offered by the local patent system, whereas learning by imitation and the acquisition of technology spillovers by local firms may be inhibited by the use of the patent system by those generating spillovers. This line of reasoning suggests that there are at least two separate but related questions whose answers may be somewhat at odds with each other when considering appropriate patent policy for developing countries. The first is whether stronger patent protection in a host country encourages technology transfer to that country. In particular, how does the presence of patent protection affect the behavior of foreign firms that may potentially invest in the country, sell technology to firms in the country, or form joint ventures with domestic firms? The second question is whether stronger patent protection encourages technology development in the country itself. That is, how does it affect the behavior of domestic firms? The first question has been easier to answer, but the second is probably more important for the economic development of the country in question.

With respect to the first question, *a priori* it seems clear that stronger IP protection in the host country should encourage (or at least not discourage) the transfer of technology by foreign firms to their subsidiaries and possibly to domestic firms, either via partnership or simple sale or licensing. Note that this argument presumes that the IP rights are enforceable, which is not an innocuous assumption. Also, note that such transfer may or may not help the local development of innovation skills and human capital. With respect to the second question, it also seems clear that stronger IP protection could encourage the innovative activities of domestic firms, but that such protection could also discourage learning via imitation and therefore inhibit technological catch-up. Thus, the impact of IP systems on technological development is ambiguous and requires further investigation.

In the next three sections, we discuss the evidence that bears on both these questions, first on technology transfer and then on the domestic impact both on innovation and then on growth.

15.4.1 Technology Transfer and the Patent System

International technology transfer typically takes place via trade, foreign direct investment (FDI), joint ventures with local partners, or simple technology licensing, although in the latter case, some tacit knowledge probably also needs to be transferred. In all of these cases, foreign firms run the risk that imitation by local firms may erode some of their profits from these activities, so the presence of enforceable IPRs should encourage all these activities. In fact, Edith Penrose goes as far as to argue that for developing countries "the only economic advantages to be gained from granting foreign patents lies in the possibility that in one way or another such grants will induce the introduction of foreign technology and capital" (Penrose 1973, p. 770).

Obviously, in the cases of more advanced technology, the imitation risk is highest when the host country has the capacity to adopt and develop such technology, which implies that the risk is generally greater in middle-income countries than in low-income countries. This risk is further increased if technologies require local adaptation in order to fit local needs and regulatory requirements and standards. At the same time, if IPR protection is strong, foreign firms may prefer to license technologies instead of choosing to be a local presence, which could decrease the amount of technology transferred, or they may choose to transfer technology that is far from the frontier. This decision may also be influenced by the ability of foreign firms to enforce licensing contracts. However, it is also conceivable that stronger IPRs increase the incentives for firms to exploit IPRs themselves instead of licensing out. It is likely that these relationships differ by industry and type of activity, that is, manufacturing or distribution.

There is some empirical evidence on the trade effects of strengthening IP laws, which suggests that they do indeed have an impact. For example, Maskus and Penubarti (1995) found that increasing patent protection had a positive impact on manufacturing imports into developing countries, an impact that was larger for the larger of these countries. Ivus (2010) used data on exports from developed to developing countries over the period that TRIPS was introduced to show that strengthening patent rights via TRIPS increased high-tech exports to developing countries by about 9%.

Using data from 158 countries during the 1993–2009 period, Delgado et al. (2013) studied the change in the trade of knowledge-intensive goods relative to other goods after TRIPS was implemented in 1995. They also made use of the fact that for some lower-income countries compliance with TRIPS was not required until 2000 and for the least developed countries it was not yet required at the time they did the study. They find that overall exports in knowledge-intensive goods increased post-TRIPS in countries at all income levels. In general, the positive impact of TRIPS compliance on developing countries was concentrated in the information and communications technology sector and the chemicals sector. Biopharmaceuticals were less strongly affected, probably because of the various pharmaceutical exceptions and delays allowed by TRIPS. Javorcik (2002) found similar results for technology-intensive investment in Eastern European countries and the former Soviet Union. Weak IPRs discouraged such investment, and foreign firms invested in distribution rather than local production in countries with weak rights.

Hall (2014) reviewed the empirical literature on the relationship between patent systems and technology transfer via trade, FDI, and technology licensing.[10] The trade literature suggested that the strength of a country's IP system did affect the willingness of developed countries to export manufacturing goods to that country, especially if the country in question had imitative capacity. The FDI literature, which is older and more voluminous, found a positive correlation between FDI and destination country patenting by multinationals as well as a correlation of FDI with the strength of IPR enforcement.

---

[10] See also Maskus (2004) and Branstetter (2004) for earlier reviews of this literature.

Looking specifically at the willingness of foreign firms to invest in R&D in other countries, Thursby and Thursby (2006) surveyed 200 R&D managers from Western European and US multinationals, asking about the factors affecting their choice of location for a new laboratory, distinguishing between location in developed and emerging or developing economies. The most important factor in an emerging economy was its growth potential. However, they found that good IP protection was important in both types of country, ranking only slightly below the factor with the highest importance, the availability of qualified R&D personnel. This result certainly suggests that IPRs will facilitate some technology transfers to middle-income countries.

However, Kanwar (2012) looked at the relation between patent strength and multinational R&D investment in the country, using data on 40 countries between 1977 and 2004. To measure patent strength, he used a modified version of the Ginarte-Park-Fraser index described in Section 15.4.2. Controlling for overall country effects, he found convincing results that overseas R&D investment was determined by market size and human capital, not by the strength of patent rights, except in high-income countries.

In summary, the literature mostly indicates a positive correlation between technology imports, FDI, and the level of IPR enforcement. Considering the extensive evidence on FDI serving as a channel for technology transfer, this implies a positive relation between IPR enforcement and technology transfer through the channel of FDI. However, the literature also points to other important factors in attracting FDI, such as country risk and the availability of low-cost high-skilled labor. It also generally emphasizes the importance of the level of development and absorptive capacity in whether patents will affect technology transfer. That is, if there is no ability to imitate in the destination country, patents will not matter as much to the firm deciding on investment strategies in that country.

15.4.2 Domestic Innovation and the Patent System

The results on IP and technology transfer seem sensible and consistent with *a priori* intuition. However, as suggested earlier, the more important question for policy is the impact of strengthened IPRs on innovation and development within a developing country. Does stronger patent protection help to enable and increase that country's own innovative capacity? This could happen because it creates greater incentives for local firms to innovate or via increased spillovers from foreign firm investment. This question has been approached empirically by economists in two different ways: looking at the relationship between IP and innovation across countries, as described earlier, and using individual country case studies of changes in patent law. For example, Kim (2003) argues that the Korean case shows that strong IPR protection in earlier stages of industrialization can hinder learning via imitation. Kumar (2003) reviews the historical relationship between IPRs, technology, and development in East Asia and concludes that "Japan, Korea, and Taiwan have absorbed substantial amount of technological learning under weak IPR protection regimes during the early phases" of their development (Kumar 2003, p. 217).

Some studies of the role of patents on innovation are historical, for example, those by Lerner (2002b), Moser (2005), and Chen (2008). The advantage of historical studies is that there are periods with no patent protection in several countries, so there is high variability in the IP environment, which helps with identification. Using 60 countries over the period 1850–2000, Lerner finds that strengthening the patent system increased patenting by foreign entities in the country, but that domestic entities patented less both at home and abroad. Moser used data on World's Fairs exhibits in the 19th century to show that the lack of a patent system led firms to specialize in inventions that could be protected with trade secrecy. Chen (2008) used lists of major inventions between 1590 and 1900 to establish the positive impact of patent systems on inventive activity.

In 1997, Ginarte and Park published an index of patent strength for 110 countries covering the period 1960–1990, updated in 2008 by Park to cover 122 countries over 1960–2005. There are five components of this index, and it is scaled to go from 1 (least protection) to 5 (highest level of protection):

1. Subject matter coverage
2. Membership in various international treaties including TRIPS
3. Duration of protection
4. Enforcement mechanisms (injunctions, etc.)
5. Restrictions on patent rights (compulsory licensing, working requirement).

This index, sometimes modified to incorporate actual ease of enforcement as opposed to legislated ease of enforcement, has been widely used in studies of the impact of patenting strength on innovation and growth.

Figure 15.10 shows a box plot for the index in the latest year it is available (2005), by income groups. Clearly, patent protection strength increases with income, although there are a few outliers among lower-income countries. Notably, these outliers include three important large developing countries: Brazil, China, and India. This suggests that a country's size may also contribute to demands for stronger IP.

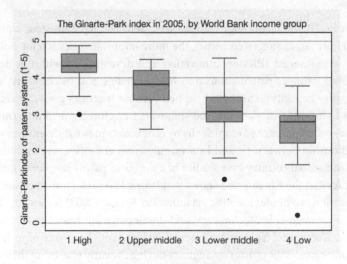

Figure 15.10 The Ginarte-Park index by country income level.

Ginarte and Park (1997) used their index to study the determinants of patent protection strength as a function of GDP per capita, R&D intensity, education, openness, and measures of market and political freedom. They found that for higher-income countries, R&D intensity and market freedom were the most important predictors of patent strength, whereas for lower-income countries, only openness and market freedom mattered, with very little impact from R&D. In regressions without these other variables, GDP per capita was positively associated with patent strength, but its importance completely disappeared when the other variables were included. This suggests that the primary channel through which patent strength has an impact is as an incentive for R&D spending.

Using the Ginarte-Park index, Kanwar and Evenson (2003) investigated its impact on R&D intensity across countries in a panel of 32 countries for the three years 1985, 1990, and 1995. They find a significant relationship controlling for GDP per capita growth, political instability, the interest rate, and random country effects. The measured coefficient suggests that a one-unit increase in patent strength is associated with an absolute increase in R&D intensity in the country of one percentage point.

There is evidence that patent strength as measured by the Ginarte-Park index has different impacts on innovative effort at different development levels, as suggested by the earlier discussion of development strategy. Allred and Park (2007) use data on firms in 35 countries during the period 1965–2000 to find that patent strength negatively affects domestic patent filings, and has little impact on domestic R&D spending. In contrast, for developed economies, increased patent strength positively impacts R&D and domestic patent filings.

Although the evidence summarized here is variable and based on data primarily selected for its availability, the main conclusion is that there is evidence patent system existence and its strength do have a positive impact on innovative activity at the country level, at least in higher-income countries. Even if it is not a fully causal relationship, there is clearly a positive association between patent strength and innovative activity.

15.4.3 Empirical Evidence on IP and Economic Growth

Does the increase in innovation associated with patents translate to higher economic growth and development? This important question has been investigated in a number of ways, with a range of approaches. Looking across countries at the firm, industry, or country level, researchers have asked how economic growth and/or innovation investments are impacted either by the strength of IP protection in the country or by the amount of patenting done within the country. The challenge in performing these tests is the usual one of simultaneity between economic development, technological development, and the choice of IP systems. To investigate this potential simultaneity, Hasan and Tucci (2010) perform Granger causality testing on GDP growth and various patent quality measures.[11] They find that causality runs in both directions, but more strongly from patent quality to growth, which is somewhat reassuring.

---

[11] Granger causality testing, for which Clive Granger earned the Nobel Prize in Economics in 2003 together with Robert Engle, is a method of using regression analysis on a set of variables to test for whether one plausibly causes another. For details of the procedure, consult most econometrics textbooks.

Studies that look at the impact of IP strength on growth have generally used the country-level index of IP strength developed by Ginarte and Park (1997) and extended by Park (2008) that we discussed in Section 15.4.2. This index is often added to a standard empirical economic growth model to examine the relationship between patent strength and growth.

Hu and Png (2013) provide a good example of the cross-country IP-growth literature, one that is greatly enriched by the inclusion of industry detail. They have data on 34 manufacturing industries in 72 countries for 1981–2000. The advantage of having data by industry is that they can measure the differential impact of patent strength within a country on industries that are more patent-intensive. That is, they look within a country and ask whether countries where patents provide stronger protection also have relatively higher growth in patent-intensive sectors. To minimize the problem of feedback from patent intensity to a country's patent strength, they measure patent intensity by using the US ratio of patents granted to an industry divided by industry sales.

The results show that patent strength does matter for industry growth, and that the impact increases somewhat between 1981–1985 and 1996–2000, after the TRIPS agreement came into force. The patent intensity variable, measured as patent grants over million dollars of deflated sales, averaged 0.018. An increase in effective patent rights of one standard deviation would have added between 0.18 to 0.75% to the industry growth rate, depending on the time period. This impact increased with the level of GDP per capita in the country, confirming others' findings that patent strength matters more at higher levels of development.

Gold et al. (2019) review the results from this line of research, finding them somewhat inconsistent, especially with regard to the variation in the relationship with the country's income level. As they suggest, some of this inconsistency may be due to the use of different models and data choices, and they construct a new IP index that is sensitive to the many changes induced by TRIPS. They then advance the interesting hypothesis that the IP-growth association is due to a placebo effect: Foreign investors believe that IP strength is good for their investment so when they see it increase, they increase their investment even though there is no actual impact of IP strength on the investment success. This hypothesis is supported by their evidence that the impact of IP-intensive imports on growth is many times that of the effect of IP on growth through domestic inventive activity (US patent applications from the country) in lower- and upper-middle-income countries, controlling for the strength of IP. Although it is not possible to truly test for the placebo effect, the finding that technology transfer rather than domestic invention is more induced by IP strength seems consistent with what other researchers have observed about the two channels.

15.5 Pharmaceutical Innovation and Patents in Developing Countries

Much of the debate over the role of patents in developing countries has centered on their use in covering pharmaceutical innovations. The weight of evidence in developed economies suggests that these patents are the most valuable for firms (Hall et al. 2005, Arora et al. 2008) and the most highly valued by managers (Cohen et al. 2000).

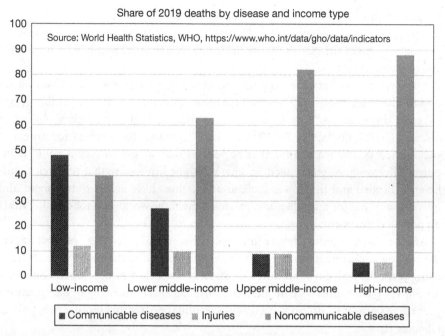

Figure 15.11 Causes of death by country income level.

Correspondingly, and as we saw in Figure 15.3, this technology is often the technology where multinationals choose to extend their patenting activity into developing countries, inhibiting the development of cheaper generic alternatives in those countries that have the relevant technological capacity (Lanjouw 1997, Scherer and Weisburst 1995). It is also often argued that patent protection in developing countries has the benefit of inducing research into neglected diseases.

The background to this debate is well described by Kremer (2002), who carefully reviews the ways in which both the use and the need for pharmaceuticals differ between developed and developing economies. He cites the small size of the markets, the different disease environment, weak health care systems, regulatory problems, and industry factors such as the high-fixed-cost/low-margin-cost structure and the importance of patents. All of this leads to underuse, overuse, and misuse of pharmaceuticals. Obviously, all this can happen in the developed world also, but these problems are worse in the developing world. Figure 15.11 shows the differences in deaths from disease types for countries at different levels of development. It is very clear that communicable diseases including HIV/AIDS, malaria, and tuberculosis are much more important in the lower-income countries, while noncommunicable, which include cancer and cardiovascular diseases, are much more important in higher-income countries.

The primary justification for the use of patents to protect pharmaceutical product innovations has been the need for firms to recoup the high costs of new pharmaceutical development in the presence of relatively low imitation costs. But many have questioned whether such a system is the best way to ensure that a socially optimal mix of pharmaceuticals is provided. For example, public health considerations may favor vaccine development, whereas private incentives may tilt research toward drugs that must be taken over a lifetime, such as blood pressure medication. In addition, patent protection can reduce access to lifesaving drugs by low-income populations, given the quasi-monopolist incentive to restrict output by raising price above marginal cost.

For these reasons, many economists point to other mechanisms for ensuring access to pharmaceuticals such as patent buyouts or prizes for desirable innovations (Kremer 1998, Stiglitz and Jayadev 2010). Recent highly publicized epidemic diseases (AIDS, Ebola, and COVID-19) have increased the demand for drug and vaccine access, and led to a number of policies such as shared patent pools, compulsory licensing, or guaranteed purchase designed to ensure that research is sufficiently funded and that lower-income populations have access to treatment and prevention.[12] But for most diseases, patents remain the workhorse for eliciting R&D on potential treatments.

Another current policy debate in the pharmaceutical patenting area that affects developing countries is whether firms are able to extend the patent life of drugs using secondary patents and how this strategy impacts less developed countries. Secondary patents are those on alternate formulations of the drug or on variations in methods of administration. We discuss secondary patenting more thoroughly in Chapter 16.

15.5.1 Empirical Evidence on the Impact of Pharmaceutical Patentability

Given the often contentious debate around this topic, which affects the health of so many, it is not surprising that a vast amount of research time has been devoted to it. We discuss a few of the recent empirical papers here. The key questions addressed are whether pharmaceutical patent availability increases pharmaceutical innovation, especially for neglected diseases, and whether such availability speeds up the diffusion of drugs to less developed countries from those where they were first introduced. In general, the focus is on pharmaceutical product patents (rather than process patents) because the former were frequently not permitted in a number of countries before TRIPS, whereas the latter were already permitted.

Cross-country comparisons of the impact of introducing product patents on pharmaceuticals during the past 4 decades or so show that they impact domestic R&D and patent filings by residents in a country only for countries with higher levels of GDP per capita (Qian 2007, Kyle and McGahan 2012). Presumably, these are the countries with enough levels of human capital and absorptive capacity to make such investments. Kyle and McGahan (2012) also found that the increased R&D effort was directed toward diseases that are prevalent in high-income countries, not toward the "neglected" diseases prevalent in low-income countries. Thus, these two studies were unable to find

---

[12] In Chapter 20, we discuss one of these mechanisms, the Medicines Patent Pool (MPP), a nonprofit organization created in 2010 by the global health initiative Unitaid.

positive innovation impacts for lower-income countries from the introduction of pharmaceutical patents. In particular, the argument that patent protection in lower-income countries will increase investment in the diseases particular to them does not seem to be supported.

Turning to the diffusion of drugs that already exist in developed countries, the results are more positive. Both Cockburn et al. (2016) and Kyle and Qian (2014) find that longer and stronger product patents speed up the launch of new drugs, regardless of the country's income level. Cockburn et al. (2016) also find that price regulation of drugs delays launch, while Kyle and Qian (2014) find that product patent availability increases both price and quantity of the drug sold. So both studies show that diffusion is increased if there is product patent protection, but that if accompanied by limits on pricing, diffusion will be delayed.

Chaudhuri et al. (2006) study quinolones (a class of antibiotics) in India, where they have been produced as generics for a long time and have the vast majority of market share in India. Accordingly, they undertake a counterfactual analysis of what would have happened to welfare (consumer surplus) if these drugs had been patented and sold in India at monopoly prices. To do this, they estimate a complex demand system for antibiotics that includes the substitutes for quinolones that are off-patent. The estimated loss to the Indian economy from patent protection for quinolones would be between US$144 and $450million annually, mostly to consumers with little loss to domestic producers. They argue that this supports the idea that introducing full TRIPS legislation in India would not be welfare-enhancing.

15.6 Summary

Economic development is often accompanied by increased attention to and use of IP rights. However, the question of which came first, the chicken or the egg, is a contentious one. The evidence mostly favors codevelopment of IP strength and economic growth. However, this link has been broken to some extent by the TRIPS agreement.

Theory tells us that there is a tendency of IP rights to harmonize upward. That is, higher-income countries and those with a greater knowledge base tend to prefer stronger and broader rights than developing countries. This appears to be confirmed by the introduction of TRIPS, which largely harmonized IP rights upward.

The relationship between patent protection and development seems to take two main forms: (1) For middle-income countries with moderate levels of human capital, patent protection seems to encourage innovation investment and catchup. Many of the most successful of these countries are East Asian and transited from relatively weak patents to strong patents during the course of their development. (2) For very low-income countries, patents are almost irrelevant, and when they are used, it is mostly by nonresidents of the country. For example, 98% of the patent applications to the African Regional Intellectual Property Office during the past decade were made by nonresidents of the country (WIPO 2022).

One area that has been studied heavily because of its importance is the role of IP, especially patents, in the production and distribution of pharmaceuticals in developing countries. The availability of patents typically speeds the launch of drugs in developing countries, but does not increase research into drugs for diseases that disproportionally affect them, nor does it increase any pharmaceutical research in lower-income countries.

16
Patents and Pharmaceuticals

Learning Objectives

After reading this chapter, you will be able to understand and explain the following concepts:

- The basic characteristics of the R&D and drug development process in the pharmaceutical industry
- The industry structure of the pharmaceutical industry
- The distinction between patent and regulatory exclusivity
- The role the patent system plays in the pharmaceutical industry
- The effect of patent protection on drug availability and the pricing of drugs
- The distinction between primary and secondary pharmaceutical patents
- The use of secondary patents to extend the scope and length of patent exclusivity
- The use of patent litigation and collusive agreements to delay generic entry

---

16.1 Introduction

The pharmaceutical industry is different from other industries. There are a diverse range of market participants: research institutions, drug developers and manufacturers, wholesalers, physicians, patients, and insurance providers. Compared to other industries, the pharmaceutical industry is subject to far-reaching regulatory intervention that promotes a variety of goals. These objectives include the development of safe, new pharmaceuticals to address therapeutic needs while also ensuring access and affordability. At the same time, innovation in the pharmaceutical industry has dramatic consequences for people's well-being and life expectancy. Innovation in pharmaceuticals also stands out because it requires very large upfront investments. In fact, the pharmaceutical industry is one of the most R&D intensive industries in any industrialized economy. It is also subject to enormous uncertainty and the development of new drugs, and their regulatory approval process takes many years before commercialization even begins. Still, new drugs that are successful are usually extremely profitable, often generating billions of dollars in profits.

Another fairly unique feature of the pharmaceutical industry is the structure of the demand it faces. In many cases, the end consumer does not actually pay for the product or even choose it. Instead, payment will generally be made by an insurance company or a government, and the choice of product(s) to be consumed is often made by a medical professional. This feature of the market generates a disconnect between willingness to pay

The Economics of Innovation and Intellectual Property. Bronwyn H. Hall and Christian Helmers, Oxford University Press.
© Oxford University Press 2024. DOI: 10.1093/oso/9780197630914.003.0016

and the price charged and that faced by the consumer. This, in turn, makes it difficult to determine the benefits to the consumer of any individual drug. In some cases, the benefits may greatly exceed the price, and in others, they may be less than the cost of the drug.

The pharmaceutical industry is also important from an aggregate economic perspective. Total health spending varies across countries, but generally accounts for a significant fraction of GDP. For example, in the United States, it accounted for nearly 17% of GDP in 2015; in Germany and Switzerland, for slightly more than 11%.[1]

There exist substantial differences between industrialized and developing countries, both in terms of health spending and access to drugs. The United States accounts for the largest share of global sales in the market for prescription drugs, followed by the EU. Developing countries account only for a small share of global sales despite being home to a much larger share of the world's population. Although these differences are to some extent explained by differences in price due to various forms of price controls in some countries as well as by price discrimination across countries with differing income levels, price alone cannot account for them.

Among drug manufacturers, there are two types of companies: so-called originator companies that conduct R&D to discover and develop new drugs, and generic companies that replicate existing drugs.[2]

Originators are the main users of the patent system in the pharmaceutical industry. They rely heavily on patent protection to appropriate returns to their drugs. Originators are vertically integrated companies; most are large multinational companies active along the entire value chain from basic R&D to sales and marketing of their products. Originators include well-known companies such as Johnson & Johnson, Pfizer, Roche, Novartis, and Merck. For these companies, drug development is very expensive and highly uncertain. For originators, the patent system plays a crucial role in the development and commercialization of their products. This is especially true because they generally rely on a few top-selling prescription drugs, so-called blockbusters, to generate the bulk of their profits. Due to the importance of these blockbuster drugs for an originator's bottom line, they carefully guard their exclusivity and employ a range of (patent) strategies to extend exclusivity in scope and over time.[3]

The business model of generic companies consists instead of making a drug that is therapeutically equivalent to the originator product as soon as the originator loses exclusivity. Such loss of exclusivity generally occurs when a patent expires, or because a generic company successfully invalidates the relevant patents or avoids infringement. Generic companies can enter the market without incurring the large R&D investment incurred by originator companies since they replicate existing drugs. Generic companies can also rely on the safety and efficacy data generated by the originator in its preclinical and clinical trials to obtain market authorization (assuming there is no data exclusivity; see Section 16.5). This saves the generic companies most of the R&D investment associated with drug development and speeds up market entry substantially. That said, generic companies may also engage in innovation, mostly extensions of existing

---

[1] *Source*: OECD Health Expenditure Indicators.

[2] In the case of biologics (see Section 16.1.2), they are referred to as biosimilars or follow-on biologics. Note that unlike generics, biosimilars are not exact copies of the original biologic product because biologics and biosimilars are made using living organisms.

[3] A single blockbuster product can account for over half of a firm's total sales (EUCOM 2009, Table 2).

drugs to differentiate their products, for example, in the form of new formulations or dosages. Generic companies also use patents to protect their new products or processes. However, patent protection is generally far less important for them than for originators.

Originators and generic companies play different roles in the pharmaceutical industry. Originators introduce new drugs or new therapeutic uses of existing drugs, while generic companies offer them at much lower prices as soon as originators lose exclusivity. The substantial drop in price following generic entry puts pressure on originators to continue to innovate to benefit from exclusivity for new drugs. However, it also creates incentives for originators to use the patent system strategically to extend exclusivity to keep generic companies at bay for as long as possible.

While most of the competition in the pharmaceutical industry occurs between originators and generic companies, originators also compete against each other. This tends to occur in particularly lucrative therapeutic areas, where originators compete over who brings a new drug to market first. Being first can be extremely profitable as it implies some time-limited market exclusivity. Originators also compete by offering different drugs in a given therapeutic area that are to some extent substitutable. Once generic entry occurs, competition occurs mostly on price. However, originators are often able to capitalize on brand recognition and customer loyalty built during the period of patent exclusivity to soften competition even after generic entry occurs (Regan 2008).

There has been a long-standing and highly contentious policy debate about the role of patents in the pharmaceutical industry. On the one hand, new drugs can have enormous therapeutic value. For example, Gilead's breakthrough drug Sovaldi, which was approved in the United States in 2013, has made it possible to cure hepatitis C, a virus that can cause severe liver damage. The value of Sovaldi to people affected by hepatitis C is hard to overstate. However, Gilead was heavily criticized for charging $1,000 per pill or approximately $84,000 for a 12-week treatment necessary to cure the virus.[4] Despite its high price tag, people in developed countries may have access to the drug through their health insurance. However, the drug at this price is solidly out of reach for almost everyone in the developing world. Gilead can only charge such high prices because it benefits from regulatory and patent exclusivity.

Given the amounts of money at stake, it is not surprising that originators such as Gilead use a broad range of patenting strategies to avoid generic competition, including strategic patenting and patent litigation. Originators also use patents strategically against other originators, employing such strategies as defensive patenting to block any type of competition. In fact, shortly before Sovaldi was approved by US health regulators, Gilead was sued by Idenix Pharmaceuticals, an originator company focused on hepatitis C drug development, for infringement of patents that cover its own hepatitis C treatment.

Patents play yet another important role in the pharmaceutical industry. They support vertically disintegrated organization of R&D. So far, we simplified the pharmaceutical industry structure by distinguishing only between originators and generics. However, research-oriented independent drug-development and drug-discovery firms as well as independent research institutions and universities play an important role in

---

[4] https://www.npr.org/sections/health-shots/2013/12/30/256885858/-1-000-pill-for-hepatitis-c-spurs-debate-over-drug-prices.

the discovery and development of new drugs. They license their discoveries to originator firms that bring them to market. This industry-internal market for technology depends heavily on the availability of patent protection.

At this point, you may ask yourself why we need to devote an entire chapter of this textbook to the use of patents in the pharmaceutical industry. You will see in Part III that the patent system works very differently in different industries. In the pharmaceutical industry, the patent system is generally considered critical in allowing firms appropriate returns to their R&D investment. This chapter reviews the different reasons why the patent system assumes such a prominent role in the pharmaceutical industry. In particular, the chapter summarizes the discussion on the effect of patents on incentives for new drug development as well as on access to drugs. We will see that the role of patent protection is quite complex, in large part because of the strategic use of the patent system by originators to obtain and maintain exclusivity.

16.2 Pharmaceuticals: A Primer

We first provide a short introduction to the drug development process (we provided a brief overview already in Chapter 2). It will help us understand the interaction of the pharmaceutical industry with the patent system.

There are two classes of drugs: nonbiologic drugs and biologic drugs (also referred to as small and large molecules, respectively). Nonbiologic drugs consist of synthetic active ingredients, while biologics are synthetized from living organisms. For example, Humira, a drug to treat autoimmune disease, is a biologic drug. It is the world's best-selling drug, with a total of $20billion in sales in 2018 alone.[5] Nonbiologics include drugs such as Bayer's Aspirin, a popular over-the-counter pain reliever. Another nonbiologic is Eliquis, an anticoagulant to prevent blood clots. This drug, marketed jointly by Bristol-Myers Squibb and Pfizer, is among the world's best-selling drugs, with nearly $10billion in sales in 2018.[6] There are important differences between nonbiologic and biologic drugs that affect their development and manufacturing process as well as regulation by health authorities. While many blockbuster drugs are nowadays biologics, the majority of drugs are still nonbiologics. To keep our discussion as simple as possible, this chapter focuses on nonbiologics.

Drugs consist of active and inactive ingredients. The active ingredient, also referred to as compound, produces the therapeutic effect of the drug. Drugs can contain one or several active ingredients. Inactive ingredients have no therapeutic effect, but they can still affect a drug's effectiveness.

Originator companies conduct basic R&D to find new active ingredients that lead to the marketing of novel pharmaceutical products. They also conduct incremental innovation through which they improve existing drugs, for example, through new formulations or delivery methods. Such follow-on research can also lead to new therapeutic uses of existing active ingredients. Examples of such second uses include

[5] https://web.archive.org/web/20220729221323/https://truecostofhealthcare.org/pharmas-50-best-sellers/.
[6] Ibid.

active ingredients bromocriptine (original therapeutic indication: Parkinson's disease; second use indication: diabetes mellitus) or finasteride (original therapeutic indication: prostate hyperplasia; second use indication: hair loss).

The research, development, and regulatory approval process of new active ingredients is long and costly. While estimates differ, reasonable estimates suggest average costs of \$800million to \$1billion and a 10- to 12-year lag between early-stage research and market authorization (EUCOM 2009).[7]

The drug innovation process starts with basic research to discover a large number of candidate active ingredients to treat a particular disease. The most promising candidate molecules reach the preclinical stage, where they are tested for safety and efficacy in the laboratory and using animals. According to estimates, only 1 out of 5,000 such candidate active ingredients that enter the preclinical phase will be successful and eventually approved for therapeutic use (EUCOM 2009).[8]

The next step in the drug development process is to assess safety and efficacy in humans. This is done in so-called clinical trials. Regulators have to grant approval for a drug to move forward with clinical trials to ensure it is safe to test the drug in humans. If approved, clinical trials proceed in four phases:

Phase 1. At this stage, the drug is administered for the first time to humans. Only healthy individuals receive the drug at this point; the goal is to test the safety and efficacy of the candidate drug. Phase 1 clinical trials take, on average, 1–3 years, and only 1 out of 3 active ingredients survives this phase.

Phase 2. In this phase, the drug is administered to individuals who have the condition it is designed to treat, in order to test its efficacy. This stage often leads to changes in formulations and dosages. This phase takes 2–5 years, and again only 1 out of 3 drugs survives this phase.

Phase 3. This phase involves large-scale randomized control trials involving both individuals with and without the relevant condition. It is by far the most expensive stage in the drug-development process. This phase often leads to changes to the drug and the way it is administered. This stage takes, on average, 2–4 years, and 2 out of 3 drugs, on average, survive this phase.

Phase 4. This phase begins only after the drug has been approved by health regulators and is actively in use. The goal is to monitor and improve its safety and efficacy by analyzing interactions with other drugs and collecting more data on potential adverse reactions, (long-term) side effects, and efficacy. This stage usually also leads to further improvements of the drug and its administration. In some cases, the additional tests also serve to obtain regulatory approval for new indications of a drug (e.g., for pediatric use).

If a drug successfully completes Phase 3, it has to obtain market approval by regulators before it can be sold and administered to patients.

---

[7] For a review of different estimates, see Table 1 in DiMasi et al. (2016).
[8] The process is improving with the availability of a full genome map and access to high-speed computing. See Tranchero (2023) for a description of the search for target genes using big data methods.

The regulatory approval process differs across countries. In the United States, a new drug is approved by the US FDA through the NDA process. An NDA requires submission of all preclinical and clinical test data. Based on these data, the FDA decides whether to grant market approval. The process is very similar in Europe. Applicants file an application with the European Medicines Agency (EMA) to obtain EU-wide market authorization through the so-called centralized procedure. EMA provides a recommendation to the EC, which then grants market authorization.

Once a drug has been approved by national regulators, the World Health Organization (WHO) issues an international nonproprietary name (INN). For example, the INN denomination for the active ingredient in Solvaldi is sovosbuvir. Individual countries such as the United States, United Kingdom, France, and Japan use generic names that are usually identical to the INN.[9]

16.3 Pharmaceuticals and the Patent System

Patents play an important role in the pharmaceutical industry. The R&D and drug approval process described in the preceding section requires enormous investments that have to be recouped during the commercialization stage. Patents in combination with regulatory exclusivity are the main tools to achieve exclusivity during a limited period of time that enables originators to recover their investments.

Indeed, when asked about the effectiveness of patents for the protection of product innovations, companies in the pharmaceutical industry are more likely to report that patents are effective than in any other industry—see Figure 16.1 (Cohen et al. 2000).

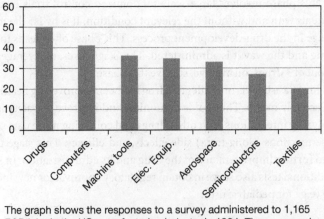

The graph shows the responses to a survey administered to 1,165 R&D labs in the US manufacturing industry in 1994. The survey asked 'respondents to report the percentage of their product ... innovations for which each appropriability mechanism had been effective in protecting the 'firm's competitive advantage from those innovations' during the prior three years.' Source: Cohen et al. (2000: Table 1).

Figure 16.1 Effectiveness of patents for product innovation.

[9] https://www.who.int/teams/health-product-and-policy-standards/inn.

Traditionally in the economics literature, the pharmaceutical industry was considered the textbook example of a discrete product industry, where one product is protected by a single patent with well-defined boundaries (Levin et al. 1987). However, this has changed substantially over time. As we will explain below, nowadays the patent landscape in the pharmaceutical industry has become much more complex, as have the products, especially biologics.

16.3.1 Patents and a Drug's Lifecycle

Patents play an important role throughout a drug's lifecycle. Originators begin filing patents on candidate compounds during the early stages of the drug development process. These patents cover the chemical compounds. The goal is to ensure freedom to operate for the originator for the development of the compound into a successful drug. Should the compound turn out to be successful in clinical trials, the patents will be critical to foreclose potential competitors. To achieve this goal, originators typically file patents with broad claims early on in the development process. That makes it more difficult for other originators to identify the specific candidate compounds and potentially create hurdles by patenting related aspects. As the drug development process progresses, originators routinely file many more patents on different aspects related to the drug, such as process or method patents.[10] Clinical trials often also reveal new information that leads to improvements in formulations or dosages.

Due to the often long lag between basic research and market authorization of a new drug, the patents on the original candidate compounds are usually filed many years before a drug reaches the market. As a result, the period of effective patent exclusivity is often much shorter than the 20-year patent term.[11] However, filing later creates risk as competitors might identify and patent the active ingredients in the meantime. There exist patent term extensions to partially compensate for the time lost due to the long drug development and regulatory approval process.[12]

16.3.2 Patents and Active Ingredients

During the drug development process, researchers search for a specific active ingredient. However, in a patent application, it is common not to seek protection for the specific active ingredient but a group of active ingredients that are related to the specific active ingredient since they might have the same effect. That can be achieved using so-called genus claims based on Markush structures. A Markush structure represents

---

[10] In the United States, such additional patents are often filed as so-called continuations. In the US patent system, continuations allow applicants to file additional patents that are based on a prior patent filing while preserving the earlier patent's priority date. At the EPO, applicants can file so-called divisional applications.

[11] Data for Europe and the United States suggest that the average effective period of exclusivity measured as the lag between the first sale of the drug and generic entry in a given market is around 12 years (EUCOM 2009, Hemphill and Sampat 2012).

[12] In the United States, a patent term extension of 5 years is available to compensate for the lengthy development and approval process. In Europe, a supplementary protection certificate (SPC) is available to also grant companies a maximum of 5 additional years of patent protection.

a collection of active ingredients, including the specific compound of interest. Compound patents often refer to and display such Markush structures where a single Markush structure can represent thousands of compounds.[13] This means that a given Markush structure does not uniquely identify the active ingredient protected by a given patent. In order to identify the patent that protects a given active ingredient, one has to identify the patents that cover a Markush structure that contains the active ingredient and to assess the specific examples provided in the patent to understand whether the active ingredient is, in fact, covered by the patent. In practice, this means that it can be challenging to identify the patents that protect a given drug.

16.3.3 Patent Types

There is a general distinction between product and process patents in pharmaceuticals. Product patents cover compounds, while process patents cover a range of subject matter, including production methods, formulations, dosages, and so forth.

Specific to pharmaceuticals, there is a related albeit more important distinction between so-called primary and secondary patents (see Table 16.1). Primary patents are patents that cover active ingredients. These patents are commonly filed during the early

Table 16.1 Patent Claim Types

Patent Type	Subject Matter	Description
Primary	Chemical compound	Active ingredients
Secondary	Processes/production methods	Methods of producing an active ingredient
	Formulation	Combination of known excipients (inactive substance) and active ingredients
	Concentrations/dosage	Therapeutic methods
	Salts	"Straightforward" derivatives of known active ingredients
	Isomers	Same molecular structure but different chemical structures
	Polymorph	Variations of known active ingredient with distinct physical properties
	Enantiomers	Nonidentical mirror images of known active ingredients
	Treatment methods	Use of a compound for treating a disease
	Second use	Different therapeutic use than originally intended
	Active metabolites/prodrugs/ester	Drug that is broken down inside the body to form an active drug (including modification of original active ingredient)

---

[13] Wagner et al. (2022) find that 23.7% of all pharmaceutical patent filings at the EPO between 1992 and 2008 contain a Markush structure.

stages of the drug development process and during the preclinical trial phase. Usually, originators file a large number of primary patents on all candidate compounds to ensure freedom to operate and to block potential competitors.

Secondary patents comprise product and process patents. Secondary process patents typically cover production processes and methods, formulations, dosages, and treatment methods. Secondary product patents usually cover alternative forms (such as salts or isomers) of existing compounds that themselves are protected by primary patents.

Kapczynski et al. (2012) found that among the secondary patents that protect drugs approved by the FDA between 1991 and 2005; 56% are formulation patents; 24% of patents cover salts, crystalline forms, and the like; and 63% of patents cover methods of use (the numbers add up to more than 100% because patents can cover more than one type of subject matter).

The combination of primary and secondary patents means that a given drug is usually protected by more than a single patent. Moreover, it means that patents that protect a given drug are filed at different stages of product development and a drug's lifecycle. Secondary patents are typically filed after primary patents and throughout a drug's entire lifecycle. Indeed, Kapczynski et al. (2012) find that most secondary patents are filed after FDA approval. Similarly, Abud et al. (2015) show that in Chile, nearly half of secondary patents are filed after drug approval by the Chilean health regulator. This has significant implications for the overall length and scope of patent protection of a given drug, which we discuss in more detail below in Section 16.7.1.

16.4 Patents and Generic Entry

Generic companies benefit from an abbreviated drug approval process. In the United States, this is referred to as abbreviated new drug application (ANDA), and in the EU, it is the abbreviated market authorization. It means that generic companies do not need to submit preclinical and clinical trial data to prove safety and efficacy. Instead, they only need to demonstrate *bioequivalence*, which means they need to demonstrate that the generic drug has the same therapeutic effect as the originator drug. This avoids duplication of clinical trials, substantially speeds up the approval process, and saves the generic company the significant expenses required by preclinical and clinical testing.

In some jurisdictions, the granting of market approval is contingent on the status of patent protection for a given drug. This is referred to as patent linkage. In the United States, for example, the FDA's Orange Book lists all relevant patents for a given drug that has received market authorization.[14] A generic drug is only approved if all of the patents that protect a drug have expired, the generic entrant can demonstrate noninfringement, or the generic company successfully invalidates the patents. In other words, market authorization of generics is contingent on the status of patent protection of the originator drug. Patent linkage creates a direct connection between market authorization of a drug and patent exclusivity. Other jurisdictions, such as the EU,

---

[14] The Orange Book does not contain biologics. Patents that protect biologics and that have been identified to biosimilar applicants are listed in the FDA's Purple Book.

India, or Brazil, do not recognize such linkage and regard market authorization as independent from patent exclusivity.

In the United States, the Drug Price Competition and Patent Term Restoration Act of 1984 (known as Hatch-Waxman Act) sets out different paths for approval for originator and generic drugs. They can enter the market if a drug is not protected by any patents listed in the Orange Book (Paragraph I certification), the relevant patents have already expired (Paragraph II certification), or they will expire at a later date (Paragraph III certification where the generic won't receive market authorization until the patents have expired). The Hatch-Waxman Act also provides incentives for generics to enter the market even before the expiration of patent exclusivity. This is done through the filing of a so-called Paragraph IV certification whereby the generic entrant demonstrates either non-infringement of the patents listed in the Orange Book or successfully invalidates them in court or through administrative proceedings.[15] In exchange for a successful Paragraph IV challenge, the generic company obtains 180 days of marketing exclusivity, that is, during those 180 days, no other generic company is granted market authorization. Empirical evidence on Paragraph IV challenges suggests that the 180-day exclusivity has a strong effect on the decision by generic companies to enter the market before patent exclusivity expires (Grabowksi et al. 2017).

16.5 Data Exclusivity

New drugs also benefit from regulatory exclusivity, which is distinct from patent exclusivity. Regulatory exclusivity results from restrictions imposed by regulators on the approval of competing (generic) drugs following the approval of a new drug. As such, regulatory exclusivity exists independently from patent protection. Regulators are able to impose such restrictions because originators and generic companies can only sell their drugs if they receive authorization to do so. While in most countries there are different types of regulatory exclusivity available to drug developers, we focus here on data exclusivity since it interacts directly with patent protection.

Data exclusivity restricts the generic company's ability to rely on existing clinical efficacy and safety data to obtain market authorization. Importantly, data exclusivity does not prevent the generic company from conducting its own tests and submitting its own test results to obtain market approval. However, this would take several years to complete and require the generic company to incur the enormous expense of conducting the necessary preclinical and clinical trials. Data exclusivity bars the generic company from relying on existing data for a limited period of time. It is worth emphasizing that data exclusivity applies irrespective of any existing patent protection. In the United

---

[15] Under a Paragraph IV challenge, the generic company has to notify the originator of its non-infringement or invalidity arguments. The originator then has 45 days to sue the generic company for patent infringement. If the originator files suit, the FDA automatically stays the ANDA for 30 months for the litigation to be resolved. This means that, in practice, in order to enter the market, the generic company usually has to invalidate the relevant patents in the course of the litigation initiated by the originator.

States, New Chemical Entity Exclusivity grants data exclusivity for 5 years after market launch.[16] This means that (generic) entrants cannot rely on the existing data for 5 years for regulatory approval. They could still generate their own data to undergo the approval process, although in practice, the cost and time it would take make the 5-year data exclusivity period an effective barrier to entry. In the EU, the EMA application, which regulates market approval of pharmaceuticals, grants 8 years of data exclusivity.[17] Data exclusivity exists in a large number of countries around the world, including developing countries. However, data exclusivity has not been harmonized internationally, and substantial differences exist in terms of length and scope of protection afforded by data exclusivity.

There are a number of differences between data exclusivity and patent exclusivity, which are summarized in Table 16.2. Patents have to be applied for and maintained in

Table 16.2 Differences between Data Exclusivity and Patent Exclusivity

Characteristic	Data Exclusivity	Patent Exclusivity
Default period of protection	5–11 years depending on jurisdiction	20 years (plus term extension depending on the jurisdiction)
Time period of protection	Fixed	Additional patents can be filed over time
Scope of protection	Data required for market approval	Flexible, multiple patents on same drug
Conditions	Automatically awarded upon market authorization	Granted by patent office in each jurisdiction separately
Fees	None	High (translation, filing, examination, grant fees, etc.)
Ongoing costs	No	Renewal fees payable in regular intervals; monitoring of market for infringement if no patent linkage
Invalidation	Not possible	Can be invalidated administratively and in court depending on the jurisdiction
Right against	Health regulators	Any infringing third party
Compulsory licenses	No	Yes

[16] In addition, 3 years of data exclusivity is available for new indications, the formulation or delivery system of an existing drug. While generics can seek FDA approval during the 3-year data exclusivity period, they are barred from doing so during the New Chemical Entity Exclusivity 5-year period. In practice, the availability of the 3-year period means that, in principle, several data exclusivity periods can be obtained for the same drug.

[17] The 2004 EU Directive 2004/27/EC, effective October 5, 2005, introduced an 8+2+1 formula. It grants 8 years of data exclusivity; during that time, generic producers can undertake testing and research required to prepare an application for market approval. However, they can only apply for market approval after the 8-year period has expired. Approval is granted only after an additional 2 years, where there is a 1-year extension available to originators for new therapeutic indications filed within the first 8 years of data exclusivity. Therefore, the minimum data exclusivity period is 8 years, with effective resulting market exclusivity of 10 years with the potential addition of 1 extra year.

force separately in each jurisdiction where protection is sought. Patents are also subject to uncertainty during the examination process and even after grant they can be invalidated. Moreover, patents have to be enforced by patent owners separately in each jurisdiction in which infringement occurs. Data exclusivity, in contrast, is automatically awarded upon receiving market authorization for a new drug. It is also automatically enforced by regulators without the need for the originator to intervene. The main disadvantage from an originator's perspective is that data exclusivity is limited to a fixed and relatively short number of years.

16.6 Patents, Drug Development, and Diffusion

It is clear that new drug development is very expensive and highly uncertain. Originators use patents in combination with regulatory exclusivity to exclude competitors, both other originators and generics. The upside of granting originators a temporary shield from competition is that it allows them to make positive profits off their new drugs. This, in turn, creates incentives for investment in the development of new drugs. On the other hand, patents restrict access to new drugs by allowing originators to choose in which markets drugs will be available and at which price. This trade-off can be easily understood by looking at the standard graph showing a monopolist's optimal pricing in Figure 16.2 (see also Chapter 11). The monopolist sets price p^M above marginal cost c, which allows the monopolist to obtain producer surplus (area A). However, this also leads to DWL (area B) because consumers who would be able to pay a price between p^M and c are excluded from the market. The producer surplus allows the monopolist to recover its investment in R&D. The DWL, however, means that a fraction of consumers are unable to obtain access to the drugs sold by the monopolist. The question therefore

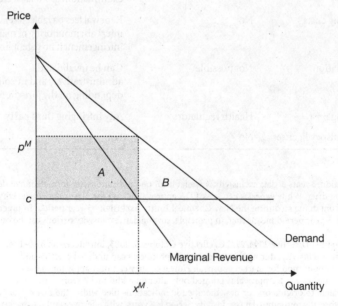

Figure 16.2 Profit maximization by monopolist.

is to what extent patent exclusivity promotes drug development, and affects the diffusion and availability of drugs.

This trade-off is clearly visible in the history of HIV/AIDS medication. Since the first cases of HIV/AIDS were detected in the early 1980s, enormous progress has been achieved in the treatment of the virus. While an infection with HIV was practically a death sentence throughout the 1980s, today, people with HIV have a life expectancy on par with HIV-negative individuals. Thanks to medical advances in the treatment of HIV, the disease has become a chronic condition that is kept in check through a single daily pill.

Despite the tremendous progress, access to anti-retroviral (ARV) medication has been fraught with controversy since the launch of the first HIV/AIDS medication azidothymidine (AZT) in 1987. The controversy intensified further when, in 1997, a combination of different ARVs, the so-called highly active anti-retroviral therapy (HAART), became available and dramatically reduced the mortality of people infected with HIV. Patents protecting HIV medication are at the core of this debate.

When AZT launched in 1987, it was sold under the brand name Retrovir by British originator Wellcome. It was available on the US market for an annual cost of US$8,000 (approximately US$18,000 today).[18] In the United States, the cost was covered by private medical insurance and publicly funded programs, in principle providing access to anyone infected with HIV. However, the same drugs were not affordable to the vast majority of people infected with HIV in the developing world. Patents prevented the production or importation of generic HIV medication in developing countries. The fact that Retrovir was patent-protected was particularly controversial because the active ingredient itself had been discovered much earlier in 1964 in the context of cancer research. However, the drug had proven ineffective in the treatment of cancer.[19]

The impact of patents on access to ARVs was significantly affected by the TRIPS agreement that came into effect in 1995. Before TRIPS, many developing countries did not grant patents on chemical compounds and had much shorter patent terms. However, as a result of TRIPS, developing countries saw themselves confronted with stringent patent rules that made it impossible to produce generic ARVs locally or import them from other countries. India was an exception as the country made use of the full 10-year transition period granted under TRIPS. It did not grant product patents until 2005. As a result, Indian generic companies were able to produce low-cost ARV medication, including the highly effective HAART combinations of different active ingredients. Indian generic company Cipla offered a triple-combination ARV for US$350 a year in 2001. The large price gap between originator ARVs and Cipla's generic ARV highlighted the impact of patents on drug pricing and access.[20] Originator companies argued that they required those high drug prices to recover their investment in R&D and to finance continued efforts to improve HIV/AIDS therapies. They were also reluctant to offer

---

[18] https://www.nytimes.com/1989/09/19/us/aids-drug-s-maker-cuts-price-by-20.html.

[19] https://www.independent.co.uk/arts-entertainment/rise-and-fall-azt-it-was-drug-had-work-it-brought-hope-people-hiv-and-aids-and-millions-company-developed-it-it-had-work-there-was-nothing-else-many-who-used-azt-it-didn-t-2320491.html.

[20] Frustrated with the high prices due to patent protection, Brazil and Thailand issued compulsory licenses in 2006 and 2007 to import and eventually produce generic ARVs. A compulsory license, which is legal under TRIPS, allows a government to produce a patented invention without the consent of the patent owner in exchange for payment of adequate compensation.

ARVs at lower prices in the developing world out of fear that it would eventually lead to lower prices in the lucrative markets in the industrialized world. However, the benefits to developing countries from access to cheap generics were enormous. Not only did life expectancy in sub-Saharan Africa increase dramatically, also GDP per capita grew significantly as a result from low-cost access to HIV/AIDS drugs (Tompsett 2020).

The example of HIV/AIDS medication illustrates the fundamental challenge in the discussion on the effect of pharmaceutical patents. If we want markets to provide incentives for investment in the development of new drugs, companies have to be able to set prices in a way to allow them to recoup their investment in R&D, as well as the drug development and approval process. However, any price above marginal cost limits access to potentially lifesaving drugs. Striking the right balance between these opposing forces is a difficult task that can have dramatic consequences for people's lives and well-being. This trade-off was also reflected in the Hatch-Waxman Act mentioned above. The law recognized on the one hand the benefits of generic competition by providing a clear pathway as well as incentives for generic entry, and a "safe harbor" provision to shield generics from infringement for development and testing purposes in preparation of applying for regulatory approval (the so-called Bolar exemption). On the other, it also recognized the need for originators to profit from their therapeutic advances by providing additional incentives in the form of patent term restoration and nonpatent, regulatory exclusivity.

In terms of the impact of pharmaceutical patents on incentives for R&D, the available empirical evidence is mixed. As we reviewed in Chapter 15, Kyle and McGahan (2012) found that stronger patent protection following the TRIPS agreement increased R&D directed at global diseases, but had no impact on R&D focused on diseases prevalent in developing countries (neglected diseases). Stronger patent rights in developing countries did not lead to more investment in research on diseases relatively more prevalent in these countries. In a similar vein, Qian (2007) found that there is no evidence stronger patent protection of pharmaceuticals leads to an increase in domestic innovative activity in the pharmaceutical industry except in high-income countries. These results suggest no change in innovative activity in response to changes in domestic pharmaceutical patent protection in developing countries.

Apart from the cross-country evidence, there is also more detailed evidence on the impact of TRIPS on innovative activities of local pharmaceutical companies in India. Dhar and Gopakumar (2006) found that the Indian pharmaceutical industry experienced an increase in R&D spending, driven mainly by the large players in the market for generics, Ranbaxy and Dr. Reddy's. Indian generics producers have developed new generic drugs and novel drug-delivery systems since the adoption of the TRIPS agreement. They also strengthened their position in the global contract research and manufacturing markets, and engaged more in collaborations and alliances with foreign originator companies. That said, despite increased R&D spending and domestic patenting activities by Indian generics producers, so far there has been little success with the development of genuinely new drugs (Athreye et al. 2009). Overall, little evidence suggests that strengthened patent protection caused domestic Indian pharmaceutical companies to switch from manufacturing generics to becoming originator companies.

The evidence on the impact of patent protection on prices is overall less ambiguous. One way to understand the impact of patents on prices is to see what happens when originators lose exclusivity and generic entry occurs. Data for Europe indicate that once generic entry occurs, prices drop, on average, by 25% within 1 year and decline further over time (EUCOM 2009). However, there is also evidence that the effect of patents on prices is heterogenous across drugs. Patents increase prices the most in lucrative therapeutic areas. Using US data, Reiffen and Ward (2006) show that the first generics company entering the market for a given drug is able to charge significant mark-ups over cost (20–30%). Mark-ups persist even when there are multiple entrants and only go to zero when 10 or more competitors exist. Larger therapeutic markets attract more entrants and generics enter the market faster. This creates more competition faster, intensifying competition and reducing mark-ups. In contrast, mark-ups are more likely to persist in less lucrative markets as they do not attract sufficient entry by generic competitors.

These findings are consistent with data for Europe that indicate generic entry occurs within 1 year of loss of exclusivity for only around 50% of drugs (EUCOM 2009), where entry is highly correlated with the sales value of the drug that lost exclusivity. Interestingly, the drop in drug price is due to price competition among generic companies. Originators often maintain their high prices by targeting the segment of the market that is less price-sensitive (Regan 2008). The lack of price sensitivity is the result of brand recognition and customer loyalty that the originator was able to build during the period of patent exclusivity. That said, originators still experience a significant decrease in their market share and revenue following generic entry. These results show on the one hand that generic entry leads to large price drops but only if competition among generic producers occurs. The absence of patents in itself does not guarantee low mark-ups. Instead, entry and ensuing competition bring down price–cost margins, and the degree to which a market attracts entry depends on its size and hence expected profitability.

Alternatively, we can also ask directly what happens to drug prices when patent protection is introduced. Duggan et al. (2016) pose this question in the context of the introduction of product patents in India to comply with the TRIPS agreement. Their findings indicate that the introduction of product patents led only to modest price increases. These relatively minor effects of product patents are to some extent explained by specific provisions of the TRIPS agreement, such as the threat of mandatory licensing, price regulation, the fact that generic producers that were manufacturing a drug before 2005 in India could continue to do so even if a patent was later granted. Potential difficulties with patent enforcement may have also constrained patent owners' ability to increase prices despite increased patent protection. Goldberg (2010) arrives at a similar conclusion. Based on empirical evidence for India by Chaudhuri et al. (2006), Goldberg argues that product patents are unlikely to lead to higher prices on pharmaceuticals in developing countries because of lower purchasing power, existing price controls, and other regulation. However, this also means that it is difficult to isolate the effect of patents on prices from these other effects. It is likely that in the absence of these other factors, the introduction of product patents could have had much larger effects on prices. These explanations also omit what is perhaps the most important reason for the limited impact of TRIPS on prices: India's TRIPS implementation excluded compound patents with priority dates prior to 1995. Sampat and Shadlen (2015) show that this effectively limited available patent protection for a significant number of drugs. Obviously, as time passes, newer drugs will be able to obtain compound protection in India, likely resulting in larger effects on prices.

While prices for patented drugs are lower in developing countries, prices fall far short from adjusting fully for income differences. Schweitzer and Comanor (2011) analyze prices of the 30 top-selling drugs in the United States over the period 2000–2007. They find that for patented drugs, middle-income countries pay, on average, 52% of the price charged in industrialized countries and developing countries pay 27%. For drugs for which there is generic competition (hence prices are lower in industrialized countries), middle-income countries pay 71% and developing countries 41% of what industrialized countries pay. For WHO-essential drugs, middle-income countries pay 28% and developing countries 6%. The results suggest that the price of generic drugs is less sensitive to differences in per capita income across countries than patented drugs, presumably because prices are already much lower.

So far, our discussion of the empirical evidence suggests that patents have a mixed effect on R&D and that they lead to significantly higher prices if they prevent generic competition. This leaves the question of whether patent protection accelerates or hinders access to new drugs. Berndt and Cockburn (2014) looked at how fast new drugs approved by the US FDA became available in the United States, Germany, and India. Drugs were launched fastest in the United States followed by Germany: 93% of drugs were launched in the United States within 3 years of market approval and 77% in Germany within the same period. In India, by contrast, only 30% were launched within 3 years, and even within 5 years only 43% had been made available. The median launch lag in the United States is less than 2 months, about a year in Germany, but around 5 years in India. While market potential appears to be the main factor, patent protection also affects launch decisions by originators. The data show that drugs introduced in India quickly faced generic competition, while there is no evidence for similarly fast generic entry in the United States and Germany. The evidence indicates that relatively weaker patent protection and enforcement may lead to no or delayed launch of new drugs, but conditional on launch, there is much faster entry of generic competition, which leads to lower prices. Berndt et al. (2011) offer similar results for a broader set of countries. The results also show that new drugs are significantly less likely to be launched in countries that afford weaker patent protection to pharmaceuticals. The results therefore suggest that weaker patent protection lessens incentives for originator companies to launch new drugs in a given market. Related analysis also suggests more specifically that the availability of product patents for pharmaceuticals increases the accessibility of new drugs (Cockburn et al. 2016).

16.7 Strategic Patenting, Litigation, and Settlement

Exclusivity obtained from primary patents filed during the early stages of the drug development process is usually short-lived because of the lengthy drug development and approval process. Regulatory exclusivity in the form of data exclusivity is equally short, offering only a few years of protection from generic competition after a new drug is launched in the market. As a result, originators resort to a set of strategies to extend both the period of exclusivity and scope of protection that they benefit from in order to limit competition beyond that granted by primary patents and regulatory exclusivity. Although originators employ a range of approaches to keep competition at bay, here we focus on patent strategies. These strategies consist of the strategic filing of patents and the strategic use of patent litigation.

16.7.1 Strategic Patenting

Strategic patenting is aimed at both generic entry and competition by other originators and achieves multiple goals. It helps companies secure freedom to operate, which enables them to conduct further R&D on the drug and related processes. Freedom to operate is particularly important in the pharmaceutical context because of the long drug development and approval process. Strategic patenting also helps directly preserve market exclusivity, which can have a large effect on a drug's overall profitability. Strategic patenting can also facilitate bargaining in IP disputes, (cross-)licensing, access to patent pools, and the financing of new drug development.

Figure 16.3 shows examples of two distinct types of patent filing strategies. The figure shows the share of patent filings that cover a given drug filed over time, where time is measured relative to the filing date of the first patent that protects the drug. In order to understand the figure, it is useful to remind ourselves that most drugs are protected by several patents where the different patents protect different aspects of the drug (see Table 16.1).

In Figure 16.3(a), we see that over 90% of all of the patents that protect a given drug are filed prior to the launch of the drug in the market. This type of patenting strategy is referred to as *prelaunch filing strategy*. Such a prelaunch strategy is often used as a form of defensive patenting to secure freedom to operate. The goal for the originator is primarily to prevent another originator from developing a related drug. Usually, the patents cover compounds similar to the originator's own candidate compounds. These similar compounds are of particular interest to other originators as they may allow them to block the originator or allow them to develop competing drugs. Here, patenting can also serve as a way of creating prior art, and its disclosure may lower the commercial interest in the compound for potential competitors since patent protection will be harder to achieve for them. Such defensive patents can sometimes also be used for (cross-) licensing negotiations.

Figure 16.3(b) shows a *postlaunch filing strategy*. Here, the majority of patents are filed after the product is launched. The graph also shows that under a postlaunch filing strategy a significant share of patents are filed even after the first patent has already expired. The postlaunch filing strategy has the obvious objective of extending the length of patent exclusivity, often by a very significant amount of time. This strategy can also help insure originators against potential loss of exclusivity should a primary patent be invalidated by a competitor or a generic entrant.

To a certain extent, the filing patterns in Figure 16.3 are not surprising. Indeed, one would expect to see the continuous filing of patents over the entire lifecycle of a drug. That is because companies continue to do research on the drug far beyond the initial R&D phase, throughout clinical trials and even after the drug is successful in the

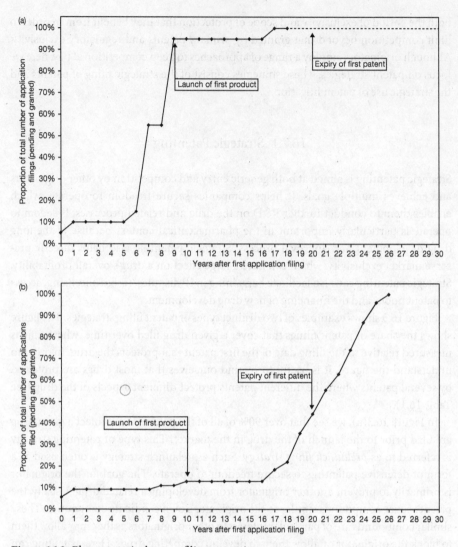

Figure 16.3 Pharmaceutical patent filing strategies.

market. This poses a challenge for regulators and policymakers: How can we distinguish between an innovation that is a complement to the existing drug or a genuine follow-on innovation, as opposed to a purely strategic move to extend patent protection in length or breadth?

So-called second-generation products illustrate this challenge. Second-generation drugs usually have the same therapeutic effect as the first-generation drug. For example, the second-generation product consists of a new formulation where the active ingredient is merely an isomer of the first-generation active ingredient. The second-generation drug will also be patented and launched shortly before the first-generation product loses patent exclusivity. The originator may even withdraw its first-generation drug from the market and invest heavily in marketing, while it still benefits from market exclusivity to switch users from its first- to second-generation drug before any generic

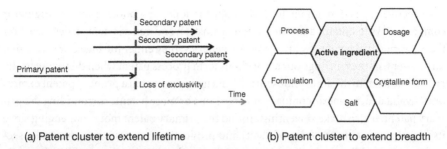

(a) Patent cluster to extend lifetime   (b) Patent cluster to extend breadth

Figure 16.4 Patenting strategies using secondary patents.

entry for the first-generation product occurs. This can help originators avoid significant price drops for the second-generation drug if it won't be perceived as a perfect substitute for the first-generation drug. This strategy is referred to as *evergreening*. Patent protection of the modified active ingredient, combinations of active ingredients, dosages, or formulations involved in such second-generation products plays a crucial role in this strategy. And even if patent protection cannot prevent competition for the first-generation product once its patent exclusivity expires, the presence of a second-generation product can make entry less attractive.

Secondary patents play an important role in patenting strategies employed by originators. As shown in Figure 16.4, secondary patents are used to (1) extend the overall length of patent protection and (2) increase the scope of patent protection. Objective (1) is achieved by distributing patent filings over time, as illustrated in Figure 16.4(a). Each patent can be maintained in force for at least the statutory patent term of 20 years plus potential term adjustments depending on the jurisdiction. Empirically, the effect of secondary patents on the length of patent exclusivity can be substantial. Data on secondary patents in the United States suggest that, on average, secondary patents have the potential to extend exclusivity by 4–5 years (Kapczynski et al. 2012). Amin and Kesselheim (2012) examine how secondary patents were used to extend the patent life of two originator HIV drugs, Abbott's Kaletra (lopinavir/ritonavir) and Norvir (ritonavir). They find that the two drugs are protected by a total of 108 patents, where the majority consists of a diverse range of secondary patents.[21] The evidence suggests that the use of secondary patents had the potential to extend the length of patent protection by at least 12 years past the expiration of the original compound patents.

However, Hemphill and Sampat (2012) show that the effective extension of patent protection achieved by secondary patents, in practice, is limited because generic companies are more likely to successfully challenge these patents through Paragraph IV entry. The Amin and Kesselheim (2012) case study also illustrates the difficulty of distinguishing between genuine follow-on innovation and purely strategic patenting. The drugs were originally sold as a soft-gelatin capsule, which was later replaced by a heat-stable tablet. This new formulation was patented and therefore has the potential to extend the length of patent exclusivity for these two drugs. That said, it also undoubtedly represents an improvement that can be of value to consumers despite no therapeutic advance in the drug itself.

---

[21] The majority of these patents are not listed in the Orange Book.

Objective (2) is best understood through the following quote from an originator company: "[W]e obtained an injunction against several generic companies based on these [secondary] patents by 'trapping' the generics: they either infringe our crystalline form patent, or they infringe our amorphous form process patent when they convert the crystalline form to the amorphous form."[22] That means, even if a primary patent expires or is invalidated, a generic company infringes one or more patents surrounding the primary patent. It also makes inventing around the primary patent more challenging since its variations (e.g., in the form of a salt) and production processes are covered by secondary patents. Ultimately, the objective is to create legal uncertainty by filing "as many patents as possible on all areas of the drug and create a 'minefield' for the generic to navigate. All generics know that very few patents in that larger group will be valid and infringed by the product they propose to make, but it is impossible to be certain prior to launch that your product will not infringe and you will not be the subject of an interim injunction."[23]

In practice, these objectives are achieved through a specific patenting strategy or combination of different patenting strategies including:

1. *Blanketing/flooding.* The originator company protects a drug in unsystematic ways by filing a large number on a wide range of aspects related to a given drug.
2. *Fencing/surrounding.* The originator files patents on different technological solutions for similar functional outcomes, effectively surrounding the patents that protect the basic active ingredient with other patents;
3. *Networking/clustering.* The originator creates an overlapping patent portfolio, akin to a web of patents, which makes it harder for generic competitors to enter with a generic version in the form of, for example, a salt or crystalline form of the active ingredient.

While the strategic use of secondary patents helps originators prevent competition, secondary patents are generally perceived as "weaker" than primary patents. The intuition is simple: Primary patents protect novel chemical compounds where patentability requirements are more easily verified, as opposed to the range of subject matter covered by secondary patents. Frakes and Wasserman (2023) show that as a result of these differences, time constraints faced by patent examiners in the examination process are more likely to limit their ability to weed out low-quality (i.e., invalid) secondary patents, rather than primary patents. Empirically, this translates into a higher likelihood of grant and invalidation of secondary patents relative to primary patents in litigation or administrative invalidity proceedings. According to data for Europe, the ratio of primary to secondary patents is 1:13 for pending patents, but only 1:5 for issued patents (EUCOM 2009). This, in turn, means that there is still significant uncertainty involved in patent protection. Evidence for the United States also shows that strategic patenting is more prevalent the higher the branded drug's sales (Kapczynski et al. 2012). This creates a situation where on the one hand originators engage more in strategic patenting for high-sales drugs by relying on secondary patents. On the other, generic companies are more likely to target these drugs due to the lucrative market opportunity and the legal vulnerability of

[22] Anonymous pharmaceutical company quoted in EU Commission (2009).
[23] Ibid.

secondary patents (Hemphill and Sampat 2012). See Box 16.1 for an important legal decision on secondary patenting in India.

Box 16.1 Secondary Patents: India's Glivec Decision

In April 2013, the Indian Supreme Court confirmed the Indian Patent Office's rejection of Novartis's patent application for Glivec. Glivec is a highly effective drug to treat chronic myeloid leukemia, a lethal disease if untreated. As such, Glivec has enormous therapeutic value to cancer patients around the world. The annual cost of Glivec in the United States at the time (in 2013) was around US$60,000, a price far beyond the reach of almost everyone in developing countries (Padula et al. 2016).

The legal question the court addressed concerned the interpretation of a clause in India's patent law (Section 3d of India's Patent Act). The clause states that "the mere discovery of a new form of a known substance which does not result in the enhancement of the known efficacy of that substance or the mere discovery of any new property or new use for a known substance or of the mere use of a known process, machine or apparatus unless such known process results in a new product or employs at least one new reactant" is not an invention and hence does not meet the requirements for patentability. This provision was added to the Indian Patent Act in 2005 as part of India's TRIPS implementation. Because TRIPS required the granting of pharmaceutical product patents, the goal of the provision was to limit the patentability of secondary patents. The active ingredient of Glivec is indeed a new form (a beta crystalline form) of a known active ingredient (imatinib mesylate). Therefore, the court held that it was not patentable. The ruling allowed generic companies to manufacture Glivec in India and to offer it at a fraction of the price charged by Novartis.

The decision upheld the constitutionality of Section 3d, which effectively restricts the ability of originators to obtain secondary patents on new forms of known active ingredients. Not surprisingly, the decision evoked strong reactions from different stakeholders and received widespread attention in the popular press around the world. Novartis cautioned that this decision would affect its decisions to invest in India and impact on its decision to introduce new drugs in India. Other stakeholders such as *Médecins Sans Frontières* (Doctors without Borders) came out in strong support of the ruling, highlighting its importance for guaranteeing access to affordable drugs in developing countries.

References
https://www.nytimes.com/2013/04/05/opinion/the-supreme-court-in-india-clarifies-law-in-novartis-decision.html?_r=0.
https://www.economist.com/schumpeter/2013/04/01/a-fools-game.
https://web.archive.org/web/20171012060037/
https://www.reuters.com/article/us-india-novartis-patent/novartis-loses-landmark-india-cancer-drug-patent-case-idUSBRE93002I20130401.

16.7.2 Litigation and Settlement

Originators also rely on the threat of litigation to avoid generic entry. In the United States, due to patent linkage, a filing of a Paragraph IV certification by a generic company (see Section 16.4) is considered an act of patent infringement. It therefore allows the originator to sue the generic company for infringement to deter it from market entry. In jurisdictions without patent linkage, generic companies can (threaten to) enter the market. To deter them or force them out of the market, originators rely on litigation in court. High litigation costs, as, for example, in the United States or the United Kingdom, and a significant threat of a preliminary injunction (which would force a generics company to stop sales of the drug), as, for example, in Germany, can help deter market entry by generics.

However, patent exclusivity involves uncertainty regarding patent infringement and validity. This creates considerable uncertainty for originators. This is especially true once the primary patents have expired and patent exclusivity relies on secondary patents. Panattoni (2011) looks at the stock market returns of originator companies following court decisions on Paragraph IV–related validity challenges in the United States. When originators won the court case, they experienced large positive cumulative abnormal returns. In contrast, when they lost, they experienced similarly large negative returns. This suggests that there is indeed substantial uncertainty around patent exclusivity and that such exclusivity is valuable.

Apart from using patent litigation to deter entry by generics, originators also use the settlement of litigation to delay entry by generics. Under this practice, known as *pay for delay* or *reverse payment*, originators pay the generic companies to settle the patent litigation. In exchange for the payment, the parties agree on a delayed market entry date for the generic version of the originator drug. The originator and generic company maximize their joint payoff by allowing the originator to remain a monopolist and share the monopoly profits until the patent expires (a straightforward result of the fact that monopoly profits exceed joint duopoly profits). Alternatively, they can agree on a payment to delay generic entry in combination with a license for the generic company to enter at a future date prior to the expiration of the relevant patent.[24] This can be profit-maximizing as a form of price discrimination. Such a settlement is attractive to both the originator and generic company because if the generic company instead successfully invalidates the originator patent, other generic companies are free to enter the market as well (in the United States only after the 180-day marketing exclusivity granted by the Hatch-Waxman Act). As a result, profits for the generic entrant would erode quickly.[25]

[24] Such entry can take the form of a licensing agreement that allows the generics company to sell a so-called authorized generic. An authorized generic is authorized by the originator and obtains market authorization under the originator's original FDA approval. As such, it is distinct from generic entry.

[25] In the United States, the 180-day exclusivity granted to the first generic entrant as a result of a Paragraph IV challenge creates strong incentives for the originator and the first generic entrant to use a settlement to avoid entry by other generic companies (Edlin et al. 2015). This is because the FDA does not grant market approval to any other generic entrant until after the first generic company has entered the market. If the pay-for-delay agreement delays that entry sufficiently, de facto no entry by other generics occurs before the patent expires.

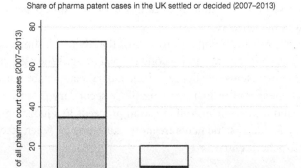

Figure 16.5 shows all patent cases involving pharmaceutical (for human use) patents filed at the Patents Court of the High Court of Justice of England and Wales between 2007 and 2013. Other: includes cases involving universities and a case only involving generic companies. All categories include infringement, invalidity, and declaratory non-infringement actions.

Figure 16.5 Pharma case outcomes in the UK by types of litigants.

In 2013, the US Supreme Court held in *FTC v. Actavis* that such pay-for-delay settlements violate US antitrust law if the purpose of the settlement is to avoid competition.[26] The court held that if the originator makes a large unexplained payment to the generic company, the settlement is considered anti-competitive. This decision marked a major shift in the perception of pay-for-delay settlements by antitrust agencies. In the case, generic manufacturer Actavis had applied for Paragraph IV certification to market a generic version of originator Solvay's AndroGel, a topical testosterone treatment. In response, Solvay sued Actavis for patent infringement. The parties settled their dispute in 2006 and agreed that Actavis would not enter the market until 2015, while Solvay's patent on AndroGel was set to expire in 2021. In exchange for the agreement, Actavis received an annual payment of between US$19 and 30 million from Solvay. If the Federal Trade Commission (FTC) had not prevailed in court, the settlement would have delayed generic entry by up to 9 years at substantial cost to consumers.

Empirically, according to the EC (2009), only a quarter of settlements involve any agreements to delay generic entry and a payment from originator to generic company. Figure 16.5 shows the outcomes of court cases involving pharmaceutical patents in the United Kingdom broken down by party type and case outcome. Figure 16.5 suggests that settlements occur in about half of all cases where originators litigate against other originators or generics. The figure does not tell us anything about whether these settlements involved any payments in exchange for delayed market entry. It does show, however, that settlements are equally likely in litigation between originators and litigation between originators and generic companies. This indicates that while pay-for-delay

[26] *FTC v. Actavis, Inc.*, 570 US 136 (2013).

settlements do occur, they are unlikely to dominate the outcome of patent litigation between originators and generics.

That said, Hemphill and Sampat (2013) show that there is a direct connection between pay-for-delay settlements and secondary patenting. When generic companies challenge originator patents, challenges of secondary patents are much more likely to settle than challenges of primary patents. Since secondary patents are more likely to be found invalid or not infringed if litigation proceeds to a judgment, the evidence suggests that pay-for-delay settlements are more likely to occur when secondary patents are the barrier to generic entry.

16.8 Summary

Patents play a crucial role in the pharmaceutical industry, perhaps more so than in any other industry. The fundamental trade-off inherent in the patent system is also particularly apparent in the pharmaceutical industry. Temporary exclusivity granted by the patent system allows originators to recoup their significant investments in the development of new drugs. However, exclusivity also means that drugs will sell at prices far above their marginal cost. This affects access to drugs. The empirical evidence suggests that this creates problems for developing countries both in terms of providing incentives for investment in diseases that are more prevalent in the developing world and access to drugs only available at high prices in markets within the industrialized world.

Strategic patenting is common in the pharmaceutical industry. This is not surprising in light of the critical role that patent exclusivity plays in securing substantial profits associated with individual drugs. Originators rely on different patenting strategies to secure their own freedom to operate and prevent competition from other originators and generics. Secondary patents are the main tool used by originators to extend patent exclusivity both in length and scope. In principle, any additional exclusivity gained through strategic patenting might also help incentivize originators to invest in R&D. However, any delay in generic entry is extremely costly to consumers and can significantly affect access.

Finally, the chapter also reviewed the anti-competitive use of settlements between originators and generic companies. Here, originators and generic companies effectively collude to maximize joint profits and foreclose other generic entrants. This situation only arises because the originator's monopoly position in the market hinges on patent exclusivity.

17

Software, Business and Financial Methods, Open Source, and Artificial Intelligence

---

Learning Objectives

After reading this chapter, you will be able to understand and explain the following concepts:

- The basic characteristics of the R&D and product development process in the software industry
- The legal and policy debate around patent protection of software as well as, business and financial methods in the United States
- The role the patent system plays in the software industry
- The effect of software, business method, and financial method patents on innovation in the software industry
- The characteristics of open-source software and its relation to proprietary software
- The current debate on the interaction between AI and the patent system

---

17.1 Introduction

In September 2014, Data Engine Technologies sued Google alleging that Google Sheets infringed six patents, known as "tab patents."[1] The patents "claim a method of implementing a notebook-tabbed interface, which allows users to easily navigate through three-dimensional electronic spreadsheets."[2] As an example of the claimed invention, Figure 17.1 which was included in patent US 5,590,259, shows an "electronic spreadsheet system [that] includes a notebook interface having a plurality of notebook pages, each of which contains a spread of information cells." To understand the invention that these patents covered, consider Claim 12 of patent US 5,590,259, which the district court considered as representative of the claimed invention that was asserted against Google:

> In an electronic spreadsheet system for storing and manipulating information, a computer-implemented method of representing a three-dimensional spreadsheet on a screen display, the method comprising:

---

[1] The patents asserted are US5,303,146, US5,416,895, US5,590259, US5,623,591, US5,784,545, US6,282,551.
[2] *Data Engine Technologies LLC v. Google LLC*, 906 F.3d 999, 1003 (Fed. Cir. 2018).

The Economics of Innovation and Intellectual Property. Bronwyn H. Hall and Christian Helmers, Oxford University Press.
© Oxford University Press 2024. DOI: 10.1093/oso/9780197630914.003.0017

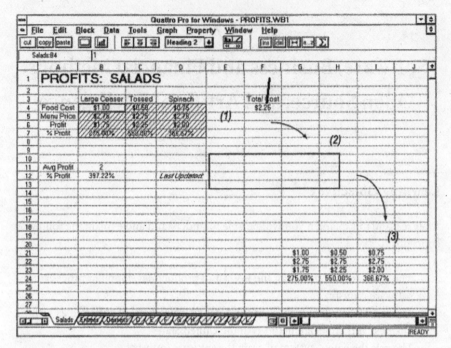

Figure 17.1 US patent 5,590,259.

displaying on said screen display a first spreadsheet page from a plurality of spreadsheet pages, each of said spreadsheet pages comprising an array of information cells
arranged in row and column format, at least some of said information cells storing
user-supplied information and formulas operative on said user-supplied information,
each of said information cells being uniquely identified by a spreadsheet page identifier, a column identifier, and a row identifier. . . .

Clearly, from today's perspective, this invention seems obvious. However, the patent
was filed in 1992. As strange as it may seem today, at the time, this was considered a
new idea. The US CAFC stated that "[a]lthough these spreadsheet interfaces have become ubiquitous, *Quattro Pro*, the first commercial embodiment of the claimed invention, was highly acclaimed as having revolutionized three-dimensional electronic
spreadsheets."[3]

The district court held that the patents were invalid because the claims were directed
to an abstract idea and hence not patentable under Section 101 of the US Patent Act.[4]
However, the CAFC reversed the district court's decision stating that Claim 12 cited
above is "directed to more than a generic or abstract idea as it claims a particular manner
of navigating three-dimensional spreadsheets, implementing an improvement in electronic spreadsheet functionality"[5] and remanded the case back to the district court.
The district court then found the patents not to be infringed by Google because Google

---

[3] 906 F.3d at 1004.
[4] The district court's decision only applied to four out of the six patents; the other two had been withdrawn
from the lawsuit.
[5] 906 F.3d at 1011.

Sheets at the time lacked three-dimensionality (three-dimensionality here means a "multipage" spreadsheet).[6]

The patents asserted against Google cover a software—or so-called computer implemented-—invention. Software patents have been a highly controversial topic since they started to emerge in the United States in the early 1970s. There are at least two reasons for the controversy.

First, the basic question whether patents should be available at all to protect software is highly disputed from a legal perspective. The legal dispute centers on the question of whether software is merely an abstract (mathematical) concept. If so, software would fall under one of the "judicial exceptions" to patent eligibility and be categorically excluded from patentability. There is also a good economic argument for exempting abstract mathematical concepts from patentability: Because of their wide applicability in a vast range of areas (some not yet known), the gap between private and social returns is particularly large.

Second, software as a technology is fundamentally different from other technologies such as pharmaceuticals or mechanical devices. Modern software consists of millions of lines of code that have to interact with lots of other components in often highly intricate ways. New code often builds and improves on existing code, that is, innovation is cumulative and sequential. As a result, software is highly complex. This makes it more difficult to precisely define the boundaries of what is claimed to be new in a patent. This undermines a patent's notice function, that is, a patent's ability to communicate its boundaries to the public. Furthermore, it increases the transaction costs of accessing and using different parts of existing software if they are owned by many different actors. This involves identifying all the relevant patents that need to be licensed, negotiating license agreements or inventing around.

Moreover, the software development process and innovation cycle are usually very short, meaning that software quickly becomes obsolete, often even before a patent is granted due to the long lag in granting patents. However, once granted, a patent can remain in place for up to 20 years counting from the filing date. As such, patent protection for software creates specific challenges, which reflect at least, in part, the fact that the current patent system was created in the late 18th century for the purposes of protecting very different types of inventions. As a result, it struggles to accommodate far more complex and fast-evolving technologies such as software.

Open-source software shows how an alternative to proprietary software looks like. Open-source developers commit to making their source code freely available, which enables others to access, use, and modify the code resulting in the free sharing of software. It turns out, however, that open-source and proprietary software are more closely linked than what one might think. They are often used as complements, not as substitutes. Each has advantages, and one is unlikely to completely crowd out the other.

There is also a closely related debate about so-called business method patents (including financial method patents). These patents protect the myriad ways of conducting business, these days mostly online. Here, the debate on the merits of granting patents on business methods has been even more contentious. Critics of business method patents argue that they overwhelmingly protect obvious and often trivial ways of conducting

---

[6] The decision was again appealed, but this time upheld by the CAFC.

business and often simply protect the obvious idea of moving existing and already widespread business practices online. Instead of protecting technical solutions to technical problems, business method patents merely protect commercial practices. Critics contend that by granting patent protection on these ideas, patent owners potentially acquire extremely broad exclusivity over ideas that do not merit exclusivity through patent protection. The counterargument is that business methods generate enormous returns for companies, and their implementation usually requires a technical solution and investment.

Figure 17.2 shows the share of software and business method filings in the United States over time. There has been a dramatic increase, with the increase coinciding with the spread of personal computers and the internet. The graph also indicates when important legal decisions occurred concerning the patentability of software. Some of these decisions appear to have had a significant impact on software and business method patent filings.

The debates on software and business method patents have been largely taking place in the United States and Europe. However, the issue has also received attention in larger developing countries, especially India, which has a large thriving software service industry. While these debates have been going on for several decades, they are far from settled. If anything, there has been renewed interest recently due to the fast-increasing importance of machine learning and AI across the entire economy. In light of the ongoing and extensive debate concerning software patents in the legal sphere and the practical realm, it is surprising that the economics literature has relatively little empirical evidence to offer on the issue.

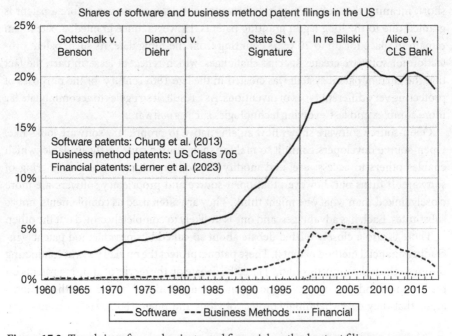

Figure 17.2 Trends in software, business and financial method patent filings.

This chapter reviews the debates about software and business method patents. It also covers the emerging discussion of the link between the patent system and AI. While this chapter focuses on patent protection, in practice, software is protected by a range of formal and informal appropriation mechanisms, including copyright, design patents, trade secrets, and contract law as well as network effects and first-mover advantage. Some of these alternative appropriation mechanisms are reviewed in our discussion of OSS. The protection of software through copyright is covered in Chapter 13.

17.2 The Legal Background

In 2009, Donald Knuth, a renowned computer scientist at Stanford University and the developer of the widely popular open-source TeX typesetting computer language, wrote a letter to Alison Brimelow, then president of the EPO, in which he states that every algorithm is a mathematical idea and, as such, should not be patent-eligible. He attached his letter from 1994 that was sent to the USPTO in which he emphasized that "[t]he basic algorithmic ideas that people are now rushing to patent are so fundamental, the result threatens to be like what would happen if we allowed authors to have patents on individual words or concepts. . . . Algorithms are exactly as basic to software as words are to writers, because they are the fundamental building blocks needed to make interesting products." He further states that "[w]hen I think of the computer programs I require daily to get my work done, I cannot help but realize that none of them would exist today if software patents had been prevalent in the 1960s and 1970s. Changing the rules now will have the effect of freezing progress at essentially its current level."

While there has been enormous progress in software development since Knuth's prediction despite a large increase in software patenting as seen in Figure 17.2, it is not possible to know what the software industry would look like today if software had been exempt from patentability. This illustrates one of the core problems with the debate on software patents. Proponents of software patents point to the spectacular developments in the software industry over recent decades, while critics argue that those developments occurred despite the existence of software patents, not because of it. Given the difficulty of assessing the counterfactual (what would have happened had software patents not been granted) empirically, this debate is far from settled.

Before getting any further into the debate on software patents, it is important to define what is meant by *software patent*. Conceptually, it may appear obvious what constitutes a software patent: a patent that claims an invention implemented through software. In practice, "pure" software patents are relatively rare since most computer-enabled inventions contain both software and nonsoftware elements. The difficulty of drawing a clear line between software as a technology and everything else is not surprising considering that software is a general-purpose technology (GPT) and nowadays part of virtually every aspect of the modern economy. It is also important to keep in mind that patents protect inventions and not the code itself that implements these inventions. Copyright, in contrast, protects the code but not the underlying idea (see Chapter 13).

There have been several attempts to define software patents. Most of the approaches rely on patent classes to filter software patents (see Box 17.1). The relevant classes were identified by looking at the patenting activity of the largest software companies in the industry, such as Microsoft, Oracle, and the like (Graham and Mowery 2003, Hall and MacGarvie 2010). The use of patent classes may result in the inclusion of both software and hardware patents even when classes are narrowly defined. To avoid this problem, other approaches have relied on keyword searches (Bessen and Hunt 2007) or even the

---

Box 17.1 Examples of Patent Class–Based Definitions of Software Patents

---

There have been different definitions of software patents in the literature. One complicating factor is that US software patent classes have changed over time and expanded overall due to the changing nature of the technology and changes in the patentability of software (this has also led to the reclassification of patents by the patent office). Here, we provide examples of different definitions:

Graham and Mowery (2003): IPC classes G06F (Electric digital data processing): 3,5,7,9,11,12,13,15; G06K (Graphical data reading, presentation of data, etc.): 9,15; and H04L (Transmission of digital information): 9.

Hall and MacGarvie (2010): US patent classes 341 (Coded data generation or conversion); 345 (Computer graphics processing and selective visual display systems); 382 (Image analysis); and 700 (Data processing: Generic control systems or specific applications).

Lerner and Zhu (2007), Noel and Schankerman (2013): IPC class G06F (Electric digital data processing).

Chung et al. (2015): US patent classes 341 (Coded data generation or conversion); 345 (Computer graphics processing and selective visual display systems); 370 (Multiplex communications); 380 (Cryptography); 382 (Image analysis); 700 (Data processing: Generic control systems or specific applications); 701 (Data processing: Vehicles, navigation, and relative location); 702 (Data processing: Measuring, calibrating, or testing); 703 (Data processing: Structural design, modeling, simulation, and emulation); 704 (Data processing: Speech signal processing, linguistics, language translation, and audio compression/decompression): 705 (Data processing: Financial, business practice, management, or cost/price determination); 706 (Data processing: Artificial intelligence); 707 (Data processing: Database and file management or data structures); 710 (Electrical computers and digital data processing systems: Input/output); 711 (Electrical computers and digital processing systems: Memory); 713 (Electrical computers and digital processing systems: Support); 714 (Error detection/correction and fault detection/recovery); 715 (Data processing: Presentation processing of document, operator interface processing, and screen saver display processing); 717 (Data processing: Software development, installation, and management); 726 (Information security); and 902 (Electronic funds transfer).

manual review of individual patent claims and descriptions (Allison and Lemley 2000, Allison and Tiller 2003). Some researchers have also used a combination of the different approaches (Hall and MacGarvie 2010).[7]

From a legal perspective, as explained in Chapter 11, certain inventions are excluded from patentable subject matter. For example, mathematical algorithms are generally not patent-eligible because they are considered an abstract idea. However, applications of abstract ideas are considered patent-eligible. The law has been grappling with the question of whether software is merely an abstract idea or whether it should be seen as a "process, machine, manufacture, or composition of matter" and hence as patentable under Section 101 of the US Patent Act. The implications are consequential because depending on where the line is drawn, software per se would either be excluded from patent-eligible subject matter or not.

Not surprisingly, the courts in the United States have been asked repeatedly over time to answer this question. As a result, they have created a long line of precedents. Box 17.2

Box 17.2 US Case Law Relevant for the Patentability of Software

1972 *Gottschalk v. Benson* [409 US 63 (1972)]: The patent under judicial review covered an algorithm to convert binary-coded decimal numbers into "true" binary numbers. The Supreme Court held that the claimed method represented an abstract mathematical algorithm and the fact that the algorithm was implemented by a computer was not sufficient to transform the claims into patentable subject matter. Since all software consists of some logical or arithmetic functions, the decision meant that all software should be considered abstract ideas that are not patentable.

1978 *Parker v. Flook* [437 US 584 (1978)]: The Supreme Court decided that a patent covering a computer program for updating an "alarm limit" to signal abnormal conditions in a chemical conversion process was not patentable. The court established that an algorithm itself was not patentable unless the corresponding claims also covered patentable hardware.

1981 *Diamond v. Diehr* [450 US 175 (1981)]: The Supreme Court regarded software to monitor the temperature of rubber-molding presses as patentable even though one step involved a mathematical expression. The court ruled that a claim is patentable despite protecting an abstract idea "when considered as a whole, is performing a function which the patent laws were designed to protect (e.g., transforming or reducing an article to a different state or thing)." In practice, the decision meant software was patentable as long as it was implemented through a mechanical or physical process.

1994 *In re Alappat* [33 F.3d 1526 (Fed. Cir. 1994)]: The Federal Circuit overturned the USPTO's rejection of a patent on a process that creates a smooth waveform display in a digital oscilloscope. The court effectively lowered the threshold of patentability by considering the transformation of data as a sufficient transformation to turn an abstract idea into a patentable claim.

---

[7] For a review of the different approaches, see Layne-Farrar (2005).

1998 *State Street Bank & Trust Co. v. Signature Financial Group* [149 F.3d 1368 (Fed. Cir. 1998)]: The Federal Circuit upheld a patent that covered a business method for a type of mutual fund that pooled assets of individual funds into a common portfolio. Its decision effectively lowered the threshold for patentability further by holding a "pure" software claim patentable as long as the software produces "a useful, concrete, and tangible result." This decision opened the door for the patenting of software and business method claims at the USPTO.

2008 *In re Bilski* [545 F.3d 943 (Fed. Cir. 2008)]: The Federal Circuit held that software has to be "tied to a specific machine or apparatus" or "transforms a particular article into a different state or thing" in order to meet the patentability threshold (the so-called machine-or-transformation test).

2010 *Bilski v. Kappos* [130 S. Ct. 3218 (2010)]: Subsequently, the Supreme Court partially overturned the Federal Circuit's decision *In re Bilski*. It held that patentability of software could not be determined solely on the basis of the machine-or-transformation test. However, the court confirmed that software protecting merely an abstract idea was not patentable. The decision also made it clear that business method patents are not categorically excluded from patentability.

2012 *Mayo Collaborative Services v. Prometheus Laboratories Inc* [132 S. Ct. 1289 (2012)]: The Supreme Court established that in order to meet the patentability threshold, a claim has to include an "inventive concept." While this case was not about software patents (rather, it was about process patents relating to medical diagnostic testing), the case had direct relevance for software patenting because it effectively raised the patentability bar for software. This decision, in combination with *Bilski v. Kappos*, created substantial uncertainty about the patentability of software claims.

2014 *Alice Corp. Pty. Ltd. v. CLS Bank Int.* [134 S. Ct. 2347 (2014)]: The Supreme Court considered whether software that managed deferred online transactions was patentable. The court found that machine transformation ("apply it with a computer") is not sufficient to render an abstract idea patentable. The court clarified the dividing line between claims directed to patent-eligible and those directed to patent-ineligible subject matter: "[I]n applying the §101 exception, we must distinguish between patents that claim the building blocks of human ingenuity and those that integrate the building blocks into something more, thereby transforming them into a patent-eligible invention. The former would risk disproportionately tying up the use of the underlying ideas, and are therefore ineligible for patent protection. The latter pose no comparable risk of pre-emption, and therefore remain eligible for the monopoly granted under our patent laws." The court established a two-step test. In the first step, the court has to determine whether a claim is directed to an abstract idea. Provided the answer in the first step is "yes," in the second step, the court has to determine whether the claim contains "enough" to transform the patent-ineligible subject matter into patent-eligible subject matter, where "enough" means an "element or combination of elements that is sufficient to ensure that the patent in practice amounts to significantly more than a patent upon the ineligible concept itself." The decision was widely interpreted as excluding many business methods claims from patentability if they are merely directed to the implementation of a common business method through a computer.

provides a summary of the most important decisions. As discussed there, the courts' opinion on the question of whether software claims are directed to patent-eligible subject matter has changed significantly over time, often moving in opposing directions. The most recent Supreme Court decision in *Alice v. CLS Bank* in 2014 does not categorically exclude software from patentability. However, it imposes a stringent test on the determination of whether software is merely directed to an abstract idea and hence raises the bar to patentability of software.

In Europe, software per se is not considered a technical invention. Because the EPO requires inventions to have "technical character" and to produce a "technical effect," software is excluded from patentability under Article 52(2) of the EPC. However, de facto this provision has been open to interpretation, in particular the question of what constitutes technical character and technical contribution, and as a result, the EPO grants thousands of software patents every year.

17.3 Software Development and the Patent System

In order to understand the debate on the economic implications of software patents, it is helpful to review how software as a technology differs from other technologies, such as pharmaceuticals and chemicals or seemingly more similar technologies such as computer hardware. First, the R&D process is more complex. In this context, complex does not mean that it is more difficult to come up with new code than, say, a chemical compound or a microchip. What it means is that to create and execute software, many different elements have to work together and communicate with each other. Complexity also gives rise to network externalities since software made by one firm usually has to be compatible with software produced by other firms because software is very rarely a closed system.

Software development is also more cumulative in nature, that is, developers routinely build and improve on existing code. This also helps explain why the software industry has a strong culture of sharing and collaboration between developers, as evidenced by the many global platforms that allow people to freely share and discuss code such as Stack Overflow or GitHub.[8] Software development also moves much faster than most other technologies. Code that is only a few years old is often already obsolete. The speed in software development creates a strong first-mover advantage. If most of the returns to new software are generated within a short amount of time, innovators can appropriate significant returns to their innovation before competitors are able to enter. Software is also different because it is not confined to a specific industry or economic activity. Instead, software is used in many different ways throughout the economy.

Finally, regarding its distribution, software development involves relatively large fixed costs, but usually relatively low marginal costs (although providing regular updates may be necessary due to the evolution and upgrading of operating systems and other software with which the particular software needs to interact; customers are often reluctant to pay much for this kind of maintenance). This also implies that copying of software is cheap, which reflects its intangible nature.

---

[8] See https://github.com/ and https://stackoverflow.com.

An understanding of these unique characteristics of software and software development is useful to understand potential challenges for the protection of software by patents. These challenges can be classified into two categories. The first category is focused on what is broadly referred to as *patent quality*, that is, the characteristics of software patents (see Chapter 11 for a discussion of patent quality).

The core argument is that the process and procedures of the patent system function relatively poorly in practice for software inventions. More specifically, because patents disclose inventions through the claim-oriented format in combination with drawings and descriptions, without any requirement to disclose code, patents may not work well in disclosing and describing precisely software inventions, potentially resulting in overly broad patents with unclear boundaries. This broad argument consists of the following more specific elements:

- *Claim boundaries.* The legal boundaries of a patent are defined by its claims (in combination with other information provided by the patent specification). Generally speaking, patentees have incentives to define broad claims in order to obtain broad coverage—they get to claim that their invention covers more "technology space." Broader claims are more likely to ensure freedom to operate and to create strategic value since competitors are more likely to "trespass" on the patent's claims. The downside of broad claims is that it might increase the chances that a patent is found invalid upon review by a court or the patent office. Another problem with broad claims is that they might make it more difficult to discern what exactly is claimed as the invention. This is particularly true for inventions that are not embodied in a physical object or process. The resulting fuzziness is compounded by the fact that there is no requirement to disclose any actual code to obtain a patent. As Burk and Lemley (2009, p. 12) put it, "[T]he patentee owns . . . what they claim, not what they actually built or described."

  The requirement to describe software in the required claim format means that it is often difficult in practice to ascertain the limits or boundaries of a software patent. One source of such overly broad claims is so-called functional claiming (Lemley 2013). Functional claiming is a specific way of describing an invention in the claims of a patent. Instead of describing the structure of the invention, the claims describe what the invention does, that is, its function (Box 17.3 provides a more detailed explanation).

  When functional claiming is used to describe software inventions, it can result in broad claims that cover any conceivable way of achieving a broad objective instead of a specific invention. This issue is, in fact, specific to software patents because by describing a function as implemented by hardware, the patent provides enough structure to avoid the limitations imposed by so-called means-plus-function claim standards. As explained in Box 17.3, means-plus-function claim standards impose certain restrictions on functional claims, which help avoid those overly broad claims. However, in practice, applicants can avoid these restrictions by referring to structural elements that implement the claimed function. For software, applicants simply recite hardware (a computer). However, it is easy to see that simply stating software is implemented by a computer does not provide much limiting structure.

Box 17.3 Functional Claiming

Under US law, there are different ways of writing claims, so-called claim formats. One way is to describe the *structure of the invention*. For example, if a new machine is invented, the structure of the machine would be described. For instance, Claim 1 of the first patent protecting a microchip, US 3,138,743 filed by Jack Kilby at Texas Instruments in 1959, describes the structure of the "miniaturized electronic circuit": "In an integrated circuit having a plurality of electrical circuit components in a wafer of single-crystal semiconductor material, a plurality of junction transistors defined in the wafer..."

Another way is to describe the *function of the invention*. In the case of the new machine, the claim would describe the function performed by the machine. In other words, the invention is described by what the invention is supposed to achieve, rather than its structure. This is referred to as functional claiming. Take a look at one of Zillow's patents, US 9,424,305 titled "Multi-faceted search," which protects software that helps users query a database. Claim 1 states, "A method in a computing system for processing a query against a set of items each having attributes of two or more of a plurality of attribute types, comprising..." Here, a method is claimed that executes a function, that is, it processes a type of query.

For the patentee, functional claiming has the advantage that it results in broader claim coverage, making it easier to cover substitute technologies. The drawback from a patentee's perspective is that the boundaries of the scope of the patent may be less clearly defined and hence the patent risks being considered indefinite and hence invalid. Simply put, functional claiming is more likely to result in broad claim scope since the invention is described "by what it does rather than by what it is." However, in the 1952 Patents Act, legislators put some limits on what is referred to as "pure" functional claiming. When an invention is described purely by its function, the patent does not cover the function itself, but only the means of implementing that function as described by the patent specification (or equivalents). This provides definition to claims that on their own do not provide a clear definition of their scope. Such claims are referred to as "means-plus-function" claims [35 USC. Section 112(6)]. In patent examination practice, an important question is whether the means-plus-function limitation applies to a given claim. If a claim is not considered purely functional, the limitation does not apply.

This allows software patents to use broad functional claims. Take, for example, patent US 6,327,579 titled "Online computer services including help desk, antivirus and/or application service features." Its first claim reads as follows:

1. A data processing method comprising:
    (a) connecting a remote computer to a host computer over a telecommunications link;
    (b) attaching, to said remote computer, at least one storage resource provided by said host computer;
    (c) allowing said remote computer to access said storage resource as if it were a physical storage device physically attached to said remote computer;

(d) providing executable anti-viral software from said host computer to said remote computer via said storage resource;

(e) executing said anti-viral software at said remote computer; and

(f) charging a fee for said step (e).

The patent claims a function, a "data processing method" that allows users to
rent software remotely over the internet. However, the way the claim is written,
the patent claims any software rental over the internet, not just one specific way
of accomplishing that. The structural elements, a computer and storage resource,
add little to define the claim in a more precise way. As a result, the patent not only
claims a specific implementation to achieve an outcome, but also any implementation that results in that same outcome.

• *Disclosure.* One of the requirements associated with obtaining a patent is to disclose the invention protected by the patent. Disclosure has to be sufficient for a
PHOSITA to make and use the invention. Because the invention is disclosed in
the claims and patent specification, fuzzy claim boundaries affect disclosure. More
generally, there is no requirement for software patents to disclose the code that
executes the patented invention because a PHOSITA is assumed to be capable of
writing the code based on the disclosure in the patent. In addition, the patentability
requirement to "reduce the invention to practice" is satisfied conceptually if the
patent merely teaches a PHOSITA to reduce the invention to practice. Therefore,
in practical terms, an inventor does not have to write any code (or even know how
to write code), and even if the inventor had produced code, there is no requirement to share it in the patent. The problem that results from such limited disclosure is a lack of notice and fewer knowledge spillovers. It becomes more difficult
for others to understand the invention protected by the patent, which increases
search costs and the risk of costly disputes. It also limits what others can learn from
the disclosure of the invention.

• *Prior art.* Software patents are more likely to be invalid because patent examiners
missed relevant prior art that would have prevented the granting of the patent or
at least narrowed the claims. Patent examiners may find it more difficult to identify
relevant prior art for software patents than pharmaceutical patents, for example.
Software as a field is less likely to be disclosed in sources conventionally considered
prior art, such as academic publications or trade journals. In the early days of software patenting, there was also a lack of expertise at the USPTO (and other patent
offices around the world) since patent offices did not hire examiners with specific
expertise in software until the mid-1990s.

The classification of patents also makes prior art search difficult. Patent offices
classify patents by technology function, where technology is defined according to
what the patented invention achieves, rather than the method/process used. This
means that if a patent protects software that is used for medical-imaging technology,
the patent will be classified under medical-imaging technology rather than software,
even though the software claims per se might be more general than just medical-
imaging technology. Hence, the challenge results from the fact that software is applicable across industries and software claims often are broad in scope. As a result,
software patents are spread across many different technology areas, making it more

difficult to find the relevant prior art. Finally, the challenges associated with prior art search are compounded by the fact that due to the legal back-and-forth described in Box 17.2, during certain periods, applicants had incentives to characterize software as hardware to avoid limitations imposed on the patentability of software.

The second set of arguments as to why the patent system functions poorly for software focuses more directly on the characteristics of software as a technology. These arguments suggest that because of the way software is developed and used in the economy, the social costs associated with patent protection potentially outweigh the benefits. There are two core arguments:

- *Complexity/cumulative.* Because software is a complex and cumulative technology, there is a risk that granting patents on specific aspects could increase transaction costs for software developers and result in risk of litigation.[9] This, in turn, could block incremental innovation. This may have a disproportionate effect on new companies since they lack experience on how to navigate a complex patent landscape and they also lack patents to help them negotiate cross-licensing agreements with other companies for patent access. It is also true that patent thickets have been shown to exist predominantly in software-related technology classes (for a more in-depth explanation of patent thickets, see Chapter 18). As a result, software patents could block entry of new firms, reduce competition, discourage recombination of existing knowledge, and hinder cumulative innovation.
- *Innovation cycle.* Software has very short innovation cycles, and as a result, it is characterized by rapid technological obsolescence. Most software is quickly updated or even superseded by new software. This is not compatible with a patent system that generally takes several years just for the patent office to examine and grant a patent. Once granted, the patent can be kept in force for 20 years (counting from the date of filing). In the software industry, 20 years is an eternity. This realization even led Jeff Bezos, the founder of Amazon, to call for a shorter statutory patent term for software and business method patents, stating that "[t]his isn't like drug companies, which need long patent windows because of clinical testing, or like complicated physical processes, where you might have to tool up and build factories. Especially in the age of the Internet, a good software innovation can catch a lot of wind in 3 or 5 years."[10] This creates a mismatch between the innovation cycle and the property rights granted by software patents.

The arguments listed above have a number of economic consequences. First, there is more uncertainty over the scope and the validity of software patents than patents in other technologies, notably pharmaceuticals or chemicals. Overly broad claims are more likely to result in patent thickets, and they mean that the claims are more likely invalid. A higher likelihood of invalidity means that there are relatively more patents on

---

[9] Bessen and Maskin (2009) show more formally how patents can block innovation in a setting where innovation is sequential and complementary. The main insight from their model is that innovators benefit from imitation in a cumulative setting, even at the expense of current profits because imitation increases the likelihood of follow-on innovations and hence increases future profits.

[10] See http://www.techlawjournal.com/intelpro/20000309bez.htm.

software that should not have been granted. However, because they have been granted, they can be asserted in court. Once they have been asserted against an alleged infringer, the burden is on the alleged infringer to demonstrate that the patents are invalid, which is an extremely costly and lengthy undertaking.

The quick innovation cycle in software adds to this problem. One might think that it just renders patents obsolete faster, and hence it should limit the ability to assert software patents. However, because of the fuzzy boundaries and the ability to claim broad software inventions, even patents that cover obsolete software may still read on newer technology and therefore have exclusionary power and could even be asserted successfully against competitors. Thus, software patents are often asserted to obtain "past damages based on infringements that no longer occur or ... to apply ... [them] to new product generations" (Burk and Lemley, 2009, p. 57). It also helps explain why the majority of patents asserted in court by nonpracticing entities (NPEs) are software patents (for further discussion, see Chapter 22).

17.3.1 Empirical Evidence on the Impact of Software Patents

The empirical evidence on the impact of software patents on companies and innovation more broadly is sparse. This is, in part, due to the difficulty of isolating the effect of patents on software development from the other major changes that the software and internet revolution has brought about. Much of the empirical evidence relies on changes observed in response to the changes in US case law relevant to software patenting. Furthermore, the available evidence does not offer clear results on the impact of software patents.

Noel and Schankerman (2013) find a large patent premium in the stock market valuation for software firms over the period 1980–1999.[11] The authors interpret the evidence as suggesting that software patents create value for firms by enhancing their ability to appropriate the returns to their innovative output. In a similar vein, Lerner and Zhu (2007) find that software firms, which were relatively more affected by a 1996 US Supreme Court decision that reduced the scope of copyright protection of software,[12] responded to the decision by filing more patents. This growth in software patenting was associated with increased sales and an expansion of a firm's product lines.

In contrast, Hall and MacGarvie (2010) do not find any clear evidence that software companies benefited from an expansion of the patentability of software. They look at private returns to publicly traded computer hardware and software firms in response to a series of court decisions that affected the patentability of software in the United States over the period 1975–2002. Their results suggest that the stock market value dropped for software companies as a result of an expansion of software patentability. Market value regressions suggest that software patents, as such, contributed little to a firm's market value. The results also suggest that the marginal returns to filing software patents were essentially zero.

[11] The patent premium is captured by the coefficient on the ratio of the patent stock to the stock of the firm's fixed assets in a market value regression that controls for the stock of R&D.
[12] *Lotus Development Corporation v. Borland International, Inc.,* 116 S. Ct. 804 (1996). For further discussion, see Chapter 13.

Using data on software companies in the United States between 1990 and 2004, Cockburn and MacGarvie (2009, 2011) find that the increase in software patenting triggered by the expansion of patentability reduced entry of new software start-up firms. They show that a 1% increase in patenting led to a 0.8% decrease in entry in software product markets. More patenting also reduced the likelihood that start-ups received outside investment. Lin and Rai (2023) find that a narrowing of the scope of software patents as a consequence of the Supreme Court decision in *Alice v. CLS Bank* led to fewer software patent filings by companies in the software industry. At the same time, these firms expanded their open-source activities as an alternative means to appropriating returns to their innovative activities. The results also suggest that software firms experienced an increase in sales because the Supreme Court decision reduced the risk of software patent litigation.

Taken together, these results do not paint a clear picture. There is some evidence that firms benefit privately from software patents, although the evidence is relatively weak. However, there is also evidence that software patents increase transaction costs especially for younger companies.

17.4 Business Method Patents

In 1997, Amazon introduced a business method for customers to shorten their purchase transaction on Amazon's online platform. The method allows customers to enter their payment information once and then retain this information such that customers do not have to reenter the information for every purchase. This significantly facilitates the purchasing process as having to reenter payment information can act as a considerable disincentive for customers to complete a transaction. If you purchase regularly on Amazon, you will be familiar with this process. Amazon patented its "Method and system for placing a purchase order via communications network" (US 5,960,411), listing Amazon founder Jeff Bezos as one of the inventors. The patent eventually became widely known as Amazon's one-click patent. Another now famous patent is online travel agency priceline.com's patent US 5,797,127. The patent, titled "Method, apparatus, and program for pricing, selling, and exercising options to purchase airline tickets," essentially covers a sealed-bid (Dutch) auction for purchasing airline tickets online.

Amazon's and priceline.com's patents are examples of business method patents. Business method inventions are discoveries that describe methods of doing business, for example, a new way of executing a business transaction. Business method patents cover a range of applications including finance, business data processing, insurance, and marketing methods. The lines between a business method and software-enabled invention can be blurry because business method patents often protect the implementation of a business method using software on the internet. Perhaps the best way to think about business method patents, as opposed to other types of patents, is that the claimed invention is commercial rather than technological. Given the explosion of e-commerce and the importance of online transactions more generally, it is not surprising that business method inventions have become much more central to many businesses.

In the United States, business methods fall into US patent class 705, which contains inventions on "Data processing: Financial, business practice, management, or cost/price determination." The class, which was created in 1997, broadly covers anything that involves data processing. A closer look at the patents covered by this class reveals substantial heterogeneity. US patent class 902 that covers "Electronic funds transfer" is often also considered to cover business methods. The definition of what constitutes a business method has changed over time, in part, as a result of various court decisions, legislative changes, and examination practice at the patent office.

The debate about business method patents is very similar to the broader debate about software patents reviewed in Section 17.2 above. However, there is a more basic question in the context of business methods: Should commercial inventions be awarded the same protection as inventions that constitute a technical solution to a technical problem?

The legal debate about business method patents has focused on whether business methods are merely an abstract idea and hence not patentable. In 1998, the CAFC issued an opinion in *State Street Bank and Trust v. Signature Financial Corporation* (see Box 17.2) that is widely seen as the door opener to a notable increase in business method patenting. The patent in that case, US 5,193,056, describes an invention where mutual funds can pool their assets in an investment portfolio organized as a partnership: "A data processing system for managing a financial services configuration of a portfolio established as a partnership, each partner being one of a plurality of funds." The pooling allowed investment managers to lower the cost of administering a fund since the fixed costs could be spread across funds. The patent describes an invention that uses computers for a business application. The court found that the claimed invention yields a "useful, concrete and tangible result" and that business method claims should be treated by the patent office as just any other type of claim. Subsequently, the court reaffirmed in *AT&T v. Excel Communications* that business method claims are indeed patentable.[13] Figure 17.2 shows that filings of business method patents indeed accelerated markedly following the *State Street* decision in 1998.

In Europe, by contrast, business methods are not patentable. The EPC explicitly excludes business methods from patentability [Article 52(2c) EPC]. That said, business methods can be patentable provided they solve a technical problem.[14]

Proponents of business method patents claim that business method inventions are critical to innovation because they cover new ways in which actions formerly carried out by humans are carried out by automated systems, including software and AI. This includes activities that humans are unable to carry out, but that machines now can. This increases the efficiency of economic transactions. Accordingly, Spulber (2011) defines a business method invention as "the discovery of a commercial technique for firms to address market opportunities, such as a transaction procedure, market microstructure, financial system, operational process, or organizational form" (p. 270). Therefore, business methods are "commercial discoveries" that build on scientific and technological discoveries. Their implementation drives "commercial innovation," that can also

---

[13] *AT&T v. Excel Communications, Inc.*, 172 F.3d 1352 (Fed. Cir. 1999).
[14] Auction Method/Hitachi, Euro. Pat. Off. Tech. Ct. App. T0258/03, April 21, 2004.

help the commercialization of other scientific and technological discoveries. As such, they increase the market value of scientific and technological discoveries. This, in turn, implies that business methods can promote technological innovation. In short, the key argument is that the granting of these patents not only provides incentives to come up with such commercial discoveries, but it also provides incentives for further innovation and investment in order to implement them.

Critics of business method patents have pointed out that they provide an opportunity to monopolize broad, abstract ideas. The argument is that business methods are intrinsically vague or abstract, which sets them apart from scientific or technological inventions. That is, business methods describe an abstract idea–a way of conducting business––not an actual technical solution. Observers have also argued that some business method patents protect methods that are trivial even to a casual observer (such as Amazon's one-click patent). Critics have also argued that prior art search is even more difficult for business method than software patents. While many ways of doing business have been used in practice before (such as priceline.com's sealed-bid auction patent), they have either been kept secret or they have simply not been codified in ways that would constitute prior art.

One example that illustrates the problem is the experience of one of the authors of this textbook with so-called one-click shopping. In the 1970s (and earlier), a small supermarket in Cambridge, Massachusetts, allowed shoppers to fill a shopping cart, add a form with their account number on it (having preregistered their billing information), and leave it to be rung up and delivered to their home, without waiting in the store. This was arguably a form of one-click shopping well before the internet, and similar services were doubtless available in many locations. Thus, this way of doing business existed prior to the internet, and it is doubtful to some that putting it online was non-obvious. However, an examiner searching for prior art would be hard pressed to find examples like this in order to reject a patent application.

A number of business method patents have attracted an enormous amount of attention and criticism due to their exceedingly broad scope, such as the Amazon one-click patent. However, a broader comparison of business method patents and patents in other technology areas indicates that business method patents are very similar in terms of standard patent quality and value metrics such as prior art references and claim counts (Allison and Tiller 2003).

17.4.1 Financial Method Patents

While there is surprisingly little evidence on the impact of the granting of business method patents on innovation and competition, an important exception is the subset of business method patents, financial method patents.

Financial method patents, like that at issue in the *State Street* case, are typically on formulas or methods of making financial transactions. These patents have been studied in a series of papers by Lerner and his coauthors (Lerner 2002a, Lerner 2010, Lerner et al. 2023). Figure 17.2 showed the trend for the financial business method patents. Note that these patents do not appear until after the *State Street* decision in 1998, which opened the door to patenting in the banking and finance sectors.

Lerner (2002a) documented that early financial patents, such as the one for the Black-Scholes option pricing formula, cited little academic literature. As in the case of software patents, patent examiners seemed unaware of much of the nonpatent prior art in this area, leading patents to be issued on methods that had long been in the literature. During the first decade following *State Street*, financial patents, especially those held by individuals and small private entities, were litigated 27 to 39 times as often as other patents. Those targeted were typically large corporations and financial institutions.

A comprehensive study by Lerner et al. (2021) shows that the patent landscape has evolved in this area as many financial transactions have moved online. During the decade 2000–2010, patented innovation in finance has shifted toward information technology and nonfinancial firms, and from New York to California. The kinds of patents now being issued are based less on the academic finance literature and more likely to concern payment methods and transaction security. The study concludes that there is a puzzle in that productivity in this sector has hardly risen, in spite of the growth in (patented) innovation activity. The authors suggest that this may be due to measurement problems: the well-known difficulties in measuring productivity in Financial, Investment and Real Estate (FIRE) as well as the fact that most innovation is coming from outside the sector, making attribution of the returns difficult. Thus, this is one of many areas where future work on productivity measurement is needed.

17.5 Open-Source Software

When you purchase Microsoft Windows, you are not actually buying the software. You are only purchasing a license from Microsoft that allows you to use their operating system. Microsoft retains full ownership over its software.

Instead, you could download for free the operating system Linux. In fact, there are many different versions, called distributions, of Linux that you can choose from. For example, you could download Canonical's Ubunto for desktop computers.

The origins of OSS, also referred to as free and open-source software (FOSS), go back to the very early days of software and computer development. Nowadays, OSS is widely used on different types of hardware. For example, an estimated 3 billion devices run on Android around the world. Other popular OSS includes Mozilla's Firefox browser and programming language Python, which has become very popular among applied researchers in many fields including economics.

The difference to proprietary software, which relies on different forms of IP protection, most importantly copyright but also patents, is that source code is made publicly and freely available. This allows other developers to modify and improve the code. Usually, the only condition for obtaining access is that any changes to the code are also made publicly and freely available. Because of the open and collaborative nature of OSS development, it is considered to be one way of implementing open innovation.

The most widely used license for OSS is the so-called GNU GPL.[15] This license allows modification of the code but requires that any modified source code also be made available under the GPL––this is what is sometimes referred to as "copyleft." This restrictive clause ensures that open-source code does not turn into proprietary software. The license also stipulates that if parts of the modified code are protected by patents, the patents must be available royalty-free to all users of the software.

Having discussed the legal wrangling over software patents above, it must seem odd that there is another approach to software development. On the one hand, by making source code freely available to the public, OSS avoids the problems associated with (temporary) exclusivity granted by the IP system. On the other, it still provides incentives for firms to innovate by allowing firms to appropriate some return on their investment.

Since companies are giving away the software free of charge, their returns come from alternative sources. For many firms, complementary sales and service revenues dominate patents for securing returns to innovation, and software is no exception. For example, Red Hat, which produces open-source operating software, was acquired in 2019 by IBM for US$34 billion. Unlike companies like Microsoft, Red Hat does not make money from selling its operating software, but from the provision of services linked to its software. Still, Red Hat clearly made enough money from these ancillary services to justify the multibillion dollar acquisition by IBM.

Red Hat is not an exception. Nowadays, for-profit companies play an important role in the creation and diffusion of OSS. As a matter of fact, the lines between developers of proprietary and OSS have become blurred, with many companies engaging in the development and use of both types of software. This reflects many different business models that successfully combine the development and sale of both proprietary and open-source code. For example, Microsoft continues to generate the bulk of its revenue through the licensing of its proprietary software such as Windows or Office. However, Microsoft also offers its own open-source Linux distribution Azure Sphere for its Azure cloud computing services. Lerner and Schankerman (2009, Table 4.2) report results from a survey of close to 2,000 firms across 15 countries that show nearly 40% of surveyed software companies engage in the development of OSS. The data also reveal that the majority of companies that develop proprietary software also engage in the development of the same type of software as open source (e.g., they develop operating software under proprietary and open-source licenses). However, it is also still true that the bulk of revenue (around 80%) comes from proprietary software.

There remain important differences between open-source and proprietary software, differences that help to explain how they continue to coexist. Take, for example, R and Stata, software programs with which you are probably at least somewhat familiar. R is open source, available under the GNU license and therefore freely available for download. In contrast, the cheapest individual Stata license costs several hundred

---

[15] It was created by Richard Stallman at the MIT Artificial Intelligence Laboratory; Stallman founded the Free Software Foundation (FSF) in the early 1980s.

dollars for a user located in the United States. Nevertheless, many applied researchers may still prefer Stata because they consider it more user-friendly or use both R and Stata depending on the task at hand. Lerner and Schankerman (2009) summarize the arguments for what they refer to as "comingling" of proprietary and OSS develop-ment: (1) There are synergies in the development and marketing of the two types of software; (2) there is heterogeneity among software users, which creates demand for both types of software; and (3) users themselves often combine the use of open-source and proprietary software, which allows firms to exploit reputational spillovers and other synergies between product types.

In general, OSS is more likely to be used in areas where the users themselves are software specialists, such as the Apache Web server, Mozilla.Firefox, email servers, or various Linux implementations. Such users are willing to contribute improvements and have the knowledge to do so. In areas where the end users are not developers, such as the Stata example above, proprietary software is more prevalent.

The comingling of open-source and proprietary code implies that open source is un-likely to act as a substitute for proprietary code. This, in turn, implies that it is unlikely to render software patents redundant. In fact, there is evidence that software patents act as complementary assets for OSS by enhancing appropriability (Fosfuri et al. 2008). Indeed, open-source developers have built up large patent portfolios themselves for de-fensive purposes. They make these patents available royalty-free (see Chapter 20 for further discussion), while still using them to safeguard their own freedom to operate (see Chapter 18 for additional discussion).

17.6 Artificial Intelligence

Let's start with a disclaimer: The discussion in this section is likely to become obsolete in the near future. That is simply because the field of AI is evolving extremely fast and the relationship of AI with the patent system is very much in flux. Before discussing the link between AI and the patent system, let's remind ourselves what we mean by AI and how it relates to the "traditional" software discussed above. The Oxford English Dictionary defines AI as "[t]he capacity of computers or other machines to exhibit or simulate intelligent behaviour; the field of study concerned with this." As implied by this definition, AI sets itself apart from traditional software through its ability to execute cognitive functions without human interference. For example, an AI system designed to recognize patterns on digital images can improve and adjust its performance—it can learn—based solely on the data input into the AI system without a human programmer having to alter the underlying code. AI is seen by many as a GPT poised to fundamen-tally change the economy and our everyday lives (see also Chapter 2). Sundar Pichai, Google's CEO, said that AI is more profound a technology than "fire or electricity or the internet."

The current state of AI is more limited. AI currently consists of systems that collect and process large amounts of data with the goal of performing discrete tasks, such as image processing or pattern recognition. Existing AI systems are capable of autono-mously learning to perform certain tasks and improve their performance without human intervention. For example, AlphaZero, a computer program developed by

Google's DeepMind released in 2017, taught itself via self-play how to play chess within just 9 hours to beat the winner of the 2016 (unofficial) world computer chess championship.[16] Self-driving cars are another application of AI. It shows the promise held by AI, but it also illustrates AI's current limitations. The advent of self-driving cars could make car ownership obsolete and thereby radically change personal mobility. Over recent years, the technology has made significant advances, to the point that many currently produced cars already incorporate self-driving features, but fully self-driving cars remain a challenge. More recently, the launch of generative AI chatbots, such as ChatGPT by developer OpenAI, boosted the general public's interest in AI. The chatbots quickly caught everyone's attention and ignited a broader, popular interest in AI due to its ability to provide detailed information across many different areas of knowledge, ranging from writing software code to legal documents.

Two aspects frame the debate around AI and patents. The first considers the patentability of AI algorithms. This debate is about whether inventions related to the development of AI algorithms or their use are patentable. This discussion resembles in many ways the debate on the patentability of computer-implemented inventions reviewed above. The second aspect, however, is new. It asks whether AI can be an inventor under patent law. This question arises because AI has the ability to autonomously create inventions. Here, the question is whether an AI system can be a natural person since only natural persons are entitled to inventorship under patent law.

With respect to patent eligibility, the question is whether there are specific considerations unique to AI. If AI is considered simply a subfield of software inventions, then AI does not require any specific considerations as it is subject to the same patent rules and regulations as software more generally. This is, for example, how the USPTO currently treats AI inventions.

The other issue concerns inventorship of AI: Can an AI algorithm produce a patentable invention? This might sound like an odd question, but several patent offices and courts around the world have been recently grappling with this issue. In 2018, Stephen Thaler filed two patent applications titled "Food container" and "Devices and methods for attracting enhanced attention" (which is essentially a flashing light) at the EPO that named an AI system called Device for the Autonomous Bootstrapping of Unified Sentience (DABUS) as the inventor. He then filed the patents in many jurisdictions around the world. So far, the EPO and national patent offices in Australia, Germany, Israel, Korea, New Zealand, the United Kingdom, and United States all rejected the patent on the grounds that an AI system cannot be an inventor (or be named as the inventor). Thaler appealed all of the decisions by the patent offices. However, they were all upheld on appeal by the national courts and EPO's Legal Board of Appeal. Only the patent office of South Africa granted the DABUS patent. However, the grant itself is not all that surprising since the South African patent office does not undertake any substantive examination. Despite these decisions, the question is far from settled. DABUS patents are still pending in a number of other jurisdictions, including China and Japan, and there are still possible appeals to decisions already made.

---

[16] https://en.wikipedia.org/wiki/AlphaZero.

That said, apart from its curiosity appeal, the practical importance and economic relevance of this debate for AI or the patent system are less apparent. From an economic perspective, the main concern is that decisions over the patentability of AI-generated inventions may impact incentives for investment in AI-driven innovation. One could take the view that AI might help reduce the costs of inventing such that patent protection is no longer necessary for appropriation. However, at least in the short run, AI is more likely to play an important role as an input in the existing innovation process rather than completely replacing it. This means that firms may still turn to the patent system to appropriate the returns to their AI-based inventions. If it turns out that patent protection is not available for certain AI-based inventions, alternative mechanisms to appropriate returns, such as secrecy and first-mover advantage, will likely become more important over time.

Finally, we note that there are many interesting issues related to AI and IP other than patents. To give just a few examples: Does the ownership of data required to train AI systems warrant the creation of a new IP right? Should copyright be available to protect creative work created by AI systems? Unfortunately, these questions go beyond the scope of this chapter. We discuss some aspects of AI and copyright protection in Chapter 13 but leave the rest perhaps for future editions of this textbook.

17.7 Summary

This chapter reviewed the debates about the relationship between software and the patent system. In doing so, we also reviewed related debates about business and financial method patents, OSS, and AI.

Our review of the legal discussion around software patents showed that the main question is whether software is an abstract idea and therefore excluded from patentability. Although US courts have been grappling with this question for half a century, it is far from settled.

We also reviewed the different arguments for why the patent system might not be well suited for the protection of software. These arguments have to do with the way patents protect inventions as well as with the particular way in which software is developed. As a result, the patent system might increase transaction costs for companies, and on balance, these costs might outweigh the benefits that arise from patent protection. However, these conclusions are largely based on theoretical arguments, rather than clear available empirical evidence.

This chapter also discussed business and financial method patents. We noted that the debate about business method patents largely mirrors that of software patents. The main question is whether business methods are more likely to simply reflect broad abstract ideas rather than technological inventions.

We also reviewed OSS, which is a thriving alternative to proprietary software. In practice, open-source and proprietary software coexist and are often used in combination. This suggests that open source is rather a complement than a substitute to proprietary software.

Finally, our discussion of patent protection and AI revealed that so far AI does not create any major new challenges to the patent system. The patentability of AI fits within the scope and framework of the debate on the patentability of software. There is also a debate about whether AI can be an inventor of a patent. However, the economic relevance of this question is still somewhat unclear.

18

Strategic Patenting, Patent Portfolio Races, and Patent Thickets

---

Learning Objectives

After reading this chapter, you will be able to understand and explain the following concepts:

- The strategic use of patents
- The competitive advantages generated by strategic patenting
- Strategic patenting in information and communication technologies
- The drivers of strategic patenting
- Different strategic motives for patenting
- Consequences of strategic patenting in the form of ownership fragmentation and patent thickets
- The effect of ownership fragmentation and thickets on firms and innovation

---

18.1 Introduction

Standard introductory microeconomics textbooks treat patents simply as a way for firms to obtain temporary exclusivity. In the most simplistic framework discussed in Chapter 11, innovation takes the form of a process innovation that lowers the innovator's marginal cost from some level c to c', where $c > c'$. A patent prevents other companies from also lowering their marginal costs to c' by adopting the same technology and hence affords the innovator a temporary monopoly.[1] The reality is a lot more complex.

It is true that patents are used primarily by firms as a legal tool to deter copying and to achieve exclusivity (Cohen et al. 2000). For example, in the pharmaceutical industry, it is possible for a single patent on an active ingredient to prevent market entry by generic competitors and to secure exclusivity for the duration of the patent's life. However, in reality, pharmaceutical originator companies do not content themselves with the filing of a single patent that protects the novel active ingredient. Instead, they file a potentially large number of additional patents, including many years after the drug was approved by regulators, usually with the goal of extending patent protection beyond the expiration of the original active ingredient patent. As a result, a new drug is usually protected

---

[1] See, for example, Tirole (1988, Chapter 10.1).

The Economics of Innovation and Intellectual Property. Bronwyn H. Hall and Christian Helmers, Oxford University Press.
© Oxford University Press 2024. DOI: 10.1093/oso/9780197630914.003.0018

not by one, but often by dozens of patents that cover a range of aspects related to the drug (see Chapter 16 for more in-depth discussion). This helps not only to prevent outright copying of the drug for longer than the life of the original active ingredient patent, it also makes it more difficult for competitors and generic producers to come up with alternative versions of the drug. Hence, while patents clearly serve their conventional function of ensuring exclusivity of the invention, they also serve a strategic function.

More generally, in our pharmaceutical example, "strategic" means that a company treats a patent as an asset, which is used to gain a competitive advantage that goes beyond the exclusivity that it would obtain if the patent protected its drug through a single active ingredient patent. Key to understanding the strategic use of a patent is precisely the "additional" competitive advantage conferred by the patent above and beyond the standard exclusivity granted by patent protection. This additional competitive advantage can take different forms, but at its core, it results from the creation of strategic options that result from a patent's "blocking power" (Granstrand 1999) that positively affect the company's competitive position in the marketplace in support of its broader business model. Jan Jaferian, former vice president of IP at Xerox, put it this way: "If you only use your patents to protect your products, which is the old paradigm, you're missing all manner of revenue-generating and other opportunities" (quoted in Rivette et al. 2000).

To see the strategic role that patents can play more clearly, take the example of Apple's patent US 8,046,721 titled "Unlocking a device by performing gestures on an unlock image" filed in 2005. The patent protects "[a] method of unlocking a hand-held electronic device, the device including a touch-sensitive display" by "continuously moving the unlock image on the touch-sensitive display" (Claim 1); see Figure 18.1. The older readers of this book might still be familiar with this *swipe-to-unlock* technology, which

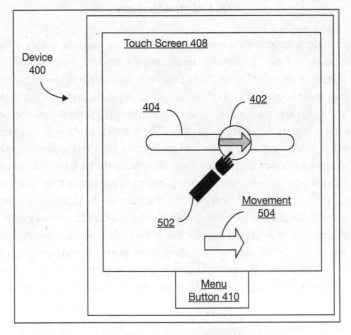

Figure 18.1 Apple's swipe-to-unlock patent (US 8,046,721).

Jury verdict in Apple Inc. v. Samsung Electronics Co., Ltd., et. al., 920 F. Supp. 1079 (N.D. Cal. Jan. 29, 2013)

4. For each of the following products, has Apple proven by a preponderance of the evidence that Samsung Electronics Co. ("SEC") and/or Samsung Telecommunications America ("STA") has infringed **Claim 8 of the '721 Patent?**

Please answer in each cell with a "Y" for "yes" (for Apple), or with an "N" for "no" (for Samsung). Do not provide an answer for any cell that is blacked out.

Accused Samsung Product	Samsung Electronics Co., Ltd.	Samsung Electronics America, Inc.	Samsung Telecommunications America, LLC
Admire (JX28B)	Y		Y
Galaxy Nexus (JX29A, JX29B, JX29C, JX29D, JX29E, JX29H, JX29I, JX72)	Y		Y
Galaxy S II (JX32C, JX32E)	N		N
Galaxy S II Epic 4G Touch (JX33A, JX33B)	N		N
Galaxy S II Skyrocket (JX34C)	N		N
Stratosphere (JX37A)	Y		Y

7. Has Apple proven by clear and convincing evidence that the Samsung entity's infringement of any of the following patents was willful?

Please answer in each cell with a "Y" for "yes" (for Apple), or with an "N" for "no" (for Samsung). Do not provide an answer for any cell that is blacked out.

Apple Patents	Samsung Electronics Co., Ltd.	Samsung Electronics America, Inc.	Samsung Telecommunications America, LLC
'647 Patent (Claim 9)	N		N
'959 Patent (Claim 25)	N	N	N
'414 Patent (Claim 20)	N	N	N
'721 Patent (Claim 8)	Y		Y
'172 Patent (Claim 18)	N		N

Figure 18.2 Jury verdict in *Apple v. Samsung.*

has been mostly replaced by biometric sensors that unlock screens through fingerprint, facial recognition, or iris scanning technology.

The patent was asserted in several court cases, including the famous *Apple v. Samsung Electronics* case litigated in the Northern District of California.[2] As shown in Figure 18.2, a jury found in 2014 that several of Samsung's devices infringed on the swipe-to-unlock patent. While the jury found a total of three of Apple's five asserted patents infringed, the swipe-to-unlock patent was the only one for which it also found willful infringement, which drastically increases payable damages (see Figure 18.2). The jury awarded Apple a total of nearly US$120million in damages (although the contribution of the swipe-to-unlock to the total was relatively small).[3]

---

[2] *Apple Inc. v. Samsung Electronics Co., Ltd., et al.*, 920 F. Supp. 2d 1079 (N.D. California, January 29, 2013).
[3] It is also true that the award was only a fraction of the damages originally requested by Apple. The case was appealed by Samsung and ultimately upheld by the CAFC.

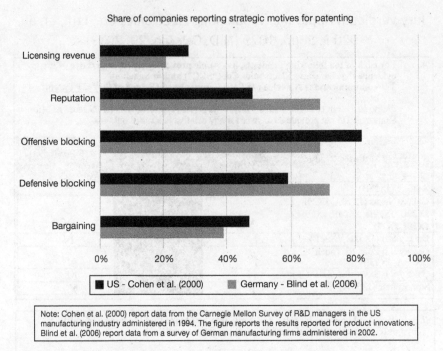

Figure 18.3 Strategic motives for patenting in the US and Germany.

While this case was litigated, the decision of a prior case between Apple and Samsung, which involved a US$1 billion damages award against Samsung, was still going through the appeals process.[4] In fact, these lawsuits were part of a global spat of patent litigation between the two companies. The swipe-to-unlock patent was clearly helpful in Apple's litigation campaign (see Figure 18.2). What does this tell us about the role and value of the swipe-to-unlock patent for Apple's business? The primary objective of the patent most likely would have been to guarantee Apple exclusivity over the swipe gesture to unlock a touchscreen. However, the swipe-to-unlock patent also gave Apple additional strategic leverage in its dispute with Samsung. The example shows that patents can serve as both legal and business assets. The focus of strategic patenting is on extracting additional value from treating patents as business assets.

The literature has, in fact, identified a range of strategic motives for patenting by firms that are distinct from the traditional motive to protect from imitation. Figure 18.3 shows the share of companies in the United States (Cohen et al. 2000) and Germany (Blind et al. 2006) that consider the different strategic motives important for their patenting decisions. For US manufacturing firms, offensive and defensive blocking (we explain what that means below) are the most important strategic motives to patent. For German manufacturing firms, a company's reputation also plays an important role. Patents are also considered important for bargaining and generating licensing revenue.

---

[4] *Apple Inc. v. Samsung Electronics Co., Ltd., et al.*, 920 F. Supp. 2d 1079 (N.D. California, January 29, 2013).

However, those motivations are less important overall than the offensive and defensive motives.

In this chapter, we review the concept of strategic patenting, its importance for companies in appropriating returns to innovation, and discuss potential consequences, including ownership fragmentation and patent thickets.

18.2 Strategic Patenting

18.2.1 Strategic Patenting in Information and Communication Technologies

Gordon Moore, the inventor of Moore's law, co-founder of Fairchild Semiconductor and Intel, stated in an interview in 2005: "What we never anticipated . . . was a lot of other participants were going to enter the business later on. So, at Fairchild we tended to patent relatively few things. . . ." As suggested by Moore's quote, the US semiconductor industry not only experienced substantial entry by specialized firms once it started to mature, but it also experienced a dramatic increase in patent filings starting in the mid-1980s.

Figure 18.4 shows patenting propensities for a number of different industrial sectors in the United States, where patenting propensity is defined as the ratio of the number of patent grants to the average of the prior 3 years' R&D expenditure (measured in real millions of US dollars). To a certain extent, these cross-industry differences

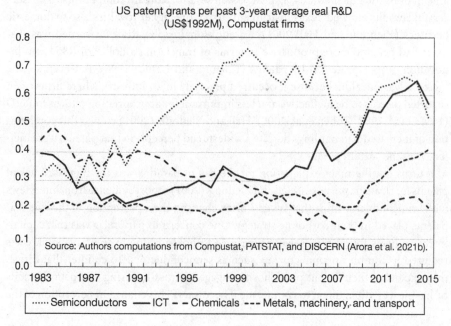

Figure 18.4 Patenting propensities across specific industries in the United States, 1980–2015.

are explained by technology-inherent differences. Patent protection is considered more effective for certain technologies and hence used more (Cohen et al. 2000), and also the productivity of R&D investment in terms of innovation output varies across technologies and industries. Figure 18.4 shows a rapid increase in patenting propensities in semiconductors beginning in the second half of the 1980s and leveling off in about the year 2000. This was a surprising development since until then, the patent system was considered largely ineffective for appropriating returns to innovation outside of the pharmaceutical and chemical industries (Granstrand 1999). It turns out that there are several explanations for this dramatic increase in patent filings per dollar of R&D spent.

Part of the explanation is an overall increase in patenting in the United States since the early 1980s. This increase was, in part, due to an institutional strengthening of the US patent system. One important change was the creation of the US CAFC, which was perceived to be pro-patent. There were also a few high-level court cases that increased the value of patents for firms. For example, in 1986, a court awarded instant camera maker Polaroid almost US$1billion in damages for patent infringement against Kodak. The court also imposed a permanent injunction against Kodak, which effectively prevented it from competing in the instant film camera market. The decision reinforced the perception that patent owners were likely to prevail in court and obtain considerable damages or valuable injunctions against competitors.

In addition, a number of large players in the market, such as Texas Instruments, AT&T, and IBM, had begun to license more aggressively to increase monetization of their patent portfolios. In particular, Texas Instruments had successfully asserted a number of patents on integrated circuits (the so-called Kilby patents) and manufacturing methods against Japanese and Korean competitors. The successful lawsuits allowed Texas Instruments to charge higher royalties also to domestic licensees (Ziedonis and Hall 2001). An additional explanation forwarded was that firms had become more productive in terms of translating a dollar of R&D into innovation output protected by patents (Kortum and Lerner 1998). But even so, the increase was puzzling because it occurred precisely in an industry where firms often reported patents to be ineffective and less important for appropriating returns to R&D (Levin et al. 1987, Cohen et al. 2000). Hall and Ziedonis (2001) coined this combination of increased patent filings despite a widespread perception that patents were ineffective as the "patent paradox."

It turns out the main explanation for the patent paradox was the increased use of patents for strategic purposes. Hall and Ziedonis (2001) report evidence from interviews with semiconductor firms that suggest firms changed their perception of the role that patents played in their corporate strategy. One concern in particular was that capital-intensive firms found themselves vulnerable to hold-up due to the large sunk costs required in complex manufacturing, such as semiconductors. To counter that threat, they expanded their patent portfolios to engage in cross-licensing and deter lawsuits by having a credible threat to countersue if necessary. This change in perception of the importance of patents for defensive purposes led to important changes in the way firms managed their intellectual property. This was also clearly reflected in the increased usage of language by managers interviewed by Hall and Ziedonis like "harvesting latent inventions," reflecting a "deeper reach into an existing pool of inventions rather than a shift in R&D activities per se" (Hall and Ziedonis 2001, p. 108). Those statements simply reflected the fact that firms increased their patent filings for a given level of innovation output.

Using data on a large sample of US semiconductor firms for the period 1975–1998, Hall and Ziedonis (2001) showed more formally that the increase in patent filings per dollar of R&D was indeed driven by strategic motives. They show that standard predictors of patent filings, above all R&D investment and firm size, explain patent filings well until the mid-1980s. However, toward the late 1980s and early 1990s, R&D spending could no longer explain patent filings. Instead, patent filings appeared to be driven by capital intensity, and more importantly, a large component of variation in patent filings could no longer be accounted for by any standard firm characteristics. The combination of the observed substantial increase in patent filings by firms and the fact that it could not be accounted for by standard predictors of patent filings lead to the conclusion that patent filings must have been driven by strategic motives. Hall and Ziedonis (2001) called this phenomenon a "patent portfolio race," more patenting by capital-intensive firms in order to reduce "concerns about being held up by external patent owners and at negotiating access to external technologies on more favorable terms" (Hall and Ziedonis 2001, p. 104).

Since the early 1990s, strategic patenting has increased dramatically and spread far beyond the US semiconductor industry (Hall 2005). The ICT industry (which includes electric machinery, electronics, instruments, computers, and communication equipment) has especially embraced the strategic use of patents that was facilitated by broader patentability of software and business methods (see Chapter 17). As a result, patenting propensities in the ICT industry (excluding semiconductors) have increased substantially. Figure 18.4 shows that although the growth was slower, patenting in the entire sector is now as high as it is in semiconductors. Interestingly, the machinery and auto sector now also shows growth in patenting propensity beginning in 2010, which reflects the increasing importance of digital technologies in this sector.

Fink et al. (2016) looked at the recent surge in patenting worldwide and found that one reason was the increase in patenting per R&D investment in the electrical machinery, computer-related, and audio-visual technologies in major patenting countries. Beginning around 1994, patents per R&D increased three- to four-fold in these technologies. Measurement of this kind is challenging because the R&D is based on country reports of aggregate R&D in broad sectors, while the patent data are based on the technological classification of the patents, which may or may not belong to the firms whose R&D is being counted. Nevertheless, the result suggests that the phenomenon is not confined to the United States.

Box 18.1 Netflix and the Changing Importance of Patents

We can also observe how the importance of patents changes over time at the firm level. Let's look at the example of the popular online streaming service Netflix. The company was founded in California in August 1997. Initially, Netflix offered a DVD mail-rental service where customers were charged per DVD rented. In 1999, Netflix introduced a flat-fee subscription service—which no longer exists today—that through clever design did away with due dates, late fees, and so on, that were traditionally associated with VHS and DVD rental services. The company went public in 2002, and in 2007, Netflix made a major technological leap by starting to stream video content on demand.

The figure below shows how Neflix's revenue grew at an exponential rate between 1998 and 2019, from slightly more than US$1.3million in 1998 to over US$20billion in 2019. The figure also indicates the number of US patents filed by Netflix since its creation up until 2019 (the last year for which we have complete data). It is clear that the company filed no patents during its first few years and then filed only a very modest number of patents, one or two annually. In its 2002 annual report, the year of its IPO, Netflix made clear that it relied primarily on informal appropriation mechanisms, stating that "[t]o date, we have relied primarily on proprietary processes and know-how to protect our intellectual property related to our Web site and fulfillment processes."

However, that filing behavior started to change soon, in step with the fast-paced growth of the company. While we don't know what caused this change of heart, the increased technological complexity of Netflix's business is certainly one factor (due to the switch to streaming technology and increased focus on content recommendation algorithms). However, another potential trigger could have been a patent infringement lawsuit that Netflix brought against competitor Blockbuster in 2006. Blockbuster, which was back then the leading video rental store company, had introduced its own DVD mail-rental service and had begun to encroach on Netflix's business model. As explained in Netflix's 2006 annual report, Netflix's "complaint allege[d] that Blockbuster willfully infringed two of the Company's patents-US Patent No. 7,024,381 entitled 'Approach for Renting Items to Customers' and US Patent No. 6,584,450 entitled 'Method and Apparatus for Renting Items.'" The lawsuit ended with a settlement in 2007 and a payment of US$7million by Blockbuster to Netflix. It is possible that the lawsuit demonstrated to Netflix the potential strategic value of patents in dealing with its competitors. Hence, another potential reason for the increased importance of patents for strategic purposes was the market entry of competitors in the streaming market, such as Hulu, launched in 2007, or HBO Go, launched in 2010.

The figure also shows the number of lawsuits in which Netflix was accused of patent infringement, and suggests that Netflix only started to become a target after it had entered the streaming business, which made the company more vulnerable to the infringement of potentially relevant software patents. Given that many of these lawsuits were filed by non-practicing entities, Netflix's success and rapidly increasing revenue also contributed to the company becoming a frequent target of patent infringement suits.

To sum up, we see in the example of Netflix that companies creating new products or even entire new markets often forgo patent protection at early stages of their development. However, as competition intensifies and the company grows, patents become more valuable from a strategic perspective. Not surprisingly, this translates into rapidly growing patent portfolios that are employed in many ways to generate a competitive advantage for the maturing company.

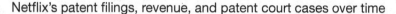

Netflix's patent filings, revenue, and patent court cases over time

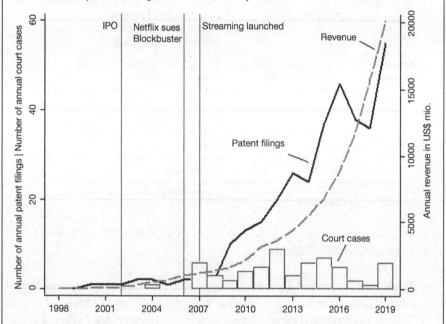

Revenue comes from Netflix's annual reports. US patents filings come from EPO's Patstat database. Court cases are patent infringement cases filed at US district courts where Netflix was the defendant accused of patent infringement. The litigation data were obtained from Docket Navigator.

18.2.2 Forms of Strategic Patenting

Nowadays across industries, firms engage heavily in strategic patenting. Take the example of Japanese tech company Konica Minolta. The company states in its 2021 IP report that "an intellectual property strategy tied closely to business strategy and technology strategy is an essential element for management." In order to create and implement its IP strategy, the company created a formal "Intellectual Property Strategy 2017–2022" with the express goal of supporting the company's business model through the strategic use of IP. Table 18.1 shows the key elements of the plan. The company has a dedicated IP division whose goal is to formulate and execute an IP strategy in addition to the traditional function of obtaining and administering the company's IP rights. It also underscores that strategic use of patents can serve diverse objectives within a broader IP strategy.

THE PATENT SYSTEM

Table 18.1 Konica Minolta's Intellectual Property Strategy 2017–2022

	Key Points	*Breakdown*
New and growth businesses	IP that supports a business model that has evolved	• Building a patent network to secure "dominant patents" and lock in "differentiating technologies" • Incorporating and using know-how and data in IP strategy
Core businesses	IP that supports profitability	• Enhancement of property value through optimization of patent portfolio • Improvement of productivity (pursuit of effectiveness and efficiency)
Across all businesses	Strengthening of IP promotion structure	• Strengthen capability in patent information analysis • Develop human resources that would lead to next-generation intellectual property IP structure • Improve and strengthen global IP structure • Improve brand value through designs and trademarks

Source: Konica Minolta 2018 IP report.

More generally, strategic patenting encompasses a number of different uses of patents that can be categorized as follows.

• **Bargaining**: A common strategic use of patents is for bargaining purposes, broadly defined. In fact, patents are in practice "typically best seen as a basis for negotiation, not a prescription for who actually uses what assets or ideas" (Farrell 2008, p. 39). Such bargaining can have many different purposes.

Patents can directly generate new or increase existing revenue streams. Rivette and Kline (2000) point to the example of Xerox's failure to patent its early graphical user interface (GUI) technology, which was eventually used by Apple's and Microsoft's operating systems. GUI technology was remote from Xerox's main line of business in the late 1970s when it made the decision not to patent its GUI technology. However, Rivette and Kline (2000) point out that even if Xerox had not pursued the development of its GUI technology and instead limited itself to licensing the technology to Apple and Microsoft, it would have earned at least half a billion dollars in royalties thanks to its patents.

Patents can also reduce costs by enabling access to other firms' patents without requiring any monetary compensation. This is usually achieved through cross-licensing agreements.

Patenting for bargaining purposes can also facilitate establishing business partnerships with competitors or upstream/downstream firms involving the joint development of new technology or products.

Bargaining also occurs in the shadow of litigation, and patents can help manage any resulting legal risk. For example, patents can avoid the escalation of a dispute to the point where the parties find themselves in court. This can be achieved either by agreeing to license, transfer, or exchange patents or by providing deterrence by credibly threatening the other party with a (counter-)suit or the prospect of protracted and costly litigation.

Patents can help achieve settlement on more favorable terms in the case where litigation occurs. Apple, for example, asserted its swipe-to-unlock patent as a counterclaim when it was sued for patent infringement by competitors Motorola and HTC in a case that eventually settled.[5] Harrington et al. (2017) recount that obtaining a more favorable bargaining position was also a major motivation for LinkedIn to start thinking strategically about its patent portfolio after going public in 2011. At the time, LinkedIn had only 1 issued patent and 35 pending patents. Such an extraordinarily small patent portfolio for a publicly traded tech company exposed LinkedIn to substantial patent litigation risk. To mitigate it, the company created a patent strategy with the help of outside consultants. The goals were to increase in-house patent filings, identify and acquire patents on the secondary market, and prepare "counter-assertion strategies" to address specific perceived litigation risks. In order increase its own patent filings, LinkedIn had to "fundamentally shift its patent culture" (Harrington et al. 2017, p. 28). The company created a legal team focused on managing its patent strategy; it set a specific target in terms of filings per dollar of R&D spent and created "invention harvesting sessions" for its engineers combined with incentive programs to help generate invention disclosures that could lead to more patent filings, similar to the ways semiconductor firms responded to changes during the 1980s. Box 18.1 discusses the example of Netflix, which serves to illustrate the changing importance of strategic patenting as companies mature.

- **Offensive/Defensive Blocking:** Firms use patents *offensively* to block competitors from pursuing certain directions of research or product development. For example, firms can patent similar, substitute technologies to make it harder to invent around their patented technology. Even if the company does not pursue the substitute technologies for its own production, it can still create obstacles for competitors and at a minimum increase costs for them. This helps create a competitive advantage for the blocking company. For example, competitors may have strong incentives to steer clear of potential patent infringement, for instance, to avoid an interim or even permanent injunction.

The successful patent lawsuit by Polaroid against Kodak for infringement of instant photography–related technology is a case in point of the magnitude of the costs that can be incurred by competitors and the ability of patents to block or shut down competitors. Kodak was ordered not only to pay close to a billion dollars in damages, but was also subject to a permanent injunction that forced it to shut down its entire instant photography business. This meant not only writing off decades of R&D investment, but also shutting down a US$1.5billion manufacturing plant, having to lay off around 700 workers, and spending almost US$500million to buy back infringing cameras already sold (Rivette and Kline 2000). The total costs to Kodak were an estimated US$3billion (Rivette et al. 2000).

Jell et al. (2017) offer another example of offensive strategic patenting that resulted in a patent portfolio race similar to what Hall and Ziedonis (2001) documented for the US semiconductor industry. Jell et al. (2017) show that in the German

---

[5] *Motorola Mobility, Inc. v. Apple Inc.*, No. 1:12-cv-20271-RNS-TEB (S.D. Florida, March 12, 2012).

newspaper-printing machine industry, where patent ownership is highly concentrated, one of the dominant firms in the industry dramatically increased its patent filings in the early 2000s to make it harder for the other firms in the industry to compete in an attempt to gain market share.

Blocking is also used as a *defensive* strategy. Instead of relying on patents to obstruct competitors' R&D, patents are employed to ensure a company's own freedom to operate—this motivation was the main driver behind the increased patenting rates observed in the US semiconductor industry discussed above. Such a defensive blocking strategy often just means ensuring options for the future, that is, ensuring that future research and product development paths are not blocked by competitors.

Defensive strategies also help ensure a company's ability to commercialize its own technology. This may seem counterintuitive: Why would a company encounter difficulties commercializing its own technology if it holds patents on its own technology? The answer is that patents only grant their owners the right to exclude others, not the right to use the patented technology (a patent is a "negative right"; see Chapter 11). Hence, patents held by other companies may still read on aspects of the company's technology (see the discussion on patent thickets below). As a result, the company may face the need to license those technologies to bring its own patented invention to market. This can be costly, especially if such licensing has to be negotiated after the company has made irreversible sunk investments in its technology and its commercialization.

Both offensive and defensive blocking strategies can be implemented through a range of specific patenting strategies. Here is a list of some of the most popular:

- *Blanketing or flooding.* Patent *blanketing* or *flooding* describes a strategy whereby a firm files a large number of patents around a competitor's (patented) technology to limit the competitor's freedom to operate (Granstrand 1999, Ernst et al. 2016).
- *Fencing or clustering.* A similar, albeit more targeted and primarily defensive strategy is referred to as *fencing* or *clustering*, whereby the innovator patents not only its core invention, which is incorporated in the innovator's product, but also specific related and in particular substitute technologies to limit a competitor's ability to invent around (Fisher and Oberholzer-Gee 2013). The outcome of this strategy is sometimes described as a *patent wall* (Rivette and Kline 2000).
- *Surrounding or bracketing.* This strategy is used to shield a core technology by patenting around it by, for example, patenting different applications or uses of the core technology (Granstrand 1999). Rivette and Kline (2000, p. 110) describe this strategy as follows: "[I]magine that your competitor has invented a new high-intensity light and has patented the filament. But . . . the filament requires a more durable glass bulb and socket housing to absorb the added heat, as well as more heat-resistant shade construction and electrical connectors. Even new manufacturing processes are required, as is new packaging. . . . Your competitor may have patented the filament, but if you patent everything else, then the competitor is locked out of much of the market." As part of this patenting strategy, follow-on inventions are also patented if they otherwise may allow competitors to build and improve on the patented core technology.
- *Networking.* Yet another strategy is *networking* whereby patents are combined in a portfolio with the express goal of increasing the protection beyond what individual patents can achieve (Granstrand 1999); see also Konica Minolta's IP strategy in Table 18.1.

- **Reputation:** Another strategic use of patent portfolios is to shape a firm's public perception and reputation. For example, firms can reinforce the public perception that they operate at the technology frontier by highlighting their number of patent filings. Because the public has little understanding of the complexities of the patent system, such simple patent counts may be effective in shaping public perception. For example, car maker Mercedes Benz advertised its E-Class series in a TV commercial in 2013 by highlighting that the company held over 80,000 patents. But even among competitors, the strategic build-up of patent portfolios may be useful in order to create a reputation for aggressively protecting one's innovation and, if necessary, enforcing it in court. This will help preempt costly conflict and litigation. It can also strengthen a firm's bargaining position in licensing negotiations.
- **Investment:** Patents can also help attract outside investment, which might be especially important for early-stage companies and projects. The strategic element here is that patents are primarily used as a credible signal targeted at outside investors, rather than as a vehicle to prevent the copying of its technology. Such patents may still accomplish exclusivity and attract investors by allowing them to recoup some of their investment in case a venture fails (they get to sell the patents). That said, the empirical evidence reviewed by Hall (2019) on whether firms engage in this use of patents is relatively weak.
- **Technology Diffusion and Standards:** Control over technology in the form of patents may help companies influence technology adoption and diffusion in an industry or market. This may be particularly helpful in order to influence or establish industrywide standards (see Chapter 21).

These strategies can be achieved by different means. Firms can adjust their own patenting decisions, that is, they can decide whether to patent a given invention, and how to craft the corresponding patent(s). They can also sell or acquire patents from other entities. In addition to outright acquisition, there are a range of other mechanisms available to firms to strategically share and exchange patents; we review these in Chapter 20. Another important element in many of these strategies is enforcement. In particular, any offensive use of patents may require a credible threat of enforcement, if necessary, in court.

Konica Minolta's IP strategy discussed above also highlighted the managerial challenges that arise when patents are treated as assets. Indeed, the strategic use of patents requires active management of patents and IP more generally. This implies, in practice, that the management of a firm's patent portfolio becomes the responsibility of not only legal counsel but also a firm's (top) management. If firms consider their patent strategy in the context of their broader business strategy, it has obvious managerial implications (Cockburn and Henderson 2003). Companies often rely on formal IP management organizations to formulate and implement patent strategies. Such organizations are usually integrated within a company's management structure, but sometimes they are also set up as external entities. This function can even be outsourced to external consulting firms, as in the case of LinkedIn discussed above. Ayerbe et al. (2014) discuss how Thales, a large French electronics company active in the defense industry, outsourced its entire IP management to an outside consultancy firm while still retaining control over strategic decisions regarding its IP.

18.2.3 Consequences of Strategic Patenting

The strategic use of patents can help create value for combinations of patents even when individual patents are of little value by themselves. This can help increase a company's profits. Chapter 16 illustrated this in the context of the pharmaceutical industry. However, it also applies to other industries that are characterized by strategic patenting. Sternitzke (2017), for example, reported that 22 interlocking patent families protect the Gillette Fusion Power razor. His analysis suggests that the interlocking characteristic of the patent portfolio successfully prevented competitors from imitating the most important features of the razor and hence resulted in a substantial competitive advantage (and hence price premium) for the Gillette razor. John Bush, former vice-president of R&D at Gillette put it this way: "We patented the key design features in the cartridge, the springs, the angle of the blades. . . . There were also patents covering the handle and some of its characteristics. We even patented the container that had the proper masculine sound and feel as it was ripped. . . . We created a patent wall with those 22 patents. And they were all interlocking so that no one could duplicate the product" (quoted in Davis and Harrison 2001).

While strategic patenting clearly has private benefits, it also generates negative externalities. As discussed in the context of patent portfolio races above, an increase in patent filings by one company can force its competitors to follow suit. Hence, increases in patent filings by one company can trigger industrywide increases in patenting (Hall and Ziedonis 2001; Jell et al. 2017). At a minimum, this may increase transaction costs for companies as they have to negotiate access to each other's patented technology and navigate any resulting legal conflicts. There is, in fact, empirical evidence that higher levels of patenting in the software industry reduce product market entry by companies (Cockburn and MacGarvie 2011). Similarly, in the US biotech industry, there is evidence that new companies perceive patent filings by competitors to increase the risk of litigation (Lerner 1995).

18.3 Ownership Fragmentation and Patent Thickets

One consequence of strategic patenting is not only a drastic increase in patent filings per dollar of R&D spent, but also a potential increase in fragmentation of ownership of technology. Especially in complex and modular technologies, where often thousands of technology components have to work together, increased fragmentation of any associated patent rights may increase transaction costs for market participants.

Fragmentation of ownership means that different patents that protect distinct components of a complex product are owned by different parties. To make the product, access to these patents has to be obtained from all the different parties. Therefore, fragmentation of patent ownership can prevent the use of the underlying patented technology because transaction costs associated with bargaining among the different patent owners to aggregate the fragmented rights become prohibitively costly--a situation described as anti-commons by Heller and Eisenberg (1998). When patent ownership is fragmented, negotiating licenses not only requires transaction costs, but also individual rights holders are likely charging too high a royalty because of the Cournot complements problem, which we discuss in Chapter 21 in the context of royalty stacking.

Noel and Schankerman (2013) offer some empirical evidence on the issue. They show that increased fragmentation is associated with lower market value for firms. They interpret this to suggest that more fragmentation indeed increases the transaction costs of settling patent disputes. Ziedonis (2004) shows that fragmentation leads firms in the semiconductor sector to increase their own patenting in response.

In the presence of technological complementarity, fragmentation of patent ownership of any corresponding patents can result in a patent thicket. Shapiro (2001) described a patent thicket as a "dense web of overlapping IP rights that a company must hack its way through in order to actually commercialize new technology" (Shapiro, 2001, p. 120). The emphasis in this definition is on "overlapping," which distinguishes thickets from fragmentation of ownership.

Indeed, thickets can occur when different patents cover the same technology and hence overlap. This implies that fragmentation fosters the emergence of thickets, but thickets can occur even in technologies with more concentrated patent ownership as long as there are overlapping patent claims. It also means that thickets can restrict company i's freedom to operate even when company i holds patents on its own technology. This situation occurs when other companies j ($i \neq j$) also hold patents that protect aspects of i's technology. In that situation, company i, in principle, requires licenses from all other right holders to commercialize its own technology.[6]

Both fragmentation and thickets are subject to a self-reinforcing mechanism. Due to strategic complementarity, patenting by one firm raises the incentives for all other firms to patent. This, in turn, increases fragmentation of technology ownership. As ownership becomes more fragmented, it increases the overall level of patenting as firms have strong incentives to accumulate large defensive patent portfolios. Moreover, in the presence of overlapping claims, the increased fragmentation exacerbates the formation of thickets. In other words, fragmentation and thickets are simultaneously a catalyst and consequence of strategic patenting.

The concept of patent thickets is not uncontroversial. Some observers see thickets as a natural consequence of fast-paced development in complex technologies (Lewis and Mott 2013). Some have pointed to the "extraordinary rates of innovation despite the fact that barriers supposedly exist" to argue that even if patent thickets existed, they do not adversely affect innovation as markets are able to resolve any blocking situations that might emerge (Teece 2018, p. 1492). As a case in point, Mossoff (2011) discusses the historical example of the sewing machine patent war in the United States in the mid-19th century. Because the sewing machine thicket was resolved through the formation of a patent pool, Mossoff argues that this historical example shows not only that thickets are not a new phenomenon (and hence not inherently associated with the modern patent system that allows for software patents), but also that thickets can be resolved by market participants without regulatory intervention.[7]

---

[6] Note that the literature has also referred to certain patenting strategies in the pharmaceutical industry as patent thickets. However, in that literature, the use of the term thicket is different from the definition used here, although clearly related. It describes a portfolio of multiple, potentially overlapping (secondary) patent filings on a given drug that have been filed by the *same* originator to extend patent exclusivity in time and scope (see Chapter 16). See, for example, Knox and Curfman (2022) who discuss the "Humira patent thicket."

[7] Chapter 20 discusses empirical evidence that arrives at less favorable conclusions regarding the impact of the sewing machine patent pool on innovation.

18.3.1 Measuring Fragmentation and Patent Thickets

There have been different approaches to measuring ownership fragmentation and thickets in the literature. A reasonable starting point is simply to count the number of granted patents within a defined product market or technology field (Cockburn and MacGarvie 2011). However, this type of measure does not work well since there are technologies and industries, such as the pharmaceutical sector, characterized by a combination of extensive patenting and relatively low levels of fragmentation and thickets. This is due to the underlying characteristics of the technology. That is, in discrete technologies such as pharmaceuticals, there is no need for many components to work together to make a product. It is also easier to define boundaries between patents even in the presence of a large number of strategic patents. However, in complex and modular technologies, such as hardware or software, many different components have to be assembled to make a product. What is more, defining boundaries between patents that cover different aspects of a given technology is much more difficult, and hence fragmentation and thickets emerge more easily.

Ziedonis (2004) proposes a measure that reflects fragmentation based on backward patent citations. She computes a *fragmentation index* as follows:

$$Frag_i = 1 - \sum_{j=1}^{J} \left(\frac{NBCITES_{ij}}{NBCITES_i} \right)^2 \quad \text{where } i \neq j$$

$NBCITES_i$ denotes the number of backward cites made by patents issued to firm i in a given year; $NBCITES_{ij}$ denotes the number of backward cites made to firm j by patents issued to firm i. The index excludes self-references, references to expired patents and nonpatent literature.[8]

Noel and Schankerman (2013) rely on a similar firm-level measure. They compute a four-firm fragmentation measure as follows:

$$Fragcite_{it} = 1 - \sum_{j=1}^{4} s_{ijt} \quad \text{with } i \neq j$$

where s_{ijt} denotes the share of the total number of citations by firm i that refer to patents held by firm j, cumulated up to year t. That means Noel and Schankerman's measure of fragmentation captures the share of backward cites by firm i that are accounted for by the top four firms that hold patents cited by firm i. The more fragmented ownership of patents, the lower the index should be. Since the measure relies on backward citations like the measure proposed by Ziedonis (2004), it captures the relevance of ownership fragmentation for a given firm i.

A different measure that captures overlapping claims and hence the core aspect of thickets more directly has been proposed by von Graevenitz et al. (2011). Their measure is also based on backward citations but in addition leverages further information

---

[8] This index is recognizable as 1 minus the HHI of backward cites by firm i.

provided by patent examiners. During the examination process, patent examiners produce search reports in which they list all relevant prior art. At the EPO, they mark prior art either with an X or Y reference (see Box 18.2). The X/Y marker indicates that the prior art unearthed by the examiner contains elements claimed by the patent under examination. In other words, the examiner identifies overlap between prior patents and

---

Box 18.2 EPO Search Reports, X/Y Citations, and Blocking Relationships

---

Examiners at the EPO issue X and Y references in their search reports after conducting a prior art search on a given application. According to Section 9.2.1 of the EPO's Guidelines for Examination, "Category 'Y' is applicable where a document is such that a claimed invention cannot be considered to involve an inventive step when the document is combined with one or more other documents of the same category, such combination being obvious to a person skilled in the art. If a document explicitly refers to another document as providing more detailed information on certain features and the combination of these documents is considered particularly relevant, the primary document should be indicated by the letter 'X.'"

Below we can see the example of patent EP 3,310,066, "Identifying media content for simultaneous playback," filed by music-streaming service Spotify. The snippet of the examiner search report shows a number of X/Y references based on prior patent filings. For example, patent application US 2010/304860, "Game execution environments," filed by Sony subsidiary Gaikai contains several elements (described in paragraphs 20 and 31-33) that are relevant for what is asserted in Claims 2, 3, and 8 of patent EP 3,310,066.

EP 3 310 066 A1

Europäisches
Patentamt
European
Patent Office
Office européen
des brevets

EUROPEAN SEARCH REPORT

Application Number
EP 17 19 6357

DOCUMENTS CONSIDERED TO BE RELEVANT			
Category	Citation of document with indication, where appropriate, of relevant passages	Relevant to claim	CLASSIFICATION OF THE APPLICATION (IPC)
X Y	US 2009/044686 A1 (VASA YOJAK H [US]) 19 February 2009 (2009-02-19) * paragraph [0010] - paragraph [0073] *	1,4-7, 9-20 2,3,8	INV. H04N21/482 H04N21/462
Y	US 2010/304860 A1 (GAULT ANDREW BUCHANAN [IT] ET AL) 2 December 2010 (2010-12-02) * paragraph [0020], [0031]-[0033] *	2,3,8	
X	US 2007/124491 A1 (HAWKINS DAX H [US] ET AL) 31 May 2007 (2007-05-31) * paragraph [0007] - paragraph [0049] *	1-20	
X	WO 2005/036875 A1 (DISNEY ENTPR INC [US]; ACKLEY JONATHAN [US]; CAREY CHRISTOPHER [US]; C) 21 April 2005 (2005-04-21) * paragraph [0028] - paragraph [0059] *	1-20	

the patent under examination. The Graevenitz et al. measure exploits this information to identify blocking relationships between patents.[9]

The idea underlying their measure is that whenever there are three firms that hold patents that block each other due to overlapping claims—which von Graevenitz et al. (2011) call a "triple"--the bargaining problem to resolve mutual blocking becomes more complicated than in bilateral blocking situations. In a triple, two firms cannot resolve the blocking situation without the third firm. Therefore, von Graevenitz et al. (2011) measure the density of patent thickets by counting the number of triples within a given technology area. While there can be many unilateral and bilateral blocking relationships, thickets only arise in situations such as the one described by firms A, B, and C in Figure 18.5, where all three firms block each other.

To see how the measure performs in practice, Figure 18.6 compares the number of triples in complex and discrete technologies as defined by Cohen et al. (2000). Complex technologies comprise technology that consists of many distinct components that can be combined in different ways and that often have to inter-operate with other components and devices. This includes technology areas such as semiconductors and telecommunications. Discrete technologies have a more direct correspondence between technology and product. In pharmaceuticals, for example, a drug often consists of only a single active ingredient. As we can see in Figure 18.6, the triple count started to increase dramatically in complex technologies toward the end of the 1980s, inline

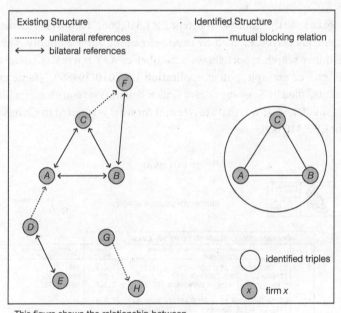

This figure shows the relationship between companies based on their mutual patent citation relationships. Source: von Graevenitz et al. (2011).

Figure 18.5 Triples-based thickets measure.

[9] The measure assumes that despite the examiner flagging the overlap, it won't be fully removed during the patent-granting process and more generally is indicative of overlapping claims between the patent cited by the examiner and the patent under examination.

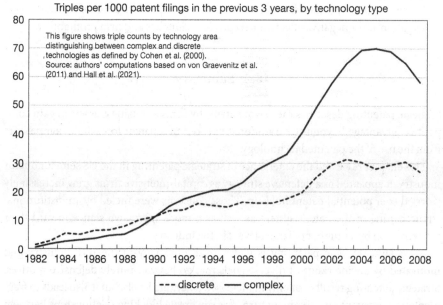

Figure 18.6 Triple counts by technology area.

with our discussion of the strategic patenting in ICT above. In contrast, in discrete technologies, the triples count increased much less over the sample period despite widespread strategic patenting in pharmaceuticals (see Chapter 16).

18.3.2 Consequences of Ownership Fragmentation and Thickets

Since the development process of complex technology is cumulative, blocking patents in the form of thickets can adversely affect innovation (Shapiro 2001). Despite this clear theoretical prediction, there is relatively little empirical evidence on the impact of thickets on firms and on innovation more broadly.

However, there is robust evidence to suggest that patenting levels are positively associated with thickets (Ziedonis 2004, von Graevenitz et al. 2013). While the available evidence also indicates that the amount of patenting reduces product market and technology entry (Lerner 1995, Cockburn and MacGarvie 2011), it does not directly capture the effect of thickets, which are distinct from the sheer amount of patenting.

Hall et al. (2021) provide direct evidence on the impact of thickets on technology entry of firms. They show that thickets affect entry by firms into new technology areas as measured by first-time patenting across a wide range of industries in the United Kingdom. The empirical analysis distinguishes between technological complexity and thicket density. Hall et al. (2021) show for a large sample of UK firms that greater technological complexity (as measured by citation network density) increases entry while thickets reduce entry. Their interpretation of the evidence is that thickets raise entry costs, which could adversely affect innovation more broadly if more radical inventions tend to come from entrants rather than incumbents. Hu et al. (2022) offer additional evidence for publicly traded firms across industries of a positive effect of patent thickets on litigation and a negative effect on new product launches and firm profitability.

18.4 Summary

Strategic patenting describes the use of patents by firms as business assets to gain competitive advantage beyond the traditional purpose of a patent to exclude competitors from the use of the patented technology.

This chapter reviewed the emergence of strategic patenting in the US semiconductor industry. It appeared as a defensive strategy as capital-intensive firms grew increasingly worried over potential patent hold-up. Those concerns were fueled by an institutional strengthening of the patent system as well as a more aggressive stance toward their monetization by a number of large players in the industry.

Nowadays, strategic patenting is widespread, especially in the ICT industry and motivated by a wide range of diverse goals that go beyond purely defensive motives. Strategic patenting results not only in increased patenting levels, but it also leads to fragmentation of patent ownership. In turn, this can create blocking relationships between different patent owners in the presence of overlapping patent claims, called patent thickets, that reinforce the need for strategic patenting and that may adversely affect technology entry and innovation more broadly.

19

Patent Litigation and Enforcement

Learning Objectives

After reading this chapter, you will be able to understand and explain the following concepts:

- The role of the enforcement system in resolving disputes
- The basic structure of patent litigation
- Economic approaches to modeling the litigation process in general
- Economic approaches to modeling the patent litigation process
- Different design choices of litigation systems
- The main characteristics of the most important patent litigation systems around the world

---

19.1 Introduction

In December 2013, iLife Technologies Inc. filed a complaint against Nintendo Inc. at the US District Court for the Northern District of Texas alleging infringement of six of its patents.[1] iLife alleged that technology incorporated in Nintendo's Wii game console to enable motion-controlled play infringed on iLife's patents. Nintendo countered by challenging the validity of the asserted patents. In parallel administrative validity challenges at the USPTO's Patent Trial and Appeal Board (PTAB), Nintendo successfully invalidated five of the six patents. However, in August 2017, the jury in the court case found that Nintendo had infringed Claim 1 of iLife's one remaining patent US 6,864,796 "Systems within a communication device for evaluating movement of a body and methods of operating the same." The jury also upheld the validity of the patent and awarded iLife a lump-sum royalty payment of US$10.1million. But the case was not over yet. Nintendo then successfully filed a posttrial motion to set aside the jury verdict. The judge ignored the jury verdict and instead found that iLife's patent was, in fact, invalid because it covered patent-ineligible subject matter and thus ultimately decided the case in favor of Nintendo.

The summary of this case omits much of the complexity of the back-and-forth that occurred in this court case. It nevertheless illustrates some of the core characteristics of

---

[1] *iLife Technologies Inc. v. Nintendo of America Inc.*, No. 13-cv-04987, 2017 WL 2778006 (N.D. Texas, June 27, 2017). iLife is categorized as a nonpracticing entity (NPE) by the Stanford NPE database (see Chapter 22 for more discussion on NPEs).

The Economics of Innovation and Intellectual Property. Bronwyn H. Hall and Christian Helmers, Oxford University Press.
© Oxford University Press 2024. DOI: 10.1093/oso/9780197630914.003.0019

patent litigation. In most cases, a patent owner alleges infringement of all or a subset of claims of one or several patents by a single or multiple defendants. As a defense, the defendant routinely challenges the patents' validity. This is an important, distinguishing feature of patent litigation because if the patent is invalidated by the court, the infringement claim is automatically dismissed. Moreover, the patent owner loses the patent as it is no longer enforceable. Questions of infringement and invalidity are complex, especially in certain technologies such as software (see Chapter 17). Patent litigation is, in fact, considered one of the most complex forms of civil litigation. Other distinguishing characteristics of patent litigation are the high costs of litigation, the long duration of the proceedings, and the often high stakes involved. Damages of US$10million are not even particularly large as the recent damages award of over US$1.9billion in *Centripetal Networks, Inc. v. Cisco Systems, Inc.* illustrates.[2]

Given the large amounts of money at stake and the fact that often well-known companies that sell popular consumer products go head-to-head with each other, it is no surprise that patent litigation regularly makes it into the headlines of the popular press. Patent litigation is also at the forefront in policy discussions on the design and functioning of the patent system. Apart from the global patent wars that occurred over the last decade in the smartphone industry, patent litigation has also been in the public spotlight in the United States for the proliferation of so-called nonpracticing entities (NPEs), also referred to as patent trolls (see Chapter 22 for more discussion). In the United States, litigation by NPEs accounts for the majority of patent assertions since 2012 and is the subject of a highly controversial policy debate (FTC, 2016). Recently, companies, policymakers, and antitrust agencies have been paying increased attention to patent litigation involving SEPs (see Chapter 21). In different jurisdictions around the world, fundamental questions about the enforceability of SEPs through injunctions and the determination of what constitutes a fair, reasonable, and nondiscriminatory (FRAND) royalty rate have had to be addressed by the courts with potentially wide-reaching consequences for patenting and innovation, especially in markets that rely increasingly on interoperability such as the IoT.

There has been a long-standing interest in the economic literature in the analysis of patent litigation from a theoretical as well as empirical perspective.[3] It is, however, probably fair to say that the theoretical analysis of litigation outweighs the empirical work. One important reason is the difficulty of obtaining data on patent litigation in most jurisdictions other than the United States. Another reason is the complexity of the patent litigation process, which creates challenges in data construction and analysis. In particular, substantial legal expertise is required to process and extract the relevant qualitative information and to convert it into data that can be used for quantitative analysis.

However, studying patent enforcement is worthwhile from a policy perspective. Enforceability of patent rights is crucial for the functioning of the patent system. In-court litigation has direct effects on the patent system as a whole. In fact, it is the ability to enforce an intangible property right if it is infringed on that confers value to it. Burk and Lemley go as far as to claim that "[t]he only relevant patents are those that are licensed or litigated . . . not the whole universe of patents" (Burk and Lemley 2009, p. 85).

---

[2] 526 F. Supp. 3d 137 (E.D. Virginia, March 17, 2021).
[3] For a review of the literature, see Weatherall and Webster (2014)

It is therefore important that patent owners can enforce a patent if it is infringed. At the same time, the litigation system has to allow alleged infringers to defend themselves in court if necessary, including by challenging a patent's validity. Regardless, the system should be designed in a way to discourage strategic behavior such as plaintiffs seeking overly broad injunctions, excessive damages, or engaging in nuisance lawsuits and defendants driving up enforcement costs to deter assertion or force settlements. In practice, therefore, courts have to strike a delicate balance between allowing patent owners to enforce their rights and to obtain appropriate remedies while avoiding incentives for excessive litigation. In short, litigation matters because of the implications for innovation that reach far beyond the courtroom.

This chapter reviews the economic theory of litigation more generally and then discusses the specific setting of patent litigation, which requires a determination of both validity and infringement. The chapter also discusses different design choices of patent enforcement systems and briefly reviews a number of patent litigation systems around the world.

19.2 Structure of Patent Litigation

The judicial system deals with disputes that could not be settled by the parties out of court and therefore require adjudication. The main objective of patent litigation is to allow patent owners to enforce their patent claims against potential infringers. There are, however, also other patent related claims asserted in court, such as disputes with regard to inventorship or ownership of a patent, issues concerning patent-licensing agreements, or declaratory actions where a party seeks confirmation from a court that a patent is invalid, not infringed, or unenforceable. In practice, these types of claims account for only a small share of all patent cases compared to infringement actions.[4]

The objective of the patent owner in patent infringement cases is to get relief in the form of a preliminary or permanent injunction against future infringement, and monetary damages compensating for past infringement. Usually, the patent owner alerts the alleged infringer to the infringement by sending a demand letter, although this step is often skipped.[5] In most cases, the dispute is either resolved through an exchange of letters or less frequently dropped by the patent owner in case no response from the alleged infringer is received. However, in case of no response or if direct communication does not lead to a resolution, the patent owner files a complaint with a competent first-instance civil court asserting patent infringement. Once the complaint has been filed, the legal process of litigation in court begins. The objective of the plaintiff is to demonstrate that the claims of one or several patents have been infringed, while the defendant counters that there is no infringement. In some jurisdictions, the defendant can also rely on an invalidity defense in court, arguing that the patent claims are invalid and

---

[4] See, for example, Cremers et al. (2016a).

[5] In the United States, one reason to skip sending a demand letter is forum shopping, that is, to avoid giving the defendant an advantage by allowing the defendant to take preemptive action and file a declaratory action with the defendant's preferred court.

therefore cannot be infringed. In other jurisdictions, patent validity can only be challenged in separate court or administrative proceedings.

There are several steps before a trial takes place, such as a case management conference, pretrial discovery, pretrial hearings, motions for a preliminary injunction, a stay, or summary judgment. The precise structure of the proceedings depends on the jurisdiction. This means that parties have ample opportunity to settle the dispute before it goes to trial and are often encouraged to do so. Even during a trial, parties usually have the opportunity to settle at any point. Only if no settlement is reached, do judges (or a jury) decide a case on the merits. Once the court has decided a case, there may be additional steps, for example, to decide the amount of damages to be paid or the allocation of litigation costs. Decisions can be appealed before a court of second instance and in some, albeit rare cases, another appeal before the highest court of the jurisdiction is possible.

There is a common (mis)perception in the economics literature that the outcome of a court case can be simply categorized as a win or loss. This ignores the complexity of patent cases. In a validity challenge, often only a subset of claims is challenged and invalidated. Depending on the jurisdiction, it may also be possible for the patent owner to amend the claims of the patent during the proceedings and thereby keep the patent alive, albeit with a narrower scope. In infringement proceedings, it is equally possible that infringement is found only with respect to a subset of asserted claims. This means that often the outcome of a case is not as clear-cut as often assumed in the theoretical literature. A related problem occurs when there are multiple unrelated defendants because case outcomes may differ across defendants. This type of within-case heterogeneity adds to the difficulty of determining the overall outcome of a case as a win or loss. Another issue concerns settlements, which are often the focus of economic analysis. There is no single definition of settlement in the literature. Often any case that does not end with a decision is simply considered to have settled. However, this ignores the possibility that some cases could have been dropped by the plaintiff, dismissed by the court for some reason, or decided by a default judgment, for example, in case the defendant does not respond. Often cases settle only after the court has reached some decision, for instance, a case settles following the court's claim construction ruling.[6] Also, usually the terms of settlement agreements are not publicly available, which means that settlements are usually difficult to interpret.

19.3 Economics of Patent Litigation

There is a large theoretical literature in economics on litigation more generally.[7] The subset of the literature that looks specifically at patent litigation is much smaller. This section first explains the general approach to modeling litigation behavior following the discussion in Spier (2007) and then discusses patent litigation more specifically.

---

[6] Claim construction is a critical step in patent litigation where parties identify disputed terms of patent claims and present arguments in support of their preferred definitions. The court then determines the definitions for these disputed terms, which play a crucial role in determining the outcome of a case in terms of validity and infringement.

[7] For reviews of the literature, see Cooter and Rubinfeld (1989) and Spier (2007).

19.3.1 Models of Litigation

In the most basic models of civil litigation, there is a single plaintiff P and a single defendant D. Both parties are risk-neutral. The plaintiff decides whether to file a claim with the court. Provided the suit is filed, the plaintiff and defendant have the option to settle their dispute. If they do not settle, the case proceeds to trial and the judge decides the case. Obviously, this simple setup is far from the complex reality of litigation. It is nevertheless a useful starting point.

Assume that plaintiff P expects to obtain a gross pay-off from litigation x. This pay-off equals the expected judgment of the trial (i.e., the probability of winning times the expected amount won). Both P and D incur positive litigation costs c_p and c_D, respectively. These costs can include court fees, attorney fees, their own opportunity costs, and the like. In this simple setup, they are assumed to be constant and exogenously determined. Also assume that the parties bear their own costs regardless of the outcome of the case. This is often referred to as the *American* cost allocation rule, as opposed to the *English* rule where the loser pays the winner's litigation cost (see Section 19.4.4 below).

First, P has to decide whether to file a complaint at the court. P will sue if its expected pay-off from doing so exceeds the cost: $x > c_p$.[8] This implies that P only sues if it is privately optimal to do so. It is possible that P's private benefits and costs diverge from the social benefits and costs of the lawsuit. This, in turn, can mean that P has excessive or insufficient incentives to file a case in court. In the context of patent litigation, this question is especially important with respect to the question of patent validity since it involves externalities (if a patent is invalidated, the invalidation does not only affect the parties to the case but everyone else as well because the patent is no longer enforceable).

Conditional on P having filed suit, the parties enter settlement negotiations before the trial takes place. In this simple model, assume that settlement is only possible before trial. If there is no settlement, the parties move to trial and the judge decides the case. A settlement is a private legally binding agreement between the parties. Assume that it involves a payment from D to P in exchange for P dropping the case. Also assume that P makes a take-it-or-leave-it settlement offer that D can accept or reject.

The minimum P would accept as a settlement is P's threat point, the net pay-off from going to trial: $\pi_P = x - c_P$. The maximum D is willing to pay as a settlement is given by $\pi_D = -x - c_D$. A settlement is therefore defined as an amount S between P's minimum acceptable amount $x - c_P$ and D's maximum acceptable amount $x + c_D$, that is, $S \in (x - c_P, x + c_D)$. Since no trial occurs if the parties settle, there is a cooperative surplus equal to the total litigation cost $c_P + c_D$.

To start with, assume that P and D have the same information about all the relevant parameters in the case. Also assume that both parties incur all their litigation costs c_P and c_D when the court case is filed. Assume that bargaining takes place over a finite number of rounds T. If P makes the last offer in round $T - 1$, D will accept it as long as it

---

[8] This assumption rules out so-called negative expected value (NEV) suits. In practice, especially within the context of NPEs, NEVs can, in fact, be profitable for the plaintiff. This can be explained by an extension of the basic model.

yields a higher pay-off than letting the judge decide. P's offer therefore is the maximum D is willing to pay

$$S_{T-1} = \delta(x + c_D) \tag{1}$$

where δ is a discount factor. Working backward, in $T - 2$, P makes an offer that is at least as great as S_{T-1}:

$$S_{T-2} = \delta^2(x + c_D) \tag{2}$$

Equations (1) and (2) imply that the case settles in the first round and D agrees to pay P the following settlement:

$$S_1 = \delta^{T-1}(x + c_D) \tag{3}$$

In this type of bargaining, the party that makes the last offer extracts the entire surplus from settling. If D were to make the last offer, the equilibrium settlement would depend on P's costs:

$$S_1 = \delta^{T-1}(x - c_P) \tag{4}$$

This illustrates that the allocation of surplus (although not the outcome) depends on assumptions about who makes the last settlement offer. A possible alternative is to randomize the sequence of settlement offers. In that case, the equilibrium settlement amount in the first round is

$$S_1 = \delta^{T-1}\left[x - 0.5(c_P - c_D)\right] \tag{5}$$

Equation (5) shows that if P and D spend the same amount on litigation, $c_P = c_D$, the settlement payment simply corresponds to the discounted expected judgment x.

A simple extension of the settlement process above is to allow parties to incur litigation costs in increments over time. The main difference to lump-sum costs is that now delaying settlement is costly and parties will settle in Round 1. With lump-sum costs, parties were, in fact, indifferent between settling in $T - 1$ and period 1, and there is no inefficiency associated with delay.

The model so far predicts a certain settlement in all cases. This makes sense given that settlement produces a cooperative surplus for the parties. But, in practice, parties do not always settle. How can we account for this reality in the model?

The reason that settlement can fail is simple. D is not willing to pay the amount S demanded by P to drop the case. But why would D disagree with P over the settlement payment?

The literature has mainly focused on two explanations for why settlement can fail. The first is the divergent expectations theory where parties have different, exogenously determined expectations about the outcome of the case (Priest and Klein 1984). The second reason why settlement can fail is asymmetric information; one party has private information relevant for the outcome of the case (Bebchuk 1984).

In the divergent expectations model, P and D differ in their beliefs about the expected judgment $x = \rho \cdot j$, where ρ denotes the probability that P wins the case and j is the amount of damages awarded to P by the court.[9] Both parties hold beliefs about the case quality q. Assume that P believes the case quality is $q_P = q + \varepsilon_P$ and D believes it is $q_D = q + \varepsilon_D$, where ε_i $(i = P, D)$ are normally distributed random variables. Furthermore, assume that there is a threshold quality q^*, where if $q > q^*$ the plaintiff wins and if $q < q^*$ the defendant wins. The parties' beliefs about the probability that the plaintiff wins the case are therefore given by the following:

$$\rho_i = Pr(q + \varepsilon_i > q^*) = \Phi\big[(q + \varepsilon_i - q^*)/\sigma\big] \text{ with } i = (P, D) \tag{6}$$

where Φ is the standard normal cumulative distribution and σ is the standard deviation of ε_i. Settlement fails if the difference in P and D's expected judgments exceeds total litigation costs $x_P - x_D > c_P + c_D$, where $x_P = \rho_P \cdot j$ and $x_D = \rho_D \cdot j$. In other words, settlement fails if P is sufficiently more optimistic than D about the outcome of the case. The model implies that cases far above or far below q^* settle, while those close to q^* go to trial. This, in turn, implies that the plaintiff win rate for cases decided by the judge predicted by the model is around 50%. This prediction is referred to in the literature as the Priest-Klein hypothesis. An important limitation of the model is it simply assumes that parties form different beliefs about the expected outcome of the case and that they are unable to change them even if new information emerges.

The other theory that can explain why settlement fails is to allow parties to have some private information over any of the parameters relevant to the case. For example, D may have better information about whether they have indeed infringed a patent. Alternatively, P may have better information on the actual amount of damages. To keep the model simple, assume there is only one-sided asymmetric information. Assume the defendant has some private information about x such that $x \sim [\underline{x}, \overline{x}]$. Furthermore, assume that the uninformed party P makes a take-it-or-leave-it settlement offer to the informed party D in period $T - 1$.[10] The take-it-or-leave-it settlement offer allows the uninformed party P to screen the informed party D into those that accept the offer for which it must be true that $S < \delta(x + c_D)$, and those that reject it for which it must be true that $S > \delta(x + c_D)$. The cutoff type is simply given by $S = \delta(x + c_D)$; hence, the cutoff settlement value is given by

$$x^* = \frac{S}{\delta} - c_D \tag{7}$$

This means that any D with $x > x^*$ accepts the settlement offer, and any D with $x < x^*$ prefers to let the judge decide. The uninformed party P then chooses equilibrium settlement offer x^* by maximizing its expected pay-off:

$$\max_{x^*} \underbrace{\int_{\underline{x}}^{x^*} \delta(x - c_P) f(x) dx}_{Trial} + \underbrace{[1 - F(x^*)]\delta(x^* + c_D)}_{Settlement = \delta(x^* + c_D)} \tag{8}$$

---

[9] Usually, the value of damages is fixed and parties only disagree about the probability that P prevails at trial.

[10] Screening models are more common in the literature. For a signaling model, see Reinganum and Wilde (1986).

The corresponding first-order condition (FOC) is the following:[11]

$$1 - F(x^*) - (c_P + c_D)f(x^*) = 0 \qquad (9)$$

Equations (8) and (9) show that the plaintiff faces a trade-off when making their settlement offer. To see this, assume that instead of $S = \delta(x^* + c_D)$ they decide to modify their offer by an amount Δ that is, $S = \delta(x^* + c_D + \Delta)$. It follows that any D with $x > x^* + \Delta$ still accepts the higher settlement. Therefore, the benefit for the plaintiff from raising their settlement demand is $[1 - F(x^*)]\delta\Delta$ which is the probability that the demand is accepted $[1 - F(x^*)]$ times the discounted increase in settlement paymen $\delta\Delta$. However, the cost to the plaintiff, which is $\Delta\delta(c_P + c_D)f(x^*)$ comes from the fact that any D that would have accepted x^* but not $x^* + \Delta$ rejects the higher settlement offer and the case goes to trial. Trial is costly to the plaintiff because they incur their own litigation cost c_P and indirectly also the defendant's cost c_D because no settlement occurs. Under the assumption that litigation costs are not too high, that is, $c_P + c_D < \dfrac{1 - F(x)}{f(x)}$, the model therefore implies that not all cases settle.

Another implication of this model is that there is selection into which cases settle. In other words, cases that settle, on average, have a higher expected judgment x than those that go to trial. It also implies that the plaintiff is, on average, less likely to prevail at trial for those cases that are actually litigated than those that are settled. This selection is one-sided (very strong cases from P's perspective settle), while selection in the divergent expectation model is two-sided (very strong and very weak cases settle). Figure 19.1 shows actual data on plaintiff win rates of both decided and settled cases.[12]

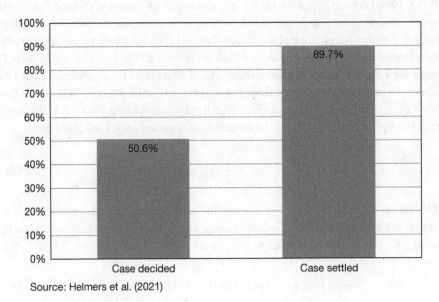

Source: Helmers et al. (2021)

Figure 19.1 Plaintiff win rate at the High Court of England and Wales.

[11] The discount rate δ drops out of the FOC, although it will still affect the level of the settlement offer.
[12] The data are from IP cases at the High Court of England and Wales, and are exceptional as they also indicate which party prevailed in a settlement agreement.

Remarkably, the plaintiff win rate is almost exactly 50%, as predicted by the Priest-Klein hypothesis. However, the plaintiff win rate in settled cases is almost 90%, providing evidence in favor of one-sided selection generated by asymmetric information.

The main limitation of models of asymmetric information is that they rely on arbitrary assumptions about who possesses private information and who makes a settlement offer. The outcome predicted by the model varies significantly based on what assumptions are made about who possesses private information.

The model also has implications for the incentives parties face when deciding whether to voluntarily share information with each other. In principle, the party that has private information could simply voluntarily reveal the information. This would lead to settlement. In practice, it can be difficult, if not impossible, to communicate information in a credible way. If the information cannot be deemed credible, it becomes impossible for the other party to make any inference based on the information that was revealed. This, in turn, implies that parties that could, in fact, credibly reveal information will refrain from doing so if the information would weaken their case.

19.3.2 A Model of Patent Litigation

Patent litigation sets itself apart from other types of litigation because it deals with not only the question of infringement but also the question of validity. Figure 19.2 shows that the question of validity is important empirically. The figure shows case outcomes for patent cases at the High Court of England and Wales where the plaintiff alleged patent infringement. As shown in Figure 19.2, the most common outcome of infringement cases is the invalidation of the allegedly infringed patents.

The fact that a patent's validity is challenged in litigation has several implications. First, it can lead to litigation even in the absence of divergent expectations or asymmetric information. The reason is that the pay-off from litigation depends on both whether the patent is ruled invalid and whether the parties agree to settle (assuming settlement means that validity is not challenged). Second, challenging patent validity in court creates strong externalities. If the patent is successfully invalidated by D, not only does D escape liability for infringement, but also the patent can no longer be infringed by any third parties.

To focus on the question of how validity affects litigation, we focus on validity and take infringement as given, that is, the patent is assumed infringed with certainty provided its validity is upheld. Furthermore, the model, which was proposed by Meurer (1989), assumes that D has not yet infringed the patent but instead clarifies its validity first before deciding whether to implement the protected invention. The patent is invalid with probability α, which is known to both parties. Assume that litigation costs are c_P and c_D, where for simplicity we impose symmetry and set $c_P = c_D = c$. P can either refuse to license the patent or make a take-it-or-leave-it settlement offer to D in the form of a licensing agreement before any litigation occurs. Under the agreement, D agrees not to challenge the validity of the patent and pays lump-sum royalties to P in exchange for using the patented technology. If D licenses the patent, D can enter the product market and compete with P.

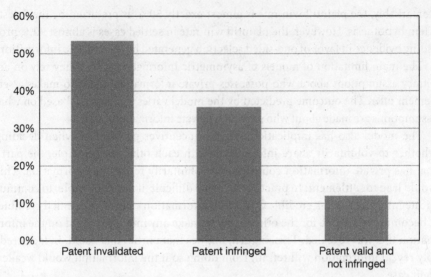

Source: Helmers et al. (2021) and authors' computations. Outcomes as a share of decided cases.

Figure 19.2 Outcomes of infringement cases decided by the High Court of England and Wales.

If D rejects the licensing offer, validity is litigated in court and D succeeds in invalidating the patent, each of the parties obtains a pay-off of $0.5 \cdot v_0 - c$, where v_0 denotes the total industry profit if both parties compete à la Cournot in the product market by practicing the patented invention.

If the case goes to trial and the patent's validity is upheld, P maintains its monopoly and gets payoff $v_1 - c$. where v_1 denotes monopoly profits ($v_1 > v_0$). D does not license the patent and pays their own litigation costs c.

If the parties settle instead, they establish a licensing agreement. P gets $v - s$, where v is a weighted average between the monopoly and competitive profits $v = \beta \cdot v_0 + (1 - \beta) \cdot v_1$ with $\beta \in [0,1]$ and s is the share of industry profits obtained by D. In equilibrium, s is equal to $0.5 \cdot v_0 - c$. Finally, if P refuses to license the patent and D does not respond, P remains a monopolist and gets monopoly profits v_1 and D gets zero.

D's threat to take P to court is credible only if their expected pay-off from challenging the patent in court is non-negative:

$$0.5 \cdot \alpha \cdot v_0 \geq c \qquad (10)$$

If equation (10) does not hold, P refuses to license the patent to D since D will not respond with litigation. Instead, if equation (10) holds, P will either refuse to license, which will lead to D challenging the patent's validity in court, or make a settlement offer that D accepts. P's decision to litigate or settle is determined by

$$\underbrace{(1 - \alpha)(v_1 - c)}_{\text{payoff if patent valid}} + \underbrace{\alpha(0.5v_0 - c)}_{\text{payoff if patent invalid}} \geq v - s \qquad (11)$$

Substituting the equilibrium settlement $s = 0.5 \cdot v_0 - c$ into (11) and simplifying yield

$$(1 - \alpha) \cdot v_1 + \alpha \cdot v_0 - 2 \cdot c \geq v \tag{12}$$

If (10) and (12) both hold, litigation occurs. If (10) holds but (12) does not, the parties settle. Figure 19.3 displays the different outcomes in the $(c - \alpha)$ space.

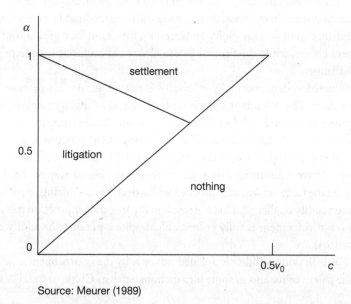

Source: Meurer (1989)

Figure 19.3 Bargaining outcomes.

The model highlights how the issue of patent validity sets patent litigation apart from other types of litigation, such as litigation over ownership of real property (e.g., a plot of land). It is easy to see that in Meurer's (1989) model, the value v realized by the patentee depends on the settlement reached and the outcome of litigation. In contrast, the value of the plot of land would be unaffected by a settlement or the outcome of litigation since the property title would not be invalidated, that is, $v = v_1 = v_0$. Therefore, if parties have common information and the same litigation costs, the dispute over a plot of land would always settle. However, in Meurer's (1989) model, litigation over patent validity can still occur.

19.4 Characteristics of Patent Litigation Systems

The economic theory of litigation is highly stylized and abstracts from much of the complexity of patent litigation systems across jurisdictions. While the basic struc-ture of patent proceedings in court is similar across jurisdictions, there are neverthe-less important differences along virtually all dimensions that characterize a litigation system. These differences are the result of differences in the law (including case law), procedures, institutions, as well as professional practice, and therefore evolve con-stantly over time. An understanding of these differences is important to gain insights about the optimal design of patent litigation systems.

19.4.1 Unified versus Bifurcated Litigation Systems

One of the most important differences between patent litigation systems is between unified and bifurcated systems (see Figure 19.4). In a unified system, infringement and invalidity are dealt with within the same proceedings, where invalidity is usually raised as a defense by the defendant to the infringement claim by the plaintiff. The judge will assess both claims, which implies that a patent that is found invalid cannot be infringed. In a bifurcated system, in contrast, there are separate proceedings in different venues to establish infringement and invalidity. In Germany, for example, regional courts decide infringement claims, while the Federal Patent Court has exclusive jurisdiction to hear validity challenges.

In a bifurcated system, normally invalidity is not an admissible defense to an infringement claim. The defendant will concentrate on a non-infringement defense while potentially attempting to invalidate the patent in parallel at the competent venue. Since the question of validity has a direct effect on infringement proceedings, courts have the option to stay infringement proceedings until validity has been decided. However, courts usually have substantial discretion in their decision to stay proceedings and, depending on the jurisdiction, may proceed with a decision on infringement regardless of a pending validity challenge. This can result in the so-called injunction gap where the judgment on infringement is fully enforceable despite a pending invalidity challenge (see Figure 19.4).

In most jurisdictions, validity is decided not only by the courts but also administratively by the patent office and in some jurisdictions, such as China or Brazil, exclusively

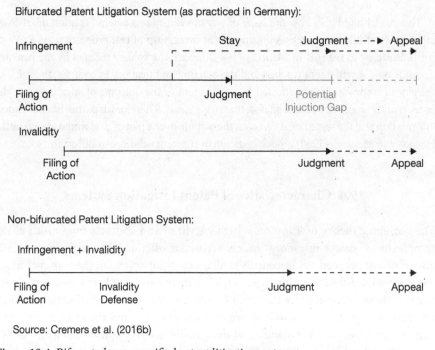

Figure 19.4 Bifurcated versus unified patent litigation systems.

by the patent office. Such administrative validity challenges can take the form of a postgrant opposition that allows third parties to challenge validity within a certain period after grant. For example, at the EPO, patents can be challenged through opposition within 9 months after grant. There are systems that allow an administrative postgrant validity challenge also after the opposition window has closed, such as *inter partes* review proceedings in the United States. These administrative proceedings interact with infringement court proceedings much in the same way as validity challenges in a court that has exclusive jurisdiction to hear validity challenges. In fact, in some jurisdictions, such as Germany, validity cannot be challenged in court as long as the window to oppose a patent at the patent office is still open or an opposition is pending. This also illustrates how administrative postgrant challenges and in-court proceedings can act as substitutes.

Whether infringement and validity are dealt with in a unified or bifurcated system has a number of important effects on patent litigation behavior and outcomes. As mentioned above, depending on the design of the bifurcated system, it is possible that the infringement decision is made before the invalidity decision. This implies that patents may be found infringed that are eventually invalidated. On the other hand, administrative proceedings can help resolve infringement court proceedings. In the United States, the *inter partes* review operates on a faster time schedule than court proceedings, which means that often they provide new information on patent validity before the parallel court proceedings do. This helps parties settle infringement disputes (Helmers and Love 2023b). Bifurcation may also directly affect litigation behavior. Evidence for Germany and the United Kingdom suggests that a bifurcated system, in which infringement is usually decided first, leads to fewer validity challenges than in a unified system. And infringement actions are more likely to settle (Cremers et al. 2016b).

19.4.2 Number of Courts and Specialization

The number of courts competent to hear patent cases differs significantly across jurisdictions. In the United States, 94 federal district courts are competent to hear patents cases. In Germany, 12 regional courts are competent to hear first-instance patent infringement claims. In other jurisdictions, such as France or the Netherlands, there is only a single court competent to hear patent cases. In the United Kingdom, there are two courts that hear patent cases where one court (Intellectual Property Enterprise Court) hears less complex cases of lower value than the other court (Patents Court). Jurisdictions also differ in terms of whether patent cases are heard by specialist courts, divisions, or judges within general civil courts. In the United Kingdom, for example, the Patents Court is a specialist court within the Chancery Division of the High Court of Justice of England and Wales. In Germany, some regional courts have specialist chambers that hear patent cases. In the United States, the court of appeal (CAFC) is a specialized court, while first-instance district courts are not.

The availability of different courts to file a claim may provide the opportunity to engage in forum and judge shopping, that is, to strategically choose a court venue or even a specific judge within a given venue. The opportunity to behave strategically arises within a given jurisdiction because individual courts and judges retain considerable discretion regarding procedural choices that affect the speed, cost, and ultimately outcome of proceedings. Plaintiffs may choose patentee-friendly venues and judges, which can lead to the strong concentration of caseloads in a single or few venues. For example, the US District Court in the Eastern District of Texas is a notoriously popular venue for US patent infringement actions, favoring NPEs (see Chapter 22) (Love and Yoon 2017, Cohen et al. 2017). Box 19.1 discusses the more recent phenomenon of judge shopping in the Western District of Texas.

Box 19.1 Judge Shopping in the Western District of Texas

On September 18, 2018, Alan Albright was sworn in as the newest member of the US District Court for the Western District of Texas (WDTX). Judge Albright, who had been a patent litigator in Austin for almost 2 decades, became the sole district judge in the Waco division of the Western District. Because of the district rules governing case allocation in effect at the time, Judge Albright automatically presided over all civil cases filed in the Waco division. Judge Albright was perceived as generally patentee-friendly. Apart from being very vocal publicly about wanting to attract patent cases to his Waco court, he adopted a number of local practices that tend to favor patent enforcers, such as aggressive deadlines to ensure a quick decision.

Case filings at the Western District of Texas by division, judge, and quarter

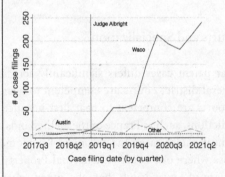 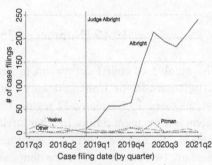

(a) Quarterly patent case filings   (b) Quarterly patent case filings in WDTX
     by division.   by judge.

Notes: The figure shows the number of cases filed at the Western District of Texas (WDTX) by division, judge, and quarter.

Source: Helmers and Love (2023c).

As shown in the figure, Judge Albright's appointment led to a dramatic increase in patent case filings at the Waco division. The figure distinguishes between cases filed across divisions within the WDTX, in panel (a), and cases assigned across the district's judges, in panel (b). The figure shows a large increase in case filings in Waco, which, in turn, were all assigned to Judge Albright. In the year prior to Judge Albright's appointment, fewer than three patent cases per quarter were filed in Waco; by 2020, Waco's quarterly average had topped 200. Patent enforcement activity in the district's other divisions remained negligible. Similarly, Judges Yeakel and Pitman, who held the highest caseloads in the Western District prior to Judge Albright's arrival, averaged just nine and four patent case filings per quarter, respectively. All other judges combined saw fewer than four new filings per quarter during the same time frame. By comparison, Judge Albright was assigned an average of nearly 230 cases per quarter in 2021, which corresponded to around 25% of all patent cases filed in the US. These numbers illustrate the effect of a litigant's ability to engage in judge shopping, that is, their ability to choose a judge who is perceived to be generally advantageous to their case.

19.4.3 Duration of Proceedings

Proceedings differ significantly in speed across jurisdictions and even within jurisdictions across venues. For example, Cremers et al. (2016a) report that infringement actions took, on average, around 14 months to a first decision in Germany but nearly 30 months in France during the period 2000–2008. To some extent, the speedier resolution in Germany is explained by the bifurcated system, which allows courts to focus on the issue of infringement. However, there are a number of other factors that also play a role such as active case management or the extent of pretrial discovery and expert testimony permitted.

The duration of proceedings has direct economic effects. They affect direct and indirect costs in the form of litigation expenses and uncertainty over the case outcome. This also creates incentives for parties to influence case duration strategically in an attempt to get the other party to drop the case or agree to a settlement.

19.4.4 Costs and Cost Allocation

The costs associated with litigation vary significantly across jurisdictions. In Germany and France, for example, cost estimates for each party range between US$90,000 to $250,000 and US$60,000 to $250,000, respectively (Cremers et al. 2016a). These costs are low compared to other jurisdictions, such as the United Kingdom or the United States, where costs commonly are well above US$1million (Helmers and McDonagh 2013, AIPLA 2017). Such large differences are explained by a number of factors, including the extent of pretrial discovery, the role of expert witnesses, as well as the length and complexity of the trial.[13]

Systems also differ in terms of whether the losing party has to cover the litigation costs of the winning party. The economic literature distinguishes between two systems that are at the opposite ends of the spectrum: Under the so-called American rule, each party pays its own litigation costs regardless of the case outcome; under the English rule, in contrast, the losing party covers its own as well as the cost of the winning party. This is, however, a highly stylized depiction of reality.

In reality, in the English system, costs are allocated on a per item basis and, as a result, the actual share of costs shifted between parties in patent cases is closer to one-half to two-thirds (Forsyth and Watts 2011, Helmers and McDonagh 2013). In the United States, under the American system, in exceptional cases courts are allowed to shift fees from the losing to the winning party although they rarely do so (Cotter and Golden 2018).[14] In other jurisdictions, such as Germany, costs are routinely shifted, though this usually affects only a fraction of total costs due to cost scales applied by the courts (Fischmann 2015).

The theoretical literature in economics suggests that the rules governing the allocation of litigation costs between parties have important effects on litigation behavior.[15] Empirically, the available evidence suggests that limiting a court's ability to award fees to the winning party results in more cases being filed (Helmers et al. 2021).

19.5 Examples of Patent Litigation Systems

This final section provides a brief overview of a number of patent litigation systems around the world. The main characteristics of these systems are summarized in Table 19.1.

19.5.1 United States

The United States is a common law system in which courts influence and change the law and legal procedures through judicial precedent. The United States has a unified litigation system, and in the first instance patent cases are heard by 94 federal district courts, as mentioned above. District courts do not have divisions or judges specialized in patent matters, and judges usually have no technical training although some judges build substantial expertise due to the concentration of patent cases on their dockets (see Box 19.1). Appeals are heard by the CAFC, which has had exclusive jurisdiction

---

[13] The 2017 AIPLA survey provides a breakdown by stage of proceedings, for example, median costs for initial case management are estimated at around $60,000 for a relatively low-value case with US$1million to $10million at risk. The median costs for discovery, motions, and claim construction are an estimated US$550,000. Pre- and posttrial median costs are an estimated US$1million.

[14] The cases *Highmark Inc. v. Allcare Health Mgmt. Sys., Inc.*, 572 US 559 (2014), and *Octane Fitness, LLC v. ICON Health & Fitness, Inc.*, 572 US 545 (2014), decided in 2014 by the US Supreme Court made it, in principle, easier for the winning party to be awarded attorney fees from the losing party.

[15] For an overview, see Spier (2007).

Table 19.1 Overview of Main Characteristics of Major Patent Litigation Systems

Characteristics	United States	China	Germany	United Kingdom
Bifurcated	No	Yes	Yes	No
Administrative postgrant review	Yes	No	Yes (EPO, DPMA)	Yes (EPO)
Jury trial	Yes	No	No	No
Preliminary injunction	Yes	Yes	Yes	Yes
Criminal liability	No	No	Yes	Yes
Average duration in first instance (months)	18-42	6-18	14	24-36
Damages amount	High	Low	Average	High
Punitive damages	Yes	No	No	No
Fee shifting	Limited	Limited	Limited	Full (item-based)
Average costs in first instance (000 US$)	1,000-6,000*	20-150	90-250	1,000-2,000
Number of courts first instance	94	18 specialized + regular courts	12 (+1 validity)	2
Specialized court/judges first instance	No	Partly	Yes	Yes
Specialized court of appeal	Yes	Yes	No	No
Separate trial for damages	No	No	Yes	Yes
Utility models	No	Yes	Yes	No
Design patents	Yes	Yes	No	No

* Median reported; *Sources*: AIPLA Economic Survey 2017; Clark (2011); Cremers et al. (2016a); Thomson Reuters Practical Law.

in patent matters since 1982. The Supreme Court hears appeals from the CAFC at its discretion.

The way in which proceedings in the United States distinguish themselves from other jurisdictions has a notable effect on case outcomes and costs involved in litigation. There are significant disclosure requirements during the pretrial discovery phase of a case, which force parties to incur substantial expenses relatively early in a case (AIPLA 2017). Most cases also include a pretrial claim construction ("Markman") hearing. Expert testimony in court also plays an important role, which can prolong a trial and raise the costs involved significantly. In patent cases that involve monetary damages, parties have the right to a jury trial despite the often highly technical nature of the subject of a dispute.

Patent owners can also file a complaint with the International Trade Commission (ITC). The ITC can grant the equivalent of injunctive relief in the form of an import ban. However, it cannot grant monetary damages to patent owners. The costs involved in a complaint before the ITC are slightly lower than at district courts but still substantial (AIPLA 2017).

Patent validity is routinely raised as a defense in court proceedings. However, there is also the possibility to challenge patents administratively. *Ex parte* reexamination allows anyone, including the patentee, to petition the patent office to reexamine the patent. The reexamination is conducted only between the patentee and the patent office without any input from third parties, even including those that have petitioned the office to initiate reexamination. The AIA in 2011 introduced *inter partes* review, covered business method (CBM) review, and postgrant review (PGR). PGR allows third parties to challenge validity within 9 months of issuance. After the 9-month period, patents can be challenged through an *inter partes* review or CBM (although CBMs were only available for an 8-year period and are no longer available). Challenged patents are reviewed by the PTAB in quasi-judicial proceedings subject to a fixed timeline, rather than patent examiners in a reexamination process.

19.5.2   China

China is a civil law jurisdiction without a rule of binding precedent. It has a bifurcated system that separates infringement and patent validity. Moreover, in the Chinese system, patents can be enforced through the civil court system as well as the patent office, which sets it apart from other patent litigation systems.

The civil court system is limited to handling infringement actions.[16] The court system in China consists of four instances: the Supreme People's Court, the Higher People's Court, the Intermediate People's Court, and the Lower People's Court. Patent infringement cases must be filed with designated Intermediate or Higher People's Courts. Appeals are heard directly by the Supreme Court. Since 2014, there are three specialist IP courts[17] and 20 IP tribunals in several provinces, which have exclusive jurisdiction over IP. In 2019, the Supreme Court created a specialized IP court to hear civil and administrative IP appeal cases.

Civil courts have the power to grant a range of remedies including pretrial and interim injunctions, the freezing of assets of the defendant, permanent injunctions, and monetary damages. In contrast to other jurisdictions including the United States, Chinese civil courts do not issue declarations of non-infringement. Chinese courts allow for only very limited discovery. In comparison with the United States or most European jurisdictions, proceedings in China are relatively fast, infringement suits take only between 6 and 18 months, and the decision on infringement and damages is made in the same court ruling. Litigation costs are relatively low in China, and court fees are computed as a percentage of damages claimed, which are generally low.

---

[16] The courts hear validity cases only on appeal to decisions by the Chinese Patent Office's Patent Review and Adjudication Board (PRAB).

[17] They are located in Beijing, Shanghai, and Guangzhou.

Decisions on patent validity are the sole responsibility of the Chinese Patent Office's (CNIPA) Patent Review and Adjudication Board (PRAB). Since 2001, there have been no opposition proceedings, so the only way to invalidate a patent is to file an invalidity claim. Since 2021, CNIPA can also hear patent infringement cases provided they have "significant influence throughout the country."[18] CNIPA can order the accused party to cease infringement and mediate financial compensation. The administrative route to enforce a patent right has a number of advantages relative to the civil court route. It is, for example, quicker and less expensive. However, one important drawback is that CNIPA cannot award any monetary damages since that requires a court ruling.

19.5.3 Europe

In Europe, since June 2023, patent enforcement occurs at the national and pan-European level. National courts are competent to hear cases involving national patents, while the UPC is competent to hear cases involving patents granted by the EPO, so-called classic, non-unitary European patents and unitary patents (for more explanation on the European patent system, see Chapter 11).[19]

This section briefly describes some of the most important national litigation systems, the UPC, as well as administrative invalidity procedures available at the EPO.

19.5.3.1 Germany

There are 12 regional courts that are competent to hear patent infringement cases. Appeals are heard by higher regional courts and at the Federal Court of Justice .

Invalidity cannot be challenged in court proceedings either as a defense in infringement proceedings or offensively in a declaratory action. There are two ways to challenge validity in Germany: administratively through opposition procedures before the patent office that granted the patent or court proceedings before the Federal Patent Court. If the patent was granted by the EPO, the patent can be challenged in an opposition during the first 9 months following the grant of the patent. If the patent was granted by the German Patent Office, the patent can be challenged in opposition proceedings before the German Patent Office. In fact, if the opposition window is still open, invalidity can only be challenged administratively at the patent office. Once the window has closed, a patent can only be challenged at the Federal Patent Court. Decisions by the Federal Patent Court can be appealed before the Federal Court of Justice, which is the only court in Germany that is competent to hear appeals of infringement and invalidity claims.

---

[18] Apart from CNIPA, local IP agencies can also hear patent infringement cases, but unlike CNIPA, they only have regional jurisdiction. In addition, the General Administration of Customs (GAC) can also enforce patent rights by seizing imports and exports of infringing products.

[19] The current European litigation system is, in fact, more complex for two reasons. First, not all members of the European Patent Convention are part of the Unitary Patent system, either because they are not part of the EU (e.g., the United Kingdom) or because they decided not to join the Unitary Patent system (e.g., Spain). Second, at least until 2030, applicants of European patents can opt out of the Unitary Patent system. Hence, patents granted by the EPO that are either opted out or validated in any of the EPC member states that are not part of the Unitary Patent system become de facto national rights. This implies that infringement as well as validity of these patents is dealt with in national courts, rather than the UPC.

19.5.3.2 United Kingdom (England and Wales)

The United Kingdom consists of separate legal systems for England and Wales, Scotland, and Northern Ireland. England and Wales is the jurisdiction among these three with by far the largest number of patent cases.

Two courts are competent to hear patent cases in England and Wales. The Intellectual Property Enterprise Court hears less complex claims of lower value. The other venue is the Patents Court, which is a specialist court of the Chancery Division of the High Court of Justice. Both courts hear both infringement and invalidity claims. Validity challenges can be raised as a counterclaim to an infringement claim or pro-actively in the form of a declaratory action. As in the US system, in England and Wales infringement and validity are decided simultaneously, which means that the invalidation of a patent leads to the dismissal of the infringement claim. Appeals from both venues are heard by the Court of Appeals. Decisions by the Court of Appeals can be challenged before the Supreme Court.

Patents granted by the EPO and validated in the United Kingdom can also be challenged in opposition proceedings during the 9-month opposition window. Although the UK IPO does not offer opposition proceedings for national patents, it nevertheless allows for administrative validity challenges through its patent opinion service. In contrast to Germany, validity challenges can be brought in court regardless of whether an opposition at the EPO is still possible or pending. However, to avoid divergent outcomes of the "invalid but infringed" type, courts can stay proceedings while the opposition at the EPO is pending.

19.5.3.3 Unified Patent Court

Prior to the Unitary Patent system, European patents had to be litigated separately and independently in each country in which they had taken effect. That system could lead to divergent outcomes where a patent was invalidated by a court in one jurisdiction, while another court in a different jurisdiction upheld the same patent (see Cremers et al. 2016a). It also happened that when the same parties litigated in several European jurisdictions, a patent was found to have infringed in one jurisdiction but not another.[20]

To address such inconsistencies, a pan-European court with unitary effect was created. After decades of planning and negotiations, the court began operations in June 2023. It has exclusive jurisdiction with respect to litigation of unitary patents as well as European patents, although there is a 7-year opt-out period for European patents. The court's decisions have unitary effect for the currently 18 EU member states in which the UPC agreement has entered into force. This means, for example. that if a patent is invalidated, the patent is invalidated in all 18 countries. Similarly, if the court imposes an injunction, the injunction automatically takes effect in all 18 countries. This sets this court apart from national courts because its decisions have truly unitary effect across multiple jurisdictions.

The court of first instance has a decentralized structure and consists of central, regional, and local divisions, which provides potential scope for forum shopping. Local and regional divisions are competent to hear infringement actions and counterclaims for invalidity (although under some conditions they may also be heard by the central

---

[20] For specific examples, see Mejer and van Pottelsberghe de la Potterie (2012).

division, which will lead to bifurcation). Declaratory actions for invalidity and non-infringement are heard by the central division. Each case in the first instance is presided over by a judge panel that consists of both legally and technically trained judges.[21] Proceedings are subject to aggressive timelines, for example, the defendant in infringement proceedings has only 3 months to file a response and counterclaim for invalidity, and the judgment in the case should be delivered within 1 year of case filing.

19.5.3.4 EPO

The EPO offers an administrative postgrant procedure to challenge the validity of unitary and non-unitary patents through opposition. If an opposition is successful, the patent is invalidated and cannot enter into effect.

Opposition procedures before the EPO differ in several ways from US *inter partes* reviews: There is no institution stage (but the EPO provides a preliminary opinion).[22] If several parties file an opposition, they are automatically consolidated into a single proceeding at the end of the 9-month opposition period and heard jointly, and the patent owner can amend the opposed patent. The proceedings end with an oral hearing, at the conclusion of which the outcome of the opposition is communicated to the parties. On average, oppositions take around 24 months and cost around US$45,000 (Chien et al. 2019).

19.6 Summary

Courts play a central role in the functioning of the patent system. Enforceability confers value to patents. At the same time, this also means that courts may offer opportunities to use patents for strategic purposes and rent seeking. The debate in the United States about the patent system over the last 2 decades reflects this ambivalent role of patent litigation in supporting the patent system and ultimately in providing incentives for innovation. In Europe, patent litigation has been largely perceived as uncontroversial, except perhaps in situations where national courts came up with divergent decisions on the same patent granted by the EPO. However, recent debates about NPEs, SEPs, and especially the design and functioning of the UPC may indicate a significant change in attitudes. In China, which has experienced a steep increase in patent filings over the last 2 decades, the patent enforcement system is gaining importance and, as a result, is receiving an increased amount of attention from the public and policymakers.

This chapter reviewed the basic structure and underlying economics of patent enforcement systems. It also discussed different design choices and their implementation, in practice, in different jurisdictions around the world. Overall, the design and functioning of patent enforcement systems have large effects on the functioning of the patent system and innovation more broadly.

---

[21] At the central division, one of three judges is by default a technically trained judge. At local and regional divisions, a technically trained judge is added to a three-judge panel in infringement actions with a counterclaim for invalidity.

[22] An *inter partes* review is initially assessed on its merits to establish its likelihood of success. If there is a reasonable likelihood that a challenged claim is invalid based on lack of novelty or obviousness, the petition is instituted and reviewed. Institution has to occur within 6 months and, upon institution, the PTAB has to hand down its final written decision within 12 months.

20

The Sharing and Exchange of Patents

Learning Objectives

After reading this chapter, you will be able to understand and explain the following concepts:

- The different mechanisms used by innovators to share and exchange patents in the market for technology including (cross-)licensing agreements, patent pools, patent pledges and patent commons, outright acquisition of patents, as well as shared ownership of patents
- Different motives for firms to share their patented technology
- The trade-off involved in licensing between revenue and rent dissipation effects
- The characteristics and economic effects of patent pools
- The characteristics and economic effects of patent pledges and patent commons
- The characteristics and economic effects of patent sales
- The characteristics and economic effects of patent co-ownership

---

20.1 Introduction

Firms routinely rely on a range of different mechanisms to share and exchange patents. These mechanisms include (cross-)licensing agreements, patent pools, patent pledges and patent commons, outright acquisition of patents, as well as shared ownership of patents.

The sharing and exchange of patents are part of what is referred to as the *market for technology*. This market distributes and reallocates the legal rights to the use of patented inventions. The market for technology encompasses other IP rights as well and even includes other forms of knowledge, such as trade secrets or technical services. Figure 20.1 shows the importance of technology trade for the US economy in terms of US dollars paid and received in IP royalties and licensing fees. While the United States has been running a large trade deficit in tangible goods since the mid-1970s, it registers a large surplus in the market for technology.

This chapter focuses on the market for patents where trade occurs in the form of the sale and licensing of technology disembodied from physical goods and protected by patents. These transactions are about the use and ownership of patented technology.

The Economics of Innovation and Intellectual Property. Bronwyn H. Hall and Christian Helmers, Oxford University Press.
© Oxford University Press 2024. DOI: 10.1093/oso/9780197630914.003.0020

US royalties and license fees in billions of US$2017

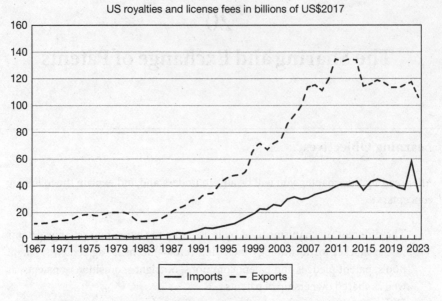

Source: FRED St. Louis Federal Reserve Bank, https:// fred.stlouisfed.org/

Figure 20.1 US international trade in intangibles.

Why do firms voluntarily share their patented technology with other firms, with or without receiving payment? Isn't the ability to exclude others from the use of a patented technology the main motivation for patenting in the first place?

The case where upstream innovators license to downstream manufacturers is perhaps the most intuitive to understand why such sharing occurs. Licensing allows the upstream innovator to monetize its invention without participating in the product market. Likewise, the downstream manufacturer can concentrate on manufacturing and selling the products that rely on the patented technology. This enables specialization.

In practice, however, product market competitors also regularly share patents with each other. The motivations for such transactions are more complex. The sharing of patented technology can avoid duplication of research. It can also enable research collaboration and resolve conflict regarding patent infringement between competitors.

Finally, some firms even make their patented technology available to the public royalty-free. This might seem puzzling at first since the patent owner incurs all the cost of invention, development, and patent ownership while forgoing all patent-licensing income. However, in some situations, there are sound technologic and strategic reasons for that type of open approach to the sharing of patents. For example, open sharing can accelerate and increase technology adoption and diffusion, and thereby increase demand for a company's products.

The sharing of patented technology can also produce significant benefits for society. It promotes the diffusion of innovation and increases the returns to innovation by creating markets. As in the case of markets more generally, the advantage is that this allows the technology to move to its best use, that is, to the entity that is willing to pay the most for it. This, in turn, increases incentives for knowledge creation more globally. That said, the sharing of technology also offers opportunities for companies to behave strategically, which could counterintuitively even delay the adoption of new technologies, limit competition, and restrict market entry.

This chapter offers an overview of the different mechanisms used by firms to share patents and discusses the underlying economics.

While the focus of our discussion here is on for-profit firms, other actors are also actively participating in the sharing of patented technology, including universities, (public) research institutions, and the government. Also note that there is a distinction between transactions that promote the sharing of existing technology and transactions that help create patentable innovations, such as R&D co-development contracts, strategic alliances, and joint ventures. The focus of this chapter is the former, the sharing of existing technology in the form of patents and possibly other knowledge assets.

20.2 (Cross-)licensing

Licensing is by far the most common way in which firms exchange patented technology. Survey evidence from the EU and Japan indicates that over a third of patenting companies engage in licensing and those that do license a large fraction of their patents (Zuniga and Guellec 2009).

Licensing means that the owner of a patent retains ownership but grants another party the right to use the patented technology, usually in exchange for a licensing fee or royalty. There are different types of licenses: sole license, exclusive license, non-exclusive license, and cross-license. A sole license describes a license where there is only a single licensee and the licensor also retains the right to practice the licensed patent. An exclusive license, in contrast, means that only the licensee is entitled to practice the patented invention and has standing to enforce the patent in court. Non-exclusive licensing agreements neither restrict the licensor from practicing the patented invention nor from licensing to other parties. As we discuss below, restrictions on licensing can have important effects on product market competition, industry profits and the incentives to license in the first place.

Cross-licensing is an agreement where parties grant each other a license for the use of their respective patents, that is, each party is simultaneously licensor and licensee. While the same goal could be achieved through a regular license, the advantage of cross-licensing is that it recognizes mutual licensing needs and can facilitate transactions by reducing the need for explicit patent valuation and exchange of monetary payments. Licenses also differ in their scope. For example, licenses can restrict the use of the patented technology to certain applications or products and/or limit the territorial scope of the license.

While patent licensing is mainly about the legal right to use a patented technology, licensing can also involve the transfer of know-how, which is especially important in situations where knowledge is more tacit and patents only disclose some but not all relevant aspects of a technology.

20.2.1 The Economics of Licensing

The licensing of patented technology allows a patent holder to grant access to the patented technology to one or potentially many third parties. That is, the licensor voluntarily relinquishes exclusivity by granting a license.

The sharing of patented technology via licensing has a number of advantages. First, it enables vertical specialization in innovation. Firms can concentrate on inventing and developing new technologies since they can appropriate returns to their inventions by licensing them to downstream firms that monetize them in the product market. This allows inventors and downstream firms to capitalize on their comparative advantage. The same is true for innovators that lack the necessary complementary assets to effectively monetize an invention (Teece 1986). Licensing allows them to appropriate greater returns to their innovation. The existence of a market for technology also affects the "make or buy" decisions of firms that shape their boundaries.[1] Indeed, a functioning market for patent licenses reduces transaction costs and thereby increases the ability of firms to source technology externally. Take the example of Dolby Laboratories, the well-known developer of audio noise reduction and encoding technology. Right from the beginning, the company made the decision to focus on the upstream development of its technology and to license it to downstream consumer product manufacturers (cassette tape recorders during the early days of the company). Importantly, Dolby licensed its technology nonexclusively and at rates that provided little incentive for downstream manufacturers to invest in the development of a substitute technology (Sherman 2018). Dolby has successfully held on to its licensing business model over time even as audio and video technology has undergone a radical transformation since the company's formation in 1965.

Licensing also affects product market competition. Access to patented technology can be an important barrier to market entry. The extreme case in point is the pharmaceutical industry, where patent protection can be an effective barrier to competition (see Chapter 16). As long as the patent is valid and in force, there is no competition from other producers using the same active ingredient. Entry can only occur if the patent owner grants a license to another company. This means that a patent owner has the ability to control market structure and competition.

Finally, licensing affects the speed and extent of technology diffusion. If patent protection is effective, in the absence of licensing, technology only reaches the market through the innovator. Licensing increases the number of companies that can bring the innovation to market, which can broaden the application of the technology across different industries and geographical areas. This also means that innovators can exploit the innovation in (geographical) markets in which they themselves are not active. This increases returns to innovation in a straightforward way.

Companies also rely on licensing for strategic and even anticompetitive purposes. For example, an incumbent firm can license to an entrant that is less efficient than another potential entrant (Rockett 1990). The purpose is to drive down industry profits by creating a competitor in order to deter the more efficient firm from entering the market in the first place. Another example of anticompetitive conduct is the use of licensing to

---

[1] The *boundaries of the firm* refer to the set of activities that take place within a firm as opposed to those transacted on markets. For more discussion, see Chapter 8.

deter innovation by competitors. By offering to license existing technology, the licensor can make licensing more attractive to other firms relative to having to invest in their own R&D (Gallini 1984). Therefore, the licensor can prevent competitors from coming up with their own potentially superior innovation. A curious example of strategic licensing is so-called second sourcing. Famously, Intel licensed its x86 microprocessors to its competitor AMD in order to protect its customer IBM from hold-up. IBM was hesitant to rely on Intel's x86 chip for fear of being subject to hold-up if Intel were the sole supplier of microprocessors. This is an example where a company (Intel) agreed to license its technology to its direct rival (AMD), which would be difficult to rationalize in the absence of strategic motives. Another strategic motive is establishing control over (de facto) standards. Network effects play an important role in standard adoption, which means that speeding up adoption is essential for the successful establishment of a standard (see Chapter 21).

Licensing and in particular cross-licensing may also be a necessity in technology areas where patent ownership is fragmented and patents are blocking access to technology components. These are also technology areas where patent thickets may occur (see Chapter 18) and firms run considerable risk of getting embroiled in patent litigation. In such settings, cross-licensing can resolve blocking situations and avoid litigation and thereby significantly reduce transaction costs. At the same time, a desire for a favorable cross-licensing bargaining position can lead to wasteful arms races in patenting (Hall and Ziedonis 2001).

20.2.2 Determinants of Licensing

Whether companies license depends on a range of factors. First, the characteristics of the patented invention. These characteristics include the type of technology (e.g., GPT) and degree to which an innovation is embodied, that is, the degree to which it is integrated into a physical product.[2] They also include the degree to which inventions are codified and the extent of tacit knowledge involved.[3] Disembodied, highly codified technology may lend itself more easily to arm's length licensing transactions, while technology with important tacit components might require additional direct knowledge transfer. Another factor concerns the commercialization aspect in downstream product markets. Commercial uncertainty, market size, and fragmentation of product markets all play a role as well.

Arora and Fosfuri (2003) offer a simple model that helps us understand the importance of the interaction between upstream technology and downstream product markets for a firm's licensing decision. The main general insight that emerges from the model is that licensing has two opposed effects:

1. *Revenue effect.* The licensor earns income from licensing in the form of licensing payments.

---

[2] A new manufacturing machine is an example of an embodied innovation, while new data-processing software is an example of a disembodied invention.
[3] The degree to which knowledge is "codified" describes the extent to which knowledge can be described in a structured and systematic manner. Codified knowledge can be more easily recorded and transferred.

2. *Rent dissipation effect.* The licensor experiences an erosion of profits as a result of licensing if the licensee competes with the licensor in the product market.

In this model, a firm licenses when the revenue effect from licensing exceeds the rent dissipation effect from creating competitors. However, when there are two or more independent potential licensors, licensing creates a negative externality for the other licensor in the product market. This effect is ignored by each licensor. This means that while it is privately profitable for each licensor to license, joint profits would be higher in the absence of licensing.

To understand how this effect comes about, assume that there are two innovators i and j with patented technologies for the production of a good. The innovators are both vertically integrated, that is, they also produce and sell in the product market. There are many potential entrants that can only enter the market if they receive a license from one of the innovators. Entry does not involve any fixed costs. If entrants receive a license, they produce the same good as the licensor.

Innovator i sells $k_i - 1$ non-exclusive licenses, while innovator j sells $k_j - 1$ licenses, where $i \neq j$.[4] The model also assumes that licensing involves fixed cost $F \geq 0$. These fixed costs represent the transaction costs involved in the licensing agreement, such as negotiating the contract and the costs involved in the actual knowledge transfer. The model assumes that the licensor obtains share $\sigma \in [0, 1]$ of the profits π earned by its licensee. That means the licensor obtains a fixed upfront fee $\sigma\pi$ from the licensee. One way to interpret σ is to treat it as the licensor's bargaining power. The more bargaining power the licensor has, the larger the share of the licensee's profits the licensor is able to extract.

The model is a two-stage game:

Stage 1. Competition in the market for technology—each innovator chooses how many licenses to sell to potential entrants.

Stage 2. Competition in the product market—the innovators and all entrants that obtained a license compete in the product market.

We solve the model by analyzing the second stage of the model first. The licensors and licensees use the technology to produce the product and compete in the product market. Any company that is active in the product market makes profits $\pi^i\left(k_i, k_j, \mu\right)$, where $\dfrac{\partial \pi^i}{\partial k_i} < 0$ and μ denotes the degree of product differentiation between i and j. The parameter μ varies between zero and 1, that is, $\mu = [0, 1]$, where $\mu = 0$ means independent products, while $\mu = 1$ implies homogenous products. We assume that profits decrease as products become more similar, that is, $\dfrac{\partial \pi^i}{\partial \mu} < 0$. Using profits $\pi^i\left(k_i, k_j, \mu\right)$

---

[4] This implies that the total number of firms that have access to technology i and j and participate in the product market are $\sum_{i=1}^{N} k_i$ and $\sum_{j=1}^{N} k_j$, respectively.

obtained from the second stage of the model, we can write each innovator's profits as

$$V^i(k_i, k_j, \sigma, \mu, F) = [1 + \sigma(k_i - 1)]\pi^i(k_i, k_j, \mu) - (k_i - 1)F \qquad (1)$$

The first part of equation (1) denotes total profits obtained from participating directly in the product market $\pi^i(k_i, k_j, \mu)$ and the licensing income from all of i's licensees $\sigma(k_i - 1)\pi^i(k_i, k_j, \mu)$. The second part of equation (1) is the sum of all transaction costs involved in i's licensing activity. Each innovator i chooses k_i to maximize its profits in equation (1). The corresponding FOC (for $k_i - 1 \geq 0$) is the following:

$$V^i_k = \underbrace{\sigma\pi^i - F}_{\text{revenue effect}} + \underbrace{[1 + \sigma(k_i - 1)]\pi^i_k}_{\text{rent dissipation effect}} \leq 0 \qquad (2)$$

where π^i_k is the derivative of π^i with respect to k_i given k_j. The FOC shows that the innovator's optimal choice of the number of licenses depends on two countervailing effects. The first term is the *revenue effect*, which captures the additional marginal licensing income of licensing the technology to one or more entrants net of the associated transaction costs. The second term is the *rent dissipation effect*. Recall that the marginal effect of an additional licensee on profits is negative: $\pi^i_k \equiv \dfrac{\partial \pi^i}{\partial k_i} < 0$, which implies that the rent dissipation effect is negative. It captures the negative impact of adding another competitor to the product market on all other firms that also compete in the

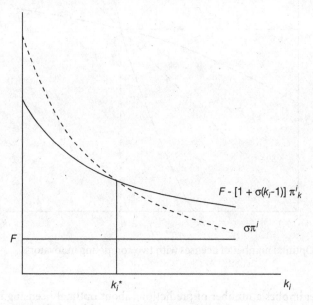

Figure 20.2 Licensor choice of the optimal number of licenses.

product market including the licensor. The equilibrium number of licenses sold by the licensor is defined by these two opposing effects. Figure 20.2 shows graphically how the equilibrium number of licenses k_i^* is determined.

Since innovators i and j compete in the product market assuming $\mu \neq 0$, in equilibrium each firm chooses the optimal number of licenses given its competitor's choice. This can be captured by reaction curves that represent each innovator's best response to the other innovator's choice of k. Figure 20.3 shows each innovator's reaction curve and the resulting equilibrium. We assume that the reaction curves are symmetric since innovators i and j are symmetric. We see that the reaction curves are upward-sloping, which implies that each innovator's optimal number of licenses increases in the other innovator's number of licenses. This is the result of an externality involved in licensing. If innovator i sells one additional license, the innovator obtains additional licensing income. This licensing income has to be balanced against the negative rent dissipation effect. However, the other innovator is also negatively affected by increased competition due to the additional licensee. Unlike the licensor, the other innovator only experiences the rent dissipation effect and no revenue effect (since all the licensing fees are paid to the licensor). The strength of this effect depends on μ since this parameter determines the degree to which i and j compete in the product market. In short, by licensing, each innovator is able to externalize part of the cost associated with licensing to the other innovator. In equilibrium, this yields more licensing than in the absence of this externality and reduces aggregate industry profits.

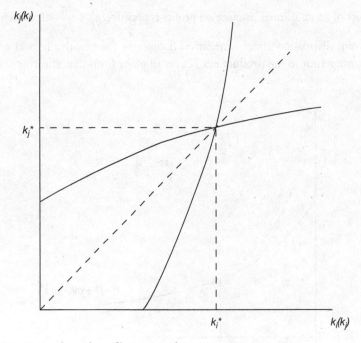

Figure 20.3 Optimal number of licenses with two competing innovators.

The model implies a number of predictions about optimal licensing behavior that are worth highlighting:

1. *Transaction costs.* Increases in transaction costs F induce firms to license less (k^* is decreasing in F). This prediction is a straightforward consequence of the fact that F depresses the revenue effect.

2. *Bargaining power.* Increases in the licensor's bargaining power σ induce firms to license more (k^* is increasing in σ). The licensor's bargaining power enters both the revenue and rent dissipation effects. However, as σ increases, its positive impact through the revenue effect outweighs its negative effect through the rent dissipation effect.

3. *Product market competition.* Licensing increases the more homogenous the products sold by companies i and j are (k^* is increasing in μ). Both the revenue effect and rent dissipation effect decrease as μ increases. However, the impact on the rent dissipation effect outweighs the impact on the revenue effect. The reason is the externality described above. The innovator externalizes more of the cost of an additional competitor to the other innovator as μ increases.

4. *Vertical integration.* Innovators that are not vertically integrated (i.e., that do not participate in the product market) license more. To see this, we can modify equation (1) for the case where innovator i does not sell in the product market:

$$V^i = \sigma(k_i - 1)\pi^i - (k_i - 1)F$$

Hence, the FOC is now

$$V^i_k = \underbrace{\sigma\pi^i - F}_{\text{revenue effect}} + \underbrace{\sigma(k_i - 1)\pi^i_k}_{\text{rent dissipation effect}} \leq 0$$

The revenue effect is the same as in equation (2), but the rent dissipation effect is smaller since adding another licensee does not create more competition for the innovator itself since it does not compete in the product market.

5. *Upstream specialization.* The presence of innovators that are not vertically integrated induces vertically integrated innovators to license more. This prediction follows directly from Prediction 4 above. Recall that firms' licensing reaction curves are upward-sloping (see Figure 20.3). This implies that if innovator i licenses more since it does not compete in the product market, in response vertically integrated innovator j also licenses more.

The available empirical evidence is consistent with these theoretical predictions. First, survey-based evidence indicates that the main motivation for firms to engage in licensing is the revenue effect, that is, the main motivation is financial (Zuniga and Guellec 2009). Evidence from the PatVal Survey shows that licensing decreases as transaction costs increase and that smaller firms license more since they have smaller market shares and are less likely to be vertically integrated (Gambardella et al. 2007). Fosfuri (2006) also finds that firms in the chemical industry license more in markets where they have a smaller market share. Fosfuri's findings also support the prediction that licensing decreases with increasing product market differentiation due to the rent dissipation effect.

20.3 Patent Pools

The Wright brothers are famous for their pioneering achievements in aviation at the beginning of the 20th century. Their breakthrough innovation was to increase lateral stability during flight by twisting the wings of an airplane in opposite directions, referred to as *wing warping*. A less well-known fact is that the brothers obtained a series of patents on their "flying machine" that they aggressively enforced in court. Their patent enforcement efforts targeted in particular one competitor, Glenn Curtiss. He had also successfully addressed the problem of lateral stability by adding wing flaps to the edges of the wings. Curtiss also applied for a patent on his invention. However, the Wright brothers claimed that their patent covered any alternative technical solution to the problem of lateral stability and hence Curtiss infringed their patent. The Wrights' stubborn attempts to enforce their patents in court and extract steep royalty payments from competitors for what was considered an overly broad patent claim stymied airplane development in the United States. The situation was such that when the nation officially entered World War I in 1917, the US government struggled to find airplanes manufactured in the United States fit for war service.

To remove this blockage, then Assistant Secretary of the Navy Franklin D. Roosevelt urged the Wright brothers and their competitors, including Glenn Curtiss, to pool their patents and make them available to each other either royalty-free or in exchange for a modest fee. The royalty was much lower than what the Wright brothers had been requesting prior to the pool's creation. The pool covered 130 patents on aircraft structures (engines and instruments were excluded from the agreement) at the time of launch in 1917. Importantly, the agreement also stipulated that any future patents would be included in the pool and available royalty-free to pool members.

The airplane patent pool, known as the Aircraft Manufacturers Association, was one of the world's first patent pools. It demonstrates one of the key advantages of patent pools: Pools remove the threat of litigation and enable affordable access to inventions protected by patent rights owned by multiple parties. The agreement lasted until 1975 when it was disbanded as a result of a consent decree with the US Department of Justice (DoJ). The DoJ asserted that the agreement had stifled competition in the airplane industry and hampered innovation. While this assertion is disputed (Bittlingmayer 1988), it illustrates another characteristic of patent pools: They enable collaboration among product market competitors, which may reduce competition and innovation.

Patent pools have gained enormously in popularity since the days of the Wright brothers. In part, the rise in popularity is due to the dramatic increase of the importance of technology standards in the modern economy and the associated fragmented ownership of often thousands of SEPs. Well-known modern patent pools include the MPEG (a digital video standard), DVD, and Bluetooth pools. Recently, there has also been a surge in new patent pool formation in pharmaceuticals. Examples include the Medicines Patent Pool (MPP, discussed in Box 20.1); the Pool for Open Innovation Against Neglected Tropical Diseases (NTD); and more recently, the WHO COVID-19 Technology Access Pool (C-TAP).

Patent pools are formal or informal setups where different companies pool their patents that are essential for a technology in order to license them to each other and possibly also to outsiders. Unlike in the case of the early-20th-century airplane patent

Box 20.1 Medicines Patent Pool

The MPP is a nonprofit organization created in 2010 by the global health initiative Unitaid. Its goal is to increase access to affordable lifesaving drugs in low- and middle-income countries. Initially, the MPP covered only HIV medication. In 2015, its mandate expanded to include hepatitis C and tuberculosis treatments, and since 2018, it has included all drugs on the WHO essential medicines list. More recently, the MPP has also become an implementing partner of the WHO's C-TAP.

The MPP negotiates non-exclusive licenses directly with originator companies. As of June 2022, the MPP had signed licensing agreements with 18 originator companies, including market leaders such as Gilead, AbbVie, and ViiV. The MPP then sublicenses the rights to generic pharmaceutical companies interested in manufacturing and selling generic versions in any of the countries covered by the MPP licensing agreement. Importantly, the MPP negotiates licenses that conceivably cover over 140 low- and middle-income countries, and licensees have to accept licenses with fixed geographic scope. The majority of these licenses are royalty-free, or if they involve royalty payments, the royalty is low, typically capped at 5% of total revenue. Presumably, the MPP is able to negotiate such low royalties due to its unique institutional setup, high public visibility, and clear public health mandate. It probably also helps that the countries covered by MPP licenses are usually countries of low or no commercial interest to originator companies.

Empirical evidence by Galasso and Schankerman (2022) and Wang (2022) suggests a large impact of the MPP on licensing. Galasso and Schankerman estimate an increase of 73 percentage points in the probability of licensing a drug that has been contributed to the MPP to generic manufacturers. However, the impact on actual launch of generic versions in developing countries is much lower. Galasso and Schankerman find only a 3-percentage-point increase of the probability of launch. Moreover, the evidence suggests that although the probability of launch increases, there is a longer delay until launch occurs, presumably because pool insiders become less active in those countries. Similarly, Wang's estimates indicate that the MPP leads to a 7-percentage-point increase in the share of generic purchases in developing countries. Galasso and Schankerman suggest that the large gap between potential launch (licensing) and actual launch is due to the fact that generics have to accept a bundle license, which includes markets where launch is not profitable. In addition, due to non-exclusive licensing, there is also the risk of excessive market entry, which could further deter entry. Still, the evidence suggests increased availability of generic drugs at lower prices as a result of the patent pool. That said, it is somewhat unclear to what extent increased licensing is driven by lower transaction costs induced by pooling of patented drugs, or rather by overall lower licensing fees negotiated by the MPP.

Wang (2022) also shows that the MPP has a positive impact on follow-on innovation by pool outsiders. She argues that the effect is driven by complementarity between patented compounds included in the pool and compounds already available to generic companies. In the context of multicompound HIV drugs, this enables drug manufacturers to develop new drug combinations. This aspect of the MPP is especially interesting as it suggests that the patent pool has a positive effect on innovation by pool outsiders.

pool, they are usually voluntary organizations set up and run by private organizations, the pool administrator. Since membership is voluntary, firms choose whether to participate in a pool. This means that the design of a pool affects participation. Moreover, companies that have chosen to join a pool can often still select the patents that they want to contribute. This means that, in practice, most pools are "incomplete," that is, they do not include all relevant patent owners and members often do not contribute all relevant patents (Layne-Farrar and Lerner 2011). For example, despite the presence of several separate pools for the High Efficiency Video Coding (HEVC) standard, there are still numerous companies with HEVC SEPs that have not joined any of the existing pools (see Box 20.2).

Patent pools have a number of benefits for both licensors and licensees. Most importantly, when patent ownership is distributed across many firms, a pool reduces transaction costs associated with licensing. The pool can act as a one-stop shop and substantially reduce the number of licensing transactions required. This avoids the so-called tragedy of the anti-commons (Heller and Eisenberg 1998). In this way, a patent pool can also help avoid royalty stacking. As explained in Chapter 21, royalty stacking results from the fact that licensors ignore the impact of the royalty that they set on all other licensors, which leads them to charge an excessive royalty. The pooling arrangement avoids this externality by enabling coordination among licensors. This also has the effect of reducing the risk of litigation. In this way, pools help promote technology adoption and diffusion. This is especially true for patents that cover technology standards since SEP ownership is commonly distributed across a large number of companies that participate in the standards-setting process (see Chapter 21). In the SEP context, a pool can also reduce asymmetric information by having an objective third party conduct essentiality checks before patents enter the pool. This can help remove a potential stumbling block in licensing negotiations and avoid costly litigation.

However, pools can also reduce competition between pool members. Typically, members of the same pool are also product market competitors, upstream or downstream. Whether a pool has anti-competitive effects depends on the relationship between the patents contributed by the different members. If the patents are substitutes that protect technologies that achieve the same effect in different ways, the pool reduces competition. However, if the patents included in a pool are complements—where complements means that they block each other in some way—the pool is unlikely to reduce competition. There is still a risk that pool members extend their collaboration outside of the pool to set prices collusively in the product market. They can also favor pool members at the expense of entrants and restrict licensing of individual pool members to outsiders. In these cases, the overall impact of a pool on competition and innovation is likely negative. Due to the fact that patent pools often involve cooperation among product market competitors, in the United States they require approval from regulators. Although antitrust agencies generally look favorably on patent pools, they may impose restrictions on pools, for example, in the form of certain rules governing licensing, such as a requirement that outsiders may license specific patents instead of only the entire pool portfolio.

An example of a patent pool that had anti-competitive effects is the Hartford-Empire pool in the early 20th century. The pool combined hundreds of patents on glassware held by the major players in the industry. The pool imposed a number of restrictions on licensees, including what could be produced and how much. The pool also included patents on substitute technologies, with the effect of limiting competition between them. The US Supreme Court found that the patent pool had engaged in licensing practices that effectively squashed competition and allowed pool members to control product prices in the glassware market. Although the US Supreme Court imposed restrictions on licensing practices, it failed to acknowledge the problem coming from the inclusion of substitute patents in the pool (Gilbert 2004).

There are also situations where there is more than one patent pool for a given technology. For example, in the case of the DVD standard, Sony, Philips, and Pioneer formed one pool and Hitachi, Matsushita, Mitsubishi, Time Warner, Toshiba, and JVC formed another pool. This example hints at the often complex process of pool formation. In practice, pools often form gradually, with one or several core members establishing the pool for other companies to then join over time if the benefits of joining the pool are sufficient. This means that usually some patent holders remain outside of a pool and license individually instead. For example, Thomson decided not to join the two DVD patent pools and instead chose to license independently. The motivation was presumably its ability to achieve higher revenue by licensing independently. It charged a royalty rate per patent family of $0.13 per DVD player, which was higher than the rates charged by the two pools of $0.09 (DVD6C) and $0.06 (DVD3C) (Mattiol 2018).

While some licensors prefer to license independently, patent pools nevertheless affect their licensing activity. One way for pools to do that is by publicly announcing royalty rates. For example, the Avanci pool offers a single patent license for its 4G mobile technology patents for US$15 per vehicle.[5] Individual licensees rarely make such announcements. Therefore, such highly visible, publicly available rates can affect the licensing rates of outsiders by setting a reference point, especially in litigation where the use of comparable licenses to determine reasonable royalties is common practice (see Chapter 22). Box 20.2 discusses another example of competing patent pools in the case of the HEVC standard, where at some point there were three competing pools and a large number of companies that did not join any of the pools.

While pools can have a number of advantages for pool members and outsiders, these benefits depend on the setup of the pool. One crucial question concerns the price for a pool license. This is a complex problem because usually no comparable market prices exist for a pool license and individual pool members might disagree about the value of the contributed patents. A related issue concerns the rules governing licensing among pool members since normally contributions by pool members differ both in quantity and value. Some pool members may be required to pay royalty fees to other pool members to compensate for such differences.

When pools license to outsiders, the question of how to divide licensing income arises. Pools adopt a variety of such sharing rules. For example, licensing payments may be a simple function of the number of contributed patents. Alternatively, such sharing rules may take into account differences in technological importance among

---

[5] https://www.avanci.com/marketplace/#li-pricing.

Box 20.2 HEVC Patent Pools

HEVC is a video compression technology. It is the successor to the Advanced Video Coding (AVC) standard. Compared to AVC, it achieves better data compression. The standard was created by the Joint Collaborative Team on Video Coding, which was formed in 2013 through collaboration of several standard-setting organizations (SSOs). The HEVC technology is protected by a large number of SEPs held by many different companies. Any device or software that uses HEVC will have to obtain a license to the relevant set of SEPs that read on the standard.

Until recently, there were three patent pools that offered HEVC licenses: (1) MPEG LA, (2) HEVC Advance, and (3) Velos Media. Apart from these pools, there are also many companies that have chosen not to join a pool and instead license their HEVC SEPs independently. The figure shows the composition of the pools as well as the outsider companies. MPEG LA was the first pool to launch in 2014. HEVC Advance was created in 2015, and the Velos Media pool was created in 2017 and dissolved in 2022. The number of SEPs differed across pools, with MPEG LA offering access to the largest number of SEPs, followed by HEVC Advance and Velos. Licensing rates also differed, with an estimated per patent royalty of $0.20 charged by MPEG LA, $0.65 by HEVC Advance, and $0.75 by Velos Media (Oliver and Richardson, 2018). The coexistence of several pools combined with the independent licensing of several large players in the HEVC technology market creates a complex licensing landscape. This is further underscored by Velos's decision to close its HEVC pool within a couple of years after its formation.

HEVC pools and independent licensors

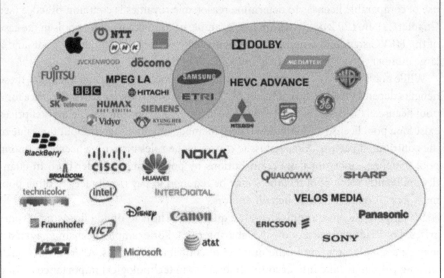

Source: Jonathan Samuelsson (2017): Current Status of HVEC. https://speakerdeck.com/stswe/current-status-of-hevc-by-jonatan-samuelsson-from-divideon?slide=4

patents. The different rules affect transaction costs since more complex rules may be more difficult to negotiate and to administer. These rules also depend on whether pool members are allowed to license independently the patents that they contributed to the pool. In this respect, pools also have to establish rules regarding individual contributions.

For example, pool members can be required to contribute all of the patents in a relevant technology or they may be allowed to only contribute a subset and license the rest independently. Pools also have to decide how to handle future patenting by pool members. This is usually done through so-called grantback clauses. These rules impose requirements on members to contribute all or specific future patents to the pool. This can be useful to prevent pool members from licensing future patents outside of the pool while still benefiting from cross-licensing within the pool. However, as shown by the airplane patent pool discussed above, grantback clauses can also affect incentives for follow-on innovation as they can limit the ability of pool members to appropriate returns to follow-on innovation. Pools may also require members to more broadly agree to so-called adjustment clauses, which allow pools to calibrate sharing rules in light of changes in members' contributions to the pool.

Empirical evidence on the impact of patent pools is largely based on the first patent pool in the United States, the Sewing Machine Combination (1856–1877). It consisted of the three main sewing machine manufacturers at the time, in addition to individual inventor Elias Howe. It contained nine complementary patents, that is, patents that stood in some blocking relationship with each other. The pool was created by Elias Howe and the three dominant sewing machine producers to solve the so-called sewing machine patent wars. As such, the pool is a good example for how patent pools can address conflict that arises from patent thickets. The pool operated until all of the nine patents expired.

The available evidence on the pool's impact suggests that it had a negative effect on innovation and patenting, especially for its members (Lampe and Moser 2010). The evidence indicates that the pool affected nonmembers by increasing the risk of litigation, thereby discouraging innovation by outsiders. This, in turn, weakened competition for members, which reduced their incentives to innovate. Moreover, outsiders were also encouraged to switch to substitute technologies that were not covered by the pool. In the case of sewing machines, the evidence suggests that outsiders switched to the *chainstitch* technology, which was clearly inferior to the *lockstitch* technology covered by the patent pool. The main reason for the reliance on an inferior technology appears to be the difference in license fees between pool insiders and outsiders (Lampe and Moser 2013). Outsiders had to pay three times as much for a license as insiders. This limited their ability to compete and drove them toward the adoption of the inferior albeit cheaper stitching technology.

Additional evidence from pools formed in a diverse set of industries during the 1930s confirms that the pooling of patents on substitute technologies reduces competition between pool members. This lessened incentives to improve the pool technology (Lampe and Moser 2016). The evidence therefore suggests that patent pools can have significant effects on outsiders and negatively affect innovation. Available evidence on modern patent pools, the MPEG and DVD patent pools, also suggests patent pool formation had a negative impact on innovation (Joshi and Nerkar 2011).

20.4 Patent Pledges and Patent Commons

20.4.1 Patent Pledges

In 2014, Tesla Motor's CEO Elon Musk publicly announced that Tesla would not enforce any of its patents against any third parties.[6] While Musk's blog post attracted an enormous amount of attention, reactions to Tesla's announcement were mixed. Some saw it merely as a public relations (PR) stunt of little practical value. Others saw it as an effective way of providing access to Tesla's electric vehicle technology, thereby promoting green car technology to grow the global market for electrical vehicles.[7] This interpretation also implied that the move could benefit Tesla directly as the adoption of its technology might ultimately increase demand for Tesla's batteries.

Tesla's announcement is an example of a *patent pledge*. Patent pledges are public, irrevocable commitments by companies not to enforce their enforceable patents against anyone that meets certain conditions. For example, in the case of Tesla, Musk stated that the pledge applied to "anyone who, in good faith, wants to use" Tesla's technology. Tesla's publicly available pledge provides a more detailed definition of what constitutes "good faith."[8] A closer look at the definition highlights a potential pitfall with a patent pledge. It can impose stringent conditions on anyone who wants to benefit from the pledge, including refraining from the assertion of any type of intellectual property against Tesla or "against a third party for its use of technologies relating to electric vehicles or related equipment" (this is referred to as a *defensive termination* right) as well as refraining from challenging the validity of any of Tesla's patents. Acceptance of these conditions can substantially limit a company's (strategic) use of its own patent portfolio.

On the other hand, these conditions provide certain defensive safeguards for the pledging firm. Tesla, in fact, sued Cap-XX, an Australian super-capacitator developer and manufacturer, in 2023 for patent infringement in spite of its patent pledge.[9] However, Cap-XX had violated the pledge provisions because it had sued Maxwell Technologies for patent infringement in 2019 shortly after Tesla had acquired the company.[10]

---

[6] https://www.tesla.com/blog/all-our-patent-are-belong-you.

[7] https://www.techdirt.com/articles/20140612/11253427557/elon-musk-destroys-rationale-patents-opens-up-all-teslas.shtml.

[8] The conditions are specifically: "A party is 'acting in good faith' for so long as such party and its related or affiliated companies have not: (a) asserted, helped others assert or had a financial stake in any assertion of (i) any patent or other intellectual property right against Tesla or (ii) any patent right against a third party for its use of technologies relating to electric vehicles or related equipment; (b) challenged, helped others challenge, or had a financial stake in any challenge to any Tesla patent; (c) or marketed or sold any knock-off product (e.g., a product created by imitating or copying the design or appearance of a Tesla product or which suggests an association with or endorsement by Tesla) or provided any material assistance to another party doing so."

[9] *Tesla, Inc. v. CAP-XX, Ltd.*, 23-cv-00334 (E.D. Texas, July 14, 2023).

[10] *CAP-XX, Ltd. v. Maxwell Technologies, Inc.*, 19-cv-01733, 2020 WL 2914497 (D. Delaware, June 3, 2020).

More generally, patent pledges differ in terms of accessibility. Some pledges are open to the public, while others are restricted to specific types of technology users. Tesla's pledge, for example, is open to the public. Car manufacturer Toyota also pledged a large number of its patents on hydrogen fuel cell and vehicle electrification technologies, but access is restricted and users have to negotiate individual royalty-free license agreements with Toyota.[11]

Patent pledges can concern a specific set of patents,[12] or they can be blanket declarations concerning all patents on a given technology or all patents held by a given company. Patent pledges are unusual as the pledging party commits not to assert a patent while still maintaining the patent in force and incurring the associated expenses. A simple alternative would be to allow the patent to lapse, which would render it unenforceable and the patented technology would enter the public domain. As such, a patent pledge is more limited in its effect. Tesla, for instance, states that its "[p]ledge is not a waiver of any patent claims (including claims for damages for past acts of infringement) and is not a license, covenant not to sue, or authorization to engage in patented activities or a limitation on remedies, damages or claims."

There can also be considerable legal uncertainty surrounding patent pledges. For example, a patent pledge may be revoked or the pledged patent might be transferred without requiring the buyer to adhere to the pledge. Either of these scenarios could put anyone who uses the technology of the pledged patent in a potentially difficult position. Patent pledges can mitigate these concerns. For example, Tesla's pledge states that any patent buyer has to "provide the same protection that Tesla provided under the Pledge and to place the same requirement on any subsequent transferee."[13]

Tesla is not the only company to make a patent pledge, nor was Tesla's pledge the first one. Pledges have been common in the OSS industry, with big players such as Sun, Red Hat, or Google routinely pledging large numbers of patents.

Why do for-profit companies pledge not to assert their patents while still incurring the full cost of their maintenance?

There are a wide range of different reasons why companies pursue patent pledges. They include product interoperability through common technology standards, promotion of technology platforms, sales of complementary products or services, and wider corporate social responsibility objectives including mitigating climate change (Contreras 2023). All of these motivations have in common that the patent holder benefits more from promoting use of its patented technology by setting the price of a license to zero than from maximizing licensing revenue or preventing any third-party use.

20.4.2 Patent Commons

In 2008, IBM together with Nokia, Pitney Bowes, and Sony launched the Eco-Patent-Commons (EcoPC). Over time more companies joined the commons, and at its height,

---

[11] https://global.toyota/en/newsroom/corporate/27512455.html.
[12] For the list of patents pledged by Tesla, see https://www.tesla.com/about/legal#patent-list.
[13] https://www.tesla.com/about/legal#patent-pledge.

a total of 13 companies contributed a total of 248 patents to the commons. The patents covered environmentally friendly technology as the stated objective of the EcoPC was the diffusion of green technology. For example, IBM pledged a patent that covered recyclable cardboard packaging for electronic components. The commons wanted to promote the adoption of the patented green technologies and facilitate follow-on innovation. Since the patented technologies were already visible to the public, these goals would be achieved by publicly committing not to assert the patents and hence enabling third parties to use and build on the patented technology.

The EcoPC is referred to as a *patent commons* since it assembles patent pledges from different companies. Therefore, patent commons can be considered a type of patent pledge. The EcoPC shared all of the characteristics of patent pledges reviewed in the previous section, for example, a public irrevocable commitment not to assert against any third party that meets certain conditions.

Patent commons are different from cross-licensing agreements and patent pools. The main distinction is that patent commons are open to third parties, that is, subject to certain limitations, anyone can use the technology covered by patents that have been placed in the commons. Often no formal contract is needed to benefit from the pledged patents; in fact, often users do not even have to notify the patent owners of their use. In contrast, cross-licensing arrangements only apply to participants of the licensing agreement. In patent pools, patents are only shared among contributing members. However, some pools also grant access to outsiders against payment of licensing fees. In any case, they require an explicit licensing agreement between licensor and licensee.

The reason patent commons exist is similar to those that motivate individual companies to make patent pledges. In the case of the EcoPC, the idea was that large companies like IBM hold large patent portfolios, which include patents that cover green technologies. Since these technologies are not at the heart of the company's business, the company can make them available to the public at little cost to its own commercial interests. Such a pledge brings potential PR benefits to the company and could even generate business by encouraging collaboration with other companies that use the pledged technologies.

The EcoPC is not the only patent commons. For example, the Patent Commons Project was created by the Linux Foundation to help protect the open-source Linux ecosystem.[14] Box 20.3 discusses a recent patent commons that provides access to patents covering technology relevant for combating the COVID pandemic.

In the case of the EcoPC, while the patents covered inventions with potential environmental benefit, empirical analysis shows that placing these patents in the commons did not increase diffusion or follow-on innovation as measured by patent citations (Contreras et al. 2019). A survey of the inventors of patents that cited patents pledged to the EcoPC indicates that royalty-free access to the cited invention played no role in the inventors' decision to rely on the EcoPC patents as prior art. This suggests that the pledge had no impact on follow-on innovation that was indeed based on the patented technology.

The EcoPC was officially discontinued in 2016, although the pledges remain valid for the remainder of the patent term. The data also revealed that participating companies

---

[14] https://patentcommons.org.

Box 20.3 Open COVID Pledge

During the COVID-19 epidemic that started in March 2020, concerns were voiced that patents could represent an obstacle to the fast response needed to combat the virus. To address such concerns, the Open COVID Pledge was created. It is a time-limited patent commons that has attracted a large number of prominent contributors, such as Intel, Microsoft, and IBM. Under the pledge, patents are available under the Open COVID License that grants a "non-exclusive, royalty-free, worldwide, fully paid-up license" to any third party. However, the pledge restricts the license by requiring that any use of the pledged IP be for "the sole purpose of ending the 'COVID-19 Pandemic' . . . and minimizing the impact of the disease." The license is set to expire 1 year after the WHO officially declares the pandemic to have ended.

The license also includes a defensive termination right. It allows the pledging party to suspend the license if a licensee asserts any of its IP against the pledger "with respect to any activity relating to the COVID-19 Pandemic" or under licensing terms specified by the pledging party. The figure here shows an example of a pledged technology. Patent US 9,772,714 pledged by IBM protects a method for eliminating pathogens from touchscreen surfaces through emission of ultraviolet light. The patent had the potential to help slow the spread of COVID by reducing the risk of transmission via touchscreens. As of May 2023, when the WHO declared the end of the global COVID pandemic, 29 companies had pledged either all or some of their patents to the COVID patent commons.

Patent US 9,772,714

| **U.S. Patent** | Sep. 26, 2017 | Sheet 1 of 10 | US 9,772,714 B2 |

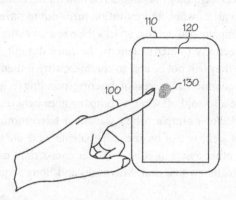

allowed the majority of pledged patents to expire. This suggested that pledging companies did not find it in their interest to maintain the pledged patents in force. While these results appear to cast doubt on the value of patent commons more generally, the evidence provided by Contreras et al. (2019) cautions against that conclusion. Interviews with various stakeholders involved in the EcoPC point to a number of specific problems with the setup of the EcoPC, which contributed to its limited impact.

For instance, the EcoPC failed to promote the diffusion of technology by, for example, linking patents to technologies or providing additional information that could have made it easier to find applications for the pledged patents. Indeed, evidence from a much broader set of patent pledges suggests that pledges can spur follow-on innovation, although there is substantial heterogeneity in the effect depending on the characteristics of the patent pledges, pledging firms, and pledged patents (de Rassenfosse and Palangkaraya 2023).

20.5 Sale of Patents

Apart from licensing either directly or through patent pools, pledges, or patent commons, patent owners also regularly buy and sell patents outright, which means a transfer of patent ownership. The transfer of the ownership interest of a patent right distinguishes the sale of a patent from licensing since licensing merely involves permission by the patent owner to a third party for the use of a patented invention. Patents are also acquired through merger and acquisitions (M&A) since patent ownership can be transferred alongside a firm's other assets. However, here we focus on independent patent transactions where patents are sold on their own.

The reasons for the sale or acquisition of patents are similar to those that motivate licensing. However, there are situations where firms prefer to outright buy or sell a patent instead of licensing it. For example, a company exits a certain market segment and has no more use for any associated patents. Given the transaction cost of licensing, companies may prefer to sell the patents instead of keeping and licensing them. This allows firms to monetize patents that they no longer commercialize themselves. A recent example for this type of transaction is the sale in 2023 of around 32,000 patents by Blackberry that protect technology no longer relevant for the company's core business.

A similar situation arises when an innovation turns out to have a different use than anticipated or the company realizes that it lacks the necessary complementary assets to monetize a patent effectively. In such situations, the innovator might be better off selling the innovation since they will not be able to commercialize it themself. Firms may also sell off a patent if the commercial success of the corresponding technology is lower than expected. Patents are also sold off when a company goes bankrupt and all remaining assets are liquidated. For example, when Canadian telecommunication equipment manufacturer Nortel went out of business, its patents were auctioned off separately from the company's other assets in 2011. A bidder consortium called Rockstar Bidco set up by Apple, Blackberry, Ericsson, Microsoft, and Sony acquired the patents for US$4.5billion.

The nonpracticing entity (NPE) business model is another motivation for standalone patent sales. NPEs specialize in the monetization and enforcement of patents (see Chapter 22). As such, they may be able to extract more value from a patent than a practicing entity could. The practicing entity may therefore decide to profit from the patent by selling it to an NPE. The sale also allows the practicing entity to disassociate itself from the NPE since the NPE business model may be incompatible with the practicing entity's business dealings or its reputation. Blackberry, in fact, sold its patents to an NPE, Malikie Innovation. The deal included a cash payment, and Blackberry will receive a share of the profits that Malikie will generate from monetizing the patent portfolio.

Patent acquisitions also allow companies to enter new markets and to overcome patent blockage, for example, in areas characterized by the presence of patent thickets. The acquisition of patents can allow companies to gain freedom to operate, for instance, by enabling cross-licensing agreements. However, firms can also buy patents with the goal of deterring the entry of new competitors. Acquiring patents is faster than building one's own patent portfolio.

The ability to trade patents as stand-alone assets also has indirect benefits. One important aspect is that it promotes access to external financing for firms. Patents can be used as collateral for a loan from a financial institution. They also promote investment in early-stage ventures since they allow investors to recoup part of their investment in case of bankruptcy.[15]

One key difference between the selling and licensing of patents is that the sale of a patent does not create a rent dissipation effect since no additional competitor is created. Instead, in the case of vertically integrated companies, the selling firm ceases to produce, while the purchasing firm starts production. In the case of an upstream firm selling to a downstream firm, the upstream firm can no longer license to other downstream firms.

In practice, patents are bought and sold either privately, directly between buyers and sellers, or through a quasi-public brokered market (Love et al. 2018). In the brokered market, patents available for sale are visible to market participants, and there are different entities that facilitate the sale of patents including patent brokers (e.g., ICAP Patent Brokerage, Vitek IP), online marketplaces (e.g., IAM Market),[16] and auction houses (e.g., Ocean Tomo). While information on patents for sale, buyers, and prices is usually not available to the general public even in the brokered market, market participants often have access to this information. This is an important distinction between the brokered and the private market for patents. In the latter, usually no information is disclosed to outside parties,[17] although patent reassignment data will still reveal that a transaction has taken place.

The empirical evidence shows that traded patents are much more valuable than untraded patents (Serrano 2018). However, on average, only a relatively small fraction of the difference in value is attributable to the trade itself. That said, the distribution of patent value due to trade is highly skewed, with a small share of patents accounting for the bulk of the gains from trade realized through the transaction (Serrano 2018).

The available evidence indicates that patent sales have increased over time (De Marco et al. 2017). Figueroa and Serrano (2019) suggest that small firms sell a higher share of their recently granted patents than large firms (8.5% vs. 5.1%). While it is true that large firms account for the overwhelming majority of patent sales, small firms buy and sell a much larger share of patents than their share in total patenting. In fact, the majority of patents sold by small firms are also bought by small firms. Akcigit et al. (2016) find that firms tend to sell patents that are more technologically distant to

---

[15] Hall (2019) reviews the rather weak evidence that patents are helpful in this way for startups.

[16] https://www.iam-media.com/market.

[17] The exception are sufficiently large ("material") transactions involving publicly traded companies that trigger reporting requirements, for example, by the US Securities and Exchange Commission.

the selling firm's patent portfolio. It is also true that patents that are bought are more similar to the buying firm's than the selling firm's patent portfolio. These empirical results indicate that the market for patents plays an important role in the reallocation of inventions to firms that are better placed to use and monetize them. A functioning market for patents can have significant positive effects on aggregate economic growth and welfare. This is an important argument in favor of the patent system because patents enable the legal transfer of ownership of an invention by turning an invention into a tradable asset (Spulber 2015).

20.6 Co-Ownership

Firms also share patents through co-ownership. Co-ownership of patents is usually the result of joint research activities.[18] Firms engage in joint research for a number of reasons. Firms can pool their knowledge and expertise if they possess complementary knowledge. Collaborations can also help reduce the risk associated with the research process, and there may be scale economies. In addition, collaboration may be a way to internalize spillovers associated with research. There is, in fact, ample empirical evidence that suggests joint research allows companies to generate more valuable innovation than what they would have achieved had they developed the innovation on their own.

However, a challenge when conducting joint research is how to appropriate returns to the innovation and how to distribute those returns. This problem is particularly challenging because parties have to make these decisions before they know the outcome or value of their joint research. These concerns can affect parties' willingness to engage in collaboration in the first place, and even conditional on having agreed to collaborate, it will affect the effort provision during the research project and knowledge exchange necessary for a successful research outcome.

One way to address this challenge is to agree *ex ante* to sharing the ownership of the patent that protects the outcome of the joint research. Co-ownership can help maximize incentives for all parties involved to invest in the joint research (Schmitz 2017). However, co-ownership can also limit the ability of co-owners to appropriate returns to the joint invention. Co-owners have equal rights to the use of the patented invention without regard to their individual contribution to the patented invention. The degree to which co-ownership affects appropriation depends on the product market relationship between co-owners. If co-owners are direct product market competitors, co-ownership implies that firms will compete in the product market. The result is a duopoly rather than a monopoly, with joint profits being lower than the profits obtained by a monopolist.

Depending on the jurisdiction, joint ownership also imposes restrictions on the licensing of the co-owned patent. In most European countries, including Germany,

---

[18] The literature distinguishes between shared and joint ownership (Hart and Moore 1990). Shared ownership means each party is free to use the asset in any way it sees fit, while joint ownership means the parties have veto power over each other's use of the asset. Here, we simply refer to both as co-ownership and distinguish between co-ownership with and without veto power where necessary.

France, and the United Kingdom, co-owners have to agree to the licensing of the patent by any of the co-owners. In these jurisdictions, co-ownership can create hurdles for the independent commercialization of a patent. In other jurisdictions, such as the United States, co-owners are free to license non-exclusively or sell the co-owned patent without consent from the other co-owners. There is no obligation to share the resulting revenue with other co-owners. Regardless of the jurisdiction, parties can use private contracts to alter the default rule to either remove or impose restrictions on the unilateral licensing of co-owned patents. That said, such contracts are not always effective since they impose contractual restrictions on statutory default rights. Moreover, writing such private contracts requires an agreement among all involved parties to alter the default rule, which may be difficult to achieve in practice (Fosfuri et al. 2017). The legal rules that govern shared ownership help explain why, empirically, joint ownership of patents is rare; estimates suggest that only a little over 1% of patents are co-owned by independent companies (Hagedoorn 2003).

Interview-based evidence reported by Belderbos et al. (2014) suggests that co-ownership of patents may limit the co-owner's ability to exploit the patents commercially. However, the evidence also indicates that appropriation is mainly a problem for firms in the same industry that share ownership. Co-ownership is less limiting for co-owners that operate in different industries or with universities. Patent citation analysis indicates that co-owned patents are associated with higher forward citation counts than individually owned patents (Belderbos et al. 2014). However, they are also associated with fewer self-citations, which may be indicative of firms being less likely to build on and further develop co-owned inventions.

Fosfuri et al. (2017) suggest that co-ownership creates a trade-off between the lack of control over the licensing and sale of co-owned patents by different owners and the increased incentives to contribute to the joint research thanks to co-ownership. Since unilateral licensing results in a rent dissipation effect (see Section 20.2) and this effect increases in product market proximity, this trade-off is more pronounced the closer co-owners compete in the product market. This mechanism implies that in legal systems where co-owners can freely license without the consent of the other co-owners, co-owners have incentives to "overlicense."

In legal systems where co-owners require permission from other co-owners to license, the result is "underlicensing" of the jointly owned patents. This happens because co-owners will veto any licensing since it erodes profits from competition in the product market (rent dissipation effect) without any licensing revenue to counteract the effect (revenue effect) since all the licensing revenue accrues only to the licensing co-owner but not the other co-owner. In contrast, in a legal regime without veto power, the same mechanism implies that the licensor can externalize some of the costs of having created an additional competitor through licensing, while obtaining all the associated benefits through the royalties paid by the licensee. The relative strength of these opposed effects again depends on the proximity of the co-owners in the product market.

Empirically, this implies that we should observe fewer co-assignments among product market competitors. However, if we observe co-ownership between product market rivals, the resulting innovation should be of higher value. Fosfuri et al. (2017) provide empirical evidence that is consistent with these predictions. Inventions that are patented at both the USPTO (no veto right to restrict licensing of co-owners) and the EPO (veto right to restrict licensing of co-owners) are less likely to be co-owned in the United States than in Europe. About 25% of patents that are co-owned in Europe are not co-owned in the United States. This effect increases in the product market proximity of co-owners. That is, the closer co-owners of the EPO patent are in the product market, the less likely they are to also share ownership of the patent in the United States.

20.7 Summary

Companies routinely share patents using a range of different mechanisms. The resulting market for patents and licenses has substantial benefits for all parties involved and society more broadly due to increased incentives to innovate. However, the sharing of patents also creates opportunities for strategic and outright anti-competitive behavior.

While there has been enormous growth in licensing and the trading of patents over recent years, the market is still developing as it is grappling with a number of problems inherent in the trading of patents. Well-functioning markets are typically characterized by the presence of many buyers and sellers and market participants can observe prices. While, in practice, firms actively trade and share patents, the market for patents is inefficient (Gans and Stern 2010). Because technologies are often highly specialized, there are relatively few licensors and licensees for a given patent. This makes it difficult for companies to identify trading partners. This problem is compounded by asymmetric information and uncertainty over the value and validity of any given patent and the need to trade patent packages rather than individual patents.

There is also a lack of price transparency since most patent transactions are not observable by the public. They are private contracts between the parties and usually kept confidential. This means that prices are generally unobservable, which, in turn, makes valuation of patents a challenging task. The challenges surrounding the licensing of SEPs, in particular the determination of what constitutes a FRAND rate, have put the spotlight on this problem (see Chapter 21). The absence of thick markets and the lack of transparency also create ample room for strategic behavior. While there have been attempts to address these issues, for example, through public patent auctions, they have not nearly reached a sufficient scale to make a material difference. This means that many patents that could be traded are currently not traded, which leaves substantial room for further growth of the market for technology.

21

Technology Standards and Standard Essential Patents

Learning Objectives

After reading this chapter, you will be able to understand and explain the following concepts:

- Technology standards and standard essential patents (SEP)
- The role of the patent system in the development and commercialization of technology standards
- The characteristics of SEPs
- Patent hold-up
- Royalty stacking
- Patent hold-out
- The computation of SEP licensing rates and the corresponding legal, economic, and policy debate

21.1 Introduction

Radio-frequency identification (RFID) is a type of wireless communication that relies on radio waves to transmit digital data. The data are stored on tags, which consist of a microchip. The tags allow the identifying, tracking, and monitoring of any object they are attached to in real time in an automated fashion. RFID tags have significant advantages over other systems such as barcodes. RFID tags do not have to be visible to be readable, and multiple tags can be read simultaneously. RFID is widely seen as a core technology that enables the IoT.[1] Passive tags in the ultra-high-frequency (UHF) band are especially cheap with a price tag of less than US$0.05 per unit. As a result, they are already widely used across many industries, including retail, manufacturing, logistics, and life sciences.

In order to perform their functions, technologies such as RFID tags require inter-operability to exchange data with other devices. Such inter-operability is enabled by technology standards.

[1] The IoT describes a system where physical devices are capable of communicating with other devices over the internet.

The Economics of Innovation and Intellectual Property. Bronwyn H. Hall and Christian Helmers, Oxford University Press.
© Oxford University Press 2024. DOI: 10.1093/oso/9780197630914.003.0021

There are, in fact, many different standards that apply to RFID tags. For example, standard ISO/IEC 18000-63:2015, which according to the International Organization for Standardization (ISO) has the goal "to allow for compatibility and to encourage inter-operability of products for the growing RFID market in the international marketplace" by defining "the forward and return link parameters for technical attributes."[2] Other relevant standards for RFID tags include GS1's Electronic Product Code Gen2v2 air interface standard,[3] which "defines the physical and logical requirements for an RFID system." This illustrates that due to their complexity, most modern communication technologies are governed by multiple technology standards developed and administered by different standard-setting organizations (SSO) such as the ISO or GS1. While there can be many different products that implement these technologies, they all have in common that in order to function, they need to comply with the relevant technology standards.

Technology standards such as those governing the RFID technology are ubiquitous in modern economies. Their number is steadily increasing, especially as ICTs continue to advance at staggering speed. Famous examples of ICT standards include wireless fidelity (WiFi), bluetooth, GPS, long-term evolution (LTE), and 5G.

Standards are crucial for enabling inter-operability between diverse technologies, components, and products. Achieving inter-operability can be a complex undertaking, but often it just means enabling the exchange of data between devices. This creates efficiencies by lowering transaction costs, allows for the creation of modular technologies, and results in strong network effects spurring the creation, adoption, and diffusion of new technologies and applications.

Most technology standards are created through a cooperative process, which is usually promoted, coordinated, and organized by an SSO, also sometimes referred to as standard development organization (SDO). That said, standards are also set through government regulation or simply evolve through market competition. In any case, the standard-setting process is complex and requires coordination among many parties with often competing interests. This creates the challenging task of developing a standard and ensuring its widespread adoption through cooperation without stifling competition between the different stakeholders involved in the process, especially downstream in the product market.

The technologies that create a standard are often protected by patents. Patents that cover technologies considered essential for a standard are called SEPs. Since standards are often developed by many different companies, ownership of SEPs is frequently fragmented. Because the purpose of standards is to reduce the use of alternative technologies, standards can result in market power for the owners of the relevant SEPs. Anyone that implements a standard by making products that are standard-compliant needs to license the SEPs that have been declared essential for the standard.[4] This sets SEPs apart from patents on technologies that are not part of a standard.

[2] https://www.iso.org/standard/63675.html.
[3] GS1 is a standard development organization.
[4] The reality of SEP licensing is a bit more complicated. Although firms may declare a patent essential, it might, in fact, not be so (this is referred to as *overdeclaration*). In addition, often not all aspects of a technology standard are necessary for a given product, which limits the share of SEPs that need to be licensed. However, there may also be patents that have not been declared standard essential that still cover relevant aspects of a standard and hence need to be licensed (so-called *undeclared* SEPs).

Most SSOs have rules in place that govern the patenting aspect of the standardization process. The rules regulate how decisions are made about which patents to include in a standard and how that information is disclosed to the public. SSOs usually also have specific requirements for SEP owners with respect to the licensing process that applies to third parties wanting to use the technology standard. The specific requirements differ across SSOs. Some SSOs, for example, require royalty-free licensing, such as the World Wide Web Consortium (W3C). Others require their members to make their SEPs available for licensing under FRAND terms (in the United States, it is also just reasonable, and nondiscriminatory, i.e., RAND).

The primary goal of FRAND is to facilitate widespread adoption of the standard. Indeed, courts around the world have interpreted FRAND as a binding commitment to share the technology protected by SEPs in order to promote diffusion of the standard. The patent owner accepts this commitment in exchange for having their patents included in a standard. FRAND licensing still implies that the patent owner is entitled to compensation in exchange for their contribution to the standard and the often substantial additional investments required by the standard development process.

However, a FRAND commitment imposes certain limitations on the compensation that can be obtained from licensing. This distinguishes SEPs from the licensing of regular patents, where the patent owner can outright refuse to license to third parties, including competitors. FRAND licensing also imposes obligations on the party that wants to implement the technology standard covered by the SEPs. Most importantly, the party has to be a "willing licensee," which means it has to be willing to negotiate a FRAND license in good faith and accept a license if the license terms comply with FRAND.

But why is there a need for FRAND licensing in the context of SEPs to begin with? Why do market participants not simply rely on the regular patent licensing framework? And what does FRAND really mean in practice?

It turns out that the answers to these questions are conceptually relatively straightforward, but extremely difficult to answer in practice. FRAND licensing exists because there is a concern that SEPs command hold-up power over potential licensees due to their ability to deny them access to the standardized technology. In addition, due to fragmentation of ownership of SEPs, there is also a concern that a lack of coordination among different SEP owners could lead to an excessive royalty burden on implementers (i.e., those that use the standardized technology), which is referred to as royalty stacking.

Hold-up power results from the fact that once a technology is chosen as an industry standard, any alternative technologies that could have been chosen instead will be less attractive commercially. Patents that cover the technology that is incorporated in the standard will command more market power than those that cover those alternative solutions. SEP owners could exclude competitors from the standardized market by refusing to license to them. And if they are willing to license, companies that use the technology standard may find themselves "locked into" the chosen technology for a number of reasons: They may have undertaken specific sunk investments into developing products that rely on the standard or they may find switching to alternative technologies more costly once the standard has been established. If not adopting a standard means incompatibility with other products and hence less value for end users, the technology gains value merely by being included in the standard relative to being a stand-alone technology. This allows the SEP owner to behave opportunistically in order to obtain royalties in excess of the incremental value of the patented technology in the absence of the standard (where incremental means relative to any other technology that existed at the time).

Problems such as hold-up and royalty stacking could lead to higher end-user prices, less adoption of a technology standard, and less innovation overall. On the other hand, if companies that develop technology standards are not appropriately compensated, they could have fewer incentives to contribute new technologies to standards and to invest in the cooperative development of new technologies. This could also have negative effects on innovation more broadly.

In practice, SEP licensing has been fraught with uncertainty over the definition of SEPs and the precise meaning and implications of a FRAND commitment. The complexity of the issue is compounded by the fact that questions concerning SEP licensing involve not only patent law, but also contract and antitrust law.[5] As a result, questions surrounding FRAND licensing have increasingly been litigated in courts in different jurisdictions around the world. While the courts have helped clarify some of the questions surrounding the interpretation and application of FRAND, many unresolved questions remain. This has also led to increased attention by policymakers and regulators.[6] Given the escalating importance of inter-operability standards especially in the context of IoT, the importance of SEPs and FRAND licensing is bound to increase in the future.

This chapter provides an overview of the licensing ecosystem of SEPs and the underlying economic concepts. It also reviews the challenges to the determination of FRAND rates and briefly discusses different approaches adopted in practice.

21.2 Technology Standards

While technology standards are the most relevant ones with respect to patent protection, standards apply much more broadly and exist in many different areas of the economy. Examples include standards that apply to freight containers to ensure compatibility across modes of transportation around the world, the SWIFT standard for international payments, the ISO 9000 quality management standards, the generally accepted accounting principles (GAAP) to harmonize corporate financial reporting, and even the ISO 3166 standard for the use of letter and number codes to refer to countries. These standards are created in different ways; some are government-mandated, others are created by individual companies or corporate consortia, and some are created by SSOs. In most of the standards just listed, intellectual property in the form of patents plays no role. That is a key distinction with technology standards where patents often

---

[5] Patent law provides relief in the form of monetary (mostly compensatory) damages and injunctive relief to stop the implementer from continuing to infringe. Contract law, in contrast, provides relief through specific performance in the form of granting a license under FRAND terms. Antitrust law provides remedies against the abuse of market power that may result from technology standards and SEPs.

[6] See, for example, the 2019 joint policy statement for SEPs and FRAND by the USPTO, the Department of Justice, and National Institute of Standards and Technology and the 2017 guidance by the EC in "Setting Out the EC Approach to SEPs."

assume a central role in incentivizing investment in the development of new technology standards as well as their adoption and diffusion.

Technology standards correspond to a set of rules and specifications that a technology has to comply with in order to function. The European Telecommunications Standards Institute (ETSI) defines a standard as "a document, established by consensus and approved by a recognized body, that provides, for common and repeated use, rules, guidelines or characteristics for activities or their results, aimed at the achievement of the optimum degree of order in a given context." Especially in ICT with its complex and modular technologies, standards are critical to guarantee inter-operability between technologies. However, technology standards serve other goals as well. They can help guarantee safety and implement government regulation among others.

In practice, standards consist of technical specifications.[7] A standard can consist of a single or many technical specifications. More complex standards usually consist of many different technical specifications, which can also evolve over time. There is enormous heterogeneity among technology standards. Some standards provide very detailed and specific sets of rules, while others focus on broader technological objectives.

21.3 SSOs and SEPs

SSOs facilitate and organize the complex standard-setting process. The process involves reviewing proposals by members for technologies to be included in a standard, the approval and publication of a standard, as well as potential revisions of the standard. While SSOs themselves assume a crucial role in the process, the standards are chosen and created by the members, not the SSOs.

Membership and participation in SSOs are voluntary. SSO stakeholders often comprise a diverse set of actors, including upstream companies focused on technology development that usually depend on royalty income from downstream licensing. Another important group are downstream technology implementers that sell products compliant with a standard to end users. There are also vertically integrated companies involved in both technology development and the production of end-user products. Many companies also participate in different standard-setting processes administered by different SSOs and often even assume different roles in different standards (e.g., technology developer vs. technology user).

Participation in the standard-setting process is associated with substantial costs. Costs arise in the form of SSO membership fees, participation in the development and negotiation process, as well as the development of technical contributions to the standard.

Most SSOs adopt IPR policies that specify the rules regarding SEPs. Specifically, IPR policies determine several core aspects of SEP ownership and licensing that are discussed next.

---

[7] For example, the technical specification for the RFID tag EPC Gen2v2 air interface standard can be found here: https://ref.gs1.org/standards/gen2.

21.3.1 Disclosure and Essentiality

Apart from managing the development of the standards, SSOs set disclosure rules that govern companies' obligations to disclose relevant SEPs to the SSO and the public. Disclosure requirements apply only to patents deemed essential to comply with a standard. This raises the question of what makes a patent standard essential. In reality, there is no single, uniform definition of essentiality. However, it is a binary assessment; there is no such thing as "degree of essentiality."

Each SSO has its own definition. Broadly, SSOs distinguish between technological and commercial essentiality. Technological essentiality means that there are no technological alternatives to implement the technology covered by the standard. In other words, the technology disclosed by patent claims is required to comply with a standard. ETSI, for example, describes essentiality as follows: "When it is not possible on technical grounds to make or operate equipment or methods which comply with a standard without infringing a SEP, i.e. without using technologies that are covered by one or more patents, we describe that patent as 'essential.'" Commercial essentiality, in contrast, is a broader concept. It means that while technological alternatives may exist, they are commercially less viable. SSO IEEE's definition covers both types of essentiality by stating that an "'Essential Patent Claim' shall mean any Patent Claim the practice of which was necessary to implement either a mandatory or optional portion of a normative clause of the IEEE Standard when, at the time of the IEEE Standard's approval, there was no commercially and technically feasible non-infringing alternative implementation method for such mandatory or optional portion of the normative clause."[8]

In practice, determining whether a patent is essential for a given standard is challenging. Often some degree of ambiguity remains. There is also the possibility that standards and patents change. SSOs generally avoid this problem by relying on self-declarations, that is, members decide themselves whether they declare their patents to read on a standard, that is, patents that protect some aspect of the technology covered by a standard. Some SSOs require members to disclose specific patents, while others accept blanket disclosures. Blanket disclosures mean that a member declares to have patents that cover a standard without providing information about specific patents. Such broad disclosures avoid the costs involved in identifying and verifying whether a given patent should be considered essential to a standard. They also have the advantage that any patent held by a licensor that is later considered essential to a given standard will be subject to the licensing commitments made by the licensor. Blanket disclosures are especially useful when the standard requires royalty-free licensing, as the cost of identifying essential patents exceeds the royalty income. Disclosure requirements often also include the patents held by affiliate companies, such as subsidiaries, to increase transparency. ETSI, for example requires that "[d]uring the proposal or development of a standard, ETSI members must inform the Director General in a timely fashion if they are aware that they hold any patent that might be essential."[9] ETSI also maintains a publicly available online database of all declared patents.[10]

---

[8] https://standards.ieee.org/about/policies/bylaws/sect6-7.html.
[9] https://www.etsi.org/intellectual-property-rights.
[10] https://ipr.etsi.org.

In addition, there is an international dimension to the disclosure requirement since often technologies are patented in many countries around the world. Commonly, disclosure of only one member of such a patent family is required if SSO rules stipulate that this implies the declaration of the entire family.[11] For example, ETSI considers as declared SEPs "all existing and future members of a patent family if ETSI has been informed of a member of this patent family. . . . Information on other members of this patent family, if any, may be voluntarily provided."[12] Some SSOs require early disclosure, although not all SSOs define what "early" or "timely" means in practice. Some SSOs require disclosure before a standard is approved but any time during the standard development process is permissible. ETSI's policy, for example, states: "[E]ach member shall use its reasonable endeavours, in particular during the development of a standard or technical specification where it participates, to inform ETSI of essential IPRs in a timely fashion." But there is no further clarification of what "timely" means in practice.

SSOs do not verify SEP declarations, and there are no penalties imposed by the SSO for over- or under-declaration. SSO IEEE, for example, states in its patent policy that it "is not responsible for identifying Essential Patent Claims for which a license may be required, for determining the validity, essentiality, or interpretation of Patents Claims. . . . Other Essential Patent Claims may exist for which a statement of assurance has not been received." This means that over- and under-declaration of SEPs are potentially common problems.

There are a number of reasons why companies may declare too many or too few of their patents as standard-essential. For example, overdeclaration may result from concerns over later being accused of patent ambush, a situation where the SEP owner keeps a patent purposefully hidden until the standard has been widely adopted in the marketplace. Overdeclaration may also occur because patents are declared essential before the standard-setting process has been finalized. Once finalized, a patent may, in fact, no longer be essential. Similarly, patent claims tend to change during patent examination. While a patent application might have been considered essential, the granted patent may no longer be essential.

However, overdeclaration and strategic declarations more generally may also occur for opportunistic reasons, such as in an attempt to inflate the share of SEPs held on a given standard. For example, Kang and Bekkers (2015) provide empirical evidence for what they call a *just-in-time* patenting strategy, whereby companies patent technologies that contribute little to a standard just before the standard's working group holds its next meeting; they then send the patent's inventors to the meeting to negotiate inclusion of the patented technology into the standard. Righi and Simcoe (2023) show that in the US patent system, licensors rely on continuations to adapt their patent filings to existing technology standards.[13] Strategies such as these designed to increase a company's number of SEPs included in a standard help improve the bargaining position of SEP owners in licensing negotiations in order to increase royalty payments. Stitzing et al. (2017) found that for SEPs declared to ETSI on the LTE standard, only a little over a

---

[11] A patent family is a set of patents that protect the same invention in different jurisdictions.

[12] https://www.etsi.org/images/files/IPR/etsi-ipr-policy.pdf.

[13] Continuations are patent applications that protect new claims based on an invention disclosed in a pending parent patent application. Importantly, continuations use the parent patent's priority date.

third of declared SEPs were considered essential by experts who performed an independent technical evaluation of each individual patent. Their evidence also confirms that patents declared standard-essential before they are granted may evolve during patent examination such that they are, in fact, no longer essential once they have been issued.

Both over- and under-declaration might affect adoption of the standard. Implementers may refrain from adopting a standard if there is concern that many essential patents are not declared and potentially not subject to a FRAND commitment. At the same time, implementers might consider royalties excessive if they are concerned that many SEPs declared to a standard are, in reality, not essential.

21.3.2 Licensing Commitments

SSOs often impose specific licensing requirements on SEP owners. Some SSOs require owners of disclosed SEPs to submit a licensing declaration; others may not have such requirements and members voluntarily make licensing declarations. Most SSOs also have standard requirements in place concerning specific licensing terms, notably FRAND, a maximum royalty, or royalty-free licensing, as well as nonroyalty terms such as grantback clauses. However, members often have the option of opting out of the default requirements. Any licensing commitments made by SEP owners are generally public and irrevocable. For example, ETSI requires that "[d]isclosure of SEP holders [be] requested to provide an irrevocable undertaking in writing that they are prepared to grant irrevocable licenses on FRAND terms and conditions."[14] Generally, licensing commitments cover the entire patent family in accordance with the automatic declaration of an entire family if a single patent is declared essential.

SSOs do not specify the royalty rate that corresponds to FRAND. Licensing and royalty rates are considered commercial issues. As such, they do not fall within the mandate of SSOs since their goal is instead to address the technological challenges associated with the standardization process. There is also a concern that facilitating the setting of royalty rates could conflict with antitrust laws as it might amount to price fixing. For example, the ISO/IEC/ITU common patent policy states that "[t]he detailed arrangements arising from patents (licensing, royalties, etc.) are left to the parties concerned, as these arrangements might differ from case to case." Lerner and Tirole (2015) suggest an alternative approach that they call *structured price commitments*. The key feature is that companies that participate in the standard-setting process commit to price caps for their SEP licensing rates before their technologies are included in a standard. Lerner and Tirole show that companies will choose prices that correspond to the *ex ante* competitive benchmark, that is, the prices they would have chosen in the absence of a standard. While conceptually appealing, the proposed approach has little in common with current practice.

Finally, there is a question regarding the transferability of licensing commitments. Patents are often transferred between parties for a number of reasons (see Chapter 20), including access to technology, defensive purposes, or the desire to monetize them.

---

[14] https://www.etsi.org/intellectual-property-rights.

SEPs are no exception. The question that arises is whether the licensing commitments made by the party that made the original declaration travel with the patent. This question has become more controversial as SEP owners have been either selling or "lending" patents to nonpracticing entities (NPEs) for different purposes, including *privateering*, where the NPEs assert the patents against competitors of the SEP owners (Helmers and Love 2023a). The main concern is that transfers could be used to circumvent (FRAND) licensing commitments. In practice, SSOs differ in the rules that they impose on their members in case of transfers. For example, ETSI states that "FRAND licensing undertakings ... shall be interpreted as encumbrances that bind all successors-in-interest."

21.4 What's So Special about SEPs?

In 2010, Microsoft sued Motorola for breach of contract.[15] Microsoft alleged that Motorola had breached its obligations to license its SEPs under FRAND terms. Motorola had requested a royalty payment of 2.25% of the end user's sales prices of Microsoft's standard compliant products including the Xbox, PCs, laptops, and smartphones.

Motorola responded to Microsoft's lawsuit by counterclaiming infringement of its SEPs and requested an injunction to stop Microsoft from selling the infringing products in the United States. Motorola had sent Microsoft demand letters alerting Microsoft to its alleged infringement of Motorola's SEP portfolios covering AVC standard H.264 and local area network (LAN) standard IEEE 802.11. Motorola also filed a patent infringement action in Germany, where Microsoft's European distribution center was located.

The case illustrates a number of challenges with implementing the policies that specify the rules regarding the licensing of SEPs. First, was Motorola's request of a 2.25% royalty on the final purchase price of Microsoft's end-user products indeed consistent with its FRAND commitment? That is, how is the appropriate FRAND royalty determined in practice? Second, should Motorola be able to obtain an injunction against Microsoft if Microsoft disagrees with the royalty requested by Motorola? Since by definition Microsoft has no alternative to using the standard, an injunction is particularly impactful. Should Motorola be able to wield so much power over Microsoft despite its FRAND commitment? To answer these questions, the following three theoretical concepts will help us understand why these questions are more complex in practice than they may appear at first glance.

21.4.1 Hold-Up

Assume there are two parties: an upstream firm and a downstream firm that uses the technology of the upstream firm in its products. If the downstream firm makes a relationship-specific investment, the upstream firm has an incentive to exploit the

---

[15] *Microsoft Corp. v. Motorola Inc.*, 696 F.3d 872 (9th Cir. 2012).

investment. Imagine, for example, that the relationship-specific investment is an investment in an assembly line that can only produce one type of product, and that the product requires the upstream company's technology. The crucial point is that because the investment is specific to the technology of the upstream company, the investment has no value outside of this relationship and is therefore sunk.

Next, imagine that before the downstream firm makes the investment, it negotiates a contract with the upstream firm over the acquisition of the technology. However, if the contract is not perfect, in other words not all future eventualities are or can be considered, the upstream firm will renegotiate the contract after the downstream firm has made its sunk investment. The reason is simple: Since the investment is sunk, the downstream firm can no longer use it when bargaining with the upstream firm. This allows the upstream firm to obtain a larger share of the surplus generated by the downstream firm than in the negotiation before the investment was made. In other words, the upstream firm is holding up the downstream firm by renegotiating the contract after the relationship-specific investment was made. It is easy to see that the concept of hold-up is not specific to the SEP context. In fact, it applies to many different situations that involve bargaining and asset ownership (Williamson 1975, 1976).

How does this concept apply to the SEP context? Lemley and Shapiro (2007) propose a simple model that illustrates its application to SEPs. Assume there is a SEP owner and an alleged infringer who negotiate a SEP patent license. The relevant parameters are the following:

- V denotes the value per unit of the patented feature to the implementer compared to the next best alternative, which is a technology that is not part of the standard.
- M denotes the implementer's profit from the patented feature, defined as sales price minus marginal costs per unit.
- θ denotes the probability that the patent is valid and infringed if litigated. θ is known to both parties.
- C denotes the cost to the implementer of redesigning its product to avoid patent infringement, as percentage of the value of the patented technology.
- L is the fraction of the implementer's total sales that would be lost if the patent owner obtained an injunction and forced the implementer to stop selling the product in the market.
- B denotes the parties' bargaining power. If $B = 0.5$, both parties have equal bargaining power. Asymmetries in bargaining power could arise for a number of reasons, such as one company is large, the other is small, and so on.

In this setting, the royalty R that results from bargaining is $R = B \cdot \theta \cdot V$. For example, assume that $\theta = 1$ (the patent is valid and infringed with certainty), $B = 0.5$ (the parties have the same bargaining power), and the value per unit of the patented feature is \$1, the benchmark royalty is equal to $R = 0.5 \cdot 1 \cdot \$1 = \$0.50$. This means that the parties split the incremental value of the patented technology equally.

Next assume that the implementer has created a product that relies on the patent, for example, the patent is a declared SEP and the product is compliant with the corresponding standard. The patent owner is suing the implementer for patent infringement.

Litigation changes the royalty that the implementer is willing to pay the patent owner. To see this, it is easiest to look at the difference between the benchmark royalty and what the implementer will agree to pay in litigation expressed as a percentage gap:

$$C + \frac{M-V}{V} L \tag{1}$$

The first term in equation (1) represents the cost of inventing around the infringing technology as a percent of the value of the patented technology. The second term is the loss from being enjoined by the court from selling the infringing product. The loss consists of the direct lost sales L and the relative importance of the infringing feature for the markup earned from selling the product $\frac{M-V}{V}$. To understand the importance of the latter, assume that $M = \$10$, while the value of the patented feature is only $V = \$1$.

This means that the markup is $\frac{M-V}{V} = \frac{\$10-\$1}{\$1} = 9$. Assume further that the direct loss in sales is 10% due to the injunction, that is, $L = 0.1$, which means $\frac{M-V}{V} \cdot L = 9 \cdot 0.1 = 0.9$. If redesigning the product costs 20% of the value of the patented technology, that is, $C = 0.2$, then $C + \frac{M-V}{V} \cdot L = 0.2 + 0.9 = 1.1$ or 110%. This implies that the royalty the implementer is willing to pay in litigation to avoid an injunction is more than twice the benchmark royalty.

This difference is entirely due to the cost to the implementer of an injunction, as shown in equation (1). This value depends strongly on the difference $M - V$ between the implementer's markup and the value of the patented feature (in our example, we assumed that the difference is very large).

The model is admittedly very simplistic, and its results are highly sensitive to the specific numbers chosen. However, the model illustrates the effect of a relationship-specific investment as the implementer incurs costs C if it wants to avoid infringement by inventing around the patent. The patent owner is also able to force the implementer to withdraw the entire product from the market (not just the patented feature). The combination of these two factors means that the patent owner is able to extract a royalty in excess of the benchmark in the absence of litigation.

In this model, hold-up arises specifically because of the patent owner's ability to obtain an injunction. A broader view of hold-up, however, includes any conduct that is motivated by the ability to enjoin unlicensed use through litigation. This type of conduct allows the patent owner to obtain royalties that exceed what the licensee would be willing to pay in its absence. Such conduct can take many forms; for example, it can involve parallel litigation in another jurisdiction, as in the *Microsoft v. Motorola* case mentioned above, or threats to sue the licensee's customers (Love et al. 2023).

While the theory is clear, establishing empirically the existence of hold-up turns out to be extremely difficult for a number of reasons. First, if companies understand the risk of hold-up, they might try to avoid or mitigate it even before it occurs. One strategy is to avoid the standardized technology altogether. This shows that hold-up can have negative private and social effects by forcing a company to adopt less efficient technology choices or forgo technology adoption altogether. Second, establishing the benchmark royalty in practice is difficult. This means establishing that a royalty is excessive is challenging. Even if it can be shown to be excessive, demonstrating that it is due to hold-up is still difficult.

There are several court cases commonly cited as evidence for the existence of hold-up. The first type of cases involved so-called patent ambush. Patent ambush describes a situation where the SEP owner purposefully hides ownership of patents essential to a standard until a downstream company sells standard-compliant products. Once the company has made the investment to develop and sell the product, the SEP owner reveals its SEPs and engages in hold-up. Examples include the *Dell Computer* case where the FTC found Dell to have hidden ownership of a patent essential for the VL-bus standard developed by the Video Electronics Standards Association (VESA).[16] In *Rambus*, the FTC also alleged that Rambus had engaged in similar conduct with respect to dynamic random access memory (DRAM)–related standards developed by the Joint Electron Device Engineering Council (JEDEC), although Rambus prevailed on appeal.[17] In Europe, the EC also alleged that Rambus had engaged in patent ambush. It specifically claimed that Rambus abused "its dominant position by claiming royalties for the use of its patents from JEDEC-compliant DRAM manufacturers at a level which, absent its allegedly intentional deceptive conduct, it would not have been able to charge."[18] Rambus settled the case with the EC by committing to royalty caps for its DRAM patents.

The element of surprise underlying patent ambush is not necessary for hold-up to occur in practice. Other cases that are often cited in the literature as evidence for hold-up include the *Microsoft v. Motorola* case discussed above. Motorola's initial FRAND offer requested royalties of 2.25% of Microsoft's final product price. After accounting for cross-licensing, Motorola's royalty demand amounted to $3.00 to $4.50, or 1.15–1.73% of the average selling price of the Microsoft Xbox. However, the court eventually only awarded a FRAND royalty of 3.471 cents per unit for Motorola's 802.11 SEP portfolio and 0.555 cents per unit for Motorola's H.264 SEP portfolio. In other words, Motorola's initial FRAND request was many times higher than what the court assessed to be the true FRAND royalty. Another example is *In re. Innovatio IP Venture LLC*, where Innovatio requested a royalty of 6% of the final sales price of products compliant with the 802.11 Wi-Fi wireless networking standard, such as laptops and barcode scanners.[19] The case was especially noteworthy because Innovatio sent its demand letters to hundreds of small end users, including coffee shops, supermarkets, and the like. The royalty amounts requested by Innovatio ranged between $3.39 and $36.90 per unit. The court, however, assessed the true FRAND rate at only 9.56 cents per unit.

[16] *In re Dell Computer Corp.*, 121 FTC 616, 618 (May 20, 1996).

[17] Opinion of the Commission, *In re Rambus Inc.*, FTC No. 9302 (F.T.C., August 2, 2006).

[18] Commission Decision COMP/38/636--Rambus of December 9, 2009, https://ec.europa.eu/competit ion/antitrust/cases/dec_docs/38636/38636_1203_1.pdf.

[19] *In re Innovatio IP Ventures*, 956 F.Supp.2d 925 (N.D. Illinois, July 26, 2013).

21.4.2 Royalty Stacking

Royalty stacking can arise in settings where multiple patents held by different owners read on a standard. It corresponds to a situation where royalties for individual patents by different owners are "stacked," and as a result, the sum of these individual royalties exceeds the royalty burden that would be charged if all patents were owned by a single company.

Theoretically, royalty stacking is a straightforward application of so-called Cournot complements. It describes a situation in which a product requires inputs from several suppliers, and demand for one input depends on demand for the other. In this situation, pricing decisions by one supplier affect the other suppliers. However, each supplier ignores their impact on the other suppliers and charges a price that exceeds marginal cost. That creates a negative externality on all other suppliers since it reduces the total number of units sold by the producer of the end product. Since each supplier sets its price independently of all other suppliers, they ignore the externality. They set a price that is, in fact, higher than the price set by a monopoly supplier that acts as a single source of all inputs. As a result, output by the producer of the end product is lower than that of a vertically integrated monopolist. This mechanism explains why fragmentation of ownership of SEPs relevant for a given standard can lead to each owner charging royalties that even exceed the price a monopolist would set. In other words, royalty stacking refers to the aggregate excessive royalty rate due to each owner individually charging an excessive royalty rate, which is a result of the fact that royalties are payable to multiple SEP owners.

Lemley and Shapiro (2007) propose a simple model of royalty stacking. Assume that there is an upstream SEP owner and a downstream implementer. The relevant parameters are as follows:

- X is the output of the firm.
- P is the price charged by the firm.
- A is the value of the product without any patented features.
- V denotes the added value of a patented feature.
- C is the firm's marginal cost (which does not include any royalty payments to the upstream firm for the use of the SEP).
- R denotes the royalty rate paid by the downstream firm to the upstream firm.

The downstream firm faces a linear demand curve:

$$X = A + V - P \tag{2}$$

Now assume that there are N different patent owners. Each patent owner holds a patent that adds value v_i; hence, $V = \sum_{i=1}^{N} v_i$.

As a benchmark, assume that a single patentee owns all N patents. The patent owner charges a combined royalty rate $R = \sum_{i=1}^{N} r_i$ for the downstream firm's use of all its patents. If we assume the downstream firm licenses the patents, it maximizes profits:

$$\pi = (P - C - R)(A + V - P) \tag{3}$$

The corresponding price is $P = (A + V + C + R)/2$, and the corresponding quantity is

$$X = A + V - P = \left[(A + V) - (C + R) \right]/2 \tag{4}$$

The patent holder sets R by maximizing royalty revenue $R \cdot X$. The optimal royalty is

$$R = (A + V - C)/2 \tag{5}$$

Substituting (5) into (4) gives the downstream firm's output:

$$X = (A + V - C)/4 \tag{6}$$

It is easy to see that the output in (6) is less than the output in a first best case, where the firm sets price equal to marginal cost $P = C$ with the corresponding output $X = (A + V - C)$. The reason is the well-known *double marginalization* problem that arises because both the downstream firm and the patent owner have market power.[20]

Royalty stacking occurs when patent ownership is fragmented. Assuming that there are now N independent patent owners, patentee i sets r_i to maximize $r_i \cdot X$. Using equation (4), the FOC is

$$(A + V) - (C + R) - r_i = 0 \tag{7}$$

If we further assume that all SEPs are equally valuable $v_i = v$, then $V = Nv$. This implies $r_i = r$ and hence $R = Nr$. Using this to substitute for R in equation (7) then yields $(A + V) - (C + Nr) = r$. Solving for r, we get

$$r = (A + V - C)/(N + 1) \tag{8}$$

Summing over all N patentees results in the equilibrium royalty:

$$R = \left[N/(N + 1) \right] (A + V - C) \tag{9}$$

The corresponding output of the downstream firm is

$$X = (A + V - C)/\left[2(N + 1) \right] \tag{10}$$

---

[20] Double marginalization refers to a situation where an upstream monopolist sells to a downstream monopolist and each charge a markup.

Obviously, expressions (6) and (10) are the same for $N = 1$. As N increases, R increases and X decreases. This shows that the total royalty the downstream company has to pay increases with the fragmentation of patent ownership, and its output decreases due to the higher price charged by the downstream firm.

It is important to highlight that the inefficiency that arises in the Cournot complements model comes from the fact that each upstream patent holder sets their own royalty rate, taking everyone else's royalty rate as given. If patent owners recognized, however, the impact that their decisions have on total output, the inefficiency could be avoided (Spulber 2019b). Such coordination among patent owners can be achieved, for example, through cross-licensing agreements and patent pools. For instance, assume that the industry consists only of vertically integrated companies. If all vertically integrated companies are symmetric, cross-licensing will be symmetric and all royalty payments cancel each other out. But even when the industry consists of vertically integrated as well as upstream-only firms, patent pooling can solve the complements and double marginalization problems (Layne-Farrar and Schmidt 2010). Ultimately, however, it is still an open empirical question to what extent royalty stacking occurs in real-world licensing negotiations.

There is relatively little direct empirical evidence on the question. Similar to the hold-up concept, there are a number of court cases commonly cited as evidence for the existence of royalty stacking in practice. In the *Microsoft v. Motorola* case, the district court noted explicitly that "Motorola's royalty request for its 802.11 SEP portfolio raises significant stacking concerns. There are at least 92 entities that own 802.11 SEPs. . . . If each of these 92 entities sought royalties similar to Motorola's request of 1.15% to 1.73% of the end-product price, the aggregate royalty to implement the 802.11 Standard, which is only one feature of the Xbox product, would exceed the total product price."

On the other hand, Galetovic and Gupta (2020) offer evidence for the 3G and 4G mobile wireless industry that questions the existence and impact of royalty stacking. They observe that the number of SEP owners in the mobile wireless industry increased dramatically over time, from only 2 in 1994 to over 130 in 2013. Similarly, the number of SEPs increased from 150 in 1994 to more than 150,000 in 2013. This drastic increase in fragmentation of ownership of SEPs should have made royalty stacking worse over time with clear implications for prices and industry structure. Nevertheless, the authors find no evidence for price increases or increased industry concentration.

However, during the 2010s, concentration indeed increased in the mobile phone industry in the United States, as shown in Figure 21.1. The HHI index of concentration has risen from 2,800 to 4,400 between 2012 and 2021, largely due to the growth of Apple's and Samsung's market shares. Average prices per mobile phone have also risen, but quality-adjusted prices have declined. This suggests that royalty stacking might not have affected the larger players in the market, but also that smaller players and entrants may have found survival difficult due to the costs of royalty negotiation.

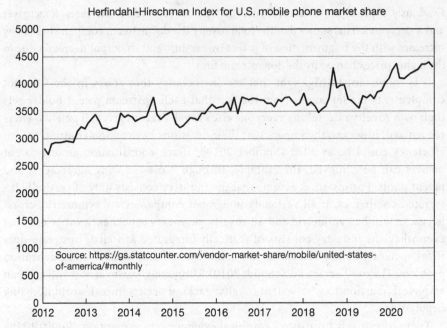

Figure 21.1 Concentration of the US mobile phone market.

21.4.3 Hold-Out

Hold-up and royalty stacking adversely affect the licensee of patented technology. In contrast, the third theoretical concept, referred to as hold-out, has the potential to adversely affect the patent owner.

In the SEP context, hold-out describes a situation where the implementer attempts to avoid licensing the relevant SEPs. In the extreme, hold-out implies that the implementer refuses a license unless forced by a court to accept one, which has also been referred to as *efficient infringement* or *reverse hold-up*. This means that the SEP owner is forced to engage in costly and lengthy litigation that also entails some risk of seeing the SEPs (partially) invalidated in the process. The implementer may also dispute essentiality in court, and even if essentiality is confirmed, the court might find that some acts of implementation are not covered by the standard and, as a result, find a lower royalty rate. Such findings might have repercussions for other subsequent licensing negotiations for the SEP owner since the use of existing comparable licenses is a common way of negotiating royalty rates (see Section 21.5 below). This situation is compounded by the mismatch between the national character of the patent system and the global business of most licensees of standard-essential technologies. Licensees can refuse to accept a global license of an entire SEP portfolio and instead engage in separate, piecemeal negotiations and litigation in each relevant jurisdiction. However, this might change in the future since in recent decisions courts in the United Kingdom and China have set global FRAND rates and determined that SEP holders can demand that an implementer practicing a national SEP take a worldwide license and an injunction can be issued if the implementer refuses.[21] The issue of portfolio licensing applies not only to the geographic but also technological scope of SEPs. Some uses of a technology standard may not require all the different components that are part of a standard. This then raises the question of whether an implementer would still be required to obtain a license for a company's entire portfolio of SEPs that read on the standard. At least theoretically, the argument is that portfolio licenses are necessary because, in principle, the SEPs are perfect complements. Because the assertion of entire patent portfolios in court is not possible, licensees may opportunistically choose to negotiate only licenses for a small subset of relevant SEPs. As a result, SEP owners may decide to at least partially forgo royalty revenue from implementers that successfully hold out.

This behavior can be optimal from an implementer's perspective if there are no punitive damages for the infringement of SEPs. An implementer may find it optimal not to voluntarily agree to a license and instead wait for the patent owner to sue for infringement. If the validity of the patent is confirmed and the implementer is found to infringe the SEPs, its maximum liability is reasonable damages, which is the same as what would have been agreed *ex ante* in a licensing agreement. This type of opportunistic behavior places the burden of successfully negotiating a license on the SEP owner. However, the effectiveness of this mechanism depends on a SEP owner's ability to obtain injunctive relief despite their FRAND commitment.[22]

In practice, determining whether the implementer is a willing or unwilling licensee is difficult as it requires distinguishing hold-out from appropriate bargaining over the appropriate royalty payment. Also, the issue of portfolio licensing may be controversial since in practice not all aspects of a standard covered by an SEP portfolio are relevant for a given end-user product.

In Europe, the CJEU laid out a framework for FRAND licensing in its *Huawei Technology Co. Ltd. v. ZTE Corp.* decision.[23] The decision set forth specific requirements for a licensee to qualify as "willing" in the context of FRAND licensing negotiations. This includes a requirement to express willingness to negotiate a FRAND license and demonstrate behavior that is "in accordance with recognized commercial practices in the field and in good faith" without engaging in delaying tactics. Moreover, should the licensee reject the SEP owner's licensing offer, it has to provide a written counter-offer on FRAND terms.

There are several examples of hold-out presented in the literature. Epstein and Noroozi (2017) point to the US case *Core Wireless v. LG Electronics*. In its decision, the district court interprets LG's behavior during licensing negotiations as a sign that LG was not negotiating in good faith. The decision stated:

[21] *Unwired Planet v. Huawei* [2020] UKSC 37 (appeal taken from Eng.); *InterDigital v. Lenovo* [2023] EWHC 539; *Optis v. Apple* [2023] EWHC 1095; and *Oppo v Nokia* (2021) Yu Minchu No. 1232.
[22] In the United States, in 2006 the Supreme Court restricted a patent owner's ability to obtain injunctive relief in its *eBay v. MercExchange* (547 US 388) decision by establishing a four-factor test for awarding a permanent injunction or monetary damages instead. In order to obtain an injunction, patent holders have to demonstrate: (1) The plaintiff suffered irreparable harm in the absence of an injunction; (2) other remedies such as monetary damages are insufficient to address that harm; (3) considering the balance of hardships between plaintiff and defendant, a remedy in equity is warranted; and (4) the public interest is not disserved by a permanent injunction. The *eBay* case criteria apply to injunctions requested by SEP owners. As a result, SEP owners have found it challenging, in practice, to obtain an injunction as they have had difficulties establishing irreparable harm (Sidak 2018).
[23] Case C-170/13, *Huawei Technologies Co. Ltd v. ZTE Corp., ZTE Deutschland GmbH.*

"[T]he Court makes note of the manner in which LG abruptly terminated licensing negotiations. After a long series of meetings between the parties, including seven meetings in Seoul, Korea, LG invited the Core Wireless representatives to Korea one last time and indicated that it would be making a monetary offer for a license. Rather than make an offer or engage in serious, good faith negotiations, LG delivered a terse one-page presentation stating that a lawsuit at that time between the parties was 'preferable' to a license. . . . It is apparent to the Court that LG's decision to terminate negotiations and continue operations without a license was driven by its resistance to being the first in the industry to take a license, and not by the merits or strength of its non-infringement and invalidity defenses."[24]

Another example is the litigation between Sisvel and Haier in Germany. Sisvel sued Haier for infringement of its SEP on wireless communication standards. In its decision in 2020, the German Federal Court of Justice allowed Sisvel to seek injunctive relief against Haier because it considered Haier an unwilling licensee. The court found Haier engaged in delaying tactics during licensing negotiations, such as taking 1 year to respond to Sisvel and declare its willingness to license. The court therefore determined that Haier was not willing to accept a license on FRAND terms.[25]

21.5 FRAND and the Licensing of SEPs

21.5.1 Licensing of Patents

Licensing of patents is usually a private transaction between the parties, and the details are not disclosed to the public. Even in court records, information concerning the terms of a licensing agreement is usually redacted. This creates the challenge that market prices for licenses are not easily observable by third parties (Helmers and Love 2022). The problem is compounded by the fact that the specific licensing terms depend to a large extent on the specific circumstances of the technologies and companies involved. For example, parties may agree to a cross-license with a balance payment if the parties agree that cross-licensing does not fully compensate one of the two parties. In a different context, the licensee may not have patents that make a cross-licensing agreement feasible. In this case, it is unclear to what extent the balance payment from the first license agreement can be used to inform the royalty payment in the second agreement as the overall licensing circumstances may be substantially different. In a third scenario, the licensee's product is a component instead of an end-user product and the component only implements some elements of a standard. In this case, it is not necessarily clear how royalties that apply to producers of end-user products translate to royalties payable by the component maker if the scope of the licenses required is narrower. Another more fundamental challenge is that for new technologies, no licensing rates have been established and market participants resort to using licensing rates for existing technologies

---

[24] *Core Wireless Licensing S.A.R.L. v. LG Electronics Inc*, No. 2:14-cv-912-JRG, 2016 WL 10749825, at *1 (E.D. Texas, November 2, 2016).

[25] *Sisvel Int'l S.A. v. Haier Deutschland GmbH*, KZR 36/17 (BGH May 5, 2020).

and adjust them to account for technology differences (e.g., using LTE licensing rates for 5G).

When parties cannot agree on a royalty payment, they can seek a determination by the courts. In the United States, for example, the law entitles patent owners to no less than a reasonable royalty for patent infringement.[26] It also is the lower bound in litigation since the patent owner may recover lost profits and potentially even punitive damages under certain conditions. In practice, proving lost profits is difficult since a causal link between infringement and lost profits needs to be established, and punitive damages require a showing of willful infringement, which is also difficult to establish. By far the most common damages imposed by US federal courts are reasonable royalties.[27]

In order to figure out what a reasonable royalty is in a given case, US courts rely on the 15 factors established in *Georgia Pacific v. United States Plywood*,[28] a case decided in 1970 (see Box 21.1). The factors are designed to help the court replicate a counterfactual negotiation between the parties––that is, as if they were negotiating before the case was resolved in court. The factors include questions about the importance of the patent to the infringing product, market demand for the product, and comparable licenses. While the factors are supposed to replicate bargaining between the parties before any lawsuit takes place, there is an important difference. In order for the court to arrive at the stage where the determination of reasonable royalties becomes relevant and it gets to apply the 15 factors, the court must have established that the patent is valid and infringed. When parties negotiate a license before any litigation takes place, uncertainty over infringement and validity should lead to a lower negotiated royalty than the one agreed on once infringement and validity have been confirmed by the court.

Courts can award a lump-sum royalty or instead a running royalty, which is a periodic payment that depends on the number of products sold in the market. In negotiating a royalty, parties and the court face the challenge of determining the royalty base as well as the royalty rate. US patent law stipulates that royalties should correspond only to the infringing features of the infringing product. This is referred to as the rule of apportionment. If a patent only covers a specific feature of a product, the question is whether the royalty base should be the sales price of the final product, which is referred to as entire market value (EMV), or should it be what is referred to as the smallest saleable patent practicing unit (SSPPU). EMV seeks to establish a royalty that corresponds to the added value of the patented feature to the entire end-user product. SSPPU instead means that the royalty base corresponds only to the added value of the patented feature to the SSPPU. The EMV is only applicable if the "patented feature creates the basis for customer demand or substantially creates the value of the component parts"[29] even if it is only part of a more complex product.

---

[26] 35 USC. §284.

[27] If the SEP owner's main source of profits is licensing, lost profits are equivalent to reasonable royalties.

[28] 318 F. Supp. 1116 (S.D.N.Y., May 28, 1970).

[29] *Virnetx v. Cisco Systems*, 767 F.3d 1308 (Fed. Cir. 2014).

Box 21.1 Georgia Pacific Factors

The court established the following factors in *Georgia Pacific v. United States Plywood* to determine the amount of a reasonable royalty for a patent license:

Established royalty: the royalties received by the patentee for the licensing of the patent in suit, proving or tending to prove an established royalty

Comparable licenses: the rates paid by the licensee for the use of other patents comparable to the patent in suit

Type and scope of license: the nature and scope of the license, as exclusive or non-exclusive; or as restricted or nonrestricted in terms of territory or with respect to whom the manufactured product may be sold

Prior licensing: the licensor's established policy and marketing program to maintain their patent monopoly by not licensing others to use the invention or by granting licenses under special conditions designed to preserve that monopoly

Relationship between licensor and licensee: the commercial relationship between the licensor and licensee, such as whether they are competitors in the same territory in the same line of business, or whether they are inventor and promoter

Effect on sales of other products by licensee: the effect of selling the patented specialty in promoting sales of other products of the licensee; the existing value of the invention to the licensor as a generator of sales of their nonpatented items; and the extent of such derivative or convoyed sales

Patent and license terms: the duration of the patent and the term of the license

Success of product covered by patent: the established profitability of the product made under the patent; its commercial success; and its current popularity

Advantage over existing technology: the utility and advantages of the patent property over the old modes or devices, if any, that had been used for working out similar results

Patented invention: the nature of the patented invention; the character of the commercial embodiment of it as owned and produced by the licensor; and the benefits to those who have used the invention

Infringer's use of invention: the extent to which the infringer has made use of the invention; and any evidence probative of the value of that use

Customary share of profit payable for invention: the portion of the profit or of the selling price that may be customary in the particular business or in comparable businesses to allow for the use of the invention or analogous inventions

Share of profit due to invention: the portion of the realizable profit that should be credited to the invention as distinguished from nonpatented elements, the manufacturing process, business risks, or significant features or improvements added by the infringer

Expert opinion: the opinion testimony of qualified experts

Hypothetical *ex ante* license: the amount that a licensor (such as the patentee) and a licensee (such as the infringer) would have agreed on (at the time the infringement began) if both had been reasonably and voluntarily trying to reach an agreement; that is, the amount that a prudent licensee who desired, as a business proposition, to obtain a license to manufacture and sell a particular article embodying the patented invention would have been willing to pay as a royalty and yet be able to make a reasonable profit and which amount would have been acceptable by a prudent patentee who was willing to grant a license

21.5.2 FRAND Overview

SEPs are different from "regular" patents because the technology they protect is required to practice a standard established by an SSO. As discussed above, in some cases declaring a patent as standard-essential is contingent on a FRAND commitment.

The FRAND commitment imposes licensing obligations on the SEP owner and also requires the implementer to be a willing licensee as discussed above in the context of hold-out. This means that the FRAND licensing framework imposes obligations on both parties to negotiate a FRAND license in good faith. An interesting practical implication is that the SEP owner and standard user can find themselves in a contractual relationship even before having agreed on a license (which would then allow a party to sue for breach of contract, as in the case of *Microsoft v. Motorola* mentioned above).[30]

As discussed above, a FRAND commitment imposes some limitations on SEP owners. Perhaps most importantly, in the United States, courts have expressed the view that if a SEP owner commits to licensing under FRAND terms, monetary damages are generally sufficient to compensate the SEP owner for infringement. That said, the courts also explicitly stated that a FRAND commitment does not automatically preclude the SEP owner's right to request an injunction. The topic of injunctive relief has been a sticking point in the determination of FRAND rates. Outside of the SEP context, injunctions are a standard relief available to patent owners to stop patent infringement. However, in the SEP context, there is a concern that licensing negotiations under the threat of an injunction will give more bargaining power (hold-up) to the SEP owner.

The critical question that SEP owners, licensees, and courts have been grappling with is how to compute a FRAND license in practice. From a theory perspective, Lemley and Shapiro (2007) suggest computing the FRAND rate as the incremental *ex ante* value of the patented invention compared to the next best alternative, taking into account infringement and validity. While this may be a theoretically appealing concept, it is not clear how to measure the theoretical concept in practice (Siebrasse and Cotter 2017). In particular, it is unclear how to isolate the incremental value of the technology before it becomes part of the standard. Identifying the next best alternative before the standard was determined is equally challenging. As a result, SEP owners, licensees, and courts have come up with alternative, more practical approaches.

In the United States and United Kingdom, there have been several high-profile court decisions that have laid out different frameworks to compute FRAND licensing rates tailored to the specific facts of a given case. For example, in the United States, in *Microsoft v. Motorola*, Judge Robart calculated the FRAND royalty using a modification of the Georgia Pacific factors to account for the importance of the SEPs to the standard and the standard-compliant product. Judge Robart noted that "it is critical to consider the contribution of the patented technology apart from the value of the patent as the result of its incorporation into the standard, the latter of which would improperly reward

---

[30] In a 2020 court decision in France, the Paris Court found in *TCL v. Philips* that a FRAND commitment under ETSI's IPR policy rules qualified as a contractual relationship between the ETSI member company and the potential licensee. [*TCL v. Philips* (Paris High Court) No. 19/02085].

the SEP owner for the value of the standard itself. Rewarding the SEP owner with any of the value of the standard itself would constitute hold-up value and be contrary to the purpose behind the RAND commitment."[31] In the United Kingdom, in *Optis v. Apple*, Justice Smith decided that "[t]he best approach . . . is to seek to price the value of the entire Stack to Apple, and then to apportion that price pro rata amongst the co-owners of the Stack in proportion with their holding . . . " and proceeded to calculate a lump-sum royalty using the information on comparable licenses provided by the parties in the case.[32]

The CJEU's *Huawei Technology Co. Ltd. v. ZTE Corp.* decision discussed in the context of hold-out above provides a procedure for the SEP owner and prospective licensee to negotiate FRAND royalties. It also sets out the conditions under which parties have recourse to legal remedies, including injunctive relief. However, the decision does not provide any specific guidance with respect to what constitutes a FRAND royalty or its specific calculation.

The existing case law has made substantial progress over the last decade in clarifying the meaning and calculation of FRAND royalties. However, it has also become clear that the determination of FRAND royalties is very specific to the facts and circumstances. Therefore, establishing a uniform framework that applies more widely beyond an individual case remains a challenge.

21.5.3 Approaches to Determine Royalties in Practice

In practice, SEP owners, implementers, and courts around the world rely mainly on three methodologies (or a combination of them) to compute FRAND royalties:

1. *Bottom-up approach.* This approach jumps directly to a determination of the value of the patents for which a license is being negotiated. There are different frameworks for establishing the value of a patent, for example in the United States, the 15 Georgia Pacific factors provide guidance. However, this approach means that the results are very fact-specific and therefore vary substantially from case to case. A potential drawback of this approach is that it often relies on ad hoc valuation criteria and royalties are computed ignoring all other SEPs that are also relevant for the same standard but not the subject of the licensing negotiation. This can potentially lead to royalty stacking.

2. *Top-down approach.* This approach first determines the aggregate SEP royalty burden of the relevant standard on a product and then determines the share of the aggregate royalty owed to an individual SEP owner. The advantage of this approach is that it explicitly takes into account the existence of other patent owners whose patents are equally relevant for implementation of the standard. In practice, this is usually done by fixing some aggregate royalty burden and then computing the share

---

[31] Paragraph 109.
[32] *Optis v. Apple* [2023] EWHC 1095 (Ch), at 237, ¶ 456 (Eng.).

of SEPs owned by a given company relative to all relevant SEPs for the standard. Additional filters can be applied to refine the analysis by, for example, evaluating standard essentiality of the patents claimed to be SEPs. The approach addresses directly concerns over royalty stacking since the total royalty burden is determined first and any given SEP owner can only get a fraction of the total as a function of the SEP owner's share of SEP ownership. The non-negligible practical challenge is to come up with a figure for the aggregate royalty burden. Courts address this problem in practice by taking into account available information on comparable licenses and sometimes also public statements made by (other) SEP owners with respect to the royalty burden. For example, Qualcomm publicly announced in 2017 that it would charge a royalty rate of 2.275% of the sales price of single-mode 5G handsets. A drawback of this approach is that it often ignores quality differences between patents as they are difficult to measure in practice, and any such quality evaluation would have to be done for all SEPs that read on a given standard. This implies that there is no guarantee either the numerator or denominator is correct when the share is computed of a given licensor among all SEPs relevant to a given standard. In addition, the top-down approach could also create incentives to overdeclare patents as essential to a standard in an attempt to obtain a larger share of the total royalty burden.

3. *Comparable licenses.* This approach relies on existing license agreements that are considered "comparable" to the agreement under negotiation. This approach assumes that royalty payments agreed to in existing licenses are "fair and reasonable," although it is worth emphasizing that this is merely an assumption. The main challenge is to define what should be considered comparable and what adjustments should be made for any relevant differences between the existing license agreements and the one being negotiated. For example, an existing agreement may have established a lump-sum royalty payment, while the current negotiation is about running royalties. Also, licensing agreements that involve cross-licensing are potentially problematic for comparison as the actual value of the license will be difficult to impute. In some situations, there may be no comparable licenses (e.g., in the case of new technologies such as 5G). In the United States, the use of comparable licenses is part of the Georgia Pacific factors and the challenge of relying on existing licensing agreements in the SEP context was recognized by Judge Robart in *Microsoft v. Motorola*: "In the RAND context, such licensing royalties for a given patent(s) must be comparable to RAND licensing circumstances. In other words, to prove an established royalty rate for an SEP, the past royalty rates for a patent must be negotiated under the RAND obligation or a comparable negotiation."

All these approaches have in common that they often require pragmatic and ad hoc assumptions about the relevance of existing data for the computation of royalty rates. This is largely due to the lack of observable market prices for patent licenses and the technological complexity involved. Another challenge is the existence of complementarities between the standard and other aspects of complex products.

21.6 Summary

This chapter provides an overview of the link between the patent system and technology standards. Patents that protect technology standards differ in important ways from other patents. The main distinguishing feature is a lack of substitutes for SEPs. This heightens concerns over the potential for patent hold-up. In addition, because ownership of SEPs is usually fragmented, there is the possibility of royalty stacking. On the other hand, SEP owners potentially face situations where implementers are delaying or evading the licensing of SEPs through hold-out. Such opportunistic behavior by SEP owners and licensees is indeed to a large extent the result of the specific characteristics of SEPs and licensing in the context of technology standards. However, even in the absence of such opportunistic conduct, the computation of SEP licensing rates is fraught with difficulties in practice. Courts around the world have been grappling with these issues, and despite substantial progress in clarifying the terms and conditions of the licensing of SEPs, important open questions remain.

22

Patent Trolls

Learning Objectives

After reading this chapter, you will be able to understand and explain the following concepts:

- The definition and business model of patent trolls, also referred to as nonpracticing entities (NPEs) or patent assertion entities (PAEs)
- The characteristics of different NPE types
- The ambiguous theoretical effects of NPEs on innovation and welfare
- The different enforcement strategies of NPEs
- The existing empirical evidence on the effect of NPEs on innovation and welfare
- The various responses to NPEs in the form of defensive aggregators, invalidation entities, and litigation insurance.

22.1 Introduction

In 2000, Research in Motion (RIM), the maker of the BlackBerry, introduced the RIM 957, its first mobile phone with push email capability, automating the transfer of emails from the mail server to the phone. Just 1 year after the phone's introduction, a patent holding company called NTP sued RIM for patent infringement in a US district court.[1] Although a cofounder of NTP was the inventor of the asserted patents, NTP was considered a so-called patent troll since it had never used (or in patent parlance "practiced") the patented inventions. The district court awarded NTP US$53.7million in damages and a permanent injunction that would have forced RIM to shut down its BlackBerry push email service, one of the main attractions of the phone. RIM appealed the case in court but was unsuccessful. RIM also challenged the validity of the patents administratively before the USPTO, but the proceedings dragged on for far too long to affect the litigation in court. In the end, RIM settled with NTP to avoid the permanent injunction and paid NTP a staggering $612.5million lump-sum royalty.

The *NTP v. RIM* case marked the beginning of a transformation of the US litigation landscape. The share of infringement cases filed by patent trolls, also referred to as nonpracticing entities (NPEs), among all US patent infringement cases rose considerably over

---

[1] *NTP, Inc. v. Research in Motion, Ltd.*, 270 F. Supp. 2d 751 (E.D. Virginia, May 23, 2023).

The Economics of Innovation and Intellectual Property. Bronwyn H. Hall and Christian Helmers, Oxford University Press.
© Oxford University Press 2024. DOI: 10.1093/oso/9780197630914.003.0022

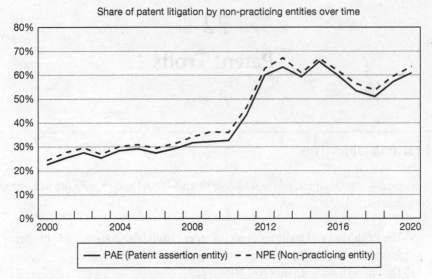

Share of patent litigation by non-practicing entities over time

The graph shows the share of US district court patent infringement cases filed between 2000 and 2020 by plaintiff type. For the definition of NPE and PAE see Table 22-1. The litigation data come from the MaxVal Patent Litigation Databank, Lex Machina, and Docket Navigator. Data on patent enforcer types come from Stanford Law School's NPE Litigation Database (Miller, 2018).

Figure 22.1 Trends in patent litigation by non-practicing entities.

the following 2 decades and, as shown in Figure 22.1, accounted for the majority of patent cases from 2012 onward. NPEs (a subset of which is also referred to as patent assertion entities, PAEs) are entities, usually registered businesses or individuals that do not make any products and instead make money from licensing patents to companies that do.[2]

The topic of patent trolls has drawn an enormous amount of attention by practitioners, academics, policymakers,[3] and even the general public and popular media outlets.[4] In the United States, arguably all major reforms of the patent system over the last 2 decades have been motivated at least, in part, by concerns over litigation by patent trolls. Still, the topic remains highly controversial. Not only is there a lively, ongoing dispute over who qualifies as a patent troll, but more importantly, the effects of patent trolls on innovation and welfare at large are heavily contested.

The controversy regarding the definition of a patent troll centers on the complexity of different business models that companies have and the fact that they may change over time. Consider two different companies. The first is a company that developed technology in the past but failed to commercialize it. It then focused on enforcing the patents it obtained on the technology it developed. The second is a company that was founded with the sole goal of acquiring patents in the secondary market and enforcing them. While

---

[2] Note that the steep increase starting in 2011 was in part driven by a change in the joinder statute enacted by the America Invents Act, which affected plaintiffs' ability to sue multiple defendants in a single lawsuit.

[3] In the United States, the Executive Office of the President issued an entire report dedicated to issue in 2013 and the Federal Trade Commission in 2016 (FTC, 2016). For an overview of relevant federal patent reform legislation, see https://www.patentprogress.org/patent-progress-legislation-guides/patent-progress-guide-patent-reform-legislation.

[4] Even popular radio and TV shows discussed the topic, for example, Ira Glass, "This American Life," July 22, 2011 (https://www.thisamericanlife.org/441/when-patents-attack), and John Oliver, "Last Week Tonight," April 19, 2015 (https://www.youtube.com/watch?v=3bxcc3SM_KA&ab_channel=LastWeekTonight).

most academics would probably agree that both types of companies are NPEs, they may still disagree about the impact these companies have on innovation and social welfare.

Some view NPEs as specialized market intermediaries that help connect up-stream inventors with downstream producers. This promotes technology transfer and increases returns for innovators. In particular, they can also help small companies and individual inventors monetize their inventions since they are better positioned to make credible enforcement threats vis-à-vis larger companies. Overall, according to this view, the impact of NPEs on innovation and welfare should be positive.

On the other hand, criticism of NPEs has focused on the claim that they do not contribute to innovation. They neither generate new ideas nor transform existing inventions into commercially viable products. Instead, critics contend that NPEs en-force patents against inadvertent infringers, and the patents that they enforce are often invalid or have little or nothing to do with the allegedly infringing technology. Critics also contend that the opportunistic conduct of NPEs is apparent from their focus on the enforcement of software patents (FTC, 2016). As discussed in Chapter 17, soft-ware patents often have broad, fuzzy claims, which means that they frequently read on inventions that have little to do with the patented claims. Patent law does not require proof of copying to demonstrate patent infringement in court. In fact, the patent owner is under no obligation to use or implement the patented technology in any way such that copying could occur.[5] Because of the way patent law is designed and because of patent-granting practice, especially in software-related areas, NPEs are able to use the threat of enforcement or actual in-court litigation to pressure companies into paying royalties. Since there is no technology transfer associated with such licensing agreements, nor did the licensee rely on the patented invention as an input prior to the agreement, the licensing fee represents a simple transfer from the innovator to the troll. This means that the costs imposed by NPEs on innovative companies exceed any potential benefits that might come from NPEs' role in secondary patent markets. Estimates suggest that the total direct cost of NPE assertions is indeed huge, US$29billion in 2011 alone ac-cording to Bessen and Meurer (2014). These arguments therefore suggest that NPEs harm innovation and decrease welfare.

Regular "practicing" companies also sometimes rely on the enforcement of patents to exclude product market rivals from competing with them by raising their rivals' costs or preventing access to or use of patented technology altogether. However, NPEs specialize in the enforcement of patents. This lowers their litigation cost relative to practicing companies. For example, the discovery stage in patent litigation will be less costly for NPEs since they do not engage in R&D or manufacturing. There may also be economies of scale and scope from filing multiple lawsuits based on the same patents against different defendants. Moreover, since they do not participate in downstream markets, they cannot be countersued and they have no interest in cross-licensing. Mark Lieberman, the managing director of NPE TM Patents, put it plainly this way: "While we can sue for infringement, we can't be countersued because we're not making or selling any products, so there's no way we could possibly be infringing anyone else's patents. Our only product . . . is intellectual property" (Rivette and Kline, 2000, p. 135). This makes standard defenses such as countersuing for infringement or cross-licensing

---

[5] Cotropia and Lemley (2009) report that copying is only established in around 2% of infringement cases.

agreements ineffective. This sets the assertion of patents by NPEs apart from practicing companies.

This chapter reviews what we know about NPEs. It discusses the ambiguous theoretical effects of NPEs on innovation and welfare and reviews the different enforcement strategies of NPEs in practice. This chapter also provides an overview of the existing empirical evidence on the effect of NPEs on innovation and welfare. In addition, it also discusses the various responses to NPEs in the form of defensive aggregators, invalidation entities, and litigation insurance.

22.2 NPE Definition and Classification of NPE Types

The term patent troll is controversial and often perceived as pejorative. According to Miller (2018), the term first appeared in a 1994 short film on the modern patent system. However, its widespread usage is credited to Peter Detkin. In 2001, Detkin, then the assistant general counsel of Intel, referred to TechSearch LLC as a "patent extortionist." The company had filed what Detkin considered an unmeritorious patent infringement suit against Intel. When TechSearch accused Detkin of libel, Detkin used the patent troll moniker to describe the company. He later explained his reasoning as follows: "When I coined the term 'troll' . . . , I was talking about people who take specious patents that were likely invalid and asserted them broadly across an industry to extract nuisance value settlements."

While the troll moniker is clearly controversial, even more descriptive terms such as NPE or PAE are contentious. To some extent, that is explained by the fact that the terms are often considered synonyms. For example, in a recent US district court case, the court held that the terms troll, NPE, and PAE all are "projective labels [that] are irrelevant, unhelpful to the jury, and in some instances carry negative connotations."[6] In addition, there is no universally agreed upon definition of any of these labels.

The literature has produced many different definitions of patent trolls. Perhaps the lowest common denominator across the different definitions used in the literature is that NPEs are entities that derive all or close to all of their revenue from patent licensing. However, conceptually, it is helpful to distinguish between two types of definitions. The first focuses on the entity that enforces a patent, while the second focuses on the patent that is enforced. According to the definition proposed by Hagiu and Yoffie (2013), patent trolls are entities that satisfy the following criteria:

1. They acquire patents solely for the purpose of payments from alleged infringers.
2. They do not undertake any research, develop technology or products related to their patents.
3. They behave opportunistically by waiting until industry participants have made irreversible investments in technology before demanding licensing payment.

Chiang (2009), in contrast, offers a definition at the patent level. A patent qualifies as a troll patent if it satisfies the following criteria:

---

[6] *Finjan, Inc. v. Cisco Systems, Inc.*, 17-cv-00072, 2018 WL 3537142, at *1 (N.D. California, July 23, 2018).

1. The patent is owned by someone who does not practice the invention.
2. The patent is infringed by, and asserted against, noncopiers exclusively or almost exclusively.
3. The patent has no licensees practicing the particular patented invention except for defendants in Criterion 2 who took licenses as settlement.
4. The patent is asserted against a large industry that is based on Criterion 2 and composed of noncopiers.

Note that the term *noncopiers* refers to companies that did not knowingly or inadvertently replicate the patented technology. As you know from Chapter 11, this is not a legal requirement to nevertheless be found to infringe on a patent.

Apart from the binary distinction between NPEs and all other entities, the literature also distinguishes between different NPE types. Those distinctions are somewhat artificial as business models change over time and some entities fall into multiple categories. Table 22.1 provides an overview.[7]

Table 22.1 NPE Types

	NPE Type	Description
1	PAE	IP licensing company, acquired patents
2	PAE	IP licensing company, started by inventor; individual
3	PAE	Corporate heritage
4		Consortium
5		University or spin-off

Source: Miller (2018).

Category 1 contains NPEs that acquire the patents that they monetize. These companies are the "purest" form of an NPE since they do not conduct any R&D and, in fact, never have conducted any R&D, and do not practice the patents that they acquire. They exist solely for the purpose of acquiring patents in order to maximize licensing revenue. Entities in this category are also often labeled PAEs. Empirically, this category accounts for the large majority of NPE patent assertions (Miller 2018).

Category 1 includes very large NPEs, also referred to as portfolio NPEs (FTC 2016) or mass aggregators (Ewing and Feldman 2012), although their vast patent portfolios may not consist exclusively of acquired patents. The most prominent aggregator is Intellectual Ventures.[8] Other aggregators include large NPEs such as Acacia Research Corporation, IP Edge, or Dominion Harbor. What sets such large portfolio

---

[7] This is a simplified version of a taxonomy originally proposed by Allison et al. (2009).

[8] Intellectual Ventures was founded by Nathan Myrvhold in 2000 and has amassed a vast patent portfolio of over 11,000 patents. Initially, Intellectual Ventures did not assert its patents in court. It only started filing infringement complaints in court at the end of 2010. Intellectual Ventures does conduct some in-house research. While this calls the NPE label into question, R&D conducted by Intellectual Ventures accounts for only a very small fraction of its business.

NPEs apart from other NPEs is their sheer size and ability to offer large-scale portfolio licensing.

Category 2 contains NPEs that were founded and are usually still owned by the inventor of the asserted patents. These registered companies only serve one function: to provide a corporate (limited liability) shell to hold the patents and assert them through (the threat of) litigation. Well-known examples in this category include the Lemelson Medical, Education and Research Foundation and Ronald A. Katz Technology Licensing LLC. This type of NPE is also considered a PAE and accounts for the second largest number of NPE patent assertions (Miller 2018). One could add to this category certain individuals who hold patents in their own name and assert those patents themselves rather than through a limited liability company. An example is Leon Stambler, who has been actively asserting several software patents that list him as the sole inventor. However, "nonpracticing individuals" are relatively rare and certainly not all cases brought by individuals qualify as NPE cases.

Category 3 contains NPEs that were at some point vertically integrated companies but then shifted their business model to focus predominantly or exclusively on the licensing of patents (Osenga 2014). These companies are also considered PAEs. An example is Conversant Intellectual Property Management, formerly Mosaid, a semiconductor company in the business of developing and making computer chips. While the company started out as a chip maker, it gradually morphed into a licensing company until it restructured in 2007 to focus on the licensing of its patents. At that point, it also started acquiring patents for its portfolio in the secondary market. Another example is Unwired Planet. Founded in 1994 under the name Libris Inc., the company developed technology enabling mobile internet access. In 2011, then operating under the name Openwave System Inc., the company sold its product business and became an IP licensing company. After becoming an NPE, Openwave changed its name to Unwired Planet. In 2013, Unwired Planet acquired a large portfolio of patents including SEPs from Ericsson, adding to its Openwave patent portfolio. These examples underscore the complexity in defining NPEs since business models often overlap and change over time.

Category 4 describes an NPE that is a consortium, that is, an association formed by different independent companies. An example is the consortium Rockstar Bidco, formed by a number of companies including among others Apple, Microsoft, BlackBerry, Ericsson, and Sony. The company won the bidding war against Google for former Canadian telecommunication company Nortel's patent portfolio put up for auction in 2011. While Rockstar has transferred a number of patents to consortium members, it has also acted as an NPE and asserted patents in its portfolio against companies that compete with its consortium members, including Google and Samsung.

Category 5 consists of universities and spin-off companies, where the spin-off companies either do not make or commercialize products or assert their patents prior to making any products. This category is more controversial since universities engage in research, and as per their mandate, they focus on education and research, not the commercialization of research. As such, technically, they are nonpracticing entities by construction, but are still distinct from PAEs. University licensing often also involves major technology transfer. An example in this category is Eolas, a company that spun off the

University of California, San Francisco (UCSF). The company has asserted a number of software patents that, in part, originated from research conducted at UCSF against a number of large companies, including Microsoft, Disney, and Facebook. In addition to spin-offs, this category also includes university-affiliated technology transfer companies that license university inventions, such as the Wisconsin Alumni Research Foundation (WARF) that serves the University of Wisconsin-Madison.[9]

22.3 The Economics of NPEs

22.3.1 Efficient Intermediary or Troll?

From a theoretical perspective, the impact of NPEs on innovation is ambiguous. NPEs could act as efficient intermediaries, assisting inventors in monetizing their inventions in the marketplace (McDonough 2006). This could increase returns to innovation, especially for smaller inventors, including individual inventors, who might otherwise struggle to license their inventions. On the other hand, NPEs could harm innovation by extracting rents from innovative firms through opportunistic litigation. In that view, NPEs exploit the weaknesses of the patent system combined with the threat of litigation to obtain licensing payments from inadvertent infringers of patents of dubious quality.

The patent system allows inventors to obtain protection for their ideas and to then sell or license the patented invention to companies that want to commercialize the technology. This enables specialization; upstream inventors can focus on coming up with new ideas, while downstream companies turn them into successful products. The existence of individuals and entities that focus on upstream innovation, while leaving the commercialization to downstream producers, is not a new phenomenon. In fact, many of America's arguably most important inventors in the 18th and 19th centuries earned money by selling or licensing their inventions downstream, especially those inventors from less affluent backgrounds (Khan 2014).

NPEs could potentially enhance technology transfer or monetize patents on behalf of inventors. They could assume the role of an intermediary, identifying promising inventions and making them available to companies that are in a position to commercialize them. As a market intermediary, they could devote effort to overcoming information asymmetry in the market, thereby enabling valuable transactions to take place that otherwise would not happen. In addition to enabling technology transfer, NPEs could also act as royalty collectors for smaller inventors whose inventions have been appropriated by companies without commensurate compensation. Because NPEs are specialized in the monetization of patents, they may be better able to force especially large technology copiers to the negotiation table by making a credible threat of a lawsuit or asserting the patents in court and, if necessary, engage in protracted and

---

[9] WARF has been involved in high-profile patent litigation. For example, in June 2016, a district court awarded WARF damages of $506million in a patent case against Apple (*Wisconsin Alumni Research Foundation v. Apple Inc.*, 135 F. Supp. 3d 865 (W.D. Wisconsin, September 29, 2015). However, the decision was overturned on appeal.

costly litigation. This argument, however, requires NPEs to channel back at least a non-negligible fraction of the returns to these small inventors.

These arguments are critical because NPEs are not engaged in the product market themselves. Therefore, they cannot use the patent system to appropriate returns to their innovation by excluding product market rivals from competing with them. The justification for the enforcement of their patents is that they enable technology transfer or at least enable inventors to collect royalty payments that they would be unable to collect otherwise, thereby incentivizing innovative activity by such inventors.

That said, even if NPEs do not enhance technology transfer or monetize patents on behalf of inventors, their presence in the secondary market for patents may still promote liquidity. If NPEs are able to accumulate information on specific technologies, they may be able to act as intermediaries in the market for patents and this will increase efficiency in the market. Yet, this might only affect incentives to patent directly rather than innovation. This, in turn, would increase the number of patents filed and potentially exacerbate potential problems associated with strategic patenting, patent ownership fragmentation, patent thickets, and royalty stacking (see Chapters 18 and 21).

On the flipside, NPEs could be seen as opportunistically abusing the patent system to extract rents from innovative companies that successfully develop and commercialize their technology. According to this view, NPEs contribute little to innovation and instead impose significant costs on society. Lemley and Melamed (2013) summarize the sources of the potential costs associated with NPEs as follows:

1. Practicing companies pay royalties for valid patents that in the absence of NPEs would not be enforced.
2. Practicing companies pay royalties for patents that are invalid or not infringed.
3. Practicing companies pay royalties in excess of the value of the patented technology.
4. Practicing companies incur litigation expenses that they would otherwise not incur.

The net social effect is ambiguous only in the case of Cost 1. It depends on the extent to which inventors of these patents see any of the returns of the NPE's successful monetization. In contrast, the impact of Costs 2–4 is clear: They increase the cost for innovative companies, which could lead to higher prices and ultimately less innovation. Regardless of the source of costs for practicing companies, the argument assumes that the alleged patent infringement by practicing companies does not involve any actual copying of technology covered by the asserted patents. Instead, if there is infringement, it is inadvertent. That is, the infringer was not aware of the existence of the patent nor the fact that they infringed it.

Such inadvertent infringement is, in fact, a common occurrence in fast-moving, cumulative technologies where simultaneous albeit independent inventions are commonplace. In these technology areas, technologies are also modular and complex, which results in substantial overlap between different components. As discussed in Chapter 18, these factors lead to companies amassing patent portfolios of such size that it is not feasible to conduct any proper patent clearance before developing new products.[10]

---

[10] For example, Mulligan and Lee (2013) calculate that in the software sector it would cost $400billion for all firms in the sector to search the full set of poorly indexed software patents, a number that was larger than the value of the sector in 2012.

This is important because it contradicts claims that without the intervention of NPEs, large companies purposefully appropriate inventions by small companies or individual inventors without compensation (which is sometimes referred to as *efficient infringement*). Instead, NPEs obtain licensing payments from companies that did not rely on the patented invention as an input, and often the patented invention has no actual relevance for the allegedly infringing product. The result is that NPEs engage mostly in so-called *ex post* licensing, that is, the licensing of patents without any associated technology transfer. This theory therefore suggests that NPEs use the patent system and litigation opportunistically to collect payments from companies that are successful not only at producing innovation but also at commercializing it. As a result, the overall effect on innovation and welfare is negative.

Scott-Morton and Shapiro (2014) offer a simple model that summarizes the main opposing theoretical arguments. In the model, there are two firms and an NPE: Firm P comes up with an invention and patents it, and vertically integrated firm M conducts R&D and commercializes products. The NPE monetizes the patent on P's behalf.

P and M choose R&D investment levels x and y, respectively, to maximize profits, denoted as $P(x)$ and $V(x, y)$.[11] Profits do not account for any royalties that M might have to pay P as a result of the NPE's monetization efforts. The model assumes that an increase in investment x by P benefits M, so $\dfrac{\partial V(x,y)}{\partial x} \geq 0$. One way to interpret this assumption is that more innovation by P benefits the economy overall due to spillovers. Finally, in the model, there are also consumers. The model assumes that consumers also benefit from more investment x because it leads to spillovers and more innovation, so $\dfrac{\partial S(x,y)}{\partial x} \geq 0$, where $S(x, y)$ denotes consumer surplus.

Now assume that P patented its invention and asserts the patent against M. The patent owner P extracts $\theta V(x, y)$ from M, where $\theta \in [0,1]$. However, a fraction α (with $\alpha \in [0,1]$) of $\theta V(x, y)$ is absorbed by the NPE as transaction costs associated with monetization, for example, to cover the litigation cost. Therefore, the profit functions for P and M are the following:

$$\begin{aligned} \pi_P(x, y) &= P(x) - x + (1-\alpha)\theta V(x, y) \\ \pi_M(x, y) &= (1-\theta)V(x, y) - y \end{aligned} \tag{1}$$

If we use the first-order conditions for profit maximization, it is easy to see that increasing θ will increase x and lower y.

Total welfare is defined as the sum of P and M's profits and consumer surplus:

$$W = \pi_P(x, y) + \pi_M(x, y) + S(x, y) \tag{2}$$

The impact of the NPE on welfare depends on θ since a higher θ denotes increased monetization by the NPE (assuming that in the absence of the NPE $\theta = 0$). Therefore,

---

[11] Profits are gross of investment levels.

the impact of the NPE on welfare can be evaluated by totally differentiating equation (2) with respect to θ (using the envelope theorem associated with the first-order conditions $\frac{\partial \pi_P}{\partial x} = 0$ and $\frac{\partial \pi_M}{\partial y} = 0$):[12]

$$\frac{dW}{d\theta} = \frac{\partial W}{\partial \theta} + \left(\frac{\partial \pi_M}{\partial x} + \frac{\partial S}{\partial x} \right) \frac{dx}{d\theta} + \left(\frac{\partial \pi_P}{\partial y} + \frac{\partial S}{\partial y} \right) \frac{dy}{d\theta} \tag{3}$$

If you look at the different components in equation (3), you see that $\frac{\partial W}{\partial \theta} = -\alpha V(x,y)$, which means that the direct effect of an increase in θ is a reduction in welfare equivalent to the transaction costs imposed by NPE enforcement. The impact of more investment x by P on M is $\frac{\partial \pi_M}{\partial x} = (1-\theta)\frac{\partial V(x,y)}{\partial x}$. Similarly, the impact of higher investment by M on P is given by $\frac{\partial \pi_P}{\partial y} = (1-\alpha)\theta\frac{\partial V(x,y)}{\partial y}$. Substituting these terms in equation (3), you get

$$\frac{dW}{d\theta} = -\alpha V(x,y) + \left((1-\theta)\frac{\partial V(x,y)}{\partial x} + \frac{\partial S}{\partial x} \right) \frac{dx}{d\theta} + \left((1-\alpha)\theta\frac{\partial V(x,y)}{\partial y} + \frac{\partial S}{\partial y} \right) \frac{dy}{d\theta} \tag{4}$$

Rearranging terms yields the following condition:

$$\underbrace{\left((1-\theta)\frac{\partial V(x,y)}{\partial x} + \frac{\partial S}{\partial x} \right) \frac{dx}{d\theta}}_{A} \gtrless \underbrace{\alpha V(x,y) - \left((1-\alpha)\theta\frac{\partial V(x,y)}{\partial y} + \frac{\partial S}{\partial y} \right) \frac{dy}{d\theta}}_{B} \tag{5}$$

If the left-hand side A of equation (5) exceeds the right-hand side B, that is, A > B, increased monetization by NPEs is welfare-enhancing. However, if the right-hand side B exceeds the left-hand side A, that is, B > A, enforcement by NPEs reduces welfare.

In order to interpret equation (5), a few more modifications are helpful. First, define the shares of M's profits received by P and M as $\sigma_P = (1-\alpha)\theta$ and $\sigma_M = (1-\theta)$, respectively. These definitions can be used to write $\frac{d\sigma_P}{d\theta} = (1-\alpha)$ and $\frac{d\sigma_M}{d\theta} = -1$, and hence,

$$\frac{dx}{d\theta} = \frac{dx}{d\sigma_P}\frac{d\sigma_P}{d\theta} = \frac{dx}{d\sigma_P}(1-\alpha)$$
$$\text{and} \tag{6}$$
$$\frac{dy}{d\theta} = \frac{dy}{d\sigma_M}\frac{d\sigma_M}{d\theta} = -\frac{dy}{d\sigma_M}$$

---

[12] For the envelope theorem, see Appendix A: Mathematics and Statistics.

Substituting these terms in equation (5) yields

$$\underbrace{\left((1-\theta)\frac{\partial V(x,y)}{\partial x}+\frac{\partial S}{\partial x}\right)\frac{dx}{d\sigma_P}}_{A1}\underbrace{(1-\alpha)}_{A2}\overset{>}{<}\underbrace{\alpha V(x,y)}_{B1}+\underbrace{\left((1-\alpha)\theta\frac{\partial V(x,y)}{\partial y}+\frac{\partial S}{\partial y}\right)\frac{dy}{d\sigma_M}}_{B2} \quad (7)$$

Let's take a look at the different elements in equation (7). The term on the left-hand side has two elements: A1 and A2. The first element A1 captures the positive effect of an increase in the patentee's investment level x on both the manufacturer M and consumers. The second term A2, which is $(1-\alpha)$, represents the share of money paid by the manufacturer to the patentee. The smaller the share that is paid to the patentee (and hence the larger the share that is paid to the NPE instead), the smaller the term A2 on the left-hand side of equation (7) and the less likely it is that the presence of the NPE increases welfare.

The term on the right-hand side also consists of two components: B1 and B2. The first term B1 represents the direct costs of NPE enforcement. The larger these costs, the more likely the welfare impact of the NPE is negative. The second term B2 captures the impact of a reduction in M's investment level y due to the costs imposed by the NPE. The impact of a reduction of y affects both the manufacturer as well as consumers. The larger this effect, the more likely is a negative effect of NPEs on welfare.

To summarize, the model shows that the net impact of NPEs on welfare depends broadly on three factors:

1. The extent to which NPEs pass on any payments from licensees to inventors.
2. The degree to which income from licensing generated by NPEs increases incentives by inventors to invest in R&D and promote innovation.
3. The extent to which the costs of NPE enforcement reduce incentives to invest in R&D and innovation by companies targeted by NPE assertions.

22.3.2 Enforcement Strategies

NPEs extract licensing payments from innovators by pursuing different patent enforcement strategies.

22.3.2.1 Nuisance Value Litigation

Some NPEs engage in nuisance value litigation. They assert patents without much if any prospect of winning a court case and instead exploit the high litigation cost the alleged infringer would have to pay to defend itself to extract a settlement payment. The patents asserted under this strategy generally would turn out to be at least partially invalid or not infringed if they were litigated all the way to a decision. Yet, defendants opt to pay a smaller settlement amount than to engage in uncertain and costly litigation.[13] The

---

[13] The median total cost of defending against an NPE infringement suit in the United States is US$1.25million. The cost of litigating only to the end of the discovery stage is still US$713,000 (AIPLA, 2017).

literature offers a number of arguments for why such negative expected value claims can be successful. In principle, if the NPE's expected value from litigation is negative, that is, the costs exceed the expected payoff, the NPE's threat is not credible and no alleged infringer should give into the NPE's licensing demands. Bebchuk (1996) showed that when litigation costs are distributed over the litigation process instead of being incurred all at once at trial, a negative expected value suit can morph into a positive expected value suit.[14] Another explanation is provided by Choi and Gerlach (2018). They show that if an NPE can sue more than one company, the NPE can leverage a win against the first defendant to increase its expected value from litigation.[15]

This nuisance value litigation strategy is particularly useful against smaller companies because, in relative terms, the litigation cost to defend themselves weighs heavier on them. A striking example of this strategy is a litigation campaign launched by NPE Innovative Wireless Solutions in 2013. Innovative Wireless Solutions filed 281 lawsuits for infringement of WiFi/Ethernet patents against end users.[16] Targeted businesses included hotels, coffee and sandwich shops, all of which do not make or sell WiFi/Ethernet devices and instead are end users that offer WiFi access to their customers.

22.3.2.2 Litigation

Other NPEs target big, successful companies and are ready to litigate the case to a judgment in the hopes of a large payout that is often tens if not hundreds of millions of dollars. These NPEs are prepared to establish that their patents are indeed valid and infringed. Their main goal is a multi-million-dollar jury award or a permanent injunction that is transformed into a lucrative settlement, rather than a quick settlement in exchange for a small payment. This strategy requires a different approach than the nuisance value litigation strategy. It starts with a more careful selection of the patents that are enforced to ensure they are sufficiently broad to read on commercially successful technology commercialized by several big players in the market while still likely valid if challenged. It also affects their behavior during litigation since a finding of invalidity will terminate the NPE's litigation campaign and hence its prospects of a big payday. An important element in this litigation strategy is that target companies should already be successfully commercializing the technology that potentially falls within the boundaries of the NPE's patents.

22.3.2.3 Timing of Enforcement

In both of the two litigation strategies discussed above, *ex post* licensing often relies on hold-up (for an explanation of hold-up, see Chapter 21). NPEs often wait until

---

[14] To see this, denote the NPE's expected value from trial as x and its litigation costs as c_p. In a negative expected value suit $x - c_p < 0$. If c_p is incurred over multiple time periods T, it is possible to get $x - (c_p/T) > 0$. See Chapter 19.

[15] To see this, assume that the probability the NPE's patent is valid and infringed is ρ. Assume the payoff from winning the case is π and litigation costs are c_p. In a negative expected value suit, we have $\rho \cdot \pi - c_p < 0$. Assume that there are two defendants who use identical technologies, so if one of the two defendants is found to have infringed the NPE's patent, the other defendant knows that it also has infringed the patent. This transforms the NPE's payoff to $\rho \cdot (\pi + \pi) - c_p > 0$. In other words, it is the NPE's ability to leverage a win against other defendants that transforms a negative expected value claim into a credible litigation threat.

[16] https://www.essentialpatentblog.com/2013/04/innovative-wireless-solutions-llc-accuses-hotels-of-inf ringing-wifiethernet-patents-formerly-owned-by-nortel.

companies have successfully developed and commercialized a technology before they assert their patents. This allows NPEs to exploit the sunk investment that firms have made in the development and commercialization of a product. This approach is more likely to succeed if target companies are unaware of the threat posed by NPEs. To accomplish this, in the past, NPEs sometimes relied on so-called patent ambush. Until 2000, in the United States, patents were not published until grant, and before 1995 the patent term was 17 years counting from grant instead of 20 years from the patent's filing date. This allowed patentees to keep their filings hidden for many years through the use of continuation filings, without losing any term for the patents that would ultimately issue. Jerome Lemelson, for example, used this so-called submarine patent filing strategy to keep his "machine vision" patents hidden for several decades.[17] In the meantime, machine vision and bar code technology had developed and been widely adopted across industries. Lemelson eventually let his submarine patents emerge and asserted them against unsuspecting companies that used bar code technology. Lemelson and his estate collected over $1.5billion in royalty payments before his core patents were invalidated and held unenforceable in 2004. The court found that Lemelson had taken an unreasonable amount of time to prosecute his patent filings.

22.3.2.4 NPE Ownership Structure

While submarine patents no longer exist, some NPEs still attempt to hide their patent ownership and assertions through their often opaque corporate ownership structure. In fact, many larger NPEs use extensive networks of shell companies, usually limited liability companies, to acquire, hold, and assert patents. Recently, for example, it came to light that several NPEs that had filed a large number of lawsuits in the District of Delaware were, in fact, controlled by IP Edge, a portfolio NPE. IP Edge had gone to great lengths to conceal that it was behind these shell companies. It recruited random individuals without any ties to IP Edge as owners of these companies (the owner of one these NPEs runs a food truck, another one is a software salesman) in exchange for a small percentage of any settlement proceeds. All relevant litigation-related decisions were still made by IP Edge via another shell company that also employed the attorneys that litigated on behalf of the shell companies.[18]

Such opaque ownership structures make it more difficult for potential licensees to assess their licensing needs (e.g., they could already have a prior licensing agreement with the parent NPE that they are unaware of) and it raises concerns that NPEs may use such ownership structures to evade potential penalties in litigation, notably fee shifting (i.e., having to pay the other party's litigation cost).

22.3.2.5 Portfolio NPEs

Portfolio NPEs, which are usually investor-backed, amass thousands of patents and often pursue multiple monetization strategies. Among others, they pressure operating companies into accepting portfolio licenses under the threat of litigation. The sheer size of the aggregator's patent portfolio makes it difficult for operating companies

[17] See Hansen (2004).
[18] https://ipde.com/blog/2022/11/04/a-wild-hearing-chief-judge-connolly-flips-over-rock-finds-mavexar-llc-crawling-around-controlling-patent-litigation-and-giving-hapless-patent-owners-just-5-10.

to defend themselves since challenging the entire portfolio is not feasible. This may enable the aggregator to pressure companies into accepting a licensing agreement without any actual litigation. The most prominent aggregator so far has been Intellectual Ventures. According to its own data, Intellectual Ventures held more than 11,000 patents in 2020, although this number almost certainly does not accurately reflect its entire portfolio.[19]

22.3.2.6 Patent Privateering

Finally, NPEs have been employed by practicing entities in what has been labeled *patent privateering* (Ewing 2012).[20] For example, as mentioned above, Ericsson transferred several thousand patents to NPE Unwired Planet, which asserted them against Ericsson's competitors. Unwired Planet and Ericsson agreed on sharing licensing revenue, with Ericsson obtaining between 20 and 70% of royalty revenue depending on the total amount of royalties collected by Unwired Planet.[21] Another example includes Nokia, which transferred patents to NPEs Acacia Research Corporation and Conversant Intellectual Property Management while receiving a share of the proceeds from the NPEs' licensing deals.[22]

Privateering has several objectives. First, it provides an opportunity for companies to monetize their patents without negatively affecting their business relationships with other companies that are unaware of the source of the asserted patents. Second, it can be used as a strategic tool to harm competitors by raising their costs without running the risk of a countersuit. In litigation between practicing companies, countersuits for infringement are a routine tool to deter litigation in the first place and, if litigation occurs, to improve one's bargaining position. This ability to countersue is, in fact, one of the main reasons why companies acquire large defensive patent portfolios. Third, companies can also use privateering to undermine the diffusion of new technologies brought to market by competitors by inducing NPEs to sue their competitors' downstream customers.

The practicing company that is selling patents to an NPE can to some extent control what the NPE does with those patents, either via contract, or by imposing constraints on the enforceability of the patents. The latter is achieved, for example, by licensing the patent to a select number of companies prior to selling the patent to the NPE. Lemus and Temnyalov (2017) suggest that the net effect of privateering on practicing companies' R&D efforts is ambiguous. On the one hand, privateering allows companies to obtain returns on their patents that might otherwise not be realized. However, privateering also renders defensive patent portfolios less useful since NPEs cannot be countersued. In addition, more generally, NPE enforcement and licensing imposes costs on companies. These effects reduce firms' incentives to invest in R&D.

[19] http://patents.intven.com/finder. In December 2020, Intellectual Ventures announced the licensing of 18,000 patents to RPX, which indicates that its true portfolio must be much larger than the patents made available on its website. See https://www.law360.com/articles/1343848/what-to-know-about-rpx-s-deal-with-intellectual-ventures. See also Ewing and Feldman (2012).

[20] The term *privateering* historically describes a practice whereby a government commissioned private ships during wartime to seize the enemy's ships at sea with force to then sell the ships. Some percentage of the proceeds usually was paid to the commissioning government.

[21] See *Unwired Planet International Ltd. v. Huawei Technologies Co. Ltd.* [2017] EWHC 711 (Pat).

[22] https://www.nytimes.com/2016/12/23/technology/daily-report-apple-hurls-the-patent-troll-insult-at-nokia.html.

22.3.2.7 Distinction from Practicing Entities

The goal of the different enforcement strategies discussed above differs from those of practicing entities. The main goal of practicing entities when they enforce their patents is to either outright prevent competitors from obtaining market access, secure freedom to operate, or raise rivals' cost while obtaining licensing revenue. Neither of these motivations applies to NPEs since they do not participate in the downstream product market.

22.4 Empirical Evidence on NPEs

In light of the ambiguous theoretical arguments and different NPE business models, this section reviews the empirical evidence to examine NPEs and their impact on innovation and welfare.

22.4.1 Opportunistic Litigation Behavior

There is substantial empirical evidence to suggest that NPEs behave opportunistically in enforcing patents. "Opportunistically" in this context means that:

1. NPEs enforce patents that are likely to be at least partially invalid.
2. NPEs enforce patents against successful companies that did not copy the patented technology, and in fact, in most cases, the technology protected by the asserted patent bears no relevance to the technology developed by the alleged infringer and played no role in the technology's commercial success.
3. NPEs assert their patents by exploiting the fuzzy boundaries that characterize in particular software patents.

By relying on such opportunistic behavior combined with the substantial cost of litigation and the uncertainty over its outcome, in practice NPEs can successfully extract settlements or win large jury verdicts.

NPEs overwhelmingly enforce software patents with relatively broad scope as measured, for example, by the number of patent classes covered by a patent. In their analysis of US district court cases filed in 2008 and 2009, Allison et al. (2017) found that 66% of NPE assertions litigated to judgment involved software patents, while only 23% of assertions by regular companies did. The data also show that NPEs avoid patents that cover chemistry or pharmaceuticals. Since technology covered by software patents is often widely used across industries, NPEs often enforce their software patents against large companies across different industries (Meurer et al. 2012), including large retailers such as Walmart or Target. The fact that NPEs assert the same patents against multiple defendants across industries, including end users, indicates that it is unlikely that all have copied the technology.[23] Instead, it illustrates the problem of fuzzy patent boundaries and broad scope, which means that the patents read on a large range of technologies used in different applications that have little to do with the patented technology.

---

[23] See also Cotropia and Lemley (2009) for evidence that actual copying is rarely alleged in these infringement cases. One could also argue that suing end users, such as retailers, instead of device or component manufacturers is in itself evidence of opportunistic behavior.

Miller (2018) also shows that court cases brought by NPEs terminate much faster because a much larger share of NPE lawsuits ends with settlement than lawsuits brought by other entities. Although it is usually difficult to interpret a settlement in a given case since the corresponding information is typically confidential, the evidence does support the view that at least some NPEs engage in nuisance lawsuits whose entire goal is quick settlement. Indeed, the FTC (2016) found that NPEs often settle for US$300,000 or less (see also Box 22.1), which is about the amount a defendant would have to spend on the initial stages of litigation.

Box 22.1 Uniloc Licensing Agreements

Uniloc is one of the most prolific NPEs with hundreds of lawsuits filed by different Uniloc entities registered in various countries including the United States and Luxembourg. In 2017, Uniloc filed several cases against Apple for patent infringement. During litigation, information surfaced that Uniloc had entered a revenue-sharing agreement with Fortress Investment Group, an investment firm owned by the SoftBank Group. Because of the critical role the revenue-sharing agreement played in the outcome of the case, the court released a number of documents submitted by Uniloc concerning the agreement (thanks to the intervention of the Electronic Frontier Foundation). The documents contain a list of Uniloc's licensing agreements including the names of the licensees, the dates of the agreements, and the corresponding payments. While the list is not exhaustive, it nevertheless offers a rare glimpse of an NPE's licensing deals. The data contain over 70 licensing agreements and the corresponding lump-sum payments received by Uniloc from accused infringers, which total over US$20million.

The figure here provides an overview of the licensing payments received by Uniloc. It is noteworthy that all licensing payments are lump-sum payments and that all cases were litigated at the Eastern District of Texas, a notoriously popular venue for NPE litigation. Figure 1 shows a highly skewed distribution of licensing payments. The median lump-sum payment was slightly less than US$110,000. In fact, 30% of licensing agreements involved a lump-sum payment of US$50,000 or less. These numbers are very close to data reported by the FTC for a much larger set of 18 NPEs similar to Uniloc (the FTC has the authority to collect such confidential information from entities). Only four agreements involved payments above US$1million. Figure 2 uses the fact that Uniloc often asserted the same patents against multiple defendants. The graph plots the distribution of lump-sum payments by different defendants for the licensing of the same set of patents. There is a lot of variation; lump-sum payments for the same patents differ substantially across licensees. For one patent (US5,490,216), the data report 45 licensing deals, with lump-sum amounts ranging from US$2,500 to US$3.5million [not shown in Figure 2]. Again, the FTC found similar variation in their larger sample of NPE licensing deals. Such variation certainly results, in part, from a lack of transparency in NPE licensing. However, there are many other potential explanations for the variation. For example, sales volumes of infringing products might differ substantially across the defendants.

Lump-sum payments received by Uniloc

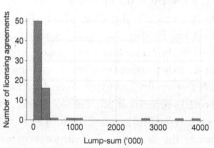

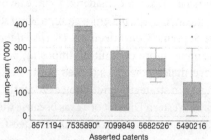

Figure 1 Number of licensing agreements by lump-sum payment (in US$).

Figure 2 Distribution of lump-sum payments (in US$) across defendants in lawsuits in which Uniloc asserted the same patents.

Note that the graph omits lump-sum payments of US$1.2 million and US$3.5million. *The relevant cases involved several patents: 7535890, 8199747, 8243723, 8724622, 8995433 and 5682526, 5715451.

Source: https://www.eff.org/document/apple-v-uniloc-unsealed-licensing-table.

NPEs are much more likely to lose than practicing companies when the case is litigated to a decision on the merits. This finding has been shown to be remarkably consistent across samples, time periods, and even jurisdictions.[24] NPEs are strikingly unsuccessful in litigation. Allison et al. (2017) find that NPEs prevail in 14% of decided cases, while practicing companies do so in 31% of cases. In particular, courts were more likely to find patents asserted by NPEs invalid due to claim indefiniteness or inadequate disclosure, both of which suggest NPEs asserted relatively low-quality patents. In fact, Feng and Jaravel (2020) show that NPEs are more prone to acquire likely invalid patents than practicing companies.[25] What is more, Risch (2012) provides evidence to show that even when NPE cases reach a decision and their patents are not invalidated, findings of infringement are exceedingly rare. These findings contrast with evidence that suggests NPEs acquire patents of higher quality, as measured by a patent's forward citations (Fischer and Henkel 2012).

Cohen at al. (2019) provide more direct empirical evidence that NPEs behave opportunistically in litigation. They show that NPEs pick their targets strategically by pursuing cash-rich companies. This contrasts with patent litigation initiated by

---

[24] Love et al. (2017) provide results for Germany and the United Kingdom similar to those obtained by Allison et al. (2017) and Mazzeo et al. (2013) for the United States.

[25] Their evidence also suggests that the low-quality patents acquired and enforced by NPEs come from patent examiners who are more "lenient" during the examination process.

producing entities. In addition, Cohen et al. (2019) also find evidence of forum shopping, that is, the strategic choice of venue. They find that during the period 2005–2015, 43% of all NPE cases were filed at the Eastern District Court of Texas. The court in Marshall, Texas, is considered a venue favorable toward IP owners (Allison et al. 2017). As a result, plaintiffs enjoyed high win rates in jury trials (Leychkis 2007). However, the Supreme Court decision *TC Heartland v. Kraft Foods Group* in 2017 made forum shopping more difficult by imposing more stringent conditions on venue choice.[26] Nevertheless, the rules turned out to be sufficiently flexible for NPEs to continue to engage in strategic venue choice. Recently, NPEs have flocked to the Waco courthouse of the Western District of Texas because the court's recently appointed sole judge, Alan Albright, has been perceived as patentee-friendly (see Box 19.1 in Chapter 19).

There is also some, albeit limited, evidence on the strategic use of corporate ownership structures by NPEs to obfuscate their patent dealings. Ewing and Feldman (2012) document that Intellectual Ventures used more than 1,200 shell companies to acquire and hold its patent portfolio. Helmers et al. (2022) found that other large NPEs also distribute their patent holdings across large networks of shell companies, such as publicly traded NPE Acacia with almost 200 subsidiaries. The use of shell companies and opaque ownership structures can be seen as an effort to conceal patent ownership in order to avoid attention and scrutiny. As discussed in Section 22.3.2, this can help limit the ability of practicing companies to avoid infringement by detecting the threat early and potentially change a product to avoid infringement or proactively invalidate the patent administratively or in court. The strategy can also be used by NPEs to avoid portfolio licensing in an attempt to extract higher royalties by exploiting royalty stacking.[27]

Finally, it is interesting to note that the dramatic increase in NPE litigation has largely remained a US phenomenon. There has been comparatively little litigation in Europe by NPEs so far (Love et al. 2017). Differences in enforcement systems, such as fee shifting in the United Kingdom (Helmers et al. 2014), lower the cost of defending a lawsuit, and smaller damage awards help explain the difference in NPE litigation between the United States and Europe.

22.4.2 NPEs as Intermediaries

The discussion in Section 22.3 suggested that NPEs could play a role in enabling technology transfer. There is survey evidence specifically about the question of whether licensing by NPEs leads to technology transfer. Feldman and Lemley (2015) obtained information from a small sample of 181 respondents to a survey of US companies. The evidence suggests that very few licensing agreements entail an actual transfer of technology and only a tiny fraction leads to the development of new products or features. Respondents reported that actual technology transfer was essentially absent in licensing agreements with NPEs. In the overwhelming majority of cases, companies only agreed to

[26] *TC Heartland LLC v. Kraft Foods Group Brands LLC*, 581 US 258 (2017).
[27] Royalty stacking refers to a situation where the combined royalties charged by different owners of patents exceed the royalty that would be charged if all the patents were owned by a single entity. See Chapter 21 for a more detailed explanation.

license patents held by NPEs in order to avoid lawsuits or to settle them. In accordance with that view, respondents also indicated that licensing requests by NPEs were more likely to come only after the NPE had initiated a lawsuit, while the opposite is the case for requests made by product market competitors. Overall, the survey evidence indicates that companies accept licenses from NPEs to ensure freedom to operate, rather than to source technology. Therefore, the evidence suggests that licensing of patents enforced by NPEs does not generate any actual transfer of knowledge to targeted firms.[28]

In line with this view, Love (2013) shows that NPEs tend to enforce patents much later during a patent's life than practicing entities. While practicing companies enforce their patents soon after they issue, NPEs assert their patents much closer to the end of the patent term. The fact that NPEs enforce patents so late indicates that they wait until technologies that broadly fall within the boundaries of their patents have become commercially successful before they assert their patents. By then, the technology originally covered by their patents is most likely already largely obsolete, which is especially true in fast-moving software-related industries.

Another theoretical argument in favor of the NPE business model suggested that NPEs create liquidity in secondary patent markets. Risch (2012) offers evidence that supports this argument. He shows that most patents asserted by NPEs originate from practicing companies that did not go out of business. This implies that NPEs promote the active trading of patents. That said, there is little evidence that this benefits smaller or startup companies' ability to obtain external financing by giving investors the opportunity to monetize patents in case a startup fails.

The other argument suggested that NPEs may act as efficient monetizers of patents, especially on behalf of small inventors. Risch (2012) provides some evidence that a significant share of patents enforced by NPEs does indeed originate from individual inventors. However, this does not provide any information on the share of revenues obtained from settlements or damage awards that was passed back to inventors. Generally, information on licensing agreements, especially by NPEs, is hard to come by (Box 22.1 discusses a rare exception), which makes it difficult to assess this claim empirically. Using information gathered from a firm-level survey, Bessen and Meurer (2014) suggest that NPEs pass through only a very small share of the proceeds from patent licensing to inventors. Although NPEs are successful in collecting licensing payments, only around 5% of the direct costs to defendants are used to reward independent inventors. This, in turn, implies that any incentive effects from monetizing inventions on behalf of inventors are most likely limited. That said, inventors certainly still benefit somewhat from the ability to sell their patents to NPEs.

22.4.3 Impact on Innovation

While there is a substantial body of evidence that describes the patent assertion behavior by NPEs and analyzes the patents that they acquire and enforce, there is a remarkable dearth of direct evidence on the impact of NPEs on innovation.

---

[28] The fact that NPEs have not been observed to grant exclusive licenses to patented technology and generally collect royalties in the form of a lump-sum payment also supports that conclusion (FTC, 2016).

There is some evidence based on survey results. Chien (2014) collected responses from a select sample of small technology companies and startups that were sued by NPEs. The results show that 40% of the companies that responded to the survey reported the NPE assertion had a significant, negative impact on their operations, including the shutdown of business lines or even the entire business. This effect was larger the smaller the company.

There is also some large-sample evidence. Meurer et al. (2012) analyze stock market reactions to NPE lawsuits. The results suggest that targeted companies experience large losses in market capitalization, on average, more than $120million. These losses dwarf the direct costs of litigation in the form of legal expenses. Cohen et al. (2019) also analyze the impact of NPE assertions on companies. Their evidence suggests that companies reduce R&D investment significantly after either losing in court or settling with NPEs. Appel et al. (2019) find that the adoption of "anti-troll" laws in the United States at the state level led to an average increase of 4.4% in employment in high-tech startups.[29] The companies also substantially increased their patenting activities in response to the law change. The effect is concentrated in information technology firms and driven mainly by improved access to external finance. These results support the view that NPEs create substantial costs for practicing companies; they make it harder for firms to obtain external financing and ultimately harm innovation.

These findings are supported by the most direct evidence available so far on the impact of NPEs on innovation. Tucker (2014) studies the effect of NPE Acacia's assertion of two software patents against medical-imaging technology companies. The analysis shows that sales of the companies' medical-imaging technology dropped by about a third relative to other products made by the same firms but not covered by the patents asserted by the NPE. This result also holds when sales by firms sued by Acacia were compared to firms that were not sued by the NPE. Importantly, the analysis also shows that the drop in sales was not driven by a drop in demand. Instead, imaging technology makers sued by the NPE stopped releasing updates of their imaging software, that is, there was a sudden stop of incremental innovation. Companies sued by the NPE halted any innovative activity of the technologies affected by the NPE lawsuit. This underscores that even NPE lawsuits per se can have negative effects on innovation regardless of their outcome.

22.5 Defensive Aggregators, Litigation Insurance, and Invalidation Entities

Practicing companies understand the threat posed by NPEs. Nevertheless, an effective response is hampered by several factors:

1. Practicing companies are the main source of patents asserted by NPEs. There are different reasons for this somewhat puzzling fact. Companies may want to

[29] States started adopting these anti-troll laws in 2013 in the form of consumer protection laws. The laws target specifically bad faith demand letters by NPEs by allowing a court to impose penalties against NPEs found to engage in bad faith patent assertions.

monetize unused patents. Selling them to NPEs may often be the best way to achieve that. Alternatively, as discussed above in Section 22.1.2, practicing companies also rely on NPEs for privateering.

2. Practicing companies face a positive externality in the invalidation of patents (Farrell and Merges, 2014). If a company successfully invalidates a patent held by an NPE, the company eliminates the threat not just for itself but also for everyone else, including the company's direct competitors. This public good aspect of patent invalidation means that companies are less willing to proactively invalidate a patent, and it affects their willingness to spend resources to invalidate a patent in litigation instead of settling.

3. For practicing companies, the value of acquiring a patent portfolio may be less than for an NPE. For example, if a company goes out of business, its patent portfolio could be acquired by an NPE and subsequently asserted. Practicing companies could preempt the NPE and acquire the patents. However, the benefits to the NPE from acquiring the patents might exceed the benefits to an individual company and hence the NPE would be willing to outbid the company. This is more likely to be true if the value of the patents to the company is primarily defensive.

Several market-based solutions to these problems have appeared over the last decade.

A new type of NPE in the form of a defensive aggregator has emerged. This entity provides a form of insurance against NPE assertions. Prominent defensive aggregators are RPX, a publicly traded company founded in 2008, and the Allied Security Trust (AST), a nonprofit cooperative founded in 2007. Practicing entities become members of RPX or AST in exchange for a membership fee. In the case of RPX, the aggregator identifies patents that might represent a threat to its members and acquires them in the secondary market or licenses them; it then issues a license to all its members, effectively neutralizing the litigation threat. It might also acquire patents directly from NPEs or challenge them in court or in administrative invalidity proceedings. RPX also makes its patent portfolio available to its members for defensive purposes, for example, to countersue other non-member companies if a member is the target of a patent infringement suit.

AST pursues a similar strategy. AST monitors the patent market closely and actively solicits patent owners to offer patents for sale or licensing. When relevant patents appear on the market, individual AST members decide whether they want to purchase those patents. The costs of the acquisition are shared among all members that decided to participate in the purchase. AST then licenses the acquired patents only to members that contributed to the purchase.

Although defensive aggregators are also NPEs, they distinguish themselves from NPEs by committing to not assert their patents to generate revenue. Defensive aggregators solve Problems 2 and 3 listed above by internalizing at least part of the positive externalities that occur from acquiring and invalidating NPE patents. That said, there is still a potential free-rider problem since non-members also benefit from the acquisition by a defensive aggregator that is committed to not assert a patent. To avoid this problem, RPX and AST engage in a "catch-and-release" strategy whereby they resell patents after having granted a license to their members. This ensures that there is still some litigation risk for non-members, while that risk has been neutralized for members.

The ability to spread the cost of patent acquisition across members means that the defensive aggregator can outbid NPEs, while individual companies would not have purchased the patents because the expected reduction in risk did not exceed the cost. A recent licensing transaction concluded in 2020 between Intellectual Ventures and RPX, where RPX agreed to license more than 18,000 patents from Intellectual Ventures, illustrates the ability of large defensive aggregators such as RPX to pool the overlapping interests of many member companies and to mitigate the threat of litigation.[30]

The License on Transfer (LOT) network is another way to address Problems 1 and 3 listed above. The organization was founded in 2014 and, according to its website, had more than 1,100 members in early 2021.[31] If a member of the network sells a patent to an NPE or becomes an NPE, all other members of the network automatically obtain a license to the affected patents. This ensures that any patent held by any of the LOT members cannot be asserted by an NPE against them. This mechanism still allows members to trade patents and even to enforce them against other members as long as the patents are not transferred to an NPE. The LOT network therefore reduces the supply of patents to NPEs. Although they can still acquire any of the patents held by a LOT member, their value will be drastically reduced if the patents cannot be enforced against any of the LOT members. This, in turn, will make the patents less attractive for purchase by an NPE in the first place.

Apart from defensive aggregators and the LOT network, there are also *invalidation entities* that focus on the invalidation of NPE patents through administrative invalidity proceedings. An example is Unified Patents, a company founded in 2012, that sells membership subscriptions. The company provides information about potentially threatening NPE patents to its members. It also directly files and litigates at the PTAB to invalidate patents held by NPEs. Unlike RPX, Unified Patents publicly committed to not pay NPEs in exchange for licenses or purchase patents from NPEs. Entities such as Unified Patents address the externality problem inherent in patent invalidation (Problem 2 above) by pooling different companies that will benefit from invalidation (although there is again a free-rider problem for non-members).

Finally, there also exist litigation insurance products that can help companies defend themselves against NPE lawsuits. There are a number of providers of defensive patent litigation policies, including Aon, IPISC, RPX, and Unified Patents. These defensive litigation products usually reimburse defendants for a share of their litigation expenses. This helps companies to litigate instead of seeking a quick settlement and thereby could deter NPE lawsuits (Helmers et al. 2022).

22.6 Summary

NPEs have attracted an enormous amount of controversy for more than 2 decades. There are compelling theoretical arguments in favor of and against patent assertions by NPEs. On the one hand, NPEs may act as market intermediaries, promoting technology transfer, and generally create liquidity in secondary patent markets. They may also help

---

[30] https://www.law360.com/articles/1343848/what-to-know-about-rpx-s-deal-with-intellectual-ventures.
[31] See https://lotnet.com.

small and individual inventors monetize their patented inventions. On the other hand, NPEs may opportunistically exploit problems in the patent-granting practice, especially in the context of software. This allows them to extract licensing payments from innovators without facilitating any type of actual technology transfer. In this way, NPEs increase costs and ultimately harm innovation.

While the effect of NPEs is ambiguous from a theoretical perspective, the existing empirical evidence is unequivocal. There is plenty of evidence to suggest that the patent enforcement behavior by NPEs is opportunistic. It harms practicing companies by imposing direct and indirect costs on them, which affect their operations and performance. There is also compelling evidence to suggest that NPE assertions harm companies' innovative activities.

While the empirical evidence suggests that NPE litigation may be socially harmful on balance, it is not obvious how to address the problem. Some have argued that the true problem is not even NPE litigation per se, but that NPEs are merely a reflection of a broader underlying problem with the patent system (Lemley and Melamed, 2013). NPEs merely opportunistically exploit these problems in the patent system. That said, a number of private organizations have emerged without policy intervention with the goal of curbing NPE activity. It remains to be seen how effective they are in addressing the challenges posed by NPEs on a larger scale. In any case, NPE assertions will likely remain an important topic for the years to come.

IV.
APPENDICES

APPENDIX A

Mathematics and Statistics

A.1 A Few Definitions

Asymptote: a line that is continually approached by a curve of interest but is never reached, even though the curve gets arbitrarily close to it.

Illustration of a function that has an asymptote

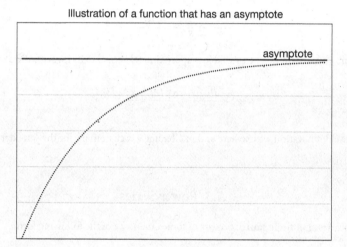

Figure A.1 Asymptote.

Support (of a distribution): the set of possible values of a random variable having that distribution; the range over which the distribution (density function) is defined. For example, the support of the normal distribution is the real line.

Affine function: a linear function plus a constant. That is, if x is a variable, a function of the form $a + bx$ that gives a straight line when plotted versus x is an affine function.

A.2 Logs and Growth Rates

In this book, log (logarithm) always refers to the natural log, that is, the logarithm such that

$$\log(e^x) = x$$

Although we could use other logarithms (e.g., base 10), the natural log has the useful property that its derivative is the exact inverse of its argument, rather than proportional to the inverse as in the case of other bases. The immediate consequence is the useful property of growth rates shown below.

Another useful consequence is that the derivative of a log of one quantity (Y) with respect to the log of another (X) measures the *elasticity* of Y with respect to X, that is, the percent increase in Y from a percent increase in X:

$$\frac{d \log(Y)}{d \log(X)} = \frac{1}{Y}\frac{dY}{d \log X} = \frac{X}{1}\frac{1}{Y}\frac{dY}{dX} = \frac{X}{Y}\frac{dY}{dX} = \frac{dY/Y}{dX/X} \equiv \text{elasticity}$$

From this equation, you can see that the log derivative of Y with respect to X yields the ratio of a small change in Y scaled by Y's magnitude to a small change in X scaled by X's magnitude.

The growth of X over a discrete interval of time (from 0 to 1) is equal to

$$\frac{X(1)-X(0)}{X(0)} = \frac{1}{X(0)}\frac{X(1)-X(0)}{(1-0)} = \frac{1}{X}\frac{\Delta X}{\Delta t}$$

As the interval of time becomes smaller and smaller, we can write this as a growth rate:

$$\frac{1}{X}\frac{\Delta X}{\Delta t} \rightarrow \frac{1}{X}\frac{dX}{dt} = \frac{d \log X}{dt}$$

Conclusion: The growth rate of a variable is approximately equal to its logarithmic derivative:

$$g_X = \frac{d \log X}{dt} = \frac{dX/dt}{X} = \frac{\dot{X}}{X}$$

Note that the dot notation we use here and in Chapter 9 is customary for the time derivative of a variable.

A.3 Power Series

A power series is an infinite sum of powers of some quantity x of the following form:

$$\sum_{t=0}^{\infty} x^t = 1 + x + x^2 + x^3 + \dots..$$

When $|x| < 1$, this series has a closed form:

$$\sum_{t=0}^{\infty} x^t \equiv \sum_{t=-\infty}^{0} x^t = \frac{1}{1-x}$$

This fact is useful in approximating the relationship between an infinite flow that is discounted at a particular rate $\beta = 1/(1 + \rho)$ and the value of the corresponding stock. For example, if an R&D investment is a continuous flow of R dollars per year and the rate of return is ρ, the stock of R&D K is given by the following:

$$K_0 = \sum_{t=-\infty}^{0} \beta^t R = \frac{R}{1-\beta} = R\left(1 - \frac{1}{1+\rho}\right)^{-1} = \frac{(1+\rho)R}{\rho}$$

A.4 Continuous Time Integral

The infinite power series above has a useful analogue in continuous time. Again, assume a constant interest rate or rate of return ρ. The PDV of a constant stream of \$1 (or any other currency unit) is the following:

$$\int_{t=0}^{\infty} e^{-\rho t} dt = \frac{1}{\rho}$$

You can easily compute that yourself. Perhaps more useful is the expression for the presented discounted value of a finite-lived stream with lifetime τ:

$$\int_{t=0}^{\tau} e^{-\rho t} dt = \frac{1 - e^{-\rho\tau}}{\rho}$$

A.5 Normal Distribution

We write the normal density function with mean μ and standard deviation σ as follows:

$$\phi(x; \mu, \sigma) = \frac{1}{\sigma\sqrt{2\pi}} \exp\left[-\frac{1}{2}\left(\frac{x-\mu}{\sigma}\right)^2 \right]$$

The cumulative normal probability function is denoted $\Phi(x; \mu, \sigma)$.

A.6 Poisson Process

This process generates a simple distribution that is useful for describing the uncertain output of R&D and innovation investment. A Poisson process describes how long one has to wait for an event to occur when the event has an arrival rate λ:

$$\text{Prob[event occurs before T]} = F(T) = 1 - \exp(-\lambda T)$$
$$\text{Corresponding density } f(T) = \lambda \exp(-\lambda T)$$

This process has several convenient properties:

- The events are independent of each other. If one happens, it does not affect the probability that another one will happen.
- The average number of events per time period is constant (and equal to λ times the time period length).
- Two events cannot happen at exactly the same time.

The fact that the expected number of events per time period is equal to λ can be used to generate the Poisson distribution. If we set the time period length to unity (typically, a year in our applications), the probability that x events will occur during that year can be written as the following:

$$\text{Prob}(x \text{ events occur}; \lambda) = \frac{\lambda^x e^\lambda}{x!}$$

where $x!$ denotes x factorial (a special case of the Gamma function):

$$x! = \Gamma(x+1) = x \cdot (x-1) \cdot (x-2) \cdots 3 \cdot 2 \cdot 1$$

The expected value and variance of a Poisson distribution are both equal to λ. Here is a picture of the Poisson probability distribution for different values of λ, the number of events per period. We also show a normal distribution with the same mean and variances as the Poisson for each value of λ, which demonstrates that the Poisson converges to the normal for large λ fairly quickly.

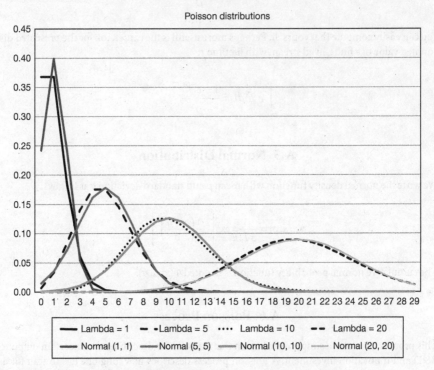

Figure A.2 Poisson and normal distributions.

A.7 Index Numbers

A.7.1 Divisia and Tornquist Indices

A Divisia index is an index number constructed from prices and quantities that allow one to aggregate them and describe the change of the aggregate over time. The derivation of a Divisia index is done in continuous time, but it is made tractable for national income accounting using Tornquist's discrete version.[1] Given a set of quantities q and prices p, at any point in time we have the following:

$$P(t)Q(t) = \sum_i p_i(t)q_i(t)$$

---

[1] A full treatment of index numbers is beyond the scope of this textbook. See Diewert (1976) for a complete discussion of the issues in creating index numbers.

Chapter 9 showed the following:

$$\frac{\dot{P}(t)}{P(t)} + \frac{\dot{Q}(t)}{Q(t)} = \sum_i w_i(t)\left(\frac{\dot{p}(t)}{p(t)} + \frac{\dot{q}(t)}{q(t)}\right)$$

If we take the price index as an example, a discrete time version of this index is

$$\frac{P(t) - P(t-1)}{P(t-1)} = \sum_i w_i(t)\frac{p(t) - p(t-1)}{p(t-1)} \tag{1}$$

The share weights are usually constructed by averaging those for the two adjacent periods:

$$w_i(t) = \frac{1}{2}\left(\frac{p_i(t)q_i(t)}{\sum_i p_i(t)q_i(t)} + \frac{p_i(t-1)q_i(t-1)}{\sum_i p_i(t-1)q_i(t-1)}\right)$$

Equation (1) yields a rate of change in prices. To obtain an actual index of prices, we can add 1 to the right-hand side. Because this is a chained index, where the current value depends on the lag of base period value, one time period will be chosen as the base with P and its components set to unity.

A.7.2 Fisher Ideal Index

The Fisher index methodology is the one currently used in the US national income accounts. It is a geometric average of the Laspeyres and Paasche indices. Recall the following formulas for these price indices (similar formulas apply for quantity indices with the roles of price and quantity interchanged):

$$\text{Laspeyres } L(t) = \frac{\sum_i p_i(t)q_i(t-1)}{\sum_i p_i(t-1)q_i(t-1)}$$

$$\text{Paasche } P(t) = \frac{\sum_i p_i(t)q_i(t)}{\sum_i p_i(t-1)q_i(t)}$$

Then the Fisher index $F(t)$ is the following:

$$F(t) = (L(t)P(t))^{1/2}$$

A.8 Internal Rate of Return

Consider a project with a sequence of cash flows every period denoted $x_1, x_2, x_3, \ldots x_T$. The internal rate of return (IRR) is defined as the discount rate ρ that solves the following equation:

$$0 = x_1 + \frac{x_2}{1+\rho} + \frac{x_3}{(1+\rho)^2} + \cdots + \frac{x_T}{(1+\rho)^{T-1}}$$
$$= \sum_{t=1}^{T} \frac{x_t}{(1+\rho)^{t-1}}$$

This equation cannot generally be solved analytically, but software to solve it is easily available (including Microsoft Excel). If all the x's are non-negative, there is a unique solution. If some of the x's are negative, there may be more than one solution.

A.9 CES Production Function

The constant elasticity of production function with constant returns and two inputs, K and L, is given by the following:

$$f(K,L) = \left[\alpha K^\rho + (1-\alpha)L^\rho \right]^{1/\rho}$$

The elasticity of substitution for this function is $1/(1 - \rho)$. In the limit as $\rho \to 0$, this becomes the Cobb-Douglas production function with an elasticity of substitution equal to 1.

A.10 Optimization

Throughout the book, we often derive the FOC of a function to find its optimum. We won't review the basics of optimization here as most students will have had at least some training in basic calculus. We only briefly review the first- and second-order conditions.

Assume we are interested in choosing x such that we maximize function $f(x)$. Then its first derivative—denoted as $f'(x)$—equals zero at the optimal x^*, and its second derivative—denoted as $f''(x)$—is smaller or equal to zero at x^*. Mathematically,

$$\text{First-order condition: } f'(x^*) = 0$$
$$\text{Second-order condition: } f''(x^*) \le 0 \tag{2}$$

If the first derivative is zero and the second derivative is greater than zero, that means you have found a minimum rather than a maximum.

Sometimes we would like to maximize a function with respect to more than one variable. For example, assume we wish to choose values of x_1 and x_2 to maximize $F(x_1, x_2)$. The corresponding first- and second-order conditions that accomplish this are the following:

$$\text{First-order conditions: } \frac{\partial F(x_1^*, x_2^*)}{\partial x_1} = 0, \quad \frac{\partial F(x_1^*, x_2^*)}{\partial x_2} = 0$$

$$\text{Second-order condition: } \begin{vmatrix} \dfrac{\partial^2 F(x_1^*, x_2^*)}{\partial x^2} & \dfrac{\partial^2 F(x_1^*, x_2^*)}{\partial x_1 \partial x_2} \\ \dfrac{\partial^2 F(x_1^*, x_2^*)}{\partial x_1 \partial x_2} & \dfrac{\partial^2 F(x_1^*, x_2^*)}{\partial x^2} \end{vmatrix} \le 0 \tag{3}$$

The vector of first derivatives is referred to as a gradient and often denoted ∇F, while the second derivative matrix is called a Hessian. The $\|\|$ notation denotes the determinant of a matrix. The extension to three or more variables should be obvious.

A.11 Envelope Theorem

In Chapter 22, we use the envelope theorem. The envelope theorem helps us answer the question of how the value of an objective function changes if one of its parameter changes. Assume a function $f(x, a)$ that has two parameters x and a. Furthermore, assume that we can only control the value of x, while a is determined outside of our control. Our goal is to choose x such that we maximize $f(x, a)$. Intuitively, the optimal choice of x depends on the value of a. In other words, for different values of a, there will be a different optimal choice of x, which we denote as $x(a)$. With this, we define the optimal value function as $V(a)=f(x(a), a)$. Now, a different way of stating our objective is to say that we want to understand how the optimal value function changes as parameter a changes. We can find out by differentiating the value function with respect to a:

$$\frac{dV(a)}{da} = \frac{\partial f(x(a),a)}{\partial a} + \frac{\partial f(x(a),a)}{\partial x}\frac{\partial x(a)}{\partial a} \tag{4}$$

Looking at equation (4), we know that $\dfrac{\partial f(x(a),a)}{\partial x} = 0$ because $x(a)$ is the optimal choice of x given a, because it is the FOC reviewed earlier. Therefore, we have

$$\frac{dV(a)}{da} = \frac{\partial f(x(a),a)}{\partial a} \tag{5}$$

Equation (5) shows that the total derivative of the value function with respect to a is equal to the partial derivative if the derivative is evaluated at the optimal choice. This is the envelope theorem.

To make our discussion less abstract, let's apply the envelope theorem within the context of a firm's profit-maximization problem (which is something you are most likely familiar with). Assume a price-taking firm that maximizes profits as follows:

$$\max_{q} \pi(q, p) = qp - c(q) \tag{6}$$

where q denotes quantity, p price, and $c(.)$ is a strictly convex cost function. You find the profit-maximizing q by deriving the FOC of (6) with respect to the firm's choice variable q:

$$\frac{\partial \pi}{\partial q} = 0 \tag{7}$$

which provides the well-known result that price equals marginal cost $p = c'(q)$. Using this result, we can write the optimal value function (which summarizes the effect of changes in p on π) of the firm as

$$V(p) = \pi(q(p), p) \tag{8}$$

Finally, in order to understand the effect of a change in p on profits, we take the derivative of $V(p)$ with respect to p:

$$\frac{dV(p)}{dp} = \frac{\partial \pi(q(p), p)}{\partial p} + \frac{\partial \pi(q(p), p)}{\partial q} \frac{\partial q(p)}{\partial p} = \frac{\partial \pi(q(p), p)}{\partial p} = q \qquad (9)$$

We get the result that $\dfrac{dV(p)}{dp} = q$ because at the optimal q, equation (7) tells us that $\dfrac{\partial \pi}{\partial q} \dfrac{\partial q}{\partial p} = 0$. In other words, at the optimum, the change in profits due to a change in q is zero. Another way to look at this is to remind ourselves that the parameter p can affect the value function directly $\dfrac{\partial \pi}{\partial p}$ and indirectly $\dfrac{\partial \pi}{\partial q} \dfrac{\partial q}{\partial p}$. The envelope theorem tells us that for small changes in the parameter p, we can ignore the indirect effect.

We can see that the envelope theorem means that if we are interested in the effect of the parameter p on the value function $\pi(q(p), p)$, we can calculate the effect by taking the derivative of the objective function with respect to the parameter and evaluating it by holding the choice variable q at its optimal value q^*.

Reference

Diewert, W. E. (1976). Exact and Superlative Index Numbers. *Journal of Econometrics* 4(2): 115–145.

APPENDIX B

List of Abbreviations

Abbreviation	Meaning
AI	Artificial intelligence
AIA	America Invents Act (US 2011)
ANDA	Abbreviated new drug application
ARV	Anti-retroviral medication
ARIPO	African Regional Intellectual Property Organization
ATP	Advanced Technology Program (US)
AVC	Advanced video coding
AZT	Azidothymidine
BEA	Bureau of Economic Analysis (US)
BEPS	Base erosion and profit shifting (OECD)
BGH	Bundesgerichtshof (Federal Court of Justice, DE)
BLS	Bureau of Labor Statistics (US)
BPatG	Bundespatentgericht (Federal Patent Court, DE)
CAFC	Court of Appeals of the Federal Circuit (US)
CBM	Covered business method
CBS	Columbia Broadcasting System (US)
CERN	European Council for Nuclear Research
CHIPS	Creating Helpful Incentives to Produce Semiconductors
CJEU	Court of Justice of the European Union
CMOS	Complementary metal-oxide semiconductor
CNIPA	Chinese National Intellectual Property Administration
CPI	Consumer price index
CRADA	Cooperative Research and Development Agreement (US)
DMCA	Digital Millennium Copyright Act (US)
DoJ	Department of Justice (US)
DRM	Digital rights management
DWL	Deadweight loss
EAPO	Eurasian Patent Organization
EC	European Commission
EcoPC	Eco-Patent Commons
EMA	European Medicines Agency
EMV	Entire market value
EPA	Environmental Protection Agency (US)
EPC	European Patent Convention
EPO	European Patent Office
ETSI	European Telecommunications Standards Institute
EWHC	High Court of Justice (England and Wales)

EU	European Union
FAA	Federal Aviation Administration (US)
FASB	Financial Accounting Standards Board (US)
FCC	Federal Communications Commission (US)
FDA	Food and Drug Administration (US)
FDI	Foreign direct investment
FOC	First-order condition
FRAND	Fair, reasonable, and nondiscriminatory (terms)
FTC	US Federal Trade Commission
G7	Group of 7, consisting of Canada, France, Germany, Italy, Japan, the United Kingdom, and the United States
GAAP	Generally accepted accounting principles
GDI	Gross domestic income
GDP	Gross domestic product
GNP	Gross national product
GPL	General Public License
GPT	General-purpose technology
HAART	Highly active anti-retroviral therapy
HVEC	High-efficiency video coding
ICANN	Internet Corporation for Assigned Names and Numbers
ICT	Information and communications technologies
IEA	International Energy Agency
IEEE	Institute of Electrical and Electronics Engineers ("I-triple E")
IMF	International Monetary Fund
INN	International non proprietary name
IoT	Internet of things
IPR	Intellectual property right
ITC	International Trade Commission
IUPAC	International Union of Pure and Applied Chemistry
JEDEC	Joint Electron Device Engineering Council
JPO	Japan Patent Office
KIPO	Korean Patent Office
LAD	Least absolute deviations (estimator)
LAN	Local area network
LTE	Long-term evolution (standard)
MPEG	Moving Picture Experts Group
MPP	Medicines Patent Pool
NA	Not available
NASA	National Aeronautics and Space Administration (US)
NCRPA	National Cooperative Research and Production Act (US)
NDA	New Drug Application
NIH	National Institutes of Health (US)
NIPA	National income and product accounts
NPE	Non-practicing entity
NRDC	National Research Defence Committee (US)
NSF	National Science Foundation (US)
NTD	Neglected Tropical Diseases
OAPI	Organisation Africaine de la Propriété Intellectuelle
OECD	Organization for Economic Cooperation and Development

OHIM	Office for Harmonization in the Internal Market (EU)
OSRD	Office of Scientific Research and Development (US)
OSS	Open-source software
OWS	Operation Warp Speed (US)
PAE	Patent assertion entity
PCT	Patent Cooperation Treaty
PDV	Present discounted value
PGR	Postgrant review
PRAB	Patent Review and Adjudication Board (CN)
PTAB	Patent Trial and Appeal Board (US)
PVP	Plant variety protection
R&D	Research and development
RAND	Reasonable and nondiscriminatory (terms)
RCA	Radio Corporation of America (US), liquidated in the 1980s
RFID	Radio-frequency identification
SBIR	Small business innovation research (US)
SCPA	Semiconductor Chip Protection Act (US)
SDO	Standard development organization
SEP	Standard essential patent
SIPO	Former name of CNIPA
SNA	System of national accounts
SPC	Supplementary protection certificate
SSO	Standard-setting organization
SSPPU	Smallest saleable patent practicing unit
STEM	Science, technology, engineering, and mathematics
TRIPS	Trade-Related Aspects of Intellectual Property
TTO	Technology transfer office
UDRP	Uniform dispute resolution policy
UHF	Ultra-high frequency
UKIPO	UK Intellectual Property Office
UPOV	International Union for the Protection of New Varieties of Plants
URS	Uniform rapid suspension
USPTO	US Patent and Trademark Office
UTSA	Uniform Trade Secrets Act (US)
VARA	Visual Artists Rights Act
VC	Venture capital; venture capitalist
VHDP	Vessel hull design protection (US)
WHO	World Health Organization
WIPO	World Intellectual Property Organization
WTO	World Trade Organization

APPENDIX C

Data

C.1 Introduction

Much of the research we discuss in this book uses data on innovative activity. This appendix provides an overview of data that might be used to analyze innovation and IP questions. It is strictly an introduction, as new data sources are constantly being created and are far too numerous for us to describe here. A useful reference is the data section of the Innovation Information Initiative (I3) website: https://iiindex.org.

This appendix is intended to allow researchers to become familiar with the main data sources available and to help them in their search for and creation of new and more specialized resources.

We first note that data come at different levels of aggregation: country, industry, firm, or invention/innovation. The types of data access range from open public access through open access via one's institution to access provided to researchers in a closed-system environment. In the latter case, usually no data export is allowed, and it can be difficult to merge with other data. Because of confidentiality reasons related to firms' strategic considerations, often detailed data at levels below the industry level are hard to come by, or only accessed in a closed-system environment. But researchers have been creative in the past, and one often encounters cases where they have persuaded firms to give them historic or anonymized data at least.

The usual innovation measures fall into four major groups: data on R&D expenditures, patent and other intellectual property data, scientific publication data, and measures derived from firm-level innovation surveys. Innovation researchers also frequently make use of related data sources on productivity, litigation, venture capital funding, and collaboration between firms, universities, and individuals. We review the main innovation data sources below. The website addresses for accessing these data are given in the references at the end of this appendix.

C.2 R&D Data

Data on R&D spending were perhaps the first innovation data to be used, after the U.S. National Science Foundation began to collect them in the early 1950s, shortly followed by other countries. In 1963, OECD member countries met for the first time to begin to establish standards and definitions for collecting such data via surveys. The Frascati Manual, now in its 7th edition (OECD 2015a), was the result.[1] This manual defines the various types of R&D spending, such as basic, applied, and development, and the scope of the activities in each one. It also specifies such things as how to count R&D personnel for survey purposes, and the collection of data spending by field and function. It has separate sections that discuss the collection of R&D data for business enterprises, governments, nonprofits, higher education, and abroad.

The Frascati Manual presents the following definition of R&D as the basic definition to be used for all the more detailed data that might be collected by particular surveys:

---

[1] The initial meeting of the OECD experts was held at the Villa Falconieri in Frascati, Italy; hence the name of the manual.

Research and experimental development (R&D) comprise creative work undertaken on a systematic basis in order to increase the stock of knowledge—including knowledge of man, culture and society—and the use of this stock of knowledge to devise new applications. (OECD 2015a, p. 44)

The manual goes on to specify activities to be excluded from the definition, such as education and training, routine software development, industrial design, and so forth. It also spends some time on the problems of measuring social science R&D and service sector R&D. The countries that have R&D surveys generally follow this definition.

For developed countries and a few large middle-income countries, a broad range of R&D spending data is generally available from the OECD. The World Bank has R&D data for all countries for which it is available. The World Development Indicators of the World Bank include the R&D–GDP ratio and the number of researchers in R&D per million population. See the references for website addresses.

At the firm level, the broadest set of R&D data that is publicly available is that reported by public firms in their accounts. US and international accounting standards have required the reporting of "material" R&D for a number of years. Most of the convenient digital sources of these data are proprietary, but many business schools and other universities have access. Key resources are Compustat and Orbis.

For the United States, some detailed government spending data by agency are available as microdata from the National Science Foundation. Firm-level R&D spending is available for confidential use at the Census Data Centers, which require an application and substantial fees.

C.3 Innovation Data

As in the case of R&D data, increased use of surveys that asked firms about their innovative activities led to demands for standards in collecting such data. The result was a meeting in Oslo, Norway, of experts from the OECD and the European Union in 1991, and the publication of the Oslo Manual. This manual defines innovation as follows:

A business innovation is a new or improved product or business process (or combination thereof) that differs significantly from the firm's previous products or business processes and that has been introduced on the market or brought into use by the firm. (OECD/ Eurostat 2018, p. 68)

Note that the manual explicitly confines its coverage to business innovation, although one might imagine that innovation by governments, nonprofits, and educational institutions is also a possibility. The manual also provides a definition of the process of innovation, which it calls innovation activities:

Innovation activities include all developmental, financial and commercial activities undertaken by a firm that are intended to result in an innovation for the firm. (OECD/ Eurostat 2018, p. 68)

Besides the basic query about whether the firm has introduced a new product or process in the past, the data discussed in the manual are the components of innovation spending, the managerial and technical capabilities of the firm, the sources of new knowledge, external and internal. It also covers methods of data collection, and different methods for identifying a focal innovation about which to ask detailed questions. Mairesse and Mohnen (2010) provide a helpful guide on using these data based on their experience.

C.4 IP Data

The most important form of IP data for studying innovation is clearly patents, which have two main advantages: (1) They are public information, so one can know who the owners and inventors are as well as their geographic location; (2) they are classified technologically by knowledgeable examiners, so they provide a great deal of technology detail that is generally not available for R&D and innovation data (Griliches 1990, Nagaoka et al. 2010). In addition, in many important jurisdictions, they contain citations to earlier patents as well as scientific and technical publications, which allows the tracing of knowledge flows. Chapter 6 of OECD (2009) contains a very useful discussion of the meaning of patent citations.

Aggregate patent, trademark, design, and utility model data for all WIPO member countries (approximately 200) are available from the WIPO IP Statistics Data Center, broken down by technology, filing office, resident and non-resident applications, and whether the application went through the PCT route. These data are obtained from the individual patent-filing offices in each jurisdiction, so more timely versions may be obtainable from them if necessary. Aggregates of EPO, PCT, and triadic (EPO, USPTO, JPO) patents by region and by technology classifications are also available from the OECD patent statistics.

For individual patent data, there are a number of sources. It is possible to obtain a great deal of information online for individual patents via Google patents or the EPO Espacenet. One can also obtain patent statistics of one's choice using Google's BigQuery on their public patent data. For US patents and their citations, they can be searched on the USPTO website, and there are also bulk downloads of the data available.

The USPTO also maintains both searchable and bulk downloadable databases for trademarks. For searchable databases of EU trademarks, designs, and Geographic Indications, see the EUIPO website. Some bulk downloading of these data may also be feasible.

Verluise et al. (2022) have created a comprehensive database of patent citations that includes not only front-page citations, but also cites to the nonpatent literature and in-text patent citations for US patents. Similar data are also available from Marx and Fuegi (2020, 2023). Also, see lens.org (below) for patent data linked to publications.

Patents generally contain citations to prior patents, and data on citations have long been used to trace knowledge flows from one patent owner to another and also as an indication of the importance of the cited patent (Harhoff et al. 1999, Nagaoka et al. 2010). Recently, advances in machine learning have enabled the analysis of patent text (abstract, claims, and written description) to produced and more refined versions of knowledge relationships among patents and of technology classifications. For an interesting example of this kind of use, see Arts et al. (2023) . For data sources, see the I3 website cited earlier.

Copyright data are more problematic, due to the lack of a registration requirement in many jurisdictions. However in the United States, a searchable database of copyright registrations is available at the U.S. Copyright Office website. The EU Copyright Office maintains a similar database, in English, French, and Spanish.

C.5 Publication Data

For a long time, the workhorse for scientific and technical journal article and citation information was the Web of Science (WoS), which contains publication information from 34,000 journals. The WoS is maintained by Clarivate. Although it has set the standard, the cost of bulk downloads of these data is prohibitive for most researchers.

Accordingly, many researchers have turned to public sources of publication data. A promising new development is OpenAlex, which is based on Microsoft's Academic Graph (which is no longer updated), but draws data from a number of sources including ORCID and PubMed. The data supplied include the publication title, author names, author institutions, concepts (a form of keywords), and citation history. OpenAlex allows bulk downloads of the entire dataset at a point in time (a snapshot).

Another possibility for publication data is Lens.org, which contains data on both patents and publications that include the citations from one to the other. Dimensions by Digital Science has a database of linked data on patents, publications, clinical trials, and other information such as funding.

C.6 Other Innovation-Related Data

Two types of data that may be useful are data on patent–product matches and data on firms matched to patenting entities. For US patents, De Rassenfosse (2018) and coauthors have collected data on virtual (internet) patent markings and provided access on the IProduct website.

Building on the work of Hall et al. (2001), Arora et al. (2020, 2021) have created a database (DISCERN) of Compustat firms matched to patent data. The database accounts for name changes and ownership changes somewhat more accurately than in the original Hall et al. dataset, which is still available at https://www.nber.org/research/data/us-patents. The period covered by DISCERN is 1980–2015.

References

Arora, Ashish, Sharon Belenzon, and Lia Sheer (2021). Knowledge Spillovers and Corporate Investment in Scientific Research. *American Economic Review* 111(3): 871–898.

Arora, Ashish, Sharon Belenzon, and Lia Sheer (2020). DISCERN (Duke Innovation and Scientific Enterprises Research Network) Database. https://zenodo.org/record/4320782#.Y9MOOHbMJUs

Arts, S., B. Cassiman, and J. Hou (2023). Position and Differentiation of Firms in Technology Space. *Management Science* 69(12): 7151–7882. https://doi.org/10.1287/mnsc.2023.00282

Clarivate (2023). Web of Science. https://clarivate.com/webofsciencegroup/solutions/web-of-science

Digital Science. Dimensions Database. https://www.digital-science.com/product/dimensions EPO (2023). Patstat Database. https://www.epo.org/searching-for-patents/business/patstat.html

EPO (2023). Espacenet Patent Search. https://www.epo.org/searching-for-patents/technical/espacenet.html

EUIPO (2023). Databases. https://euipo.europa.eu/ohimportal/en/databases

EU Copyright Office (2023). https://www.eucopyright.com/en/advanced-search

Google (2023). Patents. https://patents.google.com

Griliches, Z. (1990). Patent Statistics as Economic Indicators: A Survey. *Journal of Economic Literature* 28: 1661–1707.

Hall, B. H., A. B. Jaffe, and M. Trajtenberg (2001). The NBER Patent Citation Data File: Lessons, Insights and Methodological Tools. Cambridge, MA: National Bureau of Economic Research Working Paper Series No. 8498.

Harhoff, D., F. Narin, F. M. Scherer, and K. Vopel (1999). Citation Frequency and the Value of Patented Inventions. *Review of Economics and Statistics* 81(3): 511–515.

Innovation Information Initiative (2022). https://iii.pubpub.org

IProduct (2023). https://iproduct.io/app/#/public/page/home

Mairesse, J. and P. Mohnen (2010). Using Innovation Surveys for Econometric Analysis. In B. H. Hall and N. Rosenberg (eds.), *Handbook of the Economics of Innovation*, Chapter 26, Vol. 2, 1129–1155. Amsterdam and New York: Elsevier.

Marx, M. and A. Fuegi (2020). Reliance on Science: Worldwide Front-Page Patent Citations to Scientific Articles. *Strategic Management Journal* 41(9): 1572–1594.

Marx, M. and A. Fuegi (2023). Reliance on Science by Inventors: Hybrid Extraction of In-Text Patent-to-Article Citations. *Journal of Economics and Management Strategy* 31(2): 369–392. http://doi.org/10.1111/jems.12455

Marx, M. and A. Fuegi (2023). https://zenodo.org/record/7497435#.Y9HL1XbMJk5

Nagaoka, S., K. Motohashi, and A. Goto (2010). Patent Statistics as an Innovation Indicator. In B. H. Hall and N. Rosenberg (eds.), *Handbook of the Economics of Innovation, Volume II*: 1083–1127. Amsterdam: Elsevier.

OECD (2023). Main Science and Technology Indicators. https://www.oecd.org/sti/msti.htm

OECD (2023). Patent Statistics. https://www.oecd-ilibrary.org/science-and-technology/data/oecd-patent-statistics_patent-data-en

OECD (2009). *Patent Statistics Manual.* https://www.oecd.org/sti/inno/oecdpatentstatisticsmanual.htm

OECD/Eurostat (2018). *Oslo Manual: Guidelines for Collecting, Reporting, and Using Data on Innovation.* Paris: OECD Publishing/ Luxembourg: Eurostat. https://doi.org/10.1787/9789264304604-en

OECD (2015). *Frascati Manual 2015: Guidelines for Collecting and Reporting Data on Research and Experimental Development, The Measurement of Scientific, Technological and Innovation Activities.* Paris: OECD Publishing. http://dx.doi.org/10.1787/9789264239012-en

OpenAlex (2023). An Open and Comprehensive Catalog of Scholarly Papers, Authors, Institutions, and More. https://openalex.org

de Rassenfosse, G. (2018). Notice Failure Revisited: Evidence on the Use of Virtual Patent Marking. Cambridge, MA: National Bureau of Economic Research Working Paper Series No. 24288.

de Rassenfosse, G., H. Dernis, and G. Boedt (2014). An Introduction to the Patstat Database with Example Queries. *Australian Economic Review* 47: 395–408. https://doi.org/10.1111/1467-8462.12073

U.S. Census Bureau (2023). Federal Statistical Research Data Centers. https://www.census.gov/about/adrm/fsrdc.html

U.S. Copyright Office (2023). https://www.copyright.gov/public-records

U.S. National Science Foundation (2023). Microdata Public and Restricted Use Data Files. https://ncses.nsf.gov/explore-data/microdata

USPTO (2023). Patent Public Search. https://ppubs.uspto.gov/pubwebapp/static/pages/landing.html

USPTO (2023). Bulk Data Products. https://www.uspto.gov/learning-and-resources/bulk-data-products

Verluise, C., G. Cristelli, K. Higham, L. Violon, and G. de Rassenfosse (2022). PatCit. https://cverluise.github.io/PatCit

Wharton Research Data Services (2023). https://wrds-www.wharton.upenn.edu

WIPO (2023). IP Statistics Data Center. https://www3.wipo.int/ipstats

World Bank (2023). World Development Indicators Databank. https://databank.worldbank.org/source/world-development-indicators

Bibliography

Abbate, J. (2000). *Inventing the Internet.* Cambridge, MA: MIT Press.

Abernathy, W., and J. Utterback (1978). Patterns of Industrial Innovation. *Technology Review* 80(7): 1–9.

Abraham, R. (2007). Mobile Phones and Economic Development: Evidence From the Fishing Industry in India. *Information Technologies and International Development* 4(1): 48–56.

Abrams, D. S., and R. P. Wagner (2013). Poisoning the Next Apple: The America Invents Act and Individual Inventors. *Stanford Law Review* 65(3): 517–564.

Abramovitz, M. (1956). Resource and Output Trends in the United States Since 1870. *American Economic Review* 46(2): 5–23.

Abud Sittler, M. J., B. H. Hall, and C. Helmers (2015). An Empirical Analysis of Primary and Secondary Pharmaceutical Patents in Chile. *PLOS ONE.* doi:10.1371/journal.pone.0124257

Abud Sittler, M. J., C. Fink, B. H. Hall, and C. Helmers (2013). The Use of Intellectual Property in Chile. Geneva, Switzerland: World Intellectual Property Organization Economic Research Working Paper 11. http://www.wipo.int/publications/en/details.jsp?id=3955&plang=EN

Acemoglu, D. (2023). Distorted Innovation: Does the Market Get the Direction of Technology Right? *American Economic Review* 113: 1–28.

Acs, Z. J., and D. B. Audretsch (1990). *Innovation and Small Firms.* Cambridge, MA: MIT Press.

Adermon, A., and C.-Y. Liang (2014). Piracy and Music Sales: The Effects of an Anti-Piracy Law. *Journal of Economic Behavior and Organization* 105: 90–106.

Adner, R. (2012). *The Wide Lens: A New Strategy for Innovation.* Portfolio, Penguin Publishing.

Aghion, P., C. Antonin, and S. Bunel (2021). *The Power of Creative Destruction.* Cambridge, MA: Harvard University Press.

Aghion, P., A. Bergeaud, T. Gigout, M. Lequien, and M. Melitz (2021). Exporting Ideas: Knowledge Flows from Expanding Trade in Goods. https://scholar.harvard.edu/aghion/publications/spreading-knowledge-across-world-innovation-spillover-through-trade-expansion

Aghion, P., N. Bloom, R. Blundell, R. Griffith, and P. Howitt (2005, May). Competition and Innovation: An Inverted-U Relationship. *Quarterly Journal of Economics* 120: 701–728.

Aghion, P., and P. Howitt (1998). *Endogenous Growth Theory.* Cambridge, MA: MIT Press.

Aghion, P., and P. Howitt (1992). A Model of Growth Through Creative Destruction. *Econometrica* 60(2): 323–351. https://doi.org/10.2307/2951599

Agrawal, A., J. Gans, and A. Goldfarb (2019). Economic Policy for Artificial Intelligence. *Innovation Policy and the Economy* 19: 139–160

Agrawal, A., J. Gans, and A. Goldfarb (eds.) (2019). *The Economics of Artificial Intelligence: An Agenda.* Chicago, IL: University of Chicago Press.

Ahn. S., B. H. Hall, and K. Lee (eds.) (2014). *Intellectual Property for Economic Development.* KDI Series in Economic Policy and Development. Cheltenham, UK: Edward Elgar and KDI.

AIPLA (2017). *Survey of Costs of Patent Litigation and Inter Partes Review.* Washington, DC: American Intellectual Property Law Association

Aizcorbe, A., C. Baker, E. R. Berndt, and D. M. Cutler (eds.) (2018). *Measuring and Modeling Health Care Costs.* Chicago, IL: Chicago University Press.

Akcigit, U., and S. T. Ates (2021). Ten Facts on Declining Business Dynamism and Lessons from Endogenous Growth Theory. *American Economic Journal: Macroeconomics* 13(1): 257–298.

Akcigit, U., M. A. Celik, and J. Greenwood (2016). Buy, Keep, or Sell: Economic Growth and the Market for Ideas. *Econometrica* 84(3): 943–984.

Akcigit, U., J. Grigsby, T. Nicholas, and S. Stantcheva (2018). Taxation and Innovation in the 20th Century. Cambridge, MA: National Bureau of Economic Research Working Paper No. 24982.

Akcigit, U., D. Hanley, and S. Stantcheva (2016, rev. 2019). Optimal Taxation and R&D Policies. Cambridge, MA: National Bureau of Economic Research Working Paper No. 22908.

Akerlof, G. (1970). The Market for "Lemons": Quality Uncertainty and the Market Mechanism. *Quarterly Journal of Economics* 84(3): 488–500.

Akerlof, G. A., K. J. Arrow, and T. F. Bresnahan (2002). *Amicus Curiae* Brief in the Case of *Eldred v Ashcroft*. Cambridge, MA: Harvard University Law School Technical Report 01–618. https://cyber.harvard.edu/openlaw/eldredvashcroft/supct/amici/economists.pdf

Allen, R. C. (1983). Collective Invention. *Journal of Economic Behavior and Organization* 4(1): 1–24.

Allison, J. R., and M. A. Lemley (2000). Who's patenting what? An empirical exploration of patent prosecution. *Vanderbilt Law Review* 58: 2099–2148.

Allison, J. R., M. A. Lemley, and D. L. Schwartz (2017). How Often Do Non-Practicing Entities Win Patent Suits? *Berkeley Law Technology Journal* 32: 237–310.

Allison, J. R., M. A. Lemley, and J. Walker (2009). Extreme Value or Trolls on Top? The Characteristics of the Most-Litigated Patents. *University of Pennsylvania Law Review* 158(1): 1–37.

Allison, J. R., and E. H. Tiller (2003). The Business Method Patent Myth. *Berkeley Technology Law Journal* 18: 987–1084.

Allred, B., and W. Park (2007). Patent Rights and Innovative Activity: Evidence from National and Firm-Level Data. *Journal of International Business Studies* 38(6): 878–900.

Almeling, D. S., D. W. Snyder, M. Sapoznikow, W. E. McCollum, and J. Weader (2010). A Statistical Analysis of Trade Secret Litigation in Federal Courts. *Gonzaga Law Review* 45(2): 291–334.

Alston, J. M. and R. J. Venner (2002). The effects of the US Plant Variety Protection Act on wheat genetic improvement. *Research policy* 31(4): 527–542.

American Association for the Advancement of Science (2022). *Historical Trends in Federal R&D*. https://www.aaas.org/programs/r-d-budget-and-policy/historical-trends-federal-rd

American Physical Society (2010). Maiman Builds First Working Laser. https://www.aps.org/publications/apsnews/201005/physicshistory.cfm

Amin, T., and A. S. Kesselheim (2012). Secondary Patenting of Branded Pharmaceuticals: A Case Study of How Patents on Two HIV Drugs Could Be Extended for Decades. *Health Affairs* 31(10): 2286–2294.

Anderson G., and F. Moris (2023). Recent Increase in R&D to GDP Ratio Driven by Increases in Experimental Development. Alexandria, VA: National Center for Science and Engineering Statistics, National Science Foundation Report 23–340. https://ncses.nsf.gov/pubs/nsf23340

Andrés, L., D. Cuberes, M. Diouf, and T. Serebrisky (2007). Diffusion of the Internet: A Cross-Country Analysis. *Telecommunications Policy* 34: 323–340.

Andrews, D., C. Criscuolo, and P. N. Gal (2016). The Best versus the Rest: The Global Productivity Slowdown, Divergence across Firms and the Role of Public Policy. Paris, France: Organisation for Economic Co-operation and Development Productivity Working Papers 5.

Angeles, L. (2005). Should Developing Countries Strengthen Their Intellectual Property Rights? *BE Journal of Macroeconomics* 5 (1): article 23.

Angrist, J. D., and J.-S. Pischke (2009). *Mostly Harmless Econometrics: An Empiricist's Companion*. Princeton, NJ: Princeton University Press.

Anton, J. J., and D. A. Yao (2004). Little Patents and Big Secrets: Managing Intellectual Property. *RAND Journal of Economics* 35(1): 1–22.

Appel, I., J. Farre-Mensa, and E. Simintzi (2019). Patent Trolls and Start-Up Employment. *Journal of Financial Economics* 133: 708–725.

Arora, A. (1997). Patents, licensing, and market structure in the chemical industry. *Research Policy* 26(4): 391–403. DOI: https://doi.org/10.1016/S0048-7333(97)00014-0

Arora, A., S. Belenzon, and B. Dionisi (2023). First-Mover Advantage and the Private Value of Public Science. *Research Policy* 52(9): article 104867.

Arora, A., S. Belenzon, and A. Patacconi (2018). The Decline of Science in Corporate R&D. *Strategic Management Journal* 39(1): 3–32.

Arora, A., S. Belenzon, and L. Sheer (2021a). Knowledge Spillovers and Corporate Investment in Scientific Research. *American Economic Review* 111(3): 871–898.

Arora, A., S. Belenzon, and L. Sheer (2021b). Matching patents to Compustat firms, 1980–2015: Dynamic Reassignment, Name Changes, and Ownership Structures. *Research Policy* 50(5): article 104217. https://zenodo.org/records/4320782

Arora, A., L. Branstetter, and C. Chatterjee (2008). Strong Medicine: Patent Reform and the Emergence of a Research-Driven Pharmaceutical Industry in India. Cambridge, MA: National Bureau of Economic Research Conference Paper.

Arora, A., W. M. Cohen, H. Lee, and D. Sebastian (2023). Invention value, inventive capability and the large firm advantage. *Research Policy* 52(1): 104650. https://doi.org/10.1016/j.res pol.2022.104650

Arora, A., W. M. Cohen, and J. P. Walsh (2016). The Acquisition and Commercialization of Invention in American Manufacturing: Incidence and Impact. *Research Policy* 45(6): 1113–1128.

Arora, A., and A. Fosfuri (2003). Licensing the Market for Technology. *Journal of Economic Behavior and Organization* 52(2): 277–295.

Arora, A., and A. Gambardella (2010). Ideas for Rent: An Overview of Markets for Technology. *Industrial and Corporate Change* 19(3): 775–803.

Arrow, K. (1962a). The Economic Implications of Learning by Doing. *Review of Economic Studies* 29, 155–173.

Arrow, K. (1962b). Economic Welfare and the Allocation of Resources for Invention. In R. R. Nelson (ed.), *The Rate and Direction of Inventive Activity*, pp. 609–625. Princeton, NJ: Princeton University Press.

Arrow, K. J., Chenery, H. B., Minhas, B. S., and Solow, R. M. (1961). Capital-Labor Substitution and Economic Efficiency. *Review of Economics and Statistics* 43(3): 225–250.

Arthur, W. B. (1989). Competing Technologies, Increasing Returns, and Lock-In by Historical Events. *Economic Journal* 99(394): 116–131.

Arts, S., B. Cassiman, and J. Hou (2023). Position and Differentiation of Firms in Technology Space. *Management Science* 69(12): 7151–7882. https://doi.org/10.1287/mnsc.2023.00282

Arundel, A. (2003). Patents in the Knowledge-Based Economy, Report of the KNOW Survey. Maastricht, Netherlands: MERIT, University of Maastricht.

Åstebro, T., S. A. Jeffrey, and G. K. Adomdza (2007). Inventor Perseverance after Being Told to Quit: The Role of Cognitive Biases. *Journal of Behavioral Decision Making* 20(3): 253–272. https://doi.org/10.1002/bdm.554

Athreye, S., D. Kale, and S. V. Ramani (2009). Experimentation with Strategy and the Evolution of Dynamic Capability in the Indian Pharmaceutical Sector. *Industrial and Corporate Change* 18(4) 729–759.

Austin, D. H. (2000). Patents, Spillovers and Competition in Biotechnology. Washington, DC: Resources for the Future Discussion Papers dp-00-53. https://ageconsearch.umn.edu/rec ord/10808/files/dp000053.pdf

Autor, D., D. Dorn, L. F Katz, C. Patterson, and J. Van Reenen (2020). The Fall of the Labor Share and the Rise of Superstar Firms. *Quarterly Journal of Economics* 135(2): 645–709.

Ayerbe, C., N. Lazaric, M. Callois, and L. Mitkova (2014). The New Challenges of Organizing Intellectual Property in Complex Industries: A Discussion Based on the Case of Thales. *Technovation* 34, 232–241.

Babina, T., A. Xi He, S. T. Howell, E. R. Perlman, and J. Staudt (2023). Cutting the Innovation Engine: How Federal Funding Shocks Affect University Patenting, Entrepreneurship, and Publications. *Quarterly Journal of Economics* 138(2): 895–954.

Baker, S., and C. Mezzetti (2005). Disclosure as a Strategy in the Patent Race. *Journal of Law and Economics* 48(1): 173–194.

Bakker, G., N. Crafts, and P. Woltjer (2019). The Sources of Growth in a Technologically Progressive Economy: The United States, 1899–1941. *Economic Journal* 129(622): 2267–2294.

Balsmeier, B., L. Fleming, and S. Lück (2023). Isolating Personal Knowledge Spillovers: Coinventor Deaths and Spatial Citation Differentials. *American Economic Review: Insights* 5(1): 21–34.

Bar, T. (2006). Defensive Publications in an R&D Race. *Journal of Economics and Management Strategy* 15(1): 229–254.

Baron, J., and D. F. Spulber (2018). Technology Standards and Standard Setting Organizations: Introduction to the Searle Center Database. *Journal of Economics and Management Strategy* 27: 462–503. https://doi.org/10.1111/jems.12257

Barro, R. J. (2021). Double Counting of Investment. *Economic Journal* 131(638): 2333–2356.

Barton, J. H. (2004). Issues Posed by a World Patent System. *Journal of International Economic Law* 7(2): 341–357.

Barton, J. H. (2007). A History of Technology Transfer In and Developing World Production of Vaccines. Stanford. CA: Stanford University Working Paper.

Bass, F. (1969). A New Product Growth for Model Consumer Durables. *Management Science* 15(5): 215–227.

Baumol, W. J. (2002). *The Free-Market Innovation Machine: Analyzing the Growth Miracle of Capitalism*. Princeton, NJ: Princeton University Press.

Bebchuk, L. A. (1984). Litigation and Settlement under Imperfect Information. *RAND Journal of Economics* 15(3): 404–415.

Bebchuk, L. A. (1996). A New Theory Concerning the Credibility and Success of Threats to Sue. *Journal of Legal Studies* 25: 1–25.

Bechtold, S., and C. Tucker (2014). Trademarks, Triggers, and Online Search. *Journal of Empirical Legal Studies* 11(4): 718–750.

Becker, S. A. (1986). Legal Protection of Semiconductor Mask Works in the United States. *Computer Law Journal* 6, 589–605.

Beebe, B. (2005). Search and Persuasion in Trademark Law. *Michigan Law Review* 103(8): 2020–2072.

Beebe, B., and J. C. Fromer (2018). Are We Running ot of Trademarks? An Empirical Study of Trademark, Depletion and Congestion. *Harvard Law Review* 131(4): 945–1045.

Belderbos, R., B. Cassiman, D. Faems, B. Leten, and B. van Looy (2014). Co-Ownership of Intellectual Property: Exploring the Value-Appropriation and Value-Creation Implications of Co-Patenting with Different Partners. *Research Policy* 43: 841–852.

Belenzon, S. (2012). Cumulative Innovation and Market Value: Evidence from Patent Citations. *Economic Journal* 122(559): 265–285.

Bell, A., R. Chetty, X. Jaravel, N. Petkova, and J. van Reenen (2019). Who Becomes an Inventor in America? The Importance of Exposure to Innovation. *Quarterly Journal of Economics* 134(2), 647–713.

Bénabou, R., D. Ticchi, and A. Vindigni (2015). Religion and Innovation. *American Economic Review* 105(5), 346–351.

Benkard, C. Lanier (2000). Learning and Forgetting: The Dynamics of Aircraft Production. *American Economic Review* 90(4): 1034–1054.

Benkard, C. Lanier (2004). A Dynamic Analysis of the Market for Wide-Bodied Commercial Aircraft. *Review of Economic Studies* 71(3), 581–611.

Berndt, E. R., N. Blalock, and I. M. Cockburn (2011). Diffusion of New Drugs in the Post-TRIPS Era. *International Journal of the Economics of Business* 18(2): 203–224.

Berndt, E. R., and I. M. Cockburn (2014). The Hidden Cost of Low Prices: Limited Access to New Drugs in India. *Health Affairs* 23: 621–630.

Berndt, E. R., D. M. Cutler, R. Frank, Z. Griliches, J. P. Newhouse, and J. E. Triplett (2001). Price Indexes for Medical Care Goods and Services: An Overview of Measurement Issues. In D. M. Cutler and E. R. Berndt (eds.), *Medical Output and Productivity*, pp. 141–200. Chicago, IL: Chicago University Press.

Bessen, J. (2008). The Value of U.S. Patents by Owner and Patent Characteristics. *Research Policy* 37(5): 932–945.

Bessen, J., and R. M. Hunt (2007). An empirical look at software patents. *Journal of Economics & Management Strategy* 16(1): 157-189.

Bessen, J., and E. Maskin (2009). Sequential Innovation, Patents, and Imitation. *RAND Journal of Economics* 40(4) 611–635.

Bessen, J. E., and M. J. Meurer (2014). The Direct Costs from NPE Disputes. *Cornell Law Review* 99(2): 387–424

Bhaskarabhatla, A., and S. Klepper (2014). Latent Submarket Dynamics and Industry Evolution: Lessons from the US Laser Industry. *Industrial and Corporate Change* 23(6), 1381–1415. https://doi.org/10.1093/icc/dtt060

Bittlingmayer, G. (1988). Property Rights, Progress, and the Aircraft Patent Agreement. *Journal of Law and Economics* 31(1): 227–248.

Black, F., and M. Scholes (1973). The Pricing of Options and Corporate Liabilities. *Journal of Political Economy* 81(3): 637–654.

Blandinières, F., and D. Steinbrenner (2020). *How Does the Evolution of R&D Tax Incentives Schemes Impact Their Effectiveness? Evidence From a Meta-Analysis.* Centre for European Economic Research Discussion Paper No. 21-020. Mannheim, Germany: ZEW. https://ssrn.com/abstract=3805605

Blind, K., J. Edler, R. Frietsch, and U. Schmoch (2006). Motives to patent: Empirical evidence from Germany. *Research Policy* 35(5): 655-672. https://doi.org/10.1016/j.respol.2006.03.002

Bloom, N., and R. Griffith (2001). The Internationalisation of UK R&D. *Fiscal Studies* 22(3), 337–355.

Bloom, N., C. I. Jones, J. Van Reenen, and M. Webb (2020). Are Ideas Getting Harder to Find? *American Economic Review* 110(4), 1104–1144.

Bloom, N., M. Schankerman, and J. Van Reenen (2013). Identifying Technology Spillovers and Product Market Rivalry. *Econometrica* 81(4): 1347–1393.

Blonigen, B. A., and Taylor, C. T. (2000). R&D Intensity and Acquisitions in High-Technology Industries: Evidence from the US Electronic and Electrical Equipment Industries. *Journal of Industrial Economics* 48: 47–70.

Blundell, R., and S. R. Bond (2000). GMM Estimation with Persistent Panel Data: An Application to Production Functions. *Econometric Reviews* 19(3): 321–340.

Boldrin, M., and D. K. Levine (2004). The Case Against Intellectual Monopoly (2003 Lawrence R. Klein Lecture). *International Economic Review* 45: 327–350.

Boldrin M., and D. K. Levine (2005). *Against Intellectual Monopoly.* Cambridge, UK: Cambridge University Press.

Boldrin, M., and D. K. Levine (2013). The Case against Patents. *Journal of Economic Perspectives* 27(1): 3–22.

Bolton, P., J. F. Brodley, and M. H. Riordan (1999). Predatory Pricing: Strategic Theory and Legal Policy. Tilburg, Netherlands: Tilburg University Center for Economic Research Discussion Paper No 1999–82. https://pure.uvt.nl/ws/portalfiles/portal/533021/82.pdf

Boskin, M. J., E. R. Dulberger, R. J. Gordon, Z. Griliches, and D. W. Jorgenson (1996). *Toward a More Accurate Measure of the Cost of Living.* Washington, DC: Final Report to the U.S. Senate Finance Committee from the Advisory Commission to Study I Consumer Price Index. https://www.ssa.gov/history/reports/boskinrpt.html

Bound, J., C. Cummins, Z. Griliches, B. H. Hall and A. B. Jaffe (1984). Who Does R&D and Who Patents? In Z. Griliches (ed.), *R&D, Patents, and Productivity*, pp. 21-54. Chicago, IL: University of Chicago Press.

Bradley W. A., and J. Kolev (2023). How Does Digital Piracy Affect Innovation? Evidence from Software Firms. *Research Policy* 52(3): article 104701.

Braga C. A. O., and C. Fink (1998). The Relationship Between Intellectual Property Rights and Foreign Direct Investment. *Duke Journal of Comparative and International Law* 9: 163–188.

Bramson R. S. (1981). Intellectual Property as Collateral: Patents, Trade Secrets, Trademarks and Copyrights. *The Business Lawyer* 36(4): 1567–1604.

Branstetter, L. G. (2004). Do Stronger Patents Induce More Local Innovation? *Journal of International Economic Law* 7(2): 359–370.

Branstetter, L. G., C. Chatterjee, and M. J. Higgins (2012). Starving (or Fattening) the Golden Goose? Generic Entry and the Incentives for Early-Stage Pharmaceutical Innovation. Unpublished Paper. https://repository.iimb.ac.in/handle/2074/14571

Branstetter, L. G., C. Chatterjee, and M. J. Higgins (2016). Regulation and Welfare: Evidence from Paragraph IV Generic Entry in the Pharmaceutical Industry. *RAND Journal of Economics* 47(4): 857–890.

Branstetter, L. G., R. Fisman, and C. F. Foley (2006). Do Stronger Intellectual Property Rights Increase International Technology Transfer? Empirical Evidence from U.S. Firm-Level Panel Data. *Quarterly Journal of Economics* 121(1): 321–349.

Bresnahan, T. F. (1986). Measuring the Spillovers from Technical Advance: Mainframe Computers in Financial Services. *American Economic Review* 76(4): 742–755.

Bresnahan, T. F., E. Brynjolfsson, and L. M. Hitt (2002). Information Technology, Workplace Organization, and the Demand for Skilled Labor: Firm-Level Evidence. *Quarterly Journal of Economics* 117(1): 339–376.

Bresnahan, T. F., S. Greenstein, and R. M. Henderson (2012). Schumpeterian Competition and Diseconomies of Scope: Illustrations from the Histories of Microsoft and IBM. In J. Lerner and S. Stern (eds.), *The Rate and Direction of Inventive Activity Revisited*, pp. 203–276. Chicago, IL: University of Chicago Press.

Bresnahan, T. F., and M. Trajtenberg (1995). General Purpose Technologies "Engines of Growth?" *Journal of Econometrics* 65: 83–108.

Brouwer, E. and A. Kleinknecht (1999). Innovative Output, and a Firm's Propensity to Patent. An Exploration of CIS micro data. *Research Policy* 28(6): 615–624.

Brunt, L., J. Lerner, and T. Nicholas (2012). Inducement Prizes and Innovation. *Journal of Industrial Economics* 60(4): 657–696.

Brynjolfsson, E., L. M. Hitt, and S. Yang (2002). Intangible Assets: Computers and Organizational Capital. *Brookings Papers on Economic Activity* 1: 137–199.

Brynjolfsson, E., and C. F. Kemerer. (1994, December). Network Externalities in Microcomputer Software: An Econometric Analysis of the Spreadsheet Market. *Management Science* 42: 1627–1647.

Brynjolfsson, E., D. Rock, and C. Syverson (2021). The Productivity J-Curve: How Intangibles Complement General Purpose Technologies. *American Economic Journal: Macroeconomics* 13(1): 333–372.

Buccafusco C., J. S. Masur, and M. P. KcKenna (2023). Competition and Congestion in Trademark Law. *Texas Law Review* 102(3): 437–494.

Burk, Dan L., and M. A. Lemley (2009). *The Patent Crisis and How the Courts Can Solve It.* Chicago, IL: University of Chicago Press.

Bush, V. (1945). *Science: The Endless Frontier.* Washington, DC: U.S. Government Printing Office. https://www.nsf.gov/about/history/nsf50/vbush1945.jsp

Busom, I., B. Corchuelo, and E. Martínez-Ros, (2014). Tax incentives... or subsidies for business R&D? *Small Business Economics* 43(3): 571–596.

Butler, T. L. (1982). Can a Computer Be an Author: Copyright Aspects of Artificial Intelligence. *Hastings Communications and Entertainment Law Journal* 4(4): 707–747.

Byrne, D. M. and S. D. Oliner, and D. E. Sichel (2013). *Is the Information Technology Revolution Over?* FEDS Working Paper No. 2013-36. Washington, DC: Federal Reserve Board of Governors. https://ssrn.com/abstract=2303780

Calabresi G., and D. A. Melamed (1972). Property Rules, Liability Rules, and Inalienability: One View of the Cathedral. *Harvard Law Review* 85(6): 1089–1128.

Calboli, I., and M. Senftleben (eds.) (2019). *The Protection of Non-Traditional Trademarks: Critical Perspectives.* Oxford, UK: Oxford University Press.

Campbell, J. Y., A. W. Lo, and A. C. MacKinlay (1997). *The Econometrics of Financial Markets.* Princeton, NJ: Princeton University Press.

Cassiman, B., and R. Veugelers (2002). R&D Cooperation and Spillovers: Some Empirical Evidence from Belgium. *American Economic Review* 92(4): 1169–1184.

Cassiman, B., R. Veugelers, and S. Arts (2018). Mind the Gap: Capturing Value from Basic Research through Combining Mobile Inventors and Partnerships. *Research Policy* 47(9): 1811–1824.

Chaudhuri, S., P. K. Goldberg, and P. Jia (2006). Estimating the Effects of Global Patent Protection in Pharmaceuticals: A Case Study of Quinolones in India. *American Economic Review* 96(5): 1477–1513.

Chen, Q. (2008). The Effect of Patent Laws on Invention Rates: Evidence from Cross-Country Panels. *Journal of Comparative Economics* 36(4): 694–704.

Chesbrough, H. (1999). Arrested DevelopmenlThe Experience of European Hard Disk Drive Firms in Comparison with US and Japanese Firms. *Journal of Evolutionary Economics* 9: 287–329.

Chesbrough, H. (2006). *Open Innovation: The New Imperative for Creating and Profiting from Technology*. Cambridge, MA: Harvard Business School Press.

Chesbrough, H., S. Kim, and A. Agogino (2014). Chez Panisse: Building an Open Innovation Ecosystem. *California Management Review* 56(4): 144–171.

Chiang, T. J. (2009): What is a patent troll and why are they bad? *PatentlyO*: March 6, 2009. https://patentlyo.com/patent/2009/03/what-is-a-troll-patent-and-why-are-they-bad.html

Chien, C. (2014). Startups and Patent Trolls. *Stanford Technology Law Review* 17: 461–506.

Chien, C., C. Helmers, and A. Spigarelli (2019). Inter Partes Review and the Design of Post-Grant Patent Reviews. *Berkeley Law Technology Journal* 33(3): 817–854.

Choi, J.P., and H. Gerlach (2012). A model of patent trolls. *International Economic Review* 59(4): 2075-2106.

Chow, D. (2012). Lessons from Pfizer's Disputes Over Its Viagra Trademark in China. *Maryland Journal of International* Law 27(1): 82–110.

Chung, S., K. Han, A. Animesh, and A. Pinsonneault (2015). Competitive Impacts of IT Innovation: An Empirical Analysis of Software Patents in the IT Industry. In *Proceedings of 2015 International Conference on Information Systems: Exploring the Information Frontier, 3011-3028.* Atlanta, GA: Association for Information Systems. DOI:10.1109/HICSS.2016.643

Cimoli, M., G. Dosi, K. E. Maskus, R. L. Okediji, J. H. Reichman, and J. E. Stiglitz (eds.) (2014). *Intellectual Property Rights: Legal and Economic Challenges for Development.* Oxford, UK: Oxford University Press.

Clark, D. (2011). *Patent Litigation in China.* Oxford, UK: Oxford University Press.

Clark, K. B., W. B. Chew, and T. Fujimoto (1987). Product Development in the World Auto Industry. *Brookings Papers on Economic Activity* 18(3): 729–781.

Cockburn, I. M., and R. Henderson (1994). Racing to Invest? The Dynamics of Competition in Ethical Drug Discovery. *Journal of Economics and Management Strategy* 3(3): 481–519.

Cockburn, I. M., and R. Henderson (2003). *Survey Results from the 2003 Intellectual Property Owners Association Survey on the Strategic Management of Intellectual Property.* https://ipo.org/wp-content/uploads/2013/04/survey_results_revised.pdf

Cockburn, I. M., J. O. Lanjouw, and M. Schankerman (2016). Patents and the Global Diffusion of New Drugs. *American Economic Review* 106(1): 136–164. http://dx.doi.org/10.1257/aer.20141482

Cockburn, I. M., and M. MacGarvie (2009). Patents, Thickets, and the Financing of Early-Stage Firms: Evidence from the Software Industry. *Journal Economics and Management Strategy* 18: 729–773.

Cockburn, I. M., and M. MacGarvie (2011). Entry and Patenting in the Software Industry. *Management Science* 57(5): 915–933.

Coe, D. T., and E. Helpman (1995). International R&D Spillovers. *European Economic Review* 39(5): 859–887.

Cohen, L., U. Gurun, and S. D. Kominers (2017). Empirical Evidence on the Behavior and Impact of Patent Trolls: A Survey. In D. Sokol (ed.), *Patent Assertion Entities and Competition Policy,* pp. 27–59. Cambridge, UK: Cambridge University Press.

Cohen, L., U. Gurun, and S. D. Kominers (2019). Patent Trolls: Evidence from Targeted Firms. *Management Science* 65(12): 5449–5956.

Cohen, W. M. (2010). Fifty Years of Empirical Studies of Innovative Activity and Performance. In B. H. Hall and N. Rosenberg, *Handbook of the Economics of Innovation*, Vol. 1, pp. 129–213. Amsterdam, Netherlands: North-Holland, Elsevier.

Cohen, W. M, and S. Klepper (1996). Firm Size and the Nature of Innovation within Industries: The Case of Process and Product R&D. *Review of Economics and Statistics* 78(2): 232–243.

Cohen, W. M., and D. A. Levinthal (1989). Innovation and Learning: The Two Faces of R&D. *Economic Journal* 99: 569–596.

Cohen, W. M., R. R. Nelson, and J. P. Walsh (2000). Protecting Their Intellectual Assets: Appropriability Conditions and Why U.S. Manufacturing Firms Patent (or Not). Cambridge, MA: National Bureau of Economic Research Working Paper Series No. 7552.

Cohen, W. M., R. R. Nelson, and J. P. Walsh (2002). Links and Impacts: The Influence of Public Research on industrial R&D. *Management Science* 48(1): 1–23.

Cohen, L. R., and R. G. Noll (1991). *The Technology Pork Barrel*. Washington, DC: Brookings Institution.

Conner, K. R., and R. P. Rumelt (1991). Software Piracy: An Analysis of Protection Strategies. *Management Science* 37: 125–139.

Contagiani, A., D. H. Hsu, and I. Barankay (2018). Trade Secrets and Innovation: Evidence from the "Inevitable Disclosure" Doctrine. *Strategic Management Journal* 39: 2921–2942.

Conti, R. (2014). Do Non-Competition Agreements Lead Firms to Pursue Risky R&D Projects? *Strategic Management Journal* 35: 1230–1248.

Contreras, J. (2023). Patent Pledges as Portfolio Management Tools: Benefits, Obligations and Enforcement. In K. Blind and N. Thumm (eds.), *A Modern Guide to Patenting. Challenges of Patenting in the 21st Century*. Cheltenham, UK: Edward Elgar.

Contreras, J., B. H. Hall, and C. Helmers (2019). Pledging Patents for the Public Good: Rise and Fall of the Eco-Patent Commons. *Houston Law Review* 57 (1): 61–109.

Cooter, R. D., and D. L. Rubinfeld (1989). Economic Analysis of Legal Disputes and Their Resolution. *Journal of Economic Literature* 27: 1067–1097.

Corrado, C., J. Haskel, C. Jona-Lasinio, and B. Nasim (2015). Is International R&D Tax Competition a Zero-Sum Game? Evidence from the EU. Paper presented at 2015 National Bureau of Economic Research Conference. https://conference.nber.org/confer/2015/SI2015/PRCR/Corrado_Haskel_Jona-Lasinio_Nasim.pdf

Corrado, C., J. Haskel, J. Miranda, and D. Sichel (eds., 2021). *Measuring and Accounting for Innovation in the Twenty-First Century*. Chicago, IL: University of Chicago Press.

Corrigan R., and M. Rogers (2005). The Economics of Copyright. *World Economics* 6(3): 153–174.

Cotropia, C. A., and M. A. Lemley (2009). Copying in Patent Law. *North Carolina Law Review* 87(5): 1421–1466.

Cotter, T. F., and J. M. Golden (2019). Empirical studies relating to patents—Remedies. In P. Menell, D. Schwartz, and B. Depoorter (eds.), *Research handbook on the economics of intellectual property law*, pp. 390–421. Cheltenham, UK: Edward Elgar.

Cremers, K., M. Ernicke, F. Gaessler, D. Harhoff, C. Helmers, L. McDonagh, P. Schliessler, and N. Van Zeebroeck (2016a). Patent Litigation in Europe. *European Journal of Law and Economics* 44(1): 1–44.

Cremers, K., F. Gaessler, D. Harhoff, C. Helmers, and Y. Lefouili (2016b). Invalid but Infringed? An Analysis of the Bifurcated Patent Litigation System. *Journal of Economic Behavior and Organization* 131: 218–242.

Cunningham, C., F. Ederer, and S. Ma (2020). Killer Acquisitions. *Journal of Political Economy* 129(3): 649–702.

Cunningham, E. (2009). Protecting Cuisine under the Rubric of Intellectual Property Law: Should the Law Play a Bigger Role in the Kitchen. *Journal of High Technology Law* 9: 21–51.

Curtin, G. V., Jr. (1992). The Basics of ASICs: Protection for Semiconductor Mask Works in Japan and the United States Comments. *Boston College International and Comparative Law Review* 15(1): 113–140.

Czarnitzki, D., B. H. Hall, and R. Oriani (2006). Market Valuation of US and European Intellectual Property. In D. Bosworth and E. Webster (eds.), *The Management of Intellectual Property*, pp. 111–131. Cheltenham, UK: Edward Elgar.

Danzon, P., A. Mulcahy, and A. Towse (2015). Pharmaceutical Pricing in Emerging Markets: Effects of Income, Competition, and Procurement. *Health Economics* 24: 238–252.

Dasgupta, P., and P. A. David (1994). Toward a New Economics of Science. *Research Policy* 23(5): 487–521.

Dasgupta, P., and J. E. Stiglitz (1980). Industrial Structure and the Nature of Innovative Activity. *Economic Journal* 90: 226–293.

Datta, Hannes, George Knox, and Bart J. Bronnenberg (2018). Changing Their Tune. How Consumers' Adoption of Online Streaming Affects Music Consumption and Discovery. *Marketing Science* 37(1): 5–21.

David, P. A. (1985). Clio and the Economics of QWERTY. *American Economic Review* 75(2): 332–337.

David, P. A. (1990). The Dynamo and the Computer: An Historical Perspective on the Modern Productivity Paradox. *American Economic Review* 80: 355–361.

David, P. A. (1994). The Evolution of Intellectual Property Institutions. In A. Aganbegyan, O. Bogomolov, and M. Kaser (eds.)., *Economics in a Changing World*, Vol. 1: System Transformation: Eastern and Western Assessments. London: Macmillan. https://www.merit.unu.edu/publications/rmpdf/1993/rm1993–009.pdf

David, P. A. (1998). Common Agency Contracting and the Emergence of "Open Science" Institutions. *American Economic Review* 88(2): 15–21.

David, P. A. (2003). The Economic Logic of "Open Science" and the Balance between Private Property Rights and the Public Domain in Scientific Data and Information: A Primer. In J. M. Esanu and P. F. Uhlir (eds.), *The Role of Scientific and Technical Data and Information in the Public Domain: Proceedings of a Symposium*, Chapter 4. Washington, DC: National Academies Press.

David, P. A. (2008). The Historical Origins of "Open Science": An Essay on Patronage, Reputation and Common Agency Contracting in the Scientific Revolution. *Capitalism and Society* 3(2). https://doi.org/10.2202/1932–0213.1040

David, P. A., and S. Greenstein (1990). The Economics of Compatibility of Standards: An Introduction to Recent Research. *Economics of Innovation and New Technology* 1(1): 3–41.

David, P. A., D. C. Mowery, and W. E. Steinmueller (1992). Analyzing the Economic Payoffs from Basic Research. *Economics of Innovation and New Technology* 2: 73–90.

Davis J. L., and S. S. Harrison (2001). *Edison in the Boardroom: How Leading Companies Realize Value from Their Intellectual Assets*. Hoboken, NJ: John Wiley & Sons.

De Alessie, L., and R. J. Staaf (1994). What Does Reputation Really Assure? The Relationship of Trademarks to Expectations and Legal Remedies. *Economic Inquiry* 32(3): 477–485.

De Marco, A., G. Scellato, E. Ughetto, and F. Caviggioli (2017). Global Markets for Technology: Evidence from Patent Transactions. *Research Policy* 46: 1644–1654.

Delgado, M., M. Kyle, and A. M. McGahan (2013). Intellectual Property Protection and the Geography of Trade. *Journal of Industrial Economics* 61(3): 733–762.

Deng, Z., B. Lev, and F. Narin (1999). Science and Technology as Predictors of Stock Performance. *Financial Analysts Journal* 55: 20–32. https://doi.org/10.2469/faj.v55.n3.2269

Denison, E. F. (1972). Final Comments, *Survey of Current Business* 52(5): Part 2, 95–110.

Denison, E. F. (1969). Some Major Issues in Productivity Analysis: An Examination of Estimates by Jorgenson and Griliches. *Survey of Current Business* 49(5): Part 2, 1-27.

Dernis, H., M. Dosso, F. Hervas Soriano, V. Millot, M. Squicciarini, and A. Vezzani (2015). World Corporate Top R&D Investors: Innovation and IP Bundles. Luxembourg: Publications Office of the European Union EU Report 27129/JRC Report 94932.

DeSoucey, M. (2010). Gastronationalism: Food Traditions and Authenticity Politics in the European Union. *American Sociological Review* 75(3): 432-455. https://doi.org/10.1177/0003122410372226.

Dhar, B., and K. M. Gopakumar (2006). *Post-2005 TRIPS Scenario in Patent Protection in the Pharmaceutical Sector: The Case of the Generic Pharmaceutical Industry in India.* United Nations Conference on Trade and Development/International Centre on Trade and Sustainable Development Report. https://unctad.org/system/files/official-document/ictsd-idrc2006d2_en.pdf.

Diamond, S. A. (1983). The Historical Development of Trademarks. *Trademark Reporter* 73: 222–247.

DiMasi, J. A., H. G. Grabowski, and R. W. Hansen (2016). Innovation in the Pharmaceutical Industry, New Estimates of R&D Costs. *Journal of Health Economics* 47: 20–33.

Dimos, C., G. Pugh, M. Hisarciklilar, E. Talam, and I. Jackson (2022). The Relative Effectiveness of R&D Tax Credits and R&D Subsidies: A Comparative Meta-Regression Analysis. *Technovation* 115: article 102450.

Dinlersoz, E., N. Goldschlag, A. Myers, and N. Zolas (2018). An Anatomy of U.S. Firms Seeking Trademark Registration. Washington, DC: U.S. Patent and Trademark Office Economic Working Paper No. 2018-02.

Dixit A. K., and R. S. Pindyck (1994). *Investment under Uncertainty.* Princeton, NJ: Princeton University Press.

Dosi, G. (1982). Technological Paradigms and Technological Trajectories: A Suggested Interpretation of the Determinants and Directions of Technical Change. *Research Policy* 11(3): 147–162.

Duggan, M., C. Garthwaite, and A. Goyal (2016). The Market Impacts of Pharmaceutical Product Patents in Developing Countries: Evidence from India. *American Economic Review* 106(1): 99–135.

Eberhardt, M., C. Helmers, and H. Strauss (2013). Do Spillovers Matter When Estimating Private Returns to R&D? *Review of Economics and Statistics* 95(2): 436–448.

Economides, N. S. (1998). The Economics of Trademarks. *Trademark Reporter* 78: 523–539.

Economides, N. S., and C. Himmelberg (1995, August). Critical Mass and Network Size with Application to the U.S. Fax Market. New York: New York University, Salomon Brothers Working Paper S/95/26. http://www.SSRN.com

Edlin, A., C. S. Hemphill, H. J. Hovenkamp, and C. Shapiro (2015). The Actavis Inference: Theory and Practice. *Rutgers University Law Review* 67(3): 585–635.

Einiö, E., J. Feng, and X. Jaravel (2019). Social Push and the Direction of Innovation. https://ssrn.com/abstract=3383703 or http://dx.doi.org/10.2139/ssrn.3383703

Eisner, R., S. H. Albert, and M. A. Sullivan (1984). The New Incremental Tax Credit for R&D: Incentive or Disincentive. *National Tax Journal* 37: 171–183.

Epstein, R., and K. B. Noroozi (2017). Why Incentives for "Patent Holdout" Threaten to Dismantle FRAND, and Why It Matters. *Berkeley Technology Law Journal* 32(4): 1381–1431.

Ernst, H., J. Conley, and N. Omland (2016). How to create commercial value from patents: the role of patent management. *R&D Management* 46: 677–690.

European Patent Office (2024). How to apply for a patent. https://www.epo.org/en/new-to-patents/how-to-apply-for-a-patent

European Union Commission (2009). *Pharmaceutical Sector Inquiry: Final Report.* https://ec.europa.eu/competition/sectors/pharmaceuticals/inquiry/staff_working_paper_part1.pdf

Ewing, T. (2012). Indirect Exploitation of Intellectual Property Rights by Corporations and Investors: IP Privateering and Modern Letters of Marque and Reprisal. *Hastings Science and Technology Law Journal* 4(1): 1–108.

Ewing, T., and R. Feldman (2012). The Giants Among Us. *Stanford Technology Law Review* 8(1): 1–61.

Fagerberg, J., D. C. Mowery, and R. R. Nelson (2004). *Oxford Handbook of Innovation.* Oxford, UK: Oxford University Press.

Farley, C. H., and I. Calboli (2016). The Trademark Provisions in the TRIPS Agreement. In C. M. Correa (ed.), *Intellectual Property and International Trade: TRIPS Agreement* (3rd ed.). Alphen aan den Rijn, Netherlands: Wolters Kluwer. https://ssrn.com/abstract=3471430

Farrell, J. (2008). Intellectual Property as a Bargaining Environment, in J. Lerner and S. Stern, (eds.), Innovation Policy and the Economy 9: 39–53. Chicago, IL: University of Chicago Press.

Farrell, J., and R. P. Merges (2014). Incentives to Challenge and Defend Patents: Why Litigation Won't Reliably Fix Patent Office Errors and Why Administrative Patent Review Might Help. *Berkeley Technology Law Journal* 19: 943–970.

Fauchart, E., and E. von Hippel (2008). Norms-Based Intellectual Property Systems: The Case of French Chefs. *Organization Science* 19(2): 187–201.

Feenstra, R. C., R. Inklaar, and M. P. Timmer (2015). The Next Generation of the Penn World Table. *American Economic Review* 105(10): 3150–3182. www.ggdc.net/pwt

Feldman, M. P., and D. F. Kogler (2010). Stylized Facts in the Geography of Innovation. In B. H. Hall and N. Rosenberg (eds.), *Handbook of the Economics of Innovation*, Vol. 1, Chapter 8, pp. 381–410. Amsterdam, Netherlands, and New York: Elsevier.

Feldman, R., and M. A. Lemley (2015). Do Patent Licensing Demands Mean Innovation. *Iowa Law Review* 101: 137–189

Feng, J., and X. Jaravel (2020). Crafting Intellectual Property Rights: Implications for Patent Assertion Entities, Litigation, and Innovation. *American Economic Journal: Applied Economics* 12(1): 140–181.

Feynman, R. P. (1985). *Surely You're Joking, Mr. Feynman! (Adventures of a Curious Character)*. New York: W.W. Norton.

Figueroa, N., and C. Serrano (2019). Patent Trading Flows of Small and Large Firms. *Research Policy* 48: 1601–1616.

Filitz, R., J. Henkel, and B. S. Tether (2015). Protecting Aesthetic Innovations? An Exploration of the Use of Registered Community Designs. *Research Policy* 44: 1192–1206.

Fink, C., A. Fosfuri, C. Helmers, and A. Myers (2022). Submarine Trademarks. *Journal of Economics & Management Strategy* 31(4): 818–840.

Fink, C., B. H. Hall, and C. Helmers (2021). Intellectual Property Use and Firm Performance: The Case of Chile. *Economic Development and Cultural Change* 70(1): 321–357.

Fink, C., C. Helmers, and C. Ponce (2018). Trademark Squatters: Theory and Evidence from Chile. *International Journal of Industrial Organization* 59: 340–371.

Fink, C., M. Khan, and H. Zhou (2016). Exploring the Worldwide Patent Surge. *Economics of Innovation and New Technology* 25(2): 114–142.

Fink, C., and K. E. Maskus (2005). *Intellectual Property and Development: Lessons from Recent Economic Research*. Washington, DC: World Bank.

Fischmann, F. (2015). Patent Litigation and Cost Shifting in Europe. *Journal of Intellectual Property Law and Practice* 10(2): 98–108.

Fischer, T., and J. Henkel (2012). Patent Trolls on Markets for Technology: An Empirical Analysis of NPE Patent Acquisitions. *Research Policy* 41: 1519–1533.

Fisher, F. M., and P. Temin (1973). Returns to Scale in Research and Development: What Does the Schumpeterian Hypothesis Imply? *Journal of Political Economy* 81(1): 56–70.

Fisher, F. M., and P. Temin (1979). The Schumpeterian Hypothesis: Reply. *Journal of Political Economy* 87(2): 386–389.

Fisher III, W., and F. Oberholzer-Gee (2013). Strategic Management of Intellectual Property: An Integrated Approach. *California Management Review* 55(4): 157–183.

Flamm, K. (2021). Measuring Moore's Law: Evidence, from Price, Cost, and Quality Indices. In Corrado, C., J. Haskel, J. Miranda, and D. Sichel (eds.), *Measuring and Accounting for Innovation in the Twenty-First Century*, pp. 403–470. NBER Conference Volume. Chicago, IL: University of Chicago Press.

Flamm, K. S. (1995). In Defense of the Flat-Panel Display Initiative. *Issues in Science and Technology* 11(3): 22–25.

Foray, D., and L. Hilaire Perez (2006). The Economics of Open Technology: Collective Organization and Individual Claims in the "Fabrique Lyonnaise" during the Old Regime. In C. Antonelli, D. Foray, B. H. Hall, and W. E. Steinmueller (eds.), *New Frontiers in the Economics of Innovation and New Technology: Essays in Honour of Paul A. David*, pp. 239–254. Cheltenham, UK, and Northampton, MA: Edward Elgar.

Forman, C., and N. van Zeebroeck (2019). Digital Technology Adoption and Knowledge Flows within Firms: Can the Internet Overcome Geographic and Technological Distance? *Research Policy* 48(8): article 103697.

Forsyth, C., and J. Watts (2011). *A Guide to Patent Litigation in England and Wales.* London, UK: Freshfields Bruckhaus Deringer LLP. http://www.lexology.com/library/detail.aspx?g=6bd0f5bc-df2c-4578-8102-02c6d3c9946f

Fosfuri, A. (2006). The Licensing Dilemma: Understanding the Determinants of the Rate of Technology Licensing. *Strategic Management Journal* 27: 1141–1158.

Fosfuri, A., M. S. Giarratana, and A. Luzzi (2008). The Penguin Has Entered the Building: The Commercialization of Open Source Software Products. *Organization Science* 19(2): 292–305.

Fosfuri, A., C. Helmers, and C. Roux (2017). Shared Ownership of Intangible Property Rights: The Case of Patent Co-assignments. *Journal of Legal Studies* 46: 339–369.

Frakes M. D., and M. F. Wasserman (2017). Is the Time Allocated to Review Patent Applications Inducing Examiners to Grant Invalid Patents? Evidence from Microlevel Application Data. *Review of Economics and Statistics* 99(3): 550–563.

Frakes M. D., and M. F. Wasserman (2023). Investing in Ex Ante Regulation: Evidence from Pharmaceutical Patent Examination. *American Economic Journal: Economic Policy* 15(3): 151–183.

Franke, N., and S. Shah (2003). How Communities Support Innovative Activities: An Exploration of Assistance and Sharing among End-Users. *Research Policy* 32(1): 157–178.

Freeman, C. (1995). The "National System of Innovation" in Historical Perspective. *Cambridge Journal of Economics* 19(1): 5–24.

Friedman, D. D., W. M. Landes, and R. A. Posner (1991). Some Economics of Trade Secret Law. *Journal of Economic Perspectives* 5(1): 61–72.

Fromer, J. (2011). Trade Secrecy in *Willy Wonka's Chocolate Factory*. In R. C. Dreyfuss and K. J. Strandburg (eds.), *The Law and Theory of Trade Secrecy: A Handbook of Contemporary Research.* Cheltenham, UK: Edward Elgar;

Furman, J., and R. Seamans (2018). AI and the Economy. *Innovation Policy and the Economy* 19: 161–191.

Furman, J. L., and M. MacGarvie (2009). Academic Collaboration and Organizational InnovIn: The Development of Research Capabilities in the US Pharmaceutical Industry, 1927–1946. *Industrial and Corporate Change* 18(5): 929–961.

Furman, J. L., M. E. Porter, and S. Stern (2002). The Determinants of National Innovative Capacity. *Research Policy* 31: 899–933.

Gabble, R., and J. C. Kohler (2014). To otent or Not tIatent? The Case of Novartis' Cancer Drug Glivec in India. *Global* Health 10(3). https://doi.org/10.1186/1744-8603-10-3

Gaessler, F., B. H. Hall, and D. Harhoff (2021). Should There Be Lower Taxes on Patent Income? *Research Policy* 50(1): article 104129.

Galasso, A., M. Mitchell, and G. Virag (2018). A Theory of Grand Innovation Prizes. *Research Policy* 47: 343–362.

Galasso, A., and M. Schankerman (2022). Licensing Life-Saving Drugs for Developing Countries: Evidence from the Medicines Patent Pool. *Review of Economics and* Statistics. https://doi.org/10.1162/rest_a_01253

Galetovic, A., and K. Gupta (2020). The Case of the Missing Royalty Stacking in the World Mobile Wireless Industry. *Industrial and Corporate Change* 29(3): 827–853.

Gallini, N. T. (1984). Deterrence by Market Sharing: A Strategic Incentive for Licensing, *American Economic Review* 74(5): 931–941.

Gambardella, A., P. Giuri, and A. Luzzi (2007). The Market for Patents in Europe. *Research Policy* 36: 1163–1183.

Gambardella, A., and B. H. Hall (2006). Proprietary Versus Public Domain Licensing of Software and Research Products. *Research Policy* 35(6): 875–892.

Gambardella, A., D. Harhoff, and S. Nagaoka (2011). The Social Value of Patent Disclosure. Unpublished manusctipt. Munich, Germany: Ludwig Maximilian University of Munich.

Gambardella, A., D. Harhoff, and B. Verspagen (2008). The Value of European Patents. *European Management Review* 5: 69–84.

Gandal, N. (1994). Hedonic Price Indexes for Spreadsheets and an Empirical Test for Network Externalities. *RAND Journal of Economics* 25(1): 160–170.

Gandal, N. (1995). Competing Compatibility Standards and Network Externalities in the PC Software Market. *Review of Economics and Statistics* 67(4): 599–608.

Gandal, N., M. Kende, and R. Rob. (2000). The Dynamics of Technological Adoption in Hardware/Software Systems: The Case of Compact Disc Players. *RAND Journal of Economics* 31: 43–61.

Ganglmair, B., and I. Reimers (2019). Visibility of Technology and Cumulative Innovation: Evidence from Trade Secrets Laws. Mannheim, Germany: University of Mannheim CRC TR 224 Discussion Paper No. 119.

Ganglmair, B., W. K. Robinson, and M. Seeligson (2022). The Rise of Process Claims: Evidence from a Century of U.S. Patents. https://ssrn.com/abstract=4069994 or http://dx.doi.org/10.2139/ssrn.4069994

Gans, J. S., and S. Stern (2010). Is There a Market for Ideas? *Industrial and Corporate Change* 19(3): 805–837.

Gilbert, D., T. Walley, and B. New (2000, November 25). Lifestyle Medicines. *British Medical Journal* 321: 1341–1344. doi: 10.1136/bmj.321.7272.1341

Gilbert, R. J. (2004). Antitrust for Patent Pools: A Century of Policy Evolution. *Stanford Technology Law Review* 3: 3–31.

Gilbert, R. J. (2006). Looking for Mr. Schumpeter: Where Are We in the Competition-Innovation Debate? *Innovation Policy and the Economy* 6: 159–215.

Gilbert, R. J. (2022). *Innovation Matters: Competition Policy for the High-Technology Economy.* Cambridge, MA: MIT Press.

Gilbert, R. J., and D. M. G. Newberry (1982). Preemptive Patenting and the Persistence of Monopoly. *American Economic Review* 72(3): 514–526.

Gilson, R. J. (1999). The Legal Infrastructure of High Technology Industrial Districts: Silicon Valley, Route 128, and Covenants Not to Compete. *New York University Law Review* 74(3): 575–629.

Ginarte, J. C., and W. G. Park (1997). Determinants of Patent Rights: A Cross-National Study. *Research Policy* 26(3): 283–301.

Ginsburg J. C., and I. Calboli (2020). Overlapping Copyright and Trademark Protection in the United States. In I. Calboli and J. C. Ginsburg (eds.), *The Cambridge Handbook of International and Comparative Trademark Law*, Cambridge Law Handbooks. Cambridge, UK: Cambridge University Press.

Giorcelli M., and P. Moser (2020). Copyrights and Creativity: Evidence from Italian Opera in the Napoleonic Age. *Journal of Political Economy* 128(11): 4163–4210.

Giuri P., M. Mariani, S. Brusoni, G. Crespi, D. Francoz, A. Gambardella, W. Garcia-Fontes, A. Geuna, R. Gonzales, D. Harhoff, Hoisl, K., C. Le Bas, A. Luzzi, L. Magazzini, L. Nesta, O. Nomaler, N. Palomeras, P. Patel, M. Romanelli, and B. Verspagen (2007). Inventors and Invention Processes in Europe: Results from the PatVal-EU Survey. *Research Policy* 36: 1107–1127.

Goettler, R. L., and B. R. Gordon (2011). Does AMD Spur Intel to Innovate More? *Journal of Political Economy* 119(6); 1141–1200.

Gold, E. R., Morin, J.-F., and Shadeed, E. (2019). Does Intellectual Property Lead to Economic Growth? Insights from a Novel IP Dataset. *Regulation & Governance* 13: 107–124. doi: 10.1111/rego.12165

Goldberg, P. K. (2010). Intellectual Property Rights Protection in Developing Countries: The Case of Pharmaceuticals. *Journal of the European Economic Association* 8(2–3): 326–353.

Gompers, P., and J. Lerner (2001). The Venture Capital Revolution. *Journal of Economic Perspectives* 15(2): 145–168.

Goolsbee, A. (1998). Does Government R&D Policy Mainly Benefit Scientists and Engineers? *American Economic Review* 88(2): 298–302.

Goolsbee, A., and B. F. Jones (eds., 2021). *Innovation and Public Policy*. National Bureau of Economic Research Conference Volume. Chicago, IL: University of Chicago Press.

Gordon, R. J. (1999). The Boskin Commission Report and Its Aftermath. *Monetary and Economic Studies* 17(3): 41–68.

Gotsch, M., and C. Hipp (2012). Measurement of Innovation Activities in the Knowledge Intensive Services Industry: A Trademark Approach. *Service Industries Journal* 32(13): 2167–2184.

Grabowksi, H., C. Brain, A. Taub, and R. Guha (2017). Pharmaceutical Patent Challenges: Company Strategies and Litigation Outcomes. *American Journal of Health Economics* 3(1): 33–59.

Graham, S. J. H. (2004). Hiding in the Patent's Shadow: Firms' Uses of Secrecy to Capture Value from New Discoveries. Atlanta, GA: Technology Innovation: Generating Economic Results Faculty Working Paper. http://hdl.handle.net/1853/10725

Graham, S. J. H., A. C. Marco, and R. Miller (2017). Assessing the Representativeness of Published US Patent Records: A Research Guide. Atlanta, GA: Georgia Tech Scheller College of Business Research Paper No. 18-13. https://papers.ssrn.com/sol3/papers.cfm?abstract_id=2633710

Graham, S. J. H., and D. Hegde (2015). Disclosing Patents' Secrets. *Science* 347(6219): 236–237.

Graham, S. J. H.. and D. C. Mowery (2003). Intellectual Property Protection in the Software Industry. In W. Cohen and S. Merrill (eds.), *Patents in the Knowledge-Based Economy: Proceedings of the Science, Technology and Economic Policy Board*. Washington, DC: National Academies Press.

Graham, S. J. H., and S. Vishnubhakat (2013). Of Smart Phone Wars and Software Patents. *Journal of Economic Perspectives* 27(1): 67–86.

von Graevenitz, G., S. Wagner, and D. Harhoff (2011). How to Measure Patent Thickets: A Novel Approach. *Economics Letters* 111: 6–9.

von Graevenitz, G., S. Wagner, and D. Harhoff (2013). Incidence and Growth of PatelThickets: The Impact of Technological Opportunities and Complexity. *Journal of Industrial Economics* 61(3): 521–563.

Granstrand, O. (1999). Strategic Management of Intellectual Property. Göteborg, Sweden: Chalmers University of Technology CIM Working Paper 1999:01.

Green, J., and S. Scotchmer (1995). On the Division of Profit in Sequential Innovation. *RAND Journal of Economics* 26: 20–33.

Greene, W. H. (2008). *Econom^{et}ric Analysis* (6th ed.). Upper Saddle River, NJ: Pearson Prentice Hall.

Greenhalgh C., and M. Rogers (2006). The Value of Innovation: The Interaction of Competition, R&D, and IP. Research Policy 35: 562–580.

Greenhalgh, C., and M. Rogers (2006). The value of innovation: The interaction of competition, R&D, and IP. *Research Policy* 35(4): 562-580.

Greenhalgh, C., and M. Rogers (2010). *Innovation, Intellectual Property, and Economic Growth*. Princeton, NJ: Princeton University Press.

Greenstein, S. (2015). *How the Internet Became Commercial: Innovation, Privatization, and the Birth of a New Network*. The Kauffman Foundation Series on Innovation and Entrepreneurship. Princeton, NJ: Princeton University Press.

Greenstein, S. M. (1993). Did Installed Base Give an Incumbent Any (Measurable Advantages in Federal Computer Procurement? *RAND Journal of Economics* 24(1): 19–39.

Griffith, R., S. Redding, and J. Van Reenen (2001). Measuring the Cost-Effectiveness of an R&D Tax Credit for the UK. *Fiscal Studies* 22(3): 375–399.

Griliches, Z. (1957). Hybrid Corn: An Exploration in the Economics of Technological Change. *Econometrica* 25(4): 501–522.

Griliches, Z. (1958). Research Costs and Social Returns: Hybrid Corn and Related Innovations. *Journal of Political Economy* 76: 419–431.

Griliches, Z. (1961). Hedonic Price Indexes for uAtomobiles: An Econometric Analysis of Quality Change. In *The Price Statistics of the Federal Government*, pp. 173–196. Report of the Price Statistics Review Committee. Cambridge, MA: National Bureau of Economic Research.

Griliches, Z. (1979). Issues in Assessing the Contribution of R&D to Productivity Growth. *Bell Journal of Economics* 10(1): 92–116.

Griliches, Z. (1980). Returns to Research and Development Expenditures in the Private Sector. In J. W. Kendrick and B. N. Vaccara (eds.), *New Developments in Productivity Measurement and Analysis*, pp. 419–462. Chicago, IL: University of Chicago Press9.

Griliches, Z. (1981). Market Value, R&D, and Patents. *Economic Letters* 7: 183–187.

Griliches, Z. (1990). Patent Statistics as Economic Indicators: A Survey. *Journal of Economic Literature* 28: 1661–1707.

Griliches, Z. (1992). The Search for R&D Spillovers. *Scandinavian Journal of Economics* 94(Suppl.): S29–S47.

Griliches, Z. (1994). Productivity, R&D and the Data Constraint. *American Economic Review* 84(1): 1–23.

Griliches, Z. (2000). The Role of Education and Human Capital. In *R&D, Education, and Productivity*, Chapter 3. Cambridge, MA: Harvard University Press.

Griliches, Z., and J. Mairesse (1984). Productivity and R&D at the Firm Level. In Z. Griliches. (ed.), *R&D, Patents, and Productivity*, pp. 339–374. Chicago, IL: University of Chicago Press.

Griliches, Z., A. Pakes, and B. H. Hall (1987). The Value of Patents as Indicators of Inventive Activity. In P. Dasgupta and P. Stoneman (eds.), *Economic Policy and Technological Performance*, pp. 97–124. Cambridge, UK: Cambridge University Press.

Gross, D. P., and B. N. Sampat (2020, rev. 2023). America, Jump-Started: World War II R&D and the Takeoff of the U.S. Innovation System. Cambridge, MA: National Bureau of Economic Research Working Paper Series No. 27375.

Grossman, G. M., and E. Helpman (1991). Quality Ladders in the Theory of Growth. *Review of Economic Studies* 58(1): 43–61.Grossman, G. M., and E. Helpman (1994). Endogenous Innovation in the Theory of Growth. *Journal of Economic Perspectives* 8(1): 23–44.

Grossman, G.M., and E.L.-C. Lai (2004). International Protection of Intellectual Property. *American Economic Review* 94(5): 1635–1653.

Grossman, G. M., and E.L.-C. Lai (2006). International Protection of Intellectual Property: Corrigendum. *American Economic Review* 96(1): 456–456.

Grove, A. S. (1988). *Only the Paranoid Survive: How to Exploit the Crisis Points That Challenge Every Company.* New York: Doubleday.

Guellec, D., and B. Van Pottelsberghe De La Potterie (2003). The Impact of Public R&D Expenditure on Business R&D. *Economics of Innovation and New Technology* 12(3): 225–243.

Guellec, D., and B. Van Pottelsberghe de la Potterie (2004). From R&D to Productivity Growth: Do the Institutional Settings and the Source of Funds of R&D Matter? *Oxford Bulletin of Economics and Statistics* 66(3): 353–378.

Guellec, D., and B. Van Pottelsberghe De La Potterie (2007). *The Economics of the European Patent System IP Policy for Innovation and Competition.* Oxford, UK, Oxford University Press.

Guzman, J., and S. Stern (2017). Nowcasting and Placecasting Entrepreneurial Quality and Performance. In J. Haltiwanger, E. Hurst, J. Miranda, and A. Schoar (eds.), *Measuring Entrepreneurial Businesses: Current Knowledge and Challenges*, pp. 63–109. National Bureau of Economic Research Conference Volume. Chicago: University of Chicago Press.

Gwartney, J., R. A. Lawson, and D. Samida (2000). *Economic Freedom of the World: 2000 Annual Report.* Vancouver, BC: Fraser Institute.

Hagedoorn, J. (2003). Sharing intellectual property rights - an exploratory study of joint patenting amongst companies. Industrial and Corporate Change 12 (5): 1035–1050.

Hagiu, A., and D. B. Yoffie (2013). The New Patent Intermediaries: Platforms, Defensive Aggregators, and Super-Aggregators. *Journal of Economic Perspectives* 27(1): 45–66.

Halkos, G. E., and N. G. Tzeremes (2013). Modelling the Effect of National Culture on Countries' Innovation Performances: A Conditional Full Frontier Approach. *International Review of Applied Economics* 27(5): 656–678. 10.1080/02692171.2013.778819

Hall A. M. (2016). Standing the Test of Time. Likelihood of Confusion in Multi Time Machine v. Amazon. *Berkeley Technology Law Journal* 31: 815–850.

Hall, B. H. (1993). R&D Tax Policy During the Eighties: Success or Failure? *Tax Policy and the Economy* 7: 1–36.

Hall, B. H. (2000). Innovation and Market Value. In R. Barrell, G. Mason and M. O'Mahoney (eds.), *Productivity, Innovation, and Economic Performance*, pp. 177–198. Cambridge, UK: Cambridge University Press.

Hall, B. H. (2004). Innovation and Diffusion. In J. Fagerberg, D. Mowery, and R. R. Nelson (eds.), *Handbook of Innovation*, pp. 459–485. Oxford, UK: Oxford University Press.

Hall, B. H. (2005). Exploring the Patent Explosion. *Journal of Technology Transfer* 30: 35–48.

Hall, B. H. (2005). Measuring thIturns to R&D: The Depreciation Problem. *Annales d'Economie et de Statistique* 79–80: 341–381.

Hall, B. H. (2009). Business and Financial Method Patents, Innovation, and Policy. *Scottish Journal of Political Economy* 56(4): 443–473.

Hall, B. H. (2014). Does Patent Protection Help or Hinder Technology Transfer? In S. Ahn, B. H. Hall, and K. Lee (eds.), *Intellectual Property for Economic Development*, pp. 11–32. KDI Series in Economic Policy and Development. Cheltenham, UK: Edward Elgar and KDI.

Hall, B. H. (2019). Is There a Role for Patents in the Financing of New Innovative Firms? *Industrial and Corporate Change* 28(3): 657–680.

Hall, B. H. (2021). Tax Policy for Innovation. In A. Goolsbee and B. F. Jones (eds.), *Innovation and Public Policy*, pp. 151–188. National Bureau of Economic Research Conference Volume. Chicago, IL: University of Chicago Press.

Hall, B. H. (2022). Patents, Innovation, and Development. *International Review of Applied Economics, published online.* https://doi.org/10.1080/02692171.2021.2022295

Hall, B. H., G. von Graevenitz, and C. Helmers (2021). Technology Entry in the Presence of Patent Thickets. *Oxford Economic Papers* 73(2): 903–926.

Hall, B. H., Z. Griliches, and J. A. Hausman (1986). Patents and R and D: Is There a Lag? *International Economic Review* 27(2): 265–283.

Hall B. H., and D. Harhoff (2004). Post-Grant Reviews in the US Patent System: Design Choices and Expected Impact. *Berkeley Technology Law Journal* 19(3): 989–991.

Hall, B. H., and C. Helmers (2019). The Impact of International Patent Systems: Evidence from Accession to the European Patent Convention. *Research Policy* 48(9): article 103810. https://doi.org/10.1016/j.respol.2019.103810

Hall, B. H., C. Helmers, M. Rogers, and V. Sena (2011). *The Importance of Patents and Other Formal Intellectual Property in Comparison to Informal Protection Methods.* Newport, Wales: UK Intellectual Property Office Report. https://eml.berkeley.edu/~bhhall/papers/HHSR11_UKIPO_alternatives_report.pdf

Hall, B. H., C. Helmers, M. Rogers, and V. Sena (2013)ote Importance (or Not) of Patents to UK Firms. *Oxford Economic Papers* 65(3): 603–629.

Hall, B. H., C. Helmers, M. Rogers, and V. Sena (2014). The Choice between Formal and Informal Intellectual Property: A Review. *Journal of Economic Literature* 52(2): 375–423.

Hall, B. H., A. Jaffe, and M. Trajtenberg (2005). Market Value and Patent Citations. *RAND Journal of Economics* 36(1): 16–38.

Hall, B. H., and B. Khan (2003). Adoption of New Technology. In D. C. Jones (ed.), *New Economy Handbook*, pp. 230–251. New York, NY: Academic Press.

Hall, B. H., and J. Lerner (2010). The Financing of R&D and Innovation. In B. H. Hall and N. Rosenberg (eds.), *Handbook of the Economics of Innovation*, Vol. I, pp. 606–639. Amsterdam, Netherlands: Elsevier.

Hall, B. H., F. Lotti, and J. Mairesse (2012). Evidence on the Impact of R&D and ICT Investments on Innovation and Productivity in Italian Firms. *Economics of Innovation and New Technology* 22(3): 300–328.

Hall, B. H., and M. MacGarvie (2010). The Private Value of Software Patents. *Research Policy* 39: 994–1009.

Hall, B. H., and J. Mairesse (1995). Exploring the Relationship Between R&D and Productivity in French Manufacturing Firms. *Journal of Econometrics* 65: 263–293.

Hall, B. H., J. Mairesse, and P. Mohnen (2010). Measuring the Returns to R&D. In B. H. Hall and N. Rosenberg (eds.), *Handbook of the Economics of Innovation*, Vol. II, pp. 1034–1076. Amsterdam, Netherlands, and New York: Elsevier.

Hall, B. H., and N. Rosenberg (2010). *Handbook of the Economics of Innovation*, Vols. I and II. Amsterdam, Netherlands: Elsevier.

Hall, B. H., and J. Van Reenen (2000). How Effective Are Fiscal Incentives for R&D? A Review of the Evidence. *Research Policy* 29(4, 5): 449–469.

Hall, B. H., and R. H. Ziedonis (2001). The Determinants of Patenting in the U.S. Semiconductor Industry, 1980–1994. *RAND Journal of Economics* 32: 101–128.

Hall, R. E. (2001). The Stock Market and Capital Accumulation. *American Economic Review* 91(5): 1185–1202.

Hall, R. E., and D. W. Jorgenson (1967). Tax Policy and Investment Behavior. *American Economic Review* 57(3): 391–414.

Hanlon, W.W. (2015). Necessity Is the Mother of Invention: Input Supplies and Directed Technical Change. *Econometrica* 83: 67–100. https://doi.org/10.3982/ECTA10811

Hannan, T. H., and J. M. McDowell (1984). The Determinants of Technology Adoption: The Case of the Banking Firm. The RAND Journal of Economics 15(3): 328–335. https://doi.org/10.2307/2555441

Hansen, S. (2004, March). Breaking the (Bar) Code. *IP Law & Business*. Available at https://people.csail.mit.edu/bkph/articles/Breaking_the_Bar_Code.pdf

Harabi, N. (1995). Appropriability of technical innovations an empirical analysis. *Research Policy* 24(6): 981-992.

Harhoff, D., F. Narin, F. M. Scherer, and K. Vopel (1999). Citation Frequency and the Value of Patented Inventions. *Review of Economics and Statistics* 81(3): 511–515.

Harhoff, D., F. M. Scherer, and K. Vopel (2003). Citations, Family Size, Opposition and the Value of Patent Rights. *Research Policy* 32: 1343–1363.

Harrington, S., P. Keeley, K. Richardson, and E. Oliver (2017). How and Why LinkedIn Learned to Love Patents. *Intellectual Asset Management*: 26–33. https://www.iam-media.com/article/how-and-why-linkedin-learned-love-patents

Harris, J. E. (2021). The Repeated Setbacks of HIV Vaccine Development Laid the Groundwork for SARS-CoV-2 Vaccines. Cambridge, MA: National Bureau of Economic Research Working Paper Series No. 28587.

Hart, J. A. (2008). Flat Panel Displays. In J. T. Macher and D. C. Mowery (eds.), *Innovation in Global Industries: U.S. Firms Competing in a New World*. Washington, DC: National Academies Press. https://doi.org/10.17226/12112.

Hart, O. D., and J. Moore (1990). Property Rights and the Nature of the Firm. *Journal of Political Economy* 98: 1119–1158.

Hasan, I., and C. Tucci (2010). The Innovation-Economic Growth Nexus: Global Evidence. *Research Policy* 39(10): 1264–1276.

Hayashi, F., and T. Inoue (1991). The Relation Between Firm Growth and Q with Multiple Capital Goods: Theory and Evidence from Panel Data on Japanese Firms. *Econometrica* 59(3): 731–753.

Heather, J. M., and B. Chain (2016). The Sequence of Sequencers: The History of Sequencing DNA. *Genomics* 107(1): 1–8.

Heikkila, J., and A. Lorenz (2018). Need for Speed? Exploring the Relative Importance of Patents and Utility Models among German Firms. *Economics of Innovation and New Technology* 27(1): 80–105.

Heller, M., and R. Eisenberg (1998). Can Patents Deter Innovation? The Anti-Commons in Biomedical Research. *Science* 280(5364): 698–701.

Helmers, C., B. Ganglmair, and B. J. Love (2022). The Effect of Patent Litigation Insurance: Theory and Evidence from NPEs. *Journal of Law, Economics & Organization* 38(3): 741–773.

Helmers, C., Y. Lefouili, B. Love, and L. McDonagh (2021). The Effect of Fee Shifting on Litigation: Evidence from a Policy Innovation in Intermediate Cost Shifting. *American Law and Economics Review* 23(1): 56–99.

Helmers C., and B. J. Love (2022). Are Market Prices for Patent Licenses Observable? Evidence from 4G and 5G Licensing. *Columbia Science and Technology Law Review* 24: 55–105.

Helmers C., and B. J. Love (2023a). Are Non-Practicing Entities Opportunistic? Evidence from Litigation of Standard Essential Patents. *Oxford Economic Papers*, https://doi.org/10.1093/oep/gpae026.

Helmers C., and B. J. Love (2023b). Patent Validity and Litigation: Evidence from U.S. Inter Partes Review with Brian Love. *Journal of Law and Economics* 66(1): 53–81.

Helmers C., and B. J. Love (2023c). Welcome to Waco! The Impact of Judge-Shopping on Litigation. *Journal of Law, Economics and Organization*, published online. https://doi.org/10.1093/jleo/ewad019.

Helmers, C., B. J. Love, and L. McDonagh (2014). Is There a Patent Troll Problem in the UK? *Fordham Intellectual Property, Media and Entertainment Law Journal* 24: 509–553.

Helmers, C., and L. McDonagh (2013). Patent Litigation in England and Wales and the Issue-Based Approach to Costs. *Civil Justice Quarterly* 32(3): 369–384.

Hemphill, C. S., and B. N. Sampat (2012). Evergreening, Patent Challenges, and Effective Market Life in Pharmaceuticals. *Journal of Health Economics* 31(2): 327–339.

Hemphill, C. S., and B. N. Sampat (2013). Drug Patents at the Supreme Court. *Science* 339(6126): 1386–1387.

Helmers, C., and P. Schautschick (2013). *The Use of Intellectual Property Right Bundles by Firms in the UK*. Newport, Wales: UK Intellectual Property Office Report. https://assets.publishing.service.gov.uk/media/5a7d82efe5274a676d5327f7/ipresearch-iprbundles-report1.pdf

Henderson, R. M., and K. B. Clark (1990). Architectural Innovation: The Reconfiguration of Existing Product Technologies and the Failure of Established Firms. *Administrative Science Quarterly* 35(1): 9–30.

Henry, E., and C. J. Ponce (2011). Waiting to Imitate: On the Dynamic Pricing of Knowledge. *Journal of Political Economy* 119(5): 959–981.

Henry, E., and F. Ruiz-Aliseda (2016). Keeping Secrets: The Economics of Access Deterrence. *American Economic Journal: Microeconomics* 8(3): 95–118.

Hervé, F., and A. Schwienbacher (2018). Crowdfunding and Innovation. *Journal of Economic Surveys* 32: 1514–1530.

Herz, B., and M. Mejer (2016). On the Fee Elasticity of the Demand for Trademarks in Europe. *Oxford Economic Papers* 68(4): 1039–1061.

Herz, B., and M. Mejer (2021). The Effect of Design Protection on Price and Price Dispersion: Evidence from Automotive Spare Parts. *International Journal of Industrial Organization* 79: article 102776.

Higham, K., G. de Rassenfosse, and A. B. Jaffe (2021). Patent Quality: Towards a Systematic Framework for Analysis and Measurement. *Research Policy* 50(4): article 104215.

Hindmarch, W. M. (1851). Observations on the Defects of the Patent Laws of ust Country: ust Suggestions for the Reform of ust. Philadelphia, PA: T. and J.W. Johnson, Law Booksellers. In *The Making of Modern Law: Legal Treatises, 1800–1926*.

Von Hippel, E. (1988). *The Sources of Innovation*. Oxford, UK: Oxford University Press.

Von Hippel, E. (2006). *Democratizing Innovation*. Cambridge, MA: MIT Press.

Hirschey, M., and J. Weygandt (1985). Amortization Policy for Advertising and Research and Development Expenditures. *Journal of Accounting Research* 23(1): 326–335.

Hoisl, K., H. C. Kongsted, and M. Mariani (2021). Lost Marie Curies: Family, Education, and the Probability of Becoming and Inventor. *Management Science* 69(3): 1714-1738.

Hopenhayn, H., and F. Squintani (2021). On the Direction of Innovation. *Journal of Political Economy* 129(7): 1991-2022. DOI: 10.1086/714093.

Hu, A. G., and G. H. Jefferson (2009). A Great Wall of Patents: What Is behind China's Recent Patent Explosion? *Journal of Development Economics* 90(1): 57–68

Hu, A. G. Z., and I. P. L. Png (2013). Patent Rights and Economic Growth: Evidence from Cross-Country Panels of Manufacturing Industries. *Oxford Economic Papers* 65(3): 675–698.

Hu, P.-H., H.-H. Lee, and T. Zhou (2022). Patent Thickets, Stock Returns, and Conditional CAPM. *Management Science* 68(11). https://doi.org/10.1287/mnsc.2021.4229

Huang, N., and E. Diewert (2011). Estimation of R&D Depreciation Rates: A Suggested Methodology and Preliminary Application. *Canadian Journal of Economics* 44(2): 387–412.

Hudon, E. G. (1964). Literary Piracy, Charles Dickens and the American Copyright Law. *American Bar Association Journal* 50(12): 1157–1160. http.//www.jstor.org/stable/25723046

Hudson, J., and A. Minea (2013). Innovation, Intellectual Property Rights, and Economic Development: A Unified Empirical Investigation. *World Development* 46: 66–78.

Hufbauer G. C., and M. Hogan (2022). CHIPS Act will spur US Production but not foreclose China. Peterson Institute for International Economics Policy Brief 22-13. https://www.piie.com/publications/policy-briefs/chips-act-will-spur-us-production-not-foreclose-china

Hulten, C. R. (2010). Growth Accounting. In B. H. Hall and N. Rosenberg (eds.), *Handbook of the Economics of Innovation*, Vol. II, pp. 987–1031. Amsterdam, Netherlands: Elsevier.

Igami, M. (2017). Estimating the Innovator's Dilemma: Structural Analysis of Creative Destruction in the Hard Disk Drive Industry, 1981–1998. *Journal of Political Economy* 125(3): 625–946.

Igami, M., and K. Uetake (2020). Mergers, Innovation, and Entry-Exit Dynamics: Consolidation of the Hard Disk Drive Industry, 1996–2016. *Review of Economic Studies* 87(6): 2672–2702, https://doi.org/10.1093/restud/rdz044

Inglehart, R., C. Haerpfer, A. Moreno, C. Welzel, K. Kizilova, J. Diez-Medrano, M. Lagos, P. Norris, E. Ponarin, B. Puranen, et al. (eds.) (2014). *World Values Survey: Country-Pooled Datafile Version*. https://www.worldvaluessurvey.org/WVSDocumentationWVL.jsp. Madrid: JD Systems Institute

International Energy Agency (2017). *Fuel Economy in Major Car Markets: Technology and Policy Drivers, 2005–2017*. Global Fuel Economy Initiative Working Paper No. 19. https://www.globalfueleconomy.org/data-and-research/working-papers

Isaacson, W. (2021). *The Code Breaker: Jennifer Doudna, Gene Editing, and the Future of the Human Race*. New York: Simon and Schuster.

Ivus, O. (2010). Do Stronger Patent Rights Raise High-Tech Exports to the Developing World? *Journal of International Economics* 81(1): 38–47.

Jaffe, A. B. (1986). Technological Opportunity and Spillovers of R&D: Evidence from Firms' Patents, Profits, and Market Value. *American Economic Review* 76(5): 984–1001.

Jaffe, A. B. (2002). Building Programme Evaluation into the Design of Public Research-Support Programmes. *Oxford Review of Economic Policy* 18(1): 22–34.

Jaffe, A. B., M. Trajtenberg, and M. S. Fogarty (2000). Knowledge Spillovers and Patent Citations: Evidence from a Survey of Inventors. *American Economic Review* 90(2): 215–218.

Jaffe, A. B., M. Trajtenberg, and R. Henderson (1993). Geographic Localization of Knowledge Spillovers as Evidenced by Patent Citations. *Quarterly Journal of Economics* 108: 577–598.

Jakab, P. (2013). Leonardo da Vinci and Flight. Smithsonian Aira and Space Museum. https://airandspace.si.edu/stories/editorial/leonardo-da-vinci-and-flight

Javorcik, B. S. (2002). The Composition of Foreign Direct Investment and Protection of Intellectual Property Rights: Evidence from Transition Economies. *European Economic Review* 48: 39–62.

Jell, F., J. Henkel, and M. W. Wallin (2017). Offensive Patent Portfolio Races. *Long Range Planning* 50: 531–549.

Jensen, M. C., and W. H. Meckling (1976). Theory of the Firm: Managerial Behavior, Agency Costs and Ownership Structure. *Journal of Financial Economics* 3(4): 305–360.

Jensen, P. H., and E. Webster (2009). Another Look at the Relationship between Innovation Proxies. *Australian Economic Papers* 48(3): 252–269.

Johnston, A. W. (1974). Trademarks on Greek Vases. *Greece & Rome* 21(2): 138–152.

Jones, B. F., and L. H. Summers (2022). A Calculation of the Social Returns to Innovation. In A. Goolsbee and B. F. Jones (eds.), *Innovation and Public Policy*, pp. 13–60. Chicago, IL: University of Chicago Press.

Jones, C. I. (1995a). R & D-Based Models of Economic Growth. *Journal of Political Economy* 103(4): 759–784.

Jones, C. I. (1995b). Time Series Tests of Endogenous Growth Models. *Quarterly Journal of Economics* 110(2): 495–525.

Jones, C. I., and J. Williams (1998). Measuring the Social Return to R&D. *Quarterly Journal of Economics* 113: 1119–1135.

Jones, C. I., and J. Williams (2000). Too Much of a Good Thing? The Economics of Investment in R&D. *Journal of Economic Growth* 5(1): 65–85.

Jorgenson, D. W., and Z. Griliches (1967). The Explanation of Productivity Change. *Review of Economic Studies* 34(3): 249–283.

Jorgenson, D. W., and Z. Griliches (1972). Issues in Growth Accounting: A Reply to Edward F. Denison. *Survey of Current Business* 52(5): Part II 65-94.

Jorgenson, D. W., Z. Griliches, and E. F. Denison (1972). The Measurement of Productivity. *Survey of Current Business* 52(5): Part II. https://apps.bea.gov/scb/pdf/1972/0572cont.pdf#page=89

Jorgenson, D. W., M. S. Ho, and K. J. Stiroh. (2008). A Retrospective Look at the U.S. Productivity Growth Resurgence. *Journal of Economic Perspectives* 22 (1): 3-24.

Joshi, A., and A. Nerkar (2011). When Do Strategic Alliances Inhibit Innovation by Firms? Evidence from Patent Pools in the Global Optical Disc Industry. *Strategic Management Journal* 32(11): 1139–1160.

Kaiser F., A. Cuntz, and C. Peukert (2023). Batman Forever? The Role of Trademarks for Reuse in the US Comics Industry. *Research Policy* 52(8): article 104820.

Kang, B. W., and R. Bekkers (2015). Just-in-Time Patents and the Development of Standards. *Research Policy* 44: 1948–1961.

Kanwar, S. (2012). The Location of Overseas Research and Development and Intellectual Property Protection. *Journal of Development Studies* 48(10): 1453–1469.

Kanwar, S., and Evenson, R. (2003). Does Intellectual Property Protection Spur Technological Change? *Oxford Economic Papers* 55(2): 235–264.

Kapczynski, A. (2009). Harmonization and Its Discontents: A Case Study of TRIPS Implementation in India's Pharmaceutical Sector. *California Law Review* 97: 1571–1649.

Kapczynski, A., C. Park, and B. Sampat (2012). Polymorphs and Prodrugs and Salts (Oh My!): An Empirical Analysis of "Secondary" Pharmaceutical Patents. *PLOS ONE* 7(12): article e49470. Doi:10.1371/journal.pone.0049470

Karanikolas, M. (2020). The New Cybersquatters, the Evolution of Trademark Enforcement in the Domain Name Space. *Fordham Intellectual Property, Media, and Entertainment Law Journal* 30(2): 399–446.

Karshenas, M., and P. Stoneman (1995). Technological Diffusion. In P. Stoneman (ed.), *Handbook of the Economics of Innovation and Technological Change*, pp. 265–297. Oxford, UK: Basil Blackwell.

Katz, M. L., and C. Shapiro (1994). Systems Competition and Network Effects. *Journal of Economic Perspectives* 8(2): 93–115.

Katz, M. L., and H. Shelanski (2005). Merger Policy and Innovation: Must Enforcement Change to Account for Technological Change? *Innovation Policy and the Economy* 5: 109–165.

Keller, W. (1998). Are International R&D Spillovers Trade-Related? Analyzing Spillovers among Randomly Matched Trade Partners. *European Economic Review* 42(8): 1469–1481.

Kendrick, J. W. (1970). The Historical Development of National-Income Accounts. *History of Political Economy* 2(2): 284–315.

Khan, Z. B. (2014). Trolls and Other Patent Inventions: Economic History and the Patent Controversy in the Twenty-First Century. *George Mason Law Review* 21(4): 825–863.

Khan, Z. B. (2015). Inventing Prizes: A Historical Perspective on Innovation Awards and Technology Policy. *Business History Review* 89(4): 631–660.

Kilby, J. S. (2000). The Integrated Circuit's Early History. *Proceedings of the IEEE* 88(1): 109–111. Doi:10.1109/5.811607

Kim, L. (2003, June). Technology Transfer and Intellectual Property Rights: The Korean Experience. Geneva: International Centre for Trade and Sustainable Development UNCTAD-ICTSD Issue Paper No. 2.

Kim, J.-H., and K. Lee (2022). Local–Global Interface as a Key Factor in the Catching Up of Regional Innovation Systems: Fast versus Slow Catching Up among Taipei, Shenzhen, and Penang in Asia. *Technological Forecasting and Social Change* 174: article 121271.

Kim, J.-H., Newberry, P., Wagman, L. and Wolff, R. (2022). Local Network Effects in the Adoption of a Digital Platform. *Journal of Industrial Economics* 70: 493–524. https://doi.org/10.1111/joie.12296

Kindlon, A. E., and J. E. Jankowski (2017). Rates of Innovation among U.S. Businesses Stay Steady: Data from the 2014 Business R&D and Innovation Survey. U.S. National Science Foundation Info Brief 17-321. https://www.nsf.gov/statistics/2017/nsf17321

King, G. (2011, October 11). Edison vs. Westinghouse: A Shocking Rivalry. *Smithsonian Magazine*. https://www.smithsonianmag.com/history/edison-vs-westinghouse-a-shocking-rivalry-102146036

Kitch, E. W. (1977). The Nature and Function of the Patent System. *Journal of Law and Economics* 20(2): 265–290

Klepper, S. (1996). Entry, Exit, Growth, and Innovation over the Product Life Cycle. *American Economic Review* 86(3): 562–583.

Klepper, S. (1997). Industry Life Cycles. *Industrial and Corporate Change* 6(1): 145–182.

Klepper, S. (2016). *Experimental Capitalism: The Nanoeconomics of American High-Tech Industries*. Princeton, NJ: Princeton University Press.

Klette, T. J., J. Moen, and Z. Griliches (2000). Do Subsidies to Commercial R&D Reduce Market Failures? Micro-Econometric Evaluation Studies. *Research Policy* 29: 471–495.

Knauss, D. J., E. E. Veltenheimer, and M. Pomeranz (2019). Protecting Plant Inventions. *ABA Landslide Journal* 11(6): 44–65. https://www.cooley.com/-/media/cooley/pdf/reprints/2019/2019-08-13-protecting-plant-inventions

Knox R., and G. Curfman (2022). The Humira Patent Thicket, the Noerr-Pennington Doctrine and Antitrust's Patent Problem. *Nature Biotechnology* 40: 1761–1763.

Kogan, L., D. Papanikolaou, A. Seru, and N. Stoffman (2017). Technological Innovation, Resource Allocation, and Growth. *Quarterly Journal of Economics* 132(2): 665–712. https://doi.org/10.1093/qje/qjw040

Kortum, S., and J. Lerner (1998). Stronger Protection or Technological Revolution: What Is Behind the Recent Surge in Patenting? *Carnegie-Rochester Conference Series on Public Policy* 48: 247–304.

KPMG (2021). *Global R&D Incentives Guide*. https://assets.kpmg/content/dam/kpmg/us/pdf/2021/05/tnf-global-rd-incentives-guide-may11-2021.pdf

Krasnikov, A., S. Mishra, and D. Orozco (2009). Evaluating the Financial Impact of Branding Using Trademarks: A Framework and Empirical Evidence. *Journal of Marketing* 73(6): 154–166.

Kremer, M. (1998). Patent Buyouts: A Mechanism for Encouraging Innovation. *Quarterly Journal of Economics* 113(4): 1137–1167.

Kremer, M. (2002). Pharmaceuticals and the Developing World. *Journal of Economic Perspectives* 16(4): 67–90.

Krueger A. (2005). The Economics of Real Superstars: The Market for Rock Concerts in the Material World. *Journal of Labor Economics* 23(1): 1–30.

Kultti, K., T. Takalo, and J. Toikka (2006). Simultaneous Model of Innovation, Secrecy, and Patent Policy. *American Economic Review* 96(2): 82–86.

Kumar, N. (2003). Intellectual Property Rights, Technology and Economic Development: Experiences of Asian Countries. *Economic and Political Weekly* 38(3). doi:10.2307/4413100

Kyle, M. K., and A. M. McGahan (2012). Investments in Pharmaceuticals Before and After TRIPS. *Review of Economics and Statistics* 94(4): 1157–1172.

Kyle, M. K., and Y. Qian (2014). Intellectual Property Rights and Access to Innovation: Evidence from TRIPS. Cambridge, MA: National Bureau of Economic Research Working Paper No. 20799.

Lamoreaux, N. R., and K. L. Sokoloff (1996). Long-Term Change in the Organization of Inventive Activity. *Proceedings of the National Academy of Science USA* 93(23): 12686–12692. Doi:10.1073/pnas.93.23.12686

Lamoreaux, N. R., and K. L. Sokoloff (1997). Inventive Activity and the Market for Technology in the United States, 1840–1920. Cambridge, MA: National Bureau of Economic Research Working Paper 7107.

Lamoreaux, N. R., and K. L. Sokoloff (2001). Market Trade in Patents and the Rise of a Class of Specialized Inventors in the 19th-Century United States. *American Economic Review* 91(2): 39–44.

Lampe, R., and P. Moser (2010). Do Patent Pools Encourage Innovation? Evidence from the 19th-Century Sewing Machine Industry. *Journal of Economic History* 70: 871–897.

Lampe, R., and P. Moser (2013). Patent Pools and Innovation in Substitute Technologies: Evidence from the 19th Century Sewing Machine Industry. *RAND Journal of Economics* 44(4): 757–778.

Lampe, R., and P. Moser (2016). Patent Pools, Competition, and Innovation: Evidence from 20 US Industries under the New Deal. *Journal of Law, Economics and Organization* 32(1): 1–36.

Lancaster, T. (1990). *The Econometric Analysis of Transition Data*. Cambridge, UK: Cambridge University Press.

Landes, W. M., and R. A. Posner (1987). Trade Mark Law: An Economic Perspective. *Journal of Law and Economics* 30: 265–309.

Landes, W. M., and R. A. Posner (1989). An Economic Analysis of Copyright Law. *Journal of Legal Studies* 18(2): 325–363.

Landes, W. M., and R. A. Posner (2003). *The Economic Structure of Intellectual Property Law*. Cambridge, MA: Belknap Press of Harvard University Press.

Langlois, R. N., and W. E. Steinmueller (1999). The Evolution of Comparative Advantage in the Worldwide Semiconductor Industry, 1947–1966. In D. C. Mowery and R. R. Nelson (eds.), *Sources of Industrial Leadership*, pp. 19–78. Cambridge, UK: Cambridge University Press.

Lanjouw, J. O. (1997). The Introduction of Pharmaceutical Product Patents in India: "Heartless Exploitation of the Poor and Suffering"? Cambridge, MA: National Bureau of Economic Research Working Paper No. 6366.

Lanjouw, J. O. (2003). Intellectual Property and the Availability of Pharmaceuticals in Poor Countries. *Innovation Policy and the Economy* 3: 91–130. https://www.nber.org/books-and-chapters/innovation-policy-and-economy-volume-3/intellectual-property-and-availability-pharmaceuticals-poor-countries

Lanjouw, J. O., and M. Schankerman (2004). Patent Quality and Research Productivity: Measuring Innovation with Multiple Indicators. *Economic Journal* 114(495): 441–465.

Layne-Farrar, A. (2005). Defining Software Patents: A Research Field Guide. Washington, DC: American Enterprise Institute and Brookings Center Working Paper 05-14.

Layne-Farrar, A., and J. Lerner (2011). To Join or us to Join: Examining Patent Pool Participation and Rent Sharing Rules. *International Journal of Industrial Organization* 29(2): 294–303.

Layne-Farrar, A., and K. M. Schmidt (2010). Licensing Complementary Patents: Patent Trolls, Market Structure, and Excessive Royalties. *Berkeley Technology Law Journal* 25: 1121–1143.

Lee, K. (2013). *Schumpeterian Analysis of Economic Catch-Up: Knowledge, Path-Creation and the Middle Income Trap*. Cambridge, UK: Cambridge University Press.

Lee, K., and Y.-K. Kim (2010). IPR and Technological Catch-Up in Korea. In H. Odagiri, A. Goto, A. Sunami, and R. R. Nelson (eds.), *Intellectual Property Rights, Development, and Catch Up: An International Comparative Study*, pp. 133–167. Oxford, UK: Oxford University Press.

Lee, K., J.-H. Lee, and J.-Y. Lee (2021). Variety of National Innovation Systems (NIS) and Alternative Pathways to Growth beyond the Middle-Income Stage: Balanced, Imbalanced, Catching-Up, and Trapped NIS. *World Development* 144: article 105472.

Lee, J., and K. Lee (2021). Catching-Up National Innovations Systems (NIS) in China and Post-Catching-Up NIS in Korea and Taiwan: Verifying the Detour Hypothesis and Policy Implications. *Innovation and Development* 11(2–3): 387–411.

Lee, J.-Y., and E. Mansfield (1996). Intellectual Property Protection and U.S. Foreign Direct Investment. *Review of Economics and Statistics* 78 (2): 181–186.

Lehmann-Hasemeyer, S., and J. Streb (2020). Discrimination against Foreigners: The Wuerttemberg Patent Law in Administrative Practice. *Journal of Economic History* 80(4): 1071–1100.

Leiponen, A. and J. Byma (2009). If you cannot block, you better run: Small firms, cooperative innovation, and appropriation strategies. *Research Policy* 38(9): 1478–1488. DOI: https://doi.org/10.1016/j.respol.2009.06.003

Lemley, M. A. (2012). The Myth of the Sole Inventor. *Michigan Law Review* 110(5): 709–760.

Lemley, M. A. (2013). Software Patents and the Return of Functional Claiming. *Wisconsin Law Review* 20: 905–964.

Lemley, M. A., and A. D. Melamed. Missing the Forest for the Trolls. Columbia Law Review 113(8): 2117–2189.

Lemley, M.A., and C. Shapiro (2013). Patent Holdup and Royalty Stacking. *Texas Law Review* 85: 1991–2049.

Lemus, J., and E. Temnyalov (2017). Patent Privateering, Litigation, and R&D Incentives. *RAND Journal of Economics* 48(4): 1004–1026.

Lerner J. (1995). Patenting in the Shadow of Competitors. *Journal of Law and Economics* 38: 463–495.

Lerner, J. (1998). "Angel" Financing and Public Policy: An Overview. *Journal of Banking & Finance* 22(6): 773–783.

Lerner, J. (2002a). Where Does State Street Lead? A First Look at Finance Patents, 1971 to 2000. *Journal of Finance* 57(2): 901–930.

Lerner, J. (2002b). Patent Protection and Innovation over 150 Years. *American Economic Review* 92(2): 221–225.

Lerner, J. (2010). The Litigation of Financial Innovations. *Journal of Law and Economics* 53(4): 807–831.

Lerner, J., and R. Nanda (2020). Venture Capital's Role in Financing Innovation: What We Know and How Much We Still Need to Learn. *Journal of Economic Perspectives* 34(3): 237–261.

Lerner, J., and M. Schankerman (2009). *The Comingled Code: Open Source and Economic Development.* Cambridge, MA: MIT Press.

Lerner, J., A. Seru, N. Short, and Y. Sun (2021). Financial Innovation in the 21st Century: Evidence from U.S. Patents. Cambridge, MA: National Bureau of Economic Research Working Paper Series No. 28980.

Lerner, J., and J. Tirole (2015). Standard-Essential Patents. *Journal of Political Economy* 123(3): 547–586.

Lerner, J., and J. Tirole (2002). Some Simple Economics of Open Source. *Journal of Industrial Economics* 50(2): 197–234.

Lerner, J., and F. Zhu (2007). What Is the Impact of Software Patent Shifts? Evidence from *Lotus v. Borland. International Journal of Industrial Organization* 25: 511–529.

Lev, B. (2001). *Intangibles: Management, Measurement, and Reporting.* Washington, DC: Brookings Institution Press.

Levin, R. C., A. A. Klevorick, R. R. Nelson, and S. G. Winter (1987). Appropriating the Returns from Industrial Research and Development. *Brookings Papers on Economic Activity* 18(3): 783–832.

Levin, R. C., and P. C. Reiss (1988). Cost-Reducing and Demand-Creating R&D with Spillovers. *RAND Journal of Economics* 19(4): 538–556.

Lewellen, W. G., and S. G. Badrinath (1997). On the Measurement of Tobin's q. *Journal of Financial Economics* 44(1): 77–122.

Lewis, J., and R. Mott (2013). The Sky Is us Falling: Navigating the Smartphone Patent Thicket. *WIPO Magazine*, Vol. 1. https://www.wipo.int/wipo_magazine/en/2013/01/article_0002.html

Leychkiş, Y. (2007). Of Fire Ants and Claim Construction: An Empirical Study of the Meteoric Rise of the Eastern District of Texas as a Preeminent Forum for Patent Litigation. *Yale Journal of Law & Technology* 9: 193–232.

Li, X. (2012). Behind the Recent Surge of Chinese Patenting: An Institutional View. *Research Policy* 41(1): 236–249.

Li, Y.-D., W.-Y. Chi, J.-H. Su, L. Ferrall, C.-F. Hung, and T.-C. Wu (2020). Coronavirus Vaccine Development: ust SARS and MERS to COVID-19. *Journal of Biomedical Science* 27(1): 104–126.

Li, W. C. Y., and P. J. Chi (2021). Online Platforms' Creative "Disruption" in Organizational Capital: The Accumulated Information of the Firm. Los Angeles, CA: Moon Economics Institute Discussion Paper Series 2021 No. 1. https://drive.google.com/file/d/1mbL2KW MnsTYg7McJTVT17lJKve3kX-fL/view

Li, W. C. Y., and B. H. Hall (2020). Depreciation of Business R&D Capital. *Review of Income and Wealth* 66(1): 161–180.

Li, X., M. MacGarvie, and P. Moser (2018). Dead Poet's Property: How Does Copyright Influence Price? *RAND Journal of Economics* 49(1): 181–205.

Lichtenberg, F. R., and J. Waldfogel (2003). Does Misery Love Company? Evidence from Pharmaceutical Markets before and after the Orphan Drug Act. Cambridge, MA: National Bureau of Economic Research Working Paper Series No. 9750.

Lieberman, M. B., and D. B. Montgomery (1988). First-Mover Advantages. *Strategic Management Journal* 9(S1): 41–58.

Liebowitz, S. (1985). Copying and Indirect Appropriability: Photocopying of Journals. *Journal of Political Economy* 93(5): 945–957.

Liebowitz, S. (2006). File Sharing: Creative Destruction or ust Plain Destruction. *Journal of Law and Economics* 49(1): 1–28.

Liebowitz, S. J., and S. E. Margolis (1995). Path Dependence, Lock-In, and History. *Journal of Law, Economics, and Organization* 11(1): 205–226.

Ligon, B. L. (2004). Penicillin: Its Discovery and Early Development. *Seminars in Pediatric Infectious Diseases* 15(1): 52–57.

Lin Y.-K., and A. Rai (2023). The Scope of Software Patent Protection in the Digital Age: Evidence from Alice. *Information Systems Research*, published online. https://doi.org/10.1287/isre.2021.0137

List, F. (1841, English ed. 1904). *The National System of Political Economy*. London: Longman.

Lokshin, B. and P. Mohnen (2013). Do R&D tax incentives lead to higher wages for R&D workers? Evidence from The Netherlands. *Research Policy* 42(3): 823–830. DOI: https://doi.org/10.1016/j.respol.2012.12.004

Love, B. J. (2013). An Empirical Study of Patent Litigation Timing: Could a Patent Term Reduction Decimate Trolls without Harming Innovators? *University of Pennsylvania Law Review* 161(5): 1309–1359.

Love, B. J., C. Helmers, F. Gaessler, and M. Ernicke (2017). Patent Assertion Entities in Europe. In D. Sokol (ed.), *Patent Assertion Entities and Competition Policy*. Cambridge, UK: Cambridge University Press.

Love, B. J., Y. Lefouili, and C. Helmers (2023). Do Standard-Essential Patent Owners Behave Opportunistically? Evidence from U.S. District Court Dockets. *American Law and Economics Review* 25(1): 300–337.

Love B. J., K. Richardson, E. Oliver, and M. Costa (2018). An Empirical Look at the "Brokered" Market for Patents. *Missouri Law Review* 83: 359–408.

Love, B. J., and J. Yoon (2017). Predictably Expensive: A Critical Look at Patent Litigation in the Eastern District of Texas. *Stanford Technology Law Review* 20(1): 1–37.

Lundvall, B.-A. (ed.) (1992). *National Systems of Innovation: Towards a Theory of Innovation and Interactive Learning*. London, UK: Pinter.

Lunney, G. S. (1999). Trademark Monopolies. *Emory Law Journal* 48(2): 367–487.

Lybbert, T. J., and N. J. Zolas (2014). Getting Patents and Economic Data to Speak to each other: An Algorithmic Links with Probabilities Approach for Joint Analyses of Patenting and Economic Activity, *Research Policy* 43(3): 530–542.

MacGarvie, M. (2006). Do Firms Learn from International Trade? *Review of Economics and Statistics* 88(1): 46–60.

Machlup, F., and E. Penrose (1950). The Patent Controversy in the Nineteenth Century. *Journal of Economic History* 10(1): 1–29.

MacKinlay, A. C. (1997). Event Studies in Economics and Finance. *Journal of Economic Literature* 35(1): 13–39.

MacLeod, C., J. Tann, J. Andrew, and J. Stein (2003). Evaluating Inventive Activity: The Cost of Nineteenth-Century UK Patents and the Fallibility of Renewal Data. *Economic History Review* 56(3): 537–562.

Maddison Growth Project (2018). Maddison Project Database 2020. https://ourworldindata.org/economic-growth#economic-growth-over-the-long-run

Mairesse, J., and B. H. Hall (1996). Estimating the Productivity of Research and Development in French and US Manufacturing Firms: An Exploration of Simultaneity Issues with GMM Methods. In K. Wagner and B. van Ark (eds.), *International Productivity Differences and Their Explanations*, pp. 285–315. Amsterdam, Netherlands: Elsevier-North Holland.

Mankiw, N. G., D. Romer, and D. A. Weil (1992). A Contribution to the Empirics of Economic Growth. *Quarterly Journal of Economics* 107(2): 407–437.

Mansfield, E. (1961). Technical Change and the Rate of Imitation. *Econometrica* 29(4): 741–766.

Mansfield, E. (1986a). Patents and Innovation: An Empirical Study. *Management Science* 32(2): 173–181.

Mansfield, E. (1986b). The R&D Tax Credit and Other Technology Policy Issues. *American Economic Review* 76(2): 190–194.

Mansfield, E. (1991). Academic Research and Industrial Innovation. *Research Policy* 20(1): 1–12.

Mansfield, E. (1995). Academic Research Underlying Industrial Innovations: Sources, Characteristics, and Financing. *Review of Economics and Statistics* 77(1): 55–65.

Mansfield, E. (2000). Intellectual Property Protection, Direct Investment and Technology Transfer: Germany, Japan and the U.S.A. *International Journal of Technology Management* 19(1/2): 3–21.

Mansfield, E., J. Rapoport, A. Romeo, S. Wagner, and G. Beardsley (1977). Social and Private Rates of Return to Industrial Innovations. *Quarterly Journal of Economics* 91(2): 221–240.

Marco, A. C., M. Carley, S. Jackson, and A. Myers (2015). *The USPTO Historical Patent Data Files: Two Centuries of Innovation.* http://dx.doi.org/10.2139/ssrn.2616724

Markley, M. L. (2020). Hocus Pocus: The Magic Within Trade Secret Law. *Journal of Intellectual Property Law* 27(1): 111–136.

Marx, M., D. Strumsky, and L. Fleming (2009). Mobility, Skills, and the Michigan Non-Compete Experiment. *Management Science* 55(6): 875–889.

Maskus, K. E. (2004). *Encouraging International Technology Transfer.* Geneva, Switzerland: UNCTAD-ICTSD Project on IPRs and Sustainable Development Issue Paper No. 7. https://unctad.org/system/files/official-document/ictsd2004ipd7_en.pdf

Maskus, K. E., and M. Penubarti (1995). How Trade-Related Are Intellectual Property Rights? *Journal of International Economics* 39(3): 227–248.

Mattioli, M. (2008). Patent Pool Outsiders. *Berkeley Technology Law Journal* 33(1): 233–296.

Maurer S. M., P. B. Hugenholtz, and H. J. Onsrud (2001). Europe's Database Experiment. *Science* 294(5543): 789–790. DOI:10.1126/science.1062695.

Mazzeo, M. J., J. H. Ashtor, and S. Zyontz (2013). Do NPEs Matter? Non-Practicing Entities and Patent Litigation Outcomes. *Journal of Competition Law & Economics* 9(4): 879–904.

Mazzoleni, R., and R. R. Nelson (1998). Economic Theories about the Benefits and Costs of Patents. *Journal of Economic Issues* 32(4): 1031–1052.

McDonough III, J. F. (2006). The Myth of the Patent Troll: An Alternative View of the Function of Patent Dealers in an Idea Economy. *Emory Law Journal* 56: 189–228

Mejer, M., and B. van Pottelsberghe de la Potterie (2012). Economic Incongruities in the European Patent System. *European Journal of Law and Economics* 34(1): 215–234.

Mendoca, S., T. Santos Pereira, and M. Mira Godinho (2004). Trademarks as an Indicator of Innovation and Industrial Change *Research Policy* 33(9): 1385–1404.

Merton, R. K. (1957). Priorities in Scientific Discovery: A Chapter in the Sociology of Science. *American Sociological Review* 22(6): 635–659. Doi:10.2307/2089193.

Merton, R. K. (1968). The Matthew Effect in Science. *Science* 159(3810): 56–63.

Merton, R. K. (1973). *The Sociology of Science: Theoretical and Empirical Investigations.* Chicago, IL: University of Chicago Press.

Meurer, M. (1989). The Settlement of Patent Litigation. *RAND Journal of Economics* 20: 77–91.

Meurer, M., J. Bessen, and J. Ford (2012). The Private and Social Costs of Patent Trolls. *Regulation* 34: 26–35.

Mezzanotti F., and T. Simcoe (2023). Innovation and Appropriability: Revisiting the Role of Intellectual Property. Cambridge, MA: National Bureau of Economic Research Working Paper 31428.

Miller, S. P. (2018). Who's Suing Us? Decoding Patent Plaintiffs since 2000 with the Stanford NPE Litigation Dataset. *Stanford Technology Law Review* 21: 235–275.

Miric, M., K. J. Boudreau, and L. B. Jeppesen (2019). Protecting Their Digital Assets: The Use of Formal and Informal Appropriability Strategies by App Developers. *Research Policy* 48(8): article 103738.

Mitchell, J. T., and W. C. Terry (2011). Contesting Pisco: Chile, Peru, and the Politics of Trade. *Geographical Review* 101(4): 518–535. http://www.jstor.org/stable/23208637

Mohnen, P. (1992). *International R&D spillovers in selected OECD countries.* UQAM dept des sciences economiques cahier de recherche no. 9208. Montreal, Quebec.

Mokyr, J. (1990). *The Lever of Riches*, Chapter 7. Oxford, UK: Oxford University Press.

Mokyr, J. (1992). *The Lever of Riches.* Oxford, UK: Oxford University Press, paperback edition.

Mokyr, J. (2009). Intellectual Property Rights, the Industrial Revolution, and the Beginnings of Modern Economic Growth. *American Economic Review* 99 (2): 349-55.

Mortimer, J. H., C. Nosko, and A. Sorensen (2012). Supply Responses to Digital Distribution: Recorded Music and Live Performances. *Information Economics and Policy* 24: 3–14.

Moschini, G., L. Menapace, and D. Pick (2008). Geographical Indications and the Competitive Provision of Quality in Agricultural Markets. *American Journal of Agricultural Economics* 90(3): 794–812.

Moser, P. (2005). How Do Patent Laws Influence Innovation? Evidence from Nineteenth-Century World's Fairs. *American Economic Review* 95(4): 1214–1236.

Moser, P. (2013). Patents and Innovation: Evidence from Economic History. *Journal of Economic Perspectives* 27(1): 23–44.

Moser, P., and T. Nicholas (2013). Prizes, Publicity and Patents: Non-Monetary Awards as a Mechanism to Encourage Innovation. *Journal of Industrial Economics* 61(3): 763–788.

Moser, P., and P. W. Rhode (2012). Did Plant Patents Create the American Rose? In J. Lerner and S. Stern (eds.), The Rate and Direction of Inventive Activity Revisited. pp. 413–438. National Bureau of Economic Research Conference Volume. Chicago, IL: University of Chicago Press.

Mossinghoff, G. J. (2005). The First-to-Invent Rule in the U.S. Patent System Has Provided No Advantage to Small Entities. *Journal of the Patent and Trademark Office Society* 87(6): 514–522.

Mossoff, A. (2011). The Rise and Fall of the First American Patent Thicket: The Sewing Machine War of the 1850s. *Arizona Law Review* 53: 165–211.

Mowery, D. C. (2009). *Plus ça Change*: Industrial R&D in the "Third Industrial Revolution." *Industrial and Corporate Change* 18(1): 1–50.

Mowery, D. C. (2010). Military R&D and Innovation. In B. H. Hall and N. Rosenberg (eds.), *Handbook of Economics and Innovation*, Vol. II. Amsterdam, Netherlands: Elsevier.

Mowery, D. C., R. R. Nelson, B. N. Sampat, and A. A. Ziedonis (2004). *Ivory Tower and Industrial Innovation.* Stanford, CA: Stanford University Press.

Mowery, D. C., and N. Rosenberg (1989). *Technology and the Pursuit of Economic Growth.* Cambridge, UK: Cambridge University Press.

Moylan, C. E., and S. Okubo (2020, March). The Evolving Treatment of R&D in the U.S. National Economic Accounts. https://www.bea.gov/system/files/2020-04/the-evolving-treatment-of-rd-in-the-us-national-economic-accounts.pdf

Mulligan, C., and T. B. Lee (2013). Scaling the Patent System. *NYU Annual Survey of American Law* 68: 289–317.

Murray, F., P. Aghion, M. Dewatripont, J. Kolev, and S. Stern (2016). Of Mice and Academics: Examining the Effect of Openness on Innovation. *American Economic Journal: Economic Policy* 8(1): 212–252.

Murray, F., S. Stern, G. Campbell, and A. MacCormack (2012). Grand Innovation Prizes: A Theoretical, Normative, and Empirical Evaluation. *Research Policy* 41: 1779–1792.

Nagaoka, S., K. Motohashi, and A. Goto (2010). Patent Statistics as an Innovation Indicator. In B. H. Hall and N. Rosenberg (eds.), *Handbook of the Economics of Innovation*, Vol.II, pp. 1083–1127. Amsterdam, Netherlands: Elsevier.

Nagaraj A., and I. Reimers (2023). Digitization and the Market for Physical Works: Evidence from the Google Books Project. *American Economic Journal: Economic Policy* 15(4): 1–31.

Nelson, R. R. (1959). The Simple Economics of Basic Scientific Research. *Journal of Political Economy* 67: 297–306.

Nelson, R. R. (ed.) (1993). *National Innovation Systems: A Comparative Analysis.* Oxford, UK: Oxford University Press.

Nelson, T. H. (1965). Complex Information Processing: A File Structure for the Complex, the Changing and the Indeterminate. In L. Winner (ed.), *Proceedings of the 1965 20th National Conference*, pp. 84–100. Cleveland, OH: Association for Computing Machinery.

Noel, M., and M. Schankerman (2013). Strategic Patenting and Software Innovation. *Journal of Industrial Economics* 61(3): 481–520.

Nordhaus, W. D. (1967). The Optimal Life of a Patent. New Haven, CT: Yale University Cowles Foundation Discussion Paper No. 241.

Nordhaus, W. D. (1972). The Optimal Life of a Patent, Reply. *American Economic Review* 62(3): 428–431.

Nordhaus, W. D. (1996). Do Real Output and Real-Wage Measures Capture Reality? The History of Lighting Suggests Not. In T. F. Bresnahan and R. J. Gordon (eds.), *The Economic of New Goods*, pp. 27–70. Chicago: University of Chicago Press.

North, D. C. (1968). Sources of Productivity Change in Ocean Shipping, 1600–1850. *Journal of Political Economy* 76(5): 953–970.

Nunn, A. S., E. M. da Fonseca, F. I. Bastos, and S. Gruskin (2009). AIDS Treatment in Brazil: Impacts and Challenges. *Health Affairs* 28(4): 1103–1113.

Nuvolari, A. (2004). Collective Invention during the British Industrial Revolution: The Case of the Cornish Pumping Engine. *Cambridge Journal of Economics* 28(3): 347–363.

Nuvolari, A., B. Verspagen, and N. von Tunzelmann (2011). The Early Diffusion of the Steam Engine in Britain, 1700–1800: A Reappraisal. *Cliometrica* 5: 291–321.

Oberholzer-Gee, F., and K. Strumpf (2007). The Effect of File Sharing on Record Sales: An Empirical Analysis. *Journal of Political Economy* 115(1): 1–42.

O'Connor, A. C., Gallaher, M. P., Clark-Sutton, K., Lapidus, D., Oliver, Z. T., Scott, T. J., Wood, D. W., Gonzalez, M. A., Brown, E. G., and Fletcher, J. (2019). Economic Benefits of the Global Positioning System (GPS). Research Triangle Park, NC: RTI International and National Institute of Standards and Technology Report No. 0215471.

Ogburn, W. F., and D. Thomas (1922). Are Inventions Inevitable? A Note on Social Evolution. *Political Science Quarterly* 37(1): 83–98. Reprinted in B. H. Hall, (ed.), *Economics of Research and Development*, pp. 113–128. Cheltenham, UK: Edward Elgar.

Oliar, D., and C. Sprigman (2008). There's No Free Laugh (Anymore): The Emergence of Intellectual Property Norms and the Transformation of Stand-Up Comedy. *Virginia Law Review* 94(8): 1787–1867.

Oliner, S.D., and D. E. Sichel (2003). Information Technology and Productivity: Where Are We Now and Where Are We Going?. In D. K. Ginther, M. Zavodny, and L. H. Foley (eds.), *Technology, Growth, and the Labor Market.* Boston, MA: Springer. https://doi.org/10.1007/978-1-4615-0325-5_4

Oliver E., and K. Richardson (2018). What will TV cost you? Putting a price on HEVC licences. *IAM:* 29 March 2018. https://www.iam-media.com/article/what-will-tv-cost-you-putting-price-hevc-licences

Olson, M. (1971). *The Logic of Collective Action: Public Goods and the Theory of Groups.* Cambridge, MA: Harvard University Press.

Ondraczek, J. (2014). Are We There Yet? Improving Solar PV Economics and Power Planning in Developing Countries: The Case of Kenya. *Renewable and Sustainable Energy Reviews* 30: 604–615.

O'Neil, C. (2016). *Weapons of Math Destruction: How Big Data Increases Inequality and Threatens Democracy.* New York: Crown Random House.

Organisation for Economic Co-operation and Development. (2011). *Financing High-Growth Firms: The Role of Angel Investors.* Paris, France: OECD Publishing. http://dx.doi.org/10.1787/9789264118782-en

Organisation for Economic Co-operation and Development. (2015a). *Frascati Manual 2015: Guidelines for Collecting and Reporting Data on Research and Experimental Development, The Measurement of Scientific, Technological and Innovation Activities.* Paris, France: OECD Publishing. http://dx..org doi /10.1787/9789264239012-en

Organisation for Economic Co-operation and Development. (2015b). *Countering Harmful Tax Practices More Effectively, Taking into Account Transparency and Substance.* Action 5-2015 Final Report. Paris, France: OECD Publishing. https://doi.org/10.1787/9789264241190-en

Organisation for Economic Co-operation and Development./Eurostat (2018). *Oslo Manual: Guidelines for Collecting, Reporting, and Using Data on Innovation.* Paris, France: OECD Publishing/Luxembourg: Eurostat. https://doi.org/10.1787/9789264304604-en

Organisation for Economic Co-operation and Development. . Stat (2021). *Main Science and Technology Indicators.* https://stats.oecd.org/Index.aspx?DataSetCode=MSTI_PUB

Organisation for Economic Co-operation and Development. (2021a). *Measuring Tax Support for R&D and Innovation.* https://www.oecd.org/sti/rd-tax-stats.htm

Organisation for Economic Co-operation and Development. (2021b). *OECD R&D Tax Incentives Database Report.* https://www.oecd.org/sti/rd-tax-stats-database.pdf

Osenga, J. K. (2014). Formerly Manufacturing Entities: Piercing the "Patent Troll" Rhetoric. *Connecticut Law Review* 47: 435–479.

Ouellette, L. L. (2012). Do Patents Disclose Useful Information? *Harvard Journal of Law and Technology* 25(2): 531–593.

Padula, W. V., R. A. Larson, S. B. Dusetzina, J. F. Apperley, R. Hehlmann, M. Baccarani, E. Eigendorff, J. Guilhot, F. Guilhot, F.-X. Mahon, G. Martinelli, J. Mayer, M. C. Müller, D. Niederwieser, S. Saussele, C. A. Schiffer, R. T. Silver, B. Simonsson, and R. M. Conti (2016). Cost-Effectiveness of Tyrosine Kinase Inhibitor Treatment Strategies for Chronic Myeloid Leukemia in Chronic Phase After Generic Entry of Imatinib in the United States. *Journal of the National Cancer Institute* 108(7). 10.1093/jnci/djw003

Pakes, A. (1985). On Patents, R & D, and the Stock Market Rate of Return. *Journal of Political Economy* 93(2): 390–409.

Pakes, A., and M. Schankerman (1984). The Rate of Obsolescence of Patents, Research Gestation Lags, and the Private Rate of Return to Research Resources. In Z. Griliches (ed.), *R&D, Patents, and Productivity*, pp. 73–88. Chicago, IL: University of Chicago Press.

Panattoni, L. E. (2011). The Effect of Paragraph IV Decisions and Generic Entry before Patent Expiration on Brand Pharmaceutical Firms. *Journal of Health Economics* 30(1): 26–145.

Parchomovsky, G., and P. Siegelman (2002). Towards an Integrated Theory of Intellectual Property. *Virginia Law Review* 88(7): 1455–1528.

Park, S. (*1997*, rev. 2003). *Quantitative Analysis of Network Externalities in Systems Competition: The VCR Case.* http://ms.cc.sunysb.edu/~sanpark/NE-VCR.pdf

Park, W. G. (2008). International Patent Protection: 1960–2005. *Research Policy* 37(4): 761–766.

Pauly, S., and F. Stipanicic (2022). *The Creation and Diffusion of Knowledge: Evidence from the Jet Age.* https://fernandostipanicic.github.io/files/jmp.pdf

Pavitt, K. (1984). Sectoral patterns of technical change: Towards a taxonomy and a theory. *Research Policy* 13(6): 343–373. DOI: https://doi.org/10.1016/0048-7333(84)90018-0.

Pavitt, K. (2005). Innovation Processes. In J. Fagerberg, D. C. Mowery, and R. R. Nelson (eds.), *The Oxford Handbook of Innovation*, Chapter 4, pp. 86–114. Oxford, UK: Oxford University Press.

Peitz, M., and P. Waelbroeck (2006). Why the Music Industry May Gain from Free Downloading: The Role of Sampling. *International Journal of Industrial Organization* 24: 907–913.

Penrose, E. T. (1951). *The Economics of the International Patent System*. Johns Hopkins University Studies in Historical and Political Science. Baltimore: The Johns Hopkins Press.

Penrose, E. T. (1973, September). International Patenting and the Less-Developed Countries. *Economic Journal* 83: 768–786.

Perez, C. (1983). Structural Change and Assimilation of New Technologies in the Economic and Social Systems. *Futures* 15(5): 357–375.

Philadelphia Physicians College (2018). *Vaccine Development, Testing, and Regulation*. https://www.historyofvaccines.org/content/articles/vaccine- development-testing-and-regulation

Pisano, G. P. (1990). The R&D Boundaries of the Firm: An Empirical Analysis. *Administrative Science Quarterly* 35(1): 153–176

Plasseraud, Y., and F. Savignon (1983). *Paris 1883: Genèse du Droit Unioniste des Brevets*. Paris, France: litec.

Png, I. P. L. (2017). Law and Innovation: Evidence from State Trade Secrets Laws. *Review of Economics and Statistics* 99(1): 167–179.

Png, I. P. L. (2017). Secrecy and Patents: Theory and Evidence from the Uniform Trade Secrets Act. *Strategy Science* 2(3): 176–193.

Polanyi, M. (1962). The Republic of Science. *Minerva* 1: 54–73. https://doi.org/10.1007/BF0 1101453

Ponce, C. J. (2011). Knowledge Disclosure as Intellectual Property Rights Protection. *Journal of Economic Behavior and Organization* 80(3): 418–434.

Popp, D. (2006). International Innovation and Diffusion of Air Pollution Control Technologies: the Effects of NOX and SO2 Regulation in the US, Japan, and Germany. *Journal of Environmental Economics and Management* 51(1): 46–71.

Porter, M. E. (1985). *Competitive Advantage*. New York: Free Press.

Prager, F. (1946). Brunelleschi's Patent. *Journal of the Patent Office Society* 28(2): 109–135

Prahalad, C. K., and G. Hamel (1990) The Core Competence of the Corporation. *Harvard Business Review* 68(3): 79–91.

Priest, G., and B. Klein (1984). The Selection of Disputes for Litigation. *Journal of Legal Studies* 13: 1–55.

Prud'homme, D. (2017). Utility Model Patent Regime "Strength" and Technological Development: Experiences of China and Other East Asian Latecomers. *China Economic Review* 42: 50–73.

Qian, Y. (2007). Do National Patent Laws Stimulate Domestic Innovation in a Global Patenting Environment? A Cross-Country Analysis of Pharmaceutical Patent Protection, 1978–2002. *Review of Economics and Statistics* 89(3): 436–453.

de Rassenfosse, G. (2020). On the Price Elasticity of Demand for Trademarks. *Industry and Innovation* 27(1–2): 11–24.

de Rassenfosse, G., and A. B. Jaffe (2018). Econometric Evidence on the Depreciation of Innovations. *European Economic Review* 101: 625–642.

de Rassenfosse, G., and A. Palangkaraya (2023). Do Patent Pledges Accelerate Innovation? *Research Policy* 52(5): article 104745.

Raustiala, K., and C. Sprigman (2006). The Piracy Paradox: Innovation and Intellectual Property in Fashion Design. *Virginia Law Review* 92(8): 1688–1777.

Raymond, E. S. (2001). *The Cathedral and the Bazaar: Musings on Linux and Open Source by an Accidental Revolutionary*. Sebastopol, CA: O'Reilly Media.

Regan, T. L. (2008). Generic Entry, Price Competition, and Market Segmentation in the Prescription Drug Market. *International Journal of Industrial Organization* 26(4): 930–948.

Reiffen, D., and M. R. Ward (2006). Generic Drug Industry Dynamics. *Review of Economics and Statistics* 87(1): 37–49.

Reimer, J. (2005, December 15). Total Share: 30 Years of Personal Computer Market Share Figures. *Ars Technica* blog. https://arstechnica.com/features/2005/12/total-share/6

Reimer, J. (2012, August 14). From Altair to iPad: 35 Years of Personal Computer Market Share. *Ars Technica* blog. https://arstechnica.com/information-technology/2012/08/from-altair-to-ipad-35-years-of-personal-computer-market-share

Reimers, I. (2019). Copyright and Generic Entry in Book Publishing. *American Economic Journal: Microeconomics* 11(3): 257–284.

Reinganum, J. F. (1982). A Dynamic Game of R and D: Patent Protection and Competitive Behavior. *Econometrica* 50(3): 671–688.

Reinganum, J. F., and L. L. Wilde (1986). Settlement, Litigation, and the Allocation of Litigation Costs. *RAND Journal of Economics* 17: 557–566.

Righi C., and T. Simcoe (2023). Patenting Inventions or Inventing Patents? Continuation Practice at the USPTO. *RAND Journal of Economics* 54(3): 416–442.

Risch, M. (2012). Patent Troll Myths. *Seton Hall Law Review* 42: 457–499.

Rivette, K. G., and D. Kline (2000). *Rembrandts in the Attic: Unlocking the Hidden Value of Patents*. Boston, MA: Harvard Business School Press.

Rivette, K. G., H. R. Nothaft, and D. Kline (2000). Discovering New Value in Intellectual Property. *Harvard Business Review* 78(1): 54–66.

Robb, A. M., and D. T. Robinson (2014). The Capital Structure Decisions of New Firms. *Review of Financial Studies* 27(1): 153–179,

Rockett, K. E. (1990). Choosing the Competition and Patent Licensing. *RAND Journal of Economics* 21(1): 161–171.

Rodrik, D. (2014). Green Industrial Policy. *Oxford Review of Economic Policy* 30(3): 469–491.

Rogers, E. M. (1995, originally published 1962). *Diffusion of Innovations*. New York, NY: The Free Press.

Romer, P. M. (1990). Endogenous Technological Change. *Journal of Political Economy* 98: S71–S102.

Romer, P. M. (1986). Increasing Returns and Long-Run Growth. *Journal of Political Economy* 94(5): 1002–1037.

Rosenberg, N. (1976a). *Perspectives on Technology*. Cambridge, UK: Cambridge University Press.

Rosenberg, N. (1976b). The Machine Tool Industry, 1840–1910. In *Perspectives on Technology*, pp. 9–31. Cambridge, UK: Cambridge University Press.

Rosenberg, N. (1976c). Factors Affecting the Diffusion of Technology. In *Perspectives on Technology*, pp. 189–212. Cambridge, UK: Cambridge University Press.

Rosenberg, N. (1976d). Science, Invention, and Economic Growth. In *Perspectives on Technology*, pp. 260–279. Cambridge, UK: Cambridge University Press.

Rosenberg, N. (1976e). The Direction of Technological Change: Inducement Mechanisms and Focusing Devices. In *Perspectives on Technology*, pp. 108–125. Cambridge, UK: Cambridge University Press.

Rosenberg, N. (1982a). *Inside the Black Box*. Cambridge, UK: Cambridge University Press.

Rosenberg, N. (1982b). Learning by Using. In *Inside the Black Box*, pp. 120–140. Cambridge, UK: Cambridge University Press.

Rosenberg, N. (1982c). How Exogenous Is Science? In *Inside the Black Box*, 141–159. Cambridge, UK: Cambridge University Press.

Rosenberg, N. (1990). Why Do Firms Do Basic Research (with Their Own Money)? *Research Policy* 19(2): 165–174.

Rua, G. (2014). *Diffusion of Containerization*. US Board of Governors of the Federal Reserve System Finance and Economics Discussion Series 2014-88. Washington, DC: Federal Reserve Board of Governors. https://www.federalreserve.gov/econres/feds/diffusion-of-containerization.htm

de Saint-Georges, M., and B. van Pottelsberghe de la Potterie (2013). A Quality Index for Patent Systems. *Research Policy* 42(3): 704–719.

Saloner, G., and A. Shepard. (1995). Adoption of Technologies with Network Effects: An Empirical Examination of the Adoption of Automated Teller Machines. *RAND Journal of Economics* 26(3): 479–501.

Salter, A. J., and B. R. Martin (2001). The Economic Benefits of Publicly Funded Basic Research: A Critical Review. *Research Policy* 30(3): 509–532.

Sampat, B. N., and K. C. Shadlen (2015). Drug Patenting in India: Looking Back and Looking Forward. *Nature Reviews: Drug Discovery* 14: 519–520.

Sampat, B. N., and K. C. Shadlen (2017). Secondary Pharmaceutical Patenting: A Global Perspective. *Research Policy* 46: 693–707.

Sampat, B. N., and K. C. Shadlen (2018). Indian Pharmaceutical Patent Prosecution: The Changing Role of Section 3(d). *PLOS ONE* 13(4). https://doi.org/10.1371/journal.pone.0194714

Samuelson, P. (2005). The Story of *Baker v. Selden*: Sharpening Distinctions Between Authorship and Invention. In J. C. Ginsburg and R. C. Dreyfuss (eds.), *Intellectual Property Stories*, pp. 159–193. New York: Foundation Press.

Santoleri, P., A. Mina, A. Di Minin, and I. Martelli (2020). The Causal Effects of R&D Grants: Evidence from a Regression Discontinuity. SSRN Working Paper. https://ssrn.com/abstract=3637867 or http://dx.doi.org/10.2139/ssrn.3637867

Saxenian, A. (1996). *Regional Advantage: Culture and Competition in Silicon Valley and Route 128*. Cambridge, MA: Harvard University Press.

Schankerman, M. (1981). The Effect of Double Counting and Expensing on the Measured Returns to R&D. *Review of Economics and Statistics* 63(3): 454–458.

Schankerman, M., and A. Pakes (1986). Estimates of the Value of Patent Rights in European Countries during the Post-1950 Period. *Economic Journal* 96(384): 1052–1076.

Schautschick P., and C. Greenhalgh (2016). Empirical Studies of Trade Marks: The Existing Economic Literature. *Economics of Innovation and New Technology* 25(4): 358–390.

Scherer, F. M. (1982). Demand-Pull and Technological Invention: Schmookler Revisited. *Journal of Industrial Economics* 30(3): 225–237.

Scherer, F. M. (1984). Using Linked Patent and R&D Data to Measure Interindustry Technology Flows. In Z. Griliches (ed.), *R&D, Patents, and Productivity*, pp. 417–464. Chicago, IL: University of Chicago Press.

Scherer, F. M., and S. Weisburst (1995). Economic Effects of Strengthening Patent Protection in Italy. *International Review of Industrial Property and Copyright Law* 26(6): 1009–1024.

Schilling, M. (2020). *Strategic Management of Technological Innovation* (6th ed.). New York: McGraw-Hill.

Schmalensee, R. (1982). Product Differentiation Advantages of Pioneering Brands. *American Economic Review* 72: 349–365

Schmitz, P. (2017). Incomplete Contracts, Shared Ownership, and Investment Incentives. *Journal of Economic Behavior and Organization* 144: 153–165.

Schmoch, U. (2003). Service Marks as Novel Innovation Indicator. *Research Evaluation* 12(2): 149–156.

Schmoch, U. (2008). *Concept of a Technology Classification for Country Comparisons*. World Intellectual Property Organisation Final Report. https,//www.wipo.int/export/sites/www/ipstats/en/statistics/patents/pdf/wipo_ipc_technology.pdf

Schmookler, J. (1966). *Invention and Economic Growth*. Cambridge, MA: Harvard University Press.

Schumpeter, J. A. (1934, originally published 1911). Translated from the German by Redvers Opie. *The Theory of Economic Development: An Inquiry into Profits, Capital, Credit, Interest, and the Business Cycle*. Cambridge, MA: Harvard University Press.

Schumpeter, J. A. (1942, 1960). *Capitalism, Socialism, and Democracy*. New York: Harper Torchbooks, Harper and Row.

Schwartz, D. L., and X. Giroud (2020). An Empirical Study of Design Patent Litigation. *Alabama Law Review* 72: 417–464.

Schweitzer, S. O., and W. S. Comanor (2011). Prices of Pharmaceuticals in Poor Countries Are Much Lower Than in Wealthy Countries. *Health Affairs* 30(8): 1553–1561.

Scitovsky, T. (1954). Two Concepts of External Economies. *Journal of Political Economy* 62(2): 143–151.

Scotchmer, S. (1991). Standing on the Shoulders of Giants: Cumulative Research and the Patent Law. *Journal of Economic Perspectives* 5: 29–41.

Scotchmer, S. (2004). The Political Economy of Intellectual Property Treaties. *Journal of Law, Economics, and Organization* 20(2): 415–437.

Scott, J. T. (1989). Historical and Economic Perspectives of the National Cooperative Research Act. In A. N. Link and G. Tassey (eds.), *Cooperative Research and Development: The Industry–University–Government Relationship*. Dordrecht, Netherlands: Springer. https://doi.org/10.1007/978-94-009-2522-9_4

Scott-Morton, F., and C. Shapiro (2014). Strategic Patent Acquisitions. *Antitrust Law Journal* 79(2): 463–499.

Seabrook, J. (1993, January 3). The Flash of Genus. *The New Yorker*. https://www.newyorker.com/magazine/1993/01/11/the-flash-of-genius

Selgin, G., and J. Turner (2006). James Watt as Intellectual Monopolist: Comment on Boldrin and Levine. *International Economic Review* 47: 1341–1348.

Serrano, C. J. (2018). Estimating the Gains from Trade in the Market for Patent Rights. *International Economic Review* 59(4): 1877–1904. https,//doi.org/10.1111/iere.12338

Shah, S. K. (2000). Sources and Patterns of Innovation in a Consumer Products Field: Innovations in Sporting Equipment. Cambridge, MA: MIT Sloan Working Paper No. 4105.

Shah, S. K. (2006). From Innovation to Firm Formation: Contributions by Sports Enthusiasts to the Windsurfing, Snowboarding and Skateboarding Industries. In E. F. Moritz and S. Haake (eds.), *The Engineering of Sport* 6, pp. 29–34. New York: Springer.

Shapiro, C. (2001). Navigating the Patent Thicket: Cross Licenses, Patent Pools, and Standard-Setting. In A. Jaffe, J. Lerner, and S. Stern (eds.), *Innovation Policy and the Economy* 1: 119-150. Cambridge, MA: MIT Press.

Shapiro, C., and H. R. Varian (1999a). *Information Rules*. Boston, MA: Harvard Business School Press.

Shapiro, C., and H. R. Varian (1999b). The Art of Standards Wars. *California Management Review* 41(2): 8–32.

Shaughnessy, A. F. (2011, February). Old Drugs, New Tricks. *British Medical Journal* 342. https://www.bmj.com/content/342/bmj.d741

Shenhar, A. J., V. Holzmann, B. Melamed, and Y. Zhao (2016). The Challenge of Innovation in Highly Complex Projects: What Can We Learn from Boeing's Dreamliner Experience? *Project Management Journal* 47(2): 62–78. https://doi.org/10.1002/pmj.21579

Sherman A. (2018). Doing Intellectual Property the Dolby Labs Way. IAM. https://www.iam-media.com/article/doing-intellectual-property-the-dolby-labs-way

Sichel, D. E. (2022). The Price of Nails Since 1695: A Window into Economic Change. *Journal of Economic Perspectives* 36(1): 125–150.

Sichel, D., and E. von Hippel (2019). Household Innovation, R&D, and New Measures of Intangible Capital. Cambridge, MA: National Bureau of Economic Research Working Paper Series No. 25599.

Sidak, G. (2018). Injunctive Relief and the FRAND Commitment in the United States. In J. Contreras (ed.), *Cambridge Handbook of Technical Standardization Law*. Cambridge, UK: Cambridge University Press.

Siebrasse, N. V., and T. F. Cotter (2017). The Value of the Standard. *Minnesota Law Review* 101(3): 1159–1246.

Siegel, M., and S. Fransen (2013). New Technologies in Remittance Sending: Opportunities for mobile remittances in Africa. *African Journal of Science, Technology, Innovation and Development* 5(5): 423–438.

Slaoui, M., and M. Hepburn (2020). Developing Save and Effective Covid Vaccines: Operation Warp Speed's Strategy and Approach. *New England Journal of Medicine* 383: 1701–1703. doi:10.1056/NEJMp2027405

Snow, D. (2008). Beware of Old Technologies' Last Gasps. *Harvard Business Review*. https://hbr.org/2008/01/beware-of-old-technologies-last-gasps

Solow, R. M. (1957). Technical Change and the Aggregate Production Function. *Review of Economics and Statistics* 39: 312–320.

Solow, R. M. (1997). *Learning from "Learning by Doing."* The Kenneth J. Arrow Lectures. Stanford, CA: Stanford University Press.

Somaya, D. (2012). Patent Strategy and Management: An Integrative Review and Research Agenda. *Journal of Management* 38(4): 1084–1114.

Spier, K. (2007). Litigation. In A. M. Polinsky and S. Shavell (eds.), *Handbook of Law and Economics*, Chapter 4. Amsterdam, Netherlands, and New York: Elsevier.

Spulber, D. F. (2011). Should Business Method Inventions Be Patentable? *Journal of Legal Analysis* 3(1): 265–339.

Spulber, D. F. (2015). How Patents Provide the Foundation of the Market for Inventions. *Journal of Competition Law & Economics* 11(2: 271–316.

Spulber, D. F. (2019a). The Economics of Markets and Platforms. *Journal of Economics and Management Strategy* 28: 159–172.

Spulber, D. F. (2019b). Standard Setting Organisations and Standard Essential Patents: Voting and Markets. *Economic Journal* 129: 1477–1509.

Squicciarini, M., H. Dernis, and C. Criscuolo (2013). Measuring Patent Quality: Indicators of Technological and Economic Value. Organisation for Economic Co-operation and Development Science, Technology and Industry Working Papers 2013/03. Paris, France: Organisation for Economic Co-operation and Development Publishing. http://dx.doi.org/10.1787/5k4522wkw1r8-en

StatCounter (2021). Browser Market Share Worldwide. http://gs.statcounter.com

Stavins, J. (2003). Network Externalities in the Market for Electronic Check Payments. *New England Economic Review 2003*: 19–30.

Stephan, P. (2012). *How Economics Shapes Science*. Cambridge, MA: Harvard University Press.

Sternitzke, C. (2017). Interlocking Patent Rights and Value Appropriation: Insights from the Razor Industry. *IEEE Transactions on Engineering Management* 64(2): 249–265.

Stiglitz, J. E., and A. Jayadev (2010). Medicine for Tomorrow: Some Alternative Proposals to Promote Socially Beneficial Research and Development in Pharmaceuticals. *Journal of Generic Medicines* 7(3): 217–226

Stitzing, R., P. Sääskilahti, J. Royer, and M. Van Audenrode (2017). Over-Declaration of Standard Essential Patents and Determinants of Essentiality. https://ssrn.com/abstract=2951617

Stokes, D. E. (1997). *Pasteur's Quadrant: Basic Science and Technological Innovation*, 196. Washington, DC: Brookings Institution Press.

Stoneman, P., and F. Battisti (2010). The Diffusion of New Technology. In B. H. Hall and N. Rosenberg (eds.), *Handbook of the Economics of Innovation*, Vol. II, pp. 734–760. Amsterdam, Netherlands: Elsevier.

Stoneman, P., and O. Toivanen (2006). Technological Diffusion under Uncertainty: A Real Options Model Applied to the Comparative International Diffusion of Robot Technology. In C. Antonelli, D. Foray, B. H. Hall, and W. E. Steinmueller (eds.), *New Frontiers in the Economics of Innovation and New Technology*, pp. 439–467. Cheltenham UK: Edward Elgar.

Stoyanov, A., and N. Zubanov (2012). Productivity Spillovers across Firms through Worker Mobility. *American Economic Journal: Applied Economics* 4(2): 168–198.

Strohmeyer. R. (2008). Worst Tech Predictions. *PC World*. https://www.pcworld.com/article/155984/worst_tech_predictions.html

Suárez, F. F., and G. Lanzolla (2005). The Half-Truth of First-Mover Advantage. *Harvard Business Review* 83(4): 121–127.

Suárez, F. F., and J. M. Utterback (1995). Dominant Designs and the Survival of Firms. *Strategic Management Journal* 16: 415–430.

Suárez, F. F., S. Grodal, and A. Gotsopoulos (2015). Perfect Timing? Dominant Category, Dominant Design, and the Window of Opportunity for Firm Entry. *Strategic Management Journal* 36: 437–448.

Suri, T. (2011). Selection and Comparative Advantage in Technology Adoption. *Econometrica* 79(1): 159–209.

Sutton, J. (1998). *Technology and Market Structure.* Cambridge, MA: MIT Press.

Sveikauskas, L. (1981). Technological Inputs and Multifactor Productivity Growth. *Review of Economics and Statistics* 63(2): 275–282.

Swan, T.W. (1956). Economic Growth and Capital Accumulation. *Economic Record* 32: 334–361.

Takeyama, L. N. (1994). The Welfare Implications of Unauthorized Reproduction of Intellectual Property in the Presence of Demand Network Externalities. *Journal of Industrial Economics* 42(2): 155–166.

Teece, D. J. (1986). Profiting from Technological Innovation: Implications for Integration, Collaboration, Licensing and Public Policy. *Research Policy* 15(6): 285–305.

Teece, D. J. (2018). The "Tragedy of the Anti-Commons" Fallacy: A Law and Economics Analysis of Patent Thickets and FRAND Licensing. *Berkeley Technology Law Journal* 32: 1489–1526.

Tewksbury, J. G., M. S. Crandall, and W. E. Crane (1980). Measuring the Societal Benefits of Innovation. *Science* 209(4457): 658–662.

Thoma, G. (2019). Composite Value Index of Trademark Indicators. *World Patent Information* 56: 64–75.

Thoma, G. (2021). Composite Value Index of Trademark Indicators: A Market Value Analysis Using Tobin's q. *World Patent Information* 66: article 102064.

Thomä, J., and K. Bizer (2013). To Protect or Not to Protect? Modes of Appropriability in the Small Enterprise Sector. *Research Policy* 42: 35–49.

Thompson, N. C., K. Greenewald, K. Lee, and G. F. Manso (2021). The Computational Limits of Deep Learning. MIT Computer Science and A. I. Lab. https://arxiv.org/abs/2007.05558

Thompson, P. (2010). Learning by Doing. In B. H. Hall and N. Rosenberg (eds.), *Handbook of the Economics of Innovation*, Vol. 1, pp. 429–476. Amsterdam, Netherlands: Elsevier.

Thompson, P., and M. Fox-Kean. (2005). Patent Citations and the Geography of Knowledge Spillovers: A Reassessment. *American Economic Review* 95 (1): 450-460. DOI: 10.1257/0002828053828509.

Thomson, R. (2015). The Yield of Plant Variety Protection. *American Journal of Agricultural Economics* 97(3): 762–785.

Thursby, J. G., and M. Thursby (2006). *Here or There? A Survey of Factors in Multinational R&D Location.* Washington, DC: National Academies Press.

Tirole, J. (1988). *The Theory of Industrial Organization.* Cambridge, MA: MIT Press.

Tobin, J. (1969). A General Equilibrium Approach to Monetary Theory. *Journal of Money. Credit, and Banking* 1(1): 15–29.

Tompsett, A. (2020, March). The Lazarus Drug: The Impact of Antiretroviral Therapy on Economic Growth. *Journal of Development Economics* 143: article 102409.

Trajtenberg, M. (1989). The Welfare Analysis of Product Innovations, with an Application to Computed Tomography Scanners. *Journal of Political Economy* 97(2): 444–479.

Trajtenberg, M. (1990). A Penny for Your Quotes: Patent Citation and the Value of Innovations. *RAND Journal of Economics* 21: 172–187.

Tranchero, M. (2023). Finding Diamonds in the Rough: Data-Driven Opportunities and Pharmaceutical Innovation. Berkeley, CA: University of California Working Paper. https://www.matteotranchero.com/pdf/Matteo_Tranchero_JMP_latest.pdf

Tucker, C. (2014). Patent Trolls and Technology Diffusion: The Case of Medical Imaging. In T. Simcoe, A. K. Agrawal, and S. Graham (eds.), *Standards, Patents and Innovations*. Cambridge, MA: NBER Conference Volume. https://ssrn.com/abstract=1976593

Ugur, M., E. Trushin, E. Solomon, and F. Guidi (2016). R&D and Productivity in OECD Firms and Industries: A Hierarchical Meta-Regression Analysis. *Research Policy* 45(10): 2069–2086.

United Nations, European Commission, International Monetary Fund, Organization for Economic Cooperation and Development, and the World Bank (2009). *System of National Accounts.* New York, NY: United Nations.https://unstats.un.org/unsd/nationalaccount/docs/sna2008.pdf

U.S. Bureau of Economic Analysis (2013, March). Preview of the 2013 Comprehensive Revision of the National Income and Product Accounts. *Survey of Current Business* 93(3): 13–39.

U.S. Bureau of Labor Statistics (2014). Multifactor Productivity Trends for Detailed Industries – 2014. https://www.bls.gov/news.release/archives/prin3_09202016.pdf

U.S. Federal Trade Commission (2016). *Patent Assertion Entity Activity: An FTC Study.* https://www.ftc.gov/system/files/documents/reports/patent-assertion-entity-activity-ftc-study/p131203_patent_assertion_entity_activity_an_ftc_study_0.pdf

U.S. Government (2021). *NIPA Handbook: Concepts and Methods of the U.S. National Income and Product Accounts.* Washington, DC: Bureau of Economic Analysis. https://www.bea.gov/resources/methodologies/nipa-handbook

U.S. National Research Council (2001). *Energy Research at DOE: Was It Worth It? Energy Efficiency and Fossil Energy Research 1978 to 2000.* Washington, DC: National Academies Press.

U.S. National Science Board, National Science Foundation (2020). *Science and Engineering Indicators 2020: The State of U.S. Science and Engineering.* Publication No. NSB-2020-1. Alexandria, VA: Author. https://ncses.nsf.gov/pubs/nsb20201

U.S. National Science Foundation (2018). *Science and Technology Indicators 2018.* https://www.nsf.gov/statistics/2018/nsb20181/report.

Utterback, J. M., and W. J. Abernathy (1975). A Dynamic Model of Process and Product Innovation. *Omega* 3(6): 639–656.

Van Alstyne, M., and E. Brynjolfsson (2005). Global Village or Cyber-Balkans? Modeling and Measuring the Integration of Electronic Communities. *Management Science* 51(6): 851–868.

van den Heuvel, M., and D. Popp (2022). The Role of Venture Capital and Governments in Clean Energy: Lessons from the First Cleantech Bubble. *Energy Economics* 124 (August): 106877. DOI: https://doi.org/10.1016/j.eneco.2023.106877

van der Kam, M. J., A. A. H. Meelen, W. G. J. H. M. van Sark, and F. Alkemade (2018). Diffusion of Solar Photovoltaic Systems and Electric Vehicles among Dutch Consumers: Implications for the Energy Transition. *Energy Research and Social Science* 46: 68–85.

van Pottelsberghe, B., and F. Lichtenberg (2001). Does Foreign Direct Investment Transfer Technology Across Borders? *The Review of Economics and Statistics* 83(3): 490-497. DOI: 10.1162/00346530152480135

Varian, H. R. (2005). Copying and Copyright. *Journal of Economic Perspectives* 19(2): 121–138.

VerSteeg, R. (2018). Ancient Egyptian Roots of Trademarks. *The Antitrust Bulletin* 63(3): 283–304.

Veugelers, R., and B. Cassiman (1999). Make and Buy in Innovation Strategies: Evidence from Belgian Manufacturing Firms. *Research Policy* 28(1): 63–80.

Von Graevenitz, G. (2013). Trade Mark Cluttering: Evidence from EU Enlargement. *Oxford Economic Papers* 65(3): 721–745.

Von Graevenitz, G., R. Ashmead, and C. Greenhalgh (2015). *Cluttering and Non-Use of Trade Marks in Europe.* Newport, Wales: UK Intellectual Property Office Report 2015/48.

Von Hippel, E. (2006). *Democratizing Invention.* Cambridge, MA: MIT Press.

Wagner S., C. Sternitzke, and S. Walter (2022). Mapping Markush. *Research Policy* 51(10): article 104597.

Wang, L. X. (2022). Global Drug Diffusion and Innovation with the Medicines Patent Pool. *Journal of Health Economics* 85: article 102671.

Wang, Z. (2007). Technological innovation and market turbulence: The dot-com experience. *Review of Economic Dynamics* 10(1): 78-105. DOI: https://doi.org/10.1016/j.red.2006.10.001

Watson, J., M. MacGarvie, and J. McKeon (2022). It Was 50 Years Ago Today. Recording Copyright Term and the Supply of Music. *Management Science* 69(1): 351–376. https://doi.org/10.1287/mnsc.2022.4343

Weatherall, K., and E. Webster (2014). Patent Enforcement: A Review of the Literature. *Journal of Economic Surveys* 28(2): 312–343.

Weber, M. (1905). *The Protestant Ethic and the Spirit of Capitalism.* Translated by T. Parsons, with a foreword by R. H. Tawney. New York, NY: Charles Scribner's Sons, 1958. Republished by Dover, New York, 2003.

Webster, M., K. Fisher-Vanden, D. Popp, and N. Santen (2017). Should We Give Up after Solyndra? Optimal Technology R&D Portfolios under Uncertainty. *Journal of the Association of Environmental and Resource Economists* 4(S1): S123–S151.

Weiner, R. (2012, June 1). Solyndra, Explained. *Washington Post.* https://www.washingtonpost.com/blogs/the-fix/post/solyndra--explained/2012/06/01/gJQAig2g6U_blog.html

White, L., Jr. (1940). Technology and Invention in the Middle Ages. *Speculum* 15(2): 141–159.

White, L., Jr. (1962). *Medieval Technology and Social Change.* Oxford, UK: Oxford University Press.

Williamson, O. E. (1975). *Markets and Hierarchies, Analysis and Antitrust.* New York, NY: Free Press.

Williamson, O. E. (1976). Franchise Bidding for Natural Monopolies: In General and with Respect to CATV. *The Bell Journal of Economics* 7(1): 73–104.

Williamson, O. E. (1979). Transaction-Cost Economics: The Governance of Contractual Relations. *Journal of Law & Economics* 22(2): 233–261.

Wilson, D. J. (2009). Beggar Thy Neighbor? The In-State, Out-of-State, and Aggregate Effects of R&D Tax Credits. *Review of Economics and Statistics* 91(2): 431–436.

Wittich, C. M., C. M. Burkle, and W. L. Lanier. (2012). Ten Common Questions (and Their Answers) about Off-Label Drug Use. *Mayo Clinic Proceedings* 87(10): 982–990. https://doi.org/10.1016/j.mayocp.2012.04.017.

Wong, C. H., K. W. Siah, and A. W. Lo (2019). Estimation of Clinical Trial Success Rates and Related Parameters. *Biostatistics* 20(2): 273–286. doi:10.1093/biostatistics/kxx069

Wooldridge, J. M. (2000). *Introductory Econometrics.* Cincinnati, OH: Southwestern.

World Bank (2022). *World Bank Development Indicators.* https://datatopics.worldbank.org/world-development-indicators/

World Intellectual Property Office (2013). *World Intellectual Property Report: Brands – Reputation and Image in the Global Marketplace.* http://www.wipo.int/edocs/pubdocs/en/intproperty/944/wipo_pub_944_2013.pdf

World Intellectual Property Office (2017). *Intangible Capital in Global Value Chains.* Geneva, Switzerland: World Intellectual Property Report 2017.

World Intellectual Property Office (2021a). *Berne Convention for the Protection of Literary and Artistic Works (1886).* https://www.wipo.int/treaties/en/ip/berne/summary_berne.html

World Intellectual Property Office (2021b). *Patent Expert Issues: Layout Designs (Topographies) of Integrated Circuits.* https://www.wipo.int/patents/en/topics/integrated_circuits.html

World Intellectual Property Office (2022). *IP Statistics Data Center.* https://www3.wipo.int/ipstats/index.htm?tab=patent

World Intellectual Property Office (2023). *Patent Cooperation Treaty Yearly Review 2023.* https://www.wipo.int/edocs/pubdocs/en/wipo-pub-901-2023-en-patent-cooperation-treaty-yearly-review-2023.pdf.

Wright, B. (1983). The Economics of Invention Incentives: Patents, Prizes, and Research Contracts. *American Economic Review* 73(4): 691–707.

Yang, L., and K. E. Maskus (2009). Intellectual Property Rights, Technology Transfer and Exports in Developing Countries. *Journal of Development Economics* 90: 231–236.

Yonatan, R. (2017). 12 Accidental Innovations.https://getvoip.com/blog/2017/12/04/12-famous-accidental-innovations/

Zentner, A. (2006). Measuring the Effect of File Sharing on Music Purchases. *Journal of Law and Economics* 49(1): 63–90.

Ziedonis, R. H. (2003). Patent Litigation in the US Semiconductor Industry. In W. M. Cohen and S. A. Merrill (eds.), *Patents in the Knowledge-Based Economy,* pp. 180–218. Washington, DC: National Academies Press.

Ziedonis, R. H. (2004). Don't Fence Me In: Frated Markets for Technology and the Patent Acquisition Strategies of Firms. *Management Science* 50(6): 804–820.

Ziedonis, R. H., and B. H. Hall (2001). The Effects of Strengthening Patent Rights on Firms Engaged in Cumulative Innovation. In G. Libecap (ed.), *Entrepreneurial Inputs and*

Outcomes: New Studies of Entrepreneurship in the United States, Vol. 13, pp. 133–188. Amsterdam, Netherlands: Elsevier Science.

Zuniga, M. P., and E. Combe (2002). Introducing Patent Protection in the Pharmaceutical Sector: a First Evaluation for the Mexican Case. *Revue Région et Développement* 16: 191–221.

Zuniga, M. P., and D. Guellec (2009). Who Licenses Out Patents and Why? Lessons from a Business Survey. Paris, France: Organisation of Economic Co-operation and Development STI Working Paper 2009/5.

Index

For the benefit of digital users, indexed terms that span two pages (e.g., 52–53) may, on occasion, appear on only one of those pages.

Tables and figures are indicated by an italic *t*, *b*, and *f* following the page number.